Microsoft Office 365 Administration Inside Out

Second Edition

Darryl Kegg
Aaron Guilmette
Lou Mandich
Ed Fisher

ISBN-13: 978-1-5093-0467-7
ISBN-10: 1-5093-0467-3

Library of Congress Control Number: 2017956417

Printed and bound in the United States of America.

2 18

Trademarks

Warning and Disclaimer

Special Sales
For information about buying this title in bulk quantities, or for special sales opportunities (which may include electronic versions; custom cover designs; and content particular to your business, training goals, marketing focus, or branding interests), please contact our corporate sales department at corpsales@pearsoned.com or (800) 382-3419.

For government sales inquiries, please contact governmentsales@pearsoned.com.

For questions about sales outside the U.S., please contact intlcs@pearson.com.

Editor-in-Chief: Greg Wiegand
Acquisitions Editor: Laura Norman
Development Editor: Chris Norton
Managing Editor: Sandra Schroeder
Senior Project Editor: Tracey Croom
Editorial Production: Terrie Cundiff
Copy Editor: Kerin Forsyth
Indexer: Jack Hill
Proofreader: James Case
Technical Editor: Rozanne Whalen
Cover Designer: Twist Creative, Seattle

Contents at a glance

PART VI   SharePoint Online

Table of contents

What do you think of this book? We want to hear from you!

Microsoft is interested in hearing your feedback so we can improve our books and learning resources for you. To participate in a brief survey, please visit:

https://aka.ms/tellpress

What do you think of this book? We want to hear from you!

Microsoft is interested in hearing your feedback so we can improve our books and learning resources
for you. To participate in a brief survey, please visit:

https://aka.ms/tellpress

Introduction

Office 365 has grown up a lot since its debut as Microsoft Business Productivity Online Services in April 2009. Over the past eight years, it's evolved into the premier online suite of business services, enabling organizations as small as one-person and two-person stores to the largest multinational retailers, manufacturers, and professional services organizations to harness the power of cloud scaling and availability. Office 365 provides services to more than 100 million monthly subscribers in commercial and public sectors.

The service is evergreen—built around the ideas of continuous improvement and feature release—to ensure that customers always receive the latest capabilities and enhance their ability to be more agile and productive.

The Microsoft vision is for a cloud-enabled future, built on the capabilities of Office 365 and Microsoft Azure. This book equips you with the knowledge you need to tackle the deployment of one of the largest transformational products available as well as the insider tips that help you avoid the mistakes that might slow you down.

Who this book is for

This book is written for IT professionals responsible for deploying, migrating to, and managing some or all of an organization's Office 365 environment. Office 365 isn't just a single application or service; it's a suite of software-as-a-service tools that can touch every part of the business. As such, you might only be responsible for a portion of it and share responsibility for planning and administration with other individuals or teams.

For some people, Office 365 might seem like one more thing to learn, but in reality, if you've been administering on-premises versions of Active Directory, Exchange, Microsoft SharePoint, or Skype, you're already familiar with the concepts in Office 365. Office 365 is designed with a myriad of hybrid capabilities so that you can go to the cloud on your own terms and build on your existing knowledge of the corresponding on-premises systems. Microsoft believes that Office 365 is an extension of your data center. The management patterns and practices you've built for your on-premises environment can be updated and reused for Office 365, enabling you to achieve quicker results.

Our goal with this book is to help you at any stage of your Office 365 journey—whether you're a consultant looking for architecture and planning guidance or an IT administrator tasked with deployment.

Book features & conventions

This book uses special text and design conventions to make it easier for you to find the information you need.

Text conventions

Here are some of the text conventions and formats you'll find in this book:

- Abbreviated menu commands. For your convenience, this book uses abbreviated menu commands. For example, "Click Tools | Track Changes | Highlight Changes" means that you should click the Tools menu, point to Track Changes, and click the Highlight Changes command.

- Boldface type. Boldface type is used to indicate text that you enter or type.

- Initial Capital Letters. The first letters of the names of menus, dialog boxes, dialog box elements, and commands are capitalized. Example: the Save As dialog box.

- Italicized type. Italicized type indicates new terms.

Book Features

INSIDE OUT

These are the book's signature tips. In these tips, you'll get the straight scoop on what's going on with the software or service—inside information about why a feature works the way it does. You'll also find field-tested advice and guidance as well as details that give you the edge on deploying and managing like a pro.

TROUBLESHOOTING

The Troubleshooting sidebar highlights particular error conditions you might encounter during the configuration or deployment of a feature or service. Frequently, you'll find links to detailed articles, references to additional detailed error code information, or specific workaround instructions.

READER AIDS

Reader Aids are exactly that—additional background information on a topic, factoids, or non-essential details that provide a more rounded understanding of the topic.

Current Book Service

This book is part of our new Current Book Service, which provides content updates for major technology changes and improvements related to programming Office 365. As significant updates are made, sections of this book will be updated or new sections will be added to address the changes. The updates will be delivered to you via a free Web Edition of this book, which can be accessed with any Internet connection at MicrosoftPressStore.com.

Register this book at MicrosoftPressStore.com to receive access to the latest content as an online Web Edition. If you bought this book through MicrosoftPressStore.com, you do not need to register; this book and any updates are already in your account.

How to register your book

If you have not registered your book, follow these steps:

1. Go to www.MicrosoftPressStore.com/register.

2. Sign in or create a new account.

3. Enter the ISBN found on the copyright page of this book.

4. Answer the questions as proof of purchase.

5. The Web Edition will appear under the Digital Purchases tab on your Account page. Click "Launch" to access your product.

Find out about updates

Sign up for the *What's New* newsletter at *www.MicrosoftPressStore.com/newsletters* to receive an email alerting you of the changes each time this book's Web Edition has been updated. The email address you use to sign up for the newsletter must be the same email address used for your MicrosoftPressStore.com account in order to receive the email alerts. If you choose not to sign up, you can periodically check your account at MicrosoftPressStore.com to find out if updates have been made to the Web Edition.

This book will receive periodic updates to address significant software changes for 12 to 18 months following first publication date. After the update period has ended, no more changes will be made to the book, but the final update to the Web Edition will remain available in your account at MicrosoftPressStore.com.

The Web Edition can be used on tablets that use current web browsers. Simply log into your MicrosoftPressStore.com account and access the Web Edition from the Digital Purchases tab.

For more information about the Current Book Service, visit *www.MicrosoftPressStore.com/CBS*.

Acknowledgments

We would like to thank the teams at Pearson, Cohesion, and Microsoft Press for giving us the opportunity to share our knowledge and experiences. We'd also like to thank our coworkers and peers for content ideas, suggestions, and feedback during the writing and revising process. And, of course, we'd like to thank the countless engineers and programmers who tirelessly develop and maintain the Office 365 platform, without whom there'd be nothing for us to do.

But especially, thank you to our families for supporting and putting up with us during the process. They endured long nights, pyramids of energy drink cans piling up, and our absences at events (though, truthfully, some of us might have been happy for the excuse).

Support and feedback

The following sections provide information on errata, book support, feedback, and contact information.

Errata & support

We've made every effort to ensure the accuracy of this book and its companion content. You can access updates to this book—in the form of a list of submitted errata and their related corrections—at:

https://aka.ms/Office365AdminCBS/errata

If you discover an error that is not already listed, please submit it to us at the same page. If you need additional support, email Microsoft Press Book Support at *mspinput@microsoft.com*.

Please note that product support for Microsoft software and hardware is not offered through the previous addresses. For help with Microsoft software or hardware, go to *https://support .microsoft.com*.

We want to hear from you

At Microsoft Press, your satisfaction is our top priority and your feedback our most valuable asset. Please tell us what you think of this book at

https://aka.ms/tellpress

The survey is short, and we read every one of your comments and ideas. Thanks in advance for your input!

Stay in touch

Let's keep the conversation going! We're on Twitter at *http://twitter.com/MicrosoftPress*.

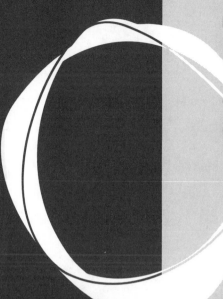

PART I

Planning, Preparing and Deploying Office 365

CHAPTER 1

Office 365 deployment milestones

Planning and deploying Office 365 is not a trivial task; a significant number of design decisions require careful planning before any implementation should begin. These decisions range from tenant naming to licensing plans, network and Active Directory readiness, mail routing, and client and user impact. Each of these deployment milestones should be reviewed and the long-term ramifications of each decision considered before proceeding to the next step, because several of these milestones include irrevocable decisions.

Deciding on a tenant: What's in a name

One of the very first decisions you make when creating your Office 365 tenant is your tenant name. In fact, you are prompted for this name during the first few pages of your initial Office 365 registration, and although that name prompt is accompanied by very little fanfare and absolutely no warning that you are about to pass the point of no return, it is the first of many deployment milestones that represent a critical decision that cannot be undone when setting up Office 365.

The tenant name selection occurs on the User ID creation page, as shown in Figure 1-1, immediately after you have selected your preferred Office 365 subscription type and you've supplied your name, phone number, email address.

Create your user ID

You need a user ID and password to sign in to your account.

| User name | @ | Yourcompany | .onmicrosoft.com |

username@Yourcompany.onmicrosoft.com

Figure 1-1 User ID creation page

The Yourcompany value provided in the User ID creation process becomes the tenant name you use to set up your Office 365 subscription and is added to the front of the onmicrosoft.com domain name suffix.

INSIDE OUT

onmicrosoft.com

All Office 365 and Microsoft Azure tenants end with the onmicrosoft.com name; this suffix cannot be changed and is visible in any Office 365 URLs and cloud logons.

The selection process tells you whether the Yourcompany portion of the sign-in ID is already in use. It won't allow you to proceed if it is not unique, as Figure 1-2 shows, but nothing indicates that this will be your Office 365 tenant name.

Create your user ID

You need a user ID and password to sign in to your account.

| dan.park | @ | contoso | .onmicrosoft.com |

Not available: contoso. Try a different name.

dan.park@contoso.onmicrosoft.com

Figure 1-2 Selecting a tenant name that is not available

When you've successfully selected a user ID, a green check mark appears beside the ID. After you click the Create My Account button, your tenant name is now permanently set for your Office 365 subscription, as shown in Figure 1-3.

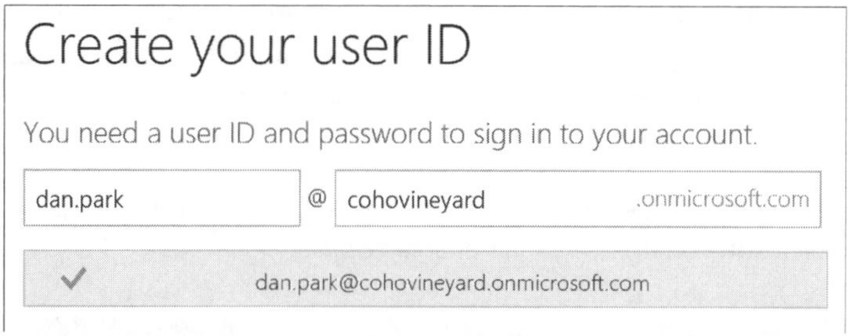

Figure 1-3 Selecting a unique tenant name

As the new subscription process is completed in the background, your new name is set up across the Office 365 tenant and appears in several locations.

INSIDE OUT

Tenant name

After you have selected a tenant name, it cannot be changed. Before creating your Office 365 tenant, discuss the ramifications of the tenant name with all the appropriate resources (such as legal and marketing) in your company.

If you are planning any merger, acquisition, or divestiture (MAD) activity, ensure that the tenant name would still be relevant after that activity has concluded.

Where to see your tenant name

When the tenant name selection is complete, each of the services in your Office 365 subscription (Exchange, Microsoft SharePoint, Skype) is branded with the name you selected. As mentioned, this branding process is permanent, and the name will be visible in several locations, both internal to the Office 365 service and your users and to external parties.

Exchange Online

Exchange Online uses your tenant name in the routing email address stamped on every mail-enabled object you create.

The Exchange hybrid process, discussed in more detail in Chapter 13, "Office 365 Hybrid Configuration Wizard," enables a recipient policy in your Exchange on-premises organization that automatically creates an email address suffix of @tenantName.mail.onmicrosoft.com for every mail-enabled object. This @tenantName.mail.onmicrosoft.com address is typically referred to as the service routing address.

This service routing address is optional and therefore might not appear on mail-enabled objects when viewed in the Exchange Online global address list (GAL). In the Exchange Online service, however, is another automatic email address assignment that is neither optional nor changeable.

As shown in Figure 1-4, Exchange Online automatically assigns an email address ending in @ tenantName.onmicrosoft.com to every mail-enabled object.

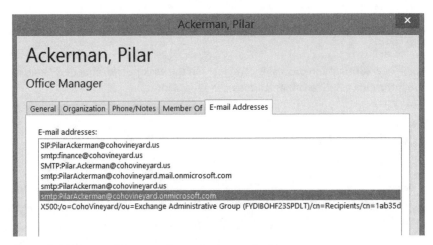

Figure 1-4 The tenantName.onmicrosoft.com email address

The email address in the example is only visible to your internal users when viewing the contact properties of another mail-enabled object. It is also important to note that this address does *not* contain the word "mail," as in the service routing address mentioned earlier.

This additional onmicrosoft.com routing address is not visible outside of your organization, nor is it present in the email header when sending messages to external recipients over the public Internet.

INSIDE OUT

mail.onmicrosoft.com

The mail.onmicrosoft.com domain suffix is not added automatically to the tenant during setup of Exchange Online. Instead, this domain suffix is added to every mail-enabled object in on-premises Exchange through an email address policy added during the Exchange hybrid setup.

SharePoint Online

Out of all the services in Office 365, your tenant name appears most prominently in SharePoint Online. It is visible in site content URLs internally as well as in the sharing URLs provided to external parties.

As Figure 1-5 shows, the tenant name is present in the URL for every external sharing request sent by email.

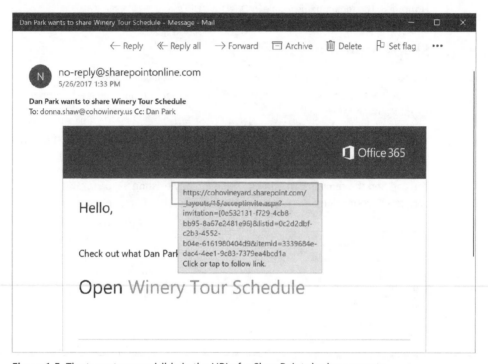

Figure 1-5 The tenant name visible in the URLs for SharePoint sharing requests

OneDrive for Business

Because Microsoft OneDrive is essentially part of the SharePoint Online service, and exists as an extension of MySites in SharePoint, your tenant name appears in any OneDrive sharing URLs sent by email to internal or external recipients. In addition, OneDrive content, viewed when navigating between folders or stored files, displays the tenant name in the URL visible in the address bar at the top of the browser, as Figure 1-6 shows.

Figure 1-6 The tenant name visible in OneDrive URLs

Skype for Business

The tenant name in Skype for Business is visible when viewing the meeting URL in meeting requests sent by email. It is the Office 365 service that contains the least number of references to your tenant name.

You can view the meeting URL by right-clicking or hovering over the Join Skype Meeting hyperlink in email invites, as shown in Figure 1-7; it displays the tenant name.

You can find the same information by selecting any existing Skype for Business meeting requests in your calendar and viewing the hyperlink for that meeting.

Figure 1-7 Viewing the tenant name in a Skype for Business sharing request

Office Pro Plus

The tenant name is not visible when viewing the properties of the Office Pro Plus applications, nor is it visible in any of the additional licensed Office suite applications such as Microsoft Visio or Project.

Office Online

Office Online applications automatically use OneDrive for Business as the default save location for newly created documents, as shown in Figure 1-8. This is visible to your user in the browser address bar, and if these documents are shared with external parties, the URL of the file will contain the tenant name.

Figure 1-8 Tenant name visibility when using Office Online applications

Selecting your licenses

When setting up an Office 365 subscription, you select a license plan as part of the setup process. This license plan can be a trial subscription, typically only valid for 30 days, after which you must either start paying for that subscription or select another; or you can sign up and pay for an annual subscription during the enrollment process and skip the free trial.

Selecting a trial subscription, as shown in Figure 1-9, enables you to start the tenant setup and even begin syncing users and assigning them licenses so that they may begin testing the service. After the trial subscription expires, you can choose to renew the licenses that you have already chosen or add completely different licenses.

Figure 1-9 Selecting a free trial subscription for an Office 365 license plan

Four basic technologies are present in Office 365: Exchange, Skype, SharePoint, and Office Pro Plus. These four technologies, along with the many other additional services available in Office 365, make the license selection process seem very complex.

Moreover, the plans are further divided into categories such as Small Business, Education, Government, Nonprofit, and even Home Use.

It is not possible to outline all the combinations of plans available, because they are constantly evolving; nor is it possible to provide a single answer as to the best possible plan.

It is important, however, for you to understand the most common plans and their fundamental differences so you can make an informed decision.

Where should I start?

If you are planning to provide all, or most, of the core Office 365 features (email, conferencing, Office applications, SharePoint) to your users, then the first decision you need to make is whether you should purchase Office 365 Business or Office 365 Enterprise.

The easiest way to make this determination is to look at your user and mailbox count in your on-premises environment. If you have fewer than 300 users, and you don't plan to exceed that number in the next one or two years, Office 365 Business might be the best option for you.

If you have, or will have, more than 300 users, consider Office 365 Enterprise to start.

INSIDE OUT

Counting your users

Office 365 requires a license for shared mailboxes that exceed 50 GB in size, so be sure to keep that in mind when adding up the cost of an Office 365 subscription or deciding between Office 365 Business and Office 365 Enterprise.

When considering Office 365 Business plans, the best approach is to examine the features that are *not* present, compared to the Office 365 Enterprise plans, to help you make the best decision about whether Office 365 Business is right for you.

Frequently, customers select Office 365 Business simply based on size and then soon discover that despite their user count, they require several of the features included by default in an Office 365 Enterprise plan that are either not available in an Office 365 Business plan or available at an added cost that makes the Enterprise plan a better value.

Office 365 Business plans

Office 365 Business plans, when compared to Office 365 Enterprise plans, have the following key differences.

- Office 365 Business plans do not provide unified communications options such as public switched telephone network (PSTN) conferencing or Cloud PBX.

- Office 365 Business plans include SharePoint Online Plan 1, which does not include enterprise search, Visio, or Excel services. Excel services should not be confused with the Excel application. Excel services are a server technology in SharePoint that enables a user to load, calculate, and display Microsoft Excel workbooks in SharePoint.

- Office 365 Business plans have a 50 GB mailbox storage limit, whereas Enterprise plans have a 100 GB limit and, in most cases, unlimited archive mailboxes.

- Office 365 Business plans have no litigation hold capability for Exchange Online mailboxes.

INSIDE OUT

Plan 1 versus Plan 2

Frequently, you see references to Plan 1 or Plan 2 for each of the major services (SharePoint, Skype for Business, Exchange Online) in Office 365.

Plan 1 in Office 365 is equivalent to the standard edition of the same product in an on-premises environment; Plan 2 is the equivalent of the enterprise edition.

If Office 365 Business is not right for your organization, based either on your size or on the features that you require, several Office 365 Enterprise options are available.

Office 365 Enterprise plans

At the time of this writing, there are four Office 365 Enterprise plans to choose from: Enterprise E1, E3, E5, and F1. Each plan adds additional features as well as additional costs for each user license.

Office 365 Enterprise E1

The Office 365 Enterprise E1 license is the most basic of the Office 365 Enterprise plans. It contains Exchange, SharePoint, Skype for Business, and OneDrive; however, it does not include Office Pro Plus and has a limit of 50 GB on user and archive mailboxes. In addition, it does not include Exchange Rights Management.

Office 365 Enterprise E3

The Office 365 Enterprise E3 license includes all the features of the E1 license and adds Exchange Rights Management, Office Pro Plus, and the eDiscovery Center and allows for the addition of paid Skype for Business add-ons such as PSTN calling and conferencing as well as Cloud PBX. These additional paid Skype for Business features cannot be added to an E1 license.

The Enterprise E3 also increases the user mailbox limit from 50 GB to 100 GB and archive mailboxes from 50 GB to unlimited, along with the addition of the Litigation and Legal Hold features.

Office 365 Enterprise E5

The Office 365 Enterprise E5 license includes all the features of the E3 license and adds Advanced eDiscovery, Customer Lockbox, PowerBI Pro, and Delve Analytics as well as the Skype for Business PSTN Conferencing feature.

Office 365 Enterprise F1

The Office 365 Enterprise F1 license, sometimes referred to as the Kiosk, Deskless, Firstline, or Front-Line Worker license, is designed to enable users to use email, calendaring, instant messaging, and other Office 365 web-based features without the need for a full-featured workstation. Office 365 Enterprise F1 licenses are targeted primarily at browser or phone use, without the need for any application software to be installed.

Office 365 Enterprise F1 licenses include a 2 GB limit on user mailboxes and support for connectivity using most browsers, as well as ActiveSync connectivity for phones and POP for some desktop clients.

F1 license users are also provided with a 2 GB OneDrive for Business storage account (compared to 1 TB for all other Enterprise licenses) and a license to use the Office Online applications. Office Pro Plus is not included in the Enterprise F1 license.

Additional Office 365 plans

In addition to the Business and Enterprise plans and the long list of additional (and constantly increasing) add-on plans such as Visio, Project, PowerBI, Dynamics, PowerApps, Stream, Flow, and Intune, a few other specialty plans, such as Nonprofit, Government, and Education, mirror the Enterprise plans but with specific eligibility requirements.

Office 365 Nonprofit

The Office 365 Nonprofit plans include the same features as the corresponding Enterprise plans; the only difference between them and the equivalent Enterprise plans is the price. Your organization must qualify for Nonprofit status to receive the discounted plan prices.

Office 365 Education

Like the Office 365 Nonprofit plans, Office 365 Education plans include the same features as their corresponding Enterprise plans; however, Office 365 Education licenses are free to students and teachers. Like Nonprofit plans, your organization must qualify to receive the plan.

Office 365 Government

The Office 365 Government plans are identical to their corresponding Enterprise plans; however, Office 365 Government plans have the following additional features and capabilities.

- All services comply with federal requirements for cloud services, including the Federal Risk and Authorization Management Program (FedRamp), criminal justice, and federal tax information systems.

- Office 365 Government complies with accreditations and certifications required for United States public sector customers.

- Office 365 Government content is logically separated from other customer content in the commercial Office 365 environments.

- Office 365 Government customer content is stored in the United States only.

- Access to customer content is restricted to screened Microsoft personnel.

Office Pro Plus

The final plan worth mentioning here is Office Pro Plus. Some of the core Business and Enterprise plans listed previously do not include any Office Pro Plus licenses; as a result, an Office Pro Plus plan should be added if those licenses are required, or the next level of Business or Enterprise plan should be considered.

In many cases, the cost of the next tier plan that includes Office Pro Plus is less expensive than buying a plan without Office Pro Plus and adding it separately.

It is also important to note that if your organization already owns Office product licenses through a volume license or other agreement, you will use a different activation mechanism for those volume license users than the users who have been assigned an Office 365 Pro Plus license. Keep this in mind when upgrading workstation software, because reactivation and possibly reinstallation of Office might be required to activate them properly.

It is also recommended not to mix Office 365 Pro Plus licenses from the Business and Enterprise plans; doing so might also cause reinstallation or reactivation issues because they use different authentication mechanisms.

Viewing and adding subscriptions

Your current subscriptions can be viewed in the Office 365 Admin Center by selecting Billing from the Admin menu and choosing Subscriptions, as shown in Figure 1-10.

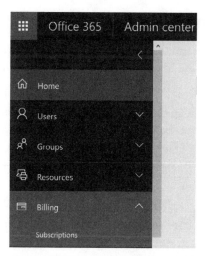

Figure 1-10 Viewing subscription and license information from the Office 365 portal

The subscription page displays each of your active subscriptions, and clicking a single subscription, as shown in Figure 1-11, displays statistics about that subscription, such as cost per user per year, total number of licenses owned and in use, and the expiration date for the subscription.

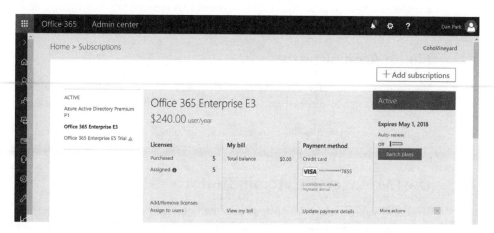

Figure 1-11 Viewing subscription information about a specific Office 365 plan

The subscription page enables you to switch plans if you decided to change all your users from one plan to another. You can also purchase additional add-on plans, assign unused licenses to your users, remove licenses, and update your payment method details.

Delegating access to your tenant

After you have created your tenant, selected at least one subscription, and started creating or synchronizing users, you might find that you need to provide access to additional administrators in your tenant.

By default, the user account that was used to set up the tenant has the Global Administrator privilege, which provides unrestricted access to all features of the tenant and underlying Azure Active Directory. There are, however, several additional administrative roles in Office 365 that enable you to delegate additional levels of permissions to the service without the need to grant unrestricted access.

Currently, there are five pre-built administrative roles: Global Administrator, Billing Administrator, User Management Administrator, Services Administrator, and Password Administrator.

Global Administrator

The Global Administrator role has all rights in the Office 365 subscription. It is like the Domain Administrator role in on-premises Active Directory and should be treated in the same manner. The number of global administrators in your Office 365 tenant should be kept to a minimum and their credentials protected. Like the Domain Administrator role, global administrators can create any of the administrative roles, including another global administrator.

Billing Administrator

The Billing Administrator role can view service settings, manage billing and subscription services, view company information, view service health, and manage support tickets.

In addition, users with the Billing Administrator privilege can view users, groups, and contacts in the tenant; however, they cannot modify or delete them, nor can they assign licenses.

User Management Administrator

The User Management Administrator role member can view users, groups, and contacts in the tenant as well as create and delete each of these object types. The user management administrator can also set user licenses and reset passwords.

User management administrators can also view service health as well as create and view support tickets.

Services Administrator

The Services Administrator role member can access service settings and subscription services, view company information and service health, and manage support tickets, but the role member cannot modify subscription or billing detail.

Users with the Services Administrator privilege can view users, groups, and contacts in the tenant; however, they cannot modify or delete them or assign licenses or reset passwords.

Password Administrator

The Password Administrator role member can view service settings, manage billing and subscription services, view company information, view service health, and manage support tickets.

Users with the Password Administrator privilege can view users, groups, and contacts in the tenant; however, they cannot modify or delete them nor can they assign licenses.

The password administrator role is like the User Administrator role, except that it cannot create users, groups, or contacts.

Administrative role summary

Table 1-1 provides an easy-to-read comparison of the five built-in administrator roles in Office 365 and the most commonly associated privileges. Each privilege is listed on the left, with any role with that permission appearing on the right.

Table 1-1 Administrator roles

View users, groups, and contacts	All roles
Create, edit, and delete users, groups, and contacts	User Management Administrator Global Administrator
View company information	All roles
Edit company information	Global Administrator
Assign licenses	User Management Administrator Global Administrator
Edit subscriptions and billing	Billing Administrator Global Administrator
Manage service tickets	All roles
View service health	All roles
Reset user passwords	Password Administrator User Management Administrator Global Administrator

View users, groups, and contacts	All roles
Add, remove, and verify domains	Global Administrator
Assign administrative roles	Global Administrator

Should you deploy hybrid?

When deploying Office 365, hybrid is one of the most common terms that you hear when discussing your Office 365 deployment options. In fact, the term "hybrid" is used not only when discussing Exchange Online, but also SharePoint Online, Skype for Business, and even directory synchronization.

Understanding what hybrid means will help you decide whether it is something you want to configure, and you should make this decision typically before the installation and configuration processes begin, because it drives additional infrastructure and setup tasks.

Exchange hybrid

When referring to Exchange, hybrid is a configuration methodology that provides for the seamless appearance and behavior of a single organization between on-premises Exchange and Office 365. The Exchange hybrid mode offers near parity of features and experience between Exchange Online and Exchange on-premises by enabling things such as cross-premises calendaring and mailbox migrations and enabling administrators to manage both environments from a single administrative interface. Figure 1-12 shows the most common features configured when using Exchange Hybrid.

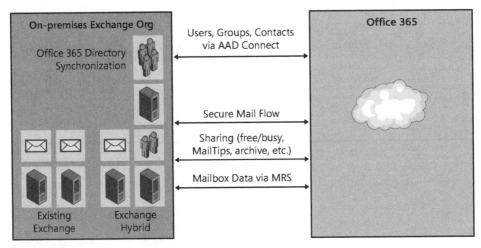

Figure 1-12 Exchange hybrid architecture overview

An Exchange hybrid configuration provides the following features.

- Enables delegated authentication between on-premises Exchange and Exchange Online

- Enables free/busy information sharing, calendar sharing, and message tracking

- Enables administrators to manage both environments from a single Exchange Administrative Center (EAC)

- Allows for online mailbox moves

- Preserves the Microsoft Outlook profile and Offline Store (OST) file after mailbox move

- Uses the Exchange Mailbox Replication Service

- Enables authenticated and encrypted mail flow between on-premises Exchange and Exchange Online

- Preserves Exchange mail headers during email transport between organizations

- Allows for a centralized transport to support compliance mail flow

Exchange hybrid mode requires an additional setup step to enable, which is explained in detail in Chapter 13, as well as several deployment prerequisites prior to running the Exchange Hybrid Configuration Wizard.

- Implementation of directory synchronization between on-premises and Office 365

- Exchange Autodiscover DNS records properly configured for each SMTP domain used in the hybrid process

- A publicly trusted certificate from a third-party certification authority (CA)

- Additional TXT records in the public DNS for Exchange federation

- Additional firewall and network configurations

- Internet-facing Exchange 2013 (or later) CAS/MBX roles

- Active Directory Windows Server 2003 forest-functional level or later

- Exchange Web Services and Autodiscover published to the Internet and secured with a public certificate

The Exchange hybrid configuration process is complex, and despite the Exchange Hybrid Configuration Wizard, many pre-setup and post-setup tasks must be performed to achieve a successful implementation.

Refer to Chapter 13 for a detailed description and walk-through of the Exchange hybrid configuration process.

SharePoint hybrid

Hybrid for SharePoint refers to a configuration by which organizational content is mixed between SharePoint Online and on-premises SharePoint. Unlike Exchange hybrid, the SharePoint hybrid configuration is much less complex, typically consisting of the two environments, with a reverse-proxy configuration that enables users to traverse links across the two environments.

There are three basic topologies when configuring SharePoint hybrid.

One-way outbound

The on-premises SharePoint farm connects one-way, outbound, to SharePoint Online, and search is supported in this topology; see Figure 1-13.

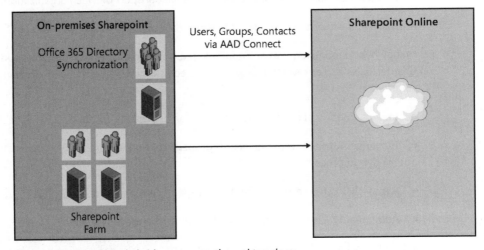

Figure 1-13 SharePoint hybrid one-way outbound topology

One-way inbound

SharePoint Online connects to an on-premises SharePoint farm, one-way, inbound, by a reverse proxy; search is supported in this topology. See Figure 1-14.

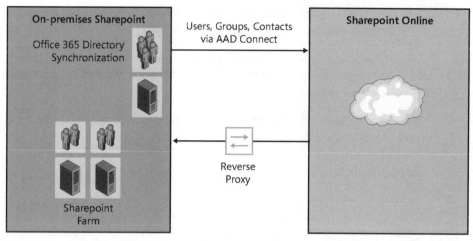

Figure 1-14 SharePoint hybrid one-way inbound topology

Two-way hybrid

SharePoint Online and the on-premises SharePoint farm are connected to one another, using a reverse proxy; search and Business Connectivity Services (BCS) are both supported. See Figure 1-15.

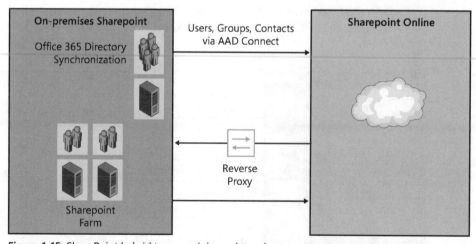

Figure 1-15 SharePoint hybrid two-way inbound topology

SharePoint hybrid provides for a somewhat homogeneous user experience; however, there are several limitations to SharePoint hybrid.

- There is no combined navigation experience between the two environments; book-marked sites and links in one environment do not appear in the other.

- Document templates, branding, and content type chaining are not shared across the two environments; they must be maintained separately.

- Although search does work across the two environments, searches are done in two stages (first one environment, then the other), and the results from each search are displayed in separate result blocks.

Please refer to Chapter 18, "SharePoint Online Hybrid," for a detailed description and walk-thru of the SharePoint hybrid configuration process.

Skype hybrid

Skype hybrid refers to a configuration in which on-premises Skype/Lync on-premises servers are connected to your Skype for Business Online environment, allowing for a split Session Initiation Protocol (SIP) domain so a single SIP address can be shared across both environments, and media connectivity is established between both environments, giving users the seamless appearance and behavior of a single configuration.

In addition, the Skype hybrid configuration enables migration of data, such as for contact lists and scheduled meetings, between the two environments.

The Skype hybrid configuration is less complex than Exchange hybrid but slightly more complex than SharePoint hybrid. As shown in Figure 1-16, it consists of connectivity between on-premises Lync edge servers and Skype for Business Online through the public Internet and requires additional configuration steps, which are explained in Chapter 16, "Deploying Skype for Business Online."

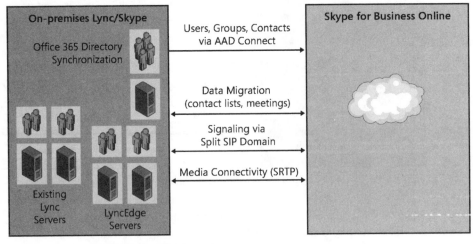

Figure 1-16 Skype for Business hybrid topology

Each of the hybrid scenarios can create additional deployment tasks when implementing Office 365. It is important to understand the benefits of each hybrid configuration and ensure that you have identified whether these scenarios are needed or wanted before beginning your Office 365 deployment, because each increases the cost of deployment as well as the project timeline.

Is your Exchange environment ready?

When beginning any Office 365 implementation that includes Exchange Online, it is important to review your on-premises Microsoft Exchange environment to ensure that you meet the minimum requirements for deployment and ascertain whether you have any configurations that might require a change in your deployment strategy or additional pre-work.

These configurations include, but are not limited to, physical Exchange server infrastructure, mail routing, spam and antivirus appliances, load balancers, proxy servers, network configurations, and firewall rules.

Physical Exchange server infrastructure

When evaluating your physical Exchange on-premises infrastructure, begin by reviewing the number of Exchange servers you have in your enterprise and each of their roles.

The Mailbox Replication Service (MRS), which is responsible for mailbox migrations to Office 365, acts as a proxy server for mailbox move requests on any existing (or additional) Exchange servers you designate during the hybrid setup.

If your user mailboxes are distributed geographically in the enterprise, but your hybrid servers, which proxy the move requests, are in another physical location across wide-area network links, you will encounter additional latency during moves and increase the possibility of timeouts or migration failures.

In some cases, depending on the distribution of mailboxes, it might be necessary to perform two-stage migrations. The first stage would migrate the mailbox over the wide area to a mailbox server closer to the hybrid MRS server, and the second stage would migrate the mailbox to Exchange Online.

Depending on the geographic difference, this approach might make the process easier, despite adding additional steps, because the net impact to the users would be mitigated. The migration, internally between servers, would enable you to move the mailbox without any user downtime, based on the way that Exchange handles MRS moves in progress. The second step, although noninvasive as well, would then be at a much lower risk for failure because the mailboxes are in the same data center or location as the hybrid server moving them to Office 365.

Mail routing

The next important physical infrastructure component is the location of any Exchange client access servers (CAS) that support mail exchange (MX) records and answer Autodiscover requests for Outlook and other email clients.

Depending on the intended mail routing and the complexity of your environment, it might be necessary to add additional endpoints for mail routing, change the location of existing public-facing endpoints, or even remove endpoints, depending on your users' locations relative to their mailboxes.

Also, it is important to note that you cannot put any additional mail transport appliances between Exchange Online and the Exchange on-premises hub or transport servers used for hybrid routing between on-premises and Office 365. Doing so strips the Exchange verbs used in message headers. If an additional mail transport is required, be prepared to install Exchange edge servers.

Mailboxes

Physical infrastructure aside, the next item to consider, which relates to both migration time and licensing, is your mailboxes. The number of mailboxes in your environment has a direct impact on the project timeline because the quantities of mailboxes and their sizes affect migration time as well as batch size limitations during migration windows.

Furthermore, you must remove any large attachments that exceed the attachment limit (150 MB when using MRS moves) from mailboxes, or the migration of the mailbox will fail. There is an option to skip large items; however, the offending messages will then be automatically removed from the mailbox during migration.

Large items

The identification of large items is typically a task that must be either assigned to your users by asking them to create Outlook views to identify large items, or done with Windows PowerShell or other utilities to create reports that then require additional action on the part of your users to remove or archive them. These tasks all require lead-time and user interaction, lengthening your migration project timeline.

Finally, when identifying mailboxes in your environment, it is recommended to sort mailboxes by type. Not only will this help with calculating the total number of licenses required—User and Shared mailboxes (over 50MB) require a license, Room and Equipment mailboxes do not—but it will help provide a better understanding of how many mailboxes of each type exist in your environment. You need this information when creating migration batches, because it is customary to move groups of users and their resource mailboxes together.

Recipient types

One additional step that should be included when reviewing mailboxes is a review of each mailbox's recipient type compared to the intended purpose of the mailbox. In past versions of Exchange, there were no Room and Equipment–type mailboxes, so it was common practice to create User mailboxes and simply delegate access differently.

Mailboxes in this state will not cause issues in on-premises Exchange; however, after they are migrated to Exchange Online, licensing requirements apply. If a mailbox that is considered a room or resource, based simply on its name or historical use, is not converted to a Room mailbox and instead remains a User mailbox, it will be deleted if it is not licensed within 30 days after that mailbox has been migrated to Office 365.

Proxy addresses and domains

Many Exchange environments evolve over time, so there are likely email domains that have either been acquired, and subsequently decommissioned, or relegated to a secondary address. There might also be domains that were purchased as part of special projects or divestiture efforts.

The migration to Office 365 requires a housecleaning of sorts to ensure that the only email domains that remain are valid and supported domains in your enterprise.

When migrating to Office 365, your users are synchronized to Azure AD, and any mail-enabled or mailbox-enabled objects (users, resources, groups) are created as mail-enabled objects in Exchange Online.

During this initial synchronization, and while the source mailbox remains in on-premises Exchange, Office 365 does not care whether the email addresses on the object are valid. In fact, many customers don't realize, until their very first pilot mailbox migrations, that they have invalid email domains configured for their users. This is because Exchange Online allows a mail-enabled user object to be created in Exchange Online because it is there simply to allow for mail flow and a complete global address list experience, with non-routable email domain suffixes in the proxy addresses array. However, the object will not be converted to a mailbox, a step that occurs during the mailbox migration, unless all the email addresses of the user are valid domains registered in Office 365.

For this reason, it is recommended that reports of all mail-enabled objects and their email addresses be generated prior to starting mailbox moves. You might find that you have a great deal of cleanup to do in Exchange before you can start migration of mailboxes.

Along with the cleanup of email addresses, it is also recommended that you review any email addressing policies (EAPs) in Exchange to ensure that older or unused domains are not still being automatically assigned to newly mail-enabled or mailbox-enabled objects in your Exchange organization.

INSIDE OUT

Other email address types

Although they will not prevent the migration of mailboxes, email addresses that begin with prefixes such as NOTES:, RFAX:, and X400: are not synchronized to Exchange Online and will not exist on mailboxes in Exchange Online.

One final note about mailboxes and migrations is that delegation of access between mailboxes does not work across the on-premises and cloud environments; so although any permissions that already existed prior to migration are retained, any new delegation can occur only if both the mailbox and the delegate exist in the same environment.

This means that when planning mailbox migration batches, it is advisable to identify any shared or delegated mailboxes within teams and departments in your organization and make sure that those mailboxes are moved to Exchange Online during the same migration batches to avoid any confusion or loss of functionality.

Public folders

The next item in your on-premises Exchange infrastructure that warrants careful review is public folders. If you have no public folders in your organization, or if you are only using public folders for free or busy data in support of older Outlook clients, you can rest easy.

If, however, you have public folders, and you require public folder data to be migrated to Office 365, you will want to learn about your options for coexistence and migration of public folder data, including mail-enabled public folders, discussed in Chapter 13.

Load balancers, network configurations, proxy servers, and firewall rules

Finally, review the network configurations related to your Exchange environment.

Server placement

The hybrid servers that support the MRS role should be located as close to the public Internet as possible, directly exposed if possible, to ensure that network connectivity, latency, or other network devices (such as stateful packet inspection applications) do not interfere with mailbox moves.

In fact, it is often recommended, based on the distribution of mailboxes as compared to hybrid servers, that you configure multiple MRS endpoints in an enterprise to enable more efficient migration of mailboxes, particularly in environments that are geographically dispersed.

Load balancers

The placement of hybrid servers supporting MRS moves behind load balancers is also an item that you should review carefully. Some load balancers might be configured to ignore or enforce sticky state as well as change header behavior, which might affect the speed at which mailbox migrations occur. Talk with your load balancer vendor and ensure that they support load-balancing Exchange hybrid servers that are used to perform MRS mailbox migrations.

Network configurations

Next, review the end-to-end network configuration of your Exchange servers relative to one another and to Active Directory. If you are adding new Exchange servers to perform hybrid roles instead of using existing Exchange servers, make sure those hybrid servers are not separated from the rest of your Exchange infrastructure, or even from Active Directory domain controller connectivity, by firewalls or network devices that might otherwise limit or block traffic.

Although it is not possible to identify every device that might cause problems in your environment simply by looking at a network map or reviewing server roles, these exercises will help you become more familiar with your environment so that you understand which configurations might require change to accomplish mailbox migrations to Exchange Online.

Proxy servers

Proxy servers, although not directly related to Exchange Online or Office 365 roles, are equally important. Before any mailboxes can be migrated to Exchange Online, your tenant directory must be fully populated by the directory synchronization tool.

Proxy servers, particularly authenticated proxies, cause issues with the synchronization of identities to your tenant. Authenticated proxies are not supported for use with the Azure AD Connect synchronization tool and should therefore either bypass the proxy configurations or change them to use non-authenticated proxy servers.

TROUBLESHOOTING

Mailbox moves in your network

If your network configuration is complex, or if you are unsure of whether any network devices or their configurations might cause issues, be prepared to deploy at least one hybrid server with a direct network address translation (NAT) from the Internet through your firewall for testing purposes.

Presenting a hybrid server directly to the Internet enables you to prove or disprove that network configurations are affecting either connectivity or mailbox migration performance issues.

As you can see from these lists, a large number of items should be carefully reviewed when discussing the placement of infrastructure in your organization that will be used for mailbox migrations.

In some cases, your environment can support migration to Office 365 with minimal effort. However, if your environment does require changes to network routing, firewall, or load balancers, or even the deployment of new servers, include these activities in the project timeline. They will increase migration time and possibly drive the need for upgrades to other supporting technologies.

INSIDE OUT

Planning your deployment

Plan time in your deployment schedule to review network and server configuration items with the appropriate teams in your organization and get them involved in Office 365 planning meetings early.

The best way to ensure success is to involve everyone responsible for your infrastructure.

Is your directory ready?

After you have had an opportunity to review your Exchange infrastructure, you must perform similar activities in your on-premises Active Directory environment.

Your Active Directory environment affects not only Exchange but all the services available in Office 365 because, in most environments, your Active Directory identities are synchronized to Azure and form the foundation of all Office 365 use cases.

User readiness

Unless your users are all cloud users, explained in more detail in Chapter 3, "Federation Services and Authentication," you must synchronize your Active Directory to Azure so that your users can log on to Azure to consume Office 365 services.

When synchronizing your users to Azure, many of the attribute values must be unique and meet certain requirements before they synchronize successfully. Many times, invalid character values in key attributes, or duplication of values between users that must be unique, create synchronization errors that must be resolved before the object will exist in Azure.

INSIDE OUT

Checking your directory

Microsoft provides a free tool, called IDFix (*http://aka.ms/idfix*), that can be run against your on-premises environment and generate a report of all known error conditions present in your directory.

The IDFix tool is not multi-forest-aware, so you must run it against each Active Directory forest and combine the results to provide a complete list of remediation activities.

UserPrincipalName

Because the UserPrincipalName attribute in Active Directory is primarily used for the user logon name in Office 365, it must meet several requirements before it can synchronize to Azure.

- The value must be unique in your environment. Two users cannot share the same UserPrincipalName value if this attribute is configured as your logon name, even in multi-forest scenarios.

- The value must not contain any spaces.

- The value must not contain any special characters.

- The value must be in the format of *prefix@suffix.xyz*. Failure to create a UserPrincipalName value in this format prevents a user from synchronizing properly to Office 365.

- A routable email domain suffix (the portion after the @ symbol) must be used.

- The UserPrincipalName cannot begin with the @ symbol.

- The UserPrincipalName cannot end with a period (.), an ampersand (&), a space, or the @ symbol.

- The value must not exceed 79 characters, 30 characters on the left side of the @ symbol and 48 characters on the right side.

- The ampersand (&) character, when present in the value, is replaced by an underscore (_).

INSIDE OUT

UserPrincipalName in older applications

Many times, organizations are required to make changes to some or all UserPrincipal-Name values in on-premises Active Directory to comply with Office 365 requirements for synchronization.

You should ensure that no older applications in your environment use the UserPrincipal-Name value before changing any values.

MailNickname

The MailNickname attribute, much like the UserPrincipalName attribute, must also meet several requirements.

- The value must not exceed 64 characters.

- The value cannot contain a space.

- The value cannot contain special characters.

- The value must be unique in each on-premises Exchange organization.

It is important to note that Exchange manages the MailNickname value. If Exchange is the only mechanism allowed to create or modify the MailNickname value, the value will never violate any of the previously mentioned conditions. If, however, Windows PowerShell scripts or third-party applications set the value programmatically, review the values to ensure uniqueness.

In a multi-forest environment in which more than one Exchange organization exists, it is necessary to compare the two environments programmatically. Neither the IDFix application nor Exchange can evaluate both environments when searching for uniqueness across them.

SamAccountName

The SamAccountName attribute in Active Directory is as important as the UserPrincipalName attribute and therefore must also meet several requirements for a user to be synchronized to Azure.

- The value must not exceed 20 characters.

- The value cannot contain any special characters.

- If the SamAccountName value is invalid, but UserPrincipalName is properly formatted, the user account will successfully synchronize to Azure.

- If both the SamAccountName and UserPrincipalName values are invalid, the user account will not synchronize.

Invalid characters

In each of the preceding lists, unless specified otherwise, invalid characters include the following.

- { and } (curly brackets)

- (and) (parentheses)

- [and] (square brackets)

- < and > (angle brackets)

- \ and / (left or right slash)

- Comma (,)

- Apostrophe (')

- Equals sign (=)

- Pound or hashtag (#)

- Ampersand (&)

- Dollar ($)

- Percentile (%)

- Asterisk (*)

Forests and domains

When evaluating your Active Directory, take care to review all Active Directory forests as well as any subdomains within each. This is particularly important because it could reduce the total number of objects that you must synchronize to Azure and possibly the synchronization server configuration by reducing the number of objects in the database and potential rules applied to those objects.

The Azure AD Connect synchronization engine can be configured during the installation process and afterward, so that only specific forests, domains, and their organizational units (OUs) are synced to Azure. Understanding your directory structure, where objects are within it, and what types of objects are synchronized to Azure enables you to prepare your environment better for synchronization to Office 365.

Forests

In some environments, it might be necessary to synchronize one or more Active Directory forests to your Office 365 tenant, perhaps because you have users in several forests or because you have a split resource model, and mailboxes exist in one forest, but the users exist in another.

In either case, it is not only important to review objects and their attributes to ensure uniqueness, it is also important to understand whether some or even all domains in the forest must be synchronized.

If you have a forest with multiple subdomains, review each domain. In some cases, an empty forest root domain contains either no objects or only administrative objects or accounts. Unless these accounts should be synchronized to Azure, the forest root can be removed from the scope of the synchronization.

Similarly, when reviewing each forest, ensure that the forest contains users, groups, contacts, or devices that should be synchronized to Office 365. If the domain lacks any of these required object types, cancel the selection of the domain during the installation of the sync tool.

Domains

Finally, when reviewing domains and OUs in your directory, note the locations of the user, group, contact, and devices. In some organizational unit hierarchies, depending on how your Active Directory was architected, you might find that all users, groups, contacts, and devices exist in OUs specifically designed for each object type.

In cases like this, you can minimize the scope of synchronization simply by selecting the OUs containing only these objects and canceling the selection of all others, as Figure 1-17 shows.

If, however, your OUs are separated either geographically or by business unit, team, or function, you might find that you need to select organizational units in which objects of all types are kept together and might contain things like servers and computers (which do not synchronize to Azure) but need to be read and evaluated by the synchronization engine, as shown in Figure 1-18.

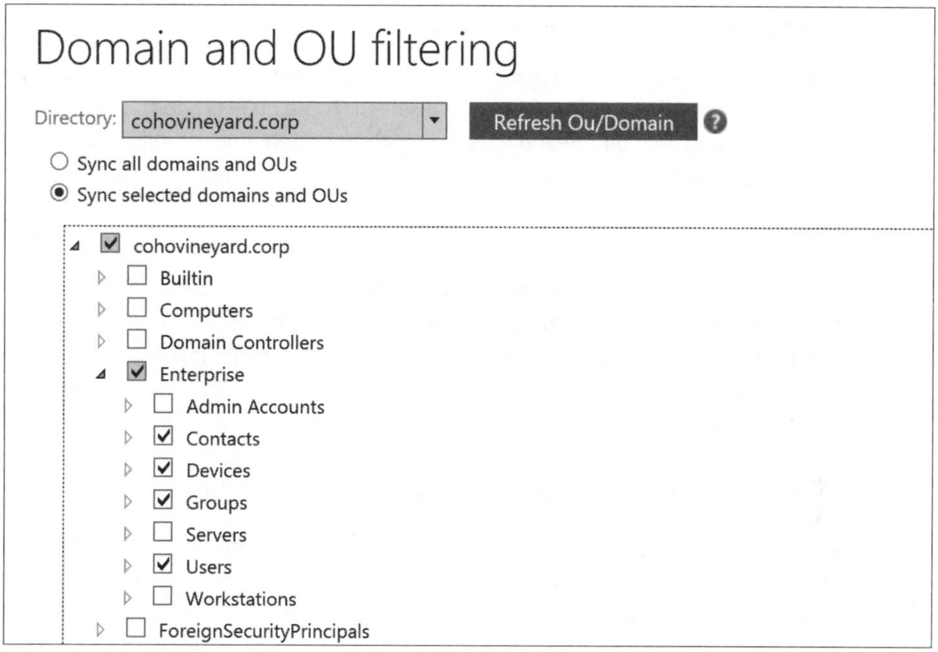

Domain and OU filtering

Directory: cohovineyard.corp [▼]   Refresh Ou/Domain ❓

- ○ Sync all domains and OUs
- ◉ Sync selected domains and OUs

▲ ☑ cohovineyard.corp
    ▷ ☐ Builtin
    ▷ ☐ Computers
    ▷ ☐ Domain Controllers
    ▲ ☑ Enterprise
        ▷ ☐ Admin Accounts
        ▷ ☑ Contacts
        ▷ ☑ Devices
        ▷ ☑ Groups
        ▷ ☐ Servers
        ▷ ☑ Users
        ▷ ☐ Workstations
    ▷ ☐ ForeignSecurityPrincipals

Figure 1-17 Selectively choosing OUs that contain desired object types

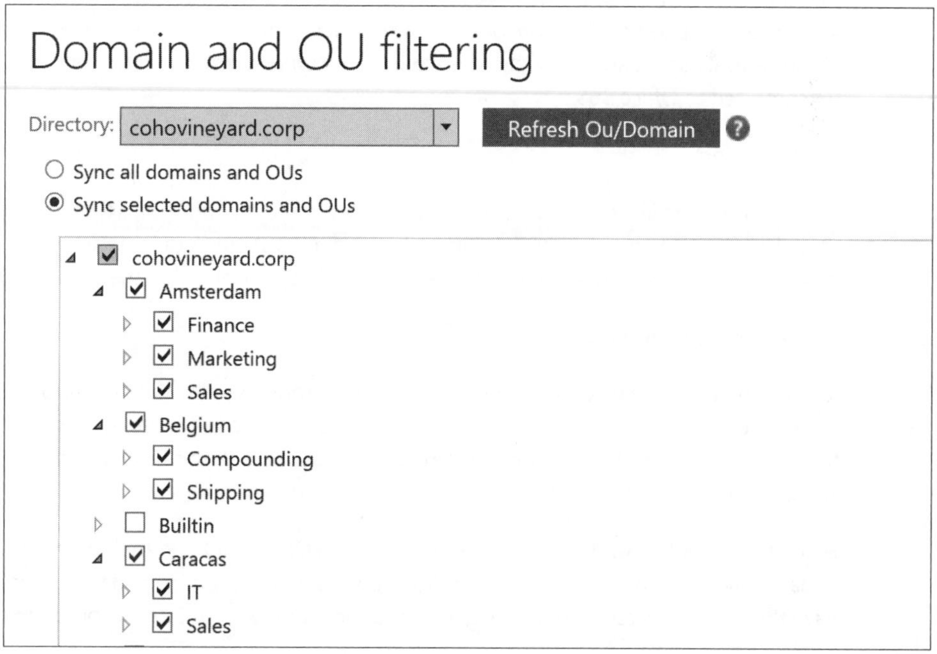

Domain and OU filtering

Directory: cohovineyard.corp [▼]   Refresh Ou/Domain ❓

- ○ Sync all domains and OUs
- ◉ Sync selected domains and OUs

▲ ☑ cohovineyard.corp
    ▲ ☑ Amsterdam
        ▷ ☑ Finance
        ▷ ☑ Marketing
        ▷ ☑ Sales
    ▲ ☑ Belgium
        ▷ ☑ Compounding
        ▷ ☑ Shipping
    ▷ ☐ Builtin
    ▲ ☑ Caracas
        ▷ ☑ IT
        ▷ ☑ Sales

Figure 1-18 Choosing OUs organized by location or function that contain all object types

Stale or disabled users and empty groups

Another area that should be reviewed prior to synchronization to Azure is groups and user accounts that might be stale, unused, or disabled. These objects add to the total object count synchronized to your tenant and increase synchronization time as well as overall clutter in your Office 365 tenant.

Stale users

Stale users are defined as unused user accounts that are still valid in Active Directory for an extended period without a current last logon attempt. Depending on your company's require-ments or legal requirements based on your industry, you might need to retain user accounts for departed users for an extended period; however, few companies review the last logon date for all user accounts and quarantine or review accounts that are out of date. At best, these accounts represent unnecessary data and, at worst, a security risk. It is therefore recommended that you identify stale accounts prior to starting synchronization to Office 365.

Although synchronization of user accounts does not automatically consume licenses, if there are accounts that have not been used in long periods (90 to 180 days), it is recommended that they not be synchronized to your Office 365 tenant to minimize risk to security. If known stale accounts are synchronized to Office 365, take care not to delegate any administrative privilege to those accounts.

Understandably, some users on leave might require their accounts to remain active; however, if an account is pending deletion, or is simply in a held state, it is recommended to move these accounts to OUs that are not within the scope of the synchronization solution and therefore not synchronized to Office 365.

Disabled users

Disabled users are like stale users, except that they are security principals that are known to be invalid and should not be used. Therefore, disabled users should not be synchronized to Office 365. Like stale users, they should be moved to OUs that are not within the scope of the sync.

Unused or empty groups

It is recommended that you review your company's groups, security and distribution alike, prior to synchronization to Office 365. Although unused groups do not represent a security threat, they do increase the object count synchronized to your tenant; this results in longer synchroni-zation times as well as a larger synchronization server database.

Evaluate distribution groups to ensure that they are still relevant and their membership is up to date. One of the best methods for auditing and evaluating groups and their validity is to have their owners recertify both the group and the membership. Often, groups are created, especially if users can create their own groups, and then forgotten when the project or event has ended. Requiring recertification of distribution groups is a great way to keep groups and their membership current and accurate.

Unused groups, when referring to security groups, means that the resource to which the group was delegated access is no longer valid. Security groups, like distribution groups, should be recertified and maintained regularly.

INSIDE OUT

Unused security groups

Unused distribution and security groups add to the object counts, synchronization database size, synchronization size, and overall clutter in your tenant.

More important, however, is that unused security groups also mean that the Kerberos token size for your users is unnecessarily large, because each security group membership counts toward the Kerberos token for a user, and excessively large Kerberos tokens can cause other access issues.

Are your users ready?

Whereas most of this chapter has been focused on the major deployment milestones and technical preparation of things like Exchange servers, network devices, firewalls, servers, and Active Directory, one of the most important steps in the move to Office 365 is user readiness—not only the user's workstation and Office software but the users themselves.

A successful implementation of Office 365 includes user communication and setting clear expectations of the process, timing, and even the possible issues that might occur. It is important for your users to understand how the process works, how their logons might change, what types of problems to expect, and when each step in the process is happening.

Although these might all sound like common activities, some customers have overlooked the value of this level of detail and experienced a deployment that was longer than originally planned.

UPN versus email address

Typically, users are accustomed to logging on to their workstation by using the standard domain\user name format, shown in Figure 1-19.

CHAPTER 1

Figure 1-19 Sign-in using the domain name\user name format

Office 365 sign-in prompts are very similar; however, instead of expecting the Active Directory domain and the user's SamAccountName shown in the preceding figure, they expect the user's UserPrincipalName, as shown in Figure 1-20.

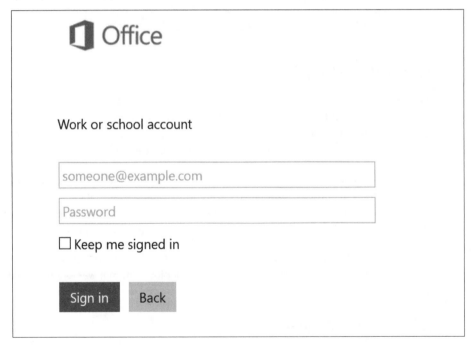

Figure 1-20 Sign-in using the UserPrincipalName format of *someone@example.com*

The UserPrincipalName value, despite being formatted like the user's email address, is a separate attribute altogether and therefore might be confusing to your users if your environment is configured to use AltId (covered in more detail in Chapter 3) or if your users have multiple email addresses that they use frequently for email communication.

It is therefore important to educate your users about the UserPrincipalName value in how it is the same as or different from their primary email address. They should also be instructed to use the UserPrincipalName whenever they are prompted for credentials, especially after you have deployed Office Pro Plus and started sharing OneDrive and SharePoint content.

Multi-forest environments

Frequently, organizations with a complex architecture that consists of more than one Active Directory forest choose to use the migration to Office 365 as an opportunity to consolidate their directories. The migration of mailboxes to Office 365 enables the elimination of on-premises Exchange infrastructure; in a multi-forest scenario where Exchange is separated from user accounts in a resource forest, you might also need to migrate user workstations as the resource forest is decommissioned.

If user workstations are migrated between forests during an Office 365 migration, it is important to communicate to your users that they might need to change the account they use to log on to their workstation, and they might receive additional logon prompts when launching Outlook.

Office versions

Depending on the version of Office installed on your users' workstations, you might have to upgrade to a newer version before the client can successfully connect to Office 365 because of the way Outlook authenticates to the Exchange Online environment.

In versions prior to the Outlook 2010 SP2 April 15, 2014, update, the client used an authentication method that is not compatible with Exchange Online. It is therefore imperative for your users to be running the most current version of Outlook possible, and if they are running Outlook 2010, it must be SP2 with the April 15, 2014, update.

One option to help with this issue is to enable Office Pro Plus licenses for your users prior to beginning migration of any Office 365 workloads and instructing your users to use their Office 365 logon to log on to the service and download the latest version of the Office products, including Outlook, prior to any mailbox migrations.

This approach enables you to acclimatize your users to the Office 365 portal experience as well as ensure that their mailbox migration does not encounter client issues that might make the experience lengthy or unpleasant.

Updating

One common problem when migrating users to Office 365, if they cannot upgrade to the latest version of Outlook, is confirming that the latest Microsoft operating system updates (including Office updates) have been applied.

Updating workstations is strongly recommended for many reasons, security included; and it is recommended that the updates be tested, approved, and deployed far in advance of the first mailbox moves.

Delegation is the primary reason that you want to make sure Outlook updates are in place before *any* mailboxes move. If a user migrates to Exchange Online, but their delegate does not, and the delegate does not have a compliant version of Outlook or the latest updates, the migrated mailbox will be inaccessible while the delegate's mailbox remains on-premises.

INSIDE OUT

Updates

When using automated updating mechanisms such as the Windows Software Update Service (WSUS), make sure that the necessary updates are approved.

Frequently, administrators claim that all updates have been applied; however, they are referring to the approved updates and not necessarily all updates.

When managing updates, ensure that any Office or Outlook updates are included in the approval process.

Mailbox cleanup

Earlier, this chapter discussed large items and their impact on mail migrations and the likelihood of data loss if they are not addressed. Another item that you can communicate to your users in advance of mailbox migrations is the identification and remediation of large items.

Ask your users to sort their mailbox, including subfolders and archives, and identify all messages with large attachments. Outlook folders can easily be sorted using message size by selecting the Size column in Outlook, as shown in Figure 1-21.

CHAPTER 1

! ⬚ ⬚ ⬚ FROM	SUBJECT	RECEIVED	SIZE ▼
▲ Size: Very Large (5 MB - 10 MB)			
🗎 Chris Ashton	Winery and Vineyard schedules for FY17	Fri 6/30/2017 1:32 PM	6 MB
▲ Size: Large (1 - 5 MB)			
🗎 Chris Ashton	Miscellaneous Documentation	Fri 6/30/2017 1:38 PM	3 MB
🗎 Chris Ashton	Misc schedule	Fri 6/30/2017 1:36 PM	2 MB
▲ Size: Medium (25 KB - 1 MB)			
🗎 Chris Ashton	Latest delivery schedules	Fri 6/30/2017 1:32 PM	179 KB
🗎 Chris Ashton	Roster	Fri 6/30/2017 1:37 PM	139 KB
🗎 Chris Ashton	Vineyard Event Flyer	Fri 6/30/2017 1:39 PM	118 KB
▲ Size: Small (10 - 25 KB)			
🗎 Chris Ashton	Winery event flyer	Fri 6/30/2017 1:38 PM	21 KB
Chris Ashton	Please clean out the break room before EOD - Holiday Weekend	Fri 6/30/2017 1:30 PM	18 KB
Chris Ashton	Team outing this weekend - late notice!	Fri 6/30/2017 1:29 PM	18 KB
Chris Ashton	Tired of getting emails from me yet?	Fri 6/30/2017 1:39 PM	17 KB
Chris Ashton	Welcome to the team	Fri 6/30/2017 1:29 PM	17 KB
Chris Ashton	Cafe closures next week	Fri 6/30/2017 1:30 PM	17 KB

Figure 1-21 Outlook Inbox sorted by message size

After the mailbox has been sorted, users can delete any large items they do not wish to keep in their mailbox. Alternatively, it is possible to right-click an email containing a large attachment, choose the attachment, and select Remove Attachment. As shown in Figure 1-22, the user is then prompted to remove the item. After removing the attachment, they are prompted to save the update to the email.

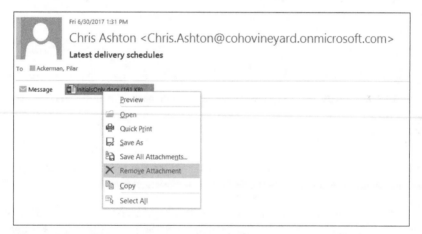

Figure 1-22 Removing an attachment from an Outlook email

Removing any large attachments but leaving the email intact enables your users to maintain their email history without adding excessive bloat to their mailbox. In fact, if your users are licensed for SharePoint Online, they could then save the attachments to a SharePoint team site (or OneDrive) before the emails are removed from the mailbox so the attachment is not lost.

Scheduling

If your Exchange environment is version 2010 or later and you have Exchange Hybrid mode set up to allow MRS mailbox moves, your users can continue to work while their mail is migrated. In fact, if mailbox migration batches are configured in Suspend When Ready To Complete (SWRC) mode, mailbox data migration might occur over several days, with a final cutover of the mailbox to Office 365 after hours or over a weekend.

The MRS mailbox move process enables you to move user mailboxes in large batches during the business day without any impact on your users, with the final cutover step happening at a more convenient time for your administrators. When the final cutover step occurs, your users receive a pop-up dialog box in Outlook, shown in Figure 1-23, prompting them to close and reopen Outlook. This is the only impact on your users as part of the migration process.

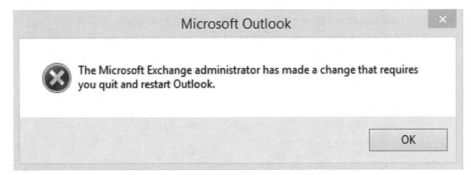

Figure 1-23 Pop-up dialog box received when Office 365 mailbox migration has completed

The global address list

After your users have migrated to Office 365, one of the first things that might look different to them is the global address list (GAL).

While their mailbox was on-premises, the global address list consisted of all mail-enabled user, group, resource, and contact objects present in Active Directory. After a user has been migrated to Office 365, however, their global address list comprises all mail-enabled user, group, resource, and contact objects present in Azure.

As part of the initial configuration of your Office 365 tenant, you implement directory synchronization, which is discussed in detail in later chapters; however, it is important to understand that decisions made during the synchronization tool implementation have a direct impact on the contents of the global address list. Failure to include the correct OUs from Active Directory, or the manual creation of cloud-based users, groups, and contacts, results in either too few or too many objects in your Exchange Online GAL.

It is therefore strongly recommended that you create pilot groups for mailbox migrations so that users can review the Exchange Online GAL and provide feedback about it when compared with the on-premises GAL before you start moving your users in bulk to Office 365.

Replying to old emails

After your users' mailboxes have been migrated to Office 365, and the global address list has been confirmed to be accurate, the appearance and behavior of the Exchange Online experience should be identical to that of the on-premises Exchange experience. In fact, some customers have actually reported that their users had no idea they had been migrated to Office 365 because the experience was identical.

One of the most common issues following migration to Office 365 is the occasional receipt of non-delivery errors when replying to some old emails or calendar appointments. Although this does not happen frequently, it can become quite an annoyance for users who do experience the issue.

This typically occurs because an x500 address is missing from the proxy addresses list for the correct recipient in Exchange Online. The x500 address, which should contain the LegacyExchangeDN value of the mailbox that should receive the email, is absent, and Exchange Online is unable to deliver the message, as shown in Figure 1-24.

From: Microsoft Outlook
Sent: Friday, April 30, 2017 8:54 AM
To: Ackerman, Pilar
Subject: Undeliverable: Vineyard renovations in FY18

Delivery has failed to these recipients or groups:

Ashton, Chris
The e-mail address you entered couldn't be found. Please check the recipient's e-mail address and try to resend the message. If the problem continues, please contact your helpdesk.

Diagnostic information for administrators:

Generating server: SATLADMDLHT510.mail.edge.coho.corp

IMCEAEX-_O=COHO_OU=North+20America_cn=W2K+20Users_cn=chris.ashton@cohovineyard.us
#550 5.1.1 RESOLVER.ADR.ExRecipNotFound; not found ##

Figure 1-24 A non-delivery report that includes the IMCEAEX error

The Synchronization process typically handles synchronization of LegacyExchangeDN values from on-premises Active Directory for all mail-enabled objects to Azure AD. Sometimes, however, there are issues with missing LegacyExchangeDN values because of direct manipulation of the attribute. In those cases, the easiest way to resolve any non-delivery report (NDR) issues related to LegacyExchangeDN is to populate the on-premises object with the missing x500 address and allow it to synchronize to Office 365 automatically. Subsequent emails then deliver successfully.

TROUBLESHOOTING

IMCEAEX non-delivery reports

You can find the process for converting the IMCEAEX non-delivery report address to an x500 address at *https://aka.ms/imceaex*.

Syncing your users and moving services

After you have successfully reviewed your infrastructure and identified any upgrades, new servers, or configuration changes, you are almost ready to start synchronizing your users and moving your services to Office 365.

There might still be a long road ahead, especially if you are planning to implement any hybrid configurations in Exchange, SharePoint, or Skype; however, the insights provided in this chapter should give you sufficient information to get started with each of those tasks. In addition, each of the major milestone activities (synchronization, hybrid, and mailbox migrations) is described in later chapters in great detail.

For the moment, however, read on. You've learned about preparing for Office 365 migration; now it's time to learn the deployment and configuration processes.

CHAPTER 2

Preparing your environment for the cloud

The previous chapter outlined each of the high-level tasks involved in an Office 365 deployment; in this chapter, you use your understanding of those tasks to start the setup of your Office 365 subscription, assign administrators, configure your network, fix up your directory, update and install client software, and start synchronizing your users to your tenant. After these tasks are complete, you can start using your Office 365 subscription and migrating your users.

Setting up your subscription

If you have not already set up your Office 365 subscription, this is the best place to start. As discussed in Chapter 1, "Office 365 Deployment Milestones," the tenant name that you select becomes permanent and branded across your subscription, so choose carefully.

Follow these steps to sign up for either a trial or paid subscription for Office 365.

1. Navigate to *https://products.office.com*.

2. Select the Office 365 plan you wish to use, either Personal or Business. When selecting Business, you can select Enterprise plans as well.

3. Select either Free Trial or Buy Now to start your Office 365 tenant creation.

4. Type a user name and tenant name when prompted to create your user ID, as shown in Figure 2-1.

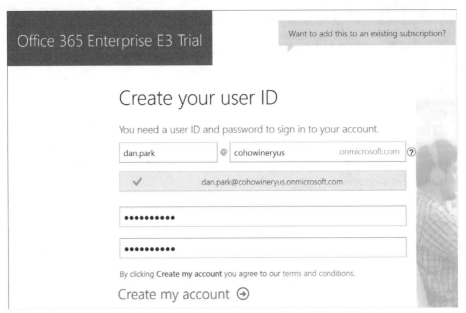

Figure 2-1 Signup for an Office subscription and selection of a user and tenant name

5. Select Create My Account to continue.

6. If you are prompted to enter captcha information, provide the necessary detail and click either Call Me or Text Me, as shown in Figure 2-2.

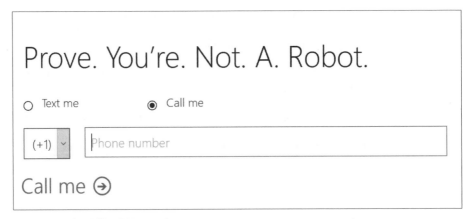

Figure 2-2 The Office 365 captcha page

7. Record your User ID when the confirmation process is complete and click You're Ready To Go.

After you have set up your new Office 365 tenant, the Office 365 portal opens, shown in Figure 2-3, where you can begin creating users, editing organizational information, and assigning licenses.

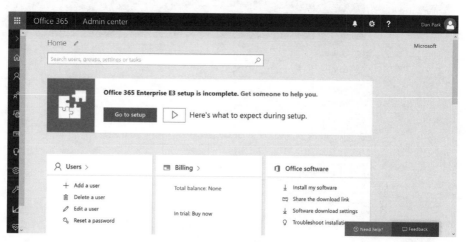

Figure 2-3 The Office 365 portal page for a newly created tenant

Assigning administrators

Using the information you learned in Chapter 1, you can either begin creating cloud accounts and delegating administrative privileges, or you can wait until you've started synchronizing your users, discussed later in this chapter, and assign permissions.

In either case, you must delegate permissions to one or more additional administrators. Keep in mind that the Global Administrator role has the rights to create other global administrators, so limit administrative delegation to one of the other administrative roles discussed in Chapter 1 and avoid creating other global administrator accounts unless necessary.

Follow these steps to create a new administrative account with User administration privileges.

1. Select Add A User from the Home page or Users view, as shown in Figure 2-4.

Figure 2-4 The Active Users view in the Office 365 portal

2. Type the necessary first name, last name, display name, and user name in the boxes provided, as shown in Figure 2-5.

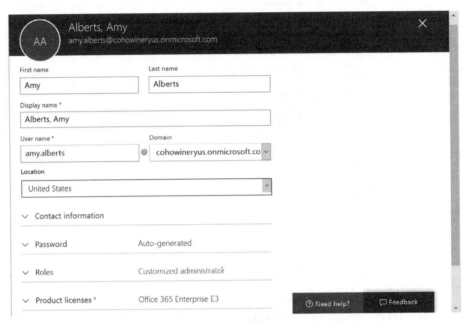

Figure 2-5 Creating a cloud user with administrative privilege

3. When creating the account, select the Roles drop-down menu, select Customized Administrator, and select the User Management Administrator check box, as shown in Figure 2-6.

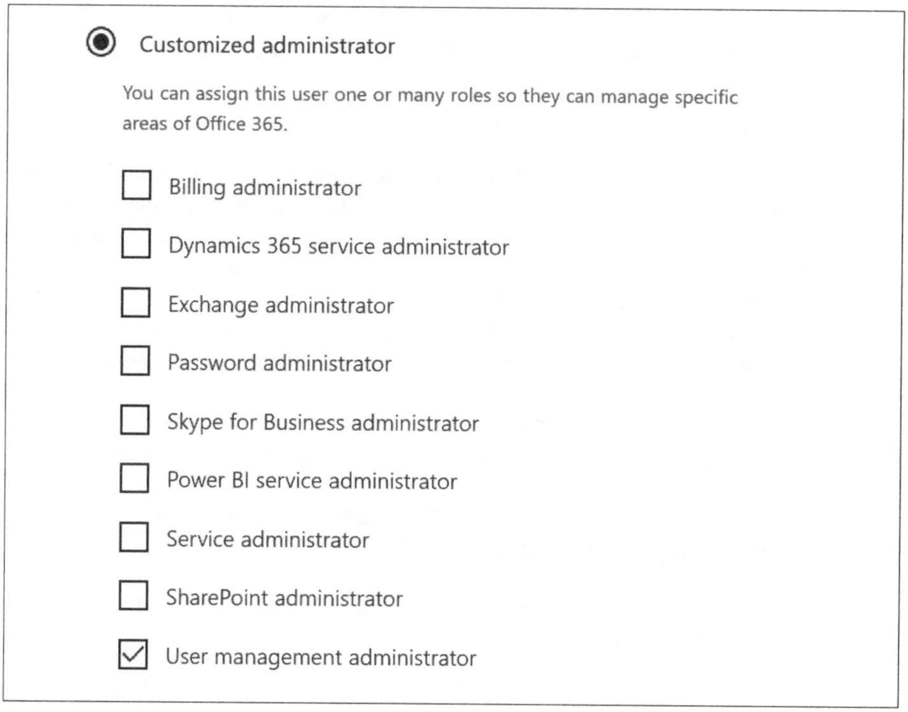

Figure 2-6 Selecting an administrator role for an Office 365 User account

4. Click Add to create the cloud user account.

You can use this process to modify existing cloud accounts, or even accounts that have been synchronized from on-premises Active Directory, by using the Azure AD Connect (AAD Connect) synchronization tool.

When you have completed the creation of any administrator accounts in your new tenant, you can move on to creating DNS records to verify your domains as well as any other services that you wish to add.

Configuring DNS, firewalls, and proxy servers

As discussed in Chapter 1, several network devices could affect your Office 365 deployment, connectivity, and continued success with the services provided. It is therefore strongly recommended that all network devices be updated to their latest versions, and you should contact each device vendor to ensure that your device supports Office 365 connectivity.

Often, it is merely a matter of upgrading your existing devices to support Office 365. This upgrade process, however, can be both time consuming and dangerous if not done correctly.

CHAPTER 2

Therefore, it is strongly recommended that any infrastructure changes required to support Office 365 be made in advance of starting your Office 365 deployment.

Public DNS records

The first configuration change you need to make is to your public DNS records; these changes enable you to verify any domain names and configure the necessary DNS records for Mail Exchanger (MX), Exchange Autodiscover, Skype for Business, and so on.

If your public DNS infrastructure is managed internally and hosted on Microsoft Windows Server through the Domain Name System role or another network appliance, the following network changes must be made manually by an authorized administrator.

If GoDaddy or another public entity hosts your public DNS, however, you can use the Office 365 portal configuration process to make the changes for you automatically.

To use the automated Office 365 portal configuration process for domain name verification, perform the following steps.

1. Click the Go To Setup button on the Office 365 Admin Center home page, shown in Figure 2-7.

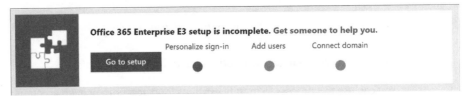

Figure 2-7 Starting the Office 365 Enterprise E3 setup process in the Office 365 portal

2. Click the Get Started button under Set Up Mail, shown in Figure 2-8.

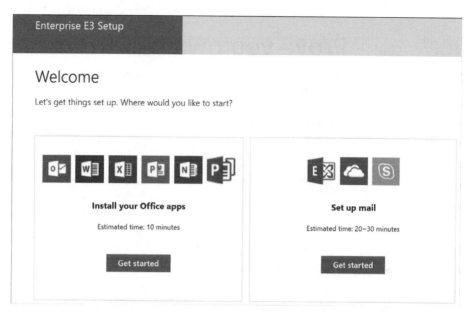

Figure 2-8 Starting the setup process by using the Office 365 Admin Center

3. Select Connect A Domain You Already Own and type the domain name in the box provided, as shown in Figure 2-9.

Figure 2-9 Selecting a domain you already own for sign-in and email personalization

4. Click Next to verify that the domain is a valid, registered domain name on the Internet.

5. Select Sign In To GoDaddy to log on to GoDaddy to prove domain ownership, as shown in Figure 2-10.

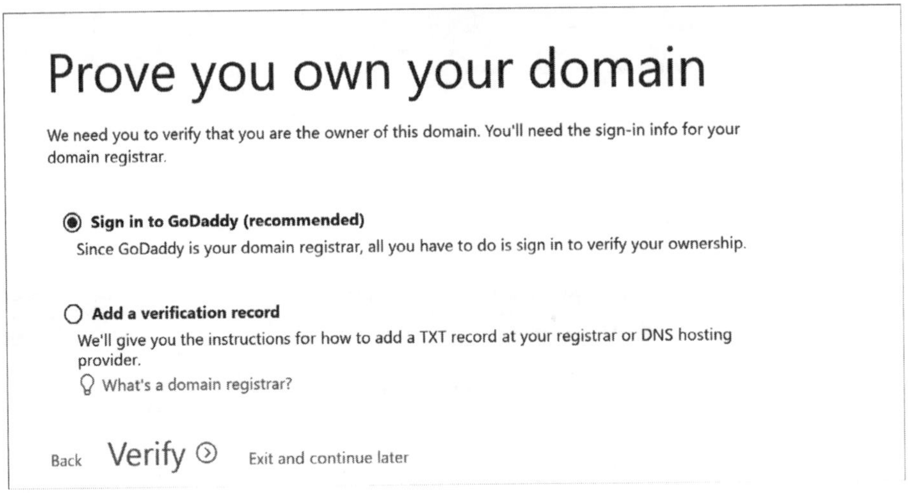

Prove you own your domain

We need you to verify that you are the owner of this domain. You'll need the sign-in info for your domain registrar.

◉ **Sign in to GoDaddy (recommended)**
Since GoDaddy is your domain registrar, all you have to do is sign in to verify your ownership.

○ **Add a verification record**
We'll give you the instructions for how to add a TXT record at your registrar or DNS hosting provider.
♡ What's a domain registrar?

Back   Verify ⊙   Exit and continue later

Figure 2-10 Proving you own your domain

6. (Optional) If your public domain registrar is not GoDaddy, or if you manage your DNS internally, select Add A Verification Record instead to be presented with the TXT record that must be manually added to DNS to verify domain ownership.

7. Click Verify.

8. Enter the account information for your GoDaddy account, as shown in Figure 2-11.

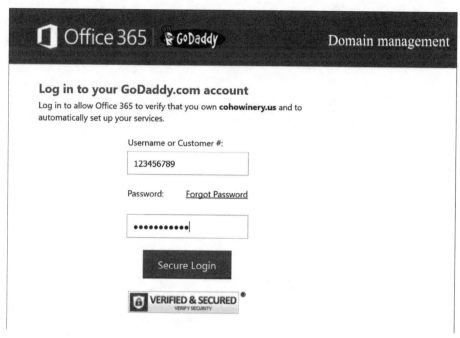

Figure 2-11 Log on to the GoDaddy logon page

9. Click Accept to confirm access.

When the sign-in verification process completes, the setup process automatically creates a TXT record in the domain DNS configuration, as shown in Figure 2-12.

Records

Last updated 7/4/2017 1:26 PM

Type	Name	Value	TTL	
A	@	50.63.202.58	600 seconds	✎
CNAME	ftp	@	1 Hour	✎
CNAME	www	@	1 Hour	✎
CNAME	_domainconnect	_domainconnect.gd.domaincontrol.com	1 Hour	✎
TXT	@	v=verifydomain MS=5083108	1 Hour	✎
NS	@	ns05.domaincontrol.com	1 Hour	
NS	@	ns06.domaincontrol.com	1 Hour	

Figure 2-12 GoDaddy DNS configuration, including verification TXT record for Office 365 domain ownership

10. Click Next to skip the addition of new user accounts.

11. Select Don't Migrate Email Messages, shown in Figure 2-13, and click Next.

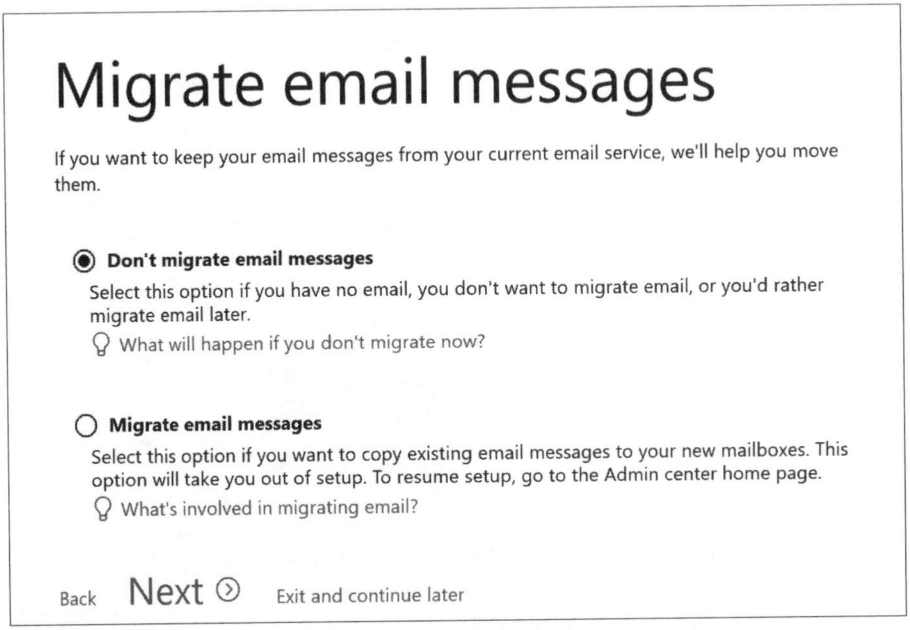

Migrate email messages

If you want to keep your email messages from your current email service, we'll help you move them.

◉ **Don't migrate email messages**

Select this option if you have no email, you don't want to migrate email, or you'd rather migrate email later.

♀ What will happen if you don't migrate now?

○ **Migrate email messages**

Select this option if you want to copy existing email messages to your new mailboxes. This option will take you out of setup. To resume setup, go to the Admin center home page.

♀ What's involved in migrating email?

Back   Next ⊘   Exit and continue later

Figure 2-13 Migrate Email Messages page that appears during the Office 365 automated setup process

12. On the Connect Your Domain page, select Add Records For Me, as shown in Figure 2-14, and click Next.

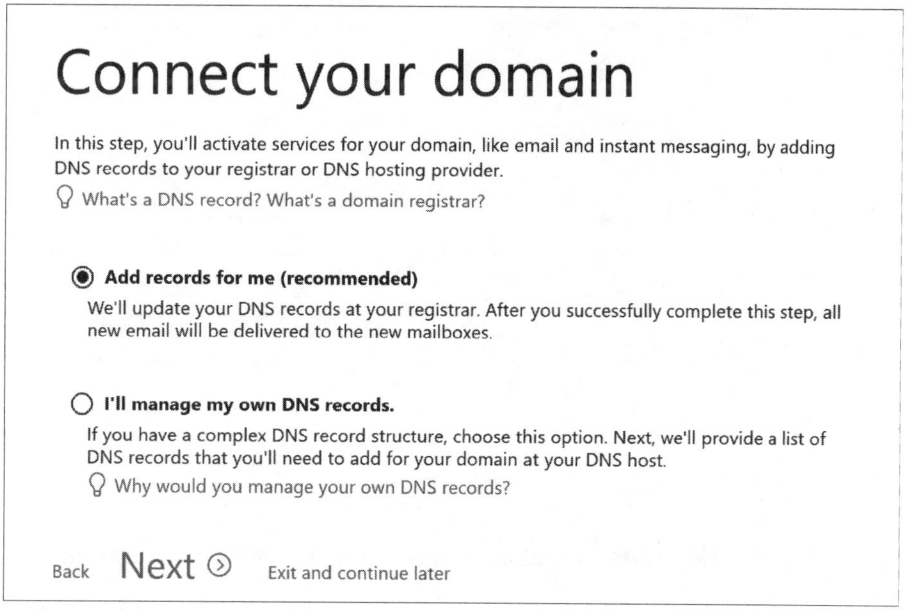

Connect your domain

In this step, you'll activate services for your domain, like email and instant messaging, by adding DNS records to your registrar or DNS hosting provider.

💡 What's a DNS record? What's a domain registrar?

🔘 **Add records for me (recommended)**

We'll update your DNS records at your registrar. After you successfully complete this step, all new email will be delivered to the new mailboxes.

⭕ **I'll manage my own DNS records.**

If you have a complex DNS record structure, choose this option. Next, we'll provide a list of DNS records that you'll need to add for your domain at your DNS host.

💡 Why would you manage your own DNS records?

Back   Next ⊙   Exit and continue later

Figure 2-14 Automatically adding DNS records for Office 365 services

CHAPTER 2

13. (Optional) If your public domain registrar is not GoDaddy, or if you manage your DNS internally, select I'll Manage My Own DNS Records to be presented with the list of records that you must manually update.

When the update process has completed, the DNS for your domain is updated to include Exchange Autodiscover, SIP, MX, and CNAME records, shown in Figure 2-15.

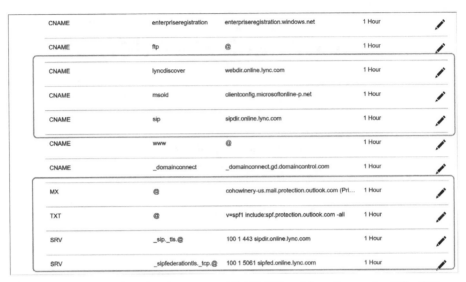

CNAME	enterpriseregistration	enterpriseregistration.windows.net	1 Hour	✏
CNAME	ftp	@	1 Hour	✏
CNAME	lyncdiscover	webdir.online.lync.com	1 Hour	✏
CNAME	msoid	clientconfig.microsoftonline-p.net	1 Hour	✏
CNAME	sip	sipdir.online.lync.com	1 Hour	✏
CNAME	www	@	1 Hour	✏
CNAME	_domainconnect	_domainconnect.gd.domaincontrol.com	1 Hour	✏
MX	@	cohowinery-us.mail.protection.outlook.com (Pri...	1 Hour	✏
TXT	@	v=spf1 include:spf.protection.outlook.com -all	1 Hour	✏
SRV	_sip._tls.@	100 1 443 sipdir.online.lync.com	1 Hour	✏
SRV	_sipfederationtls._tcp.@	100 1 5061 sipfed.online.lync.com	1 Hour	✏

Figure 2-15 DNS records updated to support SIP, MX, SPF, and Autodiscover for Office 365

Following the final step of the automated setup, shown in Figure 2-16, you are notified that setup is complete.

14. Click Go To The Admin Center to return to your Office 365 portal home page.

Figure 2-16 Completing the Office 365 Admin Center automated Office 365 setup

After you have completed the setup process, your domain is automatically registered in Office 365, and its name can be used as the domain suffix for the UserPrincipalName for user logon as well as for Exchange Online mail routing.

In addition, the Exchange Autodiscover, Sender Policy Framework (SPF), and required Server Resource (SRV) records now exist in your Office 365 tenant; these enable Microsoft Outlook and mobile client connectivity to your tenant as well as Skype client connectivity, and enable you to start sending and receiving email directly to your tenant or communicating using Instant Message (IM) and Voice Over IP (VOIP) communications through Skype for Business.

It is important to note that if your existing domain name, cohowinery.us in these examples, is already configured with MX, SIP, SMTP, CNAME, or SPF records in your public DNS and routing to your on-premises infrastructure or another email hosting provider, select the manual configuration options in the previous configuration process and make only the necessary changes to support your Office 365 setup.

Additional configuration changes for Exchange mail routing as part of the Exchange hybrid configuration, or Skype for Business hybrid, are covered in later chapters and can be performed later to avoid affecting existing functionality.

Firewall configurations

Office 365 is a cloud-based solution; therefore, your internal infrastructure must be able to communicate with your tenant without any connectivity issues created by your networking infrastructure.

If for any reason your internal infrastructure cannot communicate with Microsoft Azure, your Office 365 experience will be affected, possibly resulting in email delays and inability to authenticate and use services, add or license users, and even access cloud data.

It is strongly recommended for all network devices responsible for packet-filtering, load balancing, and network port access control to be configured to allow unrestricted outbound traffic to the Microsoft data centers.

The Microsoft data center IP ranges include all the Office 365 services and are maintained on the Office 365 support site.

The IP ranges can be viewed and downloaded at *https://aka.ms/o365-ips*, or you can subscribe to them with Rich Site Summary (RSS) feeds at *https://aka.ms/o365-ips-rss*.

Proxy servers

Proxy servers are traditionally used to proxy requests to the Internet through a single host; however, this behavior can create issues when setting up certain services for Office 365 connectivity.

Primarily, all traffic to Office 365 is outbound traffic. Some services, such as Exchange Autodiscover, Active Directory Federation Services (AD FS) authentication, and mail routing might be exceptions; however, it is important to understand that proxy server configurations can cause issues. The primary service that is affected when using proxy servers is directory synchronization.

The directory synchronization process that the AAD Connect tool performs connects regularly to Office 365 every 30 minutes to synchronize any directory updates. In addition, depending on the configuration of the tool, it also retrieves password changes and other data. If the connectivity between AAD Connect and Office 365 is affected, the synchronization might fail, resulting in incomplete data in Office 365.

It is therefore recommended to exempt the AAD Connect tool from any proxy server configurations and allow it to communicate with Azure without any proxy configuration.

INSIDE OUT
Authenticated proxy servers and synchronization

The AAD Connect tool does not support authenticated proxy servers. You must bypass any authenticated proxy servers, or you will be unable to synchronize your directories with Office 365.

If you are unable to bypass proxy servers for the AAD Connect implementation, it is recommended that you configure both Microsoft Internet Explorer and the Windows Command Shell to use the same proxy server. Both methods are used during the AAD Connect setup for communication with Office 365, so failure to enable both might result in a failed installation.

To set up Internet Explorer on the server where the synchronization tool will be installed, do the following.

1. Launch Internet Explorer.

2. Select Tools | Internet Options from the menu.

3. Select Connections | LAN Settings from the Internet Options menu.

4. Ensure that the Proxy Server check box is selected and a proxy server and port are provided in the Address and Port text boxes, as shown in Figure 2-17.

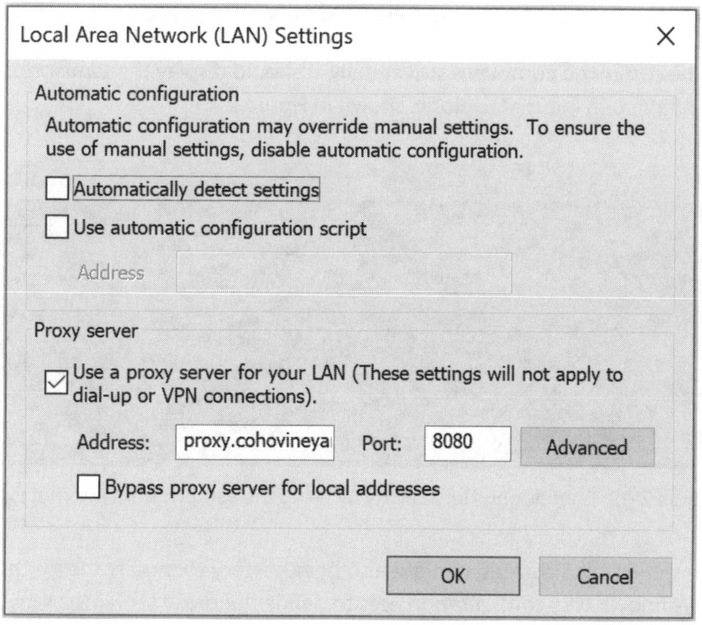

Figure 2-17 Configuring the Internet Explorer proxy server

5. Click OK to close the LAN Settings and Connections dialog boxes.

When the proxy server has been properly configured in Internet Explorer, perform the following steps to configure the proxy server for the Windows Command Shell.

1. Open an administrative command prompt.

2. Type **Netsh WinHTTP Show Proxy** and press **Enter**.

3. If the command returns Direct Access (No Proxy Server), as shown in Figure 2-18, proceed to step 4 to configure the proxy server.

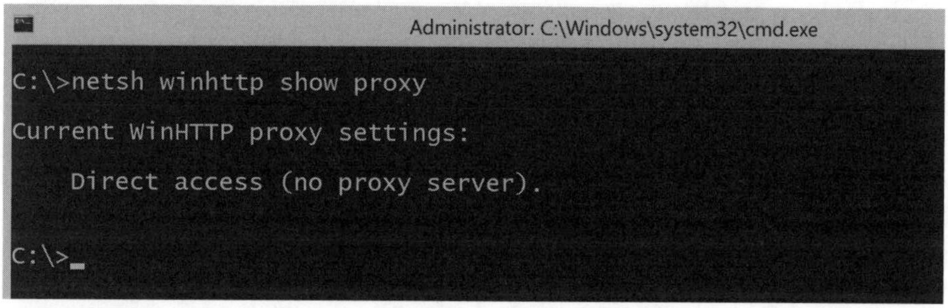

Figure 2-18 Displaying current WinHTTP proxy server configuration

4.   Type **Netsh WinHTTP Import Proxy Source=IE** and press Enter.

5.   If the command completes successfully, it should display the same proxy server that is configured in Internet Explorer, shown in Figure 2-19.

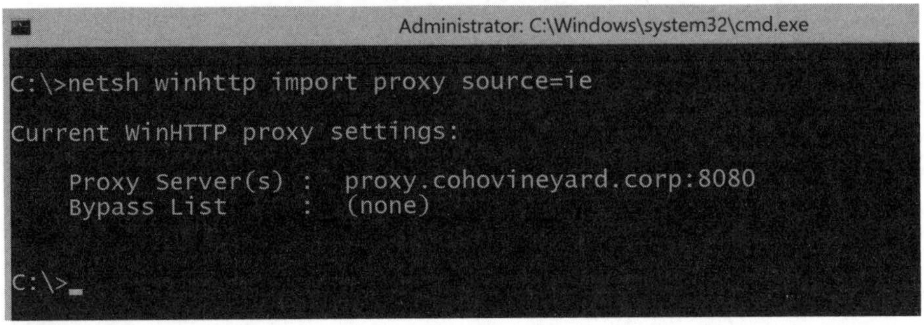

```
                                     Administrator: C:\Windows\system32\cmd.exe

C:\>netsh winhttp import proxy source=ie

Current WinHTTP proxy settings:

    Proxy Server(s) :  proxy.cohovineyard.corp:8080
    Bypass List     :  (none)


C:\>_
```

Figure 2-19 Configuring Netsh Proxy by using the settings from Internet Explorer

Finally, in some circumstances, it might also be necessary to modify the machine.config file that the Windows .NET configuration uses to define the proxy server that any .NET applications should use.

If the setup of AAD Connect fails to communicate with Azure properly, even after the settings in Internet Explorer and the Windows Command Shell have been configured, the .NET configuration file can be modified by performing the following steps.

1.   On the AAD Connect server, navigate to C:\Windows\Microsoft.Net\Framework64\ v4.xxxxxxx\Config, where x4.xxxxx is the v4.0 or v4.5 directory located in the Framework64 folder. This directory name depends on the .NET 4 version installed on your AAD Connect server.

2.   Edit the machine.config file, shown in Figure 2-20, by using Notepad.

Figure 2-20 The .NET machine.config file location

3. At the bottom of the file, insert the following block of text before the </configuration> line, substituting <PROXYADDRESS> with the name or IP address of your proxy server, and <PROXYPORT> with the correct port number.

```
<system.net>
        <defaultProxy enabled="true" useDefaultCredentials="true">
            <proxy
            usesystemdefault="true"
            proxyaddress="http://<PROXYADDRESS>:<PROXYPORT>"
            bypassonlocal="true"
            />
        </defaultProxy>
    </system.net>
```

4. Save the updated file, as shown in Figure 2-21, by clicking File | Save.

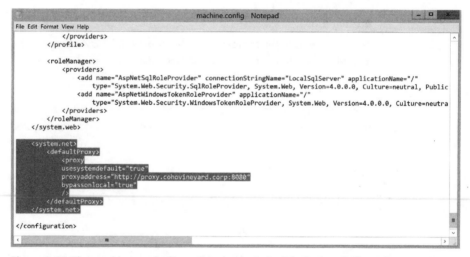

Figure 2-21 The machine.config file updated to include default proxy information

After the Proxy server configurations have been made to Internet Explorer, the Windows Shell, and the .NET configuration, you may proceed with the installation and configuration of the AAD Connect tool for directory synchronization.

Network tracing

Occasionally, during the implementation or configuration of proxy server or network firewall changes, it might be necessary to review the communication between your application and Office 365. Understanding the route that Office 365 communication must take to reach Azure will help with troubleshooting network connectivity issues.

The most common reason for connectivity tracing with Office 365, other than mailbox moves, is the synchronization process because the AAD Connect sync engine, unless configured differently, connects to Azure every 30 minutes to synchronize directory changes from on-premises to the cloud.

In addition, the AAD Connect engine, depending on the additional features selected during installation, might connect as frequently as every one to two minutes to retrieve password change requests and other authentication requests from the Azure service bus.

If you need to review traffic between your AAD Connect server and Office 365, you can use tools such as NetMon3, Fiddler, or WireShark to capture network traces from the server to ensure that no other devices are preventing proper communication.

TROUBLESHOOTING

Tracing tools

You can download the Microsoft NetMon tool from *https://aka.ms/netmon-download*, the Fiddler tool from *https://aka.ms/fiddler-download*, and the WireShark tool from *https://aka.ms/wireshark-download*.

The example uses Fiddler to capture and import from the Office 365 tenant by using the AAD Connect tool. Fiddler is installed on the AAD Connect server and is configured to decrypt HTTPS traffic.

The trace is captured as follows.

1. Launch the Fiddler tool and press F12 or select File | Capture Traffic.

2. Start the AAD Connect tool.

3. Select Connectors.

4. Select the Windows Azure Active Directory connector.

5. Select Run.

6. Choose Full Import and click OK, as shown in Figure 2-22.

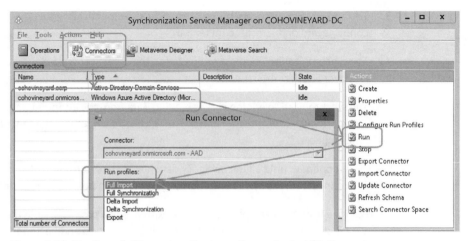

Figure 2-22 Starting a full import on the Azure Connector in AAD Connect

7. After the full import completes, review the results of the Fiddler trace, shown in Figure 2-23.

Figure 2-23 Fiddler trace of the AAD Connect Full Import run step

In Figure 2-23, each line represents a packet in the communication between the AAD Connect server and Azure Active Directory. The packets are performing the following actions.

1. Communication is established between the synchronization engine and Azure by the login.windows.net URL over secure SSL port 443.

2. Home realm discovery, a process by which the appropriate authentication provider is identified, is initiated using the Sync_COHOVINEYARD-DC_c8cd2f06f4ae@cohovineyard. onmicrosoft.com account. This account, discussed in detail in Chapter 4, "Directory Synchronization Basics," is used to authenticate with Office 365 for the purposes of synchronization.

3. The home realm discovery process results in an authentication token with the cohovineyard.onmicrosoft.com tenant.

4. The synchronization engine is redirected to the *adminwebservice.microsoftonline.com* URL over SSL port 443.

5. The synchronization engine begins reading data from the endpoint *adminwebservice. microsoftonline.com/provisioningservice.svc* URL, which returns the tenant data to the sync engine.

The process continues until all the directory data has been read from the Office 365 tenant into the Azure connector in the synchronization engine, at which point communication ceases.

As you can see from this example, despite the existence of a proxy server in the configuration, there was no impact on the traffic between the synchronization engine and the Office 365 tenant. If there had been issues with the traffic, you would have experienced retransmissions or transmission failures like the example in Figure 2-24.

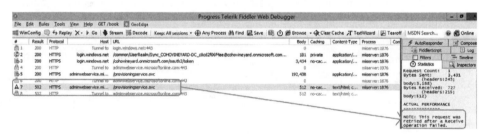

Figure 2-24 A transmission failure in a Fiddler trace

In this example, the communication with Azure AD was initiated, and the sync account authenticated properly. The transmission was interrupted, however, resulting in a retry operation that failed and stopped the import from Azure.

Tools such as Fiddler and NetMon3 can be invaluable when first setting up the synchronization process to ensure that communication is working properly and none of your network devices are affecting performance or connectivity. It is therefore strongly recommended that you become familiar with the proper functionality of the synchronization process and any other service-related connectivity (mailbox moves, Office application activation) to ensure the best possible Office 365 experience.

INSIDE OUT
Synchronization connectivity

Network connectivity between the synchronization engine and Office 365 is one of the most common troubleshooting areas, primarily related to proxy servers and any network devices that perform packet inspection.

The synchronization engine connects regularly in 30 minute intervals and, depending on additional features, as frequently as every two minutes.

Make sure you understand the network path between the sync engine and Azure, eliminate devices if possible, and be familiar with traffic patterns and troubleshooting that communication.

ExpressRoute

ExpressRoute is a frame-relay style of connection between your on-premises network and the Azure cloud. It provides direct connectivity to the Microsoft data centers through a secure and private connection and eliminates the need to traverse the public Internet for your Office 365–related traffic.

In addition to bypassing the public Internet for Office 365 traffic, ExpressRoute provides a fast and reliable connection to Azure, making replication, high availability, and data migration scenarios easier to implement.

During your implementation of Office 365, if you are considering ExpressRoute connectivity to the Microsoft cloud, it is strongly recommended that the implementation be done prior to the rest of your Office 365 readiness milestones. ExpressRoute implementation changes your network routing internally and affects things like load balancers, proxy servers, and firewalls. These changes have an impact on communication and should therefore be made prior to establishing synchronization and starting mailbox migrations.

Preparing your directories

Much like preparing your network for a successful Office 365 implementation, it is equally important to ensure that your on-premises directories are free from any issues that might affect a successful synchronization of users, groups, and contacts to your tenant.

Microsoft provides the IDFix tool, which reviews your environment and highlights any problem areas or data inconsistencies.

IDFix can be installed as follows.

1. Download the IDFix installation from *https://aka.ms/idfix*.

2. Save the ZIP file to the file system and extract the contents.

3. Launch the IDFix application by double-clicking it. Select Run if a file security warning dialog box, shown in Figure 2-25, appears.

Figure 2-25 File security warning dialog box

4. Click OK to proceed past the Privacy Statement dialog box shown in Figure 2-26.

This dialog box appears because the IDFix application reviews your data and provides reports that might contain sensitive information.

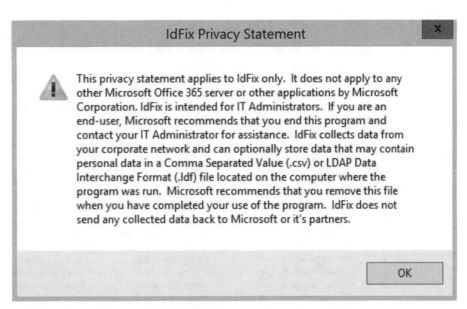

Figure 2-26 The IDFix Privacy Statement

5. Select Query from the topmost menu, shown in Figure 2-27.

Figure 2-27 The IDFix tool main menu

While the query is running, a status appears in the lower left corner of the tool.

When the query completes, a list of all issues appears, as shown in Figure 2-28, with an error description for each. The total object count and error count appear in the lower left corner.

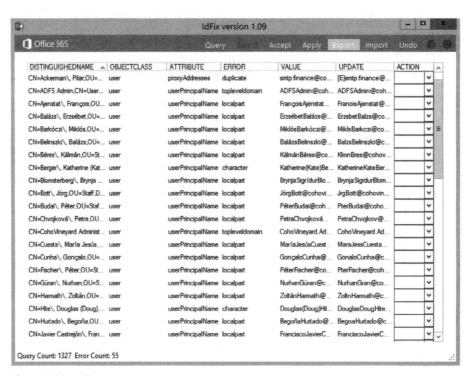

Figure 2-28 IDFix error report summary

6. Select a single error to use the Action column to define the behavior that should be used to resolve it.

7. Choose Edit, Remove, or Complete to resolve the object in question, as Figure 2-29 shows.

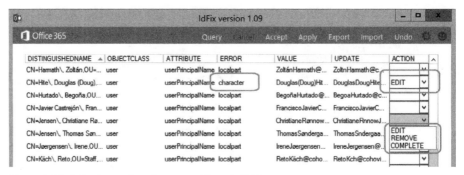

Figure 2-29 Selecting actions for error objects in IDFix

8. When you have selected the appropriate action for each object, select Apply at the top menu.

This returns a confirmation dialog box, shown in Figure 2-30.

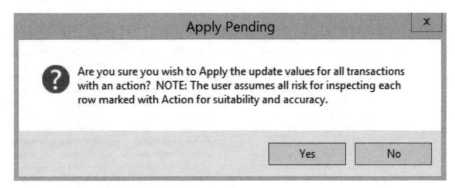

Figure 2-30 IDFix Apply Pending dialog box

9. Click Yes to apply all selected updates.

When complete, all updates that have been applied are marked Complete, as shown in Figure 2-31.

CHAPTER 2

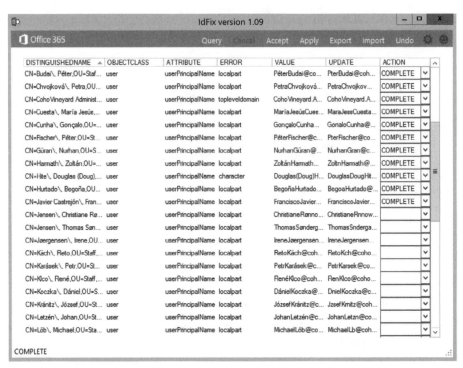

Figure 2-31 IDFix tool with Actions updated

It is important to note that when selecting Edit, you cannot manually edit the value in error; instead, the IDFix tool simply applies the update displayed in the Update column. You should review this new value that allows IDFix to make the change.

INSIDE OUT

IDFix activity

All changes the IDFix tool makes are saved as LDF files in the folder where the IDFix ZIP was extracted.

You can use these files to restore changes IDFix made to your directory, by selecting Undo in the IDFix main menu and choosing the appropriate LDF file.

10. Optionally, use Accept in the IDFix main menu to apply the updated value, shown in the Update column, automatically to each object in an error state, as shown in Figure 2-32.

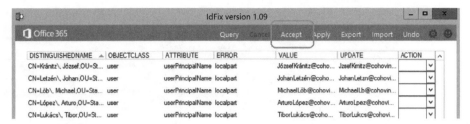

Figure 2-32 IDFix Accept

Like Apply, Accept also displays a dialog box warning that the changes being made represent a risk because they are changing data in your directory. See Figure 2-33.

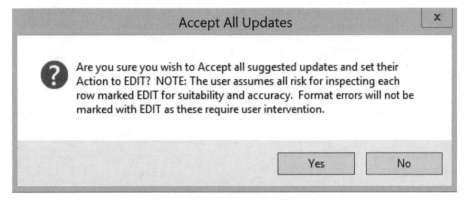

Figure 2-33 The IDFix Accept All Updates dialog box

Selecting Accept All simply changes all Action fields to EDIT; it is then necessary to use Apply to make the changes.

11. When the changes have been applied, select Query to rerun the IDFix process against your directory and confirm that no additional changes are required.

In Figure 2-34, the synchronization tool showed 46 failures on export to Azure. These failures were related to bad or duplicate data in the on-premises Active Directory.

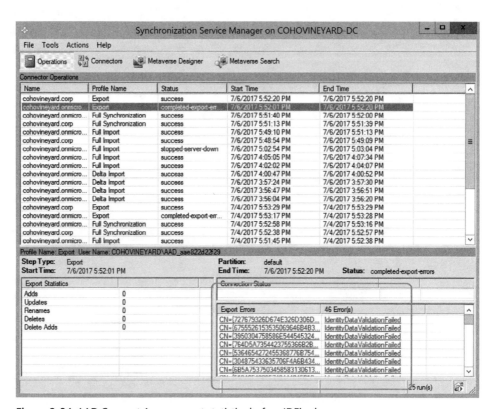

Figure 2-34 AAD Connect Azure export statistics before IDFix cleanup

After the IDFix process successfully updates all the errors reported, a resynchronization of the on-premises Active Directory results in 46 adds to Azure and zero errors, as shown in Figure 2-35.

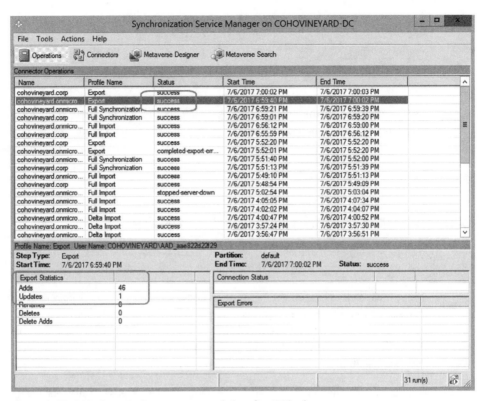

Figure 2-35 AAD Connect Azure export statistics after IDFix cleanup

The IDFix utility is an invaluable tool that you can use to identify any issues in your Active Directory prior to starting synchronization to Office 365. It is therefore recommended to run the IDFix utility against your on-premises directories, review the results, and make the appropriate changes, either manually or with the tool, before you start synchronizing your objects to the cloud.

INSIDE OUT

IDFix statistics

In the preceding examples, the IDFix tool found 55 errors but only 46 errors in the directory synchronization report, because the synchronization tool was focused on specific organizational units (OUs) in Active Directory, whereas the IDFix tool was focused on the entire directory.

> When evaluating problem objects, pay close attention to their location in the directory, because they might be in OUs or domains that you do not plan to synchronize to Azure. As a result, you might not need to modify all objects.

It's important to note that the IDFix changes affect both authentication, in the form of UserPrincipalName changes, and mail routing, in the form of email address removal and update; therefore, take care when reviewing all changes before they are applied, because the updates have the potential to modify objects and break access to other applications or affect processes already in place.

Updating and installing client software

Prior to the migration of mailboxes to Office 365, it is critical for the Outlook version levels and updates to be up to date so that there is no interruption in the user experience.

Even a mailbox that has not yet migrated to Exchange Online might experience connectivity issues or constant credential prompts if that mailbox is delegated permission to another mailbox that *has* been migrated to Office 365. It is for this reason that it is strongly recommended that Office and Windows updates be approved, applied, and up to date in advance of the Office 365 implementation.

Frequently, customers choose to apply the Office Pro Plus license to all users ahead of the mailbox moves, or even SharePoint Online and Skype for Business deployments, so that all Office versions are current and support the Office 365 workloads.

Installing Office Pro Plus

Installation of the Office Pro Plus software is extremely simple.

1. Log on to the Office 365 portal at *https://portal.office.com*.

2. When prompted, log on to Office 365, using your user name and password.

3. On the Office 365 portal page, shown in Figure 2-36, select Install Office 2016 in the upper right corner.

Figure 2-36 Installing Office 2016 from the Office 365 portal

The Office 365 portal displays additional information, shown in Figure 2-37, that assists in the Office 2016 installation.

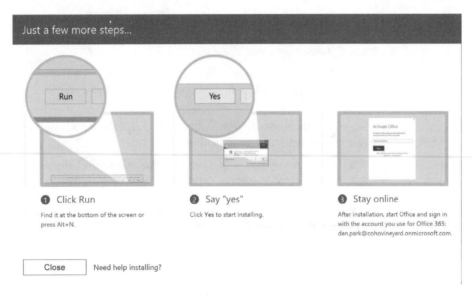

Figure 2-37 Office 365 Click To Run guidance page

When the installer has successfully downloaded from Office 365, a prompt to Save, Run, or Cancel the installation appears, as shown in Figure 2-38.

Figure 2-38 Prompt for Office 2016 Click To Run installer

4. Click Run to begin the Office 2016 installation.

   If there are any conflicting software versions already installed on the workstation, a pop-up dialog box appears, showing the application in conflict, as shown in Figure 2-39.

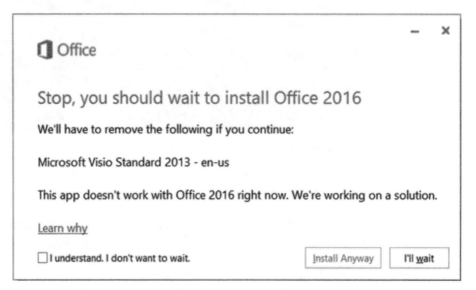

Figure 2-39 Office 2016 setup conflict with existing installed versions

5. Select the I Understand. I Don't Want To Wait check box and select Install Anyway if you wish to proceed with the installation.

   This removes the version or versions of software in conflict and proceeds with the installation. Clicking I'll Wait ends the Office 2016 installation process.

6. When the installation completes, a new window, shown in Figure 2-40, appears, indicating that the installation is complete.

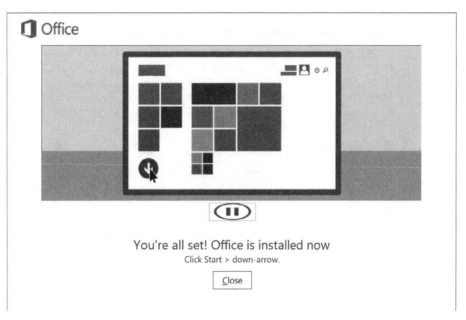

Figure 2-40 Office installation completion page

7. Click Close to complete the installation process.

When the installation completes, the Office 2016 products are available for use, and any previous documents created in past versions of Office will prompt to update the document to the latest version when applicable.

INSIDE OUT

Office Pro Plus

The Office Pro Plus installation performed by using the Office 365 portal is enabled for automatic updating. These updates occur over the Internet and not by any internal automatic update services, such as Windows Server Update Services (WSUS), configured in your organization.

Automating the installation

Although the Office Pro Plus suite can be installed manually by using the option available on the Office 365 portal page, you can also use the Office Pro Plus installation binary to create a deployment package for use with tools such as System Center Configuration Manager (SCCM).

Deployment with SCCM or other automated application deployment tools consists of downloading the Office Pro Plus binary and creating configuration files that determine the subcomponents that should be installed. The installation can be automated by push, Group Policy object (GPO), logon script, or other automation tools that you might use in your enterprise.

You can find information about deploying Office Pro Plus, using the Microsoft System Center Configuration Manager, at *https://aka.ms/ProPlusWithSCCM*.

Activation

The final step in using the Office Pro Plus suite of products is activation, a process by which the Office applications connect to Office 365 to ensure that the user is properly licensed in the tenant to use the application.

The good news is that activation is automatic. No additional action is required by the user to activate their Office installation.

Activation does, however, require the computer to have Internet access to complete the process.

After Office is installed on a user's workstation, the system tries daily to reach the Microsoft Office Licensing Service activation endpoint on the Internet. If it is unsuccessful, it retries daily for up to 30 days before the applications enter reduced functionality mode.

In reduced functionality mode, the software remains installed on the workstation, but your users can only view and print documents. Any features related to document editing or creation of new documents remains disabled until the user either types a product key or successfully authenticates with Office 365.

The reduced functionality mode displays a Product Deactivated dialog box, as shown in Figure 2-41, if Office is unable to reach the licensing service after more than 30 days.

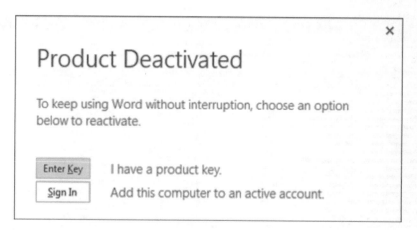

Figure 2-41 Product Deactivated dialog box

Synchronizing your users

The next step in your deployment of Office 365 is the synchronization of your users to Microsoft Azure Active Directory.

Synchronization is performed using the Azure AD Connect tool, typically referred to as AAD Connect. AAD Connect is a free download from Microsoft for Office 365 users and is based on the Microsoft Identity Manager (MIM) product line.

The directory synchronization process, although simple in theory, can be involved when installing and configuring the AAD Connect tool. In addition to the selection of objects and OUs, the AAD Connect tool can also be configured to support additional features such as pass-through authentication, group writeback, and password writeback.

You can find additional information about directory synchronization in Chapter 4, and an in-depth look into the AAD Connect installation and all options in Chapter 5, "Installing Azure AD Connect."

When the synchronization engine has been installed, pay attention to the synchronization statistics for each of the run profile steps on the Operations tab of the AAD Connect tool, shown in Figure 2-42.

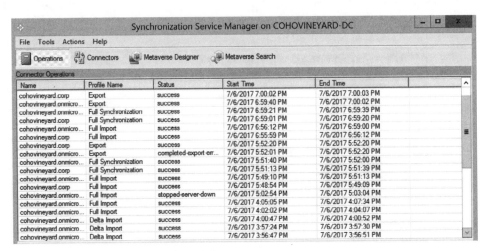

Figure 2-42 The Operations view in AAD Connect

Although it is important to review all errors reported in the Status column, those operations for the Azure connector, typically named tenant.onmicrosoft.com, should be reviewed carefully.

Any errors on the Azure connector indicate either bad or missing data in Office 365. In fact, if the IDFix tool has been run and all issues resolved prior to installation of the AAD Connect tool, the Azure connector should not show any errors related to data problems.

If errors do appear in the synchronization statistics view, the data provided there might not be sufficient to diagnose the issue adequately. In those cases, it is recommended to review the Application Event Log for more detail.

The following list, although not exhaustive of events the AAD Connect engine returned, primarily because the tool is constantly evolving and maturing, represents the most common as well as some of the most important events that you should review when present as well as included in any event-log monitoring utilities.

Informational events

The following list of informational events, found in the Windows Server Application event log, are the most common events found during normal processing of the synchronization process. They can be monitored to provide reporting on the standard operation of the AAD Connect engine, the directory synchronization process and password synchronization.

AAD Connect engine

These events are related to the AAD Connect engine, and provide detail about events related to the operation of the Azure AD Sync service.

904 – Scheduler-related informational events   Many 904 informational events are related to Scheduler starting, Scheduler settings changing, Purging AAD Connect Operations Run history, Scheduler stopping, and so on.

2001 – AAD Connect Windows Service (Azure AD Sync) Started Successfully.

2002 – AAD Connect Windows Service (Azure AD Sync) Stopped Successfully.

Directory synchronization

These events describe operations that have occurred as part of the directory synchronization process, including the start and stop of export or import cycles from Active Directory or Azure Active Directory.

104 – Export Iteration # Has Completed.

105 – Import Iteration # Has Completed.

107 – Azure AD Has Redirected The Provisioning Endpoint Service Call To *https://provisioningapi .microsoftonline.com/provisioningwebservice.svc* To An Alternate Endpoint.

114 – Export Cycle Has Competed.

115 – Access To Azure Active Directory Has Been Denied   This event is flagged as informational despite indicating that Azure Active Directory access has been blocked. This Informational event is frequently found in conjunction with a 106 Error.

116 – Informational logging that returns directory synchronization settings related to export threshold and machine name and so on.

117 – Import Prefetch Starting: Import Steps During Synchronization Cycle Will Read From Each Connector As They Start.

Password synchronization

These events describe actions the engine takes as part of the password synchronization process from on-premises Active Directory to Azure Active Directory. Each event provides detail about the starting, stopping, and progress of the synchronization process as well as any error detail.

601 – Password Synchronization Manager Has Started   This event appears for every source the Active Directory forest synchronized as a source for the Password Hash Synchronization feature.

605 – Password Synchronization Changes Have Failed For One Or More Users   This Informational event refers to an error condition but is not classified as an error.

609 – Password Synchronization Manager Has Stopped.

611 – Password Synchronization Full Sync Has Started   This event appears upon completion of the AAD Connect Installation Wizard, either during initial setup or when reconfiguring AAD Connect, when the Password Hash Synchronization feature has been enabled.

This action pauses any other password synchronization until it has completed. Changes that occur while it is running are queued and occur after this full sync has completed.

650 – A Batch Of Password Updates To Azure AD Has Started.

651 – A Batch Of Password Updates To Azure AD Has Completed   Informational events 650 and 651 occur as part of the Full Password Sync process.

656 – A Password Change Request For One Or More Users Has Been Received From The Server And Is Being Transmitted To Azure AD.

657 – A Password Change Request For One Or More Users Was Successfully Transmitted To Azure AD   Informational events 656 and 657 can contain password change requests for up to 50 users per batch. If the number of password change requests from Active Directory exceeds 50 users, multiple 656 and 657 events are generated.

658 – Windows Credentials Sync Config details.

659 – Informational logging that returns the state of the IsPasswordChangeOnLogon feature.

6201 – Server Encryption Keys Have Been Successfully Created   This event is returned during the installation of AAD Connect.

6943 – Password Sync Started For Management Agent (Connector), *ConnectorName*.

6945 – Informational logging that returns the Management Agent Run Profile settings details about Connector Name, AD Forest partition, Service Account name, and Domain.

Warning events in directory synchronization

The following event IDs are the most common warning events related to the synchronization of user, group, and contact objects from on-premises Active Directory and should be reviewed when they appear in the Windows Application Event logs.

6012 – Full Import Failed   No objects were returned from the operation.

6100 – Run Profile Step Completed With Errors   This event is logged as a warning; additional information is returned, along with this warning, in the form of Error events.

6105 – The "Exported Changed Not Reimported" Error Was Returned During An Import Run Profile Operation   This error indicates that data sent to Azure was not returned during import;

it's typically the result of other errors. This error should be skipped until all other export errors have been resolved.

6110 – The Configuration Has Changed Since The Last Run Profile Of This Type (Import Or Sync), However A Full Import Or Sync Was Not Performed   The sync engine will continue to report this warning until a full import or sync resolves the issue.

6126 – Identical to Warning 6110.

6127 – Identical to Warning 6110.

Error events in directory synchronization

The following event IDs are the most common error events related to the synchronization of user, group, and contact objects from on-premises Active Directory and should be reviewed when they appear in the Windows Application Event logs. These events enable you to identify failures in the synchronization process and remediate errors in a timely manner.

106 – Failed To Connect To Azure AD During Export Step.

109 – Failed To Connect To Azure AD During Import Step   Both error 106 and error 109 are connectivity errors when communicating with Azure Active Directory, most commonly a credential issue; however, it's possible that network communication or proxy issues are also the cause.

6801 – Error Occurred Communicating With Azure AD.

6803 – Generic   The export step encountered one or more errors.

6941 – Export Encountered One Of The Following Errors:

DataValidationFailed

InvalidSoftMatch

AttributeValueMustBeUnique

The 6941 error is logged for each error that occurs during the run step. If many export errors are visible in the AAD Connect Synchronization Manager console, there will be a large number of associated error entries. When monitoring for export failures, it's best to use the 6803 error to indicate a failure, because monitoring for 6941 returns a large number of results.

CHAPTER 2

Configuring federation

Typically, federation refers to the authentication process between your on-premises Active Directory and Azure Active Directory. The synchronization of user identities between your directory and Office 365 enables your users to authenticate with Office 365 and consume services; however, it is necessary also to configure one or more types of federation to enable this authentication process.

Chapter 3, "Federation Services and Authentication," deals with the different federation options and implementation of each. It is strongly recommended that you review each option and available features in detail before configuring federation with Office 365.

Licensing your users

After a cloud user has been created, and you have started synchronizing identities to your tenant, you must assign licenses to your users before they can begin to consume Office 365 services.

Licensing plans and subscriptions were explained in detail in Chapter 1; however, several methods are available for licensing users in Office 365, and it is important to understand each method so that you can choose the best option for you.

Currently, there are three primary methods for license assignment in Office 365.

- Group-based licensing

- Windows PowerShell licensing cmdlets included in the MSOnline PowerShell module

- Manual licensing through the Office 365 portal

Group-based licensing

One of the newest features available for licensing in Office 365 is group-based licensing, commonly referred to as GBL.

Group-based licensing requires either Azure Active Directory Premium or Azure Active Directory Basic licenses, both paid features; however, it is one of the quickest, easiest, and most effective ways to manage Azure Active Directory licenses. As the name implies, group-based licensing uses Azure Active Directory groups for the assignment of licenses to users.

INSIDE OUT

Azure group-based licensing

Azure Active Directory group-based licensing configuration can only be performed in the new Azure Ibiza portal. Group licensing configurations cannot be created, managed, or viewed in the standard Office 365 Admin portal.

Licenses are assigned to either security groups that are synchronized to Azure in the Azure AD Connect tool or to cloud-only groups created directly in Azure. Both group types require an Azure AD Basic license.

In the example in Figure 2-43, an on-premises security group and its membership has been synchronized to Azure Active Directory and the Exchange Online Enterprise E3 and Office Pro Plus licenses assigned (2 of 15 enabled services).

Figure 2-43 Group-based license assignment in Azure Ibiza portal

In addition, dynamic groups can be created in the Azure portal and configured to define membership based on synchronized attributes. The creation of Azure Active Directory Dynamic groups, shown in Figure 2-44, requires an Azure Active Directory Premium license.

CHAPTER 2

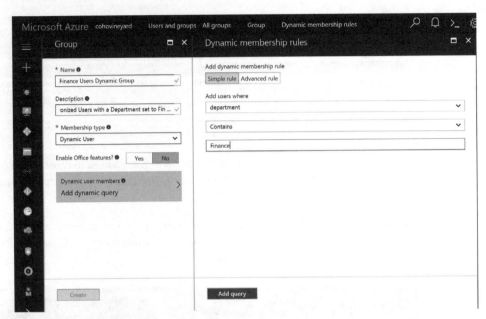

Figure 2-44 Creating a Dynamic group in the Azure Ibiza portal

After a dynamic group has been created in the Azure portal, the group can then be used for automatic license assignment through group-based licensing, as shown in Figure 2-45.

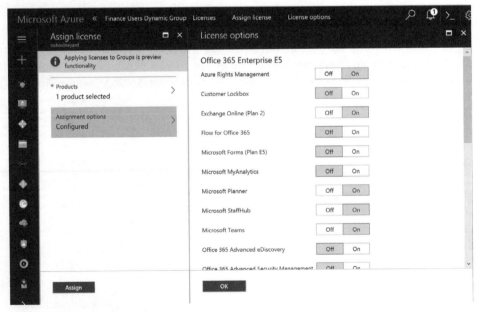

Figure 2-45 Assigning a license to an Azure Dynamic group

It is important to note the following details regarding Azure AD group-based licensing.

- All existing Azure license types are supported by Azure Active Directory group-based licensing.

- Group membership updates made in on-premises groups synced to Azure Active Directory are effective within just a few minutes of a membership change.

- Users can be members of multiple groups; licenses across groups are combined.

- If no licenses are available in the tenant, group-based licensing cannot assign licenses to a user, and no error will be returned.

- Licenses assigned through a group cannot be manually removed by Windows PowerShell or the portal.

- Users can have licenses assigned through multiple groups as well as by direct assignment (Windows PowerShell and manual).

Windows PowerShell licensing

The second method available for licensing is through use of the provided licensing Windows PowerShell cmdlets in the MSOnline PowerShell module.

The MSOnline PowerShell module includes several cmdlets you can use for user license assignment in Azure Active Directory. You can use these cmdlets to assign SKUs to users as well as to enable or disable specific plans under the SKU.

Assignment consists of three steps.

First, all users must have a Usage Location assigned to be licensed. The second step consists of defining the list of sub-plans you wish to have disabled (not enabled), and the third step consists of assigning the options directly to the user.

A user's Usage Location is set automatically by the AAD Connect tool, provided that the msExchUsageLocation value in on-premises Active Directory is populated with a valid two-digit ISO country code. If the value is not set, the AAD Connect tool can be customized to synchronize any other Active Directory attribute (such as CountryCode) as a Usage Location, provided it is a valid two-digit ISO country code.

If the Usage Location is not set by AAD Connect, it can be set programmatically by using the MSOnline PowerShell cmdlets as follows.

```
Set-MsolUser -UserPrincipalName <UserPrincipalName_value> -UsageLocation <Country_Code>
```

CHAPTER 2

In the example shown in Figure 2-46, the user, Pilar Ackerman, is being set to a Usage Location of US.

Figure 2-46 Setting UsageLocation through Windows PowerShell

The license options, or the list of disabled sub-plans, can be set as follows.

```
$licenseoptions = New-MsolLicenseOptions -AccountSkuId <SKU_Name> -DisabledPlans YAM-
MER_ENTERPRISE, RMS_S_ENTERPRISE
```

In the example shown in Figure 2-47, the LicenseOptions variable is being created to generate a set of disabled plans that includes Yammer and Exchange Rights Management. This variable will be used in step 3 to assign the license to a user.

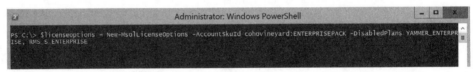

Figure 2-47 Creating a LicenseOptions variable for use by the Licensing cmdlet

Finally, the LicenseOptions variable can be used with the following Set-MsolUserLicense cmdlet to assign the license to the user.

```
Set-MsolUserLicense -UserPrincipalName <UserPrincipalName_Value> -AddLicenses
cohovineyard:ENTERPRISEPACK -LicenseOptions $licenseoptions
```

In the example in Figure 2-48, the Set-MsolUserLicense cmdlet assigns the E3 SKU to a user by using the LicenseOptions variable created previously.

Figure 2-48 Setting the user license with the Set-MsolUserLicense cmdlet

INSIDE OUT

Set-MsolUserLicense

The Set-MsolUserLicense Windows PowerShell cmdlet has two modes, depending on whether a user already has a license for the SKU being assigned.

If a user is not licensed for the SKU being assigned, the -AssignLicense switch should be used; failure to use the switch returns an error.

If the user is already licensed for the SKU being assigned, the -AssignLicense switch should not be used; use of the switch returns an error.

Manual license assignment

The final method available for license assignment is the use of the Office 365 portal to assign user licenses manually.

Manual license assignment can be done on an individual user basis by selecting the user and editing the assigned license or by selecting multiple users, as shown in Figure 2-49.

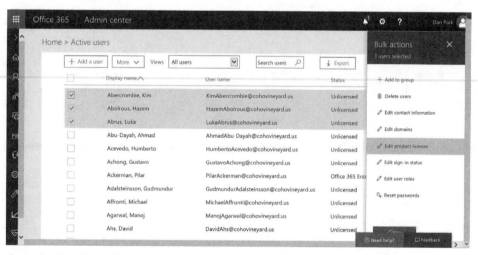

Figure 2-49 Bulk user license assignment through the Office 365 portal

Although the ability to assign user licenses is available through the Office 365 portal for both individual and bulk assignment, it does not typically scale well for large organizations with many thousands of users or with licensing requirements that might create the need to assign licenses in various combinations based on role, location, or department.

For this reason, the manual assignment of licenses is used on an ad hoc basis and as a supplement to one of the other options for license assignment.

Wrapping Up

Now that the major milestones involved in your Office 365 tenant setup have been discussed, and the chapter has provided guidance on each of these steps, you move on to more advanced topics such as federation, directory synchronization, Exchange hybrid setup, and the tasks required to help you get the most from your Office 365 experience.

PART II

Office 365 Identity and Access

Federation services and authentication

In a typical Office 365 implementation, your users exist in Azure Active Directory (AAD) primarily because of directory synchronization, discussed in detail in Chapter 4, "Directory Synchronization Basics," and Chapter 5, "Installing Azure AD Connect." However, in addition to the several identity types available, depending on how your users are created, several options are also available for user sign-in and authentication.

Each of these options has a different set of requirements and affects the implementation of directory synchronization as well as possibly driving other infrastructure requirements and even Azure AD licensed features.

This chapter discusses the different types of identities, along with the sign-in, authentication, and connectivity options available to you and how they affect your users, your environment, your implementation, and your ongoing Office 365 administration experience.

Understanding the different types of identities

"Identities" refers to security principals or users who can sign in to Office 365 and consume services. Whether it's Exchange Online or Office Pro Plus, your users must be able to authenticate with Azure AD before they can use the service, and that authentication process varies depending on the type of identity in use.

Synchronized identities

Synchronized users are exactly what that sounds like; they are users who have been synchronized to your Office 365 portal from your on-premises Active Directory. Your directory synchronization configuration dictates which users are synchronized to Azure AD, and although your users now appear in the Office 365 portal, they are still mastered on-premises and managed using the tools you are already accustomed to using.

Synchronized users are the most common user type in Office 365 and are the easiest to create and maintain. Implementation of the AAD Connect tool automatically populates your Office 365 portal with synchronized users, essentially replicas of all your existing users, as shown in Figure 3-1, and you can start using Office 365 almost immediately.

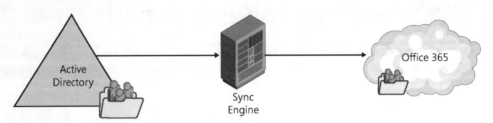

Figure 3-1 Synchronized identities

Several additional configuration options affect the user sign-in process and are discussed later in this chapter; each carries with it a different set of requirements and additional tasks that must be performed in both Azure AD and your on-premises environment.

Chapter 4 and Chapter 5 discuss synchronization of identities in detail; the following discusses the next identity type.

Cloud identities

Cloud identities are user accounts that have been created manually in the Office 365 portal. In fact, when you first set up your Office 365 subscription, the account you provided during setup is configured as a cloud user.

These accounts, like synchronized identities, can be used for sign-in to Office 365 and can use Office 365 services just like a synchronized account.

Most often, cloud identities are created by an administrator directly in the portal by entering all the necessary information, such as user principal name, display name, and email address (where applicable) and assigning a password and one or more licenses to the account. When complete, the user can start using Office 365.

To create a cloud identity, simply log on to the Office 365 Admin portal and select Add A User from the Home page, as shown in Figure 3-2.

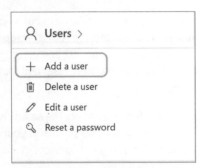

Figure 3-2 Selecting Add A User in the Office 365 Admin portal

After you have selected Add A User, the New User dialog box appears, like the one shown in Figure 3-3, where you can type the first name, last name, display name, and user name (also known as the UserPrincipalName) for the cloud user account.

The Domain drop-down list displays all the valid domains in use in your Office 365 subscription. If you've just created your subscription, it's likely that the only domain available in the drop-down list is the tenant.onmicrosoft.com domain. After you've successfully registered additional domains in your tenant, you can change this value for your cloud users.

In addition to the name information, you can also enter contact information; attributes such as address, city, state, and zip code; and values such as job title and department, as shown in Figure 3-3. Simply select the Contact Information drop-down list in the dialog box to add these details.

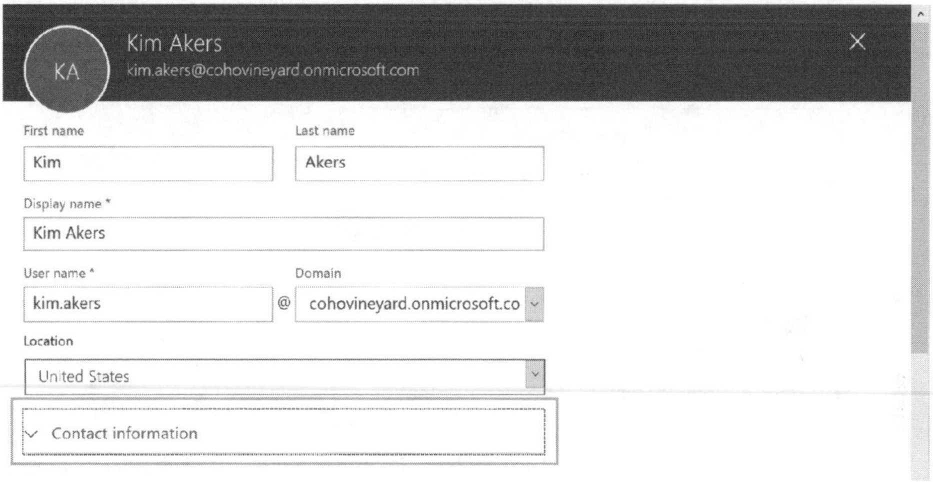

Figure 3-3 Manually creating a cloud identity

Finally, you can, during manual cloud identity creation, set a password, role, and one or more product licenses.

If you choose not to set a password, an auto-generated password will be created and sent to the email address set on your admin account.

It's important to note that the default role for all cloud identities is User. If this account is meant only to use services in Office 365, you can leave the role selection as is. If, however, this account is meant to administer Office 365, you must select the necessary role here. The different role types and their levels of access were discussed in Chapter 1, "Office 365 Deployment Milestones."

Finally, it is possible to create a cloud identity with no product licenses; however, you must select Create User Without Product License before you can complete the user creation process.

Although it is possible to create cloud identities manually, it becomes rather cumbersome and time-consuming to create more than a few. However, you can perform bulk creation of cloud identities from the Office 365 Admin portal by using a comma-separated input, or CSV, file.

By using a CSV import file, you can quickly create cloud identities when directory synchronization from on-premises is either not yet available or not applicable.

The CSV import file must contain specific header information before you can import it into the portal. The CSV header information, and even a CSV with sample data, can be downloaded from the portal with the Import Multiple Users Wizard by selecting Import Multiple Users from the More drop-down list and then selecting either Download A CSV File With Headers Only or Download A CSV File With Headers And Sample User Information, as shown in Figure 3-4.

Figure 3-4 Downloading CSV header information or sample CSV file

Each of the fields provided in the CSV has a limit to the number of characters that can be populated, as shown in Table 3-1. Values marked with an asterisk (*) are mandatory values, and you cannot leave them blank; all others are optional.

Table 3-1 Bulk user import character limits

Field	Max Length
User Name*	79
First Name	64
Last Name	64
Display Name*	256
Job Title	64
Department	64

Field	Max Length
Office Number	128
Office Phone	64
Mobile Phone	64
Fax	64
Address	1023
City	128
State or Province	128
Zip or Postal Code	40
Country or Region	128

INSIDE OUT

User name

The user name, or UserPrincipalName value, has a limitation of 79 total characters, including the @ symbol.

The alias (the left side of the user name before the @ symbol) cannot exceed 30 characters, and the domain name (the user name after the @ symbol) cannot exceed 48 characters.

After you have populated the CSV input file, you can load it by clicking the Browse button, as Figure 3-5 shows, and then click the Verify button to ensure that there are no formatting errors, that all required fields are present, and that the User Name field is populated with a valid domain in your tenant.

Figure 3-5 Importing a CSV and verifying contents

If you don't yet have domains registered in your tenant, you can use the @tenant.onmicrosoft .com suffix for the user name, and the value can be changed later from the portal.

After you have selected your CSV input file, as shown in Figure 3-5, and the file has been confirmed as valid, clicking Next enables you to set the sign-in status for your imported users as well as assign one or more product licenses, shown in Figure 3-6.

Just like manual creation of a single user, if you don't wish to assign a license to the imported users, you must select Create User Without Product License to proceed.

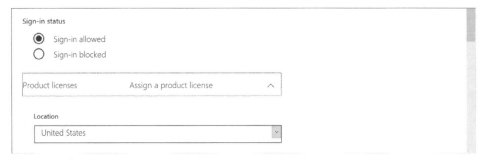

Figure 3-6 Setting user options and licenses on bulk import

Clicking Next automatically creates the users. There is no Are You Sure prompt, so you want to be sure that you've selected all the appropriate licenses and sign-in status options for your new users before clicking Next.

INSIDE OUT

Sign-in status

The sign-in status for users indicates whether the user can authenticate to Office 365 and use the services.

For synchronized identities, the sign-in status is set to reflect the UserAccountControl status in your on-premises Active Directory. When a user changes from enabled to disabled in on-premises Active Directory, the sign-in status in Microsoft Azure is changed to match.

For cloud identities, the sign-in status must be set during user creation and changed manually thereafter through the Office 365 Admin portal or the Microsoft Online PowerShell cmdlets.

It *is* possible to change the sign-in status manually for a synchronized identity from the portal and override the account status synchronized from on-premises.

When the cloud user bulk import completes, a message appears indicating the number of objects that were created, and you can download a CSV that contains the list of users and their automatically generated passwords, email the CSV to one or more administrators, or both.

The highlighted text block in Figure 3-7 is a warning that emailing the CSV with the bulk user creation results sends the temporary passwords in plaintext. Care should be taken when using Email The Results Files To These People.

View your results

Here are your results reports. You can either download and save them, or email them to yourself and others.

☑ 4 users created   ↓ Download results

☑ Email the results files to these people

Recipients *

dan.park@cohovineyard.onmicrosoft.com

⚠ If you choose to send these files by email, the passwords will be sent in plain text.

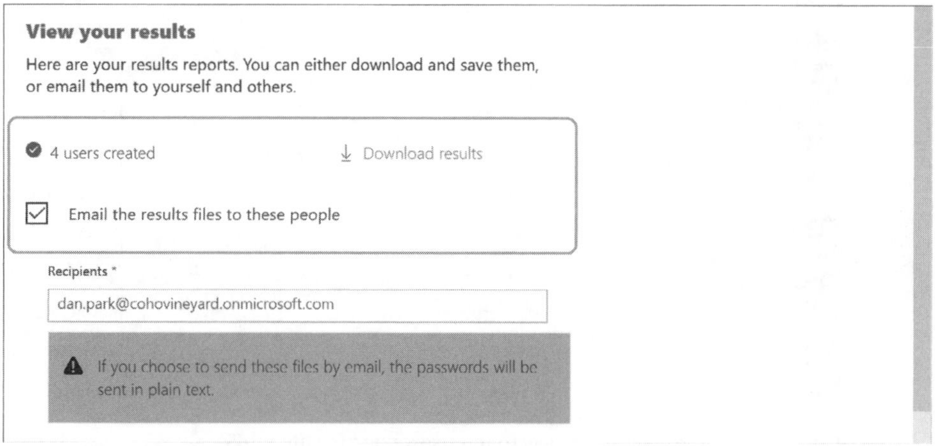

Figure 3-7 Successful bulk cloud user creation message

If you've created a combination of cloud users, possibly for administrator roles, and have also synchronized identities from your on-premises directory, it's possible that your Office 365 Admin portal is now somewhat cluttered.

It is easy to identify cloud users versus synchronized users at a glance on the Active Users page in the portal, as shown in Figure 3-8.

Figure 3-8 Identifying cloud versus synced users in the Office 365 Admin Center

Any user who was created manually in the portal, either singly or by bulk import, appears with a Sync Type of In Cloud, whereas synchronized users appear as Synced With Active Directory.

You can create custom views to organize your users on the Active Users page.

From the Active Users page, shown in Figure 3-9, select the Views drop-down list and Add Custom View, as shown.

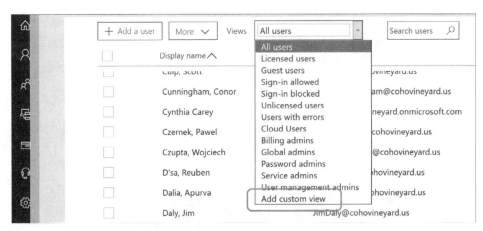

Figure 3-9 Adding a custom view to the Users page in Office 365

When the Custom View dialog box appears, as shown in Figure 3-10, enter a unique name for your view. This view will be accessible to all Office 365 administrators when using the View drop-down list on the Active Users page.

Figure 3-10 Creating a custom view in the Office 365 portal

Any of the drop-down lists or text boxes can be used to select filter criteria by which to customize the User View. In addition, the bottom of the Custom View dialog box, shown in Figure 3-11, provides additional check boxes that can also be used to filter the view.

Figure 3-11 Further customizing Custom View for users

INSIDE OUT

Filtering your view

The Custom View option in the Office 365 Admin Center gives you some flexibility in filtering the views of your users; however, it's not possible to create a view of cloud-only users. There is a filter option for synchronized users, but not the reverse.

A list of cloud-only users can be retrieved by using the MSOnline PowerShell cmdlets, or you can populate fields such as Job Title or Department with a value that you can use in the Custom View filter.

The filters available for custom views enable you to filter synchronized users, but there is no option to filter cloud users.

In most customer environments, where there are synchronized users, the cloud user accounts represent either service or administrative accounts, and those account types can be easily selected through pre-defined user views already present in the portal, as shown in Figure 3-12.

CHAPTER 3

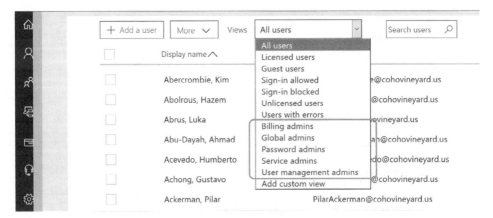

Figure 3-12 Predefined user views for admin roles

If, however, you have cloud user accounts that are not delegated any administrative access, and cannot be identified by any other means through the portal, you can use the MSOnline PowerShell cmdlets to filter these user accounts by using the LastDirSyncTime property that is present on all objects in Azure AD. If an object has been synchronized from on-premises through AAD Connect, the LastDirSyncTime property contains the date and time of that synchronization, but for any cloud user objects, that value is null.

INSIDE OUT

Connecting to MSOnline PowerShell

To make a connection to MSOnline using Windows PowerShell, you must download and install the Sign-In Assistant from *http://aka.ms/o365-sia* as well as the MSOnline PowerShell Module from *http://aka.ms/o365-psh*.

After the module has been loaded, you use the **Connect-MSOLService** command and provide credentials for an admin account in the tenant.

Connecting to MSOnline PowerShell and running the Get-MsolUser command with the -All switch and a filter of Where { $_.LastDirSyncTime -eq $null } provides a list of all cloud user accounts, as shown in Figure 3-13.

The complete command would be Get-MsolUser -All | Where { $_.LastDirSyncTime -eq $null}.

Figure 3-13 Using MSOnline PowerShell to display cloud users

Guest identities

The final identity, although not related to the synchronization process, or created manually by an administrator from the portal, is the guest account. Guest accounts are created automatically in Azure AD as the result of an invitation process in SharePoint Online to share individual documents, folders, or OneDrive content or an entire Microsoft SharePoint team site.

When a document, folder, or site is shared in SharePoint Online, your users can invite external identities, as shown in Figure 3-14.

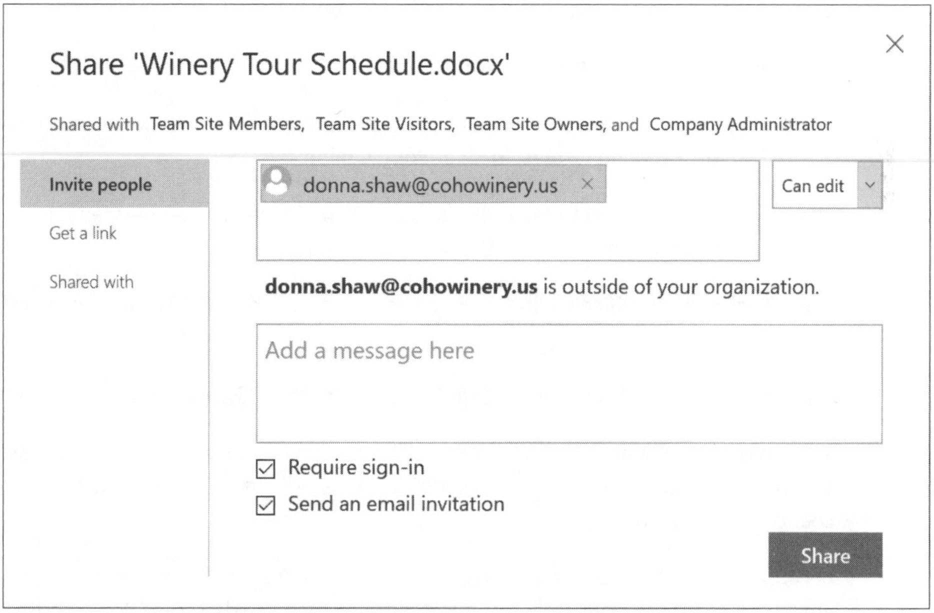

CHAPTER 3

Share 'Winery Tour Schedule.docx'   ✕

Shared with Team Site Members, Team Site Visitors, Team Site Owners, and Company Administrator

| Invite people | 👤 donna.shaw@cohowinery.us   ✕ | Can edit ⌄ |

Get a link

Shared with

donna.shaw@cohowinery.us is outside of your organization.

Add a message here

☑ Require sign-in
☑ Send an email invitation

Share

Figure 3-14 Sharing a SharePoint Online document with an external user

When the recipient accepts the sharing invite creation and authenticates to Azure AD using their email address, a guest account is automatically created in Azure AD and visible in the Office 365 Admin Center. This guest account can be seen using the custom Guest Users view in the Active Users page, as shown in Figure 3-15.

Figure 3-15 Guest user accounts in the Office 365 Admin Center

When an external or guest account has been created through the sharing process, additional sharing requests are not necessary when delegating additional permissions to the account. Instead, the guest user account appears in the User list (SharePoint People Picker) when prompting for adding members or sharing additional content.

Guest accounts are not typically licensed in your Office 365 environment and, as a result, these accounts have limited access based on whether they were created through the sharing process or were manually added to other content in your tenant.

Guest accounts have the following capabilities.

- They can access the sites, folders, or documents to which they were granted access through a sharing request in SharePoint Online.

- They can be added to team sites in SharePoint Online as members, enabling them to add, update, and delete lists and documents.

- They can use Office Online to view documents to which they have access in SharePoint Online.

Guest accounts can also be easily identified by using the MSOnline PowerShell cmdlets.

When a guest account is created in Azure AD, the email address that was used to send the sharing request is converted to the UserPrincipalName of the account; however, some minor changes are applied.

Because the UserPrincipalName can only contain one at sign (@) character, the at sign in the email address of the external account is replaced with an underscore (_), the address is followed by #EXT#, and, finally, the @tenant.onmicrosoft.com suffix is appended to the end.

The result is an easily recognizable UserPrincipalName for guest accounts, as shown in Figure 3-16.

Figure 3-16 Guest user account UserPrincipalName value

Finally, there is one other distinguishing feature of a guest identity in Azure, compared to cloud or synchronized accounts. Guest accounts, unlike the other two identity types, have a different value for the UserType property.

When viewing a guest account by using the MSOnline PowerShell cmdlets, as shown in Figure 3-17, notice that the UserType is Guest versus a cloud or synchronized account, which are set with a UserType of Member.

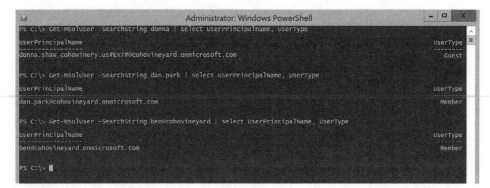

Figure 3-17 Guest user account UserType value

INSIDE OUT

Guest accounts

Whenever a guest account is created in Azure AD, the resulting UserPrincipalName is in the format of <*email_address*>_domain#EXT#@tenant.onmicrosoft.com.

A sharing request for britta.simon@contoso.com would result in a guest account with a UserPrincipalName of britta.simon_contoso.com#EXT#@youtenant.onmicrosoft.com.

CHAPTER 3

Now that you are familiar with the different types of identities used with Azure AD, it's important to understand the different types of identity federation and user authentication available for each of the identity types.

User authentication

After you have identities present in your tenant, whether they are synchronized or cloud users, you must provide a mechanism for authentication for each.

In simplest terms, authentication can be done either by password or identity federation. Both options offer several implementation methods, and the way you create your identities will have an impact on what options are available.

Password

One of the simplest methods for authentication with Azure AD is the use of cloud passwords. Essentially, each identity has a password set on the object itself in Azure AD, and that password is used for authentication purposes when sign-in to Office 365 is processed.

INSIDE OUT

Office 365 and Azure Active Directory

Office 365 and Azure AD are often used interchangeably because Azure Active Directory is the underlying directory when creating objects in Office 365.

It is important to note that passwords, federation, and authentication are all features of Azure Active Directory; Office 365 is simply one of the many services that are built on Azure Active Directory.

When signing in to Office 365, shown in Figure 3-18, you provide the UserPrincipalName (UserName) for the identity along with the password stored in Azure AD for the identity.

Figure 3-18 The Office 365 logon page

Passwords may be set in one of two ways.

- You or the user manually defines the password in the Office 365 portal.

- The password is synchronized from on-premises Active Directory through the Azure AD Connect synchronization process. Chapter 5 discusses how to do this.

INSIDE OUT

Resetting passwords

Even though the Office 365 Admin Center enables you to change the password for a synchronized user, this action will not actually work if the synchronized user account has been synchronized with a password from on-premises Active Directory.

When you enable Password Hash Sync in Azure AD Connect, only passwords for cloud user accounts can be changed using the Office 365 Admin Center.

Much like on-premises Active Directory, new user accounts are configured with a default password that must be changed on first logon, and like Active Directory, user passwords in Azure AD have an expiration policy that forces regular password changes.

Remember that the password is automatically generated when the account is created and is provided to the administrator who created the account. This is true whether the account was created individually or in bulk.

If you assign a password manually at the time of account creation, instead of relying on a randomly generated password, you have the option of forcing the user to change this password on first logon by using the Reset Password options in the New User dialog box, shown in Figure 3-19.

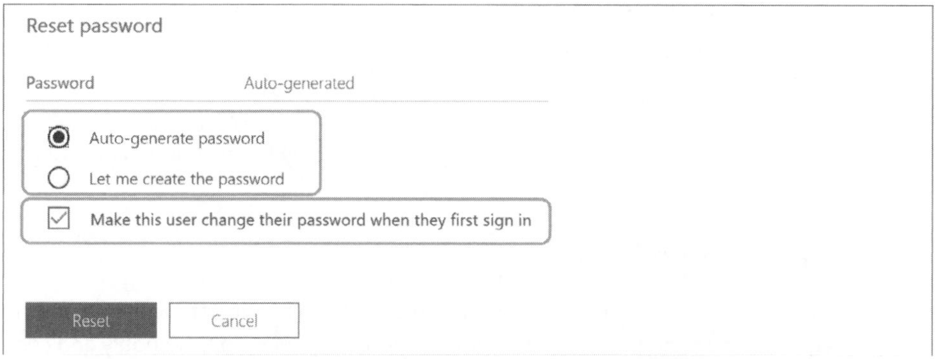

Reset password

Password   Auto-generated

○ Auto-generate password
○ Let me create the password

☑ Make this user change their password when they first sign in

Reset   Cancel

Figure 3-19 Generating or supplying a password and forcing change on sign-in

When logging on for the first time to a new cloud account, to an account whose password has expired, or to an account whose administrator has reset the password, the user is prompted to change the password, as shown in Figure 3-20.

Figure 3-20 Password change required

Any passwords that administrators created or defined during the creation of a cloud user object are subject to the same password complexity restrictions applied to users when they reset or change their password.

Office 365 cloud account passwords have the following requirements.

- 8 characters minimum

- 16 characters maximum

- Cannot contain spaces or Unicode characters

- Cannot contain a dot (.) immediately before the at sign (@)*

- Must contain a combination of three of the four following conditions*
    - Uppercase characters
    - Lowercase characters
    - Numbers
    - Symbols

The requirements marked with an asterisk (*) apply only to accounts when strong passwords are enforced.

Password policy

The password policy options in the Office 365 portal allow you to set the defaults for password expiration and complexity. These settings should be reviewed thoroughly and configured to match your company policy and existing on-premises policies where applicable.

Expiration

The Azure AD password policy that governs password expiration and notification can be configured through the Office 365 Admin Center by selecting Settings > Security & Privacy on the Home page, as shown in Figure 3-21.

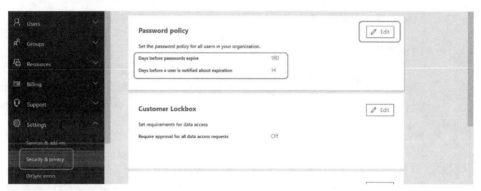

Figure 3-21 Setting Office 365 Password Policy

Selecting Edit enables you to change the password expiration interval as well as the notification settings for cloud user accounts in Office 365.

INSIDE OUT

Password policy

It is always recommended to set the password policies for expiration and notification to match your on-premises Active Directory policies. This way, even cloud identities have the same requirements.

If you enable Password Hash Sync with Azure AD Connect, the Azure AD password policies do not apply to synchronized identities.

Complexity

Unlike the settings for password expiration, strong password requirements are enabled on all cloud accounts by default and cannot be changed in the admin center.

To change the strong password enforcement for a user, or for multiple users, the MSOnline PowerShell cmdlet Set-MsolUser, with the -StrongPasswordEnabled switch must be used.

```
Set-MsolUser -UserPrincipalName sean.bentley@cohovineyard.onmicrosoft.com -StrongPass-
wordRequired $false
```

Changing the complexity requirements for a user does not force the user to make any change to their existing password, nor is the user notified in any way that their password complexity policy has changed. They are simply not required to use a complex password on their next password change.

INSIDE OUT

Complexity requirements

Changing the StrongPasswordRequired setting for a cloud user does not change the minimum or maximum password length requirements. These remain at 8 and 16, respectively.

You can view the StrongPasswordRequired setting for a user by using the Get-MsolUser cmdlet, as shown in Figure 3-22.

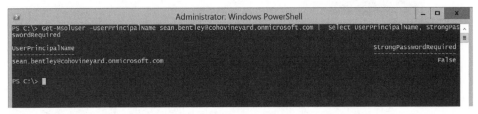

Figure 3-22 Viewing the StrongPasswordRequired property for a cloud user

Setting password complexity through Windows PowerShell rather than in the admin center means that it cannot be done automatically for new users without a custom process. This behavior is by design.

On-premises Active Directory actively enforces password complexity requirements; the same should be true for Azure Active Directory. Change password complexity requirements on a cloud user only if absolutely necessary, and never do it for admin-level accounts because this represents a security risk.

INSIDE OUT

Password for synced accounts

If you select Password Hash Sync during Azure AD Connect installation, you cannot set a password on a synced account, only on cloud accounts.

Identity federation

So far, you've examined authentication using passwords, and although this authentication method is the simplest, it might not be acceptable due to company policy or other security requirements within your organization. As a result, identity federation can be used to provide an alternate option for user authentication to Office 365.

Identity federation, often referred to as Single Sign-On, is a process by which the user accoin Azure AD use an on-premises or third-party identity provider to authenticate sign-in attempts, as shown in Figure 3-23. This removes the requirement to maintain separate passwords in Office 365 and secures the authentication process by using the source directory for your users.

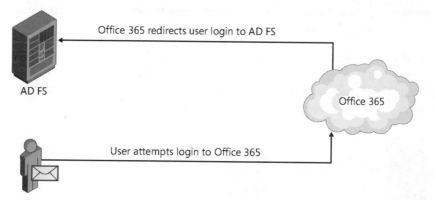

Figure 3-23 Identity federation using Microsoft Active Directory Federation Services (AD FS)

When users sign in to Office 365, they are directed back to on-premises infrastructure to verify their account, and no password data for synchronized accounts is stored in Azure AD.

INSIDE OUT

Passwords and identity federation

Implementation of both identity federation *and* password hash sync is supported. It is a simple matter of configuring identity federation for your domain names as well as selecting the optional Password Hash Sync feature during the Azure AD Connect installation.

Although the use of identity federation over passwords is a more secure authentication process, it also introduces more complexity into the sign-in process.

The Password Hash Sync feature is included in the Azure AD Connect tool, and you can easily enable it through the installation wizard, existing on the same server, whereas identity federation requires additional servers and network changes before you can use it.

Identity federation using Active Directory Federation Services (AD FS) requires a minimum of two additional servers in the environment; however, four or more are typically recommended to allow for failover and high availability.

An AD FS implementation consists of two roles, the Web Application Proxy (WAP) server and the AD FS federation server.

The WAP server is normally deployed in your perimeter network and exposed to the public Internet on port 443. It receives authentication requests when a federated user attempts to sign in to Office 365 and forwards those requests to the federation server for processing.

You deploy the federation server on your internal network, joined to your Active Directory domain, and it receives the requests that are forwarded from the WAP server. Because the federation server is domain-joined, it can communicate directly with the Active Directory domain controllers to authenticate users. See Figure 3-24.

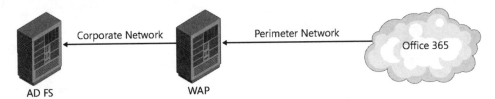

Figure 3-24 Typical AD FS infrastructure

In addition to one or more of each server type (for high availability), additional DNS, firewall, and network configurations are required to implement identity federation.

These configurations could include, but are not limited to:

- A DNS entry in your public DNS that points to the WAP server(s).

- Firewall rules in your perimeter network that allow inbound communication to your WAP servers on port 443 from the public Internet.

- A certificate for your WAP servers, provided by a trusted certificate authority.

- Load-balancing configurations for your WAP servers in your network's perimeter network.

- Firewall rules between your perimeter and internal networks, which allow inbound communication between your WAP and federation servers on port 443.

- Load-balancing configurations for your federation servers.

- An internal DNS entry for your federation server farm.

After you have installed and configured this infrastructure, you must then use the MSOnline PowerShell cmdlets to federate each of the domains registered in your tenant with your federation endpoint (the DNS name of your WAP servers on the public Internet) so that Office 365 can forward authentication requests to your on-premises infrastructure.

You can perform the installation and configuration of AD FS as part of the Azure AD Connect installation wizard; however, Active Directory Federation Services provides additional features that might not be achievable using cloud passwords.

- **On-Premises Smart-Card or Multi-Factor Authentication**   If you have an existing on-premises implementation of smart cards or other multifactor authentication (MFA) providers, these are normally integrated with Active Directory or other on-premises infrastructure. Azure AD cannot integrate directly with such providers.

    Azure AD *does* support MFA directly. You might consider switching from on-premises MFA to cloud-based MFA, which would enable the use of cloud passwords and Password Hash Sync and possibly reduce on-premises infrastructure. MFA is discussed later in this chapter. Cloud-based MFA requires an Azure AD Premium license.

- **Self Service Password Reset**   If you currently have a self-service password reset tool that is integrated with your existing on-premises Active Directory, you can modify the AD FS sign-in pages to use that service, whereas you cannot modify the forgotten-password link on the standard Office 365 sign-in page.

    Azure AD does support self-service password reset; however, it requires an Azure AD Premium license for each user and additional configuration changes to the Azure AD Connect installation to support password writeback.

- **Sign-in Restrictions**   Client Access Policy is a feature of AD FS that enables you to define rules that limit where users can authenticate from (such as from a VPN only, no public access) and even specify hours during which users can authenticate and what protocols they're allowed to use (such as ActiveSync).

- **Sign-in auditing**   Because the AD FS federation server is domain-joined and uses on-premises domain controllers for authentication, the authentication request is logged in the Windows event logs like any other authentication request when using identity federation with AD FS.

    Azure AD provides advanced logging for things like sign-in attempts; however, this feature requires an Azure AD Premium license.

CHAPTER 3

Client access policy in depth

One of the most common deciding factors when considering the implementation of federated identities is the availability of client access policies by using AD FS.

Client access policies in AD FS enable you to create custom claims rules for use with Office 365 (or other AD FS-integrated applications) that can be used to define policies that permit or deny authentication based on client location, time of day, protocol, or other attributes.

Azure AD provides for a comparable feature called *conditional access*; however, conditional access requires an Azure AD Premium license.

Federating your domain

When a domain is verified in your tenant, and you have synchronized one or more user accounts with a UserPrincipalName suffix that matches that domain, assuming you have implemented AD FS, you can convert the domain to federated.

INSIDE OUT

Federated or synchronized

For an identity to be federated, it must first be a synchronized identity, which does not have to be federated. Cloud identities cannot be federated unless they are converted to synchronized.

After your AD FS or other federation service servers are in place, a relying-party trust must be created between your AD FS infrastructure and Office 365, which you do by converting one or more of your domains to federated.

To convert a domain suffix to federated is a simple process.

1. Log on to one of the ADFS federation servers.

2. If you have not already installed the Microsoft Online Services Sign-In Assistant and Azure Active Directory PowerShell module, complete these tasks:

   - Download and install the Microsoft Online Services Sign-In Assistant from *http://aka.ms/o365-sia.*

   - Download and install the Azure Active Directory PowerShell module from *http://aka.ms/o365-psh.*

3. Open an administrative Windows PowerShell command prompt window.

4. Connect to Office 365 by typing the command Connect-MsolService, shown in Figure 3-25.

Figure 3-25 Connecting to MSOnline with Windows PowerShell

5. Provide credentials for a global administrator in your tenant, as shown in Figure 3-26.

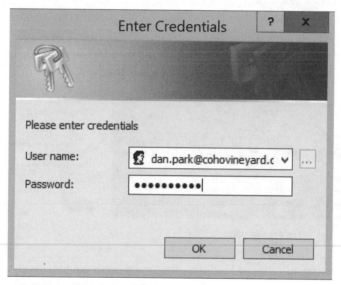

Figure 3-26 Providing credentials for authenticating to Office 365 as a global administrator

6. Enter the command (as shown in Figure 3-27):

Convert-MsolDomainToFederated -SupportMultipleDomain -DomainName yourdomain

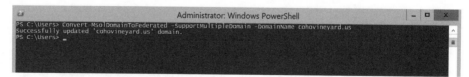

Figure 3-27 Converting MsolDomain to federated

When the domain has been successfully converted, usually in just a few seconds, the command returns a Success status.

CHAPTER 3

Your domain is now federated with Office 365, and any sign-in attempts from the portal automatically redirect you to your AD FS endpoint when the Tab key is pressed during the entry of the logon name, as shown in Figure 3-28.

Figure 3-28 Office 365 automatic redirection for federated domains

After the redirection has been successfully processed, your client sees the AD FS WAP server's forms-based logon page, shown in Figure 3-29, and the user name you supplied in the portal logon process is automatically populated in the user name field.

Figure 3-29 The AD FS sign-in page

Entry of the password, followed by clicking the Sign In button, automatically authenticates your user against your internal domain, and you can see it in the Windows Security event log on the domain controller.

The Event ID sample in Figure 3-30 from the Windows domain controller shows Audit Success from the AD FS server for the federated user sign-in.

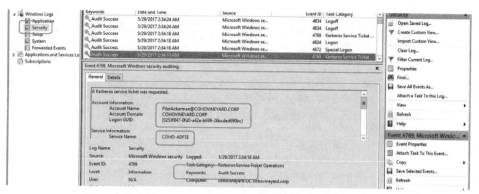

Figure 3-30 Security event log success audit for AD FS sign-in

Configuring client access policies

When you have successfully implemented AD FS and federated one or more of your domains, you can then use client access policies to apply additional rules to your configuration.

You can find the default rules that are applied to your AD FS configuration by launching the AD FS Management console on one of your AD FS federation servers, selecting Trust Relationships, selecting Claims Provider Trusts, right-clicking Active Directory, and then selecting Edit Claims Rules, as shown in Figure 3-31.

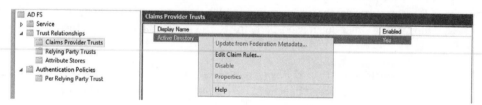

Figure 3-31 Editing the claim rules for the Active Directory provider

Each of the default claims rules appears, as shown in Figure 3-32, and additional transform rules can be applied to define the behavior of the AD FS instance. The default configuration enables all Active Directory users to authenticate and consume Office 365 services.

CHAPTER 3

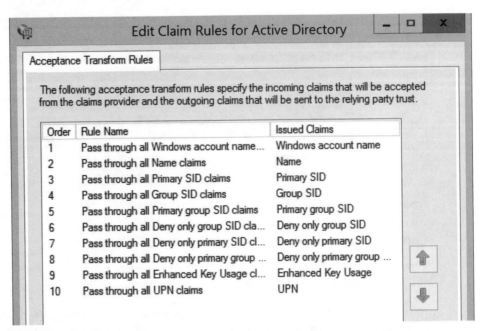

Figure 3-32 Default Acceptance Transform Rules for the Active Directory provider

If you are using AD FS 2.0, you must create five new acceptance transform rules for the Active Directory provider that will pass through the required request claim types before you can update the Office 365 relying-party trusts. This is necessary to enable client access policy with AD FS.

If you are using AD FS 2012 R2 or later, you can skip adding these five new client access policy claim types and proceed directly to the creation of the claims rules for the Office 365 relying-party trust.

To enable Client Access Policy claim types in AD FS 2.0, follow these steps.

1. Ensure that you have applied AD FS 2.0 Update Rollup2 from *https://aka.ms/adfs2-ru2*.

2. Launch the AD FS Management Console and edit the existing claims rules for the Active Directory Claims Provider Trust by selecting Edit Claims Rules.

3. Click Add Rule to start the Add Transform Claim Rule Wizard.

4. Select Pass Through Or Filter An Incoming Claim in the Claim Rule Template drop-down list and click Next, as shown in Figure 3-33.

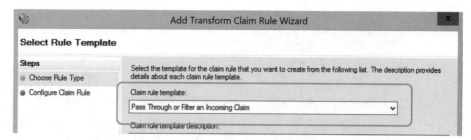

Figure 3-33 Selecting the Pass Through Or Filter An Incoming Claim template

5. Enter a display name for the claim rule, as shown in Figure 3-34, and then type *http://schemas.microsoft.com/2012/01/requestcontext/claims/x-ms-forwarded-client-ip* in the Incoming Claim Type box and click Finish.

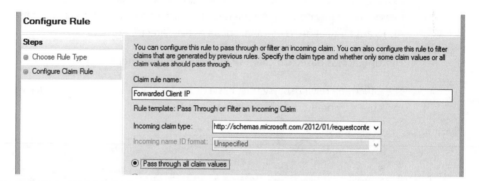

Figure 3-34 Creating an Active Directory provider claim rule

6. Repeat steps 3 through 5, using the display names and claim URLs shown in Table 3-2.

Table 3-2 Additional claims provider rules in AD FS 2.0

Display Name	Claim URL
Client Application	*http://schemas.microsoft.com/2012/01/requestcontext/claims/x-ms-client-application*
User Agent	*http://schemas.microsoft.com/2012/01/requestcontext/claims/x-ms-client-user-agent*
Proxy	*http://schemas.microsoft.com/2012/01/requestcontext/claims/x-ms-proxy*
Endpoint Path	*http://schemas.microsoft.com/2012/01/requestcontext/claims/x-ms-endpoint-absolute-path*

CHAPTER 3

INSIDE OUT

Claims provider rules

AD FS 2.0 implementations require the addition of a rollup package and five claims provider rules so that the Office 365 client access policies provided work properly.

If you are already running AD FS 2012 R2, no changes are required to the Active Directory claims provider rules.

After you have enabled the five client access policy claims types in AD FS 2.0, or if AD FS 2012 R2 is deployed, you can then create client access policies to define logon behavior.

As an example of the power of the Federation Services claims transformations, you create two rules in the following section. One rule limits access to internal users only, and the second limits AD FS authentication to members of an Active Directory group.

Limiting access based on client IP address or department

The Office 365 relying-party trust has a default Issuance Authorization rule, which allows access to all users by default, as shown in Figure 3-35.

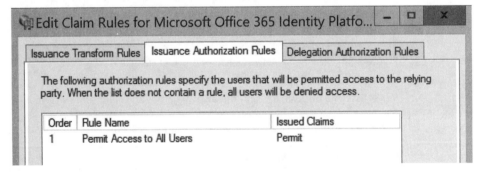

Figure 3-35 Default Issuance Authorization Rules for the Office 365 trust

To create a Claims rule that only allows access to internal IP addresses, perform the following steps.

1.   Click Add Rule to create a new issuance rule.

2.   Select Send Claims Using A Custom Rule in the Claim Rule Template drop-down list and click Next, shown in Figure 3-36.

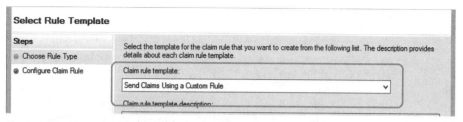

Figure 3-36 Creating a custom claim rule

3. Type the name **Permit Access To Internal Users Only** in the Claim Rule Name box.

4. In the Custom Rule box, enter the following detail, which includes a regular expression (RegEx) that defines the internal private IP address range that your users will use. There is additional detail in the following section, titled "Claims rule language and regular expressions," about regular expressions and their usage.

```
exists([Type == "://schemas.microsoft.com/2012/01/requestcontext/
claims/x-ms-proxy"])

 && NOT exists([Type == "http://schemas.microsoft.com/2012/01/requestcontext/
claims/x-ms-forwarded-client-ip", Value =~ "\b(192)\.(168)\.(0)\.(25[0-5]|2[0-4]
[0-9]|[01]?[0-9][0-9]?)\b"])

 => issue(Type = "http://schemas.microsoft.com/authorization/claims/deny", Value =
"true");
```

5. Ensure that the custom rule detail is entered correctly, as shown in Figure 3-37, and click Finish.

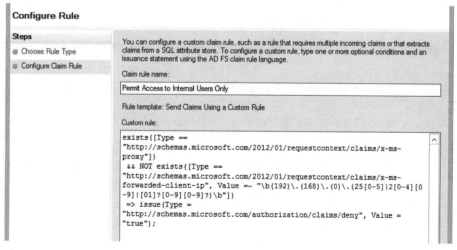

Figure 3-37 Entering the custom claim rule name and language

Claims rule language and regular expressions

The power behind this custom claim rule is the use of a RegEx to define the IP address range for your internal network and then conditional claims rule logic to determine whether the client IP address falls within that range.

The following section breaks down the claim rule language first and then discusses how the RegEx is evaluated. Finally, it expands the expression to include additional IP address ranges.

The first line in the claims rule language is the start of an IF statement:

```
exists([Type == "http://schemas.microsoft.com/2012/01/requestcontext/
claims/x-ms-proxy"])
```

This line checks for the existence of the x-ms-proxy HTTP header in the claim. The existence of this header means that your claim was sent to the AD FS server by a proxy.

Note that the statement is an EXISTS, not an EQUALS. It is effectively checking to see whether the claim came from a proxy server. In this case, the proxy server is the WAP server from the AD FS tracing debug event log from the AD FS federation server, as shown in Figure 3-38.

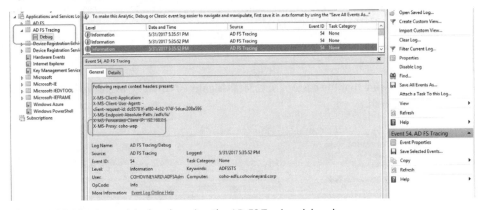

Figure 3-38 Viewing a claim header using the AD FS Tracing debug log

As the figure shows, the first portion of your claims rule IF statement has been satisfied; the claim contains an X-MS-Proxy value.

The next part is the second IF statement, preceded by && to indicate an AND condition:

```
&& NOT exists([Type == "http://schemas.microsoft.com/2012/01/requestcontext/claims/x-
ms-forwarded-client-ip", Value =~ "\b(192)\.(168)\.(0)\.(25[0-5]|2[0-4][0-9]|[01]?[0-9]
[0-9]?)\b"])
```

This condition, unlike the first condition, is a NOT EXISTS statement; it evaluates the x-ms-for-warded-client-ip HTTP header in the claim and then applies the RegEx statement.

The x-ms-forwarded-client-ip header value is important because it contains the IP address of the Forwarded client or the client that initiated the connection with your proxy (WAP) server.

If you were to use the x-ms-client-ip header instead, you would be evaluating the IP address of your WAP server, and it would be the same for every request, making it impossible to identify whether the user was internal or external.

The second IF statement, unlike the first, includes the Value= condition; it evaluates the value of the header, not just whether it is present, like the first condition. Inside the Value= portion of your rule is where the regular expression lives.

The RegEx expression consists of the following:

`\b(192)\.(168)\.(0)\.(25[0-5]|2[0-4][0-9]|[01]?[0-9][0-9]?)\b`

This expression evaluates whether the IP address of the x-ms-forwarded-client-ip falls between 192.168.0.1 and 192.168.0.255.

RegEx is a somewhat complex language; the following is a list that describes each portion of the preceding expression.

- **\b**   This is a boundary marker, it indicates the start and stop of an expression.

- **(192)**   Parentheses indicate a grouping that should be a literal match. This is the first octet of our internal IP address range (192.168.0.0/24).

- **\.**   The backslash (\) is an escape character, used so that the period (.) is evaluated literally. Without the backslash, RegEx uses the period as a wildcard character, so it needs to be preceded by a backslash because IP addresses contain a period.

- **(168)**   Parentheses indicate a grouping that should be a literal match. This is the second octet of our internal IP address range (192.168.0.0/24).

- **\.**   This is a literal evaluation of the period (.), preceded by the backslash as an escape character.

- **(0)**   Parentheses indicate a grouping that should be a literal match. This is the third octet of our internal IP address range (192.168.0.0/24).

- **(25[0-5]|2[0-4][0-9]|[01]?[0-9][0-9]?)**   This fourth grouping is the most complex. It uses a combination of set matching and literal matching to evaluate the fourth octet.

- **25[0-5]** This can be any character from 250 to 255.

- **|** This is an OR.

- **2[0-4][0-9]** This can be any character from 200 to 249.

- **|** This is another OR.

- **[01]?[0-9][0-9]?** Match between the question marks as many times as possible, matching any value between 0 and 199.

The result of the fourth grouping is an expression that will match from 0 to 255, using the OR condition (|) between each set.

TROUBLESHOOTING

Internal IP addresses

Keep in mind, when supplying internal IP address ranges for RegEx expressions, that you should include both network *and* VPN connections if you want to allow users connected through a VPN to access Office 365 services.

The final portion of the claims rule, following the two IF statements, is the action portion.

```
=> issue(Type = "http://schemas.microsoft.com/authorization/claims/deny", Value =
"true");
```

This command, preceded by =>, means that what follows is what should be added to the claim.

The claim value "deny" is set to a value of True, and the statement is closed with a semi-colon (;).

So, if you convert the claims rule, including the RegEx, to shorthand, and treat it like you would an IF statement in programming terms, you get the following.

If the claim header has an entry for the *x-ms-proxy value AND* the *ms-forwarded-client-ip* address does *not* fall between 192.168.0.1 and 192.168.0.255 (remember the statement starts with NOT Exists), *then* set the value of *http://schemas.microsoft.com/authorization/claims/deny* to *True*.

If the value of *http://schemas.microsoft.com/authorization/claims/deny* is True, then the claim is denied, and authorization fails for the user.

Using this new rule, if you test a logon attempt from a machine not on the internal 192.168.0.1-255 network, an Event ID 54 appears in the AD FS tracing log with the claim header information that will be evaluated.

As shown in Figure 3-39, the x-ms-proxy value is populated with the WAP server name, and the ms-forwarded-client-ip address is populated with the public IP address of the browser attempting logon to Office 365.

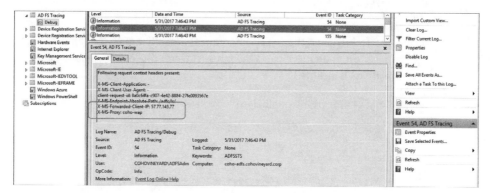

Figure 3-39 AD FS tracing debug log showing a logon attempt from an external client IP

The logon attempt is denied, and the user receives an error page from the WAP server, as shown in Figure 3-40.

Figure 3-40 AD FS WAP sign-in page showing access blocked by a claims rule

Although this rule might help for smaller organizations, where a single IP range is used for internal clients, customer IP ranges are typically much larger and include multiple subnets.

Using the preceding claims rule logic, you can update the RegEx to support the addition of a 10.0.1.1-to-255 range that could reflect a VPN, wireless, or other subnet that would be considered internal and therefore allow clients to access Office 365.

The following example reflects the change in the rule to include the 10.0.1.0/24 subnet.

```
exists([Type == "http://schemas.microsoft.com/2012/01/requestcontext/
claims/x-ms-proxy"])
```

```
&& NOT exists([Type == "http://schemas.microsoft.com/2012/01/requestcontext/claims/x-
ms-forwarded-client-ip", Value =~ "\b(192)\.(168)\.(0)\.(25[0-5]|2[0-4][0-9]|[01]?[0-9]
[0-9]?)\b|(10)\.(0)\.(1)\.(25[0-5]|2[0-4][0-9]|[01]?[0-9][0-9]?)\b"])

=> issue(Type = "http://schemas.microsoft.com/authorization/claims/deny", Value =
"true");
```

The first IF statement and the THEN statement at the end remain the same. All that changes is the RegEx expression that evaluates the x-ms-forwarded-client-ip value to determine whether the new IP range is included.

The new RegEx contains the original expression:

```
\b(192)\.(168)\.(0)\.(25[0-5]|2[0-4][0-9]|[01]?[0-9][0-9]?)\b
```

but includes a second RegEx:

```
|(10)\.(0)\.(1)\.(25[0-5]|2[0-4][0-9]|[01]?[0-9][0-9]?)\b
```

This second expression, preceded by a |, represents an OR, followed by the same logic used to specify 10.0.1.1 to 255 that was used for the 192.168.0.1-to-255 range.

The result is an updated claims rule, as viewed in the claims rule editor like the one shown in Figure 3-41.

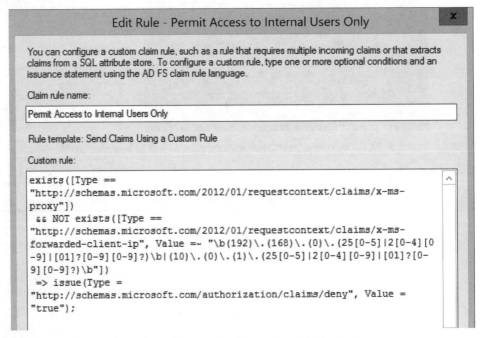

Figure 3-41 Claims rule configured for two IP address subnets in the RegEx

As you can see, the use of regular expressions in AD FS claims rules provides a method for not only filtering IP address ranges but also evaluating other user attribute values.

In the following example, you add a custom claim type for department, so that you can create a rule that prevents users in a specific department from using Office 365. You can use other attributes, but this process gives you an understanding of the methodology required.

1. Open the AD FS Management console and navigate to AD FS Service Claim Descriptions, as shown in Figure 3-42.

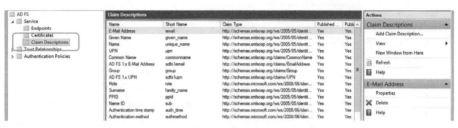

Figure 3-42 AD FS Service Management Claim Descriptions

2. In the Actions pane, click Add Claim Description and type **Department** for Claim Name and a custom claim URL (such as *http://my-claim/department*) and select both check boxes for Accepted and Offered, as shown in Figure 3-43. Click OK.

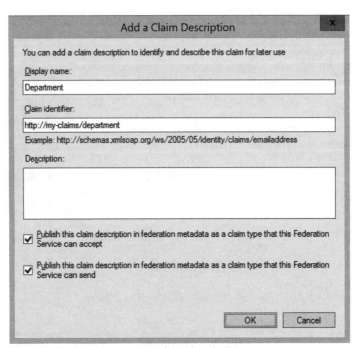

Figure 3-43 Creating a custom claim description

3. Navigate to Trust Relationships | Claims Provider Trusts. Right-click Active Directory and select Edit Claim Rules, as shown in Figure 3-44.

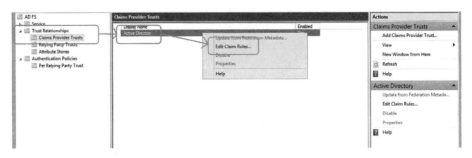

Figure 3-44 Editing the claims rules for Active Directory Claims Provider Trusts

4. Select Add Rule and choose Send LDAP Attributes As Claims, as shown in Figure 3-45. Click Next.

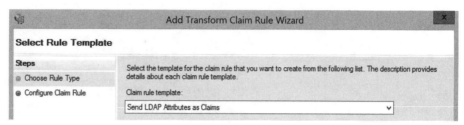

Figure 3-45 Adding a claim rule to Send LDAP attributes

5. Type **Pass Thru Department** as the Claims Rule Name. Select Active Directory in the Attribute Store drop-down list. Select Department in the LDAP Attribute drop-down list and choose Department in the Outgoing Claim Type drop-down list.

   The new claim sends the Active Directory value for Department as the claim called Department that you configured in step 2.

6. When the dialog box matches Figure 3-46, click Finish.

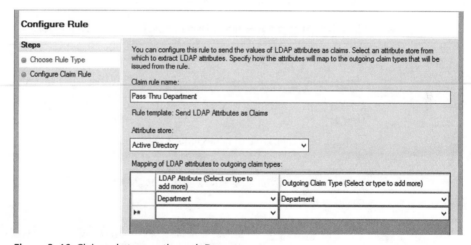

Figure 3-46 Claim rule to pass through Department

After you've added the value for department to the incoming claims, if you review the logon process for a user through the AD FS server, the AD FS debug tracing log, in the Event ID 1000 detail view, as shown in Figure 3-47, displays your new Department claim *http://my-claims /department* with the value of the Department attribute.

CHAPTER 3

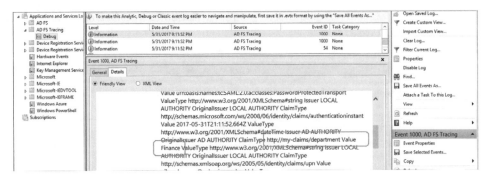

Figure 3-47 Viewing the detailed claim data in the AD FS Tracing event log

Now it's a simple matter of adding a claims rule to the Office 365 relying-party trust to deny access based on the value of the *http://my-claims/department* value.

1. Right-click the Microsoft Office 365 identity platform in the AD FS management tool, select Edit Claim Rules, and select the Issuance Authorization Rules tab.

2. Click Add Rule.

3. Select Send Claims Using A Custom Rule and click Next.

4. Type **Block Access For Finance Users** in the Claim Rule Name box.

5. Type the following content in the Custom Rule box.

   ```
   exists([Type == "http://my-claims/department", Value =~ "Finance"])
   ```

   ```
   => issue(Type = "http://schemas.microsoft.com/authorization/claims/deny", Value =
   "true");
   ```

   When the new claim rule matches Figure 3-48, click Finish.

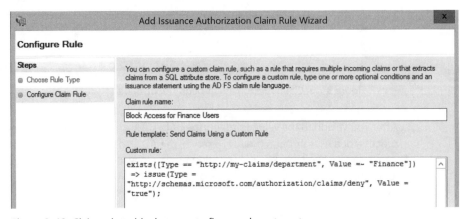

Figure 3-48 Claim rule to block access to finance department users

When the user, as a member of the Finance department, attempts to sign in, using AD FS, to Office 365, their access will be blocked.

Limiting access based on group membership

The claims rule language in AD FS is an extremely powerful tool that you can use to create very specific requirements around logon location as well as user account attributes such as department.

There are additional header values that you can use to help block access based on client type and protocol, including any LDAP attribute that exists in Active Directory—even custom schema extensions.

The final example is a bit simpler and might be more applicable, based on your business requirements.

Using group membership to permit or deny access to Office 365

So far, you have used the claims rule process to send claims to set the Authorization/Deny value to True; however, the claims rule editor also allows for a simpler, wizard-driven approach that works better for things like group membership evaluation.

In the following example, you create a rule that permits access to Office 365 through AD FS only when the user is a member of the AD FS Allowed Users security group in Active Directory.

1. Open the AD FS Management tool, right-click the Microsoft Office 365 Identity Platform relying-party trust, and select Edit Claims Rules, as shown in Figure 3-49.

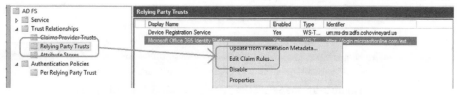

Figure 3-49 Editing the Microsoft Office 365 relying-party trust claim rules

2. Select the Issuance Authorization Rules tab and click Add Rule.

3. Select Permit Or Deny Users Based On An Incoming Claim in the Claim Rule Template drop-down list, as shown in Figure 3-50, and click Next.

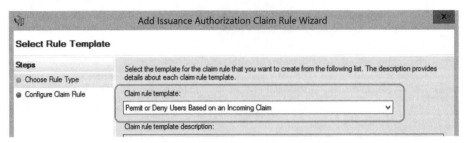

Figure 3-50 Selecting a claim rule template to permit or deny users based on incoming claims

4. Type a name for the claim rule, such as Only Permit AD FS Group Members.

5. In the Incoming Claim Type drop-down list, select Group SID.

6. Click Browse and use the Select User, Computer, Or Group dialog box, as shown in Figure 3-51, to choose the Active Directory group you want to use for this claim.

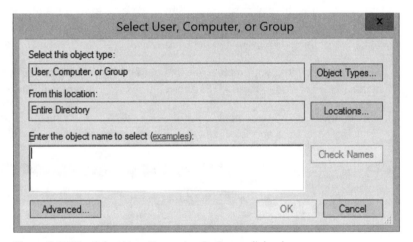

Figure 3-51 The Select User, Computer, Or Group dialog box

7. Select Permit Access To Users With This Incoming Claim.

8. When the claim rule wizard is configured, as shown in the example in Figure 3-52, click Finish to create the rule.

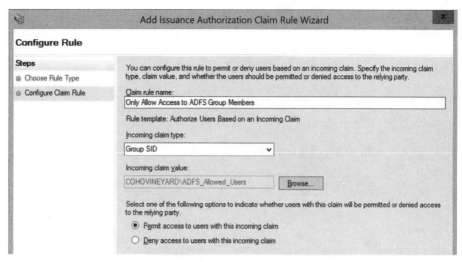

Figure 3-52 Creating a claim rule to filter based on group membership

After you add this new group-based permit rule, you must remove the default Permit Access To All Users rule; otherwise, this rule will apply to everyone, regardless of group membership, and the group-based rule will not work as intended.

CHAPTER 3

Directory synchronization basics

As a new Office 365 administrator, one of the first things you need to understand and imple-ment is directory synchronization. In fact, unless you plan to have only 10 to 20 users in your tenant, directory synchronization, and an understanding of its impact on the entire Azure Active Directory (Azure AD) experience, will be critical to a successful implementation and a continued positive Office 365 experience.

In simplest terms, directory synchronization is the process of duplicating your on-premises Active Directory objects (such as users, groups, and contacts) in Azure AD. It is, however, a bit more complex than that. There are several common misconceptions about Azure AD, and mistakes that occur during synchronization, that can make the process both cumbersome and confusing.

Directory structure

A typical on-premises Active Directory implementation is all about organization and structure. Your on-premises identity infrastructure, at a minimum, consists of one directory, and your objects are organized, typically by type or function, into containers to help ease administration.

In Active Directory, for instance, you can have one or more forests, and within each forest you have at least one additional container, the domain. Within each domain, your hierarchy consists of organizational units (OUs), enabling you to group objects, and you can nest OUs to catego-rize or subdivide your objects further.

Azure Active Directory, however, is flat. There is no discernable directory structure, nor can you dictate one. When synchronizing your objects to Microsoft Azure, all your users, groups, and contacts exist in a single container, with no organizational boundaries.

Although this configuration might seem confusing for anyone used to performing Active Directory administration, the Azure AD portal does a good job of separating object types for administrative purposes. It is true that large numbers of any particular object type might make browsing the Office 365 Admin Center portal difficult; however, the interface is designed to enable you to filter objects to help refine your search.

In Figure 4-1, note that users (active, disabled, guest), groups, contacts, and shared mailboxes are organized easily in the navigation pane. This organizational layout, coupled with the ability to search each object type, makes administration simpler despite the flat directory structure in Azure AD.

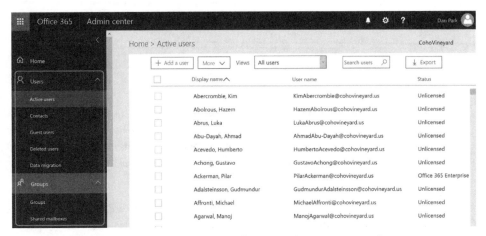

Figure 4-1 Organization of object types in the Office 365 Admin Center portal

Data uniqueness

Unlike on-premises Active Directory, where it's possible (but not recommended) to have objects with the same value populated for attributes that should be unique across your directory, Azure does not allow this. In fact, this is the most common type of error encountered when syncing objects to Azure and can be the most challenging to resolve.

The two most common types of attribute value conflict are UserPrincipalName and ProxyAddresses.

UserPrincipalName

The UserPrincipalName attribute, because it is used for authentication with Azure AD, must be unique for every object in your enterprise. Unlike the SamAccountName value, which is used for authentication to on-premises Active Directory and therefore must be unique for logon to Active Directory, the UserPrincipalName value is used for authentication to Azure AD and therefore must be unique in Azure. The SamAccountName value, for all practical purposes, is ignored.

INSIDE OUT

UserPrincipalName

Only the User and iNetOrgPerson object types have a UserPrincipalName value. Contacts and groups do not.

When an object is synchronized to Azure AD, the UserPrincipalName value is checked for uniqueness and, in the event of duplication with an existing object, special action is taken to transform that value. More information about this transformation process follows in the chapter; however, note that because UserPrincipalName is used for authentication with Azure AD, this transformation process renders the account unusable until the conflict is resolved.

Proxy addresses

Mail flow depends on proxy addresses, and just like the UserPrincipalName value, it is possible to have duplicate proxy addresses between objects in an on-premises Active Directory forest. Most commonly, proxy address conflicts appear during the initial synchronization implementation, but it is not uncommon for them to occur during the normal day-to-day administration of on-premises Exchange.

Like UserPrincipalName, when value duplication occurs between objects, Azure takes steps to remediate the duplication by using Duplicate Attribute Resiliency, as discussed in the following sidebar.

INSIDE OUT

Proxy addresses

Although not used for authentication with Azure AD, the ProxyAddress array can affect the authentication process.

If a new user is synchronized to Office 365, but the UserPrincipalName matches one of the proxy addresses of an object already synchronized to Azure AD, the UserPrincipalName will not be allowed, and authentication for that new user will be broken.

Duplicate attribute resiliency

Duplication of attribute values in the synchronization to Azure AD and the subsequent effort involved in the remediation of these scenarios has been a long-time issue in the synchronization of objects to Office 365. To help alleviate this problem, Microsoft introduced a feature in September 2016, Duplicate Attribute Resiliency.

Duplicate Attribute Resiliency operates in Azure AD, independent of the synchronization engine version, and is enabled by default on all new tenants. In fact, since its release, the feature has been enabled on all Office 365 tenants worldwide, and due to its success in remediation of sync issues, it is no longer a feature that you can turn off.

Previously, if an administrator tried to synchronize a user with a duplicate UserPrincipalName or duplicate proxy address when synchronizing users, groups, or contacts to Azure AD, the synchronization would fail, generate an error in the synchronization engine, and continue to retry the export of the object on every subsequent synchronization cycle.

This backlog of synchronization errors would increase each subsequent synchronization cycle's duration and potentially slow down the export of on-premises Active Directory changes to Azure AD. Now, however, the tenant flags those conflict scenarios, an automated email report is sent to the tenant administrator from Office 365, and the object export is marked as successful.

Duplicate proxy addresses

If a user with a duplicate email address is synchronized to Office 365, the duplicated proxy address value is simply removed from the object being synchronized and placed in a quarantined state. The value remains in this state indefinitely until the conflict is resolved manually, or the offending address is removed from the object.

When Duplicate Attribute Resiliency is triggered for a proxy address conflict, a technical notification email is sent to the tenant administrator as part of the regularly scheduled export cycle, which contains a list of all errors that occurred during that synchronization cycle.

In Figure 4-2, UserPrincipalName identifies the user with the conflict, and the details of the conflict appear. In this example, another object already uses the *finance@cohovineyard.us* email address.

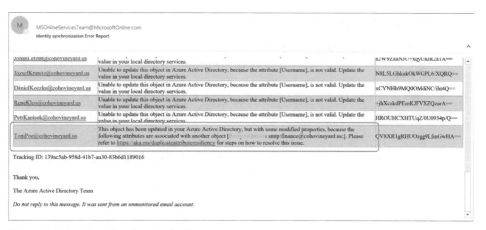

Figure 4-2 Email notification for duplicate proxy

Although the object has been successfully synchronized to Azure AD, and the offending proxy address conflict quarantined, you cannot assign an Exchange Online license to the user because of the quarantined value. Attempting to assign a license results in an error stating that the object currently has a uniqueness violation, as shown in Figure 4-3.

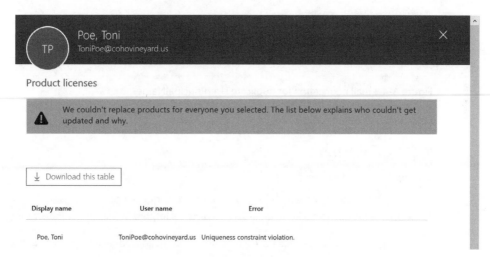

Figure 4-3 Attempt to license a user with a proxy address conflict

In this case, you can assign all the licenses beneath the SKU in question, except the Exchange Online license, until the proxy address conflict is resolved.

Duplicate UserPrincipalName

When a duplicate UserPrincipalName value is synchronized to Azure AD, Azure automatically quarantines the duplicate UserPrincipalName value, as it does for proxy addresses, and the resulting UserPrincipalName prefix for the user becomes the desired prefix, followed by a random four-digit number, and the suffix is replaced with @tenant.onmicrosoft.com, as shown in Figure 4-4.

Items remain in this state until they are manually remediated, and because the UserPrincipalName is used for authentication, this account remains unusable until the conflict is resolved.

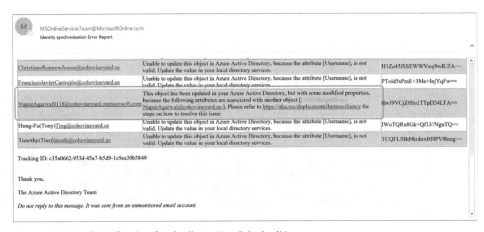

Figure 4-4 Email notification for duplicate UserPrincipalName

INSIDE OUT

Duplicate Attribute Resiliency

When the Duplicate Attribute Resiliency feature is triggered, an update is sent as part of the normal technical notification email, but no error is logged in the AAD Connect tool.

The update is sent only once for each conflict, and no additional notifications are sent.

Technical notification

Both UserPrincipalName and proxy address conflicts result in an email to the technical contact for your Office 365 tenant. Typically, this recipient is identified during tenant setup as the person who created the Office 365 subscription.

After you have successfully set up your tenant and *before* you have started synchronizing, review the technical notification setting and ensure that the email address is valid. Furthermore, it is typically recommended for the technical notification email setting to be configured to use the email address associated with a distribution list in your on-premises Exchange organization so that more than one administrator receives the notification emails from the synchronization process.

The technical notification email can be configured in the Office 365 Admin Center portal by selecting the company name (such as CohoVineyard) in the upper right corner of the main admin console page, as shown in Figure 4-5.

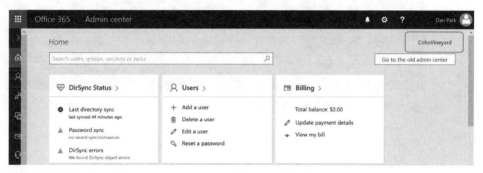

Figure 4-5 Selecting the company name to configure technical notification

This enables you to edit the organization profile for your Office 365 subscription, which includes the Technical Contact email address along with other settings such as Office 365 software release preferences, themes, and tile customizations.

If you prefer not to use the Office 365 portal to set the Technical Notification email preferences, they can also be updated by using Windows PowerShell.

The Get-MsolCompanyInformation command displays the current TechnicalNotificationEmails setting, which is a list of email addresses that receive service notifications and synchronization reports from the tenant.

You can use the Set-MsolCompanyContactInformation -TechnicalNotificationEmails command followed by a comma-separated list of email addresses that you wish to receive the updates, as shown in Figure 4-6.

CHAPTER 4

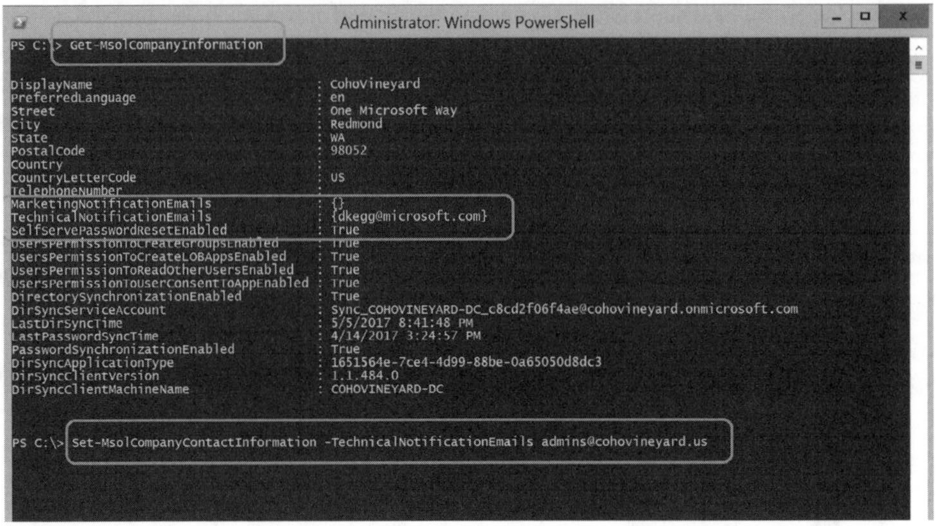

```
PS C:\> Get-MsolCompanyInformation

DisplayName                                    : CohoVineyard
PreferredLanguage                              : en
Street                                         : One Microsoft Way
City                                           : Redmond
State                                          : WA
PostalCode                                     : 98052
Country                                        :
CountryLetterCode                              : US
TelephoneNumber                                :
MarketingNotificationEmails                    : {}
TechnicalNotificationEmails                    : {dkegg@microsoft.com}
SelfservePasswordResetEnabled                  : True
UsersPermissionToCreateGroupsEnabled           : True
UsersPermissionToCreateLOBAppsEnabled          : True
UsersPermissionToReadOtherUsersEnabled         : True
UsersPermissionToUserConsentToAppEnabled       : True
DirectorySynchronizationEnabled                : True
DirSyncServiceAccount                          : Sync_COHOVINEYARD-DC_c8cd2f06f4ae@cohovineyard.onmicrosoft.com
LastDirSyncTime                                : 5/5/2017 8:41:48 PM
LastPasswordSyncTime                           : 4/14/2017 3:24:57 PM
PasswordSynchronizationEnabled                 : True
DirSyncApplicationType                         : 1651564e-7ce4-4d99-88be-0a65050d8dc3
DirSyncClientVersion                           : 1.1.484.0
DirSyncClientMachineName                       : COHOVINEYARD-DC


PS C:\> Set-MsolCompanyContactInformation -TechnicalNotificationEmails admins@cohovineyard.us
```

Figure 4-6 Using Windows PowerShell to set the technical notification contacts

Locating objects with errors

After you have successfully configured the company information in your tenant, and you have started receiving technical notification email as part of the ongoing synchronization process, you can now use both the Office 365 Admin Center portal and Windows PowerShell to review the errors present in your tenant.

This chapter discusses how to remediate different types of errors later, but it's important to understand where those errors can be located so that you don't need to rely on keeping all the notification emails you receive from the tenant.

INSIDE OUT

Getting notifications

Office 365 synchronization, after it's configured, typically occurs every 30 minutes. In the case of UserPrincipalName and proxy address conflicts, you are notified only once; however, for other validation or data integrity errors, you continue to receive an email notification each time the synchronization completes.

The email messages from your tenant can stack up quickly, and it's easy simply to ignore them as spam, but remediation of synchronization errors is the key to ensuring a healthy Office 365 synchronization experience.

Locating error objects in the Office 365 Admin Center portal

Locating objects in an error state in the Office 365 Admin Center portal is a simple matter of logging on to Office 365 and selecting Users on the main admin page.

In the Views drop-down list at the top of the page, you can then select Users With Errors, as shown in Figure 4-7.

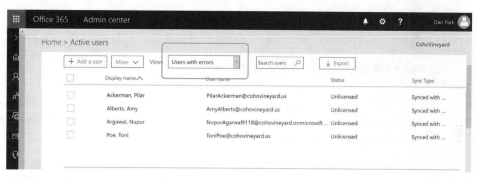

Figure 4-7 Filtering by Users With Errors

From the previous examples, you should be able to distinguish users with proxy address conflicts from those with UserPrincipalName conflicts.

> **NOTE**
>
> **Typically, UserPrincipalName conflicts have a four-digit number in the prefix and end with tenant.onmicrosoft.com.**

Although the Office 365 Admin Center portal enables you to view the objects with errors, very little additional information appears when filtering for errors in the Users view. In fact, even selecting each user individually does not provide the root cause of the error.

To reveal the cause of the error, look at the identity synchronization error report that you received by email when the error occurred, use the DirSync Status Summary page, or use Windows PowerShell.

Locating error objects by using the DirSync Status Summary page

Although the Users view in the Office 365 Admin Center portal provides limited information by using a filter view about the objects with synchronization errors, it is not the ideal method for viewing error objects. Instead, you can use the Office 365 Admin Center portal DirSync status card on the admin center Home page, shown in Figure 4-8, to drill down into individual synchronization errors.

CHAPTER 4

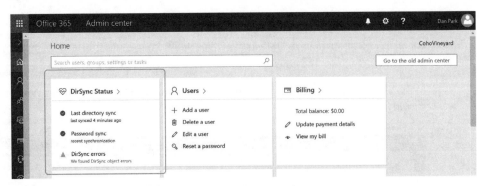

Figure 4-8 The Office 365 Admin Center DirSync Status card

Clicking DirSync errors displays a page listing each of the error objects along with the provisioning error for that object. You can then click each object and see the specific object error information you can use to remediate the error.

As shown in Figure 4-9, Azure AD detected a conflict in the finance@cohovineyard.us proxy address value; the dialog box displays both objects that were configured with that proxy address and the object whose conflicting value was removed, in this case, the *second* object to be synchronized to Azure AD with this value.

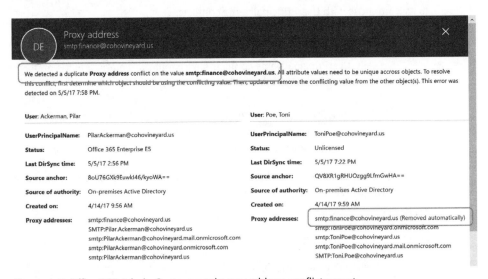

Figure 4-9 Office 365 Admin Center portal proxy address conflict report

INSIDE OUT

Conflicting objects

Although the Office 365 Admin Center portal DirSync status page displays objects with duplicate values, it removes the conflicting value for only the second, or subsequent, object synchronized to your tenant.

Azure AD does not know which object should be the winner; therefore, the value might not be removed from the correct object but only from the second object to display that value.

Locating error objects by using Windows PowerShell

When locating conflict errors in Azure AD by using Windows PowerShell, you can use a special error category called *PropertyConflict* when viewing objects. This special error category aligns with the Duplicate Attribute Resiliency feature.

To view all users with a property conflict, you can use the Get-MsolDirSyncProvisioningError -ErrorCategory PropertyConflict command.

As shown in Figure 4-10, this command returns the same four objects viewed in the Office 365 Admin Center portal.

Figure 4-10 Using Windows PowerShell to view objects with provisioning errors

CHAPTER 4

Two objects have provisioning errors on UserPrincipalName, and two have provisioning errors on ProxyAddresses.

If you prefer to sort objects based on the provisioning error type, you can use the Get-MsolDirSyncProvisioningError -ErrorCategory propertyconflict -PropertyName UserPrincipalName command to display only the UserPrincipalName errors, or PropertyName ProxyAddresses to display proxy address conflicts.

Summing up data uniqueness

A variety of methods are available for viewing provisioning and synchronization errors in your tenant. Each method provides certain conveniences when compared to the others.

For example, if you only have a few errors, you can easily navigate the portal, selecting each object in turn and identifying the root cause. When you have a larger number of errors, you can use Windows PowerShell to export a sorted list by provisioning error type to a comma-separated value (CSV) file that you can use to generate a detailed report.

In either case, understand how to access error details in the portal, and the root cause for some of the most common synchronization errors.

This chapter discusses more about detailed error tracking and remediation later; for now, it's important to understand how the synchronization engine, AAD Connect, handles the synchronization of each object type and its underlying properties.

Understanding directory synchronization

The AAD Connect tool, used to synchronize your objects to Azure AD, is based on the Microsoft Identity Manager product (and its predecessors) and uses an approach referred to as a metadirectory to maintain and synchronize your objects.

By definition, a metadirectory is simply a collection of directories—in this chapter, Azure Active Directory and one or more on-premises Active Directory domains. These individual directories are joined through a central directory that maintains information about each of the source directories. As synchronization occurs, objects from each directory are evaluated, allowing them to be filtered out, joined with objects from other directories, or transformed to create new objects that are ultimately synced to Office 365.

The ultimate goal of the metadirectory is to maintain a connection between each object and its partner as well as any new objects created as a result, so that ongoing changes in any of the directories can be updated on all the connected objects.

This network of connected directories and objects might sound a bit confusing. The following explains how metadirectory services fit into a standard deployment of AAD Connect to synchronize a single on-premises Active Directory forest to Office 365.

Figure 4-11 shows one Active Directory forest, consisting of a single domain and several OUs, which contain users, groups, contacts, and computers. This is, by all accounts, a typical on-premises Active Directory implementation.

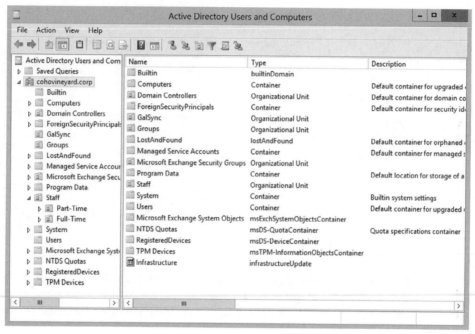

Figure 4-11 A typical Active Directory single-domain forest

The directory structure is well defined, grouping each object type.

When synchronizing this data to Azure AD, however, there are several objects, such as ForeignSecurityPrincipal objects and Trusted Platform Module (TPM) devices, that you do not want to synchronize to your tenant. The AAD Connect tool enables you, by using scoping filters (discussed in Chapter 5, "Installing Azure AD Connect"), to eliminate the objects you don't want exported to your tenant.

Filtering is the first of many functions the directory synchronization provides, and although filtering might seem simple, it's a critical first step in the transformation process. Objects filtered from the synchronization are still stored in the AAD Connect metadirectory and can be used later if necessary, based on the configuration defined.

Filtering is easy, however, so what objects do you want to export to your Office 365 tenant?

As the synchronization engine imports each object from its source directory, it's placed into a holding location in the metadirectory. This holding location, called a *connector space*, maintains all the metadirectory information about your source Active Directory forest and every object inside it. See Figure 4-12.

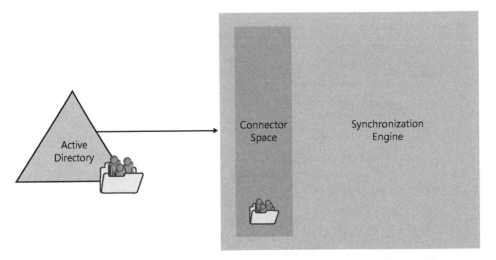

Figure 4-12 The connector space

The connector space contains a copy of each object it represents in the source directory. All the details, or attributes, of that object are maintained in the connector space and are used in subsequent steps to transform the object as it flows through the synchronization engine.

NOTE

Note that each of your connected sources (Azure AD, on-premises Active Directory) gets its own connector space. Objects do not mix between connector spaces. In fact, that's a different container, discussed in more detail shortly.

INSIDE OUT

Connector spaces

Connector spaces are a point-in-time representation of your source directory; they are not maintained in real time.

For a connector space to be updated with changes, an import from that connected data source must occur.

After the synchronization engine has imported an object and stored it in the connector space for that directory, synchronization rules are applied to the object. Depending on the rule, one of two things happens.

1. As discussed previously, the object can be filtered at this step. A filtered object never leaves the connector space; however, because it has been filtered using a rule and not excluded from the sync due to its OU, this object might be able to move on to step 2 later. For now, however, it remains in the connector space.

2. The object is allowed to flow out into the central directory, called the *metaverse*, where it can be transformed, joined with other objects, and even used to create brand-new objects in different connector spaces.

The metaverse, as shown in Figure 4-13, is the center of the metadirectory universe. It is where new objects are created and relationships are defined between existing objects from other connector spaces.

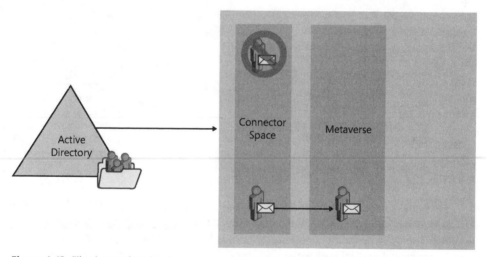

Figure 4-13 Filtering and projecting

In the diagram, the object that is not filtered from the synchronization can proceed to the metaverse and become a new object. This new object maintains a relationship with the object from the Active Directory connector space that it represents, but it is, for all intents and purposes, a brand-new object.

This process, whereby an object in a connector space is allowed through a synchronization rule to flow into the metaverse as a new object while maintaining a connection to its source, is called a *projection*.

CHAPTER 4

Much like an image on film is projected on a screen by using a bright light, the connector space object is projected into the metaverse.

The new object in the metaverse could be an exact copy of the object it represents, but it's also possible (as is typically the case) that the new object, although like the object it represents, could contain a number of new or different attribute values from its source as well as fewer attributes. See Figure 4-14.

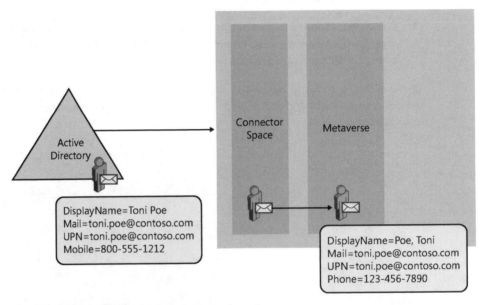

Figure 4-14 Projection from connector space to metaverse

In this example, the on-premises Active Directory object appears in the Active Directory connector space with all the same values, but as the object flows to the metaverse, the DisplayName for the object is transformed from First, Last to Last, First, the Mobile value is removed, and, instead, a new value for Phone has been created. All these changes are the result of transformation rules configured in the synchronization engine.

After our new object has been created in the metaverse, the object that it represents in the Active Directory connector space is now referred to as a *connector* simply because it maintains a connection with the metaverse object.

This connection, however, is very important. It is how the object in the metaverse is updated whenever the source object (the *connector*) in the Active Directory connector space is updated, when new proxy addresses are added to the source object, for example.

Conversely, if the source object were to be deleted from Active Directory, the metaverse object and any other object connected to it are automatically deleted as well.

So far, only the inbound synchronization rules have been discussed, the rules that deal with the projection of objects into the metaverse and any data transformations that should occur when the object is projected.

INSIDE OUT

Inbound sync rules

Everything in the metadirectory is relative to the metaverse. Inbound synchronization rules are applied to objects on their way *in* to the metaverse from a connector space. Outbound synchronization rules are applied to objects on their way *out* of the metaverse to a connector space.

The next step in the synchronization process is the evaluation of each outbound synchronization rule.

The outbound synchronization rules are applied to every object that was projected into the metaverse to determine whether that object meets specific criteria and should be allowed to proceed beyond the metadirectory.

After an object has been evaluated by an outbound synchronization rule, and if it meets the scoping filter requirements, a new object is created in the target connector space. In Figure 4-15, the target connector space is the Azure connector space.

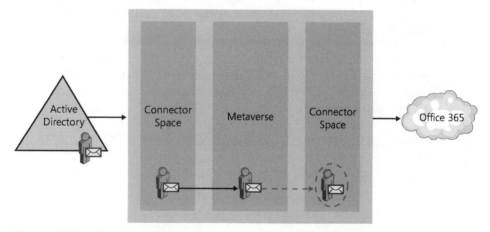

Figure 4-15 Provision from metaverse to Azure connector space

CHAPTER 4

This process, when a new object is created in a different connector space, is referred to as a *provision*. When a provision occurs, just like a projection, the resulting object can have some or all of the source object's properties, as defined by the transformations in the synchronization rule that provisioned the object.

The newly provisioned object in the target connector space maintains a connection to the source metaverse object that it was created from, which in turn has a connection from the metaverse back to the source connector space. See Figure 4-16.

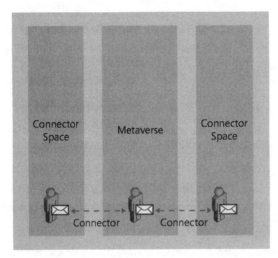

Figure 4-16 Connections from a connector space to the metaverse

After this new object has been provisioned into the Azure connector space, it is ready to be exported to Azure, resulting in an object in your tenant that looks similar to your on-premises Active Directory object.

Now that you understand the Active Directory connector space, the projection of an object to the metaverse, and the provision of a new object from the metaverse to the Azure AD connector space, review the process for a real object in Active Directory and follow its path through the synchronization engine and into Azure AD.

Your test object is a mailbox-enabled user in Active Directory, shown in Figure 4-17, that you want to sync to Azure.

Figure 4-17 Active Directory user properties

The first step in the synchronization process is to read the user from the source directory. AAD Connect does this automatically during the Import step.

INSIDE OUT

Import versus sync

Imports only read data from the source directory into a connector space. No transformation of data occurs during an import step.

Inbound synchronizations process the object, applying rules to the object as it is projected *into* the metaverse.

Outbound synchronizations process the object, applying rules to the object as it is provisioned in a connector space on its way *out* of the metaverse.

After your test user exists in the Active Directory connector space, synchronize the user to apply the rules to the object, as shown in Figure 4-18.

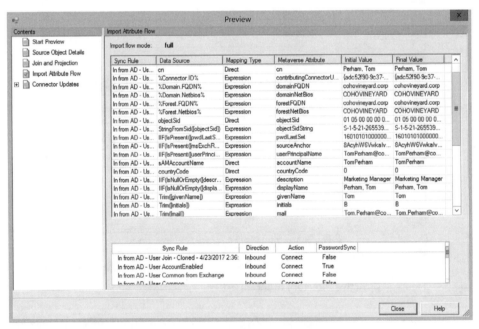

Figure 4-18 User projecting to the metaverse during synchronization

The figure shows that the user was successfully projected into the metaverse, most attributes were populated on the new object directly from Active Directory (displayName, givenName, mail), and some new attributes (domainFQDN, objectSidString) were created during the synchronization process.

In this example, you manually synchronize the objects, using the Preview button in the connector space object properties, shown in Figure 4-19, so you can see the synchronization rules applied to the test object and view the attribute values passing between the connector space object and the metaverse object. Normally, this transformation of values applies behind the scenes automatically for every object each time a synchronization step runs as part of the regular 30-minute cycle.

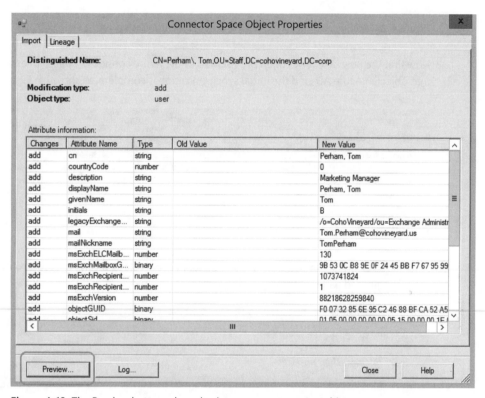

Figure 4-19 The Preview button when viewing a connector space object

While the inbound synchronization rules are being applied to project the test object to the metaverse, the outbound synchronization rules are also being applied, and in the case of the test object shown in Figure 4-20, a new object is being provisioned into the Azure connector space and staged for export to Office 365.

CHAPTER 4

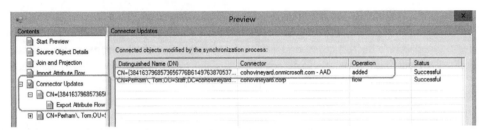

Figure 4-20 Adding a connector for Azure during synchronization

Now that the new object has been provisioned to the Azure connector space, an export places that object in Azure AD, and the initial synchronization is complete, as shown in Figure 4-21.

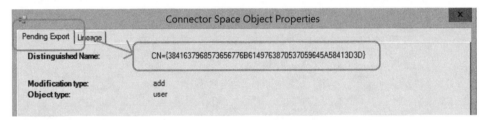

Figure 4-21 Export pending to Azure AD

Note in the example that the object is in a pending export state, awaiting export to Azure, and the distinguished name of the object appears.

INSIDE OUT

Azure distinguished name

The distinguished name of objects in the Azure connector space is not easily distinguishable, making it difficult to search for objects manually.

The value is a UTF8Hex representation of the SourceAnchor (or ImmutableID) of the user and ensures uniqueness across objects in the connector space.

You can find a script to convert the value to SourceAnchor or vice versa at *https://blogs .technet.microsoft.com/dkegg/2015/08/01/dn-value-in-aad-sync-aad-connect-the-new -format/*.

From this point on, any changes to the on-premises Active Directory object are read into the Active Directory connector space, and synchronization rules are applied and flow those changes, where applicable, to the metaverse object it is connected to, out to the object in the Azure connector space it is connected to, and, finally, out to Azure Active Directory.

This process, shown in Figure 4-22, occurs every 30 minutes for every object for the lifetime of each object.

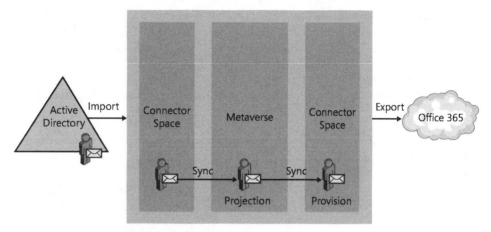

Figure 4-22 Import, sync, projection, provision, and export

The final topic that is key to the metadirectory is the *join*.

The join is absolutely critical when dealing with multiple on-premises Active Directory forests, allowing objects to be combined, but even in a single-forest implementation of AAD Connect, the join is important.

The join behaves exactly like it sounds; it glues objects together as they enter the metaverse, based on one or more criteria that you define. In the AAD Connect installation wizard, which Chapter 5 covers in depth, you select the criteria used for joins during the user matching selection process.

One of the most common join scenarios is the Exchange account forest/resource forest scenario.

INSIDE OUT

Joins

Joins only happen inside the metaverse, when two objects from two connector spaces come together during synchronization.

Joins do not occur in the connector spaces and do not occur during imports, only during synchronizations.

In a multi-forest implementation, one of the most common scenarios is the account forest/resource forest configuration. In this configuration, the account forest consists of user objects that are used for sign-in and authentication to on-premises services, and the resource forest contains the mailboxes for each of those user accounts.

There are a variety of reasons for the implementation of this configuration, and in an on-premises environment, where forest trusts exist and can be used to ensure proper authentication, it's a straightforward configuration. In Office 365, however, no forest trust exists between the cloud and on-premises, and you cannot use Kerberos for authentication.

It is therefore necessary, when synchronizing users to Azure AD, to use the synchronization process to merge the user account and mailbox account to appear as one object in Office 365.

As discussed earlier, each object in Active Directory is stored in the associated connector space, shown in Figure 4-23. In the case of a multi-forest configuration, this means that two (or more) connector spaces represent the on-premises directories.

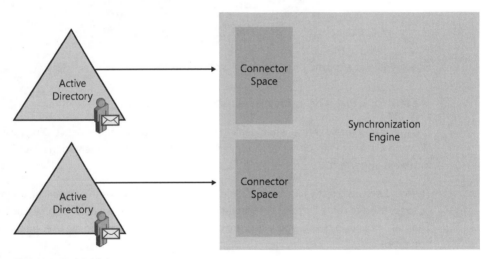

Figure 4-23 Multiple connector spaces

When a user in the account forest is mailbox-enabled, a new mailbox is created in the resource forest; this mailbox account is a disabled user account, and Exchange uses the ObjectSID of the user in the account forest to populate an attribute called msExchMasterAccountSID on the mailbox.

Now that there are two objects, one in each of the two connector spaces in Figure 4-24, there needs to be a way to identify which objects belong together during the synchronization process. This is where the join comes into play.

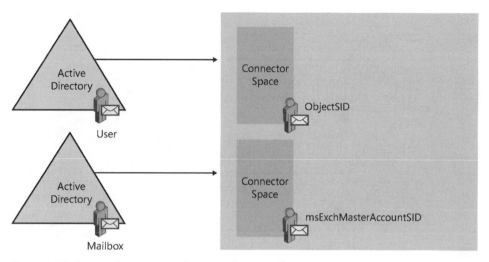

Figure 4-24 Account forest user and resource forest mailbox

AAD Connect uses the msExchMasterAccountSID attribute to join the two objects. AAD Connect populates both the account forest and the resource forest connector spaces during the import step. See Figure 4-25.

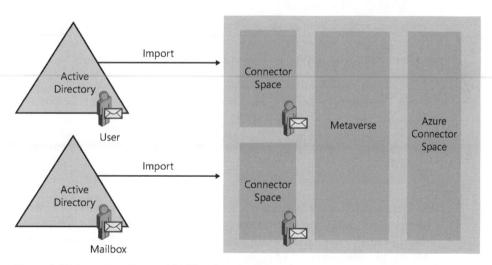

Figure 4-25 Importing User and Mailbox from both forests

During the synchronization step, one of the two objects, depending on which connector space is synchronized first, is projected into the metaverse. In Figure 4-26, the synchronization occurs on the User account first, so the User account is projected into the metaverse.

CHAPTER 4

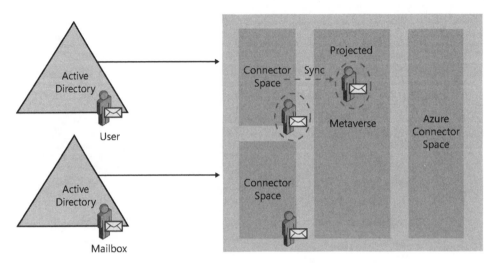

Figure 4-26 Synchronization from User forest projecting the object into the metaverse

INSIDE OUT

Controlling synchronization

When using the built-in scheduler with AAD Connect, you cannot define the order in which connector spaces are synchronized. The synchronization engine configures this during installation, and it might not match the order in which forests were added to the configuration.

To force a specific order, you would have to disable the built-in scheduler and configure a custom script.

In most implementations, the order should not matter. Synchronization rules should be created in such a way that the solution works properly regardless of synchronization order.

When the second connector space is synchronized, the matching object detects its partner in the metaverse, and the two objects merge. In the diagram in Figure 4-27, the Mailbox object from the resource forest has joined the User object from the account forest, resulting in one object in the metaverse that is a combination of both the User account and the Mailbox account. These two objects in the source connector spaces are now considered connectors, and any changes made to the source objects flow to the new joined object in the metaverse during subsequent synchronizations.

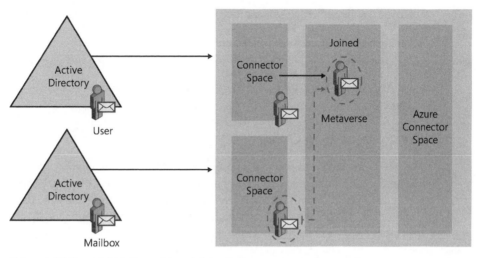

Figure 4-27 User and Mailbox objects joining in the metaverse

Finally, the new object (a combination of the two objects joined in the metaverse) is provisioned to the Azure connector space and staged for export to Office 365.

In Figure 4-28, the newly created object in the metaverse is projected into the Azure connector space for export to Azure Active Directory.

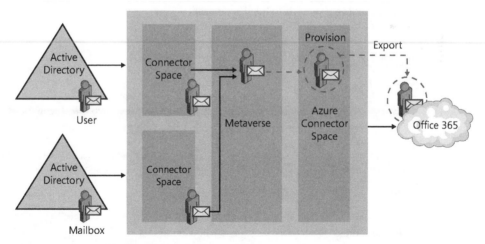

Figure 4-28 New object provisioned to Azure connector space

CHAPTER 4

This oversimplification of the join process did not mention synchronization order or attributes.

- **Synchronization order**   In the flow described previously, the User object was synchronized first. What happens if the Mailbox object is synchronized first instead?

- **Attributes**   How do you configure where the Azure connector space object's values come from?

Synchronization Order

The AAD Connect tool, as part of the normal out-of-the-box configuration that is created when you perform the installation and select the msExchMasterAccountSID and ObjectSID user-matching mode, automatically creates the necessary join rules that enable the User account and Mailbox to join. You don't need to change anything; this happens automatically, provided you select the correct User Matching option during installation.

In addition, because the mailbox account in this scenario should be disabled, it adds additional logic to the configuration to ignore the fact that the object is disabled in Active Directory. Instead, it synchronizes the object as enabled by taking that value from the account forest after they join.

Finally, and most important, because the SourceAnchor (discussed in more detail in Chapter 5) for the object cannot come from the mailbox account, additional logic is added to the synchronization engine that prevents the object from synchronizing to Azure if it's only the mailbox account and not yet joined with the user account.

INSIDE OUT

Resource forest mailboxes

For the AAD Connect default rules designed for account \ resource forest scenarios to work properly, the objects must be linked mailboxes (the default behavior) in the resource forest.

If a mailbox in the resource forest is meant to be a linked mailbox, but its msExchRecipientTypeDetails is not set to 2, then the AAD Connect synchronization rules will not work properly.

Make sure your linked mailboxes in the resource forest are stamped with the correct value in Active Directory and have not been modified manually for any reason.

Attributes

The logic behind the attributes that are populated on the newly provisioned object in the Azure connector space is a bit more complex; it is a combination of predefined behavior in the AAD Connect tool as part of the installation, but also defined by the precedence (covered in more detail in Chapter 5) assigned to the synchronization rules.

By default, when a mailbox-enabled object joins a user account, the values that are specific to the user account, such as UserPrincipalName, SourceAnchor, SecurityIdentifier (SID), and UserAccountControl (enabled or disabled), all come from the user account. Email-specific attributes, such as proxy addresses, TargetAddress, and Exchange recipient type, come from the resource account.

This flow of the obvious account-specific values is fairly straightforward and doesn't require any special consideration on your part.

What do require special consideration are the values that are used for the account-agnostic attributes, such as First Name, Last Name, Display Name, Company, and Address.

In a typical resource forest configuration, the values for these account-agnostic attributes should be used from the resource (Mailbox) object because those values are visible to all other users in the Exchange global address list (GAL).

Normally, to maintain a consistent and seamless transition from an on-premises global address list to an Exchange Online global address list, you want the values from the mailbox to be visible on the object that is synchronized to Office 365, as shown in Figure 4-29.

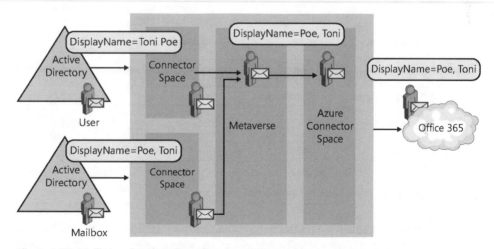

Figure 4-29 Mailbox-related attribute flow from resource forest

In the figure, the DisplayName attribute differs between the User object in the account forest and the Mailbox in the resource forest. The resource forest value for DisplayName is the value that is used on the newly joined metaverse object and flows out to Azure AD through the Azure connector space.

This attribute flow is defined by the order in which you add connectors to the AAD Connect configuration during the initial installation and affects a function of the synchronization referred to as *precedence*.

Depending on how precedence is configured, the objects that you synchronize to Office 365 could have different values than those visible in the on-premises global address list.

For example, your account forest data is maintained using a human resources (HR) system that populates things such as First Name and Last Name by using the legal first and last name of your users. Brian Albrecht, the user shown in Figure 4-30, appears in the account forest with his official first and last name.

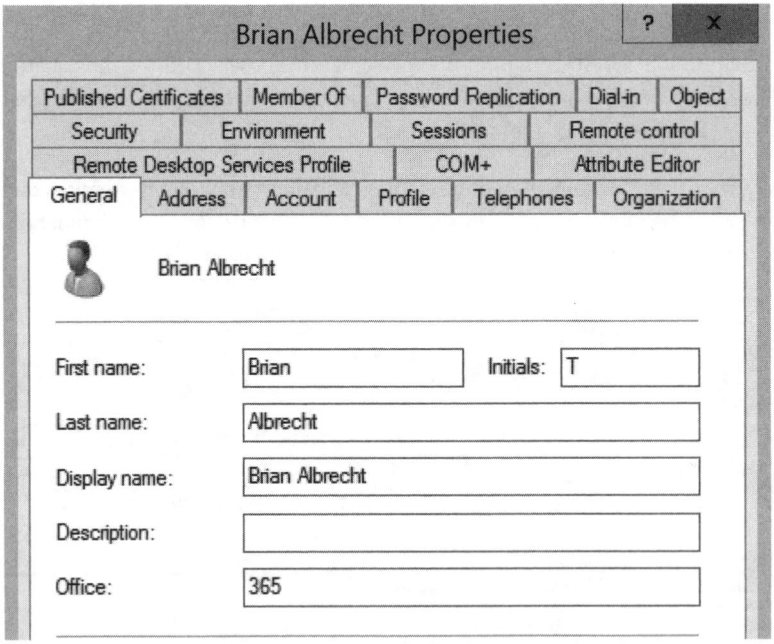

Figure 4-30 Brian Albrecht user account forest properties

However, because Brian prefers to be called Tom (his middle name), the resource forest First Name and Display Name attributes are changed to reflect this preference, as shown in Figure 4-31.

Figure 4-31 Tom Albrecht mailbox resource forest properties

Users can locate Tom in the GAL because the values in the resource forest directory are the values that appear when using Microsoft Outlook, as shown in Figure 4-32.

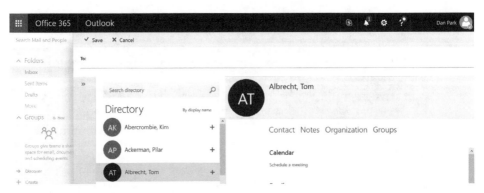

Figure 4-32 Locating a user in the Office 365 GAL

If the account forest values could flow to Azure when joining the user and resource accounts for Mr. Albrecht, the GAL in Exchange Online would show his legal first name, and the address book would look different to your users.

To correct this, the resource forest must be precedent (the winner) so that the correct values, those from the resource forest, are allowed to be the values populated in Azure.

Although the AAD Connect installation can handle the projection, provision, and join activities, you still must make important decisions that affect the Office 365 user experience, and they must be made before you start synchronizing your objects to Azure.

Managing directory synchronization enterprise-wide

Although you can manage the directory synchronization process by directly accessing the synchronization server, non-administrators can be granted access to monitor and manage health by using the Office 365 Admin Center portal. The AAD Connect health dashboard, as well as the Office 365 Admin Center portal home page, can provide additional information about the directory synchronization status.

AAD Connect health dashboard

One of the many additional features included in the AAD Premium license is the AAD Connect health dashboard. During the installation of the AAD Connect tool, discussed in detail in Chapter 5, the AAD Connect health agent is installed on the AAD Connect server and is automatically configured to send health and monitoring information to your Azure Active Directory tenant.

The AAD Connect health dashboard provides information about alerts, usage analytics, and other important information and shows you synchronization health information without needing to remote control your AAD Connect server. This enables you to maintain control over the

AAD Connect server and its configuration, but still enables other administrators to view alerts and synchronization errors.

The AAD Connect health dashboard is located at *https://aka.ms/aadconnecthealth*.

As you can see in Figure 4-33, the AAD Connect health dashboard provides a view into your synchronization configuration, including things such as the number of servers, current alerts, export status, and even the length of time required for the last export to Azure (for example, 8.56 seconds) and even the last export time (such as 8:28 A.M.).

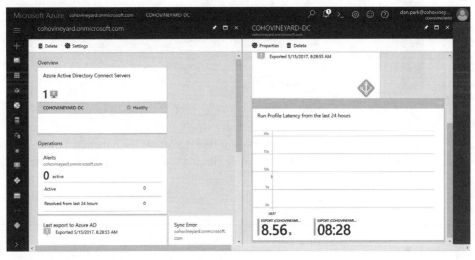

Figure 4-33 AAD Connect health dashboard

The AAD Connect health dashboard enables you to examine the errors that occurred during the last export to Azure by simply clicking the sync error count, and you can then review details about each type of error as well as a categorized view of the error types that were present during your synchronization. See Figure 4-34.

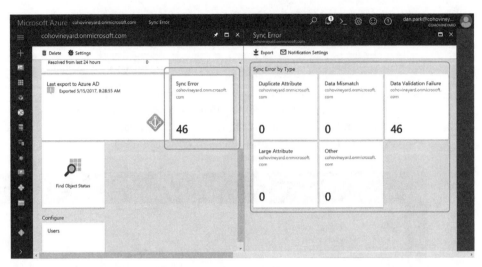

Figure 4-34 AAD Connect health Sync Error By Type

The sync error detail provided in the dashboard matches the data that is available in the AAD Connect synchronization statistics when viewing the Azure run profile, as shown in Figure 4-35.

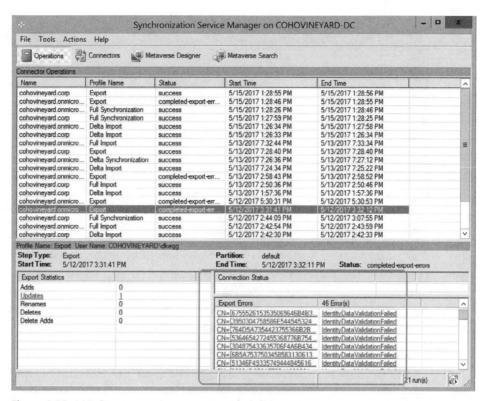

Figure 4-35 AAD Connect server export error statistics

At this level of detail, the key differences between the AAD Connect health dashboard view and the AAD Connect server statistics is that administrators in the tenant can view this information by using AAD Connect Health without the need to log on to the AAD Connect server.

Limiting access to the AAD Connect server restricts access to the AAD Connect Synchronization Rules Editor, which is the power behind the AAD Connect server configuration. Any changes to the configuration, intentional or unintentional, can have significant impact on both the data synchronized to Azure AD and the length of time that synchronization requires. Providing other administrators or management with the ability to view this information without delegating control to the server's configuration can be a valuable tool.

After you identify the synchronization errors grouped by type, you can then select each category and review those errors, as shown in Figure 4-36.

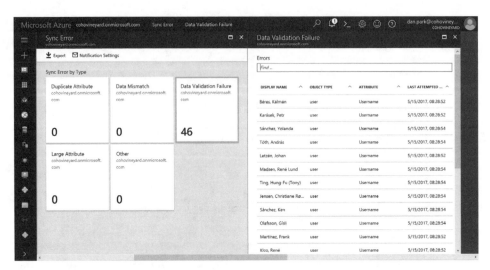

Figure 4-36 View of all errors in each sync error category

Each of the objects in an error state appears within the error category, along with the object type and the attribute that caused the validation failure.

As shown in Figure 4-37, viewing this same information in the AAD Connect synchronization manager would require you to click each object and select the Detail button to provide the error detail. This view does not provide the object type or actual object name, nor does it provide the detail in a single view like you find in the AAD Connect health service dashboard.

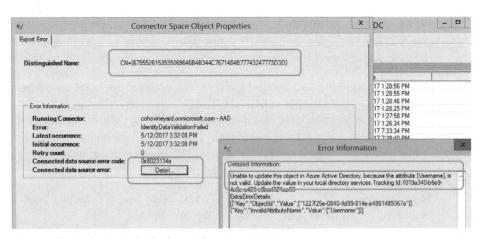

Figure 4-37 Reviewing individual errors by using AAD Connect

Finally, in addition to a detailed list of all the validation errors, you can click each object in the AAD Connect health dashboard view and see a description of the error, details about the error, and key attributes about the object in question to help make it easier to identify in your on-premises Active Directory. See Figure 4-38.

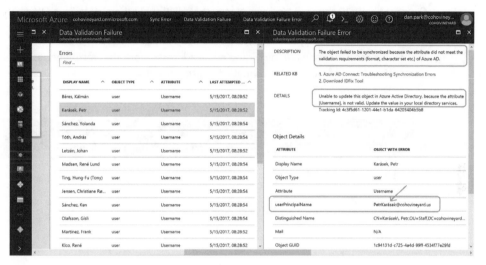

Figure 4-38 Viewing individual object details in the AAD Connect health dashboard

As the screenshot in the figure shows, the user name (UserPrincipalName) attribute contains invalid data, the diacritic above the letter A in the user's UserPrincipalName.

You would then need to remediate the invalid data in your on-premises Active Directory before the object(s) would successfully synchronize to Azure AD.

Two additional features are available on the Sync Error page, Export and Notification Settings, as shown in Figure 4-39.

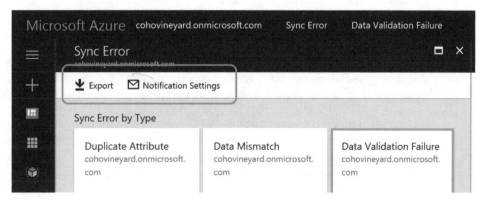

Figure 4-39 AAD Connect health dashboard Sync Error page with Export and Notification Settings

CHAPTER 4

Export enables you to export all the export errors from every category into a comma-separated value (CSV) file that provides not only the error type and object type, but all the other data provided for each object when viewed individually in the dashboard.

Notification Settings enables you to define who should receive notifications from the AAD Connect health dashboard. You can specify that all global administrators in Office 365 receive notifications as well as provide the email address for other recipients.

It is recommended that when providing email addresses for other recipients, especially if you don't select the option to notify global administrators, that you use the email address of a group. See Figure 4-40.

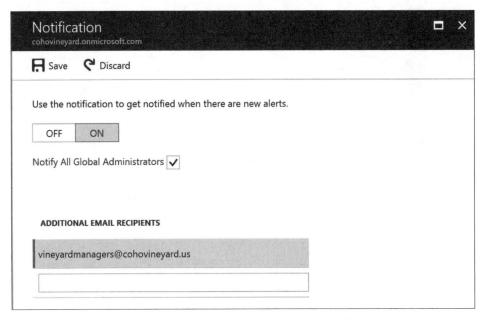

Figure 4-40 Notification settings in the AAD Connect health dashboard

Managing directory synchronization without AAD Connect health

As the preceding examples show, the AAD Connect health dashboard in Azure can be an invaluable tool in the management of directory synchronization to Office 365. It provides an aggregated view of all directory sync activities, errors, performance statistics, and status at a glance.

It is important to note, however, that the AAD Connect health dashboard requires an Azure AD Premium license for your users. Without the AAD Premium license, you still receive reports about object-level sync errors by email each time a synchronization occurs. These error reports and the technical notification email settings were explained earlier in this chapter.

Even without the AAD Connect health dashboard, you can still monitor your directory synchro-nization health for a large enterprise. It simply requires a bit more work on your part, and as discussed earlier, it requires access to your AAD Connect server.

The following explains how you would review and remediate synchronization errors by using the AAD Connect tool for the Coho Vineyard tenant.

First, you would rely on the technical notification email you receive from the tenant each time the AAD Connect synchronization process occurs. See Figure 4-41.

These synchronizations occur every 30 minutes, so if you're not receiving any emails, and you are confident you have errors, start by configuring the technical contact for your tenant.

Figure 4-41 Directory synchronization error report

When you receive the synchronization error report from the tenant, as shown in Figure 4-41, identify the object in an error state and then log on to your AAD Connect server and perform the following steps.

1. Launch the Synchronization service and select Metaverse Search, as shown in Figure 4-42.

Figure 4-42 The Metaverse Search option

2. Use the SourceAnchor value from the email error report to select Add Clause on the right side of the screen in the Actions pane. Select the SourceAnchor attribute in the Attribute drop-down list on the left. Leave the Operator drop-down list set to Equals and paste the SourceAnchor from the email report into the Value field and click Search on the right.

    As shown in Figure 4-43, the search results page should return the object that is causing an error.

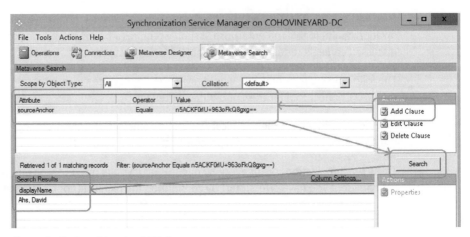

Figure 4-43 Searching the AAD Connect metaverse

3. When you have located the object, you can double-click it in the Search Results view to display all the properties of the object.

    The Metaverse view, however, will not tell you what the problem is.

4. Instead, click the Connectors tab and select the Azure connector to view the properties of the Azure object that is failing export, shown in Figure 4-44.

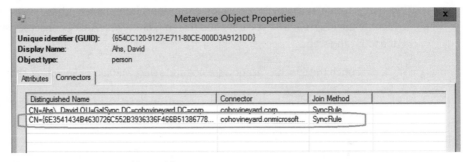

Figure 4-44 Metaverse object with connectors

TROUBLESHOOTING

Metaverse Object connectors

The Metaverse object properties Connectors tab shows all the connectors it has to other objects in the metadirectory. In this case, there are two. One is the on-premises Active Directory connector, which represents the source object from your forest; the other is the object in the Azure connector space, which the synchronization rules provisioned.

The Azure connector contains most of the attributes found in the metaverse; however, it is not clear from the connector space object alone what the cause of the error is, and selecting the Details button on the Export Error tab only provides similar information to that found in the error email report. See Figure 4-45.

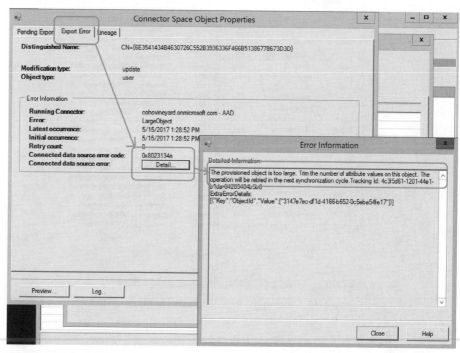

Figure 4-45 Export Error tab details in the Azure connector space

Export Error Details

Even in the AAD Connect health dashboard, the root cause of this export error is not apparent. Instead, Error Information states that the provisioned object is too large. The object-too-large error doesn't actually refer to this object itself, or to the number of attributes on the object; instead, it refers to the number of values populated on a multi-valued attribute present on the object.

In this case, the object-too-large error refers to the ProxyAddresses attribute, shown in Figure 4-46.

CHAPTER 4

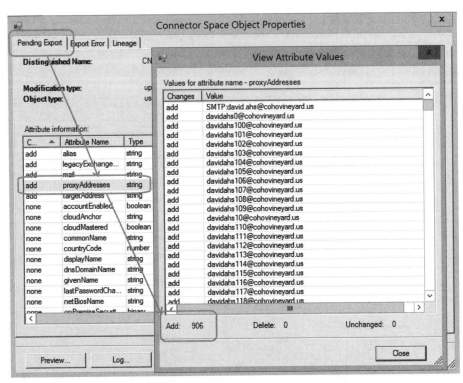

Figure 4-46 Viewing the ProxyAddresses attribute on the Pending Export tab

5.   Clicking the Pending Export tab for the object and selecting the ProxyAddresses array shows that you are trying to export a user to Azure with 906 email addresses. The limit for proxy addresses on an object in Exchange Online is 500.

INSIDE OUT

exports

Any object that generates an error during export to Azure AD remains in a pending export state in AAD Connect.

Every 30 minutes, when the synchronization engine exports to Azure, these pending exports retry, and depending on the number of errors, a large portion of your export time could be spent retrying failed objects.

It's important to resolve export errors as quickly as possible to keep synchronization cycles short.

Removing excessive email addresses or, in the case of a group or shared account, moving them to another object in on-premises Active Directory clears the error for this object and allows it to export successfully to Office 365.

Interpreting the directory synchronization status

Some errors, such as diacritics in the UserPrincipalName, are relatively easy to identify in the error reports, whereas others such as the object-too-large error don't provide all the necessary details to remediate the root cause quickly.

As the Office 365 service and the AAD Connect synchronization engine evolve, additional reporting mechanisms are added to help make the troubleshooting and remediation processes easier, so it is important to upgrade your implementation, not only for improvements in sync reporting but also in the synchronization process itself as new versions of the AAD Connect synchronization tool are released.

As each new version of AAD Connect is released, new features are added that improve the speed of synchronization, error reporting, and integration of other service-wide features such as pass-through authentication and group writeback.

You can find the AAD Connect version release history at *http://aka.ms/aad-versions*.

Summary

As you can see, the directory synchronization process can be quite complicated when it comes to syncing different objects as well as objects from multiple directories. The concepts covered in this chapter should help you identify many of the common problems that could result from an improper implementation of the directory synchronization process or errors that may result from bad data in your directories. The next chapter discusses the installation of the AAD Connect synchronization tool in detail as well as demonstrates several options to help remediate some of the most common issues encountered when configuring directory synchronization.

CHAPTER 4

Installing Azure AD Connect

The installation of Azure Active Directory Connect (AAD Connect), like other configuration milestones when deploying Office 365, is not a trivial event. The initial installation requires not only planning for service accounts, directory hierarchy, filtering, and permissions, but also for features such as password synchronization, hybrid writeback, Azure Active Directory (Azure AD) application, and attribute filtering as well as several features related to authentication.

Many of the features selected during the installation can be enabled or disabled later with the Azure Active Directory Connect Wizard; however, a few key decisions must be made during initial installation that cannot be undone and would subsequently require a re-installation of the tool if they needed to be changed.

The custom and express installation experience

The latest version of the AAD Connect installation can be downloaded from *http://aka.ms /aad-connect*. Save the installation MSI file to the server where AAD Connect will be installed and launch the installer as a local administrator.

After the typical license agreement and welcome pages, the first thing you must decide is whether you want to do an express or custom installation.

The express installation is intended for configurations that have only one Active Directory forest in your environment (although it can contain multiple child domains), and you intend to enable password synchronization.

Express mode installation is the best method for getting your Office 365 synchronization up and running quickly and provides a limited number of questions regarding your intended configuration; however, if you intend to scope your synchronization to specific organizational units (OUs) or want to enable features such as group writeback or attribute filtering, you cannot select those settings during initial setup in an express mode installation.

You can customize the installation further, however, after the wizard has finished.

In addition, the use of express mode enables the auto-upgrade process, which enables AAD Connect to upgrade its binaries automatically to the latest version of the software as it is released, without any intervention on your part. Auto-upgrade is not an option when using the customized installation method.

The express option is *not* available if your AAD Connect server is not joined to an Active Directory domain. Figure 5-1 shows the Express Settings details during the installation process.

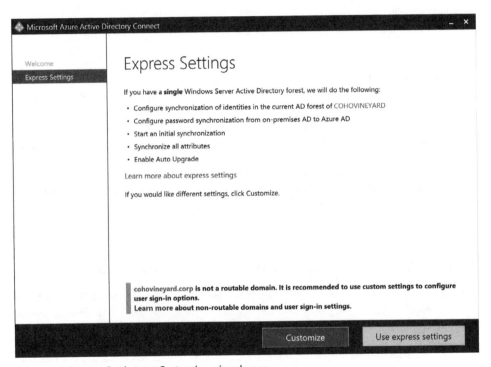

Figure 5-1 Express Settings or Customize wizard page

As part of the express settings setup, the wizard examines the UserPrincipalName suffixes configured for your forest. If your forest is not configured to use any suffixes that represent a routable domain, a warning appears, suggesting a customized deployment because AAD Connect uses the default UserPrincipalName value when synchronizing users to your Office 365 tenant. A non-routable UPN suffix such as **.local** or **.corp** would result in a UPN in the tenant of @yourtenant.onmicrosoft.com. This *onmicrosoft.com* UPN means that your users would be unable to log on to Office 365 by using their UPN or email address, and it would be impossible to use an Identity Provider such as Active Directory Federation Services (AD FS) to authenticate logons.

Refer to Chapter 1, "Office 365 Deployment Milestones" for more details about UserPrincipalName considerations and Chapter 3, "Federation Services and Authentication," for more information about federated logon options.

INSIDE OUT

Express or custom?

If your environment consists of more than one Active Directory forest or more than 100,000 objects, you plan to use AlternateID, the UserPrincipalName of your users does not contain an Internet-routable domain suffix, you don't want password synchronization, or you intend to enable features such as Group Writeback, AD FS, or pass-through authentication, you must use the custom installation method.

Express installation

After you have selected express installation, you are prompted for credentials for your Office 365 tenant, as shown in Figure 5-2.

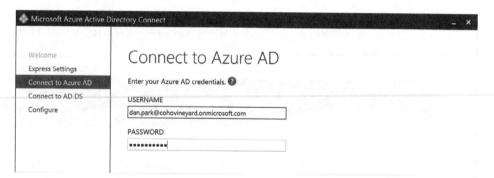

Figure 5-2 Azure AD credential page

The credentials provided here are not used permanently as part of the synchronization process; they simply ensure that you have the Global Administrator privilege in your Office 365 tenant.

The installation credentials used here must be for a Global Administrator so that the installation wizard can automatically create a directory synchronization account in your Azure AD tenant, as seen in Figure 5-3.

CHAPTER 5

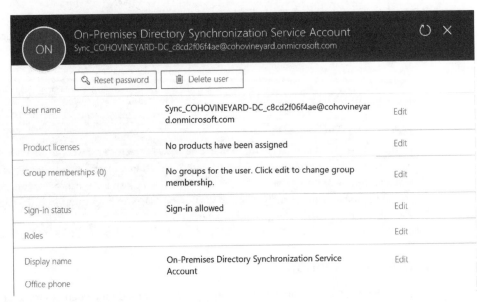

Figure 5-3 Automatically created directory synchronization account

The *On-Premises Directory Synchronization Service Account* installer, shown in Figure 5-4, is named Sync_SERVERNAME_randomGUID@yourtenant.onmicrosoft.com and is a standard user account, not a Global Administrator account.

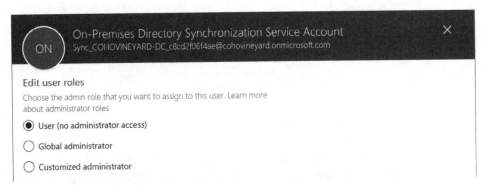

Figure 5-4 On-Premises Directory Synchronization Service Account tenant permissions

After supplying credentials to connect to Office 365, you must provide credentials for your on-premises Active Directory forest, as shown in Figure 5-5.

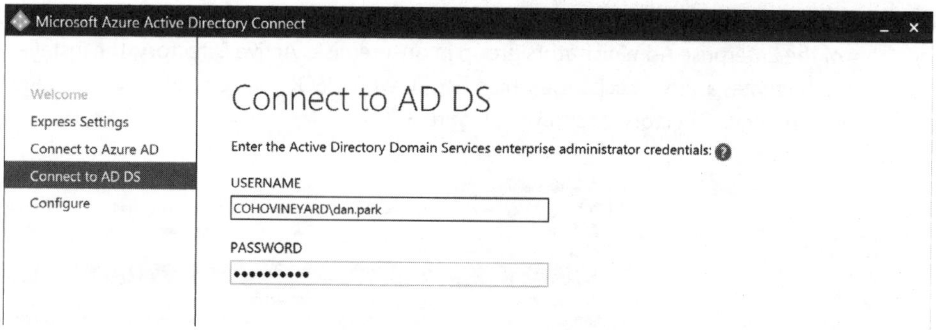

Figure 5-5 Connection to Active Directory

The on-premises Active Directory account that you provide must be a member of the Enterprise Administrators group in Active Directory because the account provided is not used for the permanent synchronization process but, rather, to create a service account in on-premises Active Directory that will be used for the permanent synchronization process.

If the Active Directory account provided is not a member of the Enterprise Administrators group, a warning appears at the bottom of the page, as shown in Figure 5-6, and installation will not continue.

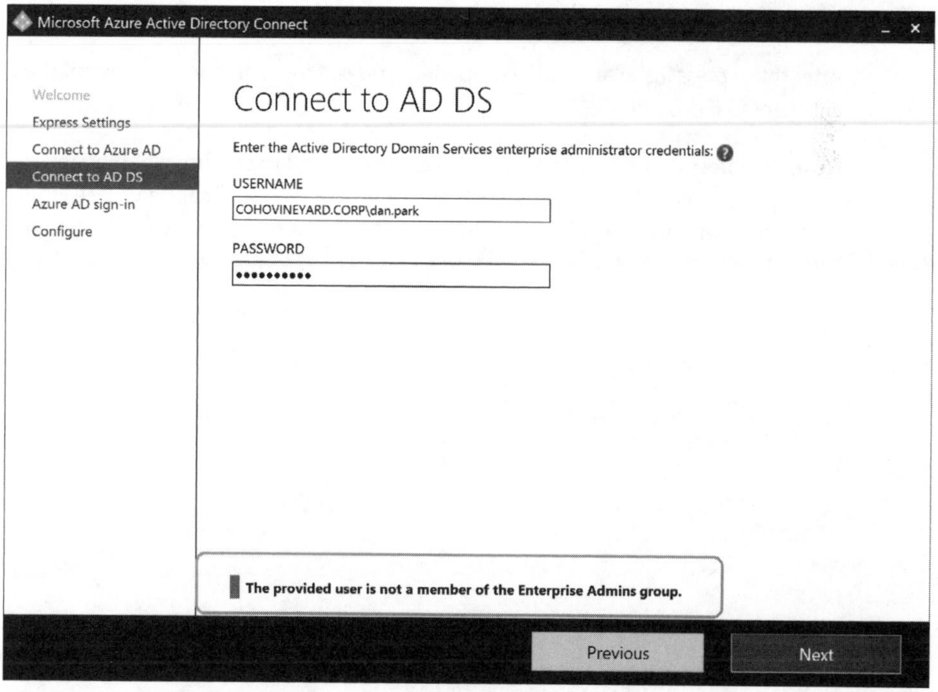

Figure 5-6 Error showing account is not a member of the Enterprise Admins group

CHAPTER 5

After the installation wizard has successfully confirmed that the account provided is a member of the Enterprise Administrators group in on-premises Active Directory, the installer automatically creates a service account, which begins with MSOL_ and a random GUID value, in the Users OU in Active Directory, as shown in Figure 5-7.

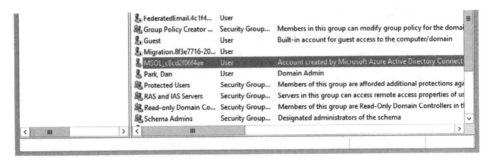

Figure 5-7 Automatically created service account in Active Directory

This automatically generated service account is set with a password that never expires, and the password will not be provided to you.

In addition, the service account is granted the Replicating Directory Changes and Replicating Directory Changes All permissions at the top level of the forest, as shown in Figure 5-8. These permissions are necessary to support password synchronization.

After the express installation has completed, you can move this account out of the Users OU to another OU if desired.

Next, the forest UserPrincipalName suffixes are checked to confirm whether any can be used for authentication with Office 365. Each Active Directory UPN suffix appears (see Figure 5-9), along with confirmation, if the suffix is a valid Azure AD domain registered in your tenant.

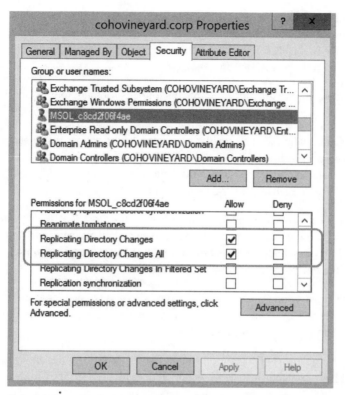

Figure 5-8 Permissions required for password synchronization

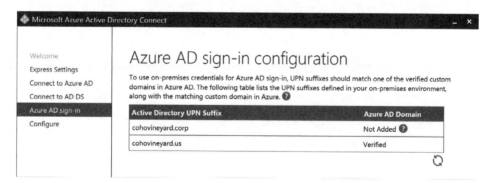

Figure 5-9 Active Directory UPN suffix verification

If any of your domains are marked Not Added, a warning appears, stating that your users will not be able to sign in to Azure AD by using their on-premises credentials.

This is only a warning because the wizard cannot confirm whether any of your users are using the unverified UPN suffixes that it found. If your users are already using a verified UPN suffix, or if you plan to change user UPN suffixes later, you can ignore this warning, and no further action regarding UPN suffix and Azure AD logon is required.

For more information, refer to Chapter 2, "Preparing Your Environment for the Cloud," for details about the IDFix tool and user account preparation for synchronization to Office 365.

Finally, the express installation wizard provides a summary of the actions that the installer will take to enable directory synchronization with your Office 365 tenant, as Figure 5-10 shows. The final two options available during the express installation are the ability to defer synchronization until later and enable Exchange hybrid deployment.

It is at this point in the process that you might want to clear the *Start The Synchronization Process When Configuration Completes* check box so that you can make changes to the automatically selected OUs, add additional UPN suffixes to your forest, update your users' UPN values, or simply wait to synchronize your users until you're ready.

Selecting the Exchange Hybrid Deployment check box adds additional rules to the configuration that enable writeback of select Exchange-related Active Directory attributes from Azure Active Directory to on-premises Active Directory.

The version of Exchange installed in your forest determines which attributes are written back, and if you do not have Exchange installed, this option does not appear. See Figure 5-10.

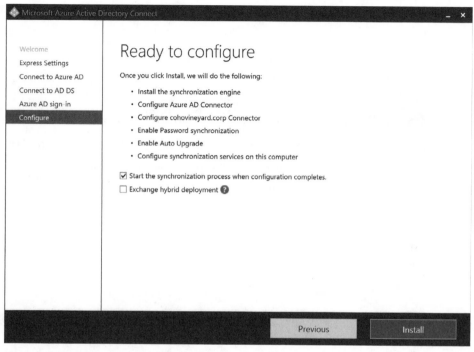

Figure 5-10 Ready to configure AAD Connect

After you click **Install**, the wizard begins by installing SQL Server Express and creating the SQL database files in the **C:\Program Files\Microsoft Azure AD Sync\Data** directory. It then installs the Synchronization service, the connectors for Azure Active Directory, and on-premises Active Directory; creates the custom Sync account in the tenant; and installs the Azure AD Connect Health service.

It is now safe to click *Exit*, and if you selected *Start The Synchronization Process* on the summary page, your AAD Connect installation is already busy synchronizing your users to Office 365. See Figure 5-11.

CHAPTER 5

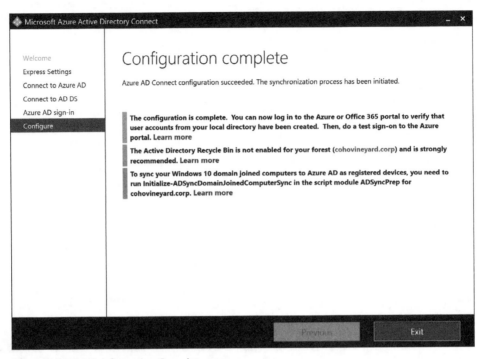

Figure 5-11 The Configuration Complete page

Custom installation

The custom installation process differs significantly from the express installation. In the express installation, you are presented with a minimum of installation choices, quite literally three to four pages, and the installer makes certain assumptions about your preferred configuration options so that you can complete the installation quickly and easily.

The custom installation, however, enables you to customize every aspect of the AAD Connect installation, and it is in the custom installation mode that you are presented with a few options that cannot be changed after you complete the installation, without a complete re-installation of the tool.

Selecting Customize on the initial installation page provides you with the first of many configuration pages on which you can specify your own custom installation options. See Figure 5-12.

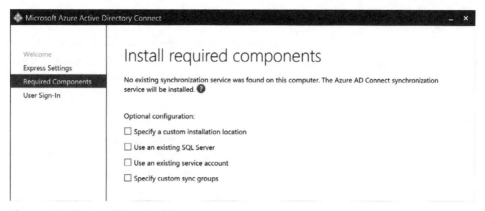

Figure 5-12 The Install Required Components page

Installation location

At this point, you can specify a custom installation for the AAD Connect binaries. The default location is *C:\Program Files\Microsoft Azure AD Sync* and cannot be changed during express installations; however, in custom mode, you can specify an alternate drive and or file path for the installation.

Selecting Specify A Custom Installation Location enables manual entry of the installation location, or you can use the Browse button to navigate the file system to find a suitable directory, as shown in Figure 5-13.

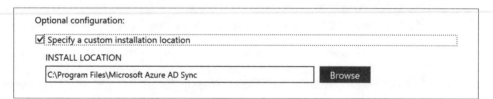

Figure 5-13 Specifying a custom installation location

It is important to note that although you can select an alternate installation location for the AAD Connect product binaries, a separate directory named Microsoft Azure Active Directory Connect in the C:\Program Files directory is installed automatically when the AAD Connect installation is launched, because of the installation MSI file you downloaded, automatically extracting its contents. This installation option does not allow you to move that directory, and it should not be deleted after installation has concluded, or the AAD Connect customization wizard will not successfully launch if you want to make changes to an existing configuration.

CHAPTER 5

Using SQL Server

AAD Connect, in both express and custom modes, can support up to 100,000 Active Directory objects, using the included Microsoft SQL Server Express edition that is installed as part of the AAD Connect setup process. If your environment has more than 100,000 objects, or if it is close to that number, the AAD Connect tool must be installed using a full version of Microsoft SQL Server.

AAD Connect does not count objects or tell you whether you need to use full SQL Server versus SQL Server Express. It is up to you to review your directory or directories to determine whether you can proceed with SQL Server Express or require the full version of SQL Server.

When using a full version of SQL Server, it is not necessary to implement any of the SQL Server high-availability technologies such as log shipping or clustering; however, those technologies are supported. Typically, it is recommended that in lieu of high-availability configurations like those mentioned, you should install a second AAD Connect server in staging mode to eliminate the need for a more complex back-end SQL Server implementation. More about staging mode appears at the end of this chapter.

INSIDE OUT

100,000 objects

The 100,000-object limit advertised when using SQL Server Express edition with AAD Connect is a theoretical limit. The actual limit is the size of the SQL database, which is restricted to 10 GB. The 100,000-user object limit is a recommended limit, based on other implementations of the AAD Connect tool and should be carefully considered during installation.

The 100,000-object limit refers to the total number of objects, not the total number of users. When calculating the number of objects, you must consider users, groups, and contacts as well as OUs across every domain in the forest.

If your company is within 10,000 or 15,000 of the object limit, if you have any upcoming merger or acquisition activity, or if you are synchronizing multiple forests to Office 365, it is recommended to err on the side of caution and install AAD Connect by using a full version of SQL Server.

An upgrade from the included SQL Express edition to a full version of SQL Server post-installation is not supported and would require a complete uninstallation and reinstallation of the AAD Connect tool.

Selecting Use An Existing SQL Server enables you to provide the name of a SQL Server and instance for the AAD Connect database. The SQL server can be located on a remote server or on the AAD Connect server itself; both scenarios are supported. If you are using the default MSSQLSERVER instance on the SQL server, you can leave the Instance Name text box blank, as shown in Figure 5-14; otherwise, the Instance Name must be provided. If you are using an alternate port for the SQL server, you must provide the Instance Name, followed by a comma (,), and the port number, even if the Instance Name is the default MSSQLSERVER name.

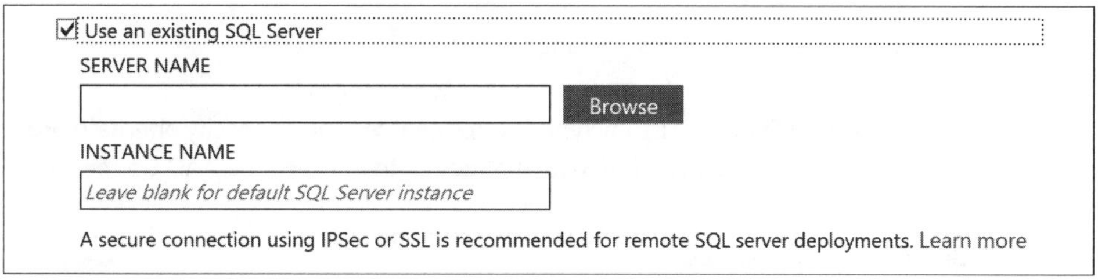

Figure 5-14 Using an existing SQL server

The installation of SQL Server creates a database named ADSync on the server, along with the associated stored procedures.

> TROUBLESHOOTING
>
> **SQL permissions**
>
> **When installing AAD Connect by using an existing SQL server, either local or remote, the account that you are currently logged on to the server with must have administrative permissions (SQL SA) within SQL, or the installation will fail.**

Selecting a service account

Selecting Use An Existing Service Account (see Figure 5-15) enables you to select a domain service account that will be used for the Azure AD Sync Windows service when the AAD Connect installation concludes. This service account is also automatically granted DB Owner and Public rights on the ADSync database as part of the installation process.

If the SQL server is local to the AAD Connect server, a service account does **not** need to be specified. Instead, a local account is created on the server automatically; this account is used for the Windows service and is granted DB Owner and Public rights on the ADSync database.

CHAPTER 5

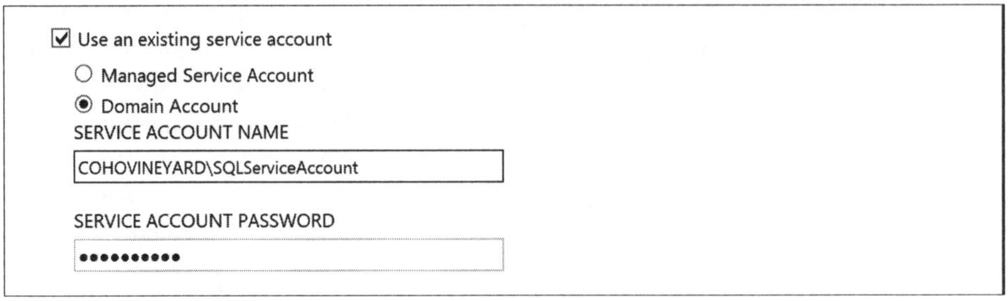

Figure 5-15 Selecting a service account

Finally, selecting Specify Custom Sync Groups enables you to specify alternate group names for the four groups, shown in Figure 5-16, that delegate rights to the AAD Connect implementation.

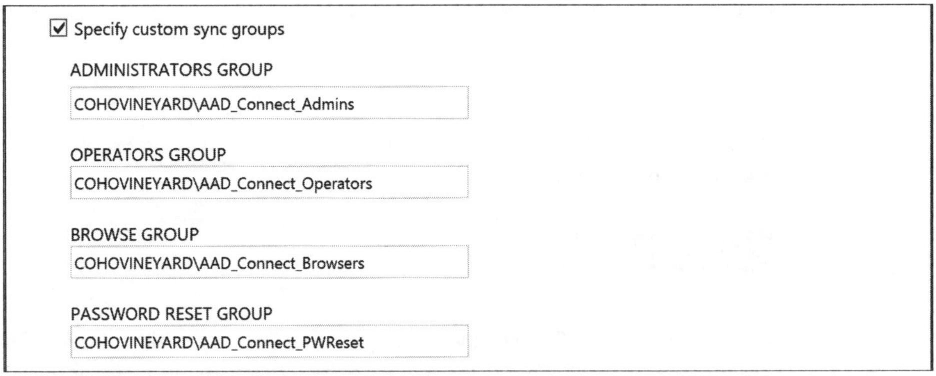

Figure 5-16 Specifying custom sync groups

These four groups can be domain groups if you are installing AAD Connect on a domain controller (as shown in Figure 5-16) or group names that are local to the AAD Connect server; however, in either case, if you specify custom sync groups, you need to create them prior to beginning the installation. Failure to create the groups prior to installation causes the installer to fail and an entry to be logged in the Application event log, indicating that the groups could not be found.

If you do not provide custom sync groups, the installer automatically creates the following four groups, which are used to secure AAD Connect and are granted the following permissions.

Group Name	Permissions
ADSyncAdmins	Full rights to the AAD Connect tool
ADSyncOperators	Able to view operations run history; cannot view connectors or objects; able to view sync rules but unable to edit or delete
ADSyncBrowse	No access to the Sync service console and cannot view Synchronization rules
ADSyncPasswordSet	No access to the Sync service console and cannot view Synchronization rules

The only group that is populated at the time of installation is the ADSyncAdmins group. The user account used to perform the AAD Connect installation is placed in this group automatically when the installation completes.

Selecting your authentication method

Another critical milestone when installing and configuring AAD Connect is the selection of the authentication method your users will use to access Office 365. Several options are available during the installation of the AAD Connect tool in custom mode on the User Sign-In page.

Although the selection of an authentication method is important in the overall design and deployment of Office 365 and your directory synchronization, you can run the configuration wizard on the desktop at any time to change these settings. As a result, you might want to choose Do Not Configure and bypass the authentication configuration steps during initial installation and return to change them later.

Password synchronization

Selecting Password Synchronization on the User Sign-In page, shown in Figure 5-17, configures the AAD Connect tool to synchronize user passwords automatically from on-premises Active Directory to Azure Active Directory. This synchronization process occurs independently of the regularly scheduled 30-minute synchronization cycle the AAD Connect server uses to synchronize on-premises Active Directory object properties (for example, Name, eMail address, and so on), so that password changes in on-premises Active Directory are replicated to Office 365 every 1 to 2 minutes.

CHAPTER 5

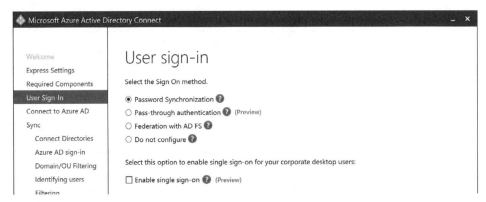

Figure 5-17 The User Sign-In page

> ## INSIDE OUT
>
> *Password encryption*
>
> Passwords synchronized to Office 365 are not transmitted in clear text. Instead, the hash of the user's password is encrypted a second time, using an MD5 key and a salt. A salt is a cryptographic term for random data.
>
> The result is a hash of a hash, or salted hash, and is transmitted by an encrypted HTTPS session between the AAD Connect server and Office 365.
>
> The user authentication and hash expansion\decryption then takes place in Azure Active Directory, not in on-premises Active Directory.

Scope

When you enable the password synchronization feature as part of the AAD Connect installation, there is an initial synchronization of all passwords to Office 365 for any users configured within the scope of the solution.

In an express mode configuration, *all* user objects are automatically within the scope of the solution; however, when performing a custom installation, the organizational unit configuration selected, and any enabled group filtering, define the users who fall within the scope of the configuration and, subsequently, what passwords are initially synchronized.

Permissions

When password synchronization is automatically enabled as part of express mode, the service account (for example, MSOL_xxxxxxx) that is generated in on-premises Active Directory is automatically delegated the Replicating Directory Changes and Replicating Directory Changes All permissions at the top level of the forest.

When performing a custom installation, however, there is no automatic account creation, and therefore no rights are delegated automatically. The service account that you create for the Active Directory forest connector must be delegated the rights manually to the top level of each domain in the forest.

INSIDE OUT

Password policies

It is important to note that when you use password synchronization, the cloud account password is set to Never Expire. An expired password in on-premises Active Directory that remains unchanged is still valid in Office 365 and can be used for logon to the tenant.

Pass-through authentication

Pass-through authentication can be selected during the AAD Connect installation, as shown in Figure 5-18. Optionally, after installation has concluded, it may be added by running the AAD Connect Wizard located on the desktop.

Figure 5-18 Selecting Pass-Through Authentication

Overview

Pass-through authentication is an alternative to password synchronization if your company policies prohibit the transmission of passwords, even in encrypted format, over the public Internet. Instead of syncing user passwords to the cloud and relying on Office 365 to process logons, pass-through authentication allows the on-premises Active Directory infrastructure to process authentication requests, without the need to transmit passwords or deploy identity providers such as AD FS.

The implementation of pass-through authentication requires the deployment of a processing agent, added to the AAD Connect server automatically when you select this option, which operates using outbound-only communication. The agent can be deployed on more than one server for the purposes of high availability, provided the server is joined to the domain where the users being authenticated reside and the server is running Windows Server 2012R2 or later.

Pass-through authentication behaves similarly to AD FS, although instead of redirecting authentication requests back to an on-premises server, the request is placed in a queue in Microsoft Azure and then picked up by a regularly scheduled process initiated by the processing agent running on-premises. The processing agent sends the request to an Active Directory domain controller, it is processed by the domain controller, and the results are returned to the processing agent to be sent back to Azure. Upon receipt, Azure issues a token to the user, who can then access Office 365 services.

Requirements

Although Azure AD pass-through authentication eliminates the need to synchronize passwords to Office 365 and simplifies the authentication process when compared to the implementation of AD FS or other identity providers, pass-through authentication does have several key requirements that must be met to ensure that it operates properly.

- The AAD Connect server and underlying pass-through processing agent must be installed and joined to a domain within the forest where the authentication requests are directed. All servers running the processing agent must also be running Windows Server 2012R2 or later.

- Pass-through authentication is supported in a multi-forest configuration, but a forest trust is required.

- The UserPrincipalName value used for synchronization to Office 365 must be the value from the UserPrincipalName attribute in on-premises Active Directory and must be a routable UPN suffix. Alternate Login ID is not supported with pass-through authentication.

- The AAD Connect server, and any servers running the processing agent, must be able to reach Azure Active Directory on several additional TCP/IP ports and should not be located behind a proxy server or network devices that perform SSL inspection or URL filtering.

You can find the list of prerequisites for pass-through authentication at *https://docs.microsoft .com/en-us/azure/active-directory/connect/active-directory-aadconnect-pass-through -authentication#azure-ad-pass-through-prerequisites*.

Selecting pass-through authentication deploys the processing agent as part of the AAD Connect Custom installation. Any additional installations of the processing agent require download of the processing agent from *https://go.microsoft.com/fwlink/?linkid=837580*.

Federation with AD FS

Selecting Federation With AD FS on the User Sign-In page adds several additional pages to the installation wizard, as shown in Figure 5-19. These additional pages enable you to perform the installation of the AD FS and Web Application Proxy server roles in your organization.

Figure 5-19 Federation with AD FS

The AD FS installation is executed by the AAD Connect Wizard; however, the installation of AD FS does *not* occur on the AAD Connect server. You must have at least two additional servers ready for the AD FS Federation server role and the Web Application Proxy server role. The AD FS federation server should be joined to the domain; the Web Application Proxy server can be a member of either the domain or a workgroup, based on your company's requirements. Both servers should be running Windows Server 2012R2 or later.

In addition to the two servers required for AD FS, you also need an SSL certificate with your Federation Service name defined (for example, adfs.cohovineyard.us) or a wildcard certificate that can be used to secure the Web Application Proxy server role.

On the AD FS Farm page, shown in Figure 5-20, you can choose to configure a new AD FS farm, or you can select an existing AD FS farm already configured in your environment.

When selecting Configure A New AD FS Farm, you must provide a PFX certificate file that secures the Web Application Proxy.

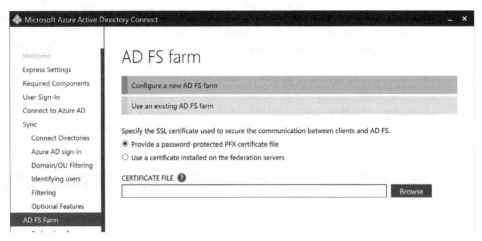

Figure 5-20 AD FS Farm page

Clicking the Browse button returns a File Explorer window, from which you can navigate to the PFX file you intend to use for the Web Application Proxy server. After you have selected the PFX file, you are prompted to supply the password for the certificate file before you can proceed.

In the Subject Name drop-down list, select the certificate subject name that you wish to use for the Federation Service name, as shown in Figure 5-21. If your certificate is a wildcard certificate, you must instead provide a subject name prefix for the federation endpoint. The resulting Federation Service name appears at the bottom of the page. This should be the name that you use for the communication between the Web Application proxy servers and the federation servers as well as the name that you configure in your public DNS and inbound firewall rules for the Web Application Proxy server.

See Chapter 2 for more details about the networking requirements for the AD FS Web Application Proxy server role.

Figure 5-21 Selecting a subject name prefix

After supplying the certificate information, you are prompted to provide the name of the server where the AD FS service should be installed. This is the federation server and should be joined to a domain within the Active Directory forest where authentication takes place.

You can provide a server name or IP address, or you can use the Browse button to search Active Directory for a server by using its name or IP address.

After you have selected the server name and entered the credentials for a domain administrator, your AD FS federation server appears in the Selected Servers list, as shown in Figure 5-22. Repeat this for each AD FS federation server you want the installer to configure for you.

CHAPTER 5

Figure 5-22 Selected AD FS server

You are then prompted to enter the name or IP address of the Web Application Proxy server. Like the AD FS Federation server selection page, you can enter the name or IP address directly or click the Browse button to search Active Directory for the server.

You are prompted for credentials, but unless the Web Application Proxy server is joined to the domain, you must provide credentials for a local administrator on the server. Your Web Application Proxy server name appears in the Selected Servers list after you select it, as shown in Figure 5-23.

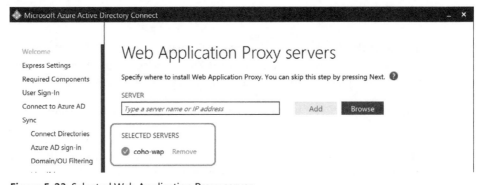

Figure 5-23 Selected Web Application Proxy server

INSIDE OUT

PSRemoting

The installation of the AD FS role and the Web Application Proxy role depends on remote Windows PowerShell connectivity to both servers.

First, confirm that the Windows Remote Management service is running on all target servers and then enable PSRemoting on each server by the Windows PowerShell command:

```
Enable-PSRemoting -Force
```

If installing the Web Application Proxy role on a server that is not a member of the domain, you must also add that server name to the WSMan trusted hosts list on the AAD Connect server by using the Windows PowerShell command:

```
Set-Item WSMan:\localhost\Client\TrustedHosts -Value <hostname> -Force -Concatenate
```

Enter the credentials for a domain administrator account as shown in Figure 5-24; this enables the AAD Connect installation wizard to complete the AD FS configuration on the remote servers.

Figure 5-24 Entering domain administrator credentials

Provide a service account for the AD FS service. This service account can be either a standard domain user account or a group Managed Service Account (gMSA).

The group Managed Service Account options are not available if your domain is not running Windows Server 2012 or later.

The wizard can be used to create a group Managed Service Account, you can provide an existing gMSA, or you can provide an existing domain user account.

The service account provided must be a member of the Enterprise Admins group if you are selecting an existing domain user account. See Figure 5-25.

CHAPTER 5

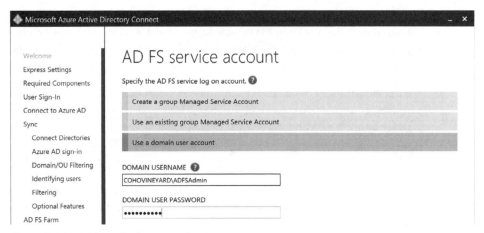

Figure 5-25 AD FS service account selection

You are prompted to select the domain that should be used for the federation process, and a list of all the domains that have been registered in your Office 365 tenant appears.

After you have selected a domain, that domain is converted to a federated domain in your tenant. Afterward, any time a user logon ending in that UPN suffix is presented during logon to Office 365, the authentication request is redirected to the Web Application Proxy server, using the Federation Service Name that you selected when adding the certificate, as shown in Figure 5-26.

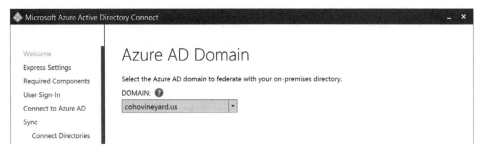

Figure 5-26 Azure AD domain selection

Clicking Next opens the final configuration page, where you can review your selected installation options and then click Next to proceed.

When enabling either password synchronization or pass-through authentication, you can enable Single Sign-On (SSO) as well. Single Sign-On forces the authentication process with Azure AD to behave like integrated Windows authentication, using the on-premises Active

Directory domain controllers to create tokens automatically for authenticated users who are accessing Azure resources.

The beauty of Single Sign-On is that the user is never challenged for credentials. Their authentication request is presented to Azure AD and redirected to an on-premises domain controller; a token is generated and then automatically provided to Azure AD to authorize access, all without any user intervention.

INSIDE OUT

Single Sign-On

The Single Sign-On feature can be used with both password synchronization and pass-through authentication; however, when using Single Sign-On, the user must be using a computer that is a member of the domain, and that computer must be running a supported client. Supported clients include most current browsers and any applications configured to use modern authentication.

Some examples of modern authentication–enabled applications include the Office 2013 and Office 2016 suites and the Microsoft Outlook application for IOS and Android phones. The Office 365 team maintains a current list of modern authentication–enabled applications at *https://blogs.office.com/en-us/2015/11/19/updated-office-365-modern-authentication -public-preview/*.

After you have selected the appropriate authentication method for your environment, click *Next* to proceed.

Connecting to your directories

During the AAD Connect custom installation process, after you have selected your authentication method, you are prompted for credentials for your Azure AD tenant.

These credentials ensure that you are a global administrator in your tenant and retrieve a list of domains registered in your tenant. The installation wizard uses these details in later installation pages.

The credentials you provide in this step are not stored, however, nor are they used for the ongoing synchronization process. If necessary, you can remove the global administrator role from this account, following successful installation of the AAD Connect tool. See Figure 5-27.

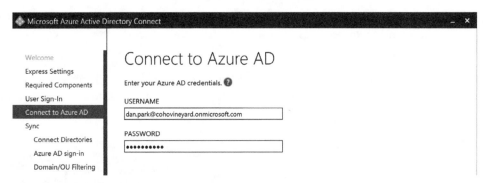

Figure 5-27 Connecting to Azure AD

The next step in the custom installation process is the selection of all the directories that contain objects (users, groups, contacts, devices) that you plan to synchronize to your Office 365 tenant.

Currently, the AAD Connect installation wizard offers only one option in the Directory Type drop-down list: Active Directory. In future versions, the wizard will be updated to include options such as Active Directory Lightweight Directory Services (AD LDS), which uses the Lightweight Directory Access Protocol (LDAP), and other identity sources.

The forest drop-down list displays the name of the forest to which the AAD Connect server is currently joined. You must provide credentials to connect to that forest in the form of DOMAIN\ *UserName*.

If the AAD Connect server is not a member of a domain, you must manually enter the forest name because it will not be automatically populated.

TROUBLESHOOTING

Domain/Username

The AAD Connect installation wizard requires the forest user name credentials in the DOMAIN*UserName* format because these credentials are stored in the properties of the on-premises Active Directory connector for ongoing synchronization.

Providing the credentials in the UPN format (for instance, dan.park@cohovineyard.corp) in this step returns an error, and the installation wizard exits, requiring you to start the entire installation over again.

After you have entered the user name and password for the service account, click the Add Directory button. AAD Connect examines the forest, using the service account credentials provided, to ensure that it can reach the forest and the provided service account is valid. In addition, the wizard examines the forest schema to determine whether additional options for features (for example, Exchange hybrid) can be added as part of the installation process.

The credentials entered in this step are stored in the AAD Connect configuration and will be the permanent service account used to connect to the forest for the ongoing synchronization process.

INSIDE OUT

Service account permissions

The service account used for each directory that you synchronize needs, at a minimum, membership in the Domain Users group in Active Directory. If your Domain Users group has been modified in any way, you must ensure that the account has LDAP read permissions to your forest(s).

Other features such as Group Writeback also require additional permissions for the connector service account. You can find those additional features and requirements at *https://docs .microsoft.com/en-us/azure/active-directory/connect/active-directory-aadconnect-accounts -permissions#custom-settings-installation*.

You can add additional forests or directories to the configuration by manually typing the name of the forest in the Forest text box, providing service account credentials in that forest with the necessary permissions, and clicking Add Directory. See Figure 5-28.

CHAPTER 5

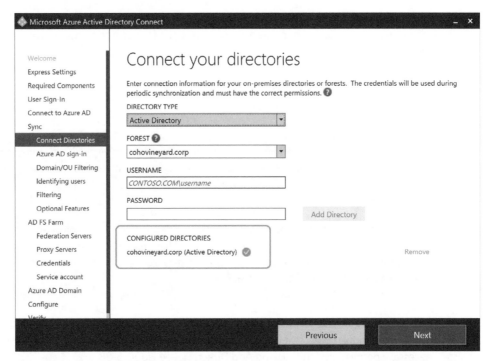

Figure 5-28 Connect Your Directories page

INSIDE OUT

Adding directories

The order in which you add multiple directories to the AAD Connect configuration is critical and represents another decision that could require reinstallation of the AAD Connect tool.

The synchronization rules the wizard creates are applied in the order in which you add the directories during this step. If you are in a multi-forest scenario where linked mailboxes exist across forests, or you plan to join user objects between forests, you add the forest that should be precedent for user attributes first.

Precedence, and more detail about synchronization rule ordering, is discussed later in this chapter.

After you have successfully added all the directories to your configuration, click the Next button to proceed.

The UserPrincipalName and SourceAnchor attributes

The next page of the custom installation wizard provides a list of all UPN suffixes that exist across the forest or forests you entered on the Connect Your Directories page.

Each UPN suffix is compared against the domains that are currently verified in your Office 365 tenant, and if any UPN suffixes do not exist as a verified domain, you see a warning at the bottom of the screen, stating that users might not be able to log on to Office 365 if they are configured to use an unverified domain.

This warning is meant to serve as a reminder that additional work might be required in either your tenant, such as the registration of additional domains, or in your on-premises Active Directory, such as changing your users' UPN values to match verified domains, before authentication will work properly during user logon.

It is safe to proceed, even with unverified domain suffixes, because they can be added later, and it will not affect the installation process or require you to run the wizard again.

The other option on this page, the User Principal Name selection drop-down list, represents yet another of the critical installation milestones that cannot be undone after the installation has concluded.

The User Principal Name drop-down list enables you to choose the value to use as the UserPrincipalName value for logon and authentication with Azure AD. In most cases, you accept the default value of UserPrincipalName from the on-premises Active Directory schema; however, it is possible that in some environments an alternate value is used.

In some environments, the UserPrincipalName value might already be used by older applications and prevent you from changing the value to use a UPN domain suffix registered in Office 365. In other environments, company or security policy might prohibit the use of this value for the purposes of authentication.

In those cases, the most common alternate attribute used for UserPrincipalName is the Mail attribute because the Mail value and UserPrincipalName value both use the commonly accepted format of *name@domain*.

Use great care when deciding to use an alternate attribute for the UserPrincipalName value. This process is typically referred to as Alternate Login ID and not only does it require additional changes to the AD FS implementation, but it might also render other applications incapable of authenticating with Office 365 because they expect the UserPrincipalName value to be used (as, for example, in pass-through authentication). See Figure 5-29.

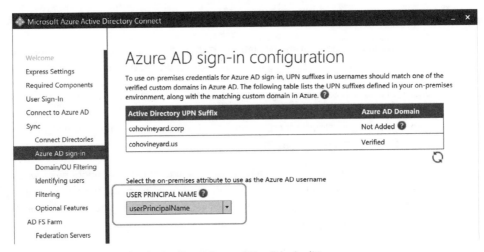

Figure 5-29 Azure AD Sign-in Configuration and UserPrincipalName page

You can find additional details regarding Alternate Login ID and supportability at *https://docs .microsoft.com/en-us/azure/active-directory/connect/active-directory-aadconnect-accounts -permissions#custom-settings-installation*.

INSIDE OUT

UserPrincipalName

Selection of the UserPrincipalName value in the AAD Connect custom installation wizard is an action that you cannot undo after you complete the installation.

If you need to change the UserPrincipalName attribute, you must uninstall AAD Connect and reinstall it.

After you have confirmed the attribute that should be used for UserPrincipalName and have reviewed the list of domain suffixes, click Next to proceed.

The Domain and OU filtering page enables you, on a per-directory basis, to select or clear the domain partitions and organizational units (OUs) that you want in the scope of the solution.

Any OU that you select automatically includes all objects in that OU and any sub-OU in the scope of the synchronization. In the case of multiple forests, the Directory drop-down list enables you to choose OUs for each, as shown in Figure 5-30.

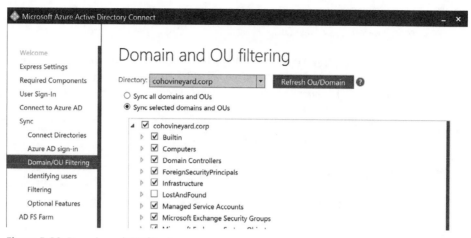

Figure 5-30 Domain and OU filtering

The status of each check box is important because it provides detail about whether the OU and any sub-OUs beneath it will be included or excluded from the scope of the synchronization.

An empty check box indicates that the OU is excluded from the scope of the synchronization, and a check box with a check mark indicates that the OU is included in the scope of the synchronization.

Any selected OU that contains sub-OUs automatically includes those sub-OUs, as shown in Figure 5-31.

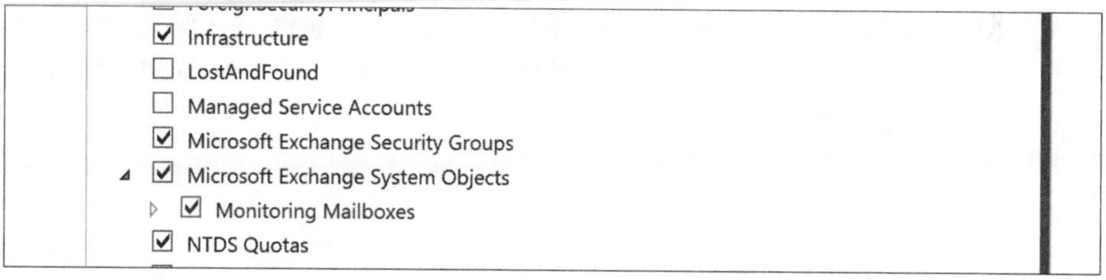

Figure 5-31 Selected boxes and empty boxes for OUs

Although the presence or absence of a check mark might seem obvious, there are two additional states that are distinctly different and affect how changes to the OU structure post-installation affect synchronization.

A check box with a gray background *and* a check mark indicates that one or more sub-OUs beneath that OU have not been selected. It also means that following deployment of the AAD Connect tool, any new OUs added beneath that OU in the future are automatically included in

CHAPTER 5

the scope of the synchronization. No changes are required in the AAD Connect configuration to accommodate these new OUs.

A check box with only a gray background indicates that one or more sub-OUs beneath that OU have not been selected but also means that, following deployment, any added new OUs beneath that OU will *not* be included in the scope of the synchronization.

It would require an update to the AAD Connect configuration, using the wizard or changes to the connector properties, to include the new OU. See Figure 5-32.

Figure 5-32 Gray selected and gray empty OU boxes

If you prefer not to make changes to the domain and OU filtering for your directories during the AAD Connect Custom installation, leave this page unchanged. You can rerun the wizard or manually edit the properties of the connector at any time.

After you have selected your OU filtering preferences, click Next to proceed.

Uniquely identifying your users

The final set of configuration options that irrevocably affect your AAD Connect installation, requiring reinstallation if you get them wrong, are on the *Uniquely Identifying Your Users* page, shown in Figure 5-33.

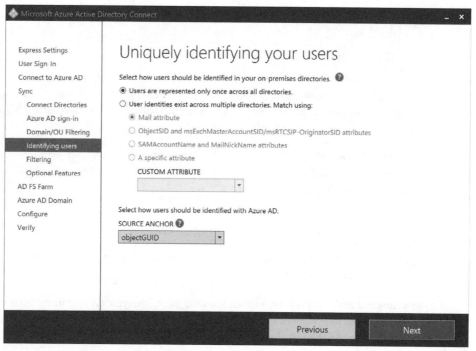

Figure 5-33 Uniquely Identifying Your Users page

User matching

On the Uniquely Identifying Your Users page, select the method that AAD Connect uses to join your users together. If you have a single directory, your best option is the Users Are Represented Once Across All Directories button. This setting tells AAD Connect that user objects should not be joined in any way, resulting in a one-for-one mapping of users to Azure AD user objects after successful synchronization with your tenant.

If, however, you have more than one forest in your enterprise, give careful consideration to the user-matching options offered here. Failure to choose the correct option not only requires a reinstallation of the AAD Connect tool, but might also result in objects synchronized to your tenant that you would also need to delete. If you discover this error too late, and have already migrated mailboxes to your tenant or started creating Microsoft SharePoint content, you not only need to reinstall AAD Connect, you might also need to migrate mailboxes back to on-premises and even risk loss of SharePoint Online and One Drive for Business content.

When reviewing the user-matching options available on this page, consider how your users appear across your on-premises directories. If user joins are required, you must then select the appropriate user-matching configuration.

CHAPTER 5

INSIDE OUT

mailNickname

The presence of the mailNickname attribute is critical when configuring AAD Connect to synchronize Exchange mailbox objects to Office 365, because it identifies the account as a mail-enabled object. Make sure that all your mail-enabled and mailbox-enabled users in Active Directory have a valid mailNickname.

If your users are missing the mailNickname value, the AAD Connect synchronization rules related to most Exchange attributes will not apply, and the resulting object in Exchange Online will not be correctly decorated.

ObjectSID/msExchMasterAccountSID

The ObjectSID/msExchMasterAccountSID user-matching option is designed for use in Exchange resource forest deployments.

In a standard Exchange resource forest scenario, there are typically two forests. It is possible to have a resource forest linked to more than one account forest, but at a minimum, two forests are required for a linked mailbox scenario.

One forest contains the security principals (user objects) and is referred to as the user forest; the other forest contains linked mailboxes and is called the resource forest. When linked mailboxes are created, Exchange automatically populates the value of an Active Directory attribute called msExchMasterAccountSID on the linked mailbox object. The msExchMasterAccountSID attribute contains the security identifier (or ObjectSID) of the user account from the account forest that the mailbox is linked to and is populated automatically when the Exchange admin tools create the linked mailbox.

The AAD Connect user-matching dialog box automatically includes an option for Exchange-linked mailbox scenarios by the ObjectSID And msExchMasterAccountSID button, as shown in Figure 5-34.

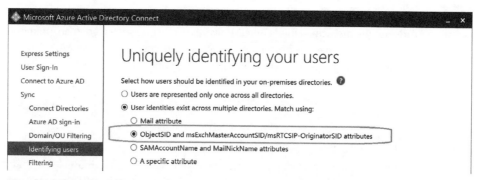

Figure 5-34 Joining linked Exchange mailboxes

This option configures AAD Connect to join objects based on their ObjectSID value in the account forest with the object containing the associated msExchMasterAccountSID value in the resource forest.

There is no need to identify which forest is which in your configuration; the presence of the msExchMasterAccountSID value identifies which forest is the resource forest, and the joins happen automatically during the synchronization process.

It is important to note a few assumptions related to the Exchange resource forest, primarily related to the linked mailbox objects' configuration.

First, in Exchange Server 2007 and later, when a mailbox is created as a linked mailbox, the resulting user object associated with that mailbox in the Exchange Server resource forest is disabled in Active Directory, whereas the user object in the account forest is left enabled and used for logon to the mailbox cross-forest.

AAD Connect assumes, as a result, that any linked mailbox objects it synchronizes consist of two user objects that it must join. The user account is enabled and used for logon; the second mailbox account is disabled. This assumption is reflected in the synchronization rules (discussed later in this chapter) created during the installation that apply to enabled and disabled objects.

If the Exchange-linked mailbox account is enabled in Active Directory, an unsupported but all-too-common occurrence, the synchronization rule behavior might be effected.

Second, when a linked mailbox is created in Exchange, the msExchRecipientTypeDetails value in Active Directory for that account is set to a value of 2. If for any reason this value is changed to a value other than 2, the synchronization rules related to the SourceAnchor for the object will behave differently and likely result in the wrong data being synchronized to Azure AD for the linked mailbox pair.

CHAPTER 5

If the wrong SourceAnchor is synchronized to Azure, not only must the object be deleted from Azure, but the msExchRecipientTypeDetails value must be corrected in on-premises Active Directory and the mailbox object then removed from the scope of the AAD Connect server and re-added so that the proper synchronization rules apply to that object.

INSIDE OUT

Linked mailboxes

If your environment consists of Exchange-linked mailboxes, you must ensure that the linked mailbox accounts are disabled and the msExchRecipientTypeDetails attribute in Active Directory is set to a value of 2.

If either of these conditions is not met, the synchronization of the linked mailboxes to Azure will most likely include data from the wrong forest and require deletion of the object from the cloud and removal from the scope of the AAD Connect server before it can be corrected.

Mail

When no traditional Exchange resource forest/account forest model is in use, but the Mail attribute is populated with the same information in both forests, you can use Mail Attribute as shown in Figure 5-35 to configure AAD Connect to perform joins between objects using the Mail attribute.

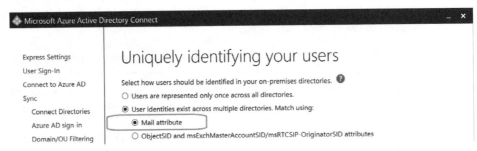

Figure 5-35 Joining using Mail Attribute

The Mail Attribute user join configuration is most commonly used when two or more directories contain Exchange mailboxes, and they are configured to use the Microsoft Identity Manager or Forefront Identity Manager product to perform global address list synchronization (GalSync) between those forests.

sAMAccountName and mailNickname

An alternate method for joining user objects is using the sAMAccountName and mailNickname attributes. When you use this option, AAD Connect attempts to join user accounts cross-forest using the sAMAccountName first, followed by the mailNickname, as shown in Figure 5-36, in the In From AD – User Join rule's join criteria.

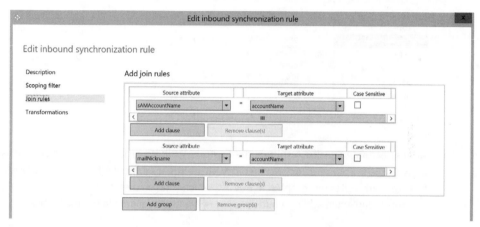

Figure 5-36 User join rules when selecting sAMAccountName or mailNickname

The purpose of this configuration is to accommodate those organizations where the mail value is not unique or not populated cross-forest; however, the customer has created objects that share an sAMAccountName, a mailNickname, or both.

It's important to note that the sAMAccountName and mailNickname values are expected to be unique in their own forests.

Custom Join attribute selection

The final option available during the user matching configuration is the selection of a custom attribute for user joins, using the A Specific Attribute option, shown in Figure 5-37.

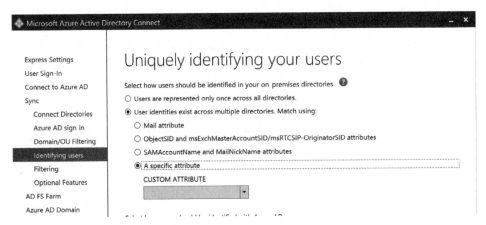

Figure 5-37 Selecting the A Specific Attribute option

After selecting A Specific Attribute, the Custom Attribute drop-down list presents a list of all available on-premises Active Directory attributes. It's important to note that most Active Directory attributes represented in this list, which is taken directly from the Active Directory schema it read when adding your directories, are also available in the metaverse.

Several restrictions are important to note when manually selecting an attribute to use for joins between objects.

First, if you wish to use the sAMAccountName attribute, be sure to click the sAMAccountName *and* mailNickname options and not sAMAccountName from the drop-down list.

The pre-built selection for sAMAccountName and mailNickname ensures that the joins use the AccountName attribute in the database, which is where the AAD Connect configuration synchronizes the sAMAccountName value. If you choose sAMAccountName manually, you will receive an error, shown in Figure 5-38, because there is no sAMAccountName attribute in the AAD Connect metaverse.

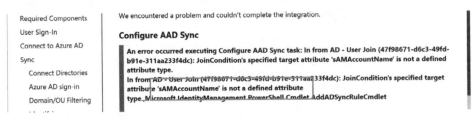

Figure 5-38 Error when selecting sAMAccountName manually

The drop-down list does not allow the use of any multi-valued attributes in Active Directory (for example, ProxyAddresses), because the join condition only works for single-valued attributes. It is not capable of performing joins using a multi-valued attribute because it cannot enumerate the individual values.

Furthermore, if you have extended your Active Directory schema with custom attributes, you should not select any of these custom attributes. They behave similarly to the selection of sAMAccountName in Figure 5-39 and return an error stating that the attribute is not a defined attribute and the installation will fail.

Last, any time you select a custom join criterion on the Uniquely Identifying Your Users page, the value in the SourceAnchor drop-down list, typically ObjectGUID, is cleared and must be re-selected before you can proceed.

In fact, the Next button remains inactive until you select a value for SourceAnchor.

INSIDE OUT

Selecting a custom join

When selecting a custom join, whether it's Mail, sAMAccountName, or even a custom attribute, the AAD Connect tool will not synchronize that user if the selected value is null.

This is not typically an issue in multi-forest configurations, but if you select Mail as the join criteria, only users with the Mail attribute populated will be allowed to synchronize to Azure AD.

Keep this in mind when selecting a join condition.

SourceAnchor

The SourceAnchor attribute selection is the last setting that you are prompted for as part of the installation that cannot be changed after you have completed the setup process. Like the other critical decision milestones mentioned previously, if you select the wrong value during this step, AAD Connect must be uninstalled and reinstalled to correct the error.

More important, if you have already synchronized objects to Azure AD by using the wrong SourceAnchor attribute, you will most likely need to delete those objects from Azure as well.

The selection of the SourceAnchor value is extremely important because the value represents a key component of each object's life cycle and its synchronization to Azure AD.

Other key values, such as UserPrincipalName and eMail address, which are used for critical services such as authentication or mail routing, can be changed during the life of a user, and AAD Connect flows those updated values to Azure.

SourceAnchor, however, is permanent because it uniquely identifies the object and anchors it to the source object that it represents in the on-premises directories.

INSIDE OUT

Changing SourceAnchor

Changing the SourceAnchor value for an object in Azure AD causes the object to be deleted and re-created as a net-new object, even if every other attribute of the object is identical.

In fact, changing the SourceAnchor value for an object carries so much impact that if AAD Connect detects that the SourceAnchor for an object is changing, it will display an error and prevent the change.

The SourceAnchor attribute in AAD Connect, by default, is derived from the ObjectGUID value in on-premises Active Directory because the ObjectGUID value for an object in Active Directory is unique for the lifetime of that object. It cannot be changed, either programmatically or from the GUI, and if the object is deleted and subsequently recovered from the Active Directory recycle bin, the ObjectGUID is preserved.

The ObjectGUID value is a binary value, and like the security identifier or ObjectSID, it is generated at the time of creation. The GUID, or globally unique identifier, is generated on an Active Directory domain controller, is unique within the forest, and never changes for the lifetime of that object.

NOTE

In fact, due to the way the GUID is generated, using the object's creation date; time; MAC address of the network card on the domain controller that created the object; and a 12-digit, random hexadecimal value, some argue that the ObjectGUID value created for an object is universally unique and not just unique across the Active Directory forest where it exists.

As part of the synchronization process, AAD Connect uses an object's ObjectGUID, converted from a binary object to a base64 encoded string, to populate the SourceAnchor value in the metaverse. The SourceAnchor value is then synchronized to Azure AD and represented as the ImmutableID value of the object, as Figure 5-39 shows.

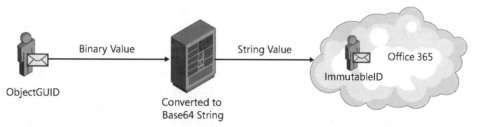

Figure 5-39 ObjectGUID to SourceAnchor to ImmutableID transition

Selection of the ObjectGUID as the origin of the SourceAnchor value in AAD Connect was done to ensure that objects remain unique, and although you have the option to select an alternate Active Directory attribute to represent the SourceAnchor for your objects, great care should be given to the selection process.

When selecting an alternate attribute, consider the following factors.

- **Select an attribute that will never change.** Changing the value in Active Directory, either purposely or accidentally, breaks the synchronization of the object.

  Some examples of possible attributes might be EmployeeID or Badge Number.

  EmployeeID number or other unique company identifiers, provided you have a mature Identity Management system that prevents any duplication and prohibits reuse, are good candidates for SourceAnchor.

  > NOTE
  > Social Security Number, although intentionally unique, represents personally identifiable information (PII); it is used in U.S. privacy law, and its use carries very specific laws and requirements. If you do not store PII today, you should work with your legal and corporate security teams before using this data in the synchronization to Office 365.
  >
  > Because the SourceAnchor value is converted to base64 from its source and then written to Azure AD, it is very easy to reverse engineer the value. Anyone with rights to your tenant (such as global administrators or user administrators), and even Microsoft Premier Support, would have access to that PII.

- **Select an attribute that will be unique for every object everywhere.** Duplication of the value on two or more objects breaks the synchronization of all but the first object synchronized to Azure with that value.

  Most organizations select an alternate SourceAnchor because they are multi-forest in nature or involved in frequent merger, acquisition, or divestiture activities and expect to move objects across forests regularly, or at least once during an object's life cycle. Consideration must be given to such values as EmployeeID or other *potentially* unique alphanumeric or numeric values that are sequential in nature, because although they are unique within *your* organization, it's possible that an acquisition or merger with another Office 365 customer can result in duplication of values that were thought to be unique.

As you can see, using an attribute other than ObjectGUID for the SourceAnchor carries with it some design considerations that are likely to involve several groups within your organization and might not result in a quick decision. Waiting to decide *whether* you should use an alternate attribute and *which* attribute to use is something that should be done well in advance of the AAD Connect implementation.

Filtering users and devices

During the installation of the AAD Connect tool, you can select one group from each forest that can be used to filter users, groups, contacts, or devices for synchronization to Azure AD.

By default, all users present in the OUs you selected earlier in the installation process are synchronized to Azure AD. This group is meant to serve as a method for piloting your deployment to Office 365, so only the objects in the group are synchronized to your tenant. It further limits the number of objects that are synchronized to Office 365. See Figure 5-40.

Figure 5-40 Filtering users and devices

Selecting Synchronize Selected enables you to type the name of a group in on-premises Active Directory in the GROUP box.

If the group name can be located in Active Directory, clicking the Resolve button displays the complete distinguished name of the group and a green check mark to indicate success, as shown in Figure 5-41.

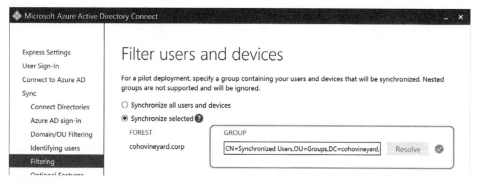

Figure 5-41 Successfully resolving a group

INSIDE OUT

Filtering groups

Any group used for filtering must reside in an organizational unit that is within the scope of the solution.

No error appears during group selection in the wizard or during synchronization afterward; group filtering simply fails to function and no objects will be synchronized to Azure.

The group filtering option does not support nested groups; it is intended to be used for piloting only and removed when the solution is placed in production use.

In addition, the associated rules that the selection of this option created cannot be removed by rerunning the AAD Connect wizard post-pilot, so you must either delete or manually disable the rules in the Synchronization Rules Editor to go live with the solution. See Figure 5-42.

CHAPTER 5

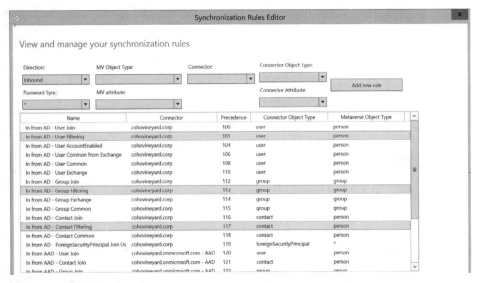

Figure 5-42 Synchronization rules related to filtering

Optional features

On the Optional Features page, you can enable enhanced functionality as part of the AAD Connect installation process. These features range from hybrid writeback, discussed earlier, to password synchronization and attribute filtering.

The options presented on the Optional Features page can be changed at any time, using the AAD Connect wizard located on the desktop after installation has completed, and this list of enhanced features grows with each release of the AAD Connect tool.

Any features that are flagged as (Preview) indicate that they are not finalized features and might change between versions.

It's also important to note that some features require additional subscriptions (such as Azure AD Premium licensing) for you to use them.

As each version of AAD Connect is released, you can find further information about the optional features at *http://go.microsoft.com/fwlink/?LinkId=532861*.

Exchange hybrid deployment

Exchange hybrid, discussed earlier in this chapter because it has a direct impact on user matching and subsequent GAL synchronization in multi-forest scenarios, is a feature that enables the AAD Connect tool to write back into on-premises Active Directory a select number of attributes.

These attributes are determined by the version of Exchange installed in the target forest and include, but are not limited to the following ones.

- **Proxy Addresses**   The cloudLegacyExchangeDN value from Exchange Online is written back into the Proxy Addresses array of User, Group, and Contact objects as an x500 address. This writeback occurs so that if mailboxes are migrated out of Office 365 back to on-premises, any messages sent internally while in Office 365 can be replied to without risking delivery errors after migration.

- **Safe Senders, Blocked Senders, Safe Recipients**   These values are hash values stored in Active Directory and updated whenever a user makes changes to these settings in their Outlook client. After a user's mailbox has been migrated to Office 365, these values are then managed in Azure AD and written back to on-premises Active Directory so that if the mailbox is ever migrated out of Office 365, those on-premises values will be up to date.

- **VoiceMail settings**   Like the safe and blocked senders lists, these values are updated in Azure AD when a user enabled for Skype for Business Online makes changes to their settings and then their account is migrated back to on-premises.

- **Archive status**   Although a mailbox resides in Exchange Online, it is possible for the mailbox not to have had an archive prior to migration and was only activated afterward. This attribute tells on-premises Exchange whether an archive exists.

The Proxy Addresses writeback is automatically configured for groups, users, and contacts, whereas the remainder of the attributes applies only to user objects.

These rules are created as part of the installation process but can be modified or disabled manually afterward, as discussed earlier in the chapter. However, subsequent upgrades of the AAD Connect tool might modify the rules or restore them to their original state, so it is important to review all rule modifications prior to upgrade, and it is always recommended to clone existing rules instead of modifying them directly, so that their settings are maintained during upgrade.

Azure AD app and attribute filtering

Selection of the Azure AD App And Attribute Filtering feature provides an additional set of wizard pages that enable you to tailor your installation to either a specific Office 365 workload (such as Exchange Online only) or set of workloads, or to exclude one or more attributes specifically from the synchronization to Azure AD.

The first of these additional pages is Azure AD Apps filtering, shown in Figure 5-43.

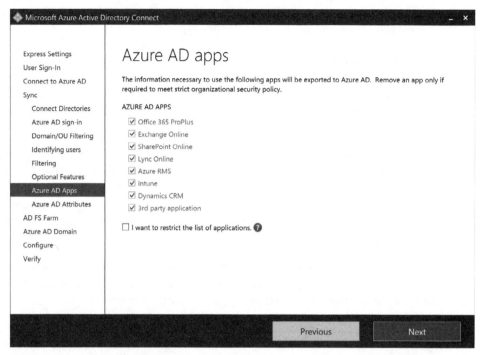

Figure 5-43 Azure AD Apps filtering

Azure AD apps filtering enables you to identify the Azure AD applications for which you wish to synchronize relevant attributes to Office 365. Clearing an application check box removes all the outbound rules from the configuration related to that Azure AD application, preventing the attributes in on-premises Active Directory from reaching Office 365.

As Figure 5-44 shows, a default installation of AAD Connect with no Azure app filtering enables outbound synchronization rules for Exchange Online, Dynamics, Lync Online, SharePoint Online, Intune, AzureRMS, and the common attribute sets.

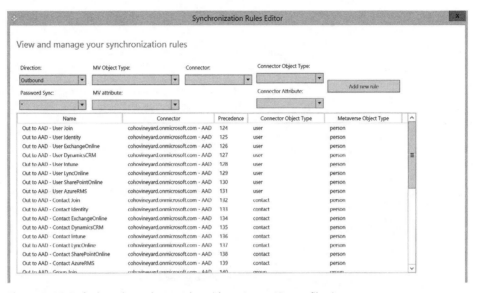

Figure 5-44 Default outbound sync rules with no Azure AD app filtering

However, Figure 5-45 shows that with Azure app filtering enabled to allow only Exchange Online, all other applications are now absent from the synchronization to Azure AD.

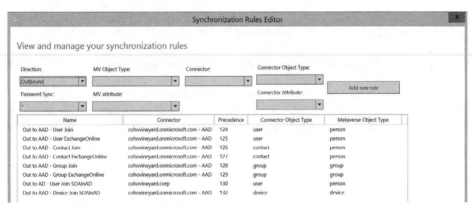

Figure 5-45 Outbound sync rules with Azure App filtering

As an alternative, if you don't wish to eliminate a particular Azure app from the synchronization to Office 365 but, instead, wish to prevent the synchronization of one or more attributes, you can select the Azure AD Attributes filtering page, shown in Figure 5-46.

CHAPTER 5

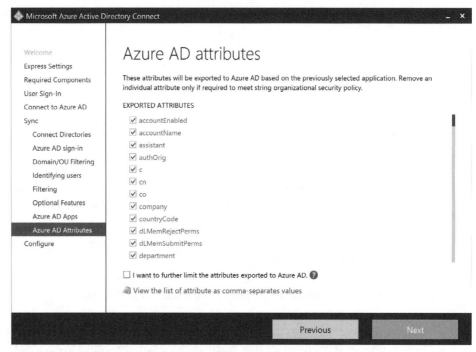

Figure 5-46 Azure AD Attributes filtering page

Azure AD attribute filtering is provided because it might be necessary to filter some attributes your organization uses that are included in the default set of attributes for a particular workload (such as Exchange Online) but contain data that you might not want synchronized to Azure AD.

Those individual attributes' check boxes can be cleared, and any synchronization rules the installation creates that normally contain those attributes will be modified so they are not included, as shown in Figure 5-47.

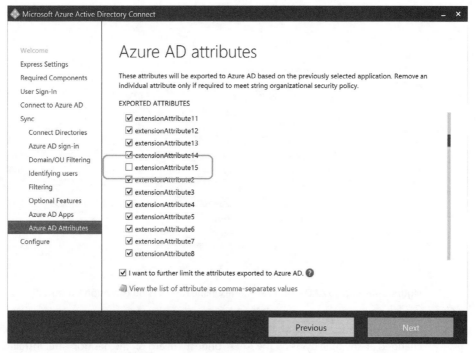

Figure 5-47 Clearing the extensionAttribute15 check box

Note in Figure 5-48 that extensionAttribute15 was excluded from the configuration by the Azure AD Attributes filtering page. As a result, the Out To AAD – User Exchange Online synchronization rule pictured in Figure 5-48 has no attribute flow for extensionAttribute15.

CHAPTER 5

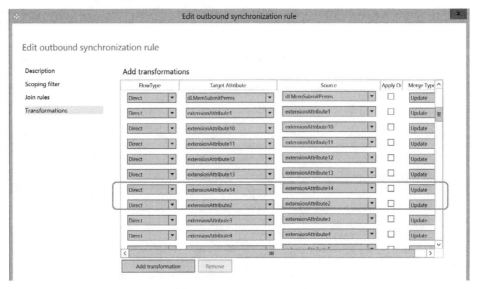

Figure 5-48 Out To AAD – User Exchange Online rule missing extensionAttribute15

Any customizations made on the Azure AD app and attribute filtering wizard pages can be changed at any time by using the AAD Connect Wizard on the desktop after installation has completed.

Password synchronization

Even though the Password Synchronization option appears earlier in the configuration process, on the User Sign-In page, it also appears on the Optional Features page.

If you selected Password Synchronization previously, it is selected for you automatically, and its check box cannot be cleared, as shown in Figure 5-49.

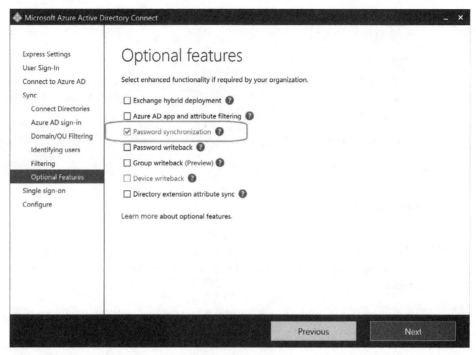

Figure 5-49 Password Synchronization selected automatically

If, however, you chose another option on the User Sign-In page, such as pass-through authentication or AD FS, it is possible to add Password Synchronization here as an additional option.

Password synchronization, in conjunction with alternate user sign-on options, is a supported scenario and provides for a fail-safe configuration in the event that your primary user sign-in option is not working. You can find additional information about the use of password synchronization as a backup for AD FS at *https://docs.microsoft.com/en-us/azure/active-directory /connect/active-directory-aadconnectsync-implement-password-synchronization#what-is -password-synchronization*.

As discussed previously in this chapter, implementing password synchronization by using the Customize AAD Connect implementation requires the service account selected during the Connect Your Directories process to be delegated Replicating Directory Permissions and Replicating Directory Permissions All at the top level of the forest.

CHAPTER 5

INSIDE OUT

Password synchronization

Unlike the regularly scheduled 30-minute sync cycle for Active Directory attributes, the AAD Connect password synchronization process happens automatically in the background, independently of the scheduler.

You should expect password changes in Active Directory to replicate to Azure AD within 1 to 2 minutes.

Password writeback

Another feature related to passwords that can be enabled on the Optional Features page is Password Writeback, which enables your users to change their password in Azure Active Directory by using the portal, and that password automatically is updated in on-premises Active Directory.

This writeback feature has several limitations and requirements, however, for it to be deployed in an enterprise.

Requirements

First, the use of the Password Writeback feature requires the user to be licensed for Azure AD Premium. An Azure AD Premium P1 or P2 license, or the Enterprise Mobility Suite (EMS) license qualifies for this feature and enables your user to use the Password Writeback feature.

Second, password writeback is supported for synchronized users, with or without Password Sync enabled, as well as for federated users using AD FS and users configured to use pass-through authentication. Cloud-only accounts do not qualify for password writeback.

Finally, any users wishing to use password writeback and the password reset portal must have the Password Writeback feature enabled for their account, and they must have the challenge data required for the organization populated on their account.

Enabling password writeback

Enabling password writeback consists of the following high-level steps.

1. Enable password reset for the Azure AD tenant.

2. Configure the password reset policy for the Azure AD tenant.

3. Type the registration data for each user.

To enable password reset for the Azure AD tenant, follow these steps.

4.   Log on to the Office 365 portal by navigating to *https://portal.microsoftonline.com* and select the Admin tile from the Office 365 app launcher as shown in Figure 5-50.

Figure 5-50 Office 365 Admin tile

5.   On the lower left side of the Admin page, expand Admin Centers and select Azure AD to open the Azure portal, shown in Figure 5-51.

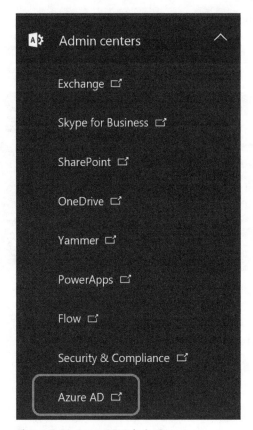

Figure 5-51 Azure AD Admin Center

6. Choose Azure Active Directory from the menu on the left side of the Azure portal and then choose Password Reset, as shown in Figure 5-52.

    You are prompted to enable password reset for Everybody or for a specific group.

    If you select the group option, you are prompted to select a group that has been synchro-nized to your tenant. If you have not yet synchronized any groups from your on-premises Active Directory, you can select Everybody and return to the portal later to change to a specific synchronized group.

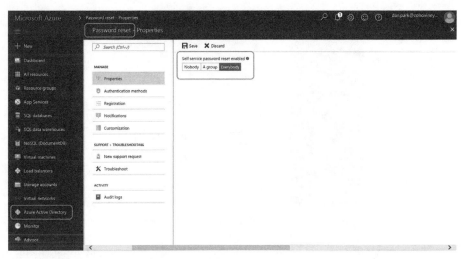

Figure 5-52 Azure AD admin portal dashboard

7.   Click the Save button at the top of the screen to save your changes.

INSIDE OUT

Password policy

Password policies selected in the Azure AD admin portal apply to users only; administrators are secured differently, and their settings cannot be changed.

Administrator accounts require both mobile phone and email address for the challenge questions.

To configure the password reset policy for the Azure AD tenant, follow these steps.

1.   Select Authentication Methods on the left side of the admin portal to select the number of methods required to reset a password.

2.   Below the selection for number of methods, select the box for each method type that you want to allow and, if you are enabling password reset for the first time, click the red exclamation point to configure the security questions, as shown in Figure 5-53.

Figure 5-53 Configuration of password reset policy authentication methods

If you select Security Questions, additional options appear that enable you to identify the number of questions required to register versus the number required to reset a password, and the current list of configured security questions appears, as shown in Figure 5-54.

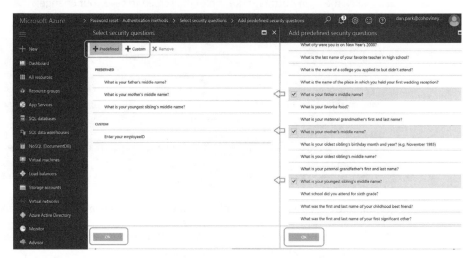

Figure 5-54 Selection of password reset security questions

On the top of the page, you are prompted to select from a list of predefined questions or to enable your own custom questions.

Clicking either option displays additional options on the right side of the screen, and you can select from the predefined list of questions or enter your own custom questions.

3. After you have completed the selection, click OK.

You are returned to the authentication methods screen, and the number of security questions you selected appears at the bottom of the screen.

4. Click Save.

After you have enabled the password reset options in the tenant, you must ensure that the data selected for registration (for example, email, mobile phone, office phone) has been populated in your on-premises Active Directory so that it synchronizes to Azure AD. Do this with the AAD Connect tool, using on-premises Active Directory as the source for this data. It is important, therefore, for the data populated in Active Directory to be accurate, or the password reset process will not work properly.

As an alternative, you can direct your users to *https://aka.ms.ssprsetup* to register their authentication methods manually. See Figure 5-55.

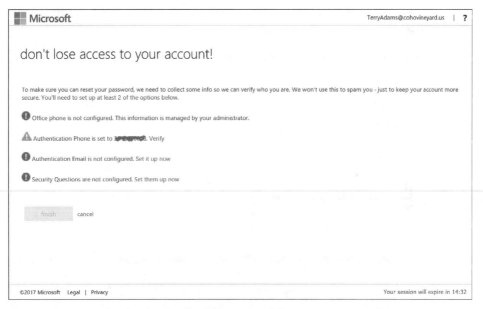

Figure 5-55 Entry of authentication detail for password reset

Any authentication methods registered manually through the Self Service Password Reset portal are maintained in Azure AD only; they are not written back to on-premises Active Directory.

After all the appropriate authentication methods have been successfully configured, users can reset their password through the Office 365 portal by selecting Can't Access Your Account on the sign-in page, shown in Figure 5-56.

Figure 5-56 Selecting Can't Access Your Account on the sign-in page

They are then redirected to the password reset portal, where they are prompted for their User ID and asked to provide Captcha information.

After that has been successfully confirmed, they are prompted for their challenge information, as shown in Figure 5-57.

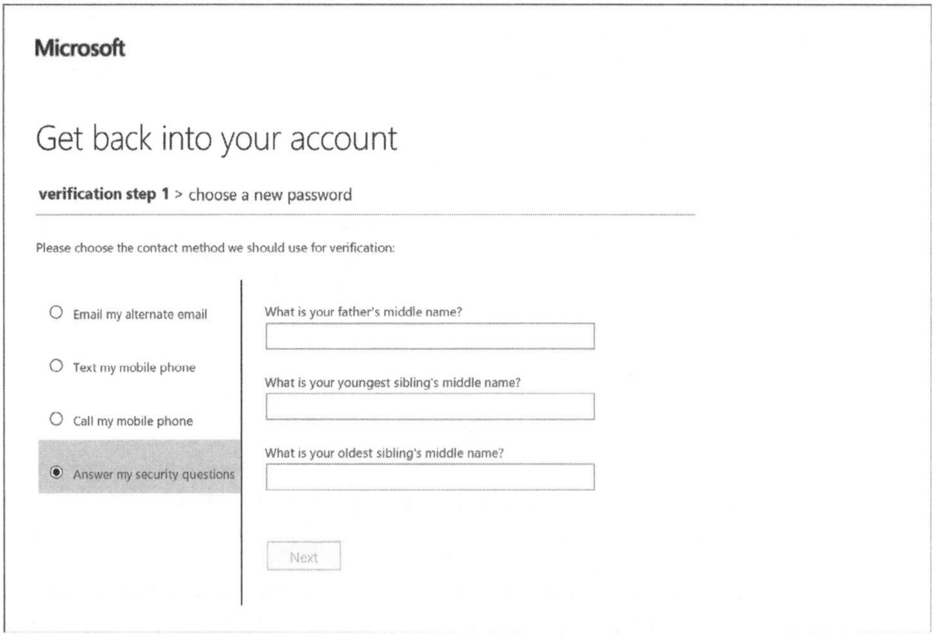

Microsoft

Get back into your account

verification step 1 > choose a new password

Please choose the contact method we should use for verification:

○ Email my alternate email

○ Text my mobile phone

○ Call my mobile phone

● Answer my security questions

What is your father's middle name?

What is your youngest sibling's middle name?

What is your oldest sibling's middle name?

Next

Figure 5-57 Password reset portal options

Successful entry of your challenge information enables you to reset your password in the portal, and that password change is written back to on-premises Active Directory.

Group writeback

The Group Writeback option, available on the Optional Features page, enables you to configure AAD Connect to write back Office 365 groups that are created in the portal into on-premises Active Directory.

Selecting Group Writeback enables Office 365 groups to be written back to on-premises Active Directory as Exchange distribution groups so that on-premises mailboxes can send and receive email from the group.

Group writeback has the following requirements and limitations.

- The Group Writeback feature requires Azure AD Premium licenses to be available in your Azure AD subscription.

- Group writeback requires the on-premises Exchange organization to be a minimum of Exchange 2013 CU8 or later.

- Groups written back into on-premises Active Directory are not visible in the on-premises Exchange global address list (GAL) unless the objects are manually updated using the Update-Recipient Exchange Windows PowerShell cmdlet.

- Group writeback is only supported for single Exchange forest deployments.

- The Group Writeback feature is for Office 365 groups only; security and distribution groups are not supported.

It is important also to note that if none of your on-premises Active Directory forests contain the Exchange schema, this option will not be available on the AAD Connect Optional Features page.

Selecting Group Writeback displays an additional wizard page that enables selection of the organizational unit in on-premises Active Directory that should be used for any Office 365 groups written back, as shown in Figure 5-58.

CHAPTER 5

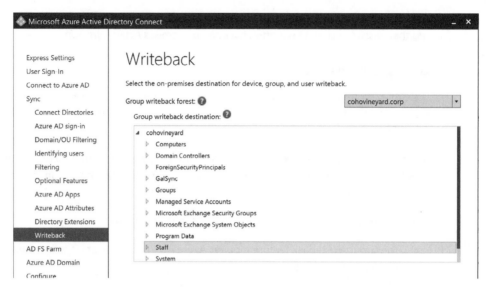

Figure 5-58 Selecting the group writeback location

Only one organizational unit can be selected for the writeback of groups, and if that OU was not selected in the Domain/OU filtering page earlier in the installation process, an error appears, stating that the OU selected is currently excluded.

You can select an alternate OU, or you can click the Previous button to return to the Domain/OU filtering wizard page and the OU included in the scope of the synchronization.

Device writeback

Device Writeback, located on the Optional Features page, enables you to configure AAD Connect to perform a writeback of devices that have been joined to your Azure AD tenant.

This writeback is provided so that conditional access to AD FS can be configured to secure applications by allowing access only from trusted devices you have successfully registered in Azure AD. These devices, however, must exist in on-premises Active Directory so that the AD FS on-premises infrastructure can use them for conditional access.

Selecting Device Writeback displays an additional wizard page that enables selection of the on-premises forest that should be used for any devices written back, as shown in Figure 5-59.

In a multi-forest configuration, only one forest can be selected as a target for device writeback. Using device writeback to more than one Active Directory forest is not supported.

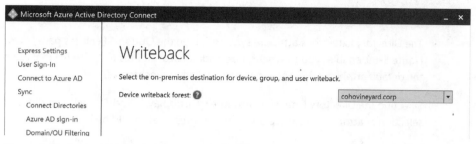

Figure 5-59 Device Writeback forest selection page

Device writeback has the following requirements and limitations.

- The Device Writeback feature requires Azure AD Premium licenses to be available in your Azure AD subscription.

- Device writeback does not support a multi-forest implementation of AAD Connect.

- The devices written back to on-premises Active Directory must be in the same Active Directory forest as the users.

- Conditional access to AD FS requires AD FS 2012R2 or later.

- Device writeback can take up to 3 hours to write back newly registered devices successfully to on-premises Active Directory.

- At least one Windows Server 2012 R2 must be joined to Active Directory.

- It is necessary to use the MSOnline Windows PowerShell module to enable device writeback in Active Directory.

- Enabling device writeback in Active Directory creates an OU named RegisteredDevices at the top level of the forest.

After you have enabled device writeback, you must configure additional conditional access policies in your AD FS infrastructure before the devices can be used to secure applications, and issuance rules for your applications must be modified to support the IsRegisteredUser claim type.

Refer to the following link for a step-by-step guide to enabling conditional access in AD FS 2.0 with device writeback: *https://docs.microsoft.com/en-us/azure/active-directory/active-directory-device-registration-on-premises-setup*.

CHAPTER 5

Directory Extensions attribute sync

The Directory Extensions attribute sync option on the Optional Features page, shown in Figure 5-60, enables you to synchronize additional attributes to Azure AD that are not part of the default attributes the AAD Connect installation synchronizes.

Selecting the Directory Extension attribute sync displays an additional wizard page that enables selection of attributes from the on-premises forest that should be included in the sync.

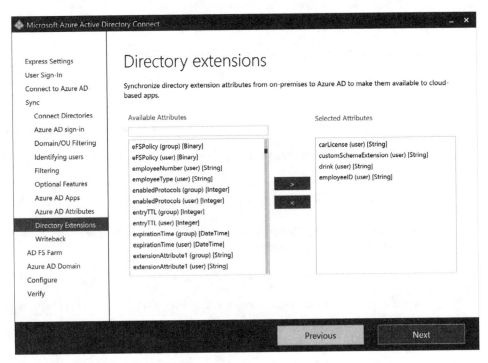

Figure 5-60 Directory Extensions page

The Directory Extensions attribute sync has the following requirements and limitations.

- The directory extensions attribute sync is limited to a total of 100 additional attributes.

- Attributes can only be 250 characters or fewer in length; characters beyond 250 are truncated during the synchronization.

- Attributes that are synchronized in this manner are not visible in Exchange, SharePoint, and so on and are visible only when using Microsoft Graph or GraphAPI.

- Any attribute synchronized by using the AAD Connect Directory Extensions attribute sync are considered mastered on-premises and cannot be modified in Azure AD.

After the Directory Extensions attribute sync has been configured, the AAD Connect installation adds new inbound and outbound synchronization rules, which contain the selected attributes, to the configuration, as shown in Figure 5-61.

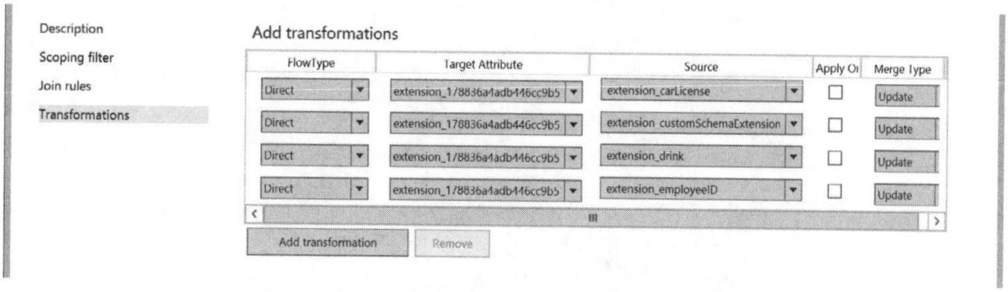

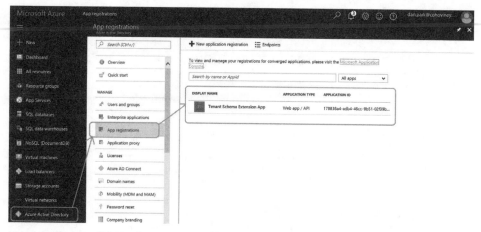

Figure 5-61 Additional outbound rule for directory extension attributes

If additional attributes are required, these rules cannot be edited; you must use the AAD Connect Wizard located on the desktop to add additional attributes to the configuration.

Finally, the Directory Extensions attribute sync also registers a new application in Azure AD that you can find by selecting Azure Active Directory in the portal and selecting App Registrations, as shown in Figure 5-62.

Figure 5-62 Azure AD application for the directory extension sync

It's important to note the application ID for the new tenant schema extension app; it is used in the naming for all custom schema attributes created in Azure AD. A GraphAPI view of the new

CHAPTER 5

attributes synchronized for the user is shown in Figure 5-63. The attributes are in the Extension_ApplicationID_On-PremAttributeName format.

Figure 5-63 GraphExplorer view of custom attribute sync values

Finalizing the installation

After you have completed the Optional Features selections, clicking Next presents the Ready To Configure page, shown in Figure 5-64, which provides a summary of the selections you made in the installation wizard and two final options before proceeding with the installation.

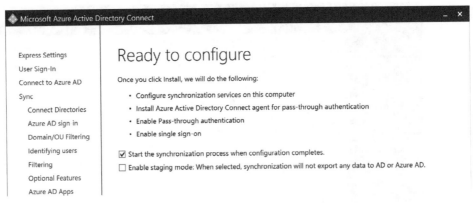

Figure 5-64 Ready To Configure page

The Start The Synchronization Process When Configuration Completes check box tells the AAD Connect installation wizard to start the synchronization process automatically as soon as the installation completes.

Leave this box clear if you plan to edit synchronization rules, add additional rules, enable device writeback, or make any other changes that might require you to run the AAD Connect Wizard on the desktop.

Finally, the Enable Staging Mode check box enables you to put the AAD Connect server in read-only mode.

If you are installing your first AAD Connect server in the enterprise but wish to make changes, or if you simply aren't ready to start exporting users and groups to Azure, you can enable staging mode. Staging mode enables the server to read from Active Directory and apply synchronization rules to your objects, but nothing will be exported to Azure AD. This enables you to review the results of your configuration and make changes without ever exporting to Office 365.

More information about staging appears at the end of this chapter.

Configuration complete

After the AAD Connect installation completes, the installation wizard presents a summary screen that displays the status of the installation as well as any warnings about the environment, along with synchronization status. See Figure 5-65.

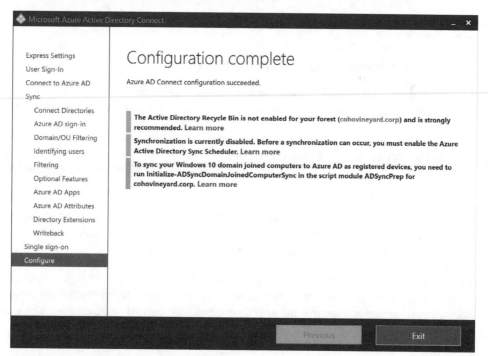

Figure 5-65 Configuration Complete page

Review all notifications and warnings the installer displays and take any additional action if required.

If synchronization was disabled (the check box was left cleared) on the final installation screen, you are reminded to re-enable the scheduler before synchronization will occur.

It is now safe to click Exit.

INSIDE OUT

AAD Connect documenter

After you have successfully completed the installation of the AAD Connect tool, making a backup of the configuration is recommended.

This backup can then be used with the AAD Connect configuration documenter tool to generate an HTML report of your configuration at *https://github.com/Microsoft/AADConnectConfigDocumenter*.

The configuration documenter also enables you to report on differences between configuration backups and generate a script that can be used to migrate differences between two servers.

Precedence, and why it matters

Precedence is defined as *priority in importance, order, or rank*, and this definition, when referring to directories or synchronization rules in AAD Connect, could not be more relevant.

Ordering of the Active Directory forests when performing a multi-forest installation of AAD Connect is critical to the precedence of values as they are synchronized. However, even in a single-forest configuration, precedence could be a concern if configuration changes are planned after deployment.

Although it might not be obvious during the installation of the tool, the resulting synchronization rules dictate the value synchronized to Azure AD for each object, so it's important to understand precedence and its impact on the configuration.

Each object that falls within the scope of the AAD Connect implementation, through organizational unit membership or even group filtering, is subject to the precedence order of the synchronization rules that the AAD Connect installer created based on selections you made through the setup wizard.

Synchronization rules, as shown in Figure 5-66, are ordered first by direction (inbound vs. out-bound), second by object type, and finally by order of importance, or precedence.

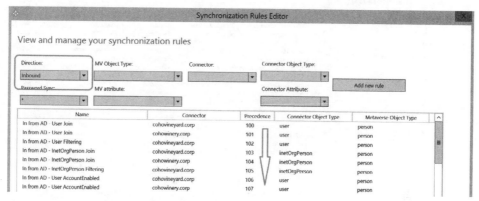

Figure 5-66 Precedence of synchronization rules

Each rule is assigned a precedence value, typically starting from 100 and increasing in value as order of importance decreases. As a result, the lower the numerical value of a rule, the higher its precedence.

When a new object enters the scope of the AAD Connect sync, each rule is applied to the object, based on its object type, visible in the Connector Object Type column, starting at the top of the precedence list and working downward.

Some rules might not apply to an object, depending on their purpose. For example, an Exchange synchronization rule will not apply to an object that is not mail-enabled.

The rules that are applied to an object can be found at the bottom of the preview pane for a user (discussed in Chapter 4, "Directory Synchronization Basics"), and the rule that contributed each attribute is visible in the Sync Rule column, as shown in Figure 5-67.

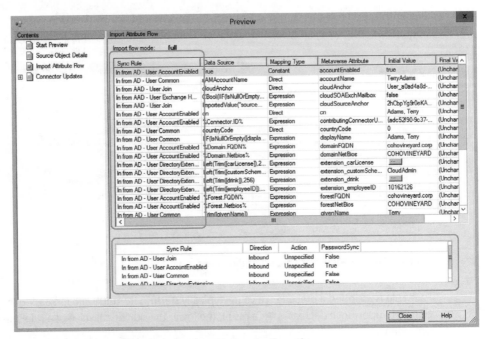

Figure 5-67 Preview dialog box showing synchronization rules

In Figure 5-68, you can see that the value for AccountEnabled, visible in the Metaverse Attribute column, is set to True and was set in the In From AD – User AccountEnabled rule.

The In From AD – User AccountEnabled rule has a precedence value of 106, so if you wanted to create a new rule that forced the value of AccountEnabled to False, your new rule would need a precedence that is higher (that is, numerically lower) than rule number 106, as shown in Figure 5-68.

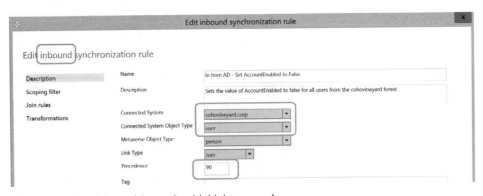

Figure 5-68 New Inbound Sync rule with higher precedence

The new synchronization rule is an Inbound rule, as appears in the top left corner, and it is configured to apply to User objects from the CohoVineyard.corp forest, with a precedence value of 90.

This means that the AccountEnabled value (not shown here but configured on the Transformations page) will be set to False when you resynchronize your user account as shown in Figure 5-69.

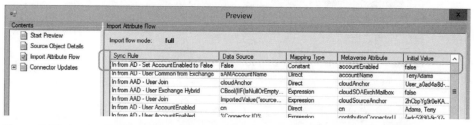

Figure 5-69 AccountEnabled value changed to False

Synchronization rule precedence can be used to change one or more attribute values for objects by creating new synchronization rules or customizing the rules the AAD Connect installation wizard created. However, it is even more important to understand the ordering of synchronization rules in a multi-forest configuration where objects are configured to join on attributes such as Mail, because the order in which the forests were added to the AAD Connect Wizard affects the resulting objects synchronized to Azure AD.

In Figure 5-70, two Active Directory forests are configured to synchronize to Azure. Each forest is enabled for Exchange and contains a combination of mail users and mailboxes; a join on the Mail attribute was selected in the AAD Connect installation wizard.

If you compare the precedence value of the In From AD – User Join rules, you can see that the CohoVineyard.corp forest was added first in the installation wizard, because it has a precedence value that is higher (that is, numerically lower) than the precedence value for the CohoWinery.corp forest.

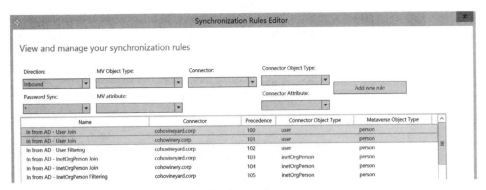

Figure 5-70 The In From AD – User Join rules for two forests

INSIDE OUT

Identifying precedence

It is easy to identify the order in which forests were added to the AAD Connect configuration, by reviewing the In From AD – User Join rules.

As each forest is added, the In From AD – User Join rule, the provisioning rule that is responsible for determining whether an object should be synchronized, is inserted in the configuration after the previous forest's In From AD – User Join rule.

As more forests are added, all the rules are renumbered, but the In From AD – User Join rules, starting at 100, remain at the top of the rules list and show the precedence order for each forest.

When you can recognize the precedence order the synchronization engine uses to process objects, you can quickly identify where problems might occur. It is best to understand this rule-ordering process prior to installation; however, in some cases, you might inherit an existing installation of AAD Connect and do not have the luxury of re-installation.

Under those circumstances, it might be necessary to clone existing rules to change the behavior of the synchronization rules or create new rules to force an alternate precedence configuration.

In Figure 5-71, two objects are joining on the Mail value to create a single object that will be synchronized to Office 365. A mailbox from the CohoWinery.corp forest joins with a mail user from the CohoVineyard.corp forest.

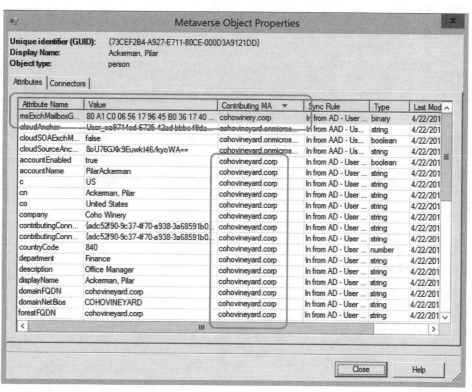

Figure 5-71 Metaverse object properties for a joined user

In the Contributing MA column, all the attributes for the user are coming from the CohoVineyard.corp forest except for the msExchMailboxGUID value, which comes from the CohoWinery.corp forest. This is because the CohoVineyard.corp forest is the precedent forest, its In From AD – User Join rule has a value of 100, and it is therefore higher in precedence than CohoWinery.corp for *all* values.

The only reason msExchMailboxGUID is coming from the CohoWinery.corp forest is because the CohoVineyard.corp object is a mail user and has no msExchMailboxGUID in CohoVineyard.corp.

In this example, provided that the properties for values from CohoVineyard.corp were the values expected in Azure AD, nothing further would be needed. The synchronization process would flow the object to Office 365 as a mail user, the object type in the precedent forest, and the msExchMailboxGUID attribute would be ignored.

If, however, there were values that should be precedent from the CohoWinery.corp forest, it would be necessary to make changes to the synchronization rules so that those values were precedent.

Two methods are available for achieving this goal.

- Clone the synchronization rule(s) that flow those attributes as a higher precedence (lower numeric value).

- Create a new inbound synchronization rule with a higher precedence for the attributes in question.

In this example, you would select the second option because you are only concerned with the Title and Department values.

First, create a new inbound synchronization rule with a precedence higher than 100 for user objects from the CohoWinery.corp forest. See Figure 5-72.

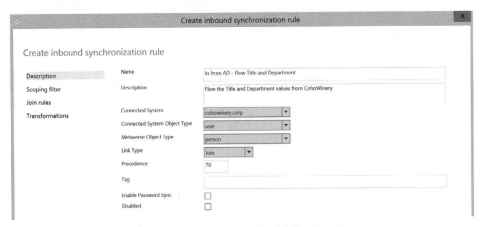

Figure 5-72 Creation of a new synchronization rule for Title and Department

Add the attribute transformations for the Title and Department values, as shown in Figure 5-73.

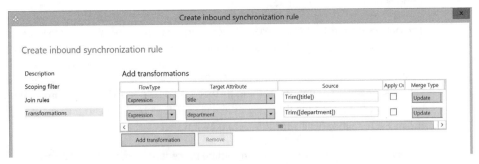

Figure 5-73 Transformations for Title and Department attributes

Note that the attribute transformations are not direct flows, but are instead expressions, primarily because the AAD Connect tool takes certain precautions to help ensure that the data synchronized to Azure AD is free from formatting errors.

In the case of the Title and Department values, the Trim() function eliminates any leading or trailing white space.

In addition, you would not need to create the expressions used in this rule. Instead, you would search the synchronization rules for the rule that would ordinarily flow those two values (that is, In From AD – User Common) and copy the existing transformation expression to your new rule.

Searching the synchronization rules is simply a matter of using the drop-down lists at the top of the Synchronization Rules Editor. Selecting the connector, object type (for instance, User), and attribute (that is, Title) drop-down lists causes the editor to filter all rules that do not meet those criteria. You can then edit these rules and review the transformation for the attribute in question and duplicate that transformation in your new rule. See Figure 5-74.

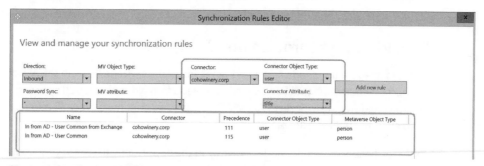

Figure 5-74 Filtering in the Synchronization Rules Editor

After the new synchronization rule has been saved, re-synchronization of the user object shows that the values being synchronized to Azure AD for Title and Department are now coming from the CohoWinery.corp forest through the new synchronization rule that was created, as shown in Figure 5-75.

CHAPTER 5

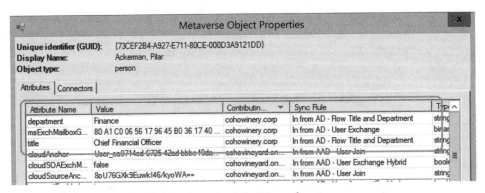

Figure 5-75 Attribute values flowing from the CohoWinery forest

Although it is possible to make precedence changes by cloning rules or creating new rules, depending on the number of customizations, it might ultimately make more sense to uninstall and reinstall the AAD Connect tool because it will keep the number of customizations to a minimum and simplify the configuration.

Should you synchronize now?

If you enabled staging mode at the end of the installation wizard, you can safely start the AAD Connect scheduler. The tool begins reading objects from your directories, applying synchronization rules and staging exports to Azure AD. This process continues every 30 minutes, but nothing is exported until you are ready.

This is the beauty of staging mode. It gives you the opportunity to review your configuration, especially if you are not completely sure that all your selections are correct or you are aware of unique configurations in your environment, but you are not sure what the tool will do with your data and how those objects will sync to Azure—all without writing any data to the cloud or making any changes to your environment!

Now take your time, review as many objects as possible and consider the following scenarios.

- **Do you have data that should *not* leave your on-premises Active Directory (such as that EmployeeID is the user's Social Security number)?**   If so, either remove that data from your environment or use the Azure App And Attribute filtering option in the AAD Connect Wizard to remove the attribute from the configuration.

- **Do you have objects that should be synchronized to Azure but are not being staged for export?**   Confirm that you have selected the correct OUs and, if necessary, run the AAD Connect Wizard and use domain/OU filtering to include the missing OUs.

- **Do you have too many objects staged for export to Azure?**   Confirm that you have selected the correct OUs or use group membership filtering to reduce the object count. Depending on your directory hierarchy, it might be necessary to create additional synchronization rules to filter these objects in other ways.

- **Are you joining user objects across forests properly?**   Take careful note of the attributes flowing to Azure when joining object types between your forests. It might be necessary to use the sync rule editor to change precedence for one or more synchronization rules or create your own.

It's often said that nothing shines the light of day on your directory data like synchronizing it to Azure. Conditions that are possible in on-premises Active Directory, such as duplicate values for attributes such as Mail, are not allowed in Azure AD, and the AAD Connect tool flags these conditions as errors during the export process.

Remember that after you start synchronizing objects to Azure AD, it becomes increasingly difficult to make changes to the configuration, especially if there are changes to the SourceAnchor value, and data cleanup is critical to get your data to the cloud.

Starting synchronization

Now that you've reviewed your configuration thoroughly and tested as many of your objects as possible, you're ready to start exporting your data to the cloud.

1.   If you enabled staging mode, disable it by using the AAD Connect Wizard on the desktop.

2.   Launch the AAD Connect Wizard and select Configure on the welcome screen.
     Several options appear.

3.   Select Configure Staging Mode and click Next, as shown in Figure 5-76.

CHAPTER 5

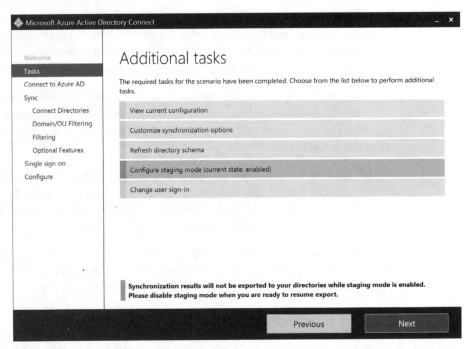

Figure 5-76 Configuring staging mode

4. Type credentials for a global administrator in the tenant and click Next.

   These credentials are not stored in the configuration; they are used simply to ensure that you have the proper privileges to enable synchronization of objects to your Azure AD tenant.

5. Clear the check mark from the Enable Staging Mode check box shown in Figure 5-77 and click Next.

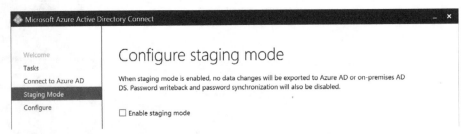

Figure 5-77 Configure Staging Mode page

The Ready To Configure page appears, with the option to start the synchronization immediately, as shown in Figure 5-78.

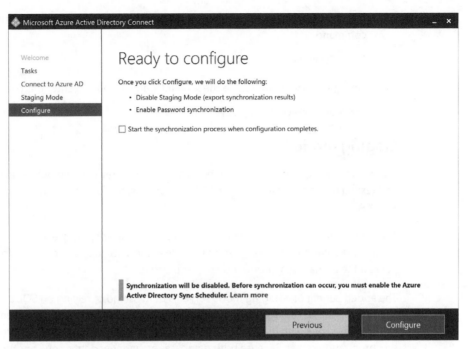

Figure 5-78 Ready To Configure staging mode page

6. Click Configure to complete the change.

If you selected Start the Synchronization Process, the synchronization starts immediately, and objects begin exporting to your Office 365 tenant. No further action is required.

If, however, you did not immediately enable synchronization but are ready to do so sometime later, you can start the synchronization process by using Windows PowerShell.

7. Open an administrative Windows PowerShell prompt and issue the following command.

`Start-ADSyncSyncCycle`

This starts the synchronization process immediately; however, it executes only one time, leaving the scheduled sync cycle disabled.

During initial population of the Azure AD tenant, this single export to Azure helps identify any issues with data, in the form of export errors, but allows you time to review and correct the data before a second synchronization cycle occurs.

8. When you are ready to enable the regular 30-minute sync cycle, enter the following Windows PowerShell command.

`Set-ADSyncScheduler -SyncCycleEnabled $True`

This enables the scheduler for a regular 30-minute synchronization interval.

CHAPTER 5

9. If at any time, you want to view the status of the scheduler, you can use the following command.

```
Get-ADSyncScheduler
```

10. Finally, if you want to disable the scheduler again, you can enter this command.

```
Set-ADSyncScheduler -SyncCycleEnabled $False
```

Staging mode

Previously, staging mode was discussed as an option for reviewing synchronization of objects and testing the configuration of the AAD Connect installation prior to the first export of data to Azure AD.

The staging mode server, however, has an equally important purpose in a typical Azure AD synchronization strategy. It is designed to provide a warm-standby server to use for failover purposes if the primary synchronization server is down.

The added benefit of a staging mode server is that instead of relying on SQL Server high-availability features such as log shipping or clustering, AAD Connect can be installed on a separate stand-alone server with its own SQL database without any need to interact with the primary synchronization server. Because both databases are independent of one another, any SQL database corruption on the primary server would not be replicated to the staging server.

Migrating from the primary synchronization server to the staging server is simply a matter of running the AAD Connect Wizard on the desktop and disabling staging mode. It is assumed that the primary server is down or unavailable when this action is performed, and you must ensure that prior to bringing the primary server back online, the secondary server is returned to staging mode.

Two AAD Connect servers both synchronizing to the same tenant is not supported.

Summary

The installation of AAD Connect, as discussed in this chapter, is not a simple task. Many customization options are available during the setup, and some of these customizations are permanent, requiring a complete re-installation if they need to be changed. It is therefore important for you to read and understand each of the customization options available in the installation wizard before proceeding with the installation of the tool.

When you have completed the installation of AAD Connect, you can start synchronizing objects to Office 365 and using other workloads such as Skype for Business, Exchange Online, and SharePoint Online. Just remember to review all your available options before starting the installation so you avoid redoing work and correcting mistakes that might cost you time and money.

PART III

Inside the Office 365 Admin Portal

The Office 365 portal, dashboard, and admin centers

The Microsoft Office 365 portal is the launching pad to administering most of the service's features. To log on to the Office 365 portal, navigate to *http://portal.office.com*. There, you can log on with either a managed tenant ID or a federated identity. For more information on managed and federated identity, see Chapter 3, "Federation Services and Authentication."

Setting up your Office 365 subscription

Before you have anything to administer, you need an Office 365 subscription. Office 365 subscriptions are available for a variety of organizations, ranging from just a few employees to schools and universities, midsized companies, and global enterprises. To get started, launch a browser and navigate to *http://www.office365.com*.

You can set up a trial for either home or business use and, for business, you can choose between midsize and enterprise options. If you navigate to the enterprise plans, you can choose to start an Enterprise E3 trial, as shown in Figure 6-1.

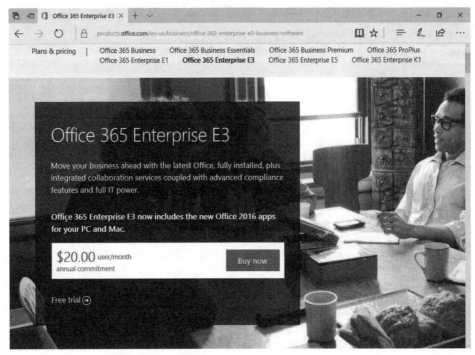

Figure 6-1 Free trial link to begin an Office 365 Enterprise E3 trial

When you initiate a free trial of Office 365 Enterprise E3, you're prompted to fill out basic information. At the top of the form is a drop-down list from which to choose your region. This is one of the two configurations of your Office 365 subscription that you cannot change. (The other is the Tenant or Subscription name.)

When selecting the region for your Office 365 subscription, take into consideration where your organization conducts business as well as where your sites and users are distributed. Some organizations might have restrictions on where their data can be physically located, so you might need to verify data processing requirements with your organization's legal team.

INSIDE OUT

Microsoft Online Services

Microsoft operates a number of data centers globally, and your data will be stored or distributed among many of them. For organizations that have specific geographic restrictions for data storage, Microsoft provides a general list of the countries where data centers servicing a given region are located, at *http://www.microsoft.com/online/legal/v2/?docid=25*. Overall information, including links to privacy statements and trust centers, is located at *http://www.microsoft.com/online/legal/v2*.

The regional setting dictates where your information will be stored and what services are available; not all services are available in all regions. It also determines what regional privacy laws affecting your subscription are in effect. See Figure 6-2.

Figure 6-2 Office 365 new tenant signup

After you select a region and fill out the basic information, you are asked to create a user ID. The left side of the @ symbol is the user alias, and the right side is the tenant name. All tenant names end in .onmicrosoft.com. You cannot change the tenant name later, so make sure you pick something that reflects your business name, branding, or ideals.

After you've filled out the information, you can click Create My Account. A captcha screen appears, asking you to verify your identity with a phone call or text message.

After your identity has been verified, the sign-up page displays your account information, as shown in Figure 6-3.

Figure 6-3 Office 363 tenant creation confirmation page

Click You're Ready To Go to begin the tenant logon process. The main portal admin page appears.

If you close out of your browser window instead of clicking You're Ready To Go and then decide to navigate back to the portal logon page, you are most likely to be greeted with the Additional Info Required screen after entering your credentials.

Clicking Next redirects you to a page to set up reset options if you need to reset your password. By default, the portal prompts you for two forms of backup verification: an email address and a phone number. If you click Cancel before completing either of them, you're redirected to the logon page. If you complete one of the methods, you'll enter the portal but be prompted to set up a second recovery authentication method on the next logon.

INSIDE OUT

Provisional tenants

Basic education subscriptions are free but generally require you to verify an .edu domain in your Office 365 tenant. To drive adoption rates, Microsoft enables users at educational institutions to create their own tenants. To start the process, users only need an email address ending in .edu. From there, a tenant is provisioned with 1,000,000 licenses for Power BI and Office 365, and users can begin consuming some services right away.

A limited number of services are available initially in the provisional tenant (sometimes called viral tenants), with options to add both more free and paid-for subscriptions. Any additional services must be provided by an administrator after the provisional tenant has been created. For example, students may obtain licenses to use Microsoft OneDrive and Office Online, but Exchange Online cannot be configured. Users cannot change their own license assignments in a provisional tenant.

Frequently, administrators might not even know that a provisional tenant has been created on their behalf; the first indication is usually when they attempt to confirm their educational domain in their new tenant. They receive a warning that the domain is configured for another tenant, which then results in confusion and usually leads to a support call.

Fortunately, there is an easy solution to this problem—the Admin Takeover process. Using this process, an IT administrator can claim a provisional or viral tenant and convert it to a normal IT-managed tenant.

To perform an IT admin takeover of a provisional or viral tenant, follow these steps.

1. Log on to *https://portal.office.com* with an identity ending in your educational institution's email domain.

2. Select the Become An Admin link at the bottom of the page.

3. At the prompt, begin the domain verification process.

    The domain verification process for a provisional tenant is identical to the domain verification process for any other tenant; simply verify the domain ownership through the use of a DNS record.

After confirming the tenant, your account is elevated to global administrator and will be able to log on to the Office 365 Admin Center.

Getting started in the Office 365 portal

Depending on the licenses that have been assigned to your account, different icons (called tiles) might appear on the landing page. This account has been given all the licenses available in the tenant, which include Exchange Online, SharePoint Online, Office ProPlus, Yammer, Planner, Delve, Office 365 Video, Sway, Flow, Teams, PowerApps, and Dynamics, as shown in Figure 6-4.

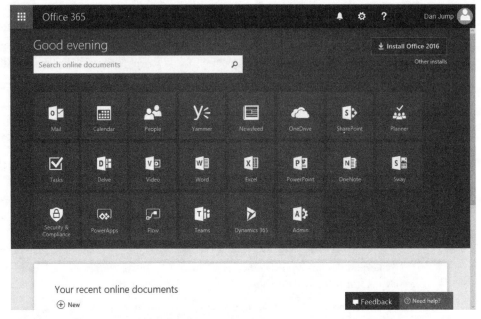

Figure 6-4 Office 365 portal landing page

Clicking any of the tiles opens the relevant individual applications, with the exception of the Mail, Calendar, People, and Tasks tiles. Those tiles are linked to parts of Outlook on the Web (the online branding of Outlook Web App). The Admin tile is only displayed for administrators and opens the Office 365 Admin Center.

The Office 365 portal landing page

The starting page of the Office 365 portal provides access to many parts of the service.

The following list describes the parts of the portal.

- **App Launcher**   This link in the upper-left displays all the tiles on the portal screen and provides a search box for locating custom apps or tiles that might not show up on the home page.

- **Notifications**   The bell icon lists notifications for activities happening in the portal. The creation or completion of a migration batch and subscription alerts are examples of things that might be displayed here.

- **Settings**   The gear icon takes you to your personal settings, where you can configure a few general settings or delve deeper into individual Office 365 app settings. It also provides a search box so you can locate individual configuration items. You manage the settings for the Office 365 tenant from the admin center, which you access from the Admin tile.

- **Help**   The question mark exposes a menu of help choices. In some admin centers, it also provides context-sensitive help.

- **My Accounts**   Clicking the user icon or name shows the My Accounts menu, giving you options to access your About Me page in Delve and your account and profile settings or to sign out of Office 365.

- **Search**   The search box enables you to search for content you have access to across OneDrive, Microsoft SharePoint, and email.

- **Software Installs**   This enables you to install the Office ProPlus media. The Other Installs link opens your individual software download page, where you can download other applications licensed for your account.

- **Application tiles**   Each application has its own tile. All the tiles in this section open user-licensed applications, with the exception of Security & Compliance and Admin, which link to admin applications.

The admin center

Clicking the Admin tile on the portal landing page launches the Office 365 Admin Center, as shown in Figure 6-5.

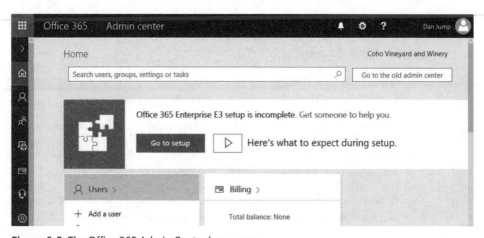

Figure 6-5 The Office 365 Admin Center home page

When you first launch the Admin Center, the navigation menu is collapsed. Hovering over an icon exposes that menu's actions and tasks. Clicking the > arrow at the top of the navigation (left) pane expands the menu to show a description for each icon.

Selecting the Home icon at any point in the admin center takes you back to the home page view.

The Office 365 Admin Center home page has cards for common tasks, including user administration, billing, software downloads, domains, and service notifications, as shown in Figure 6-6.

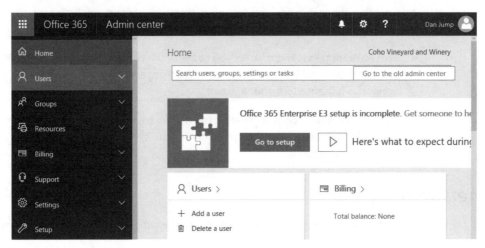

Figure 6-6 Office 365 Admin Center, navigation expanded

Expanding each menu displays links for additional activities. The menus are listed here, followed by a deeper look into what each menu offers.

- **Users**   From the Users menu, you can choose to administer objects under Active Users, Contacts, Guest Users, Deleted Users, and Data Migration.

- **Groups**   The Groups menu contains groups as well as shared mailboxes.

- **Resources**   The Resources menu includes Rooms & Equipment as well as SharePoint Sites and Public Website development partners such as GoDaddy.

- **Billing**   The Billing menu includes options to manage your subscriptions, view existing bills, view licenses, purchase additional services, and review billing notifications.

- **Support**   Under Support, you can open and track tickets with Office 365 support.

- **Settings**   The Settings menu enables you to manage options for directory synchronization, multifactor authentication (as well as other service add-ins), and security and privacy settings; add and remove domains; participate in feature releases and other global organization configurations; and perform Microsoft Partner configuration.

- **Setup**   The Setup menu displays a list of your purchased products and tutorials on how to configure them, a link to managing your domains (which links to the same section as Domains in the Settings menu), and Data Migration (which points to the same menu as Data Migration in the Users menu).

- **Reports**   Under Reports, you find dashboard-style reports regarding your Email, OneDrive, SharePoint, and Skype activity as well as security and compliance reports.

- **Health**   The Health menu enables you to monitor the service status of Office 365 services and view messages and alerts that have been posted in the Message Center.

- **Admin Centers**   The Admin Centers menu opens the admin centers for Exchange, Skype For Business, SharePoint, OneDrive, Yammer, PowerApps, Flow, and Azure Active Directory. In addition, there is a link to Security & Compliance (which is the same destination as the Security & Compliance tile displayed for administrators on the initial Office 365 landing page).

Users

The Users menu enables you to administer a few types of objects as well as discover and perform migrations.

Active Users

Active Users includes any object that could access Office 365 services and can contain a mix of managed and synchronized users. Users can be licensed, unlicensed, or blocked from accessing services altogether.

The Active Users page enables you to search for users based on name or email address as well as filter users based on built-in roles or other custom criteria, as shown in Figure 6-7.

CHAPTER 6

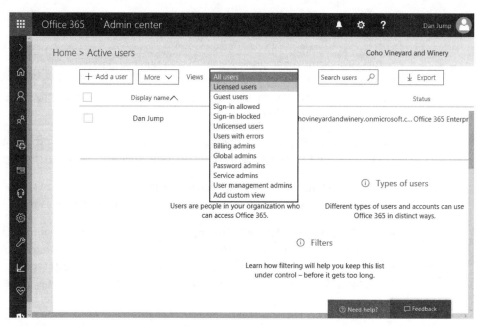

Figure 6-7 Office 365 Active Users drop-down filter list

Users can be filtered by the criteria listed in Table 6-1.

Table 6-1 Active Users filtering criteria

User type	Description
Licensed users	Users who have been assigned an Office 365 license and can use Office 365 services.
Sign-In allowed	Users who can sign in to Office 365 to access services.
Sign-In blocked	Users who cannot sign in to Office 365. When Directory Synchronization is enabled, these are typically user accounts that are disabled on-premises.
Unlicensed users	Users who have no assigned Office 365 license. These might be normal users or special resource accounts such as shared mailboxes or administrative accounts.
Users with errors	Users who have errors associated with their accounts such as users who might be missing attributes.
Billing admins	Users who have been granted the Billing Admin role. Billing admins can make purchases, manage subscriptions, open tickets, and monitor service health.
Global admins	Users with full access to the Office 365 tenant. The individual who creates the Office 365 tenant becomes the first global admin.

User type	Description
Password admins	Users who have been granted the Password Admin role. Password admins can reset passwords, manage service requests, and monitor Office 365 service health.
Service admins	The Service Admin role enables those users to manage service requests and monitor service health.
User management admins	User admins are delegated the rights to reset passwords (except for accounts that are global, billing, or service admins), monitor service health, manage users and groups, and manage service requests.
Add Custom View	This option enables you to create a custom view for filtering users, including domain, location, licenses, sign-in status, whether the user is synchronized, whether the users have errors, users who have mailbox data with no licenses (common after a migration), or location and address properties.

Contacts

You can create shared contacts in the Office 365 Admin Center. Users can see contacts in the global address list. To create contacts, you must be a global administrator or an Exchange administrator. Exchange administrators can create contacts through the Exchange Admin Center. In an environment with directory synchronization enabled, any on-premises administrator with appropriate rights can create contacts in the on-premises directory and they will be synchronized to Office 365.

Guest users

The Guest Users page shows external users who are members of Office 365 groups. Guest users are added by the owners of Office 365 groups and are not created directly here.

Deleted users

The Deleted Users page shows users who have been removed from the service. Users can be deleted through a variety of methods: manually from the Office 365 Admin Center or by the Remove-MsolUser cmdlet from Windows PowerShell, or, in an environment with directory synchronization, by deleting the user on-premises or moving the user out of synchronization scope. Deleted users can be restored up to 30 days after they have been removed.

INSIDE OUT

Restoring deleted users

From time to time, accounts might need to be restored in the tenant. Restoring synchronized accounts is a much more complex topic and is discussed in Chapter 4, "Directory Synchronization Basics."

CHAPTER 6

Managed accounts (accounts whose source of authority is Office 365) can be easily restored through the portal by following these steps.

1. Sign in to Office 365 with an admin account.

2. Navigate to Admin Center | Users | Deleted Users. See Figure 6-8.

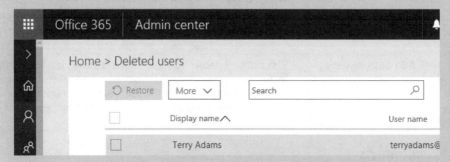

Figure 6-8 Office 365 Deleted Users page

3. Select one or more users whom you want to restore and then click Restore. If you have only a single user account to restore, the user object opens, and you can then click the Restore button.

4. Select the appropriate password option and click Restore, as shown in Figure 6-9.

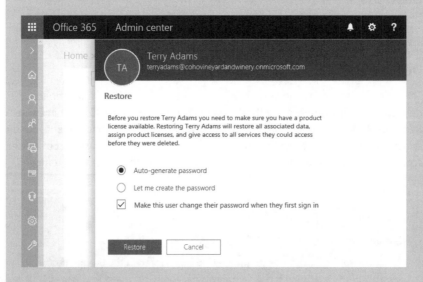

Figure 6-9 Office 365 Restore dialog box to restore a deleted user

5. Close the dialog box.

If there is a conflict when restoring a user (for example, a new user who has the same sign-in name or proxy email address as the user you are attempting to restore), Office 365 alerts you. At that point, you can cancel and rename the existing user that is in conflict and start the restore process again, or you can continue and type a new primary email address. If the value in conflict is a proxy address for the user you are restoring, Office 365 automatically drops the conflicting addresses.

Data Migration

The Data Migration page is where you can find information about performing various migrations (PST, IMAP, Exchange staged or hybrid, and OneDrive for Business). It also has links to quick-start guides for other Office 365 services.

Groups

The Groups menu in the navigation pane contains two related entries: Groups and Shared Mailboxes.

Groups

The term "groups" in Office 365 now includes both Office 365 groups (referred to in some places as modern groups or unified groups) and more traditional distribution lists. Distribution lists can be created in-cloud through the portal or Windows PowerShell or synchronized from your on-premises environment. Office 365 groups can only be created and managed in Office 365. You can find detailed information about managing groups in Chapter 11, "Understanding the Office 365 Resource Types."

Shared mailboxes

The other option on the Groups menu is Shared Mailboxes. On the Shared Mailboxes page, you can add, search, and modify shared mailboxes. Shared mailboxes, like other resources, can be created in the Office 365 tenant directly or synchronized and migrated from on-premises Active Directory.

Resources

The Resources menu includes Rooms & Equipment (special types of shared mailboxes in Exchange Online), Sites (SharePoint sites), and Public Website.

Room and equipment mailboxes

Room and equipment mailboxes are shared mailboxes that are configured as a specific recipient type in Exchange Online. Certain calendar-processing and delegate information is applied to

CHAPTER 6

them that is not available for regular user mailboxes or standard shared mailboxes. Room and equipment mailboxes enable you to reserve resources through Outlook or Outlook Web App. See Figure 6-10.

Figure 6-10 Office 365 Rooms & Equipment page

From this interface, you can create a room or equipment mailbox as well as manage them.

Sites

The Office 365 product suite includes SharePoint Online. Through the Sites page, shown in Figure 6-11, you can perform basic site operations, such as creating a SharePoint site collection (logical grouping of documents and web applications) and administering external sharing.

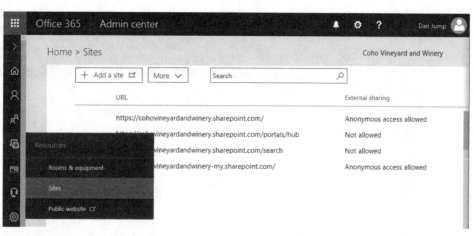

Figure 6-11 Office 365 Sites page

By selecting a site, you can configure a few options, as shown in Figure 6-12.

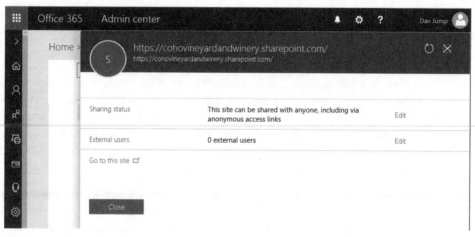

Figure 6-12 Administer basic site options

Clicking the Edit button next to Sharing Status, for example, displays a dialog box that enables you to configure sharing settings for the entire site, as shown in Figure 6-13.

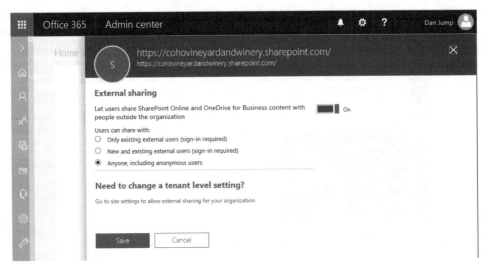

Figure 6-13 Configuring external sharing for a site

More advanced sharing options for SharePoint site collections and sites are available in the SharePoint Admin Center.

Public website

In previous versions of Office 365, you could host a public website in SharePoint Online. Although there were many advantages of that (such as being able to use similar templates and styles and configure authentication and external sharing), there were some limitations in how you could use your domain name in the service as well as the order in which you could activate services. This had the potential to create confusion for users and administrators and required planning to make sure that things were activated in the correct order.

Customers who subscribed to the Office 365 service after March 9, 2015, have access to a new feature that integrates third-party offerings with the Office 365 interface. Microsoft has partnered with both GoDaddy and Wix to provide customers with platform administration and hosting tools. See Figure 6-14.

When you select the Public Website menu in a tenant created after March 9, 2015, you arrive at a page that presents two options to begin working with third-party partners to develop and host content for your organization, as shown in Figure 6-15.

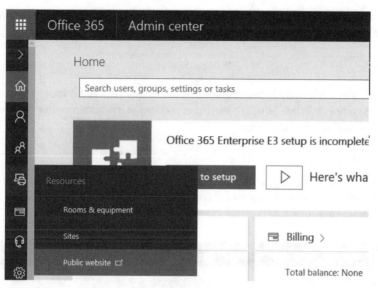

Figure 6-14 Launching the public website page

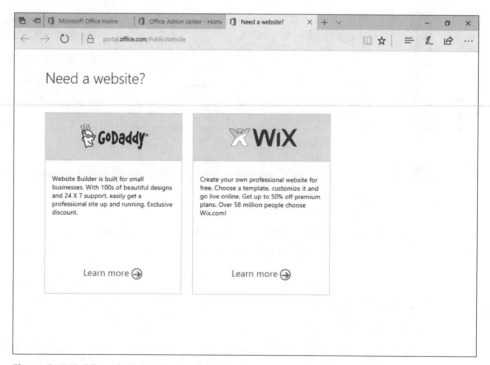

Figure 6-15 Public website partner options

Clicking the Learn More links below either partner opens its respective onboarding sites for Office 365 customers.

Billing

The Billing menu contains options to purchase and manage your subscriptions. Some of the options and choices overlap. As with a few other sections in the admin center, there are links to tasks that are available on other menus.

Subscriptions

The Subscriptions page is very simple; it lists the purchased subscriptions or stock-keeping units (SKUs), number of license units purchased and assigned for each SKU, a description, and the pricing, as shown in Figure 6-16.

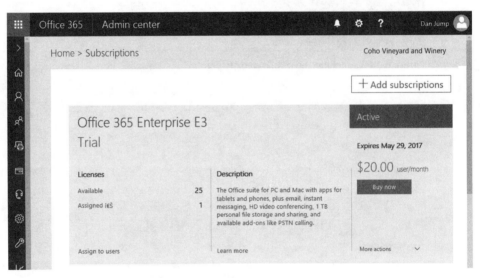

Figure 6-16 Subscriptions page

Clicking the +Add Subscriptions button at the top of the page opens Billing | Purchase Services. Under the More Actions drop-down list, you can cancel or add a partner of record.

INSIDE OUT

Partner of record

The partner of record or subscription advisor is a Microsoft partner that you might be working with to help configure, support, or maintain your Office 365 subscription. The partner of record can be delegated access to your subscription and earns a commission from

Microsoft. You can designate a subscription advisor during the purchase of services or at any time through this portal. You can also change or remove a subscription advisor at any time.

Some partners might use the commission incentive from Microsoft to perform basic services for free or reduced costs if you assign them to be your subscription advisor. You need the partner Microsoft Partner ID to complete this task.

1. Sign in to Office 365 with an account authorized to make service changes (such as a global administrator or billing administrator).

2. Select the App Launcher icon and then click Admin.

3. Point to Billing and select Subscriptions.

4. Select the More Actions drop-down list next to the subscription you want to modify and then select Add Partner Of Record.

5. Type the partner ID in the dialog box and click Check ID.

6. After the Partner ID has been verified, click Submit.

Bills

The Bills page, as shown in Figure 6-17, shows you bills that you have incurred. Bills are available in both HTML and PDF format.

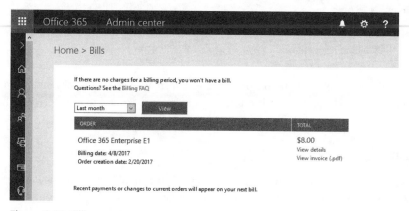

Figure 6-17 Billing center

Licenses

The Licenses page under Billing provides a high-level snapshot of the licenses available in your Office 365 tenant.

CHAPTER 6

The data provided on this page is for reference only. There are no activities you can perform against the licenses.

Purchase services

The Purchase Services page enables you to purchase any services for which your tenant is eligible, based on your tenant type (commercial, small business, government, education) and region.

Purchasing a service only requires you to expand the ellipsis and select Buy Now. Depending on how your tenant is registered, you might have the option to pay monthly, yearly, or by purchase order. The purchase order option is only available to volume license subscribers or customers who purchased Office 365 services through a large account reseller (LAR).

Billing notifications

The Billing Notifications page shown in Figure 6-18 lists the administrators who will receive invoices and reminders.

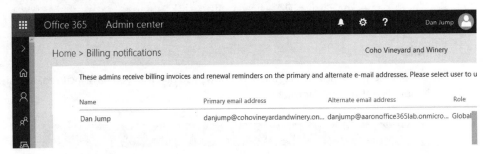

Figure 6-18 Billing notifications

The list of users is not configurable on this screen. Instead, it is dynamically built from global administrators and billing administrators. To modify the list of users who receive notifications, add them to the global or billing administrator roles.

Support

The Support menu is a little different from others. Rather than linking to a new page, a panel appears on the right of whichever page you're working on, exposing the support options, as shown in Figure 6-19.

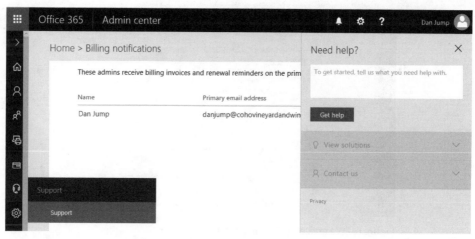

Figure 6-19 Office 365 Support page

When the Support panel is exposed, you can enter search criteria to begin the process. Potential solutions and tasks matching your input keywords appear. Depending on the keywords supplied, you might also see an option to run diagnostics or open a support case with an engineer.

Settings

The Settings menu contains many options for configuring your tenant.

Services & Add-Ins

Navigating to the Services & Add-Ins page gives you access to many built-in add-ins as well as the ability to upload additional add-ins from the Office Store or an XML file.

To upload an add-in from the Office Store, follow these steps.

1.   Sign in to Office 365 with a global administrator account.

2.   In the Office 365 Admin Center, navigate to Settings | Services & Add-Ins.

3.   Click the Upload Add-in button, as shown in Figure 6-20.

CHAPTER 6

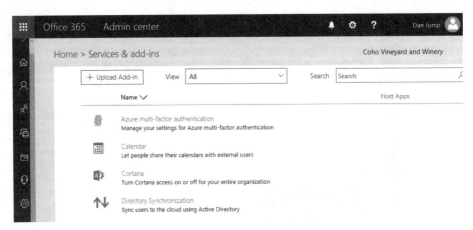

Figure 6-20 Services & Add-Ins page

4. Select the source for the add-in (browse the Office store, an XML manifest located locally, or a publicly available URL for a manifest file) and click Next. See Figure 6-21.

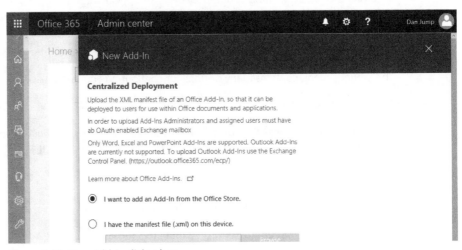

Figure 6-21 New Add-In dialog box

5. If the Office Store is selected as the source, follow the prompt to select an add-in from the catalog and click Add.

6. Select the options on the Add-In page to turn the add-in on or off and select which users have access to the add-in. Click Save, as shown in Figure 6-22.

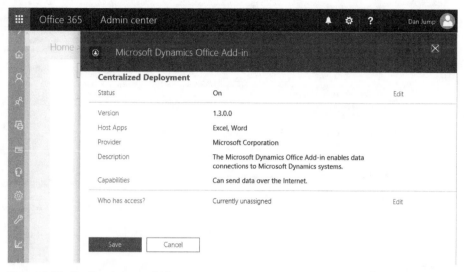

Figure 6-22 Configuring an add-in

7. After the add-in is imported, click Close.

In addition to being able to upload and import add-ins, you can manage several service features on the Settings | Services & Add-Ins page.

Azure multifactor authentication

The Azure multifactor authentication service controls how users can access your tenant. Multifactor authentication can be enabled per-user individually or by selecting various filters based on Office 365 administrative roles. On the Services & Add-Ins page, select Azure Multi-Factor Authentication and then click Manage Multi-Factor Authentication to open the Azure Multi-Factor Authentication page shown in Figure 6-23.

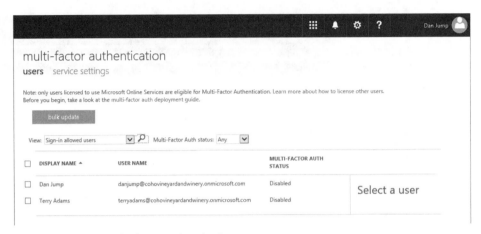

Figure 6-23 Azure multi-factor authentication management

Calendar

The Calendar service configuration item enables you to change general Calendar sharing permissions for the Exchange Online organization. See Figure 6-24.

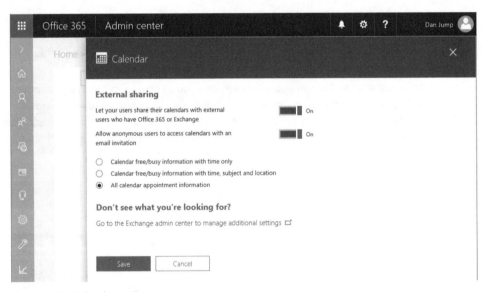

Figure 6-24 Calendar settings

The Go To The Exchange Admin Center To Manage Additional Settings link opens the Exchange Admin Center Organization page, where you can manage organization-level sharing and individual sharing policies.

Cortana

You can use the Cortana service to enable or disable Cortana services for your users. The toggle enables or disables the feature tenant-wide, as shown in Figure 6-25.

Figure 6-25 Cortana service setting

Cortana features require Windows 10 desktop devices, Cortana for Windows Phone, or the Cortana app for iOS or Android. For Windows 10 devices, Cortana has to be configured to allow access to your Office 365 data. For Windows 10 devices, you must configure Cortana to access your Office 365 account. Cortana can be used on Windows 10 devices to search Office 365 content if you have integration configured.

1. On a Windows 10 device, click inside the search bar and then click the Notebook icon (directly under the Home icon), as shown in Figure 6-26.

Notebook
icon →

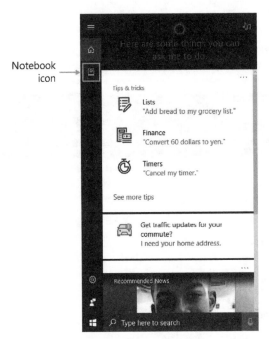

Figure 6-26 Windows 10 Search bar

2.   If this is the first time you have configured the Notebook, you are prompted to sign in. Type an existing personal account from Live or Outlook.com or create a new one.

If you create a new one, you shouldn't use your Office 365 email address.

3.   Select Connected Services.

4.   Select Add A Service.

5.   Select Office 365.

6.   Select Connect.

7.   In the Connecting To A Service pop-up menu, type your Office 365 user name and password and then click Sign In.

Directory Synchronization

Directory Synchronization on the Services & Add-Ins page provides information about preparing your environment for Office 365 directory synchronization, as shown in Figure 6-27.

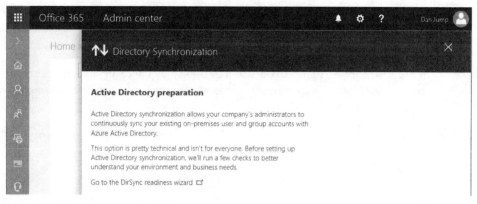

Figure 6-27 Directory Synchronization settings

Directory synchronization involves downloading, installing, and configuring Azure AD Connect. Clicking the link to launch the DirSync Readiness Wizard launches a planning wizard that asks you questions about the size of your organization and verified domains and then guides you through downloading and installing Azure AD Connect. Directory synchronization and Azure AD Connect are discussed in depth in Chapter 4 and Chapter 5.

Docs.com

Docs.com is a Microsoft service that enables your organization's users to publish Office documents. Documents published to Docs.com are available publicly or can be restricted to users inside your organization, as shown in Figure 6-28.

Figure 6-28 Docs.com settings

With Docs.com, you can collect and publish Microsoft Excel workbooks, Office Mix and Microsoft PowerPoint presentations, Sway stories, Microsoft OneNote notebooks, PDF files, Minecraft worlds, and Word documents. Docs.com integration is disabled by default.

If a user attempts to sign in to Docs.com by using their Office 365 ID and Docs.com has not been enabled, an error appears stating that the service has been turned off for their organization, as shown in Figure 6-29.

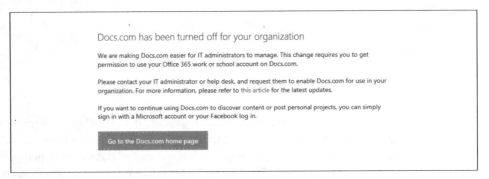

Figure 6-29 User error when Docs.com is not enabled for a tenant

IMPORTANT

Beginning on June 19, 2017, a migration service became available to move content elsewhere, and on August 1, 2017, you can no longer upload content to docs.com. On December 15, 2017, the service will be turned off.

GigJam Preview

GigJam is a service that enables users to mark up and modify content on the fly for sharing with peers, vendors, partners, or customers. GigJam is either enabled or disabled for the entire tenant and is disabled by default. Figure 6-30 shows the configuration.

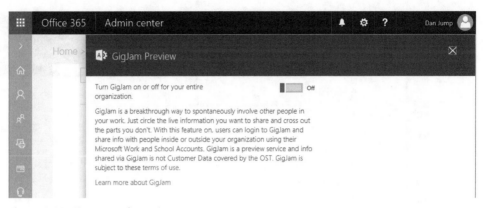

Figure 6-30 GigJam configuration

GigJam requires a client to be installed on compatible Windows, MacOS, iOS, or Android devices and supports integration of the following types of data.

- **Calendars**   From Office 365, Microsoft Outlook, or Google

- **Contacts**   From Office 365, Outlook, Google, Salesforce, or Dynamics CRM

- **Email**   From Office 365, Outlook, or Google

- **Opportunities and Accounts**   From Salesforce or Dynamics CRM

- **Files**   From OneDrive, OneDrive for Business, Google Drive, Box, and DropBox

- **Tasks**   From Asana, Wunderlist, or Trello

Integrated apps

When the Integrated Apps feature is turned on, users in your organization can allow third-party apps to access their Office 365 information. For example, an app might ask for permission to access a user's calendar or files that are in a OneDrive folder.

Integrated apps are enabled by default.

Mail

The Mail settings page provides a dashboard of many common Exchange Online settings. All the links in the Mail settings open the corresponding configuration inside the Exchange Admin Center. Links are provided to configure auditing reports, manage and track mail flow, and adjust filtering policies, as shown in Figure 6-31.

CHAPTER 6

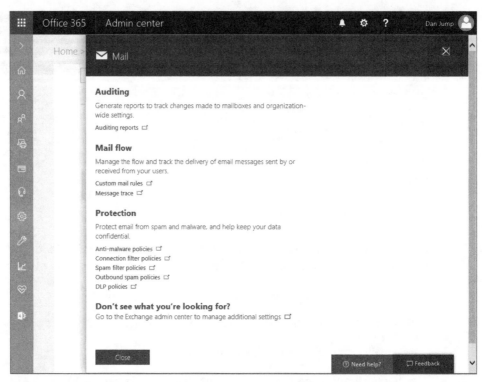

Figure 6-31 Mail settings

Managing Exchange Online settings is covered in Chapter 14, "Managing Exchange Online."

Microsoft Azure Information Protection

Azure Information Protection (also known as Rights Management), shown in Figure 6-32, is a service that enables you to sign, encrypt, and manage content in a variety of ways. Rights can be applied to email messages by the sender, through transport rules, or to individual documents to control distribution.

Figure 6-32 Azure Information Protection

Azure Information Protection requires a license that includes Azure Rights Management Services (RMS).

Microsoft Teams

Microsoft Teams, shown in Figure 6-33, is a chat-based collaboration hub that enables you to conduct scheduled or ad hoc meetings with audio, video, and content sharing. Teams are groups of people working together and can be organized by products, lines of business, interests, reporting structure, geography, or any method that makes sense.

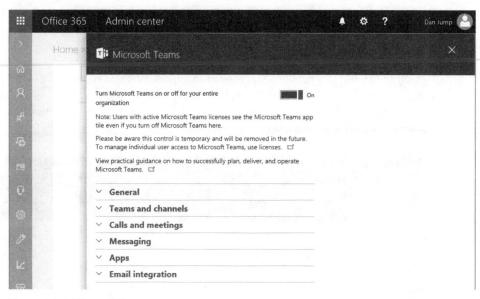

Figure 6-33 Microsoft Teams

You must have a separate user license to use Microsoft Teams.

Office 365 Groups

Office 365 Groups, shown in Figure 6-34, is a collaborative feature that combines concepts of a mailbox and a distribution list. Groups has several features and manageable options, such as external membership and access to content.

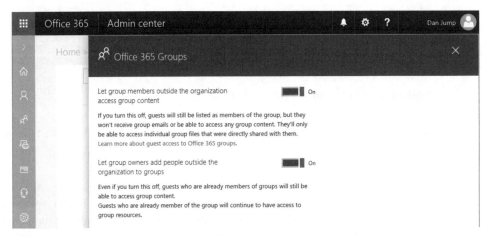

Figure 6-34 Office 365 Groups settings

The Office 365 Groups settings page only enables you to manage external access to groups. Other configuration options for groups are discussed in Chapter 7.

Office Online

As Office 365 and other online services grow in popularity and users work with other organizations, users might need to collaborate by using third-party applications. By enabling this feature, Office Online users can access supported document types stored in third-party storage service providers. See Figure 6-35.

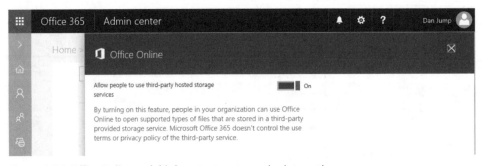

Figure 6-35 Office Online and third-party storage service integration

By default, Office Online is configured to work with third-party storage services.

Office software download settings

For organizations that have Office ProPlus SKUs in their tenant, you can control which versions of the Office installation media are available for user download. See Figure 6-36.

Figure 6-36 Office software download settings

The Software Download Settings dialog box is updated as newer versions of Office ProPlus become available for both Windows and Mac. This does not manage Office mobile software downloads available in the Google Play, Apple App, or Windows Phone stores.

Office Store

The Office Store contains applications that can be added to your Office 365 subscription. Microsoft does not own or manage applications available in the Office Store. Third-party services, fees, and support are acquired outside of the Office 365 subscription.

The Office Store is enabled by default for Office 365 tenants. When the Office Store is enabled, it can be accessed from a tile in the Office 365 app launcher.

Reports

The Reports setting manages whether user information appears in Office 365 reports. Names are used by default. If this setting is enabled, names are replaced with an anonymous identifier. See Figure 6-37.

Figure 6-37 Reports settings

Sites

The Sites settings page, shown in Figure 6-38, controls basic external sharing options for SharePoint and OneDrive sites.

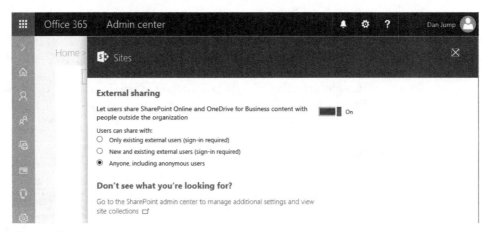

Figure 6-38 Sites settings

The Go To The SharePoint Admin Center To Manage Additional Settings And View Site Collections link opens the top level of the SharePoint Admin Center. The SharePoint Admin Center is discussed in more detail in Chapter 17, "Overview of SharePoint Online," and Chapter 18, "Implementing the SharePoint Online Hybrid Configuration."

Skype for Business

The Skype For Business settings page, shown in Figure 6-39, has a few general organization settings that can be managed, such as enabling external federation and communication with other organizations by using Skype for Business.

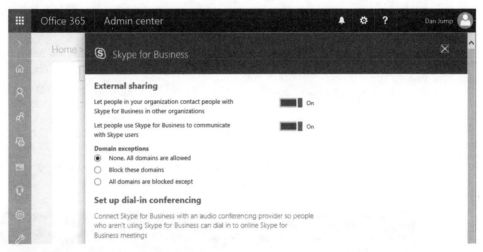

Figure 6-39 Skype For Business settings

Under Set Up Dial-In Conferencing, the Go To The Skype For Business Admin Center To Setup Dial-In Conferencing link opens the Skype Admin Center in a new browser window. The Go To The Skype For Business Admin Center To Manage Additional Settings link under Don't See What You're Looking For opens a new browser window to the Skype For Business Admin Center Organization settings page.

StaffHub

StaffHub, shown in Figure 6-40, is a deskless-worker IT solution focused primarily on service industries where users might not have full-time workstations. StaffHub uses Office 365 Groups to provide access to resources.

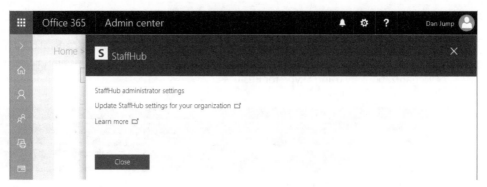

Figure 6-40 StaffHub settings

The only configuration option for StaffHub is a link to manage the StaffHub settings for your Office 365 tenant, which opens a new window to *https://staffhub.office.com/admin*. From there, you can enable or disable StaffHub for your tenant, enable self-provisioning, and customize URL links for internal resources, as shown in Figure 6-41.

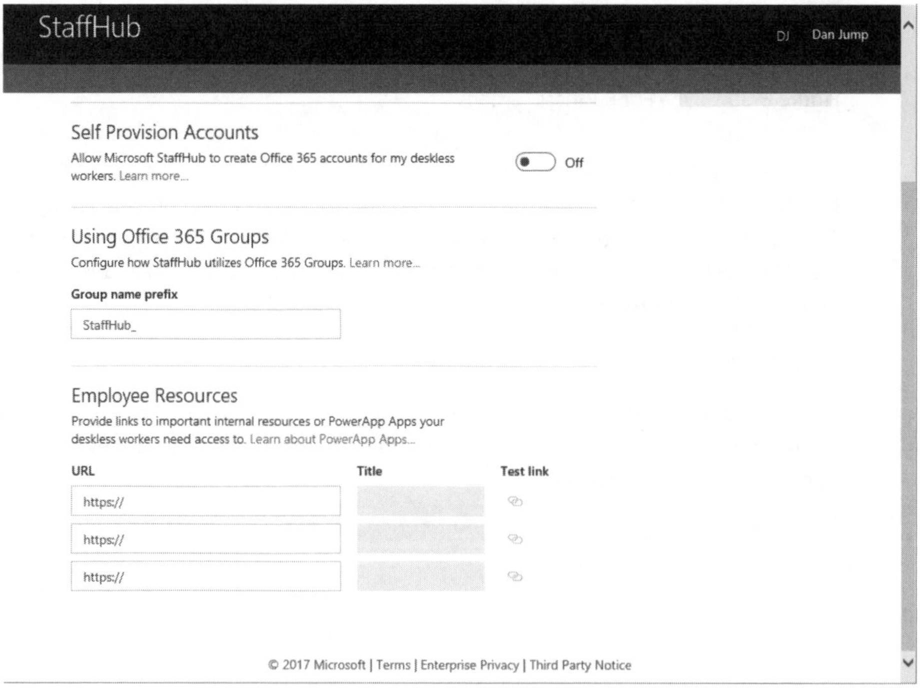

Figure 6-41 The StaffHub Admin site

Self-provisioning is a feature that enables users to create their own accounts by using the application interface (browser or mobile app–based). By default, user accounts are created in the *firstname.lastname@<domain>* format, with a number appended if a duplicate user name exists.

Sway

Sway is a content-creation tool that enables users to create presentations. Users can generate and import their own content as well as import content from external sources to create their story within a web browsing session. Sways can be shared with your organization users only or posted publicly to be discovered by external users, as shown in Figure 6-42.

Figure 6-42 Sway settings

Access to Sway is configured by user licensing. To enable or disable Sway for a user, assign or remove their Sway license.

To-Do Preview

Microsoft To-Do is a Preview tenant app, shown in Figure 6-43, that can be used to manage tasks, which can be grouped into categories. To-Do synchronizes Exchange tasks.

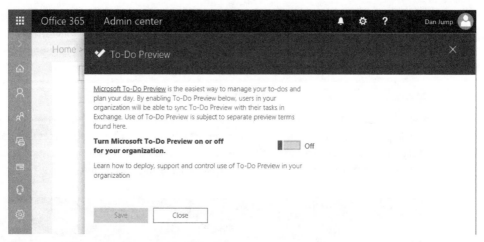

Figure 6-43 To-Do Preview settings dialog box

To-Do is governed by a separate set of terms. To-Do is not enabled by default.

Security & Privacy

Another option you can select from the Settings menu in the Office 365 Admin Center is Security & Privacy, shown in Figure 6-44. The Security & Privacy page enables you to configure two basic settings: the password policy for managed (cloud-only) accounts and global external sharing for SharePoint sites. The third option is a link to review information about enabling self-service password reset so that users can change their own passwords.

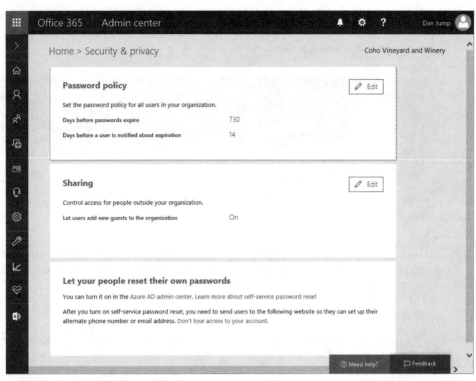

Figure 6-44 Security & Privacy page

Selecting Edit in the Password Policy section, shown in Figure 6-45, enables you to set the time limits for password expiration and notification or, optionally, configure them never to expire.

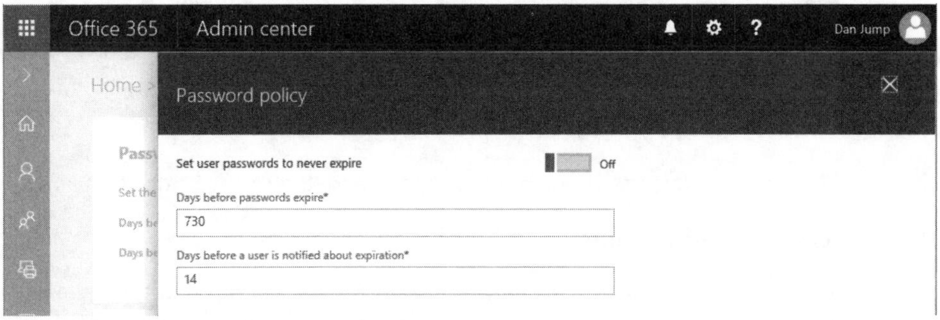

Figure 6-45 Password Policy dialog box

Selecting Edit in the Sharing section, shown in Figure 6-46, opens a simple dialog box to enable or disable adding guests to the organization. This setting affects whether users can add external recipients to Office 365 Groups.

Figure 6-46 Sharing dialog box

Self-service password reset is an Azure AD Premium feature and requires an additional license. More information about enabling self-service password reset is in Chapter 5, "Installing Azure AD Connect."

Domains

The Domains setting, shown in Figure 6-47, enables you to add or remove domains for your organization.

Figure 6-47 Domains page

The Settings | Domains option displays the same content as the Setup | Domains menu.

Organization Profile

The Organization Profile page, shown in Figure 6-48, enables you to configure high-level general information for your tenant, such as organization name and address, release preferences, language, and display themes.

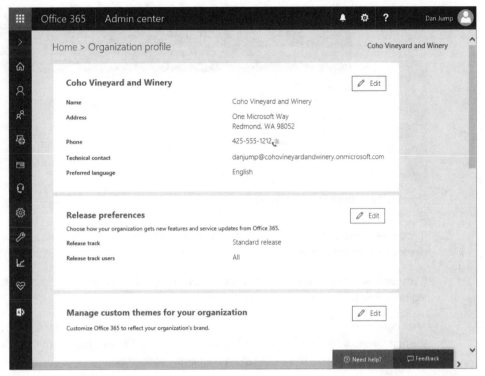

Figure 6-48 Organization Profile page

Organization information

Edit the organization information to reflect your organization's name, address, phone number, and technical contact email address.

Release preferences

Modify the Release Preferences setting, shown in Figure 6-49, to configure when tenant features are available. The available options are Standard Release (when Microsoft releases the settings to general availability), First Release For Everyone (get updates at the earliest release date organization-wide), and First Release For Selected Users (specify users to preview updates for the organization).

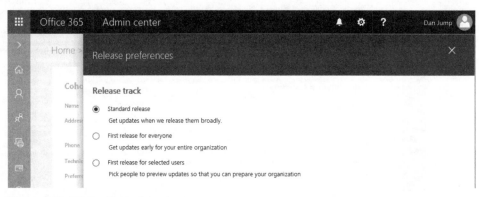

Figure 6-49 Release Track dialog box

If you select First Release For Everyone, you are asked to confirm that you are applying this change organization-wide,

If you select First Release For Selected Users, you are asked to confirm your choice before moving on to select users from your organization.

After confirming your selection, you are notified that you need to select individuals to receive the first release updates. Click the Add People button and add the users from the picker by either scrolling through the list or typing their email addresses.

Users that you select from the picker appear as Release Track Users on the Settings | Organizational profile page.

Manage custom themes for your organization

You can apply branding and theme customization to Office 365 to match your organization's branding. See Figure 6-50.

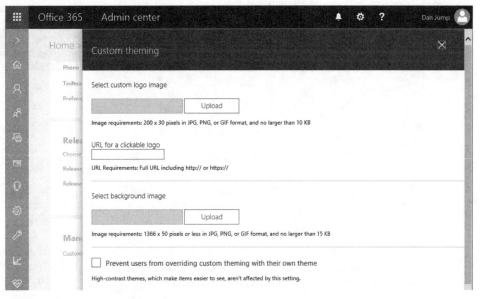

Figure 6-50 Custom theming dialog box

Add custom tiles for your organization

You can create a custom tile that appears in the My Apps list of the App Launcher for each user. To create a custom tile, specify a name for the tile, a URL that the tile will open, a description of the tile or application, and a URL for the image that will be used on the tile.

To add a tile, click the +Add A Custom Tile button, fill out the required information, and click Save, as shown in Figure 6-51.

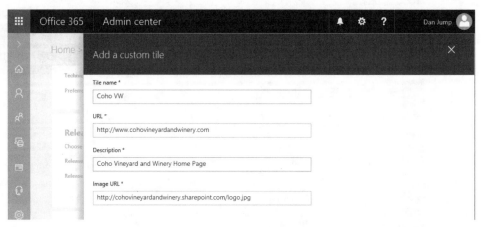

Figure 6-51 Add A Custom Tile dialog box

After your change has saved, you can view the newly created tile by clicking the app launcher, navigating to New or All, and then locating the tile. See Figure 6-52.

Figure 6-52 New custom tile

Provide customized help desk information

You can customize the portal with your own help desk information. To do so, first click Edit and then move the slider for Help Desk Card to On. Edit the information with your organization's details, as shown in Figure 6-53.

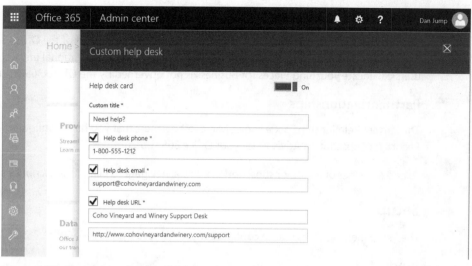

Figure 6-53 Customizing help desk information

The customized information appears when users click the question mark (?) icon in the upper right portion of the Office 365 portal, shown in Figure 6-54.

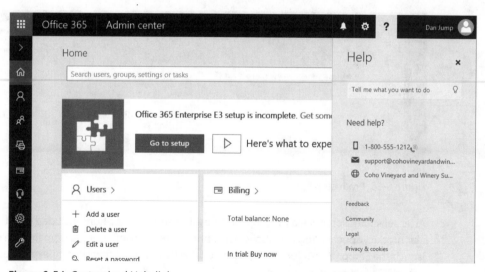

Figure 6-54 Customized Help links

Data location

The data location widget only shows the data center regions where your data is located. This is assigned when you create your tenant and cannot be changed.

Bing Places for Business

Clicking the Edit button under Bing Places For Business takes you out of the Office 365 portal. From here, you can search for your organization or create an organizational entry so Internet users can locate you. Bing Places for Business is not governed by the Office 365 Trust Center.

Partner relationships

The Partner Relationships page shows Microsoft partners that you have configured as Partner of Record (or Subscription Advisor) for your Office 365 subscriptions.

To add a partner of record or subscription advisor, navigate to Billing | Subscriptions.

Setup

The Setup menu enables you to configure the initial settings for your Office 365 tenant.

Products

Your subscriptions are listed under Products. Clicking a product on the page shown in Figure 6-55 displays the options available for that product (Assign Licenses, Buy More, Close) as well as suggested next steps.

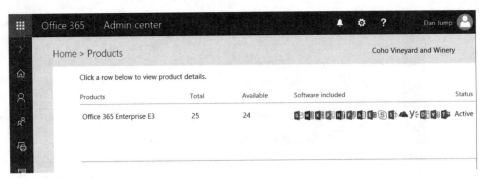

Figure 6-55 Products page

After selecting a product, a list of all the software and service options included with that particular product appears. You can also watch a brief video on configuring a domain with Office 365, launch the Setup Wizard for your services, chat with a support specialist, or explore additional Office 365 configuration guides.

Domains

On the Domains page, you can view existing domain settings, add a new domain, or remove a domain from your tenant.

Selecting a configured domain shows you the records you need to configure in DNS to make your services available to your users. If you haven't yet verified a domain in your tenant, you can start that process here as well. Chapter 2, "Preparing Your Environment for the Cloud," covers adding and verifying domains in your tenant.

Data migration

Data Migration on the Setup menu redirects you to the same Migration page as when you choose Data Migration on the Users menu. It also enables you to perform the same activities.

Reports

Office 365 provides a number of reports and metrics that you can use to gauge usage, trouble-shoot problems, or investigate trends and adoption in your organization.

Usage

The Usage reports, shown in Figure 6-56, provide a dashboard-style view of usage in your Office 365 tenant.

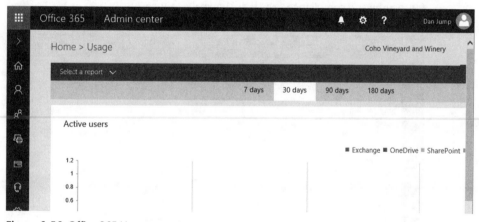

Figure 6-56 Office 365 Usage reports page

Each of the cards on the Usage page can be clicked for further information. Data is available for up to the past six months.

By selecting the Select A Report drop-down list on the Usage page, you can choose from 17 pre-built reports covering Office 365 general statistics, Office 365 groups, Exchange Online, OneDrive, SharePoint, Skype, and Yammer, as shown in Figure 6-57.

CHAPTER 6

Figure 6-57 Office 365 Usage reports

Security & Compliance

In addition to statistical Office 365 tenant data, you can also view a number of reports designed for security and compliance review, as shown in Figure 6-58.

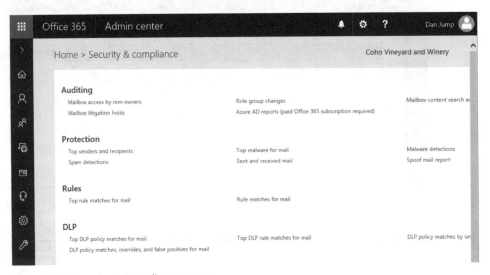

Figure 6-58 Security & Compliance reports

The reports under Reports | Security & Compliance are built from data in Exchange Online and Exchange Online Protection. To get the most out of the auditing reports, enable mailbox auditing in Exchange Online.

Some reports, such as Mailbox Content Search And Discovery, have undergone transformation, have more robust features, and are available in the Security & Compliance admin center.

Health

The Health menu contains an overview of current and past service health conditions as well as notifications for new and upcoming features or changes to the service.

Service health

The Service Health page, shown in Figure 6-59, has an overview of current service status, incidents that are currently being managed by Microsoft that affect your tenant, or advisories that might be affecting your tenant.

Figure 6-59 Service Health page

Message Center

Although summary data from the Message Center appears on the portal dashboard, as shown in Figure 6-60, there is a lot more to be found in the Message Center itself.

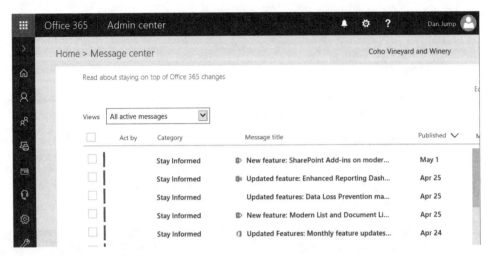

Figure 6-60 Message Center page

Notifications in the Message Center can be classified in a few ways.

- **Plan for Change**   Messages categorized as Plan for Change mean that a change is coming for how to deploy or manage a feature. For example, it might mean that a service feature will be deprecated and replaced with a new feature. In such a case, you are notified that a change is coming and given appropriate planning tools. A service change might have a lock-down period during which you'll no longer be able to use the previous process, tool, or feature or be able to create new instances of the feature being retired while existing items continue to work. You'd then be provided with a transition or retirement date along with an upgrade path.

- **Prevent or Fix Issues**   This notification class contains messages that are intended to help identify and fix existing on-premises issues, such as duplicate proxy addresses in mailboxes.

- **Stay Informed**   A notification that is classified as Stay Informed typically has to do with a new or update feature that will soon be available to your tenant. Stay Informed messages include monthly update summaries, subscription notifications, and any other messages not specifically related to upcoming changes or resolving existing issues.

Service admin centers

To this point, the admin center has focused primarily on tenant-wide objects and configurations—users, groups, software downloads, domains, add-ins, reporting, and health. The Office 365 Admin Center also contains links to the admin centers for the individual cloud services in your tenant, such as Exchange Online, Skype for Business, and SharePoint, as shown in Figure 6-61.

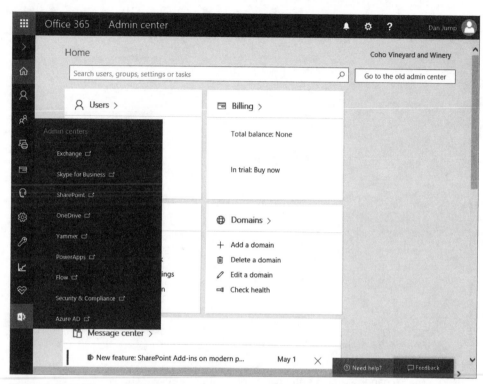

Figure 6-61 Service admin centers

Many of the services are large and complex and have entire chapters dedicated to them elsewhere in this book. Some services, such as Exchange, Skype for Business, SharePoint, and Azure Active Directory, have components that you can integrate with your on-premises environment, creating a mesh of services and features for your organization and users.

Exchange

The Exchange Admin Center is where many administrators spend most of their time because messaging is a crucial application for nearly every organization.

Unlike Exchange on-premises, an administrator in Exchange Online does not need a mailbox to administer the service. Launching the Exchange Admin Center opens the Exchange Admin Center page, which presents an expanded view of all the menus and options available under them, as shown in Figure 6-62.

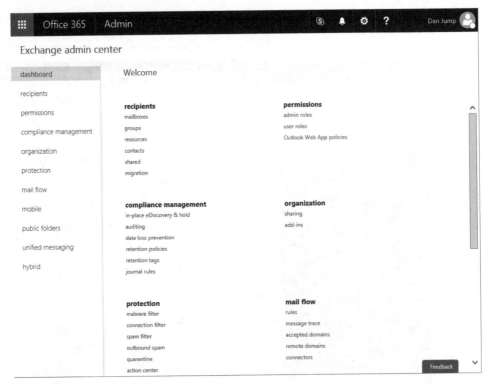

Figure 6-62 Exchange Admin Center

The Exchange Admin Center has several administrative sections.

- **Recipients**   Recipients covers the various types of recipients in the organization, including user and shared mailboxes, groups, resources, and contacts. It is also where migration endpoints are configured and onboarding or offboarding are handled.

- **Permissions**   The Permissions area enables you to grant admin roles (such as Compliance or Recipient Management), user roles (management role assignments, determining which attributes and properties a user can change through Outlook), and Outlook Web App policies (which features are available in the web client).

- **Compliance Management**   Although some features have overlap in the Security & Compliance Center, you can still create and manage retention policies and tags, manage data loss prevention policies and templates, run auditing reports, place holds on data, and configure journaling.

- **Organization**   The Organization options you can configure include relationships with other federated Exchange Online or Exchange on-premises organizations and add-ins for Exchange Online.

- **Protection**   The Protection options control malware, content and spam filtering, connection filtering, and DomainKeys Identified Mail (DKIM) configuration. You can also manage the user quarantine configuration and release held messages.

- **Mail Flow**   The Mail Flow settings enable you to configure your accepted domains (domains your organization owns), transport rules, and connectors to on-premises or other organizations. You can also trace messages through the Exchange Online and Exchange Online Protection environments.

- **Mobile**   Use the Mobile options to control access by mobile device management. These settings can be used instead of or in addition to policies configured elsewhere, such as Office 365 Mobile Device Management (MDM), InTune, or a third-party mobile-device management platform.

- **Public Folders**   Public Folders contains options to manage the public folder mailboxes (data storage location for public folders) as well as the public folder hierarchy (the list of folders).

- **Unified Messaging**   Configure unified messaging dial plans (or telephone number formats) and connectivity to on-premises session border controllers.

- **Hybrid**   The Hybrid link enables you to start the Office 365 Hybrid Configuration Wizard (which must run from your on-premises Exchange environment) and provides a link to download the Exchange Online PowerShell module, which supports multifactor authentication.

INSIDE OUT

Show Command Logging

Windows PowerShell is the tool of choice for automating repetitive tasks, ensuring standard results, and performing advanced tasks, but sometimes, the shell can be a little daunting, and if you're learning a new task, you might not even know what cmdlets you need to use, much less their syntax

That's when Command Logging comes in handy. With Command Logging, you can see exactly what to do. When you enable Command Logging, the admin center opens a new window and displays the Windows PowerShell commands it's running behind the scenes.

CHAPTER 6

To enable Command Logging, select the question mark (?) icon, shown in Figure 6-63, from the Exchange Admin Center menu bar and then select Show Command Logging.

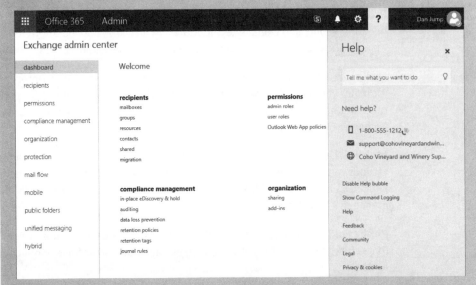

Figure 6-63 Enabling Command Logging in the Exchange Admin Center

After you enable Command Logging, a new window pop-up appears on the desktop. You can select any option in the Exchange Admin Center or perform any task (such as creating a new rule), and Command Logging shows you the associated steps in Windows PowerShell.

In the example shown in Figure 6-64, Get-MessageTrace is selected with starting and ending dates, and Command Logging shows the cmdlet with syntax that was run.

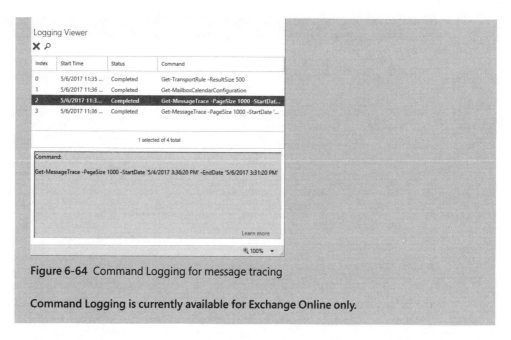

Figure 6-64 Command Logging for message tracing

Command Logging is currently available for Exchange Online only.

More information about configuring and managing Exchange Online, using both the admin center and Windows PowerShell, can be found from Chapter 10, "Preparing an On-Premises Environment to Connect to Exchange Online," through Chapter 14, "Managing Exchange Online."

Skype for Business

Launching the Skype For Business Admin Center opens the dashboard. The Skype for Business dashboard is arranged similarly to the Exchange Admin Center dashboard. See Figure 6-65.

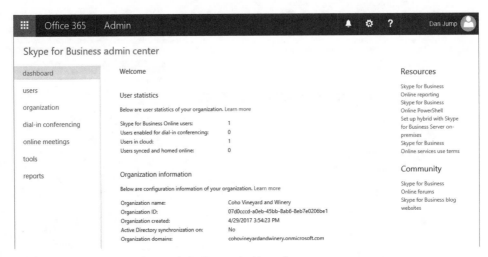

Figure 6-65 Skype For Business Admin Center dashboard

The Skype for Business Admin Center has six configuration areas as well as a list of links to additional resources and community support and information.

- **Users**   The Users menu enables you to manage individual user settings, such as whether a user can use audio or video features in Skype for Business.

- **Organization**   In the Organization menu, you can modify the tenant-wide configuration for displaying presence, mobile phone notifications, and with which external organizations you allow communication.

- **Dial-in Conferencing**   The Dial-in Conferencing menu presents options to configure PTSN bridge conferences (if you have purchased them) and assign dial-in numbers to users.

- **Online Meetings**   Online Meetings refers to the scheduled meetings your organization's users create. You can specify global settings for the meeting invites as well as enable and configure Skype broadcast meetings.

- **Tools**   Microsoft provides an ever-expanding array of downloadable and online tools to troubleshoot Skype sign-in and connectivity issues as well as call quality tools to help diagnose and troubleshoot networking.

- **Reports**   The Reports section provides an interactive reporting dialog box that enables you to build usage reports for your organization, as shown in Figure 6-66.

Figure 6-66 Skype For Business Reports

For in-depth Skype for Business Online deployment, configuration, and management topics, see Chapter 15, "Skype for Business Online Concepts and Implementation," and Chapter 16, "Deploying Skype for Business Online."

SharePoint

The SharePoint Admin Center, in terms of configurable options, has nearly as many as the rest of the admin centers combined. SharePoint has a robust set of collaboration features, and with this latest version, SharePoint online is getting close to parity with its on-premises counterpart. See Figure 6-67.

Figure 6-67 SharePoint Admin Center

After you launch the SharePoint Admin Center, you are directed to the Site Collections page.

SharePoint Online settings are broken into 13 menu options.

- **Site Collections**   The site collection is the basic unit of organization for SharePoint and a permissions boundary. Site collections contain sites, libraries, and documents. The Site Collections settings page enables you to create sites and allocate resources.

- **InfoPath**   On the InfoPath page, you can control basic user settings around InfoPath forms.

- **User Profiles**   The User Profiles page enables you to manage settings for user profiles (MySites) as well as organization properties and attributes that SharePoint can work with.

- **BCS**   With Business Connectivity Services (BCS), you can configure your SharePoint Online tenant to connect to either other online services or data repositories.

- **Term Store**   From the Term Store settings page, you can configure term sets for use in your SharePoint tenant.

- **Records Management**   Use the Records Management page to configure Send To Connections for the Content Organizer.

- **Search**   Configure SharePoint online search options on the Search settings page.

- **Secure Store**   Use the secure store to manage credentials used to connect to external applications and data sources, such as those configured in Business Connectivity Services.

- **Apps**   Add, remove, purchase, and configure SharePoint apps in the Apps setting.

- **Sharing**   Although you can configure basic site-sharing settings from the Office 365 Admin Center (under Resources | Sites), you can use the Sharing options to manage much more granular settings.

- **Settings**   General settings for SharePoint Online are managed here, such as enabling or disabling the Office Graph, setting Yammer to be used as the default collaborative social experience, and many OneDrive settings.

- **Hybrid**   The Hybrid settings page presents a link to the Hybrid Picker, a tool to help you choose which hybrid features to use to link your SharePoint on-premises and SharePoint Online environments.

- **Device Access**   Use Device Access to control which devices can connect to Office 365, based on authentication protocols (modern or older authentication) and IP address ranges.

For more information about configuring and managing SharePoint Online, see Chapter 17, "SharePoint Online." SharePoint Hybrid configuration is covered in Chapter 18, "SharePoint

Online Hybrid." You can learn more about OneDrive for Business in Chapter 19, "OneDrive for Business," and Yammer in Chapter 20, "Yammer."

OneDrive

OneDrive (formerly, the SharePoint MySites storage component) is an online file storage service integrated with Office 365. OneDrive for Business has a multiplatform sync client, enabling users to store, update, and manage content online and offline. See Figure 6-68.

Figure 6-68 OneDrive for Business Admin Center

The OneDrive for Business Admin Center is new to Office 365 and gives administrators a number of new ways to manage the OneDrive experience for users. Launching the OneDrive Admin Center opens Home, a landing page that describes the purpose of the admin center. Other menu links enable you to manage other features of the service.

- **Sharing**   Control OneDrive sharing options, such as allowing sharing with external users.

- **Sync**   Use the Sync settings page to enable or disable synchronizing only to domain-joined workstations or to block certain file types.

- **Storage**   Use the Storage settings to control the amount of storage allocated to a user and how long to keep deleted files.

- **Device Access**   Similar to the SharePoint Online Device Access feature, the OneDrive Device Access settings enable you to configure which devices can access content stored on OneDrive.

- **Compliance**   The Compliance setting provides links to the Security & Compliance Center so you can configure auditing and preservation policies as well as alerts.

- **Notifications**   Use the Notifications settings to configure when users are notified about OneDrive sharing activities.

More information about configuring OneDrive for Business can be found in Chapter 19.

Yammer

The Yammer Admin Center, shown in Figure 6-69, is divided into four administrative sections.

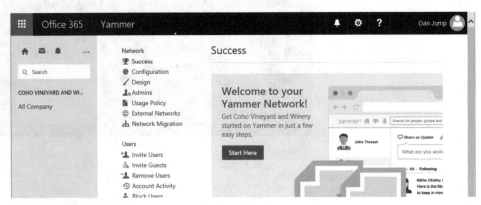

Figure 6-69 Yammer Admin Center

- **Network**   The Network section contains seven items relating to the network and organization configuration. The Success page is the first page that appears when you navigate to the Yammer Admin Center. The subsections enable you to configure your networks and domains, designate admins, create a usage policy, and initiate a migration from another Yammer network.

- **Users**   The Users section contains configuration items relating to adding, removing, importing, updating, synchronizing, disabling, and exporting users and guests.

- **Content And Security**   The Content And Security section enables you to manage and monitor content in your Yammer network. You can maintain a list of keywords to be notified on, various network and identity settings, and the data retention policy and export your network data.

- **Analytics**   In the Analytics section, you can analyze information such as how many users your network has, the number of messages posted, the number of active groups, and how users are posting data.

Chapter 20, "Yammer," discusses Yammer configuration and management topics in depth.

PowerApps

PowerApps is a codeless application development platform that enables to you link data from a variety of Office 365 services to create interactive apps for mobile and web browser users.

INSIDE OUT

PowerApps primer

When you first launch the PowerApps Admin Center, you only have access to Data Policies configuration, which you use to create a data loss prevention policy for your PowerApps environment. See Figure 6-70.

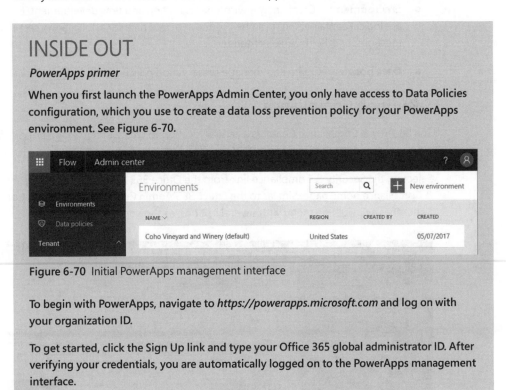

Figure 6-70 Initial PowerApps management interface

To begin with PowerApps, navigate to *https://powerapps.microsoft.com* and log on with your organization ID.

To get started, click the Sign Up link and type your Office 365 global administrator ID. After verifying your credentials, you are automatically logged on to the PowerApps management interface.

Flow

The Flow Admin Center, much like the PowerApps Admin Center, has only a few configurable options, as shown in Figure 6-71.

Figure 6-71 Flow Admin Center

- **Environments**   Create new environments for app and flow development. Environments are logical containers that can be used to separate data for applications, security roles, locations, or other business criteria.

- **Data policies**   Create and manage preservation policies for your Flow data.

Security & Compliance

The Security & Compliance Center is a central location to create and manage policies for your data as well as create reports and export data for discovery purposes.

Selecting the Security & Compliance link from the Office 365 Admin Center opens the Security & Compliance home page. Similar to the Office 365 Admin Center, the Security & Compliance Center has a navigation menu with several options, as shown in Figure 6-72.

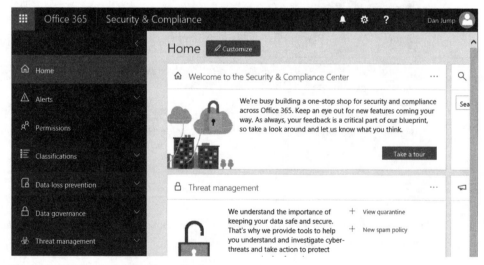

Figure 6-72 Security & Compliance Center

- **Alerts**   The Alerts menu has two features, which enable you to create and manage alerts and audit activities as well as view the alerts that have been generated.

- **Permissions**   Permissions enables you to manage most aspects of activity in the Security & Compliance Center, although you must grant additional permissions in either the Exchange or SharePoint admin centers.

- **Classifications**   Labels are a new way of classifying data types and can be applied manually or automatically to data in Outlook, OneDrive, and SharePoint.

- **Data Loss Prevention**   Sometimes called data leakage policies, the Data Loss Prevention section enables you to create intelligent policies that scan for sensitive data types in your organization and perform activities on them.

- **Data Governance**   Although the concepts of retention are not new to Office 365, the data governance process is. This area of the Security & Compliance Center helps you create policies to manage the life cycle of your data, as shown in Figure 6-73.

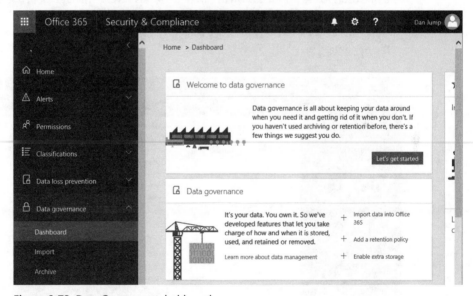

Figure 6-73 Data Governance dashboard

- **Threat Management**   The Threat Management tools enable you to configure mail filtering and malware policies, manage the quarantine, and manage the Domain Keys settings for your organization.

- **Search & Investigation**   Search & Investigation provides a consolidated way to search data across your Office 365 tenant for eDiscovery purposes.

CHAPTER 6

- **Reports** The reporting dashboard shows you all the reports that are available for download.

- **Service Assurance** The Service Assurance area features a collection of data from various Microsoft sources for reporting on audit controls. Much of this data is available in the Microsoft Trust Center.

For an in-depth look at the Security & Compliance center, please see Chapter 7, "Inside the Security & Compliance Center: Alerting, Threat Management, and Reporting," and Chapter 8, Inside the Security & Compliance Center: Data Classification, Loss Prevention, Governance, and Discovery."

Azure Active Directory

The Azure Active Directory Admin Center gives you a behind-the-scenes look at the directory objects enabled in your Office 365 tenant.

The Microsoft Azure portal, shown in Figure 6-74, has several management areas because it also is the management interface for other Azure workloads (such as SQL databases or virtual machines). The key area is Azure Active Directory. To view this area, select Azure Active Directory in the navigation pane.

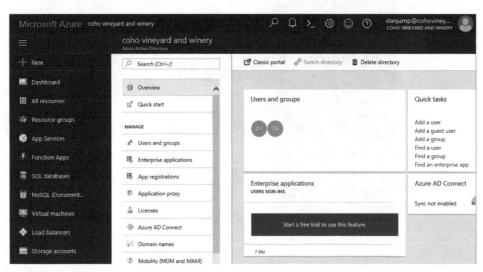

Figure 6-74 Azure Active Directory portal

Many of the areas in the Azure Active Directory portal overlap areas in the Office 365 Admin Center (such as management of domain names or Azure AD Connect). These settings can be managed in either location because not all Azure customers might be Office 365 customers.

- **Overview**   Overview is a dashboard of the current Azure AD configuration and settings.

- **Quick Start**   For new Azure AD subscriptions, you can move through a series of initial steps to get the most out of your subscription.

- **Users And Groups**   You can manage the user and group settings, as well as devices and branding, through this menu. In addition, you can view sign-in and audit logs and configure self-service password reset options.

- **Enterprise Applications**   This view gives you insight into how your directory service is being used. You can initiate a trial, but continued usage requires purchase of additional services.

- **App Registrations**   App Registrations shows you which Office 365 applications are connected to your tenant.

- **Application Proxy**   Application Proxy is a feature that enables you to publish applications to the Internet that are located behind your corporate firewall. It requires the addition of an Azure AD Basic or Azure AD Premium license.

- **Licenses**   The Licenses menu shows an overview of licenses available in your tenant. You can apply licenses to users individually (which is a free option) or through Groups, which requires an Azure AD paid subscription.

- **Azure AD Connect**   From the Azure AD Connect page, shown in Figure 6-75, you can view the status of directory synchronization or download and install Azure AD Connect to synchronize your on-premises directory to Azure Active Directory and make it available to cloud applications and services such as Office 365.

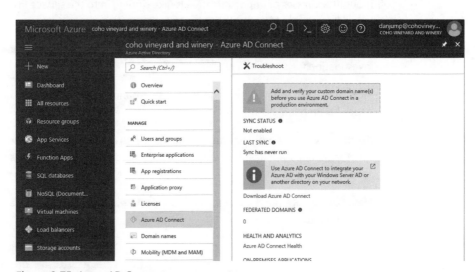

Figure 6-75 Azure AD Connect management screen

- **Domain Names**   Similar to the Settings | Domains page in the Office 365 Admin Center, this page enables you to register and verify domains for use with Azure Active Directory and applications or services that use it.

- **Mobility**   This management screen enables you to configure and manage enrollment for mobile device and application management platforms such as InTune. Automatic enrollment requires an Azure AD Premium subscription.

- **Password Reset**   Configure options for self-service password reset.

- **Company Branding**   Use the Company Branding page to configure themes and branding for Azure Active Directory applications.

- **User Settings**   The User Settings page enables you to configure settings for users such as the ability to register applications or access the Azure Active Directory admin portal.

- **Properties**   From the Properties page, configure basic settings about your Azure Active Directory subscription (such as the name and whether to allow global administrators to manage the subscription).

- **Notifications Settings**   Subscribe to notifications such as status and feature availability.

- **Conditional Access**   Conditional Access enables you to configure policies to control access to Azure Active Directory services. Conditional access requires an Azure AD Premium license.

- **Users Flagged For Risk**   This security view shows users what the service thinks might have been compromised through analysis of things such as sign-in attempts from anonymous IP addresses or impossible travels (like signing in to the service in one country followed by a sign-in from another country).

- **Risky Sign-Ins**   These sign-ins are individual sign-ins that the service has flagged for investigation.

- **Sign-Ins**   This setting shows sign-ins for an organization. Use of this feature requires an Azure AD Premium license.

- **Audit Logs**   The Audit Logs menu enables you to search and return auditable events for users, groups, applications, and devices.This page has guided options to help troubleshoot common issues.

- **New Support Request**   Use the New Support Request page to create a ticket with Microsoft Azure services.

INSIDE OUT
Azure Active Directory

Although most features in the Azure Active Directory management portal are included as part of your Office 365 subscription, there are additional features that require an Azure AD Basic, Azure AD Premium, or Enterprise Mobility Suite license.

Previously, when connecting to the Azure Active Directory management interface the first time, you were required to enter credit card details for any charges that you incurred for using features in the portal. That requirement has been removed, and now you can just sign in with your existing Office 365 global administrator account.

After a brief setup, your Azure Active Directory subscription is set up, and you can log on and select Azure Active Directory from the navigation menu on the left.

For configuring and managing Azure Active Directory and Azure AD Connect, see Chapter 4 and Chapter 5.

Summary

As you've seen throughout this chapter, the Office 365 Admin Center is the starting point for all of the Office 365 management and configuration activities. All of the service admin centers use a similar theme, so once you understand and can successfully navigate one, you'll be able to find the features and options in any of the them.

To learn more about the admin centers for Office 365 services, please see those services' respective chapters in this book.

CHAPTER 6

Inside the Security & Compliance Center: Alerting, threat management, and reporting

The Security & Compliance Center, shown in Figure 7-1, is the hub for security reporting, discovery, and data protection across all the products and services in the Office 365 suite. Many options are available in the Security & Compliance Center—several of them only available with optional products and services. The standard features are available in service plans up to Enterprise E3. The advanced features, designated here with an asterisk (*), under Alerts, Data Loss Prevention, Threat Management, and Search & Investigation, are accessible after you have activated service plans that include Advanced Threat Protection or Advanced eDiscovery.

This chapter discusses the features in the following sections of the Security & Compliance Center.

- Alerts

- Permissions

- Threat Management

- Reports

- Service Assurance

Figure 7-1 Security & Compliance Center

Alerts

You can configure alerts to notify you when certain types of activities or behaviors are detected in your environment. Alerts can be triggered by a variety of things, including suspicious logon activity or changes in roles or permissions.

Dashboard*

The Alerts Dashboard, one of the features available with an Enterprise E5 subscription, initially presents you with an option to configure analytics. The Alerts Dashboard is shown in Figure 7-2.

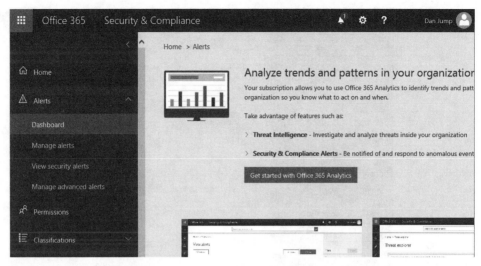

Figure 7-2 Alerts Dashboard page

To get started with with analytics, follow these steps.

1. To configure analytics, select **Get Started With Office 365 Analytics**.

2. On the Threat Explorer page, click **Next**.

3. On the Threat Dashboard page, click **Next**.

4. On the Alerts page, click **Enable Office 365 Analytics**.

5. Review the updated dashboard under Alerts. See Figure 7-3.

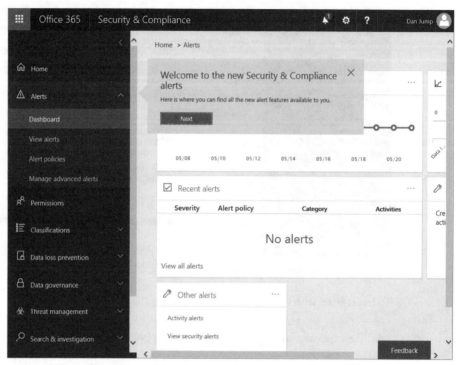

Figure 7-3 Updated Alerts dashboard after enabling Office 365 analytics

View alerts*

If you have licenses that include Advanced Security Management, the **View Alerts** menu replaces **View Security Alerts**. View Alerts (Figure 7-4) enables you to filter the list of alerts shown as well as export them to a comma separated values (CSV) file for further analysis.

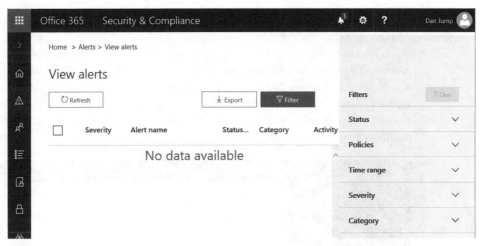

Figure 7-4 Filter alerts

Manage alerts

To start generating alerts on activities, enable recording of activities in the Security & Compliance Center. Click **Start Recording User And Admin Activities** (Figure 7-5) to enable the collection of auditable activities. After you turn auditing on, you can begin creating activity alerts.

Figure 7-5 Enabling activity alerts

WHERE ARE MY ALERTS?

If you have an Enterprise E5 or Advanced Security Management SKU, Manage Advanced Alerts And Alert Policies replaces Manage Alerts. You can still access the standard **Manage Alerts** and **View Security Alerts** pages by navigating to **Alerts | Dashboard** and selecting **Activity Alerts** or **View Security Alerts, as shown in Figure 7-6,** in the Other Alerts section. When you select Activity Alerts, you then have access to the Start Recording User And Admin Activities link.

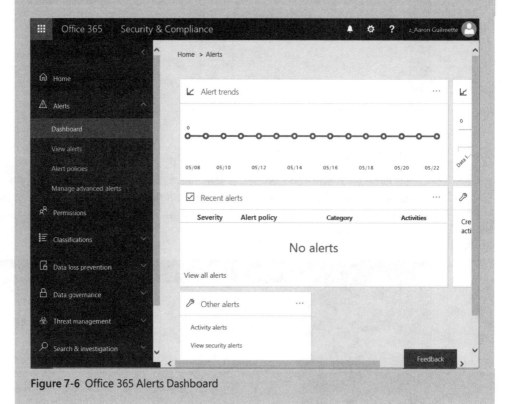

Figure 7-6 Office 365 Alerts Dashboard

After you enable recording, confirm the action by clicking **Turn On**. See Figure 7-7.

Figure 7-7 Confirming the enabling of security auditing

A dialog box might appear to update your organization settings. This is the same as running Enable-OrganizationCustomization from Windows PowerShell. Click **Yes** to allow the update. Depending on the number of objects in your tenant, it might take a while to run. See Figure 7-8.

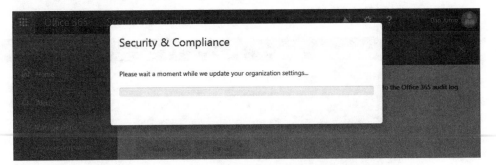

Figure 7-8 Enable-OrganizationCustomization preparing the environment

NOTE

To capture audited events in Exchange Online, you must enable mailbox auditing for Exchange Online mailboxes. Mailbox auditing is a per-user setting, so if you are configuring alerts for ExchanOnline, consider enabling mailbox auditing as part of your provisioning process. To enable auditing for all mailboxes, connect to the Exchange Online PowerShell endpoint and run the following cmdlet:

```
Get-Mailbox -ResultSize Unlimited -Filter {RecipientTypeDetails -eq "UserMail-
box"} | Set-Mailbox -AuditEnabled $true
```

When the organization update is complete, you can begin creating policies for alerts. To create a new policy, follow these steps.

1. Launch the Security & Compliance Center and navigate to **Alerts | Manage Alerts**. If you have an Office 365 E5 subscription, navigate to Alerts | Alert Policies.

    The wizard steps and interface might be slightly different, depending on whether you are creating your policy in a tenant with an E3 or an E5 subscription.

2. Click **+New Alert Policy**.

3. Type a name for the policy and a description.

4. Expand Send This Alert When.

5. Under Activities, select the events that you want to audit. See Figure 7-9.

    For a complete list of auditable activities, see *https://support.office.com/en-us/article /Search-the-audit-log-in-the-Office-365-Security-Compliance-Center-0d4d0f35-390b -4518-800e-0c7ec95e946c?ui=en-US&rs=en-US&ad=US#auditlogevents&PickTab =Audited_activities*.

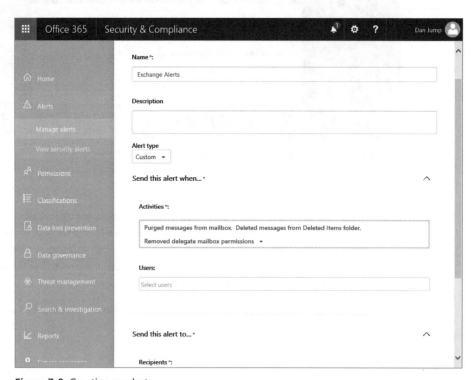

Figure 7-9 Creating an alert

6. Under Users, type individual users whose activities you want to audit or leave blank to configure the alert for all users.

7. By default, the user who is creating the alert is added to the notification list. To change who is alerted, expand Send This Alert To and then update Recipients with the appropriate alert recipients.

8. Click **Save** to create the alert.

You can also use the New-ActivityAlert and Set-ActivityAlert cmdlets when connected to the Security & Compliance Center PowerShell endpoint. If you create an alert through PowerShell that contains activities not included in the New Alert Policy Wizard or SMTP recipients not available in the global address list, a message appears on the Properties page of the alert, stating that it contains custom operations not listed in the picker.

INSIDE OUT

PowerShell endpoints for Office 365 services

There are a number of PowerShell management endpoints for various Office 365 services. You can import the commands from many of them into the same PowerShell console session. The most common endpoints are the following.

- **Exchange Online Protection** *https://ps.protection.outlook.com/powershell-liveid*

- **Exchange Online** *https://outlook.office365.com/powerhshell-liveid*

- **Security & Compliance Center** *https://ps.compliance.protection.outlook.com /powershell-liveid*

You can access any of them by instantiating a new PSSession object.

```
$Session = New-PSSession -ConnectionUri <PowerShell Endpoint> -Configuration-
Name Microsoft.Exchange -Credential (Get-Credential) -Authentication Basic
-AllowRedirection

Import-PSSession $Session
```

View Security Alerts

View Security Alerts shows you the two types of alerts available in a standard Office 365 subscription: Account Protection and Spam Submission.

For each alert displayed, you see information regarding the level of risk, type of alert, and available actions. For example, if an account has been disabled or locked out, an action you might take would be to review the alert and unlock the account.

Alert policies*

After you enable Office 365 Analytics under the Alerts Dashboard (for Enterprise E5 or Advanced Security Management SKUs), you can refresh the security portal and see that a number of default alert policies have been created. See Figure 7-10.

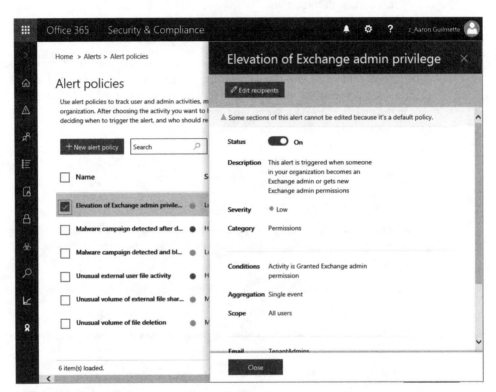

Figure 7-10 Alert policies.

Manage Advanced Alerts*

If you have an Enterprise E5 or Advanced Security Management SKU, **Manage Advanced Alerts** has replaced **Manage Alerts**. You can access the advanced alerts by turning on Advanced Security Management. See Figure 7-11.

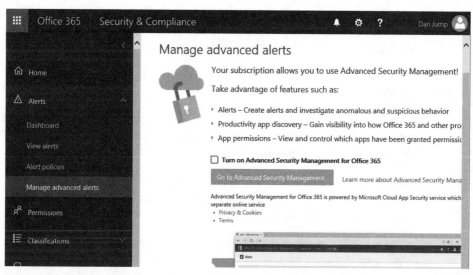

Figure 7-11 Manage Advanced Alerts page

After turning on Advanced Security Management, you are redirected to the Office 365 Cloud App Security portal, as shown in Figure 7-12.

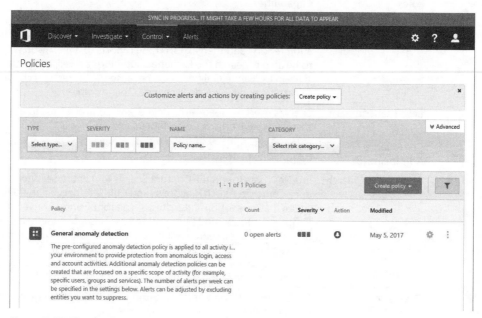

Figure 7-12 Cloud App Security portal

You can configure activity or anomaly detection policies to alert on behaviors. You can also view the built-in templates, create policies from them, and conduct investigations on audited activities or apps.

Permissions

The Office 365 Security & Compliance Center enables you to grant permissions to users who perform Security & Compliance tasks such as device management, data loss prevention, data labeling, retention, and discovery.

Users can perform only the tasks for which they are granted access. To access the Security & Compliance Center, users must be an Office 365 global administrator or a member of one or more Security & Compliance Center role groups.

The Permissions page enables you to assign a set of permissions or rights to users to perform certain actions. Each of the built-in permissions is made up of individual roles.

Each of the 29 built-in roles grants a specific right, as listed in Table 7-1.

Table 7-1 Security roles and capabilities

Roles	Capabilities
Audit Logs	Enables users to turn on and configure auditing for their Office 365 organization. This role also enables users to view the organization's audit reports and then export these reports to a file. If you want users to be able to search the Exchange audit logs as well, assign the permissions in Exchange Online. This is because the underlying cmdlet used to search the audit log is an Exchange Online cmdlet.
Case Management	Enables users to create, edit, delete, and control access to eDiscovery cases in the Security & Compliance Center.
Compliance Administrator	Enables users to view and edit settings and reports for compliance features.
Compliance Search	Enables users to run the Content Search tool in the Security & Compliance Center to search mailboxes and public folders, SharePoint Online sites, OneDrive for Business sites, Skype for Business conversations, Office 365 groups, and Microsoft teams. This role enables a user to get an estimate of the search results, but additional roles are needed to perform actions such as previewing, exporting, or deleting search results. This role also enables users to perform searches across mailboxes and get an estimate of the results.
Device Management	Enables users to view and edit settings and reports for device management features.
Disposition Management	Controls permissions for accessing Manual Disposition in the Security & Compliance Center.

Roles	Capabilities
DLP Compliance Management	Enables users to view and edit settings and reports for data loss prevention (DLP) policies.
Export	Enables users to export the results of a content search to a local computer. It also enables them to prepare search results for analysis in Advanced eDiscovery.
Hold	Enables users to place content in mailboxes, public folders, sites, Skype for Business conversations, and Office 365 groups on hold. When on hold, a copy of the content is stored in a secure location. Content owners can still modify or delete the original content. When content is on hold, content owners can still modify or delete the original content, but the content will be preserved until the hold is removed or until the hold duration expires.
Manage Alerts	Enables users to view and edit the settings and reports for alerts.
Organization Configuration	Enables users to run, view, and export audit reports and manage compliance policies for DLP, devices, and preservation.
Preview	Enables users to view a list of items that were returned from a content search. They can also open and view each item from the list to view its contents.
Record Management	Enables viewing and editing configuration and reports for the Record Management feature.
Retention Management	Enables users to manage retention policies.
Review	Enables users to see and open the list of the cases on the eDiscovery page in the Security & Compliance Center of which they are members. They can't perform any other case management tasks. This role also enables users to use Office 365 eDiscovery or Advanced eDiscovery to track, tag, analyze, and test documents that are assigned to them.
RMS Decrypt	Enables users to decrypt RMS-encrypted email messages when exporting search results or preparing search results for analysis in Advanced eDiscovery.
Role Management	Enables users to manage role group membership and create or delete custom role groups.
Search And Purge	Enables users to perform bulk removal of data matching the criteria of a content search.
Security Administrator	Enables viewing and editing configuration and reports for security features.
Security Reader	Enables viewing configuration and reports for security features.

Roles	Capabilities
Service Assurance View	Enables users to access the Service Assurance section in the Office 365 Security & Compliance Center. Users can download the documents available in the Service Assurance section. Content includes independent auditing and compliance documentation and trust-related guidance for using Office 365 features to manage regulatory compliance and security risks.
Supervisory Review Administrator	Enables users to create and manage the policies that define which communications are subject to review in an organization.
View-Only Audit Logs	Enables users to view and export their organization's audit reports. Because these reports might contain sensitive information, this role should only be assigned to those with an explicit need to view this information. If you want users to be able to search the Exchange audit logs as well, you have to assign the permissions in Exchange Online, because the underlying cmdlet used to search the audit log is an Exchange Online cmdlet.
View-Only Device Management	Enables viewing configuration and reports for the Device Management feature.
View-Only DLP Compliance Management	Enables users to view the settings and reports for data loss prevention (DLP) policies.
View-Only Manage Alerts	Enables viewing configuration and reports for the Manage Alerts feature.
View-Only Recipients	Enables users to view information about users and groups.
View-Only Record Management	Enables viewing configuration and reports for the Record Management feature.
View-Only Retention Management	Enables viewing configuration and reports for the Retention Management feature.

Compliance administrator

The Compliance Administrator role has management permissions within the Office 365 Security & Compliance Center and Exchange Admin Center as well as access to read audit logs. The compliance administrator can also manage settings for device management, data loss prevention, reports, and preservation.

eDiscovery manager

The eDiscovery Manager role group has two subgroups—eDiscovery Manager and eDiscovery Administrator. Members of this role group (either manager or administrator) can create and manage eDiscovery cases. They can add and remove members to a case, place content locations on hold, create and edit content searches associated with a case, export the results of a content search, and prepare search results for analysis in Advanced eDiscovery.

eDiscovery manager

Members of the eDiscovery Manager subgroup can view and manage the eDiscovery cases they create or are a member of, but not cases that other eDiscovery managers create if they are not added as a member of the case. This applies to both eDiscovery and Advanced eDiscovery.

eDiscovery administrator

Members of the eDiscovery Administrator subgroup can perform all case management tasks that an eDiscovery manager can do for any eDiscovery case, including those to which they are not currently members. To manage cases for which they are not a member, they must first add themselves as a member. eDiscovery administrators can also perform administrative tasks in Advanced eDiscovery.

Organization management

Members of the Organization Management role can control permissions for accessing features in the Security & Compliance Center and grant permissions to other users. Members can manage settings for device management, data loss prevention, reports, and preservation. Global administrators are automatically added as members of this role group.

Reviewer

The Reviewer role has the most restrictive eDiscovery-related permissions. Members of this group can see and open only the list of the cases on the eDiscovery page in the Security & Compliance Center that they are members of and have been granted access to view. Reviewers cannot create or modify cases, searches, or holds. They can't export search results or prepare results for Advanced eDiscovery. However, members can access cases to which they've been added in Advanced eDiscovery to perform analysis tasks.

Security administrator

Membership in the Security Administrator role group is synchronized across services. This role group is not manageable through the administrator portals. Members of this role group can include cross-service administrators as well as external partner groups and Microsoft Support. By default, this group is not assigned any roles. However, it is a member of the Security Administrators role group and inherits the capabilities of that role group.

Security reader

Members of the Security Reader role group have read-only access to a number of security features of the Identity Protection Center, Privileged Identity Management, Monitor Office 365 Service Health, and Office 365 Security & Compliance Center.

Service assurance user

Users who are members of the Service Assurance User role can review the Service Assurance documents in the portal, such as information regarding Office 365 service audits and certifications.

Supervisory review

Users who are granted the Supervisory Review role can create and define supervision policies, which can be used to capture communications for internal or external review.

Threat management

The Threat Management menu collects, displays, and provides analytics about threats detected in your Office 365 environment and enables you to configure policies to manage message security further.

Dashboard*

If you have licenses that include Advanced Threat Protection, you have access to the Threat Management dashboard.

The first time you launch the dashboard, if you have not already enabled Office 365 Analytics elsewhere, click **Get Started With Office 365 Analytics**, as shown in Figure 7-13.

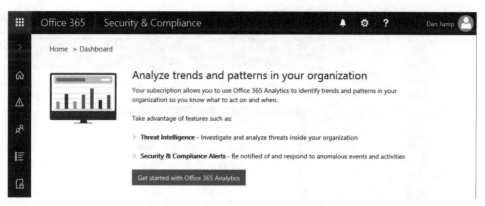

Figure 7-13 Threat Management dashboard

After clicking the Get Started With Office 365 Analytics button, you click through a few informational fly-outs that highlight some of the features of Threat Analytics. See Figure 7-14.

Figure 7-14 Office 365 Analytics informational page for Threat Explorer

On the final page, you are prompted to enable the feature. Click **Enable Office 365 Analytics** to complete the initial configuration, as shown in Figure 7-15.

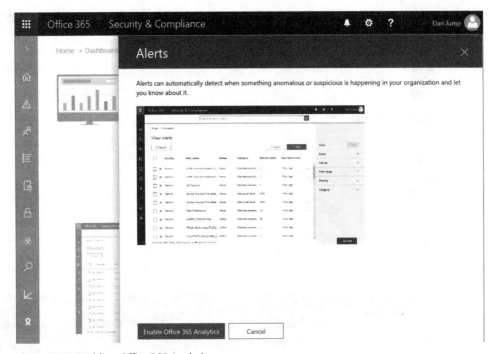

Figure 7-15 Enabling Office 365 Analytics

When Office 365 Analytics has been enabled, you are redirected to the Threat Management dashboard shown in Figure 7-16.

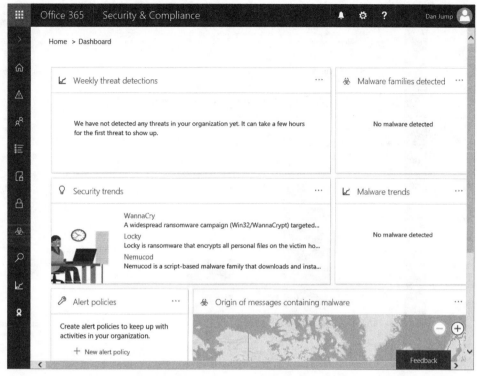

Figure 7-16 Threat Management Dashboard page after Office 365 Analytics has been enabled

The dashboard contains both informational and actionable items. You can view reports and trend lines for threats detected or blocked in your environment. The dashboard also has short-cuts to create and manage alert policies (which link to the **Alerts | Alert Policies** page).

Threat Explorer*

The Threat Explorer feature enables you to review details about individual threats in your organization. You can create and filter your search based on many message attributes. Figure 7-17 shows Threat Explorer.

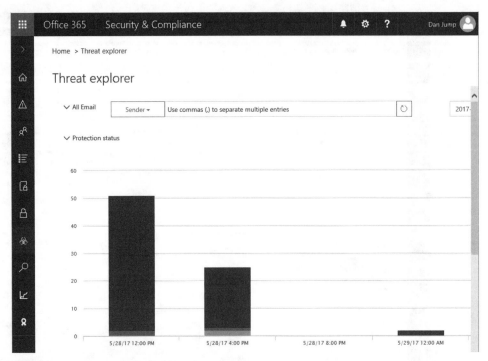

Figure 7-17 Threat Explorer dashboard

If you are investigating or experiencing an attack against your Office 365 environment, you can use Threat Explorer to analyze threats; it shows you the attacks over time, and you can analyze this data further by threat families.

The Threat Explorer view in Figure 7-18 shows malware families detected.

Figure 7-18 Threat Explorer top malware families

The Threat Explorer page has tabbed links for Top Malware Families, Emails, and Email Origin. Clicking the Emails tab displays information about the individual messages that triggered the alerts. You can also mark any suspicious email for follow-up. Marked emails shows up on the Incidents page. The Email Origin tab shows where messages are coming from geographically, based on information contained in the message headers.

To create an incident, select one or more messages from the list and click **+Add Mails To Incident**. See Figure 7-19.

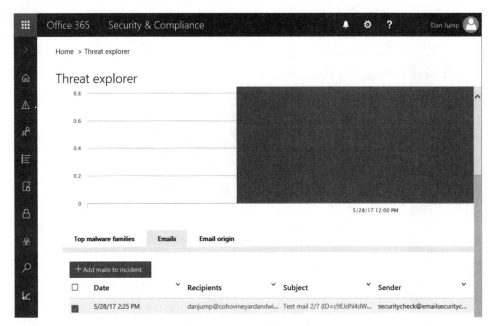

Figure 7-19 Add Mails To An Incident

You can either create a new incident based on the selected emails or, if you are already tracking an incident, add the selected emails to that. After clicking +Add Mails To Incident, you are prompted, as shown in Figure 7-20.

Figure 7-20 Creating an incident or updating an existing incident

You can provide a name and severity ranking for the incident. See Figure 7-21.

Figure 7-21 Entering a name for the incident

After you have created the incident, you can review and manage the incident on the Incidents dashboard.

Incidents*

Incidents are used to track activities in the Threat Management application. After adding messages to an incident, you can explore the open incidents on the Incidents dashboard. Incidents can be viewed, as shown in Figure 7-22, by navigating to **Threat Management | Incidents**.

Figure 7-22 Incidents dashboard

If you click an incident, an informational fly-out appears. You can edit the details of the incident or delete it. Clicking the details of a mail submission opens another fly-out (Figure 7-23) with the individual messages related to the incident. From there, you can perform actions on the individual messages such as removing them, placing them in the user's Junk mail folder, removing the attachments, or allowing the messages to be delivered.

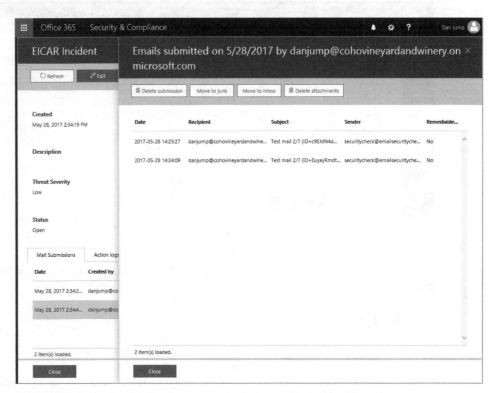

Figure 7-23 Reviewing details of message submissions on the Incident fly-out

Mail filtering

Mail filtering in the Security & Compliance Center configures many of the same options in Exchange Online Protection that you can configure through the Exchange Admin Center. If you have a subscription that includes Advanced Threat Protection, you have additional options for spoof intelligence. Spoof intelligence enables you to create allow and block lists of senders that might be spoofing your domain.

Anti-spam settings, shown in Figure 7-24, are set to Standard by default. You can configure custom settings by turning the toggle for Standard Settings to Off or by selecting the Custom tab and turning the toggle for Custom Settings to On.

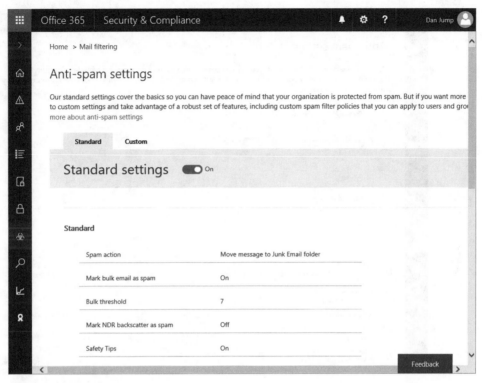

Figure 7-24 Anti-spam Settings page

Although many of the default policies are always set to On, you can edit them to tune them specifically to your organization or industry. See Figure 7-25 for additional settings that you can configure.

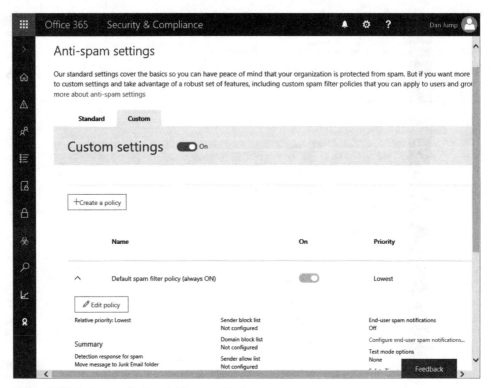

Figure 7-25 Anti-spam Custom Settings enabled

You can create new spam filtering policies and apply them to custom lists of users, groups, or domains.

Anti-malware

The Anti-malware page (Figure 7-26) enables you to configure the Exchange Online Protection anti-malware settings. Like Mail filtering, the default policy cannot be removed or disabled, although some of its settings can be modified (such as email notifications and whether to delete only affected attachments or the entire message).

Anti-malware policies can be scoped and applied to individual users or groups. You can also configure common attachment-blocking filters, shown in Figure 7-27, to discard attachments of known file types automatically.

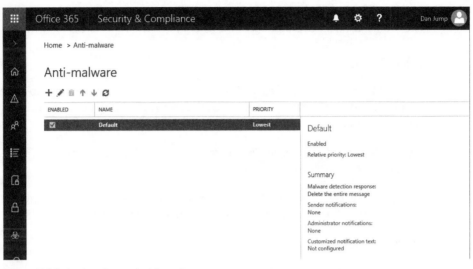

Figure 7-26 Anti-malware dashboard

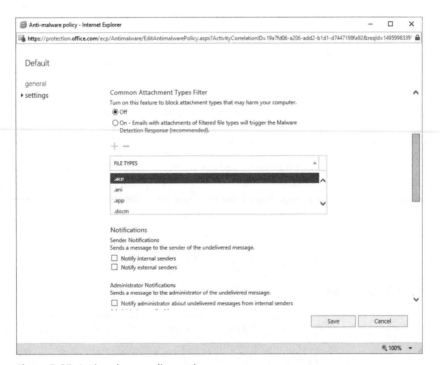

Figure 7-27 Anti-malware policy settings

If you have licenses for Advanced Threat Protection, more configuration options for attachment and link handling are available under the Safe Attachments and Safe Links menus.

DKIM

DKIM, or DomainKeys Identified Mail, is an authentication process designed to protect you against forged email. DKIM signatures are used to verify message authenticity by verifying that the messages originated from your organization and users.

DKIM requires configuring DNS CNAME records for each domain that you want to have signed and then enabling DKIM signing for your domains in Office 365.

The first step in configuring DKIM is to ensure that you have the required records in DNS. Office 365 performs automatic key rotation based on these CNAME values.

The format of the records is shown in Table 7-2.

Table 7-2 DKIM DNS record format

Host name	selector1._domainkey.<domain>
Value	selector1-<domainGUID>._domainkey.<InitialDomain>
TTL	3600

Host name	selector2._domainkey.<domain>
Value	selector2-<domainGUID>._domainkey.<InitialDomain>
TTL	3600

The value for <domainG> is the value used in your customized MX record for Office 365. For example, if your domain is cohovineyardandwinery.com, your MX record would be cohovineyardandwinery-com.mail.protection.outlook.com, and the domainGUID value would be cohovineyardandwinery-com. InitialDomain refers to the tenant domain name registered when you first set up Office 365.

Using that format, you can create the selector records for DKIM shown in Table 7-3.

Table 7-3 Sample DKIM DNS records for cohovineyardandwinery.com

Host name	selector1._domainkey.cohovineyardandwinery.com
Value	selector1-cohovineyardandwinery-com._domainkey.cohovineyeardandwinery.onmicrosoft.com
TTL	3600

Host name	selector2._domainkey.cohovineyardandwinery.com
Value	selector2-cohovineyardandwinery-com._domainkey.cohovineyeardan-dwinery.onmicrosoft.com
TTL	3600

When you have published the DKIM CNAME records in your organization's DNS, you're ready to enable DKIM in Office 365.

1. From the Security & Compliance Center, navigate to **Threat Management | Dkim**.

2. Select the domain for which you wish to enable DKIM signing (Figure 7-28) and click **Enable**.

Figure 7-28 DKIM enabled

If you do not have the CNAME records published, you receive an error that says:

CNAME record does not exist for this config. Please publish the following two CNAME records first. selector1-<domainGUID>._domainkey.<InitialDomain> selector2-<domainGUID>._domainkey.<InitialDomain>

You can also enable DKIM signing through Exchange Online PowerShell by running:

```
New-DkimSigningConfig -DomainName <domain> -Enabled $true
```

Safe Attachments*

The Safe Attachments menu is only available if you have purchased licenses that include Advanced Threat Protection.

Advanced Threat Protection (ATP) helps you prevent zero-day malware attacks in your email environment. ATP can be used to protect either Office 365 Exchange Online environments or on-premises environments. ATP provides a way for you to create policies that help ensure that your users access only links in emails or attachments to emails that have passed additional layers of inspection.

Safe Attachments uses Dynamic Delivery to ensure that users can continue working with email while attachments are being scanned. Dynamic Delivery replaces attachments with a place-holder attachment notifying the recipient that the attachment is still being scanned. If the attachment passes scanning, it is reattached to the message in the recipient's mailbox. If ATP detects that the attachment is malicious, it is blocked.

To configure a safe attachments policy, follow these steps.

1. From the Security & Compliance Center, navigate to **Threat Management | Safe Attachments**.

2. Click + to create a new policy.

3. Type a name for the policy and configure the options desired, as shown in Figure 7-29.

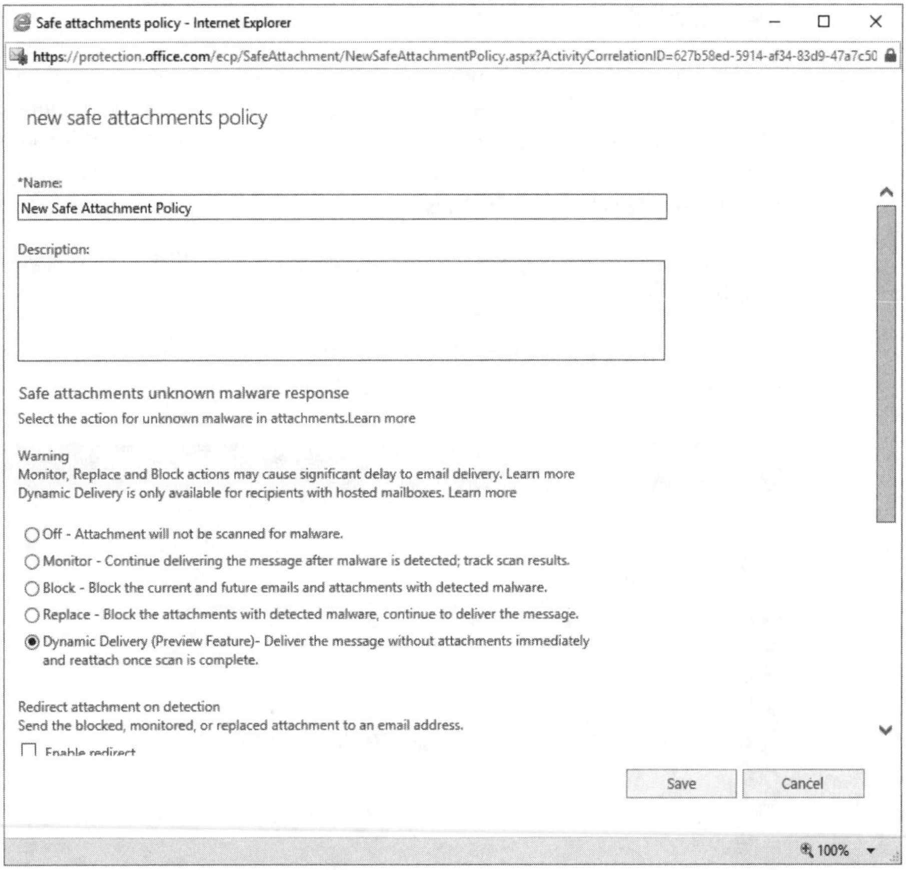

Figure 7-29 Configuring a safe attachments policy

For Replace and Block actions, messages are not delivered to the recipients until scanning has finished.

If you have selected Dynamic Delivery, it will work only with mailboxes hosted in Office 365. If you have selected Dynamic Delivery and the mailbox is on-premises, the policy falls back to Replace, and the message won't be delivered until the scan has completed.

The policy also can be configured to redirect the blocked, monitored, or replaced attachment to another mailbox for administrator review.

4. Select recipients to whom the policy will apply.

5. Click Save.

Safe Links*

The Safe Links menu is presented only if you have purchased licenses that include Advanced Threat Protection. Safe Links helps prevent users from following links in email that link to websites recognized as malicious. For messages in HTML, Safe Links identifies any link that uses the *<href>* attribute; for messages that are delivered in plaintext, Safe Links identifies URL construction and attempts to verify the links.

Safe Links also includes reporting that enables you to see which users have followed potentially malicious links.

When you purchase Advanced Threat Protection, a default Safe Links policy setting object is deployed for your entire organization. See Figure 7-30.

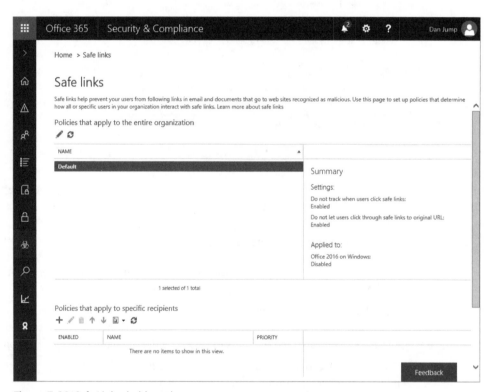

Figure 7-30 Safe Links dashboard

The default policy has tracking disabled and blocks links to malicious sites when clicked through Outlook Web App or Outlook 2016. It is not applied to users, however.

You can edit the organization-wide default Safe Links policy to specify URLs that you always want to block as well as to enable Safe Links behaviors for other Office 2016 desktop apps (Word, Microsoft Excel, Microsoft PowerPoint, and Microsoft Visio). Safe Links is not currently supported in Office Online applications or on Office for Mac, iOS, or Android.

To get protection for your users, you must create a new policy and then apply it to users, using the conditions in the policy. In addition, users must have an Advanced Threat Protection license for Safe Links to work.

Quarantine

Quarantine holds messages that were blocked due to bulk mailing, spam, phishing, or transport rules. Quarantine is shown in Figure 7-31.

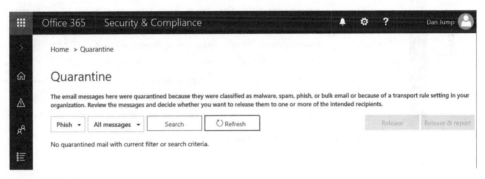

Figure 7-31 Quarantine page

You can review the items in quarantine by navigating to **Threat Management | Quarantine** in the Security & Compliance Center.

You can filter the quarantined messages based on type (Bulk, Spam, Transport Rule, Phish) and scope (All Messages, Only My Messages). If messages appear here, you can select them and release them to users when you've determined they're safe.

Advanced Threats*

The Advanced Threats page is available only if you have an Advanced Threat Protection license. From the Advanced Threats page, you can schedule reports for threats and usage of advanced threat protection features in your environment. Threats are shown in Figure 7-32.

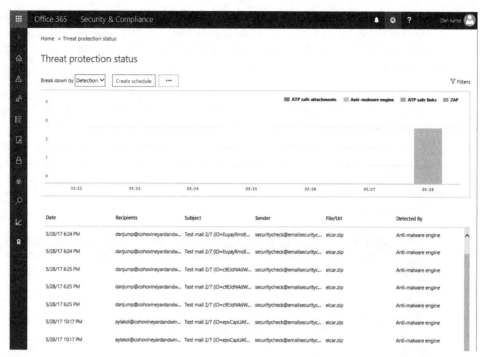

Figure 7-32 Advanced Threats Threat Protection Status dashboard

Reports

The Reports section of the Security & Compliance Center enables you to view, download, and, in some cases, schedule automatic reports.

Dashboard

The Reports dashboard, shown in Figure 7-33, displays interactive widgets for a number of common reports.

CHAPTER 7

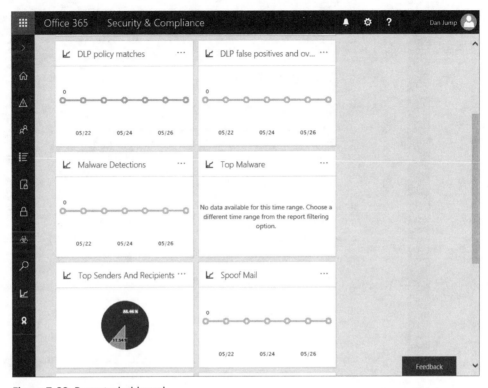

Figure 7-33 Reports dashboard.

Clicking the ellipsis (…) for a widget opens a pop-up menu to pin it to the Security & Compliance Center home page dashboard. Clicking the data portion of the widget displays additional detail about the report.

Inside the report view (Figure 7-34), you can view a graph, filter the items based on a number of criteria, or sort the data. Depending on the report, you might be able to download data to a CSV or create a scheduled report.

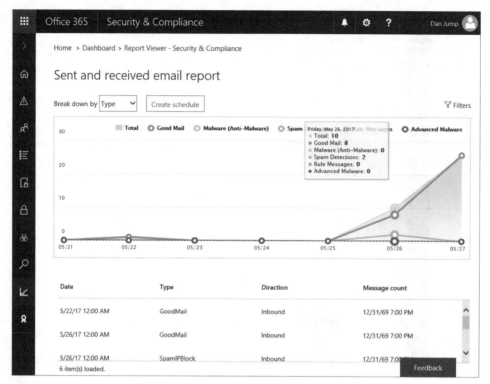

Figure 7-34 Detail of Sent And Received Email Report

Manage schedules

For reports that support scheduling, you can view and edit the scheduled reports. Report schedules are shown in Figure 7-35.

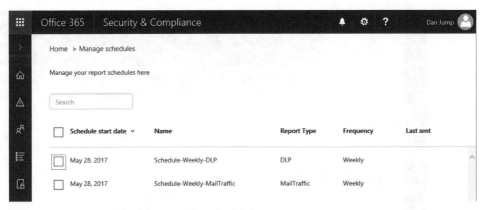

Figure 7-35 Manage Schedules page for scheduled reports

By selecting a report, you expose the report fly-out menu, which enables you to edit the schedule and report options.

Reports for download

Items that you have requested an additional report for (by selecting Report in a report's widget) show up under Reports For Download. See Figure 7-36.

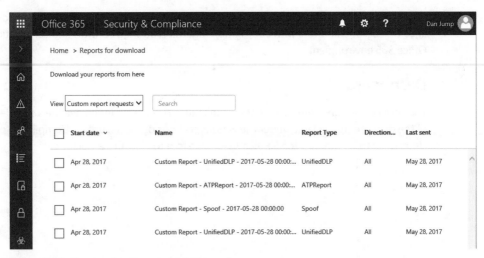

Figure 7-36 Reports For Download dashboard

Clicking a report opens the detail fly-out, shown in Figure 7-37, with a summary and link to download the report.

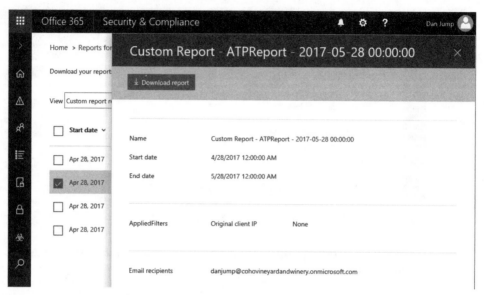

Figure 7-37 Custom report fly-out

Service assurance

Service assurance is a collection of reports and documents that you can use to provide compliance officers and auditors with information regarding audited controls and certifications for the Office 365 environment.

Dashboard

The Service Assurance dashboard, shown in Figure 7-38, provides an overview and description of the documents available under the various sections of the Security & Compliance portal. Users need to be granted the Service Assurance role to view these documents.

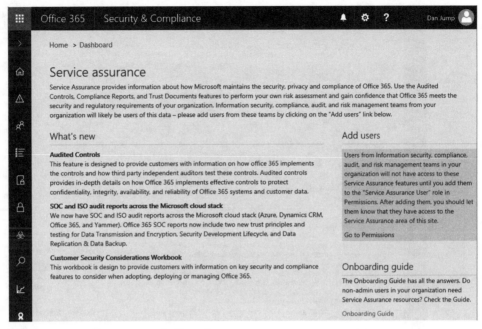

Figure 7-38 Service Assurance dashboard

Compliance reports

The Compliance Reports page shows a number of audit and certification reports available for download. See Figure 7-39.

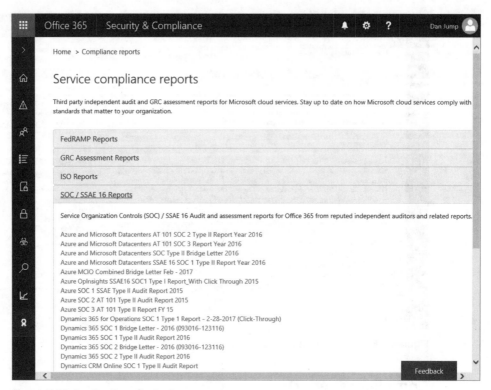

Figure 7-39 Service Compliance Reports page

Trust documents

Trust documents (Figure 7-40) display general information documents that outline how Microsoft protects your data in cloud services and meets compliance regulations.

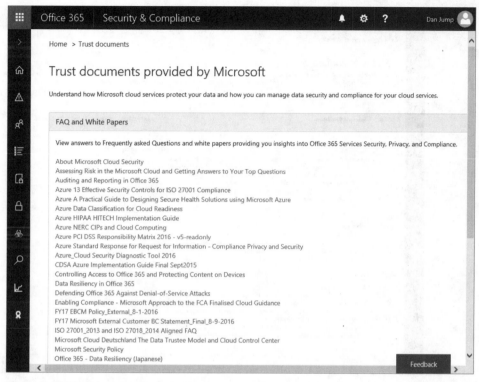

Figure 7-40 Trust documents

Audited controls

The Audited Controls page shows the standards that Office 365 services have been audited and tested against. From this page, you can select which documents you want to download. See Figure 7-41.

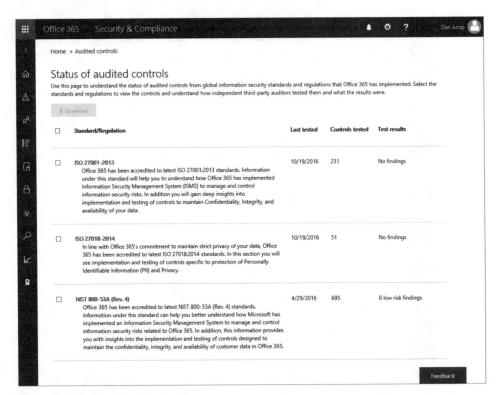

Figure 7-41 Audited controls reports

Settings

On the **Service Assurance | Settings** page, shown in Figure 7-42, you can select which types of assurance documents you want displayed in the portal, based on your region and industry. You can select multiple industries and regions. After updating your selection, click **Save**. Your view will be filtered the next time you return to view documents.

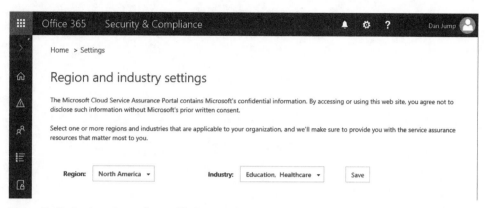

Figure 7-42 Settings for region and industry selections

Summary

This chapter reviewed the monitoring and reporting aspects of the Security & Compliance Center, as well as some of the threat management capabilities. Other features of the Security & Compliance Center are covered in Chapter 8, "Inside the Security & Compliance Center: Data Classification, Loss Prevention, Governance, and Discovery."

Inside the Security & Compliance Center: Data classifications, loss prevention, governance, and discovery

The Security & Compliance Center, shown in Figure 8-1, has three core functions: alerting, tracking, and managing threats; managing permissions and roles in Office 365; and managing the data life cycle.

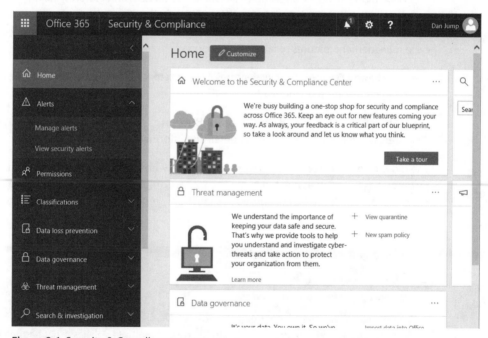

Figure 8-1 Security & Compliance center

This chapter discusses the data management tools available, including data classifications and labels, loss prevention policies, governance, and eDiscovery.

Classifications

Classifications enable you to specify labels and policies you use to categorize and manage the life cycle of information.

Labels

Use labels to categorize or classify information. After a label has been created and published, it's available to users in applications such as Microsoft Outlook, Microsoft OneDrive, and Microsoft SharePoint. When labels are applied to email or documents (either manually or automatically), the content is categorized, retained, or deleted based on the settings you specify in policies. You can create labels to retain content for a certain length of time or delete it when it reaches a certain age.

Labels are global features, applying to all Office 365 services and features, including user and resource mailboxes in Exchange Online, SharePoint Online, OneDrive for Business, and Office 365 Groups. Due to their global nature, you should start transitioning older per-service data life cycle management features to labels. This includes:

- **Exchange Online**   Specific features such as retention tags, retention policies, and messaging records management.

- **SharePoint Online and OneDrive for Business**   Specific features such as in-place records management, Records Center, and information management policies.

The older features will continue to work side by side with labels, but moving forward, Microsoft recommends using labels created in the Security & Compliance Center for your data governance needs. Labels can be configured in a label-only mode as well as with retention and deletion actions.

INSIDE OUT

Understanding retention precedence

Content can have a number of retention policies or labels applied to it, each with different criteria, actions, and retention periods. In the case of multiple policies, what happens to your data? Figure 8-2 shows the precedence of policy application.

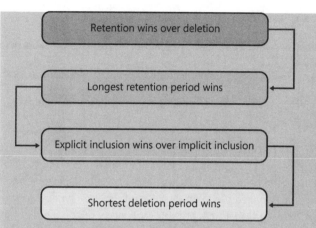

Figure 8-2 Retention precedence

Retention wins over deletion   For example, Retention Policy 1 retains email for 1 year and then deletes it, and Retention Policy 2 says retain email for 5 years and then delete it. After 1 year, the email would be deleted and hidden from the user's view (Retention Policy 1) but retained in the Recoverable Items folder until the content reaches 5 years (Policy 2).

Longest retention period wins   If content is subject to multiple policies with retention actions, the content is retained for the longest period. In the previous example, Retention Policy 1 deleted email after 1 year, but the Retention Policy 2 action was to retain for 5 years. Policy 2 has the longest retention period, so the content will be retained for 5 years.

Explicit inclusion wins over implicit inclusion   If User 1 applies Label 1 with a retention action of 10 years but the configuration of Retention Policy 2 is to delete after 5 years, the content will be retained for 10 years as long as the user manually applies Label 1 before the message has been permanently deleted. Labels that are applied by policy are considered implicit. Explicit is also conferred in the concept of specificity, meaning that if Retention Policy 1 retains content in all mailboxes for 1 year, but Retention Policy 2 specifically retains content in User 1's mailbox for 5 years, the content in User 1's mailbox will be retained for 5 years.

Shortest deletion period wins   If content is subject to multiple policies that delete content (with no retention), it will be deleted at the end of the shortest retention period.

Labels are reusable classification mechanisms that you can use as part of multiple label policies. Only one label can be applied per piece of content (such as an email or document), and an explicit label always takes precedence over an auto-apply label. The following are key points regarding label application.

- If a user assigns a label manually, they can change or remove the label.

- If content has an automatically applied label, a user can replace the label manually.

- If a user applies a label to content manually, an auto-apply label cannot replace it.

- If content is subject to multiple policies that auto-apply labels, the label for the oldest rule is assigned.

Labels cannot be applied to Exchange Online public folders or Skype data and can only be automatically applied to content that matches a keyword search or a sensitive data type. Labels that are published to users can be applied to Exchange, SharePoint, OneDrive, and Office 365 Groups. Labels that are auto-applied based on sensitive information types can only be applied to SharePoint and OneDrive, and labels that are auto-applied based on a query can be applied to Exchange, SharePoint, OneDrive, and Office 365 Groups.

Creating a label

Labels are created from the Classifications menu. In this example, you create two labels—one label that will be published for users to apply manually to content they want to retain, and then one label that will be published and automatically applied to email to be retained for a year and then deleted. To create the labels, follow these steps.

1. In the Security & Compliance Center, expand Classifications and select **Labels**.

2. Select + **Create A Label**.

3. Type a name and a description for the label and click **Next, as shown in Figure 8-3**.

Figure 8-3 Creating a label

4. Turn the Retention slider on, select the **Don't Retain The Content** button, select 1 Day, and then click **Next**. See Figure 8-4.

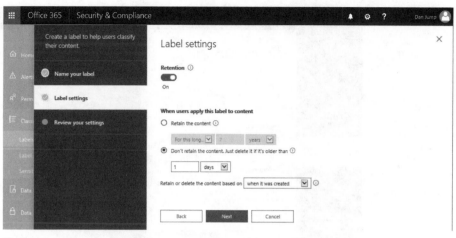

Figure 8-4 Adjusting label settings

5. Confirm the settings and click **Create This Label**. See Figure 8-5.

Figure 8-5 Reviewing label settings

6. Click **Close**.

7. Create a second label named Retain Data For 10 Years, but select 10 years as the retention period with no delete option. Compare your settings to Figure 8-6.

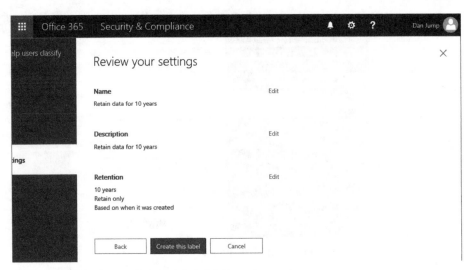

Figure 8-6 Reviewing settings for label with 10-year retention

Publishing a label for manual application

Publishing a label makes it available for users to use in applications. Labels can be published in two ways—for manual or automatic application. Publishing one or more labels creates a label policy with the selected labels as members. Labels that you want to apply automatically must be based on keyword searches or sensitive data types.

1.   On the Labels page, select the check box next to **the previously created Retain Data For 10 Years** label.

2.   Select **Publish Label**. See Figure 8-7.

Figure 8-7 Publishing a label

3. Click **Next after confirming the label to publish**.

4. Select the **All Locations. Includes Content In Exchange Email, Office 365 Groups, OneDrive And SharePoint Documents** button and click **Next**. See Figure 8-8.

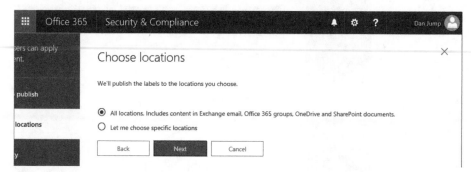

Figure 8-8 Choosing locations to publish labels

5. Type a description and a name for the policy, as shown in Figure 8-9, and click **Next**.

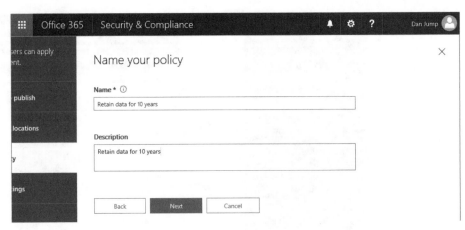

Figure 8-9 Naming the label policy being published

6. Confirm the settings and click **Publish Labels, as shown in Figure 8-10**.

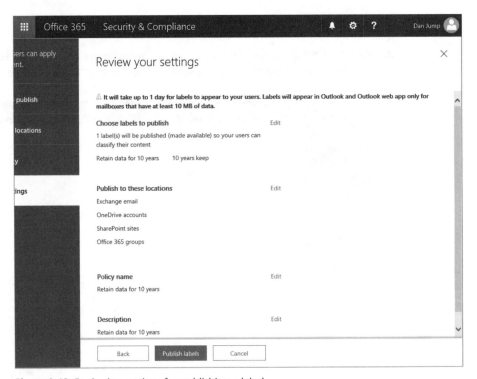

Figure 8-10 Reviewing settings for publishing a label

7. Click **Close**.

Publishing a label for automatic application

In this example, you create a label that automatically applies to content based on a sensitive-content type of template.

1. On the Labels page, select check box next to the **Delete Sensitive Data** label.

2. Click the **Auto-Apply Label** button, as shown in Figure 8-11.

Figure 8-11 Auto-applying Delete Sensitive Data label

3. Click **Next**.

4. Select the **Apply Label To Content That Contains Sensitive Information** button and click **Next**. See Figure 8-12.

Figure 8-12 Choosing auto-apply label settings

5. Select **Custom** (Figure 8-13) and click **Next at the bottom of the page**.

Figure 8-13 Selecting Custom to create a new custom policy template

6. Click the **Add** button and then select one or more check boxes from Sensitive Information Types, shown in Figure 8-14. Click **Add** when you are finished.

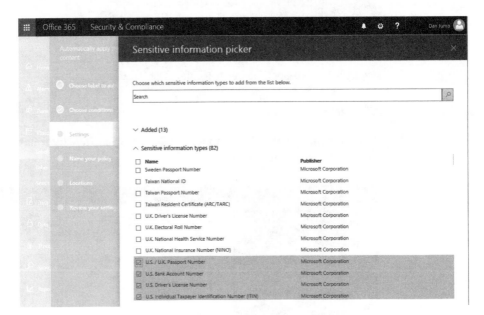

Figure 8-14 Adding sensitive information templates to custom policy

7. Click **Done**.

8. Confirm the list of items to detect and click **Next**.

9. On the Name Your Policy page, shown in Figure 8-15, type a name and description for the policy and click Next.

Figure 8-15 Naming the policy

10. Select the **All Locations** button and click **Next**.

11. Click the **Auto-Apply** button, as shown in Figure 8-16.

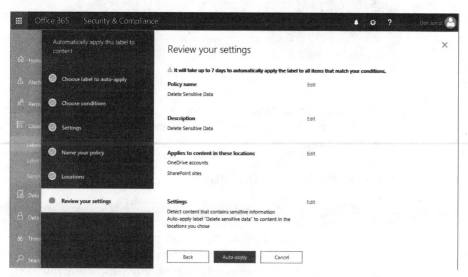

Figure 8-16 Reviewing the settings for the policy

12. Click **Close**.

Label policies

Label policies can be used to assign labels and specify actions (such as retain or delete) automatically.

Label policies are automatically created when you publish a label for either manual or automatic application. See Figure 8-17.

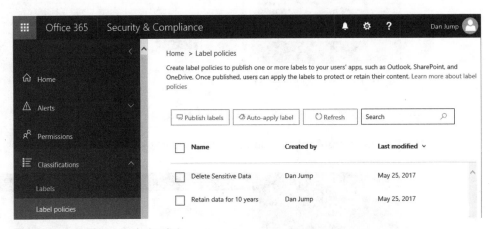

Figure 8-17 Configured label policies

On the Label Policies page, you can choose to publish or auto-apply labels that you've already created. Label policies that contain labels with the retention action also appear under **Data Governance | Retention**.

Sensitive information types

The Sensitive Information Types page (Figure 8-18) displays the collection of data types that can be used to classify data. Although Office 365 comes with many default sensitive information types, you can also create a custom type based on your organizational requirements (for example, a part number format, unique identifier format that you give customers, or other content that you can search for based on regular expressions). Sensitive information types can be used in labels, retention policies, and data loss prevention policies.

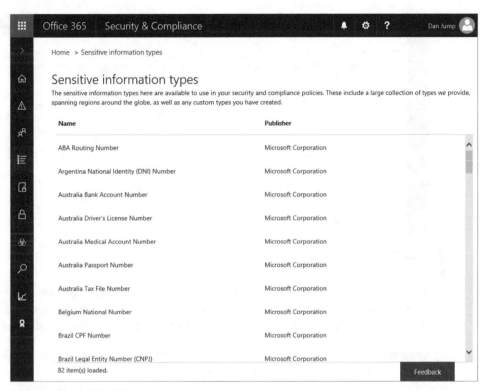

Figure 8-18 Sensitive information types

Custom sensitive information types are specified by an XML file. You can find the specifications for the file structure at *https://support.office.com/en-us/article/Create-a-custom-sensitive -information-type-82c382a5-b6db-44fd-995d-b333b3c7fc30* if you want to create a sensitive information type template based on unique patterns and document structures.

Data loss prevention

Data loss prevention (DLP) helps you identify and protect your organization's sensitive data. You can configure policies based on keywords, sensitive information types, or document fingerprints to restrict distribution of content or perform other actions, such as forcing encryption. A DLP policy can identify data across many locations, including Exchange Online, SharePoint Online, and OneDrive for Business. Figure 8-19 shows the Data Loss Prevention page.

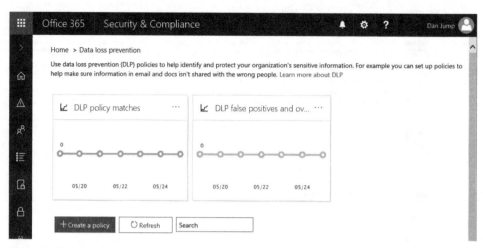

Figure 8-19 Data Loss Prevention page

A DLP policy comprises one or more locations and one or more rules. Locations are the services where sensitive data is stored, such as Exchange Online or OneDrive, and rules contain conditions that content must meet and actions to take when content matching conditions is found.

Conditions examine content and context. For example, sensitive content might be deemed lower risk if it is shared internally versus externally.

Depending on where content is being accessed, Actions restricts content from being accessed or sent.

When a document meets a policy's conditions for OneDrive or SharePoint content, access is blocked for everyone except the site collection owner and the last user to modify the document. After the document is brought back into compliance, the original permissions are restored. When access to a document is blocked, the document appears with a policy tip icon overlaid on the document's original icon.

For email content, the action blocks the email from being sent. Depending on the DLP transport rule configuration, the sender might receive a non-delivery report (NDR), a policy tip, or an email notification that their message was found to be noncompliant.

There might be instances when users have a business justification to handle sensitive data or transmit it outside the organization. User notifications and user overrides can notify a user that the content violated a policy and present them with an option to override if they have a business justification.

A DLP policy can also include incident notifications. An incident notification can be sent to a compliance officer; it includes information about the item that was matched, the content that matched the rule, and the name of the person who last modified the content. In the case of an email message that triggers a DLP rule, the report also includes information regarding the sender and attaches the message that matched the policy.

Policy

The first step in creating a DLP policy is determining the type of content to protect. Office 365 includes a number of templates (based on sensitive data types) that can be used to give your policy a starting point.

To create a policy from a template, follow these steps.

1. In the Security & Compliance Center, click Data Loss Prevention and select **Policy**.

2. Click + **Create A Policy**.

3. Select a policy template from the default templates, such as U.S. Financial Data shown in Figure 8-20, and click **Next**.

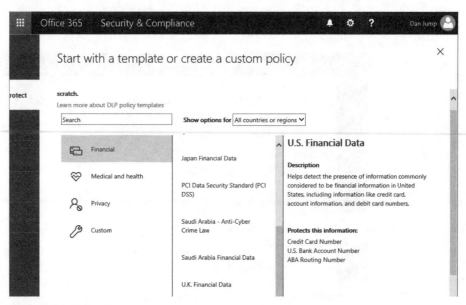

Figure 8-20 DLP policy creation

4. Type a name and description for the policy and click **Next**.

5. Select the **All Locations In Office 365. Includes Content In Exchange Email And OneDrive And SharePoint Documents** button and click **Next**. See Figure 8-21.

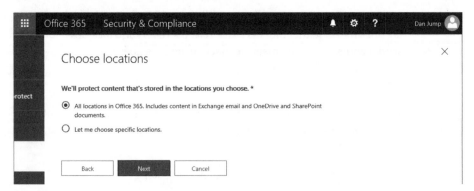

Figure 8-21 Choosing locations to apply a data loss prevention policy

6.   Choose how to protect the data.

The default option is to detect when the content is shared outside the organization, but you can also choose With People Inside The Organization or configure advanced selection settings.

7.   Click **Next** when finished. See Figure 8-22.

Figure 8-22 Choosing options for protecting data

If you choose advanced settings, you can edit the individual rule settings in the template or add your own, as shown in Figure 8-23.

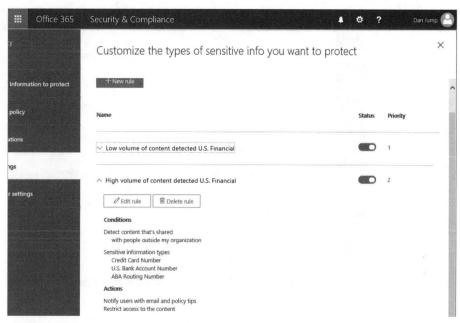

Figure 8-23 Configuring advanced settings for a DLP policy

8. After making your selection (either for the default or to modify the rule settings through advanced settings), click **Next**.

9. Select options for how to respond to sensitive data being detected. Options include configuring a policy tip (a notification displayed in the user interface) as well as the thresholds for content sharing, whether to block the user from sending, or whether to deliver an incident report to an administrator or compliance officer. See Figure 8-24.

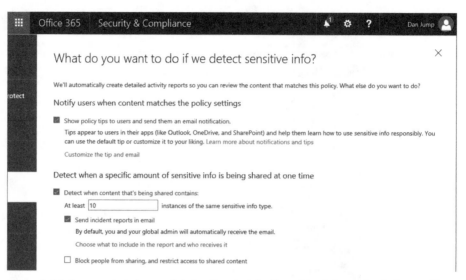

Figure 8-24 A screenshot shows a list of actions to take if sensitive information is detected by the DLP policy.

10. Select the **I'd Like To Test It Out First** button to enable the DLP policy in test mode. Click Next.

POLICY APPLICATION MODES

If you're creating DLP policies with a large potential impact, consider rolling the policy out gradually.

Configure the policy in test mode without Policy Tips   Use the DLP reports to assess the impact. You can use DLP reports to view the number, location, type, and severity of policy matches. You can use the reports to tune the queries and policies. In test mode, users will be unaware that DLP policies are scanning their activities. DLP policies will not affect the productivity of people working in your organization. To turn on this mode, select the I'd Like To Test It Out First button when configuring the policy.

Show Policy Tips while in test mode   After you have configured the policy to your liking, you can edit the policy and enable Policy Tips. With Policy Tips enabled, users are notified while they are accessing data that matches the policy. At this stage, you can also ask users to report false positives so that you can refine the rules further, such as by excluding document libraries, users, or recipients of data. To enable Policy Tips, edit the policy, click Edit in the Status section (Figure 8-25), and then select the Show Policy Tips While In Test Mode button.

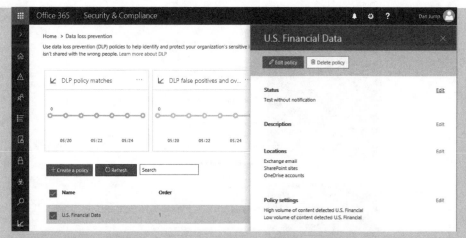

Figure 8-25 Editing DLP policy

Yes, turn it on right away   After you are confident about the configuration, you can begin full enforcement of the policies so that the actions in the rules are applied. To enable the policy fully, edit the policy, click Edit in the Status section, and then select the Yes, Turn It On Right Away button.

You can turn off a policy at any time. If your policy has multiple rules, you can also disable individual rules of the policy if they are having an adverse effect on your organization.

11.   Confirm the settings and click **Create**. See Figure 8-26.

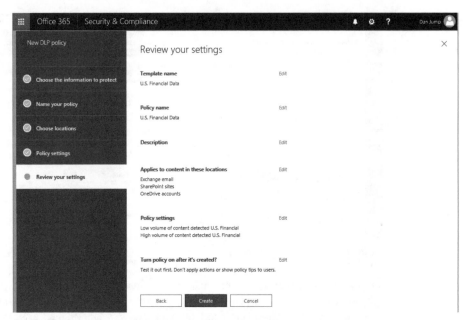

Figure 8-26 Reviewing DLP policy settings

App permissions*

App permissions are part of Advanced Security Management. App permissions enable you to configure policies for applications connected and authorized to use your Office 365 subscription. See Figure 8-27.

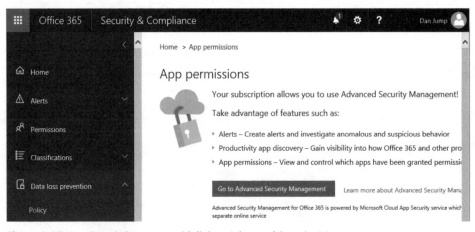

Figure 8-27 App Permissions page with link to Advanced Security Management

When Advanced Security Management has been activated in your tenant, you can click the Go To Advanced Security Management button to be redirected to *https://portal.cloudappsecurity .com/#/app-permissions*. From there, you can create and manage policies and reports for applications connected to your Office 365 subscription. See Figure 8-28.

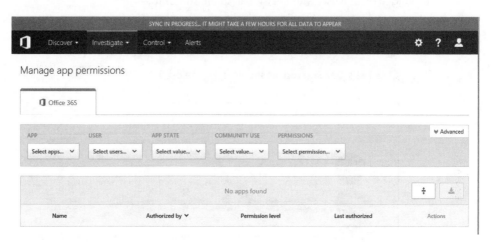

Figure 8-28 Cloud App Security App permissions page

Device management

The built-in Mobile Device Management (MDM) for Office 365 service helps you secure and manage mobile devices such as iPhones, iPads, Android phones and tablets, and Windows phones. You can create and manage device security policies, remotely wipe a device, and view detailed device reports.

To configure MDM for Office 365, you need to go through several steps.

- Activate the Mobile Device Management service.

- Set up Mobile Device Management.

- Configure domains for Mobile Device Management.

- Configure an APN certificate for iOS devices.

- Set up multifactor authentication.

- Manage device security policies.

- Enroll devices.

Activating the Mobile Device Management service

Before you can begin creating policies for device management, you must first activate the Mobile Device Management service. To create mobile device management policies, you must be logged on as a user with the Global Administrator role.

1. In the Security & Compliance Center, click Data Loss Prevention and then select **Device Management**.

2. Click **Let's Get Started**, as shown in Figure 8-29.

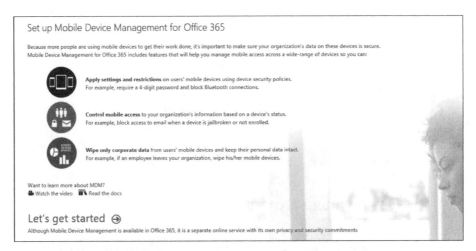

Figure 8-29   Office 365 Mobile Device Management configuration start page

3. If desired, update the name of the MDM security group and then click **Start Setup**. See Figure 8-30.

Figure 8-30 Office 365 Mobile Device Management setup

4. After the setup completes, and you are redirected to the Office 365 Admin Center, begin typing **mobile device management** in the Search box. When it appears, click it.

5. Wait for the MDM service activation, shown in Figure 8-31, to complete.

    This can take up to a few hours to complete. If you accidentally close the page or navigate away from it, you can return to the page through the Security & Compliance | Data Loss Prevention | Device Management menu.

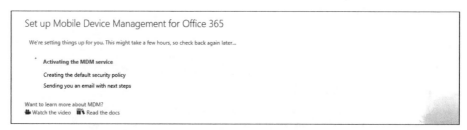

Figure 8-31 Activating Office 365 Mobile Device Management

After it has completed, you are directed to the Mobile Device Management For Office 365 page, shown in Figure 8-32.

Figure 8-32 Mobile Device Management home page

Configuring domains

If you have custom domains configured for your tenant, you configure additional DNS records for your tenant. If you will not use Windows-based devices with MDM for Office 365, or just use the default tenant name, you can skip this section.

After these configuration steps, users of Windows devices are redirected to enroll in MDM for Office 365.

1. Under Settings on the right side of the page, click **Manage Settings** to display a list of four tasks. See Figure 8-33.

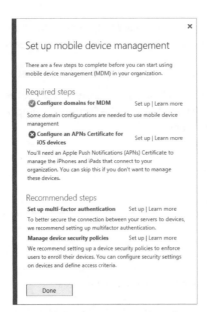

Figure 8-33 Setting up Mobile Device Management for Office 365

If you have already added all your domains and configured the DNS records for your tenant (including the EnterpriseEnrollment and EnterpriseRegistration DNS records), you can skip to the next step. Clicking the **Set Up** link next to Configure Domains For MDM opens the Domain Management page of the Office 365 Admin Center.

2. If you have added your domains but have not created the necessary DNS records for MDM, add these records to your organization's external DNS, based on the information in Table 8-1.

Table 8-1 MDM for Office 365 DNS records

Host name	Record Type	Target Address	TTL
EnterpriseEnrollment	CNAME	EnterpriseEnrollment-s.manage.windows.com	3600
EnterpriseRegistration	CNAME	Enterpriseregistration.windows.net	3600

Configuring Apple Push Notifications service

If you intend to manage Apple iOS devices, you must configure MDM for Apple Push Notifications service (APNs). The Apple Push Notifications service enables third-party application developers to send notification data to applications (such as MDM for Office 365) installed on Apple devices.

INSIDE OUT

Apple push notifications

Configuring Apple push notifications requires an Apple ID. To create an Apple ID for your organization, follow these steps.

1. Create a shared mailbox or distribution list in Office 365 that is not tied to a particular administrator configuring push notifications. If you create a mailbox, grant yourself permissions to the mailbox so you can access it in step 5.

2. Open a browser and navigate to *https://appleid.apple.com*.

3. Click Create Your Apple ID.

4. Fill out the form, using the details of the shared mailbox created in step 1. Record the answers to the security questions. See Figure 8-34.

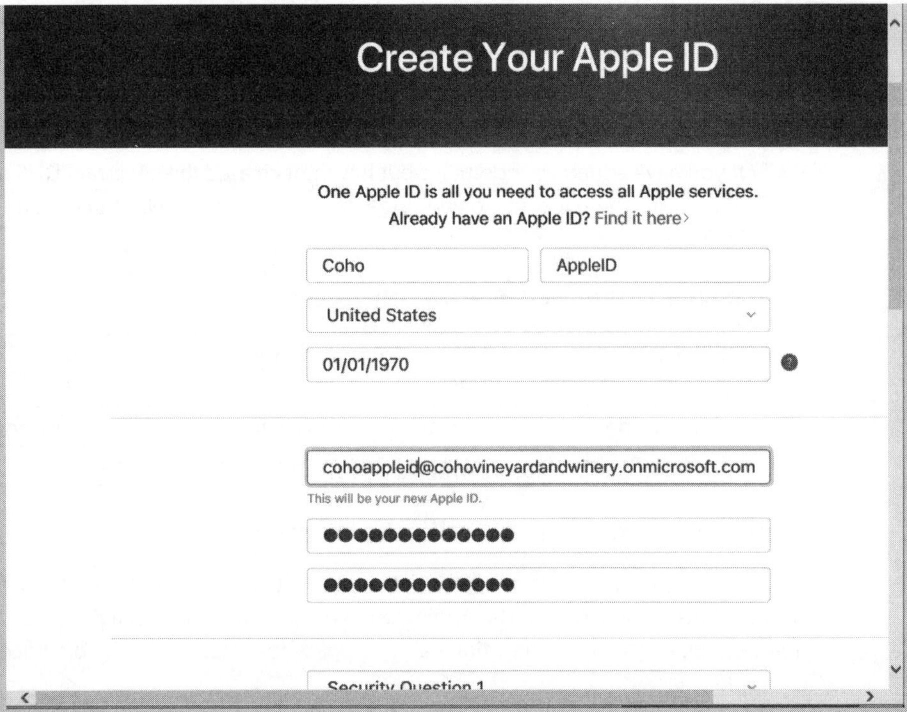

Figure 8-34 Creating an Apple ID

5. Type the confirmation code you received in the email and click Continue to confirm your new Apple ID.

To configure APNs, follow these steps.

1. Next to Configure An APNs Certificate For iOS Devices, click Set Up.

2. On the Install Apple Push Notification Certificate page, click the **Download Your CSR File** link. Save it to a location on your computer and then click **Next**.

3. Click the **Apple APNS Portal** link, shown in Figure 8-35.

Figure 8-35 Creating an APNs certificate

4. Click the Sign In With Your Apple ID link. Type your corporate Apple ID and password and click **Sign In**. See Figure 8-36.

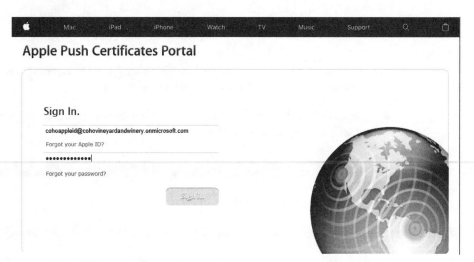

Figure 8-36 Apple Push Certificates Portal

5. Click **Create A Certificate**, select the check box to agree to the terms and conditions, and click **Accept**.

6. Browse to the CSR file you saved previously and click the **Upload button, shown in Figure 8-37**.

Figure 8-37 Uploading CSR for the Apple Push notifications certificate

7. If prompted, cancel the Download The Generated.json File in *identity.apple.com*. If the page doesn't refresh, click the browser refresh button.

8. Click the **Download** button next to the Mobile Device Management certificate (Figure 8-38) and save it to a directory on your computer.

Figure 8-38 Downloading the certificate

9. Navigate back to Office 365 and click **Next** on the Create An APNs Certificate page.

10. Browse to the .pem certificate file downloaded from the Apple Push Certificates portal and click **Finish**. See Figure 8-39.

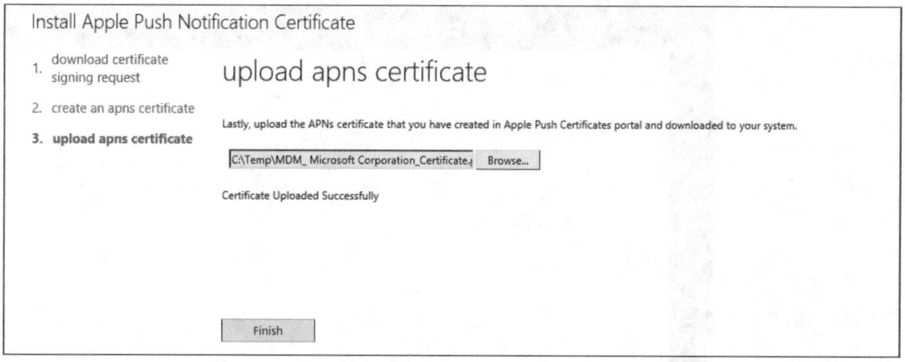

Figure 8-39 Uploading the APNs certificate

11. Navigate back to the Mobile Device Management portal (**Security & Compliance | Data Loss Prevention | Device Management**) and click **Manage Settings**.

SET UP A REMINDER TO RENEW THE APN CERTIFICATE

The APN certificate expires one year from the day you configure the Apple Push Notifications service. Set a reminder for a year from the date of configuration to renew the certificate. To renew the certificate, go through the same steps you used to create and install the initial certificate.

Configuring multifactor authentication

Click the **Set Up** link next to *Set Up Multi-Factor Authentication To Configure Multi-Factor Authentication* (if it hasn't already been configured). For more information about configuring multifactor authentication, see Chapter 3, "Federation Services and Authentication."

To configure device security policies, follow these steps.

1. Create a Security Group for testing Office 365 MDM Device security policies. For more information about configuring security groups, refer to Chapter 7, "Inside the Security & Compliance Center: Alerting, Threat Management, and Reporting."

2. Click the **Set Up** link next to *Manage Device Security Policies to manage and configure a device security policy.* (The link opens the Security & Compliance Center.) Navigate to **Data Loss Prevention | Device Security Policies**.

3. Click the + button to create a new device security policy. See Figure 8-40.

Figure 8-40 Device security policies page

4. Type a name and description for the new policy and click **Next**. See Figure 8-41.

Figure 8-41 New Device Security Policy Wizard

5. Select the requirements to apply, such as requiring a password and an inactivity lock.

6. Scroll to the bottom of the page and choose either Allow Access And Report Violation (which allows noncompliant devices to access Office 365) or Block Access And Report Violation. Click **Next**. See Figure 8-42.

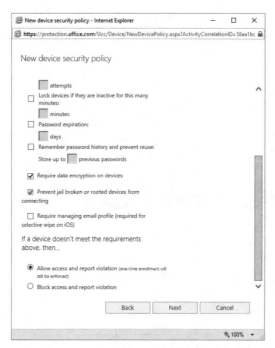

Figure 8-42 Second page of the New Device Security Policy Wizard

7. Configure any of the additional options shown in Figure 8-43 and click **Next**.

Figure 8-43 Third page of the New Device Security Policy Wizard

8. Click the **Yes** button to specify a group to test the policy deployment against and then click the plus sign (**+)** to add a security group to test the policy against. Click **Next**. See Figure 8-44.

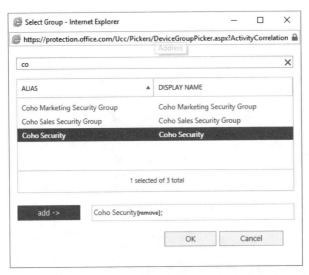

Figure 8-44 Selecting a group to apply the device security policy to

9. Confirm the settings shown in Figure 8-45 and click **Finish**.

Figure 8-45 Confirming device security policy settings

Device security policies

After you have activated Office 365 Mobile Device Management, the Device Security Policies page becomes available. Use this page to configure additional security policies or organization exclusions from MDM.

Organization-wide device access settings

On the Device Security Policies page, select **Manage Organization-Wide Device Access** settings.

Use the buttons shown in Figure 8-46 to allow MDM-compatible devices to connect to Office 365 or block them from connecting. You can also exclude certain groups from being managed through MDM policies.

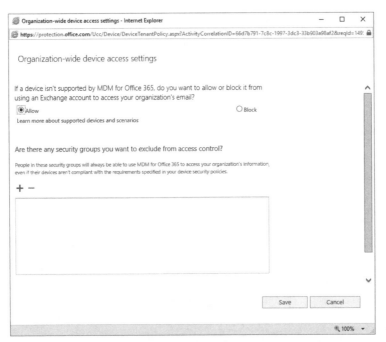

Figure 8-46 Organization-wide device access settings

INSIDE OUT

Effects of device security policies

Configuring device security policies has different effects on different devices. Table 8-2 lists some common settings and their related effects.

Table 8-2 Available device security policy options

Security Policy	Windows Phone 8.1+	Android 4+	Samsung Knox	IOS 6+	Notes
Require encrypted backup	✕	✕	✓	✓	IOS encrypted; backup required.
Block cloud backup	✕	✓	✓	✓	Block Google backup on Android (dimmed), iCloud backup on iOS.
Block document synchronization	✕	✕	✕	✓	iOS: Block documents in the cloud.

Security Policy	Windows Phone 8.1+	Android 4+	Samsung Knox	IOS 6+	Notes
Block photo synchronization	✕	✕	✕	✓	iOS (native): Block Photo Stream.
Block screen capture	✓	✕	✓	✓	Blocked when attempted.
Block video conference	✕	✕	✕	✓	FaceTime blocked on iOS; not Skype or others.
Block sending diagnostic data	✕	✕	✓	✓	Block sending Google crash report on Android.
Block access to app store	✓	✕	✓	✓	App store icon missing on Android home page, disabled on Windows, missing on iOS.
Require password for app store	✕	✕	✕	✓	iOS: Password required for iTunes purchases.
Block connection to removable storage	✓	✕	✓	N/A	Android: SD card is dimmed in settings, Windows notifies user, apps installed there are not available
Block Bluetooth connection	✓	*	*	✕	*Office 365 MDM cannot disable Bluetooth as a setting on Android. Instead, MDM disables all the transactions that require Bluetooth: Advanced Audio Distribution, Audio/Video Remote Control, hands-free devices, headset, Phone Book Access, and Serial Port. A small toast message appears at the bottom of the page when any of these is used.

CHAPTER 8

Blocking Exchange ActiveSync for unsupported devices

To secure your organization further, you can block Exchange ActiveSync access to Office 365 for mobile devices that Office 365 MDM does not support. When you are satisfied that your device security policy works, edit the policy to block access for devices not compatible with Office 365 MDM.

1. Navigate to **Data Loss Prevention | Device Security Policies** and select **Manage Organization-Wide Device Access Settings**.

2. Choose the **Block** button to prevent unsupported devices from accessing Office 365 and click **Save**.

List of managed devices

Clicking **View List Of Managed Devices** opens the Mobile Device Management page and displays the default view.

Data governance

The Data Governance section covers how to handle data over the life cycle of your data, from creation or ingestion through retention and deletion.

Dashboard

Launching the Data Governance dashboard, shown in Figure 8-47, presents several options to learn about data governance concepts, topics, and tasks.

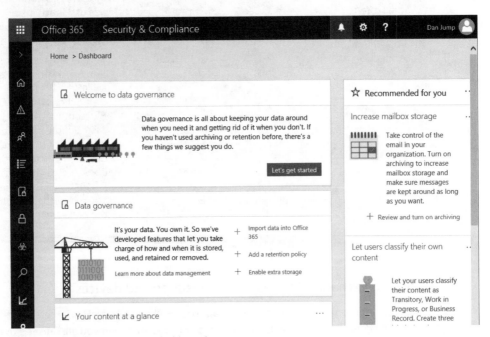

Figure 8-47 Data Governance dashboard

Import

The **Data Governance | Import** page, shown in Figure 8-48, is a dashboard for import tasks that you have configured to import your organization's PST files into Office 365. Office 365 supports two types of import tasks—network upload and drive shipping.

Drive shipping requires you to purchase hard drives, create a mapping file that describes which PST is to be imported into which mailbox or archive, copy the PSTs to the hard drives, and encrypt the drives with BitLocker and then send the drives by courier to an Office 365 data center for upload to an Azure storage blob by Office 365 support personnel.

Network upload requires you to upload all the PSTs to import to an Azure shared access signatures (SAS) storage blob where Office 365 can access them and create a mapping file that associates the PSTs with the user mailboxes or archives.

In either case, PSTs can be imported into user primary mailboxes, archive mailboxes, or inactive mailboxes. After PST files are imported to an Office 365 mailbox, the Retention Hold setting for the mailbox is turned on for an indefinite duration, and the retention policy assigned to the mailbox won't be processed until you turn off the retention hold or set a date to turn off the hold to ensure that the mailbox owner or administrator has time to configure appropriate retention settings for the mailbox.

Figure 8-48 Import service dashboard

PREPARING FOR PST IMPORT

Before starting the import process, gather your PSTs to a central location, such as a file share on a server. If you are planning to perform a network upload, it would be best if that server has access to the Internet so you can run the upload directly from it. If PSTs are in use in your network, you might need to use a script to disconnect them from Outlook before copying them. For a sample script, see *https://gallery.technet.microsoft.com/Disconnect -PSTs-from-939d7a5f.*

Network import

The network import process requires you to stage your data on an Azure storage blob, create a mapping file to associate the content with users, and then create an import job responsible for importing the content.

Generate a SAS URL and install AzCopy.

1. Log on to the Security & Compliance Center by using an account that has the Organization Management permission (such as a global administrator) in the Security & Compliance Center as well as the Exchange Online Mailbox Import Export role, and navigate to **Data Governance | Import**. For best performance, perform these tasks on the file server where the PSTs are currently stored.

2. On the Import page, click **+ New Import Job**.

3. Type a name for the import job and click **Next**.

   Note that the import job name cannot have uppercase letters or spaces.

4. Click the **Upload Your Data** button, as shown in Figure 8-49, to select the network import job type and click **Next**.

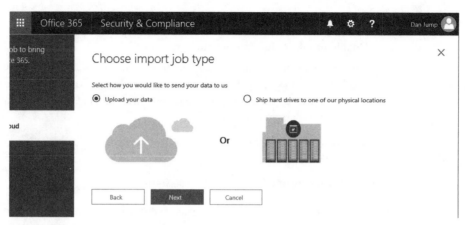

Figure 8-49 Choosing the import job type

5. Click **Show Network Upload SAS URL,** copy the displayed URL, and save it to a text file for later. See Figure 8-50.

Figure 8-50 Copying the SAS URL to the clipboard and saving it to a text file for later

6. If you don't already have it installed, download the Azure AzCopy tool from the link provided on the page and install it to the default location. (The AzCopy tool requires 64-bit Windows.)

7. Cancel the upload wizard.

    You restart the wizard after staging and preparing the files.

TROUBLESHOOTING

Unable to select New Import Button

The **+ New Import Job** button does not appear until you have granted your account the Mailbox Import Export Role (even if you are already a global admin) in the Exchange Administrative Center or through Windows PowerShell. In Exchange Online PowerShell, run the following cmdlet.

```
New-ManagementRoleAssignment -Role "Mailbox Import Export" -Name "PST Import"
-User <identity>
```

To copy PSTs to Microsoft Azure, follow these steps.

1. Launch a command prompt on the computer where you have installed the AzCopy tool and change to the directory where AzCopy is installed. (The default location is %ProgramFiles(x86)%\Microsoft SDKs\Azure\AzCopy.)

2. Run the following command to upload the PST files to Office 365. See Figure 8-51.

   ```
   AzCopy.exe /Source:<location of PST files> /Dest:<SAS URL> /V:<Log file location>
   ```

   For example, if you have saved the PSTs in D:\PSTs on the computer from where you're running AzCopy.exe and want to save the log file to C:\LogFiles, the syntax would look like this:

   ```
   AzCopy.exe /Source:D:\PSTs /Dest: "https://b9a17028e9174c9e92421bc.blob.core.win-
   dows.net/ingestiondata?sv=2012-02-12&se=2017-06-25T17%3A51%3A31Z&sr=c&si=Ingestion
   SasForAzCopy201705261751288693&sig=SqVSSykF09Yyww2p4g2TMJmsrvmgTcCRxZfVY2mMezw%3D"
   /V:C:\Logfiles\AzCopyUpload.log
   ```

   If you are accessing the PSTs through the remote share PSTs on the server FILESERVER, the syntax would look this:

   ```
   AzCopy.exe /Source:\\FILESERVER\PSTs /Dest: "https://b9a17028e9174c9e92421bc.blob.
   core.windows.net/ingestiondata?sv=2012-02-12&se=2017-06-25T17%3A51%3A31Z&sr=c&si=
   IngestionSasForAzCopy201705261751288693&sig=SqVSSykF09Yyww2p4g2TMJmsrvmgTcCRxZfVY-
   2mMezw%3D" /V:C:\Logfiles\AzCopyUpload.log
   ```

Figure 8-51 Copying files to Azure SAS URL with AzCopy

The PST import file is used to assign the uploaded PSTs to users. To prepare the PST Import mapping file, follow these steps.

1. Download a copy of the PST import mapping file from *https://go.microsoft.com/fwlink /p/?LinkId=544717*. Alternatively, create a CSV file with the following columns:

   Workload,FilePath,Name,Mailbox,IsArchive,TargetRootFolder,ContentCodePage,SPFileCo ntainer,SPManifestContainer,SPSiteUrl

2. Modify the PST import file, creating one line per PST that you uploaded. Use the information in Table 8-3 to populate the CSV appropriately and save it to a directory on your computer.

Table 8-3 CSV template parameter values

Parameter	Description	Example
Workload	Specifies the Office 365 service that data will be imported to. To import PST files to user mailboxes, use Exchange.	Exchange
FilePath	Specifies the folder location in the Azure storage location where PST files are uploaded.	
Name	Specifies the name of the PST file that will be imported into the user mailbox. This value is case-sensitive.	danjump.pst
Mailbox	Specifies the email address of the mailbox that the PST will be imported into. If the destination is an inactive mailbox, you must specify the mailbox GUID of the inactive mailbox.	danjump@cohovineyardan- dwinery.com or 0ba887ee-f7a5-4765-8a40- 9a787193fccc
IsArchive	Specifies whether the target mailbox is primary or archive. TRUE is archive, FALSE is primary mailbox.	FALSE or TRUE
TargetRootFolder	Specifies where in the target mailbox to import data. If left blank, items will be imported from the PST to a new folder called ImportedPST at the root level of the mailbox. If you specify / , then items will be imported into the user's inbox folder. If you specify /<foldername>, items will be imported into a new folder named <foldername>.	<blank> / /foldername

Parameter	Description	Example
ContentCodepage	Optional parameter to specify numeric value for codepage to use for importing PSTs in the ANSI file format. This is used for importing PSTs from Chinese, Japanese, and Korean sources because these languages typically use double-byte character sets.	See Code Page Identifiers at *https://msdn.microsoft.com /en-us/library/window s/desktop/dd317756(v=vs.85). aspx* for values that can be used.
SPFileContainer	For PST Import, leave this field blank.	Not applicable
SPManifestCon-tainer	For PST Import, leave this field blank.	Not applicable
SPSiteURL	For PST Import, leave this field blank.	Not applicable

A sample PST Import mapping file might look like the example in Figure 8-52.

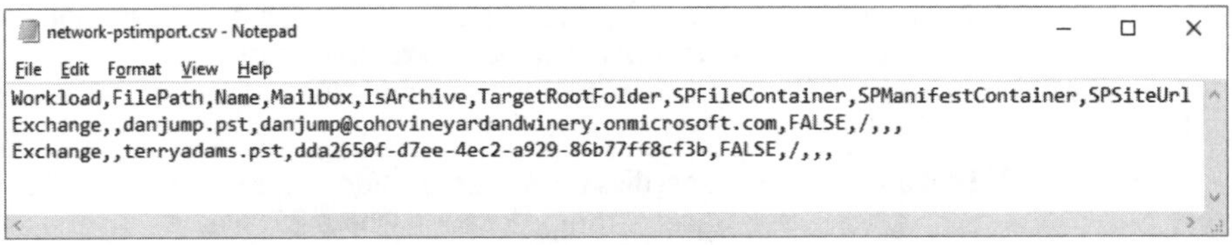

Figure 8-52 PST import mapping file for network upload

To create the import job, follow these steps.

1. Navigate to **Security & Compliance Center | Data Governance | Import** and click **+ New Import Job**.

2. Type a name for the job and click **Next**.

3. Choose the **Upload Your Data** button and click **Next**.

4. Select both check boxes on the page to indicate that you have finished uploading files and have created the mapping file, click the **Show Network Upload SAS URL** link, and then click **Next**. See Figure 8-53.

Figure 8-53 Continuing the PST upload process

If you don't click Show Network Upload SAS URL, you get an error when clicking Next, stating that you need to fill out all fields.

5. Click **+ Select Mapping File** and browse to the mapping file you have created.

6. Click **Validate** to check for errors in the CSV.

7. Select the check box to agree to terms of service and click **Save**. See Figure 8-54.

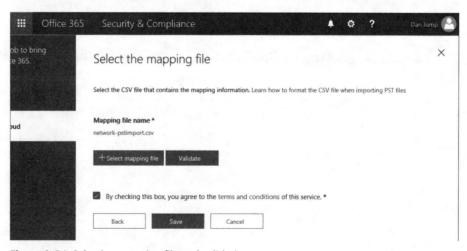

Figure 8-54 Selecting mapping file and validating

8. Click **Close** and view the informational fly-out, shown in Figure 8-55, that shows the status of the import. Click **Close** after you have reviewed the information.

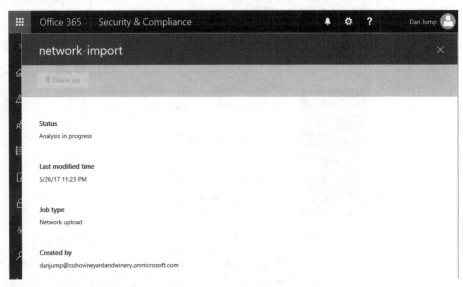

Figure 8-55 Network upload informational fly-out

9. Monitor the status of the analysis on the **Data Governance | Import** page.

10. After analysis has completed, click the **Ready To Import To Office 365 link shown in Figure 8-56**.

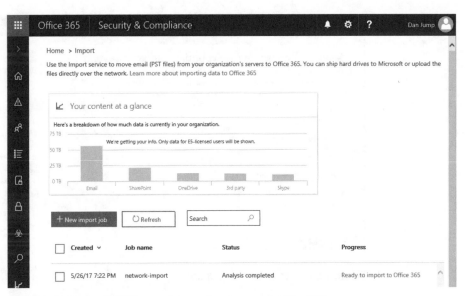

Figure 8-56 Network PST import job ready to import to Office 365

11. Click the **Import To Office 365 button shown in Figure 8-57**.

Figure 8-57 Beginning the import to Office 365

12. Choose whether to filter the import (Figure 8-58). If you select the **Yes** button, clicking **Next** opens the filtering criteria page. If you select the **No** button, clicking **Next** opens the final confirmation.

If you choose to filter the data, you are presented with options to select the types of data to import and exclude content based on date or senders.

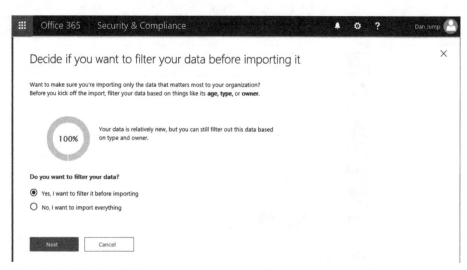

Figure 8-58 Choosing filtering option

13. Click **More Filtering Options** to see the additional filtering criteria shown in Figure 8-59.

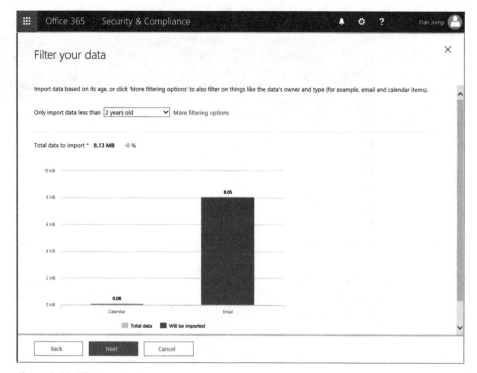

Figure 8-59 Filter Your Data page

14. Review, set any additional filtering options, and click **Apply**. See Figure 8-60.

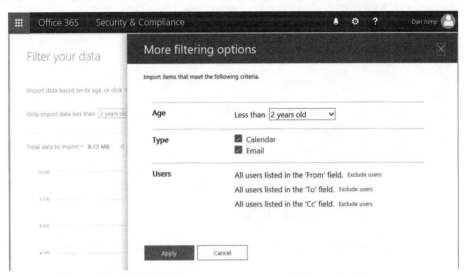

Figure 8-60 More filtering options

15. If you are filtering data, complete your filtering selections and click Next.

One of two screens appears based on whether you chose to filter data. Figure 8-61 shows the result of choosing to filter data.

Figure 8-61 Import data page if no filtering was selected

If you choose not to filter data, the Review Your Filter Settings page appears, as shown in Figure 8-62, showing the result of choosing not to filter data.

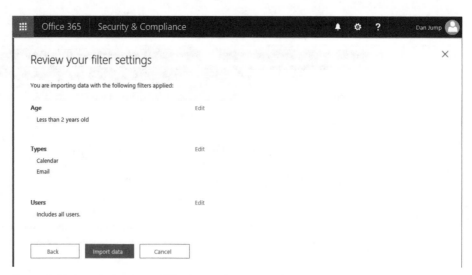

Figure 8-62 Import data page if filtering options were selected

16. Click **Import Data**.

17. Click **Close** on the confirmation page, shown in Figure 8-63.

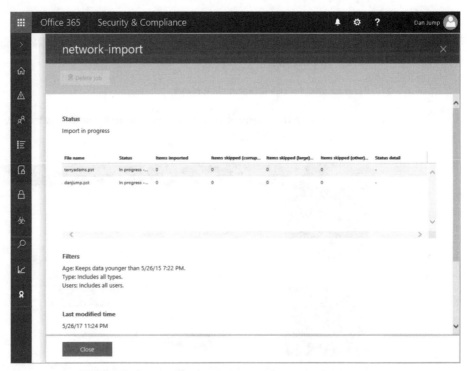

Figure 8-63 Import batch confirmation page

18. You can monitor the import progress by selecting the import job on the **Data Governance | Import** page.

After the import job has completed, the mailboxes are configured with the Retention-HoldEnabled parameter. When you are certain that your retention policies are correct and want to enable the processing of retention policies on the mailbox, you can connect the Office 365 Exchange Online PowerShell endpoint and run this cmdlet on the mailboxes with retention hold enabled:

```
Set-Mailbox -Identity -RetentionHoldEnabled $false
```

Drive shipping

If you have a large volume of data to import, you can use a drive shipping import job to ingest your data into Office 365. The overall process is very similar to the Network Import method, except that you are staging data on physical hard drives instead of in an Azure storage blob.

To use drive shipping, you need to prepare the hard drives, and you must use internal SATA or SAS hard drives for drive shipping. External USB hard drives are not accepted.

To download the PST import tool and secure storage key, follow these steps.

1. From the Security & Compliance Center, navigate to **Data Governance | Import** and click **+ New Import Job**.

2. Type a name for the job and click **Next**.

3. Select the **Ship Hard Drives To One Of Our Physical Locations** button, shown in Figure 8-64, and click **Next**.

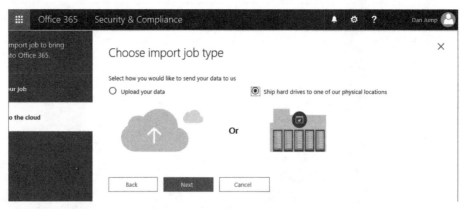

Figure 8-64 Choose Import Job Type page for drive shipping

4. Click **Copy The Drive Shipping Key** and then copy the value and save it in a text file.

5. Click **Download Tool**, shown in Figure 8-65, to download the Azure Import/Export tool.

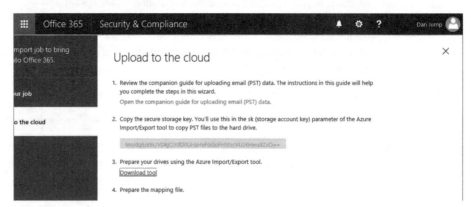

Figure 8-65 Upload To The Cloud page for drive shipping

6. Cancel the wizard because you restart the wizard after the hard drives are staged and the PST import mapping file has been created.

To copy the PST files to the hard drive, follow these steps.

1. Extract the downloaded WaImportExportV1.zip file to a directory on your computer.

2. Open an elevated command prompt on the computer to which the WaImportExportV1. zip was downloaded and extracted and change to the directory to which the WaImportExportV1.zip file was extracted.

3. Run the following command to prepare the first hard drive and copy the PST files to it. See Figure 8-66.

```
WAImportExport.exe PrepImport /j:<Name of journal file> /t:<Drive letter> /
id:<Name of session> /srcdir:<Location of PST files> /dstdir:<PST file path> /
sk:<Storage account key> /encrypt /logdir:<Log file location>
```

For example, if your hard drive is mounted as Drive D and the PSTs are stored in the C:\ PSTs local path, and you want to save the log file to C:\Logging, the syntax would look like the following:

```
WAImportExport.exe PrepImport /j:DriveShip1.jrn /t:D /id:driveship1 /srcdir:C:\
PSTs /dstdir:"ingestiondata/" /sk:"zbNIIs2Uy7g25Yoak+LlSHfqVBGOeNwjqtBEBGqRMoidq6/
e5k/VPkjOXdDIXJHxHvNoNoFH5NcVUJXHwu9ZxQ==" /encrypt /logdir:c:\Logging
```

Figure 8-66 Running the WAImportExport tool to prepare the hard drives

4. WAImportExport.exe spawns a new window. Read the contents and press any key to continue or Ctrl-C to cancel if your hard drive does not meet the requirements. See Figure 8-67.

CHAPTER 8

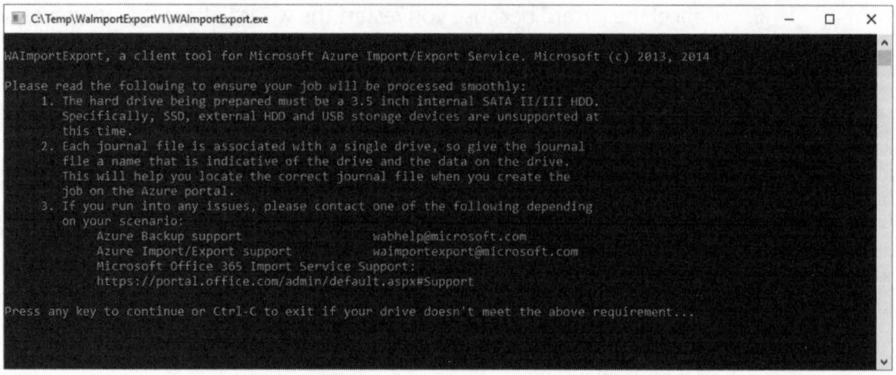

Figure 8-67 Confirming running the WAImportExport tool to prepare the hard drives

5. Depending on your system configuration, you might see an additional prompt for the 8dot3 file name creation. Type **Yes** to let the tool disable it and continue. See Figure 8-68.

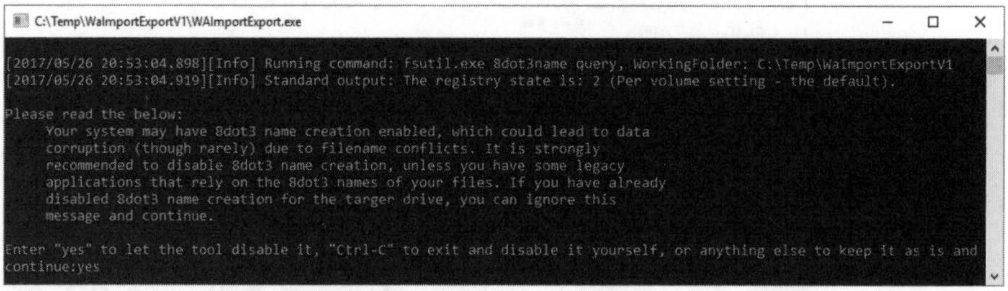

Figure 8-68 Confirming disabling of 8dot3 file naming

6. When the process completes, a command prompt is returned. See Figure 8-69.

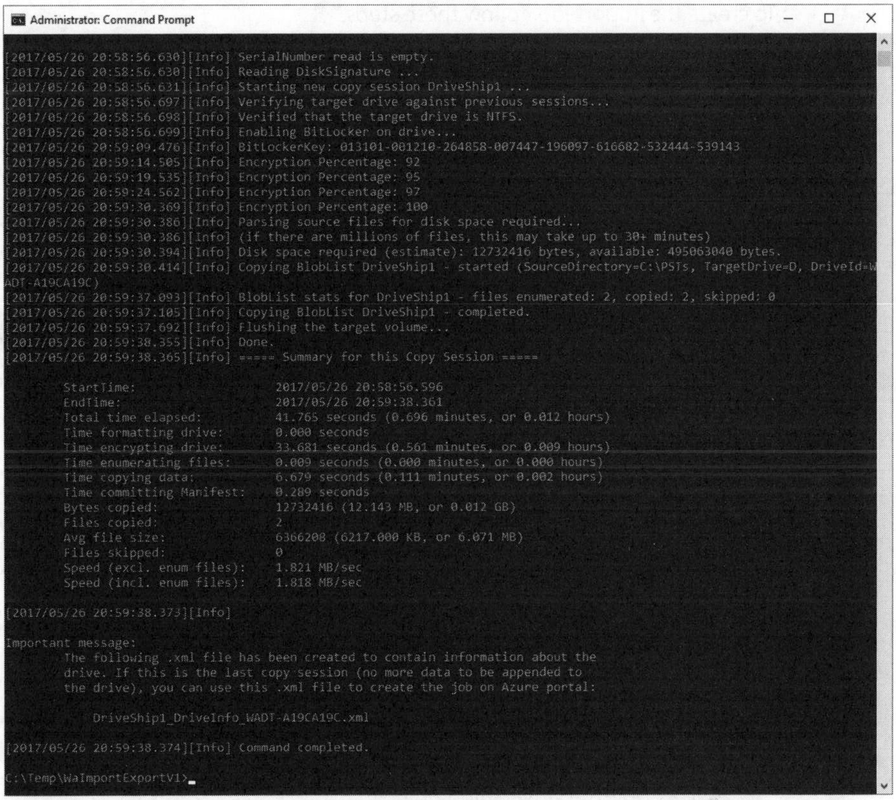

Figure 8-69 WAImportExportTool completes drive encryption and copies data to drive

7. For subsequent copies to the same hard drive, update the /id: parameter with a new session ID and leave the journal name the same. The WAImportExport process appends to the existing journal file. If you start using a new hard drive, update the Journal parameter (/j:) with a new journal file name and a new session ID (/id:) value.

You use the PST import file to assign PSTs to users. To prepare the PST Import mapping file, follow these steps.

1. Download a copy of the PST import mapping file from *https://go.microsoft.com/fwlink /p/?LinkId=544717*. Alternatively, create a CSV file with the following columns:

   Workload,FilePath,Name,Mailbox,IsArchive,TargetRootFolder,ContentCodePage,SPFileCo ntainer,SPManifestContainer,SPSiteUrl

2. Modify the PST import file, creating one line per PST that was uploaded. Refer to Table 8-3 for the parameters and examples.

To create the import job, follow these steps.

1. From the Security & Compliance Center, navigate to **Data Governance | Import** and click **+ New Import Job**.

2. Type a name for the job and click **Next**.

3. Select the Ship Hard Drives To One Of Our Physical Locations button, as shown in Figure 8-70, and click Next.

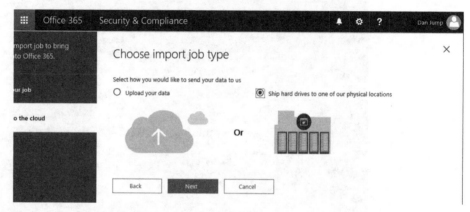

Figure 8-70 Choosing import job type for drive shipping

4. Click Copy The Drive Shipping Key.

    If you do not click the Copy The Drive Shipping Key link, an error states that not all of the fields are populated.

5. Select the check boxes to indicate you have prepared the hard drives, the journal files, and the PST Import mapping file and click **Next**. See Figure 8-71.

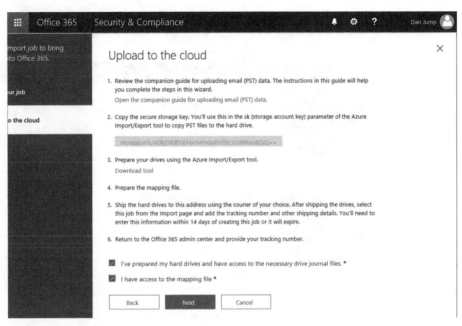

Figure 8-71 Upload To The Cloud drive shipping page

6. On the Select The Drive File page, click **+ Select Drive File** and select the journal file that was specified with the /j: parameter. Click **Validate** to check the file for issues. Upload a journal file for each hard drive being shipped. See Figure 8-72.

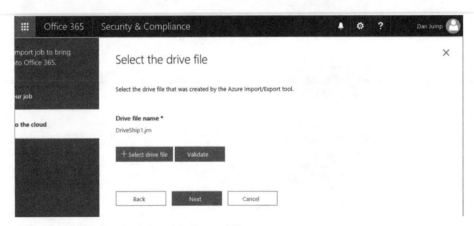

Figure 8-72 Select and validate drive journal file

7. Click **Next**.

8. Click **+ Select Mapping File** and select the mapping file created earlier. Click **Validate**, check for syntax errors (Figure 8-73), and then click **Next**.

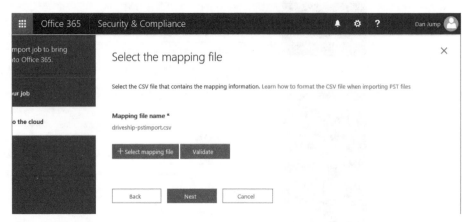

Figure 8-73 Select and validate PST import mapping file

9. Type contact information, as shown in Figure 8-74, select the check box agreeing to the terms of the Azure Import Service, and click **Save**.

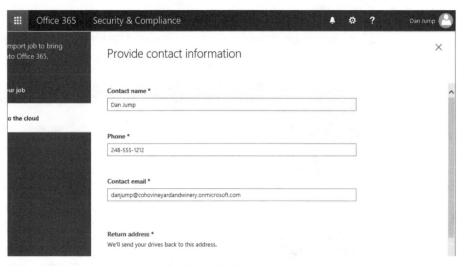

Figure 8-74 Contact information for drive shipping

10. Click **Close** to dismiss the page.

11. When you have a tracking number for the shipment, edit the import job and click **Enter Tracking Number**, fill out the carrier, tracking number, and your return shipping account number and click **Save**. See Figure 8-75.

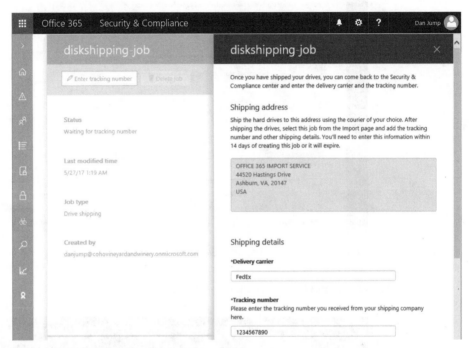

Figure 8-75 Diskshipping-job details dialog box

After Microsoft receives your drives, data center personnel begin importing your data into the Azure storage space, and the status on the Import page updates to Import In-Progress.

After all PSTs have been imported, the status changes to Analysis In Progress to identify the age and types of items contained in the PST.

After the analysis is complete, the status is updated to Analysis Complete, and the progress area says Ready To Import To Office 365.

12. Click **Ready To Import To Office 365**, as shown in Figure 8-76.

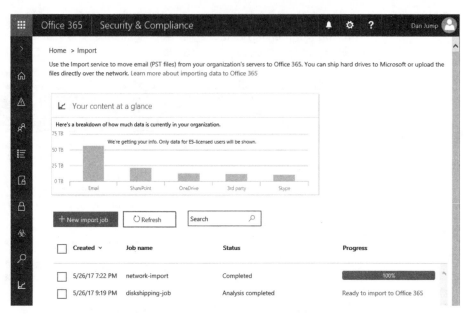

Figure 8-76 Ready to import drive shipping job

13. Click **Import To Office 365**. See Figure 8-77.

Figure 8-77 Beginning drive shipping import

14. Choose whether to filter the import. If you select **Yes**, click **Next** to open the filtering criteria page. If you select **No**, click **Next** to open the final confirmation. See Figure 8-78.

Figure 8-78 Choosing the filtering option

15. If you choose to filter the data, you are presented with options to select types of data to import and exclude content based on date or senders. Click **More Filtering Options** to see the additional filtering criteria shown in Figure 8-79.

Figure 8-79 Filter Your Data page

16. Review and set any additional filtering options and click **Apply**. See Figure 8-80.

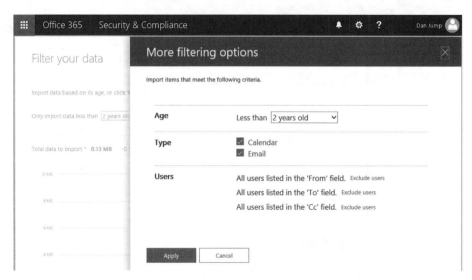

Figure 8-80 More Filtering Options dialog box

17. If you are filtering data, complete your filtering selections and click **Next**.

One of two screens appears, based on whether you chose to filter data. If you chose not to filter, you see the page in Figure 8-81.

Figure 8-81 Import data page if no filtering was selected

If you chose to filter data, you see the page shown in Figure 8-82.

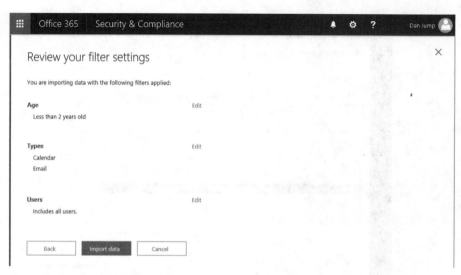

Figure 8-82 Import data page if filtering options were selected

18. Click **Import Data**.

19. Click **Close** on the confirmation page.

20. Monitor the import progress by selecting the import job on the **Data Governance | Import** page, if desired.

    After the import job has completed, the mailboxes are configured with the Retention-HoldEnabled parameter.

21. When you are certain that your retention policies are correct and want to enable the processing of retention policies on the mailbox, you can connect the Office 365 Exchange Online PowerShell endpoint and run this cmdlet on the mailboxes with retention hold enabled.

    ```
    Set-Mailbox -Identity -RetentionHoldEnabled $false
    ```

Archive

Archive mailboxes provide additional storage to users with Exchange Online Plan 2 or Exchange Online Archiving licenses applied to them. If a user has an archive mailbox enabled, content older than 2 years old is automatically moved from the primary mailbox to the archive mailbox if no other policies are configured. Figure 8-83 shows the Archive page.

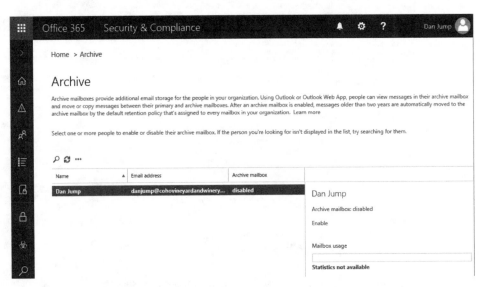

Figure 8-83 Archive page

To enable archives for individual users, follow these steps.

1. On the **Data Governance | Archive** page, select the user for whom you want to enable an archive mailbox. Click Enable.

2. Click **Yes** to enable the archive. See Figure 8-84.

Figure 8-84 Enabling the archive for a user

Archive mailboxes can be enabled for all users from the dashboard in the Security & Compliance Center. To enable archives for all users, follow these steps.

1. In the Security & Compliance dashboard, as shown in Figure 8-85, select **Online Archive Mailbox** from the list of widgets and then select **Manage**.

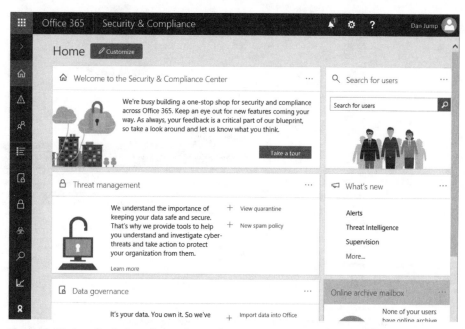

Figure 8-85 Security & Compliance Center dashboard with Online Archive Mailbox highlighted

2. Click **Enable Archives**. See Figure 8-86.

Figure 8-86 Enabling archives for users

3. Alternatively, from a Windows PowerShell session connected to an Exchange Online session, run:

```
Get-Mailbox -ResultSize Unlimited | Enable-Mailbox -Archive
```

Retention

Retention policies are programmatic ways to manage or govern the accumulation, retention, and deletion of content. Depending on your organization's industry, you might find that you need one or more retention policies configured to:

- Comply proactively with industry regulations and internal policies that require you to retain content for a minimum period of time—for example, the Sarbanes-Oxley Act might require you to retain certain types of content for seven years. In other regulated industries, you might need to retain certain documents pertaining to consumer data for up to 30 years.

- Reduce your exposure in the event of litigation or a security breach by permanently deleting old content that you're no longer required to keep. Your organization's legal team might have policies to reduce the amount of data you store and manage organizationally to reduce the scope of data that could be discovered in a lawsuit.

Retention policies in Office 365 can help you by retaining content so it can't be permanently deleted before a specified period or by deleting content permanently at the end of a retention period to manage the data life cycle.

Office 365 retention policies enable you to create rules to retain; delete; or retain and delete content based on time frames, locations, or search criteria. You can deploy policies to cover certain data sources (such as Skype, Exchange, or SharePoint) or just certain types of data, based on keywords or specific sensitive information types.

Some highly regulated industries might require compliance with Securities and Exchange Commission (SEC) Rule 17aa-4, which requires that after a retention policy is enabled, it cannot be disabled or made less restrictive. By using the Preservation Lock feature of a retention policy, you can ensure that no one can turn off the policy.

RETENTION POLICIES IN EXCHANGE ONLINE

To apply retention policies to Exchange Online content, mailboxes must be configured with an Exchange Online Plan 2 license or an Exchange Online Plan 1 license with the Exchange Online Archiving add-on license.

Overview of retention policies for content types

When you include a location such as a SharePoint site or mailbox in a retention policy, the content remains in its original location. Users can continue to work with their documents or mail. If the user edits or deletes content that's covered in the policy, a copy of the content as it existed when you applied the policy is retained.

For sites, a copy of the original content is retained in the Preservation Hold library when users edit or delete it. If the Preservation Hold library doesn't exist for the site when a retention policy is enabled, a new Preservation Hold library is created. The Preservation Hold library is only visible to the site collection administrator.

If the content being protected is modified or deleted during the retention period, a copy of the original content as it existed when the retention policy was assigned is created in the Preservation Hold library. There, a timer job runs periodically and identifies items whose retention period has expired, and these items are permanently deleted within seven days of the end of the retention period.

If the content is not modified or deleted during the retention period, it's moved to the first-stage Recycle Bin at the end of the retention period. If a user deletes the content from there or purges this Recycle Bin, the document is moved to the second-stage Recycle Bin. A 93-day retention period spans both recycle bins. At the end of 93 days, the document is permanently deleted from wherever it resides, in either the first- or second-stage Recycle Bin.

For a retention policy to maintain copies of versions of documents in a site or library, versioning must be turned on for the site or library. If a document is deleted from a site that's being retained and document versioning is turned on for the library, all versions of the deleted document are retained.

If document versioning isn't turned on and an item is subject to several retention policies, the version that's retained is the one that's current when each retention policy takes effect. For example, a document named Doc1.docx dated June 1 exists in a site when the first retention policy is applied to a site. Doc1.docx has been edited several times since the initial retention policy was applied. On July 1, a new retention policy is applied to the same site, and the July 1 version of Doc1.docx is also preserved.

A retention policy can retain content either indefinitely or for a specific period of time. For content to be retained for a specific period, the retention policy can be configured to retain the data based on when it was created or last modified. A retention policy can also delete the content at the end of the retention period. Finally, a retention policy can simply delete old content without having a requirement to retain it for a period of time.

For mailboxes and public folders, the copy is retained in the Recoverable Items folder. These secure locations and the retained content are not visible to users. In the case of a mailbox, the Recoverable Items folder is at the mailbox level. For Public Folders, the Recoverable Items folder is per-folder. Only users who have been granted the eDiscovery role have access to the Recoverable Items folder.

By default, when a user deletes a message in a folder other than the Deleted Items folder, the message is moved to the Deleted Items folder. When a user deletes an item in the Deleted Items folder, the message is moved to the Recoverable Items folder. If the user deletes an item by using Shift+Delete in any other folder, the item is moved directly to the Recoverable Items folder. Content in the Recoverable Items folder is retained for 14 days by default (and can be extended up to 30). At the end of the Recoverable Items retention period, the content is purged permanently unless a retention policy is configured to retain the content for longer.

If a mailbox is deleted or the license removed while governed by a retention policy, or is on Litigation Hold, the mailbox becomes an inactive mailbox. The contents of an inactive mailbox are still subject to any retention policy that was placed on the mailbox before it was made inactive, and the contents are available in an eDiscovery search to users with the eDiscovery role.

Creating a policy

Consider the following requirements.

- You need to preserve content for a minimum of 3 years from when it's created across all data sources and repositories in Office 365.

- Content can be optionally retained for up to 5 years but must be purged after that.

To achieve these business requirements, you must create two policies—one to preserve content for 3 years from when it's created and one to delete content older than 5 years.

1. In the Security & Compliance Center, click Data Governance and select **Retention**.

2. On the Retention page, shown in Figure 8-87, click **+ Create**.

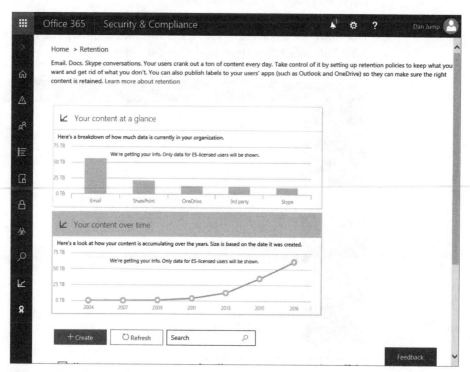

Figure 8-87 Retention dashboard

3. Type a name and description for your 3-year retention policy and click **Next**. See Figure 8-88.

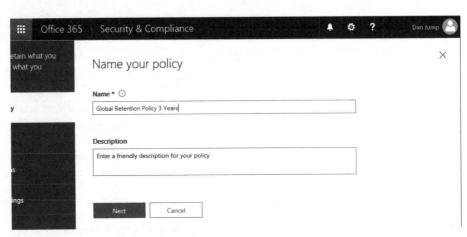

Figure 8-88 Naming the retention policy

4. Type the retention period of 3 years and select **No** under *Do You Want Us To Delete It After This Time?* Click **Next**. See Figure 8-89.

Figure 8-89 Retain content options

5. Select **All Locations. Includes Content In Exchange Email And Public Folders, Office 365 Groups, And OneDrive And SharePoint Documents** button and click **Next**. See Figure 8-90.

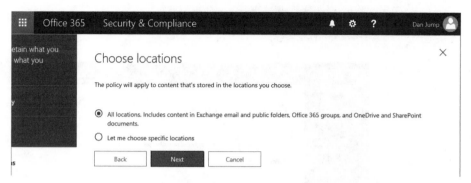

Figure 8-90 Choose locations to include in retention policy

6.   Ensure that the **Don't Turn On Preservation Lock** button, shown in Figure 8-91, is selected and click **Next**.

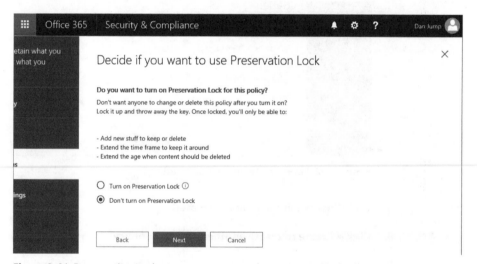

Figure 8-91 Preservation Lock

PRESERVATION LOCK

Preservation Lock is intended to help organizations comply with SEC Rule 17a-4. It's disabled by default. If you enable Preservation Lock for a policy, you cannot ever remove the policy or modify it, except to extend the retention period. Content that the policy applies to cannot be removed until the retention period expires.

7. Review the settings for the retention policy, as shown in Figure 8-92, and click **Create This Policy**.

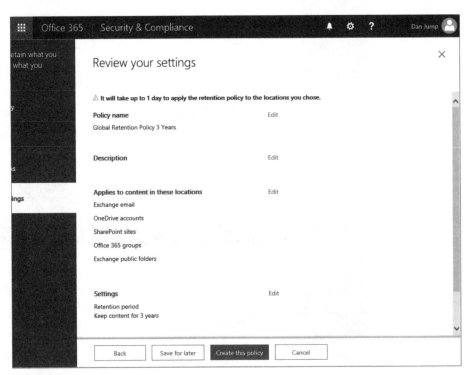

Figure 8-92 Reviewing retention policy settings

8. Click **Close when the policy is created**.

9. Click + **Create to create another retention policy**.

10. Type a name and description for the Delete After 5 Years policy and click **Next**.

11. Select the **No, Just Delete Content That's Older Than** button and configure the setting to reflect 5 years. Click **Next**. See Figure 8-93.

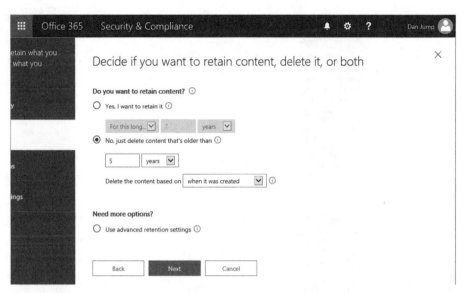

Figure 8-93 Configuring retention settings

12. Select the **All Locations** button and click **Next**.

13. Ensure that **Don't Turn On Preservation Lock** is selected and click **Next**.

14. Confirm the settings and click **Create This Policy**. See Figure 8-94.

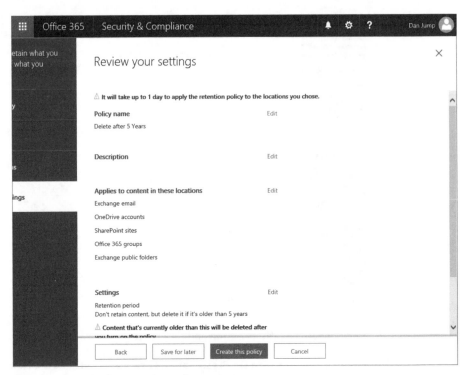

Figure 8-94 Reviewing retention policy settings

15. Click Close.

INSIDE OUT

Labels or retention policies

On the surface, labels and retention show a lot of overlap. Both can be used to manage data, and both can be automatically applied to content. So, which should you use?

Use labels when:

- You want to be able to categorize data automatically.
- You want users to be able to categorize data in Outlook, OneDrive, or SharePoint.

Use retention policies when:

- You want or need to layer multiple retention and deletion policies on top of one another.
- You have SEC 17a-4 requirements for data preservation policies.

- You need to apply retention policies automatically to all content types in Office 365, including Exchange Online mailboxes and public folders, Skype, Office 365 groups, SharePoint, and OneDrive content.

Labels cannot be configured to auto-apply across all content in email—they can only be automatically applied to content matching keywords or sensitive data types. In addition, labels do not apply to Exchange Online public folders.

Labels and retention policies can be used in conjunction with one another. For example, you could have a retention policy that retains for 3 years and then deletes data but also publish a label that enables users to keep data for up to 10 years by manually applying it to content. Depending on your organization's compliance requirements and direction from the legal team, you might need to limit the ability of users to retain data beyond the periods established by policy.

Supervision

You can configure supervision policies to capture employee communications for examination by internal or external reviewers. Some highly regulated industries might require auditing of communications.

Preparing to configure supervision policies

Before configuring supervision policies, identify users or groups of users whose communication must be reviewed, as well as users or groups of users who will perform the reviewing.

You also might need to add yourself to the Supervisory Review role group to be able to create policies. To do this, from the Security & Compliance Center, point to Permissions, select Permissions, and then edit the membership of the Supervisory Review group.

To configure a supervision policy, follow these steps.

1. From the Security & Compliance Center, navigate to **Data Governance | Supervision**. See Figure 8-95.

CHAPTER 8

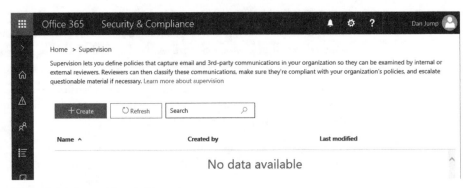

Figure 8-95 Supervision dashboard

2.   Click + **Create**.

3.   Type a name and description for the policy and click **Next**.

4.   Select the users or groups to supervise and click **Next**. Type users or groups in the Exclude These Users box to prevent their mail from being captured for review. See Figure 8-96.

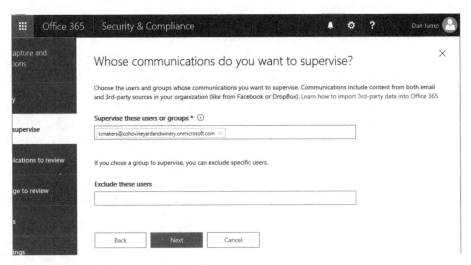

Figure 8-96 Configuring users to supervise

5.   Specify review criteria. In addition to Inbound and Outbound, you can filter content based on keywords, message size, or the presence of attachments. After you've selected criteria (Figure 8-97), click **Next**.

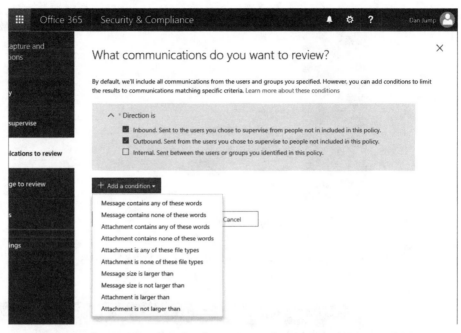

Figure 8-97 Configuring direction of mail to review and additional selection conditions

6. Choose what percentage of content to review and click **Next**. See Figure 8-98.

Figure 8-98 Configuring percentage of communications to review

7. Choose users or groups who should review the communications from the picker, shown in Figure 8-99, and click **Next**.

Figure 8-99 Choosing reviewers

8. Review settings, shown in Figure 8-100, and click **Finish** to complete the supervision policy configuration.

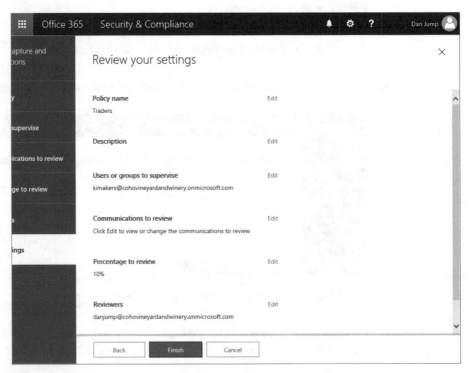

Figure 8-100 Review Your Settings page for supervision policy settings

Reviewing supervised content

After a supervision policy has been configured, reviewers can monitor and review the communications through either Outlook Web App or the Outlook desktop application.

Outlook Web App

A special mailbox is automatically mounted, and the Supervision add-in for Outlook Web App is automatically configured in a supervisor's Outlook Web App mailbox.

After the add-in has loaded into the mailbox, reviewers can mark messages as compliant, non-compliant, questionable, resolved, or not reviewed by clicking the message and then clicking the **Supervisory Review** add-in link inside the message, as shown in Figure 8-101.

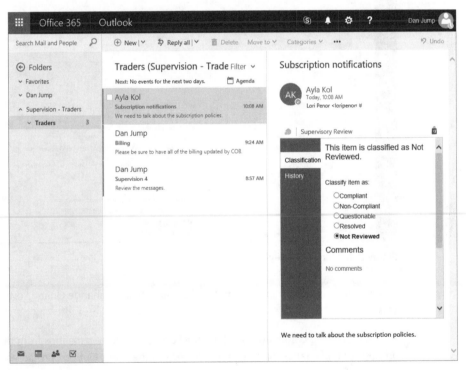

Figure 8-101 Supervisory review in Outlook Web App

Outlook desktop

To connect to the supervisory review mailbox in Outlook, the mailbox must at least be temporarily unhidden from the global address list so reviewers can add the mailbox to their Outlook profile.

1. From the Security & Compliance Center, navigate to Data Governance | Supervision and click a supervision policy to open the policy dialog box.

2. Under Supervision Mailbox, select the email address displayed for the policy's supervision mailbox and copy it. See Figure 8-102.

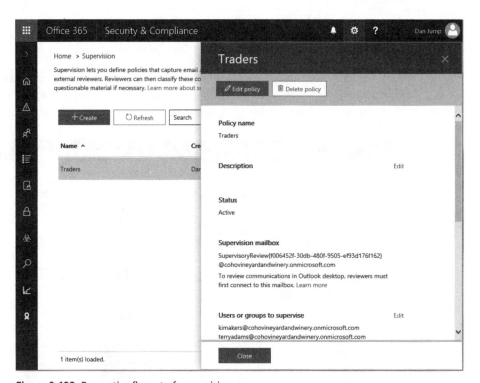

Figure 8-102 Properties fly-out of supervision group

3. Open a Windows PowerShell prompt and connect to an Exchange Online PowerShell session.

4. Run the following command to unhide the SupervisoryReview mailbox from the global address list and enable you to add the mailbox to the user's Outlook profile, as shown in Figure 8-103.

```
Set-Mailbox -identity "SupervisoryReview{guid}@domain.com" -HiddenFromAddressList-
sEnabled $False
```

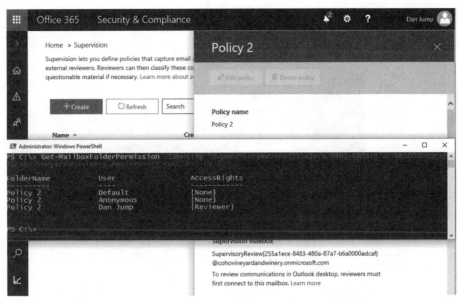

Figure 8-103 Viewing folder permissions on the SupervisoryReview mailbox

INSIDE OUT

Supervisory Review mailbox

The Supervisory Review mailbox is a special mailbox that is hidden from users, including the administrators. However, you can still perform some activities against it if you know how.

To expose the mailbox so Outlook can mount it, it must be unhidden from the global address list. Other commands that work against the mailbox include Set-MailboxPermission, Get-MailboxFolderPermission, and Set-MailboxFolderPermission.

For each supervision policy you create, a new SupervisoryReview{guid} mailbox is created, a corresponding folder named for the policy is created inside that mailbox, and the reviewer is given Reviewer permissions to the mailbox.

For example, if you create a policy named Policy 2 in the Security & Compliance Center and assign the user Dan Jump as the reviewer, you can verify the permissions on the folder with the Get-MailboxFolderPermission cmdlet.

5. From the user's Outlook profile, select **File from the Outlook ribbon and then click +
    Add Account**. See Figure 8-104.

Figure 8-104 Outlook File menu

6. In the Add Account Wizard, select the **Manual Setup Or Additional Server Types** button, shown in Figure 8-105, and click **Next**.

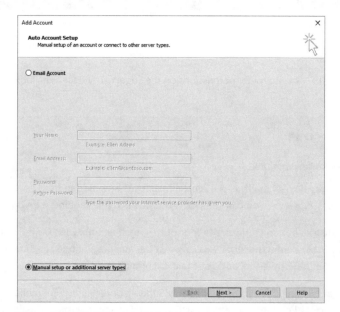

Figure 8-105 Add Account Wizard

7. Select the **Office 365** button, paste the email address of the SupervisoryReview mailbox (SupervisiorReview{GUID}@domain.com) in the Email Address field, and click **Next**.

8. If prompted for credentials, type the credentials of the user who was granted the supervisory review role and click **OK**. See Figure 8-106.

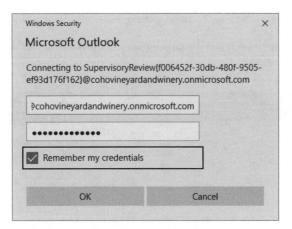

Figure 8-106 Outlook security dialog box

9. After the configuration is complete, as shown in Figure 8-107, click **Finish**.

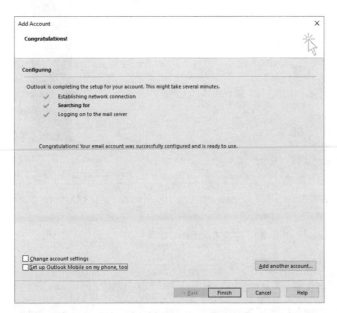

Figure 8-107 Completed Add Account Wizard

10. Close and restart Outlook.

11. Click the ellipses (...) at the bottom of the navigation pane, select **Folders**, and scroll down the navigation pane. Notice that the SupervisoryReview{guid}@domain.com mailbox has been added to the user's profile.

12. Browse to the folder named for the policy configured under Supervision and expand it.

13. Select a message and then select the **Supervisory Review** add-in in the message preview. See Figure 8-108.

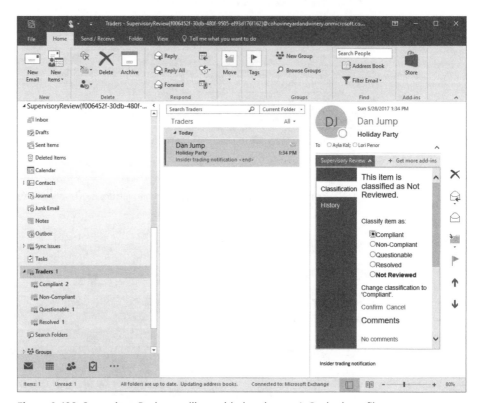

Figure 8-108 SupervisoryReview mailbox added to the user's Outlook profile

14. Select a classification and click **Confirm**.

HIDING THE SUPERVISORYREVIEW MAILBOX

After the mailbox has been successfully added to reviewers' profiles, you can re-hide it from the global address list if desired. If you add new users to the Supervisory Reviewer role, you must unhide the mailbox again so the new reviewer can add it to their Outlook profile.

Reviewing supervision reports

You can see both summary and more detailed reports regarding the disposition of reviewed messages.

To view the summary statistics report, navigate to **Data Governance | Supervision** and click a supervision policy. Scroll to the bottom of the dialog box to see the summary statistics (Figure 8-109) for messages reviewed for the policy.

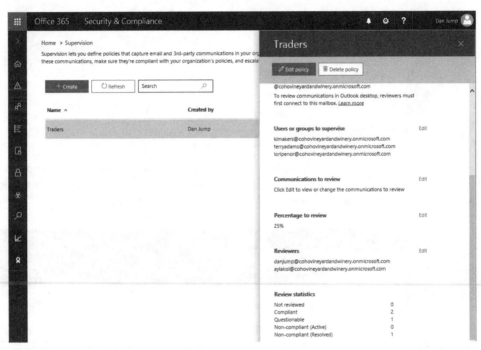

Figure 8-109 Supervision summary statistics

To view more detailed reports, navigate to **Reports | Dashboard** and select the Supervision widget. See Figure 8-110.

Figure 8-110 Supervision reports

Click the ellipses (…) to open the Export Conditions fly-out and download a report as a comma-separated values (CSV) file. In the Export conditions fly-out, you can select a date range as well as specific policies or reviewers to include in the export. See Figure 8-111.

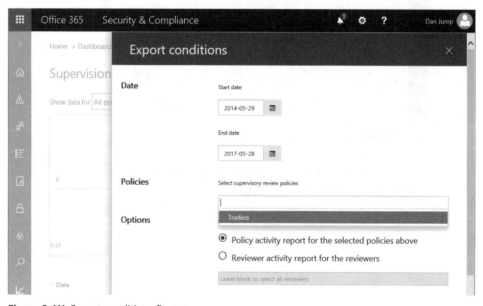

Figure 8-111 Export conditions fly-out

Search & Investigation

From the Search & Investigation menus, you can perform Content, Audit Log, and eDiscovery searches across all Office 365 services.

If you previously used the Exchange Online Admin Center to create searches or in-place holds, Microsoft recommends that you begin using the Security & Compliance Center to perform those actions. Starting July 1, 2017, you can no longer create in-place eDiscovery searches in Exchange Online directly, although you can still modify existing in-place eDiscovery searches.

Content Search

Use Content Search to discover content in email and documents stored in SharePoint or OneDrive, Skype for Business conversations, and Teams. Search results can be previewed and exported for download and delivered as documents, files, and email archives.

Access Content Search by navigating to **Search & Investigation | Content Search** in the Search & Compliance Center. Figure 8-112 depicts the Content Search page.

Figure 8-112 Content Search

To perform a search, follow these steps.

1. On the Content Search page, click **+**.

2. Provide a name for the search and then select search locations. You can search everywhere or select specific data sources. After finalizing your selection, click Next. See Figure 8-113.

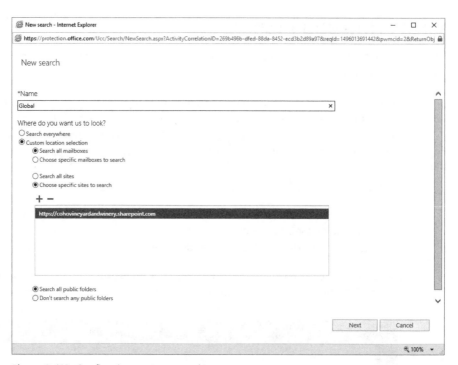

Figure 8-113 Configuring content search parameters

You can search for all content or specific keywords and patterns. You can also add conditions such as message participants (senders or recipients), document authors, item types, and date ranges.

3.   After you've added the conditions, click **Search**. See Figure 8-114.

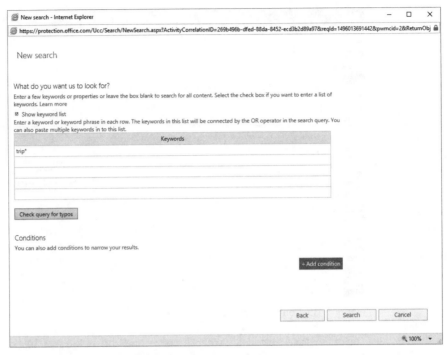

Figure 8-114 Configuring search keywords and conditions

After starting the search, the Content Search page reopens, as shown in Figure 8-115. When the search completes, the results appear.

CHAPTER 8

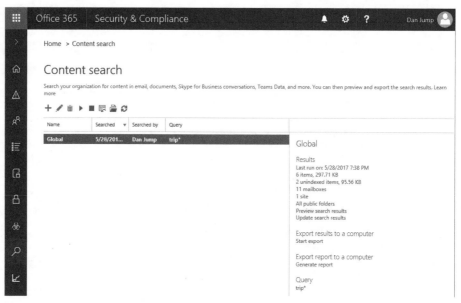

Figure 8-115 Content Search dashboard with results

The options available include Start (to rerun and update the search), Preview The Search Results In The Browser, Download The Results, and Download The Report.

To export and download results, follow these steps.

1. On the Content Search page, click **Start Export on a completed search**.

2. In the Export Search Results dialog box, choose your export options and click **Start Export**. See Figure 8-116.

Figure 8-116 Export The Search Results For Global dialog box

If you are not a member of the eDiscovery Manager role group, you won't be able to export results, and an error appears. If you are a member of the Organization Management role group, you can add yourself as a member of the eDiscovery Manager role, sign out of the Security & Compliance Center, sign back in, and retry the export.

3. When the export has finished processing, click **Download Exported Results**.

4. On the Download Exported Results page, copy the export key to the clipboard and then click the **Download Results** link at the bottom of the page, shown in Figure 8-117.

Figure 8-117 Download page for exported search results

After a moment, the Microsoft Client Discovery Unified Export Tool runs. See Figure 8-118.

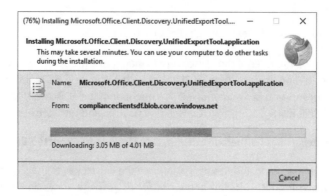

Figure 8-118 Export download tool

SUPPORTED BROWSERS

The application requires the Internet Explorer or Edge browser to run. It will not run with Firefox or Chrome.

5. Paste the export key into the export key text box, type or browse to a directory to save the downloaded files, and then click **Start**. See Figure 8-119.

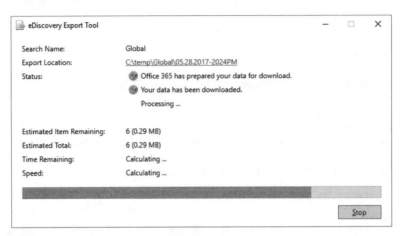

Figure 8-119 eDiscovery Export Tool dialog box

6. After the files have downloaded, navigate to the path listed in Export Location (Figure 8-120) and close the application.

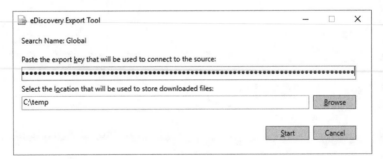

Figure 8-120 eDiscovery Export Tool status screen

The files are saved in a subdirectory named for the search specified in the eDiscovery Export Tool. A separate subdirectory is created for exports from each service.

Audit Log Search

The Audit log search enables you to search for audited events by both users and administrators. The Security & Compliance Center presents a unified audit log, so you can search the following types of user and admin activity.

- User activity in SharePoint Online and OneDrive for Business

- User activity in Exchange Online (Exchange mailbox audit logging must be enabled.)

- Admin activity in SharePoint Online

- Admin activity in Azure Active Directory

- Admin activity in Exchange Online (Exchange admin audit logging)

- User and admin activity in Sway

- User and admin activity in Power BI for Office 365

- User and admin activity in Microsoft Teams

- User and admin activity in Yammer

Before you can search the audit log, audit logging must be turned on, and you must be a member of a role group that includes either View-Only Audit Logs or Audit Logs roles. Figure 8-121 shows the Audit Log Search page.

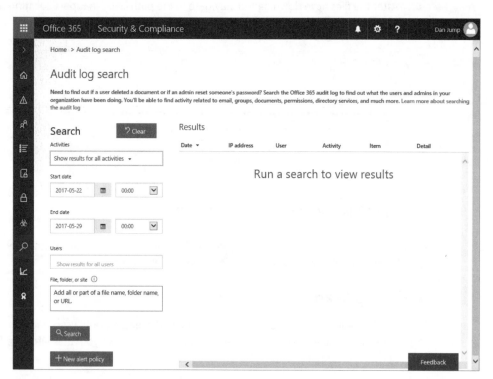

Figure 8-121 Audit Log Search page

Performing a search simply requires selecting the types of activities to view and a date range. To refine results further, you can specify users or part of a file name, folder name, or URL. The audit log can be searched for as far back as 90 days.

After you have performed the search, you can filter the results further by clicking the Filter Results button. See Figure 8-122.

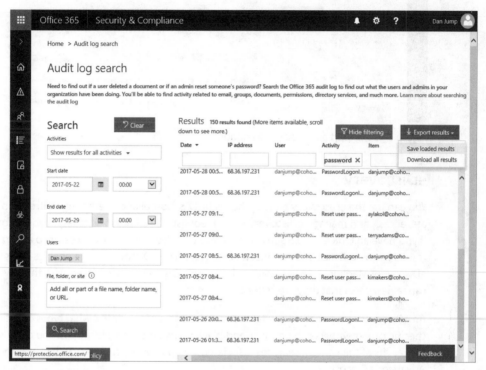

Figure 8-122 Audit log search with filtering applied

After clicking the Filter Results button, you can add criteria in the column header areas. For example, if you want to filter by activities that involved passwords, type **password** in the activity field, and the list will filter in-place. You can click an individual event for more details or select Export Results to download them to your computer. You can download either the filtered list of results shown on screen or the original results before filters were applied.

Figure 8-123 shows the filtering text entry areas with the Export Results button selected.

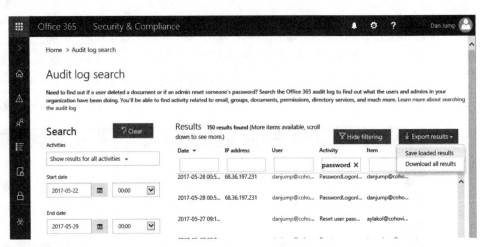

Figure 8-123 Export audit log results options

eDiscovery

You can use the eDiscovery page in the Security & Compliance Center to control who can create, access, and manage eDiscovery search requests (also known as cases) in your organization. If you have an Office 365 E5 subscription, you can also use eDiscovery cases to analyze search results by using Office 365 Advanced eDiscovery. The eDiscovery page enables users with the eDiscovery Manager role to create and manage eDiscovery cases. Users with the Reviewer role can review cases that they are assigned to.

An eDiscovery case enables you to add members to a case, control what types of actions that specific case members can perform, and place holds on content locations. You can also export the results of the content searches associated with a case or prepare search results for analysis in Advanced eDiscovery.

Assigning eDiscovery permissions to case members

Before users can perform eDiscovery searches, review cases, or export results, they must be granted eDiscovery-related permissions. Only users who have membership in an eDiscovery-related role group or a custom role group that has the Reviewer role can be added to an eDiscovery case.

You have to be a member of the Organization Management role group (or be assigned the Role Management role) in the Office 365 Security & Compliance Center to assign eDiscovery permissions. Role permissions are discussed under the Permissions topic in Chapter 7.

INSIDE OUT

OneDrive permissions

Although eDiscovery and Content Search do allow you to search OneDrive for Business sites, you can't do it without first granting permissions to the account that will run the searches. By default, neither Office 365 global admins nor compliance managers have the required permissions to search OneDrive for Business sites.

To grant access to search OneDrive for Business sites, install and configure the SharePoint Online admin tools and follow the steps at *https://support.office.com/en-us/article /Assign-eDiscovery-permissions-to-OneDrive-for-Business-sites-422858ff-917b-46d4 -9e5b-3397f60eee4d?ui=en-US&rs=en-US&ad=US&fromAR=1.*

As an overview, the process involves:

- Generating a list of OneDrive for Business sites that you want to be able to search.
- Running a script to grant the eDiscovery user permissions to the sites.
- Performing the eDiscovery search.
- Removing the eDiscovery user's OneDrive permissions.

Creating a case and adding members

To create a case, you must be a member of the eDiscovery Managers role or role subgroup.

1. From the Security & Compliance Center, navigate to **Search & Investigation | eDiscovery** and then click **+ Create A Case**.

2. In the New Case dialog box, give the case a name (unique in your organization) and a description and then click **Save**.

3. After the case has been created, click the case to open the **Manage This Case** dialog box, as shown in Figure 8-124.

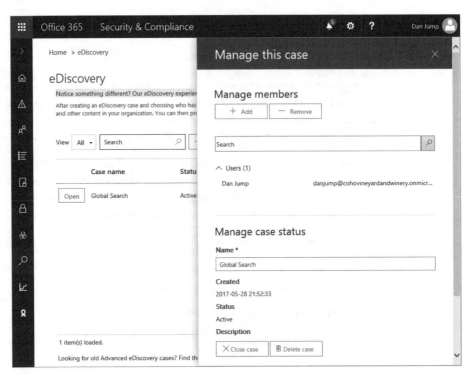

Figure 8-124 Manage This Case eDiscovery dialog box

4. Click **+ Add** to add additional members to the case and then click **Save**.

Only users who have been assigned to a group that has the Reviewer role group membership appear.

INSIDE OUT

Limiting the scope of whom users can search

There might be instances when you don't want users with the eDiscovery manager role to search organization-wide. For example, if your organization has multiple business units, you might need to restrict the ability of eDiscovery users in each organization to search mailboxes, SharePoint Online, or OneDrive for Business sites in their own business unit.

You can do this with the New-ComplianceSecurityFilter cmdlet.

Suppose you need to restrict the eDiscovery manager David Hamilton so that he can only search and export content for user mailboxes that belong to members of the Marketing distribution group and content located in the Marketing SharePoint site.

> **You could create a compliance security filter similar to the following.**
>
> ```
> $DG = Get-DistributionGroup "Marketing"
>
> New-ComplianceSecurityFilter -FilterName Marketing -Users DavidHamliton@cohovineyar-
> dandwinery.onmicrosoft.com -Filters "Site_Site -eq 'https://cohovineyardandwinery.
> sharepoint.com/sites/Marketing' -and Mailbox_MemberOfGroup -eq '$($DG.Distinguished-
> Name)'" -Action All
> ```
>
> **For more information, see the New-ComplianceSecurityFilter cmdlet help.**

Placing content on hold

You can use an eDiscovery case to create holds to preserve content that might be relevant to proceedings such as a legal inquiry. You can place holds on mailboxes and OneDrive for Business sites for users, the group mailbox, SharePoint site, and OneDrive for Business site for an Office 365 group and the mailbox and site associated with a Microsoft Team resource. The content is held until you remove the hold from the content location or the hold is deleted.

When creating a hold, you can control the held content's retention within a date range (sent, received, or created), an indefinite hold for all content in a site or mailbox, or a query-based hold that only retains content matching the query terms.

To create a hold, follow these steps.

1. From the Security & Compliance Center, navigate to **Search & Investigation | eDiscovery** and then click **Open** next to the case you want to manage.

2. Select the **Hold** tab. See Figure 8-125.

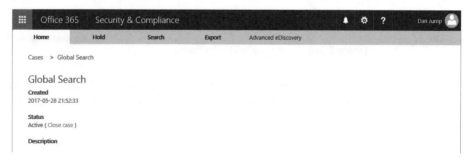

Figure 8-125 eDiscovery case

3. On the Hold page, click **New +**.

4. On the Create A New Hold page, name the hold with a name unique in your organization.

5. Add the mailboxes and sites to search.

   If you add a distribution group, members of the distribution group will be searched.

6. Click Next. See Figure 8-126.

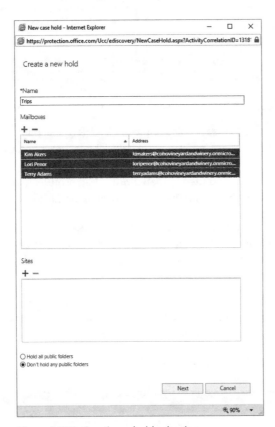

Figure 8-126 Creating a hold selection

7. Type keywords and conditions to create a query-based hold or leave blank to hold all content in the mailboxes and sites. Click **Finish** to create the hold. See Figure 8-127.

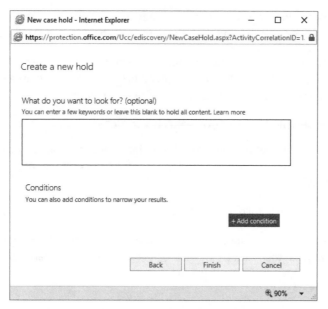

Figure 8-127 Entering keywords or conditions for a hold

After the hold has been created, you can refresh the Hold page to display updated statistics, shown in Figure 8-128. The statistics include the number of mailboxes and sites on hold and data about the content that was placed on hold, such as the total number and size of items placed on hold and the last time the hold statistics were calculated.

Figure 8-128 eDiscovery case hold

The number of items indicates those from all content sources that are placed on hold. If you've created a query-based hold, this indicates the number of items that match the query.

The number of items on hold also includes unindexed items found in the content locations. If you create a query-based hold, all unindexed items in the content locations are placed on hold, potentially including content that doesn't match the search query.

Creating and running a content search for a case

After an eDiscovery case has been created and content placed on hold, you can create and run additional content searches. Content searches run in the context of the case are restricted to the members of the case.

To create a content search, follow these steps.

1. From the Security & Compliance Center, navigate to **Search & Investigation | eDiscovery** and then click **Open** next to the case you want to manage.

2. Select the **Search** tab.

3. On the Search page, click **New +**.

4. On the New Search page, type a name for the search.

   Content searches associated with a case must have names that are unique across your Office 365 organization.

5. Choose the content locations that you want to search.

   You can search mailboxes, sites, and public folders in the same search. You can choose to search all content locations or specify a custom set based on the requirements of the search. Remember, you can create multiple searches per case, so you might want to perform different sets of keyword queries on the same content to return different results.

6. Click **Next** when you have finished your content location selection. See Figure 8-129.

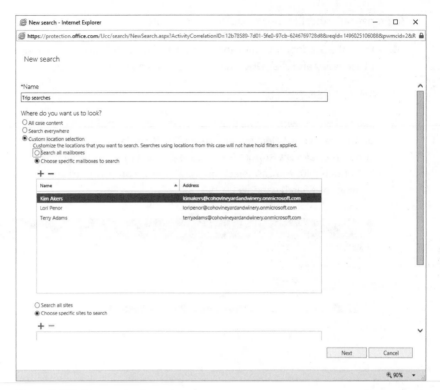

Figure 8-129 New content search

VERIFY THE SEARCH SCOPE

Only the first button, All Case Content, searches in-scope content. If you select Search Everywhere or a custom location selection by specifying particular mailboxes or sites, any query-based searches or existing holds for the case are not used.

7. Add search terms and conditions if desired. If you want to return all content, leave the keywords and conditions blank. Click **Search** to complete and run the search with the specified parameters.

Exporting the content search results

After the search has completed, you can create an export of the results. Exporting from an eDiscovery case is the same as exporting from a content search outside of a case.

To prepare an export for download, follow these steps.

1. From the Security & Compliance Center, navigate to **Search & Investigation |
    eDiscovery** and click **Open** next to the case you want to manage.

2. Select the **Search** tab.

3. Select the case with results that you want to export and then click the **Export** button
    on the menu bar. Select either **Export The Results** (to prepare an export of the actual
    content) or **Export Report** (to prepare a report of items included in the export), as shown
    in Figure 8-130. You can select multiple cases by pressing Ctrl and clicking the individual
    cases in the Search window.

Figure 8-130 Exporting content search results

When you export the results of multiple searches, the search queries from all the searches
are combined by using OR operators in a single content search. If your searches contain
keywords, you are limited to 500 across all searches, which is the same limit for a single
content search.

The search results that are exported are organized by the content source. If multiple
searches return different items in the same data sources, they are grouped together in
the export. For example, if different keyword searches return different email items in the
same mailbox and you selected the option to export each mailbox to an individual PST,
the results from multiple searches would be saved to the same PST.

If the same email item or document from the same content location is returned by more
than one of the searches that you export, only one copy of the item will be exported.

4. Select the options to suit your needs and then click **Start Export**.

Just like performing a content search and export outside of an eDiscovery case, if you are not a member of the eDiscovery Manager role group, you won't be able to export results and will receive an error. If you are a member of the Organization Management role group, you can add yourself as a member of the eDiscovery Manager role, sign out of the Security & Compliance Center, sign back in, and retry the export.

5. Click the **Export** tab, as shown in Figure 8-131.

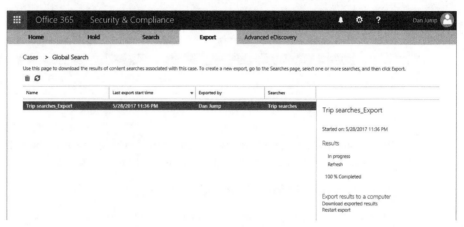

Figure 8-131 eDiscovery Export tab page

6. When the export has finished processing, click **Download Exported Results**.

7. On the Download Exported Results page, copy the export key to the clipboard and then click the **Download Results link**.

    After a moment, the Microsoft Client Discovery Unified Export Tool runs. The application requires Internet Explorer to run. It will not run in Firefox or Chrome.

8. Paste the export key into the Export Key box, enter or browse to a directory to save the downloaded files, and click Start.

9. After the files have downloaded, navigate to the path listed in Export Location and close the application. See Figure 8-132.

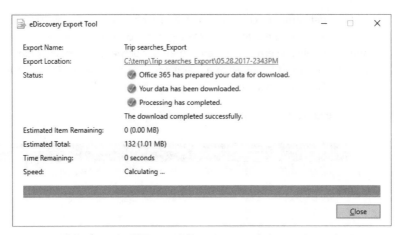

Figure 8-132 eDiscovery Export Tool data download complete

The files are saved in a subdirectory named for the search specified in the eDiscovery Export Tool. A separate subdirectory is created for exports from each service.

Preparing results for Advanced eDiscovery

If Advanced eDiscovery licenses are assigned to mailboxes in the search scope, you can also perform Advanced eDiscovery searches against them to refine further the content being returned.

In large cases, when hundreds of thousands or millions of records might be returned, advanced eDiscovery can be used to process the results further and limit the data set that is exported. Advanced eDiscovery can also perform optical character recognition to extract text from images, which can be useful on scanned documents, and enables you to apply the text and analytic capabilities of Advanced eDiscovery to text recognized from images.

Although you can prepare multiple searches at once for export, you can only prepare the results of a single search for analysis in Advanced eDiscovery at a time.

To analyze content in Advanced eDiscovery, follow these steps.

1. From the Security & Compliance Center, navigate to **Search & Investigation | eDiscovery** and then click **Open** next to the case you want to manage.

2. Select the **Search** tab.

   Select the case with results that you want to process using Advanced eDiscovery and click **Prepare Results For Analysis**. If you have not assigned an E5 or Advanced eDiscovery license to any users in your tenant, the Prepare Results For Analysis link displays a blank page after clicking.

3.   Select options for preparing results for Advanced eDiscovery, as shown in Figure 8-133.

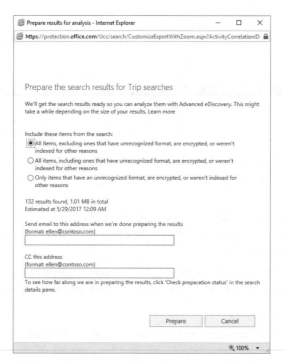

Figure 8-133 Preparing results for Advanced eDiscovery

4.   Select the preparation options and click **Prepare**.

Reviewing the case in Advanced eDiscovery

After you have selected an eDiscovery case to be prepared for Advanced eDiscovery, you can view its status in the Advanced eDiscovery Center.

1.   From the Security & Compliance Center, navigate to **Search & Investigation | eDiscovery** and click **Open** next to the case you want to manage.

2.   Click the **Advanced eDiscovery** tab.

The Advanced eDiscovery tab is shown in Figure 8-134.

Figure 8-134 Advanced eDiscovery Prepare workflow tab

3. If you have more than one search that was prepared for Advanced eDiscovery, select the appropriate search under Contains and then click **Process**. If you need to customize the processing, click **Advanced**.

In addition to file data, metadata such as type, extension, creation date and time, author, owner (or custodian), and subject can be loaded into Advanced eDiscovery and saved for the case.

4. Wait while Advanced eDiscovery processing takes place. See Figure 8-135.

Figure 8-135 Advanced eDiscovery processing

Advanced eDiscovery provides system metadata values such as near-duplicate groupings or relevance scores. The administrator can add other metadata, such as file annotations.

After processing has completed, Advanced eDiscovery displays the summary page, shown in Figure 8-136.

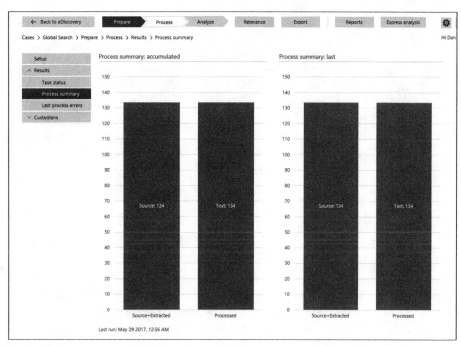

Figure 8-136 Completed Advanced eDiscovery processing

5. Expand Custodians and click Manage to view current custodians, as shown in Figure 8-137. Edit custodians if necessary. Click the **Analyze** button in the workflow at the top of the screen when finished.

Figure 8-137 Advanced eDiscovery Process workflow tab

6. Configure the analysis options for near-duplicates and email threads.

   A higher percentage of similarity results in more unique documents being returned. A lower percentage of document similarity results in fewer returns.

7. Click the **Analyze** button. See Figure 8-138.

Figure 8-138   Advanced eDiscovery Analyze workflow tab

8.   Review the Near-Duplicates (ND) and Email Threads (ET) results, as shown in Figure 8-139.

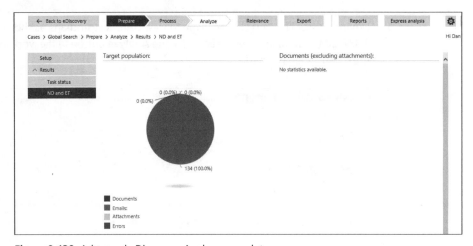

Figure 8-139   Advanced eDiscovery Analyze complete.

9.   Click the **Export** button on the workflow.

10.   Click the **Create Export Session button at the bottom of the page, as shown in Figure 8-140**.

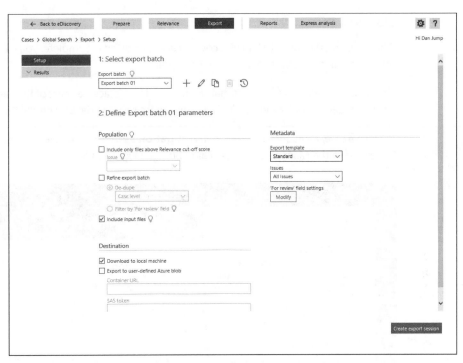

Figure 8-140 Advanced eDiscovery Export

11. In the fly-out that appears with the export key, click **Copy To Clipboard**. Paste it into a text file and save a copy of the key. Click **Close**. See Figure 8-141.

    The eDiscovery Export tool used for normal content searches and eDiscovery exports launches automatically.

Figure 8-141 Advanced eDiscovery Download Files fly-out with export key

12. Paste the export key into the Export Key box and enter or browse to a location to save the export.

13. Click **Start**.

14. Click **Close** and browse to the export location to view the processed files.

Closing a case

When the investigation that an eDiscovery case supported is complete, you can close the eDiscovery case in the Security & Compliance Center.

Closing a case releases any holds that might have been placed as part of the case. Depending on your organization's retention policies, this might result in data being deleted.

To close a case, navigate to **Search & Investigation | eDiscovery**, select the case and click Close Case in the Manage This Case dialog box. See Figure 142.

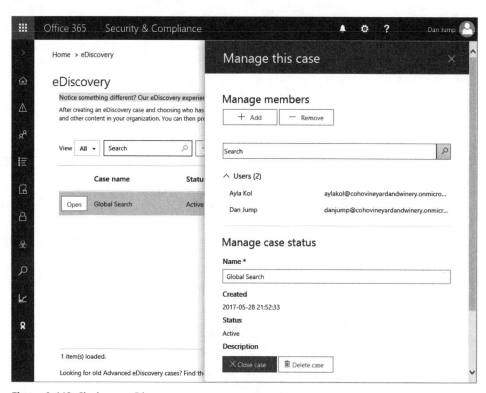

Figure 8-142 Closing an eDiscovery case

Productivity App Discovery*

Productivity App Discovery, shown in Figure 8-143, is available only if you have Advanced Security Management licensing. Productivity App Discovery enables you to see how Office 365 and other cloud service apps are being used in your organization.

Figure 8-143 Productivity App Discovery launch page

To access Productivity App Discovery, click the **Go To Advanced Security Management** button. A new browser window or tab opens in *https://portal.cloudappsecurity.com*.

To use Productivity App Discovery, create a new report and upload traffic logs from your firewall, proxy, or other network appliances. Click the Create A New Report button, shown in Figure 8-144, to get started.

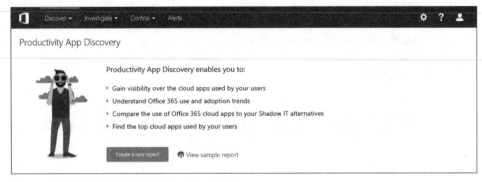

Figure 8-144 Productivity App Discovery landing page

Type a report name and a description and select the type of logs that you will upload, as shown in Figure 8-145.

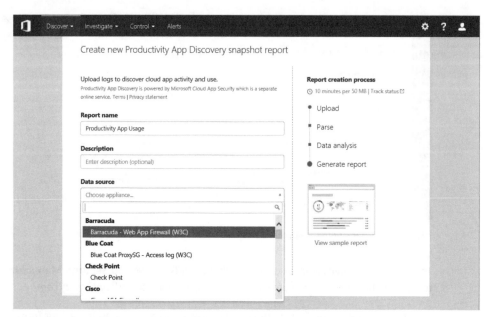

Figure 8-145 Creating a new Productivity App Discovery snapshot report

After you have uploaded the logs, Productivity App Discovery analyzes the logs and generates a report for you to download. Productivity app reports can be used to give you insight into how your users are consuming cloud services outside of the Office 365 suite, providing a more holistic view of the application landscape.

Summary

The Office 365 Security & Compliance Center offers a number of discovery and reporting tools to provide insight into your organization's data and users' activities. In addition, you can use policies to protect data against accidental or intentional deletion.

CHAPTER 9

Office 365 service health reporting and support

Office 365 provides several service health reporting and notification tools for administrators and users. There are status notification pages, reporting in the dashboard, status as well as RSS feeds, and a management pack available for the system center operations manager.

Admin roles for service health

Before users can view service health features, they must be assigned a role that includes service health. Global administrators have this role by default. To assign it to another user, follow these steps.

1. Sign in to the Office 365 portal with your Office 365 global administrator account.

2. In the admin center, select Users.

3. On the Active Users page, choose the user whose administrator role you want to change. The dialog box for the user opens.

4. Next to Roles, select Edit, as shown in Figure 9-1.

CHAPTER 9

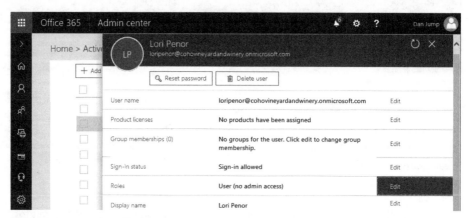

Figure 9-1 Screenshot of editing an active user

5. You can choose the Global Administrator role by selecting the Global Administrator button (to grant full access to all features of the tenant) or, to choose the least-privileged administrative role, by selecting the Customized Administrator button and then selecting the Service Administrator check box. See Figure 9-2.

Figure 9-2 Selecting an admin role for the user

6. Click Save.

7. Click Close to close the confirmation message.

8. Click Close to close the user properties dialog box.

After a user has been granted the appropriate roles (either Global Administrator or another role with Service Health administrator rights), they will be able to log on to the portal and navigate through the health pages.

Service Health dashboard

There are two views of data in the Service Health dashboard—the General Availability view and the v2 view. As Microsoft develops newer features and data visualizations, it will release them into the v2 view. Eventually, the v2 view will become the default view available to administrators.

V1

The v1 view is the current view presented to administrators in the Service Health dashboard. To see it, log on to the admin center, point to Health, and then select Service Health.

Service Health

The Service Health page, shown in Figure 9-3, displays a status of services in the tenant with three tabs: All Services, Incidents, and Advisories.

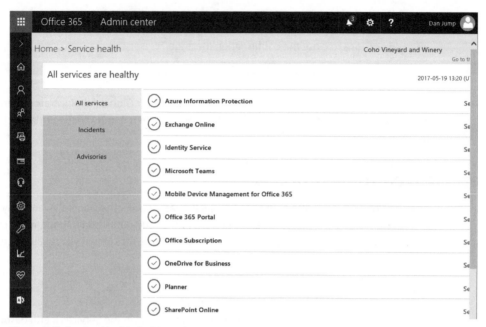

Figure 9-3 Service Health dashboard

The All Services tab presents the current status of all services currently available in the tenant (whether they are available to users or not).

Service incidents are events that affect the delivery of a feature or service. Service incidents can be caused by hardware or software failure in the data center, a failure in the network connectivity between you and the Microsoft data centers, or regional catastrophes such as fire or flood. Most service interruptions are resolved quickly; however, some might result in longer outages.

Service incidents can be broken down into two categories.

- **Planned Maintenance**   Planned maintenance events are scheduled instances when Microsoft has communicated (by the Message Center) that infrastructure delivering a service will be unavailable or in a degraded state. Planned maintenance usually occurs during times when such services are predicted to be at their lowest rate of usage.

  - In the Americas, this is from 21:00 to 03:00 Pacific Time (GMT -8) on Fridays and Saturdays.

  - In Europe, the Middle East, and Africa, this time is 20:00 to 02:00 (GMT) on Fridays and Saturdays.

  - In the Asia-Pacific region and China, the lowest usage time is Saturdays from 01:00 to Sundays at 16:00 (GMT +8).

- **Unplanned Downtime**   An incident is categorized as unplanned when a service is unavailable or not operational outside of a planned maintenance window.

Advisories are service degradations resulting in a lower-performing service. Service degradations can include situations such as delays in message-tracking results or inability to access settings for an application or service. See Figure 9-4.

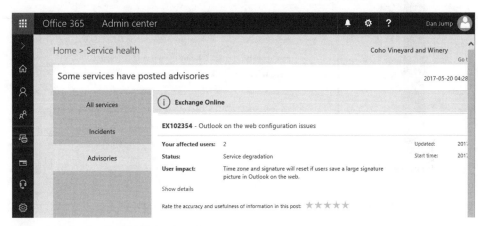

Figure 9-4 Service Health Advisories tab

Message Center

The Message Center, pictured in Figure 9-5, is the central hub of notifications for Office 365 services. Summaries of items in the Message Center are presented on the portal home page. In the Message Center, content can be displayed by group or by event category, which can help when searching for events.

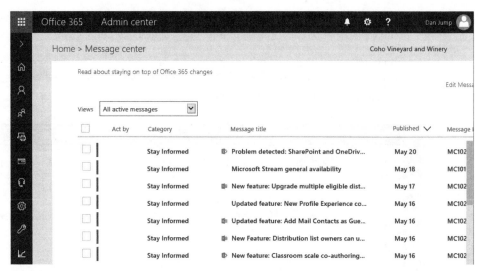

Figure 9-5 Message Center dashboard

Message Center notifications are arranged in three categories.

- **Plan for Change**   Messages categorized as Plan for Change announce that a change is coming for how to deploy or manage a feature. For example, it might say that a service feature will be deprecated and replaced with a new feature. In such a case, you'll be given appropriate planning tools. A service change might have a lock-down period during which you'll no longer be able to use the process, tool, or feature or create new instances of the feature being retired while existing items continue to work. You'd then be provided with a transition or retirement date along with an upgrade path, information about consuming a new feature, or suggestions for how to mitigate the retirement of a feature. See Figure 9-6.

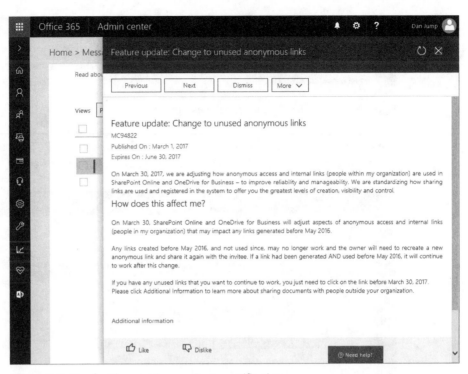

Figure 9-6 Plan for Change Message Center notification

- **Prevent or Fix Issues**   This notification class contains messages that are intended to help identify and fix existing on-premises issues, such as duplicate proxy addresses in mailboxes or repeated connectivity problems in your on-premises environment.

- **Stay Informed**   A notification that is classified as Stay Informed typically has to do with a new or update feature that will soon be available to your tenant. Stay Informed messages include monthly update summaries, subscription notifications, and any other messages not specifically related to upcoming changes or resolving existing issues.

V2

As Microsoft develops newer features and views of data, it might periodically release updated user interfaces. To access the v2 interface for the Service Health dashboard, click the Go To The V2 Service Health Page *link* at the upper right top of the Service Health page, as shown in Figure 9-7.

Figure 9-7 Link to the v2 Service Health dashboard

The v2 Service Health page currently has a combined all-services view (Figure 9-8) that shows services with incidents and advisories overlaid, but new features will be added to it.

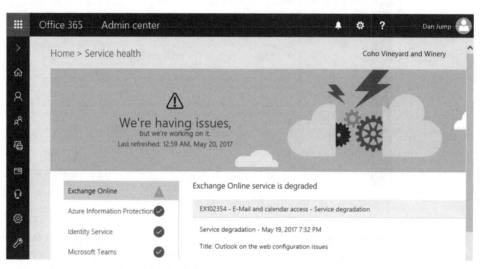

Figure 9-8 V2 Service Health dashboard

Status page (status.office365.com)

The Office 365 Service Health Status page, shown in Figure 9-9, can be used to track availability of the Office 365 portal sign-in page.

Figure 9-9 Office 365 Service Health Status page

Office 365 mobile app

The Office 365 admin mobile app gives you access to a variety of tools at your fingertips. Monitoring service health and availability is one of the many features that the mobile app offers. It can be configured to deliver pop-up notifications to your mobile device and display messages from the Message Center. See Figure 9-10.

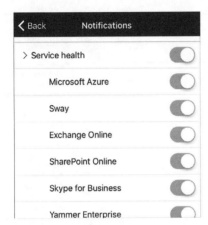

Figure 9-10 Office 365 admin mobile app

The Office 365 admin mobile app can be downloaded from *http://go.microsoft.com /fwlink/?LinkID=627216*.

CHAPTER 9

System Center Operations Manager management pack for Office 365

In addition to the native tools and services provided, Microsoft also provides a management pack for System Center Operations Manager. Figure 9-11 shows the System Center Operations Manager management pack for Office 365 configured.

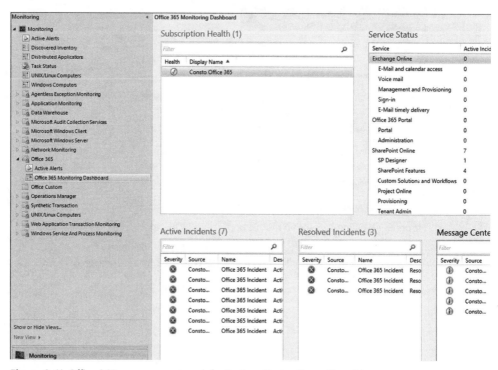

Figure 9-11   Office 365 management pack for System Center Operations Manager

You can configure alerts and monitors for various services, review active and resolved incidents, and read notifications in the Message Center. In addition, the Office 365 management pack can monitor and alert on multiple Office 365 subscriptions.

The management pack is available at *http://www.microsoft.com/en-gb/download/details .aspx?id=43708* and can extend System Center Operations Manager 2012 SP1, System Center Operations Manager 2012 R2, and System Center Operations Manager 2016.

Summary

This chapter identified ways that you can monitor alerts for service availability and performance in Office 365. The service alerts and notifications that appear in the Service Health dashboard and the Office 365 portal can help you prepare for changes in the Office 365 service.

CHAPTER 9

PART IV

Exchange Online Configuration and Management

Preparing an on-premises environment to connect to Exchange Online

The Exchange Online component of Office 365 supports cloud-only deployments; hybrid coexistence; and staged, cutover, and hybrid migration paths. Before configuring your existing Exchange on-premises environment to connect to Office 365, plan to take a step back to evaluate the current state of your Exchange organization. Ensuring that you meet all the prerequisites prior to undergoing coexistence or migration steps will help save time and reduce the risk of failure.

Exchange Online deployment concepts

If you are familiar with Exchange on-premises, you might already have a good basis for understanding how Exchange Online works. Just as Exchange on-premises uses an Active Directory environment to store attributes and properties for configuration and recipient objects, Exchange Online also stores its configuration information in Active Directory. In the case of Exchange Online, the Active Directory component is Azure Active Directory, a multitenant directory service designed to scale to billions of objects.

Recipients

Exchange Online has many types of recipients, and all of them have some relationship to an underlying Active Directory object. Mailboxes, contacts, and distribution groups build on a corresponding Active Directory object by adding Exchange-specific attributes (mail, proxyAddress, and mailNickname are a few examples) and exposing them to the Exchange interfaces.

For more information about the various object types used in Exchange Online (and Office 365 in general) and how to interact with them, see Chapter 11, "Understanding the Office 365 Resource Types."

Mail routing

Similar to Exchange on-premises, Exchange Online uses the concept of connectors to manage mail flow. You can scope connectors to send traffic for one or more domains on a specific route or receive from one or more hosts by using a specific configuration. In Exchange on-premises, you designate connectors as either Send Connectors (which control outgoing mail flow from a server) or Receive Connectors (which control incoming mail to a server). In Exchange Online, the analogous connectors are Outbound (Send) and Inbound (Receive) and are labeled from the perspective of the Office 365 tenant.

In addition to connectors, Exchange Online also enables you to define connection filters to allow or block connections from specific IP addresses or ranges as well as transport rules to filter or modify inbound and outbound traffic further.

When establishing mail flow with a foreign system (Exchange Online or an external messaging environment), you might configure one or more connectors and filters to control the mail flow.

For more advanced mail flow configurations and scenarios, see "Mail flow best practices for Exchange Online and Office 365 (overview)" at *https://technet.microsoft.com/en-us/library /jj937232(v=exchg.150).aspx*.

Autodiscover

Autodiscover is the process that Microsoft Outlook uses to determine the location of a user's mailbox. Autodiscover can be configured to use one or more methods, including looking for specific DNS records or service connection points (SCPs) in Active Directory.

Autodiscover is also used as part of the free/busy lookup process whereby a user's calendar is queried to check availability for meeting requests. In previous versions of Exchange, it was not necessary to configure Autodiscover to configure Outlook. However, Office 365 requires the use of Autodiscover to configure mailboxes correctly.

Depending on your configuration and business requirements, you can configure Autodiscover differently than the recommended records in the Office 365 portal. In hybrid configurations, you should configure Autodiscover DNS records to point to the on-premises mail system because Exchange on-premises can redirect requests to Office 365 but not vice versa. When all mailboxes are migrated, you can choose to update your Autodiscover records to point to Office 365.

Each Outlook client goes through a predefined Autodiscover lookup order:

1. **Service connection point**   The class service connection point is defined in the Active Directory schema. SCP objects published in Active Directory contain information that clients can use to bind to a particular service or host offering a service. Exchange Service Connection Point objects are created under the CN=Autodiscover,CN=Protocols,CN=< Exchange Server>,CN=Servers,CN=Exchange Administrative Group,CN=Administrative Groups,CN=<Exchange Organization>,CN=Microsfot Exchange,CN=Services container. The value in the serviceBindingInformation attribute is configured as *https://<Exchange Server FQDN>/autodiscover/autodiscover.xml*.

2. **HTTPS root domain query**   When Outlook is running on a machine that is not joined to an Active Directory domain, the client constructs a URL based on the domain portion of the user's email address. For example, if your email address is danjump@cohovineyardandwinery.com and you are attempting to configure Outlook on a computer that is not domain-joined, it attempts to query the Autodiscover service at *https://cohovineyardandwinery.com/autodiscover/autodiscover.xml*.

3. **HTTPS Autodiscover domain query**   If the previous queries don't return the location of an Autodiscover service, Outlook uses the domain portion of the user's email address to try a new URL. Using the previous domain as an example, Outlook tries *https://autodiscover.cohovineyardandwinery.com/autodiscover/autodiscover.xml*. This is the default Autodiscover record format that appears on the Office 365 Domains configuration page.

4. **HTTP redirect method**   If an HTTPS Autodiscover domain query fails, Outlook retries the same URL, using HTTP instead of HTTPS.

5. **SRV record query**   The next method Outlook uses to locate a user's mailbox is by querying DNS for a service locator (SRV) record, using a predefined format. The record is configured as *_autodiscover._tcp.domain.com*, with the host name pointing to the Exchange server hosting the Autodiscover service and the port value configured as 443.

6. **Local XML**   Outlook can also be configured to use a local XML file, which requires manually creating an autodiscover.xml file and modifying the local computer's registry to point to the path of the XML file.

7. **Cached URL**   Introduced in Outlook 2013, if all other discovery methods fail, Outlook attempts to use the location of the last Autodiscover service that it used (if a profile had successfully been configured before).

You can use Group Policy or modify the registry to disable specific Autodiscover methods. For more information, see *https://support.microsoft.com/en-us/help/2612922/how-to-control -outlook-autodiscover-by-using-group-policy*.

Migration and coexistence methodologies

When planning a coexistence with or migration to Exchange Online, you will want to consider both your long-term and short-term goals in addition to your current Active Directory, Exchange, desktop configuration, and network topologies. Depending on your business requirements and environment, you might be able to choose one or more of these migration coexistence strategies.

- **Cutover migration**   If your on-premises environment is running Exchange 2003, Exchange 2007, Exchange 2010, or Exchange 2013, and you have fewer than 2,000

CHAPTER 10

mailboxes, you can use a cutover migration. Due to the nature of a cutover, you have to migrate everyone together. Although 2,000 mailboxes is the maximum number of users that can be migrated with this method, it's more realistic to limit it to environments with 150 mailboxes or fewer.

- **Staged migration**   If your on-premises environment is running Exchange 2003 or Exchange 2007 and you have more than 150 mailboxes, you can run a staged migration. Staged migrations require the use of Azure Active Directory Connect (AAD Connect).

- **Express migration**   If your on-premises environment is running Exchange 2010, Exchange 2013, or Exchange 2016, you don't plan to use any directory synchroniza-tion technologies to migrate your users, and don't need to maintain the ability to look up free/busy status between Office 365 and on-premises users, you can use an express migration. Express migrations can also be referred to as minimal hybrid migrations.

- **Hybrid migration**   If your on-premises environment is running Exchange 2010, Exchange 2013, or Exchange 2016, you can use a hybrid migration. You can also use hybrid migrations in Exchange 2003 or Exchange 2007 environments if you deploy an Exchange 2010 or Exchange 2013 server. Hybrid migrations support the idea of online mailbox migrations if mailboxes are hosted on Exchange 2007 or later servers, meaning that the user's mailbox stays mounted and online until the moment of cutover, and then the user's Outlook profile can be redirected to Office 365. If mailboxes are hosted on Exchange 2003, the mailbox is locked and unavailable until the migration for that mailbox is completed. Public folders hosted on Exchange 2003 must be migrated to Exchange 2007 before hybrid coexistence or migration can be performed.

- **IMAP migration**   If your source environment is running a version of Exchange prior to 2003 or a foreign email system, you can use an IMAP migration. IMAP migrations are typ-ically unable to migrate calendar and contacts. Most organizations that need to perform migrations from non-Microsoft or hosted platforms work with a partner that specializes in migrations or uses third-party tools.

You can find more information about choosing migration methods in Chapter 12, "Mailbox Migration Types." If you know you are going to perform a hybrid configuration for either mail-box migration or long-term coexistence, see Chapter 13, "Exchange Online Hybrid."

Planning considerations

From the planning perspective, you'll need to analyze each of the types of recipients you want to migrate as well as transport rules, business requirements, and your existing environment.

Exchange and Active Directory on-premises environment

At the core of your migration planning will be your existing Exchange and Active Directory environments. To ensure a smooth coexistence or deployment, make sure you spend time reviewing your current environments.

Active Directory versions and configuration

The minimum requirement for configuring AAD Connect is that your Active Directory is upgraded to at least Windows Server 2003 forest functional level. If you are planning to use the password writeback feature of AAD Connect, your domain controllers must be running Windows Server 2008 or later with current updates.

READ-ONLY DOMAIN CONTROLLERS

The read-only domain controller (RODC) was introduced with Windows Server 2008 as a way to provide authentication services in environments that needed an extra layer of security, such as extranets or facilities without good physical security.

If you have deployed read-only domain controllers (RODCs) in your environment, you'll want to avoid using them for directory synchronization to Office 365 because they can create difficult troubleshooting scenarios. You might even consider creating a new Active Directory site that does not have RODCs or specifying a custom list of domain controllers to ensure that you don't contact them.

You must take special consideration to ensure that AAD Connect is not using RODCs for password writeback. If you will be configuring password hash synchronization, you must also make sure that the passwords are cached on read-only domain controllers in the event that an RODC is queried. Finally, if AAD Connect is using read-only domain controllers, make sure that the filtered attribute set contains all the attributes that you will be synchronizing to Office 365.

Autodiscover

A properly configured Autodiscover service is necessary for access to Office 365. In addition, if you are going to configure hybrid coexistence for public folders, on-premises Autodiscover is necessary so that the Public Folder proxy mailboxes can locate the on-premises Exchange Public Folder tree.

In topologies with mixed versions of Exchange, the Autodiscover service should be configured to point to the latest version of Exchange.

INSIDE OUT

Autodiscover advanced configurations

Although the best-practices recommendation is to configure external Autodiscover to point to the latest version of Exchange, there might be situations when that's not possible due to existing network configurations, custom integrated software deployments, or shared infrastructure resources. In these cases, it is possible to configure parameters in Office 365 through the Set-OrganizationRelationship cmdlet to control how services that require those features will respond.

You can use the TargetAutodiscoverEpr parameter to set the specific Autodiscover URL of Exchange Web Services for the external organization (in this case, the on-premises Exchange organization).

The TargetSharingEpr parameter can be used to control the exact endpoint for Exchange Web Services requests. If both TargetAutodiscoverEpr and TargetSharingEpr are configured, TargetSharingEpr takes priority, and TargetAutodiscoverEpr is ignored. More information about the TargetSharingEpr and TargetAutodiscoverEpr parameters is located in Chapter 14, "Managing Exchange Online."

Certificates

Confirm that a third-party certificate has been installed and configured correctly and is used in publishing Exchange services, including Exchange Control Panel (ECP), Exchange Web Services (EWS), Offline Address Book (OAB), and Outlook Web App (OWA). Occasionally, the certificate file that has been installed might seem to be fine but causes problems with the hybrid configuration setup. To check your certificate, run the following cmdlet in the on-premises Exchange Management Shell against the thumbprint of the certificate that you use for hybrid configuration, as shown in Figure 10-1.

```
Get-ExchangeCertificate -ThumbPrint <thumbprint> | Format-List
HasPrivateKey,IsSelfSigned,RootCAType,Status
```

Figure 10-1 Exchange certificate details

Exchange versions, service packs, cumulative updates, and rollups

Prior to starting a migration or hybrid configuration, verify that the most recent Exchange service packs, cumulative updates, and rollups are applied. This is especially important for Exchange hybrid deployments, because the Hybrid Configuration Wizard implements features and connectors in the Exchange environment and performs compatibility tests. For every version of Exchange Server supported in a hybrid topology, the servers must be at N-2 current (current version and up to two previous versions of cumulative updates or rollups) to be successfully configured.

Your organization's long-term management strategy should dictate which version of Exchange you deploy for Exchange Online coexistence or migration. For example, if you decide to transition to a purely cloud-based environment or have an existing Exchange 2003 deployment, you might choose to do the bare minimum to transition to Office 365. You can use the following information in Table 10-1 to help determine which versions of Exchange are supported for your environment.

Table 10-1 Exchange support matrix

On-premises environment	Exchange 2016–based hybrid deployment	Exchange 2013–based hybrid deployment	Exchange 2010–based hybrid deployment
Exchange 2016	Supported	Not supported	Not supported
Exchange 2013	Supported	Supported	Not supported
Exchange 2010	Supported	Supported	Supported
Exchange 2007	Not supported	Supported	Supported
Exchange 2003	Not supported	Not supported	Supported

You can find information about Exchange updates at *https://technet.microsoft.com/en-us /library/hh135098(v=exchg.150).aspx.*

Exchange Best Practices Analyzer

Depending on your version of Exchange, the Best Practices Analyzer might be included or available as a separate download. Run the Exchange Best Practices Analyzer to identify potential configuration issues. The Exchange Best Practices Analyzer can make recommendations for memory or logging configurations, identify databases that haven't been backed up in a long time or network or storage drivers that are out of date, or point out other less favorable configurations.

For Exchange 2003, the most current Best Practices Analyzer is available at *https://www .microsoft.com/en-us/download/details.aspx?id=22485*. Starting with Exchange 2007, the Best Practices Analyzer is included in the product.

IDFix

Microsoft provides the IDFix tool to help identify and resolve common directory attribute errors in your on-premises Active Directory and Exchange environments. Common issues might include invalid characters in the UserPrincipalName (UPN) or mailNickname attributes or instances when two or more users have been configured with the same SMTP proxy address.

There are certain error conditions that it can't detect yet, such as identifying when a user and a group might share the same SMTP address. These errors are frequently discovered when you synchronize your environment to Office 365 with AAD Connect. IDFix can identify when user objects have UPNs that have non-public, top-level domains (TLDs) but cannot identify whether you have UPNs or proxy addresses that have not been configured in your Office 365 tenant.

If you begin receiving errors such as duplicate proxy addresses during synchronization by AAD Connect, you can use the script at *https://gallery.technet.microsoft.com/Find-Duplicate-Values -in-6b012059* to identify the conflicting objects. The script identifies all instances of the conflicting address across all object types.

SSL offloading

Some organizations might configure Secure Sockets Layer (SSL) offloading, using one or more network devices to terminate the SSL connections. This is frequently configured in large organizations that have deployed server farms so that administrative teams don't have to manage certificates across many servers. Although SSL offloading is supported for Outlook Web App traffic as well as for some other Exchange Web Services calls, it is not supported for Mailbox Replication Service (MRS) traffic. MRS is used for the mailbox migrations to and from Office 365 and expects end-to-end SSL encryption of the traffic. If your organization uses SSL offloading, you will most likely need to configure a separate virtual IP (VIP) interface for the servers used for hybrid mailbox moves.

Windows updates

An often-overlooked basic environment check is to make sure your servers are up to date with both Windows and Exchange updates. Updates can include performance, security, or feature enhancements that your migration or coexistence environment needs to function optimally.

Recipients

From a coexistence or migration perspective, some objects might be fully migrated, whereas others might be only synchronized. Depending on your long-term business and technology objectives, you might have a deployment that has objects directly managed in Office 365, objects that are managed on-premises, or both.

For example, you might decide after your migration is done that you just want to manage objects in the cloud, and you disable directory synchronization and decommission Exchange from your on-premises environment; you might continue to manage your Active Directory objects on-premises, synchronize them to Office 365, and manage Exchange features through either the Office 365 and Exchange admin centers or through Windows PowerShell; or you might even choose to migrate some objects to Office 365 for full cloud management but keep other objects on-premises.

Contacts

A contact is a mail-enabled recipient that is used to provide visibility in the global address list for an external recipient. Contacts can represent foreign users, resources, or distribution groups. Contacts can be synchronized from your on-premises directory to Office 365 and managed on-premises, or they can be created in Office 365 as stand-alone objects.

Mailboxes

The mailbox object, whether user, shared, or resource, is a data storage object that will exist in either the on-premises environment or Office 365. In deployments with synchronized identity, the Exchange properties for a mailbox might be configured in the on-premises environment and synchronized through AAD Connect to Office 365, or they might be managed directly in Office 365.

Relationship between mail-enabled users and mailboxes

If you are new to Exchange or have never migrated objects between Exchange organizations, you might have noticed that objects in synchronized environments can appear differently, depending on which interface you're using.

When you synchronize on-premises users who have mailboxes to Office 365, it's important to understand the relationship between the on-premises and cloud objects. From the Active Directory perspective, the on-premises user's objectGuid value is converted to a base64 string value and stored as the ImmutableID on the object's corresponding Azure Active Directory object.

The relationship between the on-premises objectGuid and the cloud ImmutableID values can be expressed this way, as shown in Figure 10-2:

```
[system.convert]::ToBase64String(objectGuid).ToByteArray()
```

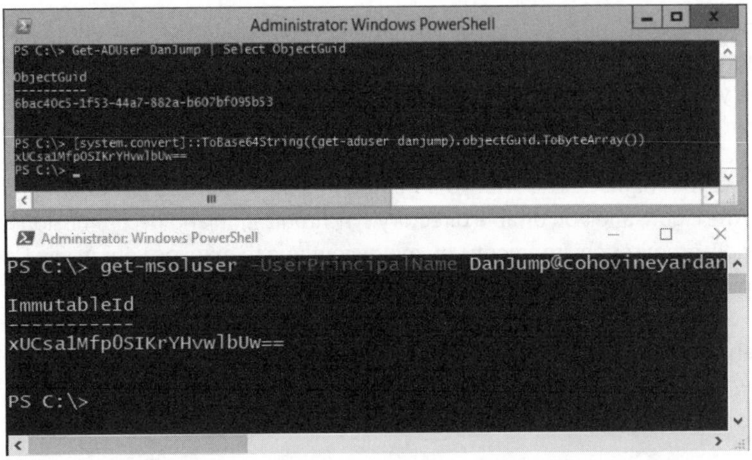

Figure 10-2 Active Directory objectGuid and Office 365 ImmutableID

From the Exchange perspective, every on-premises mailbox user who is synchronized is represented by a mail-enabled user in Exchange Online. The primary differences are that mail-enabled users have the idea of a targetAddress (a type of forwarding address) and values for msExchRecipientTypeDetails and msExchRecipientDisplayType that tell Exchange it's only a mail-enabled object, whereas mailbox users do not have a targetAddress value and instead have a value for homeMDB. Mailbox users have a value in msExchRecipientTypeDetails and msExchRecipientDisplayType that indicates that they are mailboxes.

Prior to migration, when you look at a mailbox user from Exchange on-premises, they are seen as a local mailbox user. That same user, when viewed from the perspective of Exchange Online, is displayed as MailUser. When you view a migrated user from Exchange on-premises, their Recipient Display Type indicates they are a MailUser, and their Recipient Type Details indicates they are a Remote Mailbox User (a subtype of MailUser). When looking at migrated users from Exchange Online, they appear as Mailbox User.

Message sizes and attachments

If you are migrating from an Exchange on-premises environment to Office 365, using either a cutover or hybrid migration, you can migrate messages that are up to 150 MB each. However, if you are migrating using IMAP or Exchange Web Services (third-party tools typically use Exchange Web Services), the maximum message size that can be migrated is 35 MB. Depending on your migration strategy and how your users communicate, you might want to evaluate your mailboxes for large attachments so you can notify users that those objects will not migrate successfully.

Accepted domains and addressing

Accepted domains are the domains over which your organization claims ownership. Although you can add any domains you like to your on-premises Exchange organization, you may only add and confirm domains in your Office 365 environment for which you can prove ownership through DNS record registration. You can synchronize users and contacts with any email addresses to Office 365, but you can only migrate mailboxes for users that have verified domains in your tenant. If you have a mailbox that has proxy addresses for domains that are not confirmed in your tenant, the migration will fail. As part of a migration process, make sure your Office 365 tenant has all the domains added to it that your environment uses.

Any domains not matching must be removed from mailboxes prior to migration. The script at *https://gallery.technet.microsoft.com/exchange/Remove-Exchange-Proxy-eb5be217* can help you remove addresses from objects.

To migrate mailboxes to Office 365 and enable successful Autodiscover and cross-premises mail routing, mailboxes need to have a proxy address matching *<tenant>.mail.onmicrosoft.com*. Mailboxes without a tenant proxy address will fail migration.

One of the tasks that the Hybrid Configuration Wizard performs is adding the tenant mail routing domain to all the email address templates that contain domains selected in the hybrid setup. In Exchange 2010, this can cause a large address book update to occur that has unexpected results if you have many email address templates or have manually configured primary SMTP addresses for users and have not set the EmailAddressPolicyEnabled attribute to False for those users. To avoid the automatic address book rebuild during Hybrid Configuration Wizard, you might want to update your email address templates beforehand. If you have many templates, this can be a daunting task. You can use the script at *https://gallery.technet.microsoft .com/exchange/Bulk-or-Selectively-Update-be06b784* to bulk update your email address templates.

The corollary to that is that if you have users with EmailAddressPolicyEnabled set to False, those users will not get the tenant proxy address stamped on them and thus fail mailbox migration. You can use the script at *https://gallery.technet.microsoft.com/exchange/Add-Office-365 -Tenant-93391e4c* to stamp mailboxes with the necessary tenant proxy address, or add an Out-To-AD rule to AAD Connect to update users automatically. You can use the script at *https:// gallery.technet.microsoft.com/exchange/Create-an-AAD-Connect-Rule-45ea6591* to modify AAD Connect to perform this function.

Mail-enabled users

Your organization might have on-premises security principals that have been configured as mail-enabled users. Mail-enabled users are not the same as mailbox users, because they do not have local mailbox storage in your organization. You can think about a mail-enabled user as a combination of both a security principal (user) and a contact—the result being a user who might have logon privileges to your network and a display entry in the global address list.

By default, mail-enabled users are synchronized to Office 365. If you have a mail-enabled user with a value in msExchMailboxGuid that is synchronized to Office 365, the object will be flagged as a mailbox awaiting migration in Office 365.

Groups

Groups, quite simply, are collections of mail-enabled objects—whether they are mailboxes, mail-enabled users, contacts, or other distribution groups.

When synchronized from an on-premises environment, most group properties can only be managed from the on-premises environment. Some organizations are accustomed to managing distribution groups through the Outlook interface, giving end-users the ability to add or remove group members as they need to without assistance from the service desk.

As far as considerations go, this is important to decide on. If groups are mastered on-premises and synchronized to Office 365, then Office 365 users will be unable to use Outlook to manage group membership. To continue to enable users to manage distribution groups through Outlook, groups must be re-created in Office 365, which can pose problems for mail-enabled security groups that are used as both distribution lists for mail recipients and a mechanism for granting permissions to network resources on-premises.

In these instances, you might need to make a break between the security and distribution list functions, create a script to copy members from one group to another on a regular basis (so that the group membership is the same between both cloud and on-premises), or manage two groups separately. If you choose to maintain separate groups, you can filter those particular groups from being synchronized.

Dynamic distribution groups

Although dynamic distribution groups are supported in Office 365, they are only supported when they are created directly in Office 365. On-premises dynamic distribution groups cannot be synchronized to Office 365.

If you have dynamic distribution groups on-premises that you want to show up in Office 365, you can create a mail-enabled contact in Office 365 to provide global address list visibility for the group or convert the dynamic group to a static group and manage it as a normal group.

Office 365 Groups

Office 365 groups (also known as modern or unified groups) are a new type of group object in Office 365 and do not exist in the on-premises versions of Exchange. If your organization decides to use Office 365 groups, they will exist only in-cloud.

A feature in AAD Connect enables you to write a mail-enabled object back on-premises to provide global address list visibility to on-premises users for these objects. Object writeback is discussed in detail in Chapter 4, "Directory Synchronization Basics," and Chapter 5, "Installing Azure AD Connect."

INSIDE OUT

Office 365 Group Writeback Sender Authentication

AAD Connect enables you to configure a mail-enabled object to be written on-premises for Office 365 groups. However, the value for msExchRequireAuthToSendTo, which controls whether external users may send to an Exchange recipient, supplies the constant TRUE value in the AAD Connect attribute transformation. If you have configured Office 365 groups to allow external mail *and* have group writeback enabled *and* have configured your MX record to point to your on-premises environment, external senders attempting to deliver mail to an Office 365 will receive an non-delivery receipt (NDR). To work around this issue, either manually modify the msExchRequireAuthToSendTo attribute for the on-premises object representing the Office 365 group or create an AAD Connect rule to populate that attribute manually with FALSE.

Permissions and delegation

Part of the email migration planning exercise is determining the migration schedule. Although it's important to map out the schedule from the perspective of end-user communication, it's also important for another reason: permissions and delegation. It's critical to make an effort to move delegators and delegates together because not all the permissions work cross-premises. Although full mailbox access permissions should work, on-premises users won't be able to exercise certain rights (such as Send-As) against cloud mailboxes and vice versa.

Typically, users are delegated rights to other mailboxes or resources in their own work group or department, so that might be one way to attempt to organize and map out migration groups to preserve permissions and mailbox access.

Public folders

Depending on how long your on-premises Exchange organization has existed, you might have public folders (either older or modern). You can migrate both types of public folders to Office 365. However, just like mailbox migrations, there are several things to check prior to migration, such as folder uniqueness and proper attribute validation.

The standard IDFix tool does not detect mail-enabled public folders. If you are planning to migrate a significant number of mail-enabled public folders, you might find it helpful to validate that they don't have any invalid characters or improperly formatted SMTP addresses. You can use the script at *https://gallery.technet.microsoft.com/IDFix-for-Public-Folders-341522d6* to help identify potential problems with your mail-enabled public folders.

Mail routing

Mail routing between on-premises and cloud environments is a crucial component of a migration or coexistence. It is important to ensure that the servers designated for hybrid transport can send to and receive from Exchange Online.

Data loss prevention

Office 365 offers data loss protection features that are integrated with Exchange Online protection. Data loss prevention templates can be implemented to scan for sensitive data types such as Social Security numbers or credit cards and perform block, notify, redirect, or encrypt actions on those messages.

In addition, your organization might have an existing investment in data loss prevention technologies that meets specific requirements, and you might need to configure Office 365 to route outbound mail through that environment. If that is a requirement, you will most likely use a centralized mail transport configuration, criteria-based routing transport rules, or a combination. For more information about centralized mail transport, see Chapter 13.

Message encryption

Your organization might have a requirement to encrypt messages sent to particular recipients or that contain certain types of data. In these instances, you might need to configure forced-TLS connectors or enable Office 365 message encryption settings. For more information about Office 365 message encryption, see Chapter 14.

Message hygiene

Most organizations have some sort of message hygiene (anti-spam, anti-malware, heuristic analysis) products or services configured, either on-premises or hosted by a service provider. Depending on your organization's configuration and investment in those technologies, you might wish to continue using them or transition fully to Exchange Online Protection (EOP).

Although it is possible to configure multiple products for message hygiene in succession, it is not recommended. Exchange Online Protection uses, among other technologies and algorithms, IP reputation to determine whether a sending system is safe. Chaining multiple filtering products can have an adverse effect on the ability of EOP to provide the highest level of service.

Instead, you might consider cataloging rules and filters in your existing system and prepare to configure similar rules and filters in Exchange Online Protection.

Networking

When planning a migration of a core service such as messaging to an external system, consider how you will connect to that system both during the migration process and as you transition to operational management.

Bandwidth

One of the core questions surrounding network requirements is discovering how much bandwidth your users will consume post-migration. You can use a tool such as the Exchange Client Network Bandwidth Calculator to help estimate your bandwidth based on client profile and location or time zone data.

You can download the calculator from *https://gallery.technet.microsoft.com/Exchange-Client -Network-8af1bf00*.

Firewall

For mailbox migrations, free/busy lookups, Autodiscover, and mail transport to work correctly between on-premises and cloud environments, you must work with network administrators to enable the necessary communications.

From the perspective of the Exchange servers configured with hybrid connectivity, you need to ensure communication on port 25 inbound and outbound for mail transport; port 443 inbound for Autodiscover, Mailbox Replication Service, and free/busy; and ports 80 and 443 outbound for Exchange Federation and Certificate Revocation List checking.

For a complete list of hybrid endpoints, please refer to "Office 365 URLs and IP address ranges" at *https://support.office.com/en-us/article/Office-365-URLs-and-IP-address-ranges-8548a211 -3fe7-47cb-abb1-355ea5aa88a2*.

Load balancing

Many large organizations use either software or hardware load balancers as part of a solution to provide highly available access to services. Load balancers can be configured to work with Office 365. However, there are several things to consider, depending on the version of Exchange that is being used for hybrid transport and mailbox migration.

SSL offloading, termination, or bridging is not supported for Mailbox Replication Service traffic. In addition, for configuring hybrid migration endpoints, it is recommended that you create one-to-one Network Address Translation (NAT) addresses for each server used for mailbox migrations. This provides the most granular method to manage mailbox migration endpoints.

Several hardware and software vendors have whitepapers and guides to assist in configuring their load balancers to work with Exchange. You can find resources for Exchange 2010-qualified load balancers at *https://technet.microsoft.com/en-us/office/dn756394*.

Proxy

Microsoft recommends that you bypass proxy environments for Office 365. If your outbound traffic uses proxies, you might experience performance problems or service connection problems when attempting to use Office 365 services.

Proxy services are typically used either to perform web-filtering requests (to ensure users' traffic conforms to the organization's acceptable usage policy) or to provide caching and accelerate performance for frequently accessed resources. All traffic between on-premises and Office 365 endpoints is encrypted by SSL, so most proxy implementations are unable to view or cache the traffic (without sophisticated man-in-the-middle or SSL bridging capabilities).

For further information about how Office 365 works with proxies and methods of deploying proxy automatic configuration scripts to workstations, please see *https://blogs.technet.microsoft .com/undocumentedfeatures/tag/proxy-automatic-configuration/*.

DNS

Many tasks performed in Office 365 require you to configure specific DNS records to enable or complete service enablement.

Autodiscover

Autodiscover is the service whereby clients (whether they are desktop, web, or mobile clients or remote Exchange systems) locate Exchange resources. For most Office 365 deployments, Autodiscover is configured through a DNS CNAME record that points to either the on-premises Exchange organization (prior to migration) or Office 365 (post-migration).

Domain verification records

To make a domain available to use in Office 365, you must add it and then confirm ownership with a DNS TXT record. You can find more information about how to configure DNS TXT verification records in Chapter 1, "Office 365 Deployment Milestones."

Microsoft Federation Gateway

When configuring Exchange on-premises to share free/busy information with Exchange Online or other Exchange on-premises organizations or as part of the Hybrid Configuration Wizard, you must confirm ownership of your Exchange organization for the Microsoft Federation Gateway. You can generate the DNS verification record prior to running the Hybrid Configuration Wizard to streamline the process.

For more information about configuring DNS records for the Microsoft Federation Gateway, see Chapter 13.

MX record

The Mail eXchanger (MX) record tells mail transport agents where to route mail. Prior to migration, your MX record points to either your on-premises mail gateway or, perhaps, a hosted mail gateway service that provides antivirus and antispam services.

Post-migration, it's recommended that you update your MX record to point to Exchange Online Protection.

SPF, DKIM, and DMARC records

These records help prove the authenticity and authority of sending email systems. Although they are not required, it is recommended that you configure them.

In addition, if you are already using them in your environment, plan to include Office 365 services to ensure that recipients can continue to receive your mail.

For more information about configuring DKIM, see Chapter 7, "Inside the Security & Compliance Center: Alerting, Threat Management, and Reporting." For information about configuring SPF, DKIM, and DMARC in Office 365, see *https://technet.microsoft.com/en-us/library/mt734386(v=exchg.150).aspx.*

Network security appliances

In addition to firewalls and proxies, many organizations deploy network security appliances that inspect traffic, looking for suspicious activity. You can deploy intrusion detection systems (IDSs) and intrusion protection systems (IPSs) to monitor, alert, and take action on network traffic based on rules and activity profiles.

In some instances, these can slow or stop the flow of migration activities. Two such features of security appliances that can cause considerable delay or troubleshooting activities are flood mitigation and exfiltration protection. The exact terminology might vary, depending on the vendor, but the features restrict or deny the continued outbound data flow from your on-premises servers to Office 365, detecting the continuous stream of traffic to an off-premises destination as anomalous activity that might indicate data compromise or theft.

If your organization has deployed these types of devices, you will want to exclude traffic between the hybrid migration endpoints and Office 365 from any policies that interrupt the flow of migrating data.

Things that don't migrate

Although the directory synchronization and hybrid migration process have become increasingly complete, there are still things that don't translate between environments and, if you are using third-party tools to migrate from hosted or older systems, you'll need to capture parameters and attributes in the source environment that did not make it to the target system.

Access protocol configuration

Certain mailbox parameters, such as what access protocols are allowed, are not migrated in hybrid or third-party migrations. If you are using CASMailbox settings to control access to ActiveSync, POP3, IMAP, or Exchange Web Services, you will find that those settings do not persist between on-premises and cloud environments.

Calendar processing information

Calendar processing is the set of rules that is typically applied to shared and resource mailboxes, such as automatic booking, delegates, and scheduling horizons. These settings are not migrated in either hybrid migrations or third-party migrations.

You can build your own method to export and import these properties or use a script such as at *https://gallery.technet.microsoft.com/Export-and-Import-Calendar-123866af* to capture and reapply those configurations.

Forwarding addresses

If you have mailboxes configured with forwarding addresses (ForwardingAddress or ForwardingSmtpAddress), those values are not maintained in either hybrid or third-party migrations.

You can use the script at h*ttps://gallery.technet.microsoft.com/exchange/Forwarding-Address -Import-5b3ead8e* to export the data from your on-premises environment and re-apply it to cloud objects post-migration.

Retention tags and policies

Retention policy tags and retention policies are not synchronized or transferred between environments automatically. If you are using Exchange retention policy tags on-premises and wish to continue using them in Office 365, you must export them from your on-premises environment and import them to Office 365 before migrating mailboxes.

The scripts Export-RetentionTags.ps1 and Import-RetentionTags.ps1 are available in *%EXCHANGEINSTALLDIR%\Scripts*.

INSIDE OUT
Journaling retention tags

Although journaling as a feature is supported in Office 365 and Exchange Online, retention policies and retention policy tags with journaling cannot be imported. Depending on your version of Exchange, you might need to modify the Import-RetentionPolicyTags.ps1 script.

To make the necessary changes to the Import-RetentionPolicyTags.ps1 script, locate the lines that contain the following text and comment them out:

- tagExists.LabelForJournaling
- tagExists.MessageFormatForJournaling
- LabelForJournaling
- MessageFormatForJournaling

You can find more information about exporting and importing retention policy tags at *https://technet.microsoft.com/en-us/library/jj907307(v=exchg.150).aspx*.

Transport rules and configurations

Transport rules and configurations are not migrated between environments. Depending on your organization, these might or might not be necessary. Many organizations, when migrating to Office 365, take the opportunity to create new rules. However, if your organization has a high degree of customization, you might find it helpful to transfer those settings and then remove what is unnecessary.

In addition, if you are in a position to need to migrate to a new Office 365 tenant, you might need to export and import transport rules as well.

You can use a script such as you can find at *https://gallery.technet.microsoft.com/exchange/Migrate-EOP-Settings-9d480325* to help with this task—either from on-premises to cloud or between cloud organizations.

Additional tools

In addition to the tools and scripts mentioned in this chapter, Microsoft provides planning, deployment, and troubleshooting tools to help you plan and complete your migration.

Remote Connectivity Analyzer

The Exchange Remote Connectivity Analyzer is a web-based tool that can be used to troubleshoot Autodiscover, free/busy, and mail flow issues and works with both Office 365 and Exchange on-premises deployments.

You can access the tool at *https://testconnectivity.microsoft.com*.

Exchange Server Deployment Assistant

The Exchange Deployment Assistant is a web-based tool you can use to determine which components you need to install and steps to follow to complete a hybrid migration. The Exchange Deployment Assistant is available from *https://technet.microsoft.com/en-us/office/dn756393*.

Summary

This chapter focused on preparing your on-premises Exchange environment for an Office 365 migration plan for how to transition services to Office 365. Not all services you use on-premises might have a direct translation to a service offered in Office 365, and you might need to update third-party applications or processes to adopt Office 365 fully.

Understanding the Office 365 resource types

When performing nearly any action in Office 365, you perform it against some type of object, whether it's a user, a contact, a group, or a resource mailbox—the list goes on. Depending on the type of environment (managed domains with cloud ID or synchronized from an on-premises directory) and type of workload (Exchange, Skype, Microsoft SharePoint, Azure Active Directory), you might need to manage one or more object types or an object type in different contexts (managing the object properties of an Azure AD user versus the email properties of a mail-enabled user).

The Office 365 Admin Center displays several types of objects, as shown in Figure 11-1.

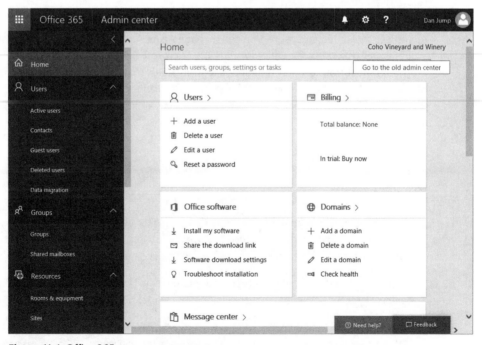

Figure 11-1 Office 365 resource types

The objects presented are a composite view, displaying properties from Azure Active Directory as well as Exchange Online and Skype for Business Online.

When you explore the details of a user, for example, this is evident. See Figure 11-2.

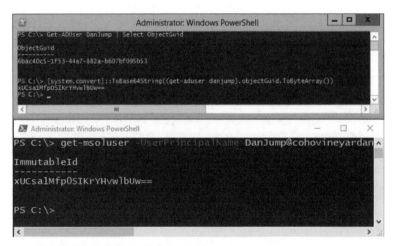

Figure 11-2 Active user properties

As you can see in the screenshot, you can manage Azure Active Directory and Exchange properties (as well as settings for Office ProPlus and Microsoft OneDrive). For example, on a user's properties sheet, you can view or manage Sign-In Status (Azure Active Directory), Group Memberships (Azure Active Directory or Exchange), Product Licenses (Azure Active Directory), Roles (Azure Active Directory), User Name (Azure Active Directory), Email Address (Exchange), and Aliases (Exchange).

INSIDE OUT

Building the Office 365 Admin Center, one cmdlet at a time

The Office 365 Admin Center provides a nice at-a-glance view of operations, but as you get into the daily administration of Office 365, you'll probably be looking for more efficient ways to do things. That's where Windows PowerShell comes in.

Depending on the types of objects you want to manage (Azure Active Directory, Exchange Online, Skype for Business Online, or SharePoint Online), you might have to download different modules.

Although you can access Exchange Online by importing an Exchange Online session into a standard Windows PowerShell environment, the other online services need specific modules to make the necessary commands available.

- For Skype for Business, download and install the module from *www.microsoft.com /en-us/download/details.aspx?id=39366*.

- For SharePoint Online, download and install the module from *www.microsoft.com /en-us/download/details.aspx?id=35588*.

- Azure Active Directory requires multiple components, including the Microsoft Online Services Module (*http://connect.microsoft.com/site1164/Downloads/Download-Details.aspx?DownloadID=59185*) and the Azure AD Preview Module (*https:// docs.microsoft.com/en-us/powershell/azure/install-adv2?view=azureadps-2.0*).

After you install the modules, you can connect to any of the online services to retrieve information about objects in your tenant. To make your administration easier, consider connecting to multiple services from a single Windows PowerShell console—that will enable you to use cmdlets from any of the modules available for use.

Azure Active Directory

Just as Active Directory is the foundation for on-premises services such as Exchange and Skype for Business, Azure Active Directory plays the analogous foundational role for online services. Before you can manipulate Azure AD objects with Windows PowerShell, you must download and install the necessary components.

Some features require the older version of the cmdlets (Azure Active Directory 1.0 or MSOnline), and some features require Azure Active Directory 2.0. Eventually, all features will be migrated to the newer module, but as of the time of writing, you still need both sets of modules to administer all the object types and settings fully.

- Download and install the .NET Framework 4.5 or later (if you don't already have it) from *https://www.microsoft.com/en-us/download/details.aspx?id=42642*.

- *Install* PowerShellGet, available in Windows 10, the Windows Management Framework 5.0 (*http://go.microsoft.com/fwlink/?LinkId=398175*), or through the MSI Installer package for PowerShellGet at *http://go.microsoft.com/fwlink/?LinkID=746217&clcid=0x409*.

- Install the Azure AD PowerShell 1.0 module from *http://connect.microsoft.com/site1164 /Downloads/DownloadDetails.aspx?DownloadID=59185*.

After you install these components, launch an elevated Windows PowerShell prompt and run the following command to install the Azure Active Directory 2.0 PowerShell module:

```
Install-Module AzureADPreview
```

If this is the first time you've used Install-Module or PowerShellGet, you might be prompted to install NuGet or allow it to download from untrusted repositories.

After you've installed the necessary components, you can launch a new Windows PowerShell window and connect to Azure Active Directory, as shown in Figure 11-3:

```
Import-Module MSOnline,AzureADPreview

$Credential = Get-Credential

Connect-MsolService -Credential $Credential

Connect-AzureAD -Credential $Credential
```

Figure 11-3 Connecting to Azure and MSOnline PowerShell endpoints

From here, you have several avenues to view, create, manage, or delete objects. This section focuses mainly on cloud ID users. Because many synchronized users' details are managed on-premises, you won't be able to run most Set- commands on them. For purposes of this discussion, the MSOnline module cmdlets are referenced because the newer Azure Active Directory and Azure AD Preview modules don't have all of the capability at this time.

INSIDE OUT

Windows PowerShell profiles and functions

As an administrator, you'll likely find yourself using Windows PowerShell to work with objects in Office 365. You can create functions and store them in your Windows PowerShell profile so you can access them more easily.

A function is essentially a script that's pre-loaded into memory and can be accessed by typing the function name. For example, you can create a function by typing the following:

```
Function o365Logon($Credential)
{ Import-Module MSOnline,AzureADPreview
Connect-MsolService -Credential $Credential
Connect-AzureAD -Credential $Credential }
```

This would enable you to save a credential object (Get-PSCredential) and then run the function and pass the stored credential $Credential to it:

```
$Credential = Get-Credential
o365logon -Credential $Credential
```

For an example of a Windows PowerShell profile, see *https://blogs.technet.microsoft.com /undocumentedfeatures/2016/01/22/customizing-the-windows-powershell-console/.*

Object types

In Azure Active Directory, you can manipulate several object and resource types. Here's a list of types of common objects you can work with.

- **Users**   Security principal that allows logon. Licenses for services are applied to users, and the licenses that those services grant might attach additional properties to the Azure Active Directory user object.

- **Groups**   A collection of objects, such as users, contacts, or other groups.

- **Contacts**   A contact that represents a recipient, typically in an external organization, that does not have logon privileges.

Managing the objects

As mentioned earlier, there are many ways to interact with objects in Office 365, including the Office 365 admin centers and Windows PowerShell.

Users

Users are the basic security principals in Azure Active Directory. The main cmdlets for managing users are:

- New-MsolUser

- Get-MsolUser

- Set-MsolUser

- Remove-MsolUser

CHAPTER 11

As you might expect, New-MsolUser is used for creating security principals, Get-MsolUser returns objects, Set-MsolUser sets properties on the objects, and Remove-MsolUser removes a user object from Azure Active Directory.

In these next two examples, you can see how the process of creating a new user is a relatively simple task in either the Office 365 Admin Center or Windows PowerShell.

To create a user in the Office 365 Admin Center, follow these steps.

1.   Navigate to Office 365 Admin Center.

2.   From the Home screen, click + Add A User (shown in Figure 11-4) or, in the navigation pane, select Users | Active Users and then click + Add A User.

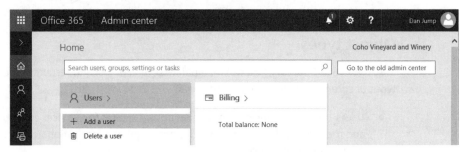

Figure 11-4 Adding a user

3.   Fill out the user details. Optionally, specify a password (one is randomly generated if you don't select the option), whether you want any administrative roles granted, and licensing.

    If licensing is selected, additional features are enabled, such as an Exchange mailbox or access granted to download the Office ProPlus Click-To-Run media. See Figure 11-5.

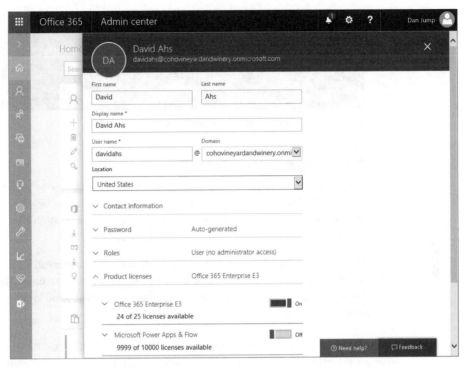

Figure 11-5 Office 365 Admin Center Add User dialog box

4. Close the Add User dialog box.

To do the equivalent new user creation task in Windows PowerShell, follow these steps.

1. Launch a Windows PowerShell window and connect to Azure Active Directory with the Connect-MsolService cmdlet.

2. Use the following cmdlet and parameters shown in Figure 11-6 (replacing the UserPrincipalName and LicenseAssignment for your environment) to create a new user with the same options you selected in the Office 365 Admin Center:

```
New-MsolUser -UserPrincipalName kimakers@cohovineyardandwinery.onmicrosoft.com
-FirstName Kim -LastName Akers -DisplayName "Kim Akers" -UsageLocation US -Licen-
seAssignment cohovineyardandwinery:ENTERPRISEPACK
```

CHAPTER 11

Figure 11-6 Creating a new user with New-MsolUser

NOTE NEW-MSOLUSER PARAMETERS

The Location property you see when you add a user in the Office 365 Admin Center maps to the -UsageLocation parameter in the New-MsolUser or Set-MsolUser cmdlets. A location is required when you assign a license to a user. The location is intended to indicate the country where the services are consumed.

The Office 365 Admin Center automatically displays licenses available in your tenant. To retrieve a list of available licenses, use the Get-MsolAccountSku cmdlet. The license will be displayed as tenant:LICENSENAME, and you can use that value for the LicenseAssignment parameter.

For more information on license assignment in Office 365, see Chapter 2, "Preparing your environment for the cloud," as well as *https://blogs.technet.microsoft.com /undocumentedfeatures/2016/06/21/office-365-license-assignment/*, "Office 365 License Assignment."

You can use the Get-MsolUser cmdlet to look at the properties of a user. For example, if you want to return the list of properties that appear in the Office 365 Admin Center default view of an active user, you can run these commands when connected to Office 365 by Windows PowerShell.

```
$FormatEnumerationLimit = -1

$User = Get-MsolUser -UserPrincipalName DanJump@cohovineyardandwinery.onmicrosoft.com

$Groups = @()

$Roles = @()

$GroupsMembers = @()

$RolesMembers = @()

$Groups = Get-MsolGroup

$Groups | % { $data = Get-MsolGroupMember -GroupObjectId $_.ObjectID | ? { $_.ObjectId
-eq $User.ObjectId }; $data | Add-Member -Type NoteProperty -Value $_.DisplayName -Name
"Groups"; $GroupsMembers += $data }
```

```
$Roles = Get-MsolRole

$Roles | % { $RoleName = $_.Name; $data = Get-MsolRoleMember -RoleObjectID $_.ObjectId
| ? { $_.ObjectId -eq $User.ObjectId }; $data | Add-Member -Type NoteProperty -Value
$RoleName -Name Roles; $RolesMembers += $data }

$User | Add-Member -Type NoteProperty -Value $GroupsMembers -Name Groups

$User | Add-Member -Type NoteProperty -Value $Rolesmembers -Name Roles

$User | Format-List @{Name="User Name"; Expression={$_.UserPrincipalName}}, @
{Name="Aliases"; Expression={$_.ProxyAddresses}}, Licenses, @{Name="Group Member-
ships"; Expression={$_.Groups.Groups}}, @{Name="Sign-in Status"; Expression={If
($_.BlockCredential -eq $false) {"Sign-in Allowed"} Else {"Sign-in Blocked"}}}, @
{Name="Roles";Expression={$_.Roles.Roles}}, @{Name="Display Name"; Expression={$_.Dis-
playName}}, @{Name="Office Phone";Expression={$_.PhoneNumber}}
```

The resulting output in Figure 11-7 shows you the same data that you see in the portal, with the exception of Office Installs (because there currently is no Windows PowerShell cmdlet you can use to return that data).

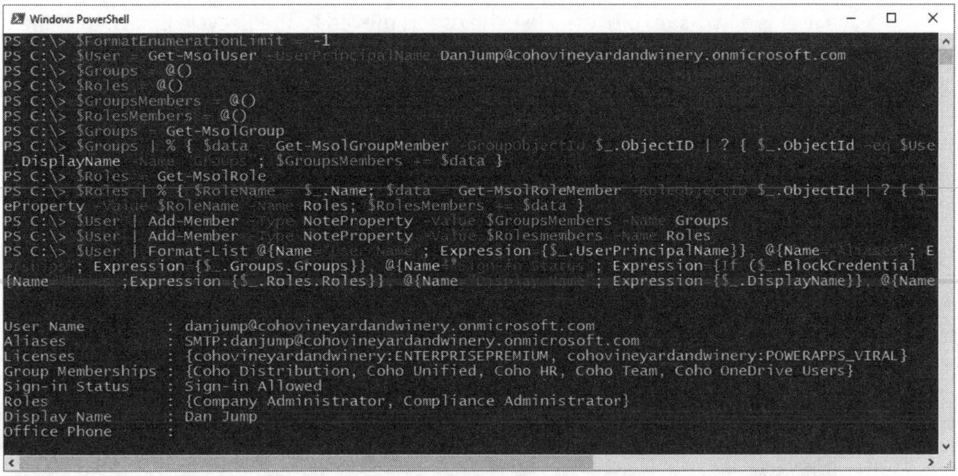

Figure 11-7 Windows PowerShell script to display user information similar to Office 365 Admin Center

WHAT IS THIS OBJECTID?

Although most of the Microsoft Online cmdlets enable you to manage objects by using the email address of an object, there are a few (such as Get-MsolRole, Get-MsolRoleMember, Get-MsolGroup, and Get-MsolGroupMember) that require you to use an object ID. The

CHAPTER 11

object ID is the globally unique identifier (GUID) of the object in the tenant. You can use the -SearchString parameter to search for an object if you don't know its GUID.

As the newer Azure Active Directory cmdlets replace the older MSOnline cmdlets, using ObjectId will become a more common parameter, and you'll have to replace parameters such as UserPrincipalName or EmailAddress with ObjectId or SearchString if you want to continue locating objects by a friendly name. For Get-AzureADUser, you can use either -ObjectID <GUID> or -ObjectID <emailaddress> to locate an object.

Just as you can navigate and edit the properties of a user through the admin center, you can also update the properties by using the Set-MsolUser command. For example, you could use the following command to change the Department property for a user.

```
Set-MsolUser -UserPrincipalName kimakers@cohovineyardandwinery.onmicrosoft.com -Department "Marketing"
```

The Remove-MsolUser cmdlet is the corollary to deleting a user in the admin center. Deleting a user is a two-step process. First, the user is moved to the Recycle Bin. Then, if the user is not recovered in 30 days, an Azure Active Directory cleanup job removes the object. Alternatively, you can run the Remove-MsolUser cmdlet with the RemoveFromRecycleBin parameter to delete the user fully, as shown in Figure 11-8.

```
Remove-Msoluser -UserPrincipalName DavidHamilton@cohovineyard.onmicrosoft.com
```

```
Remove-Msoluser -UserPrincipalName DavidHamilton@cohovineyard.onmicrosoft.com
-RemoveFromRecycleBin
```

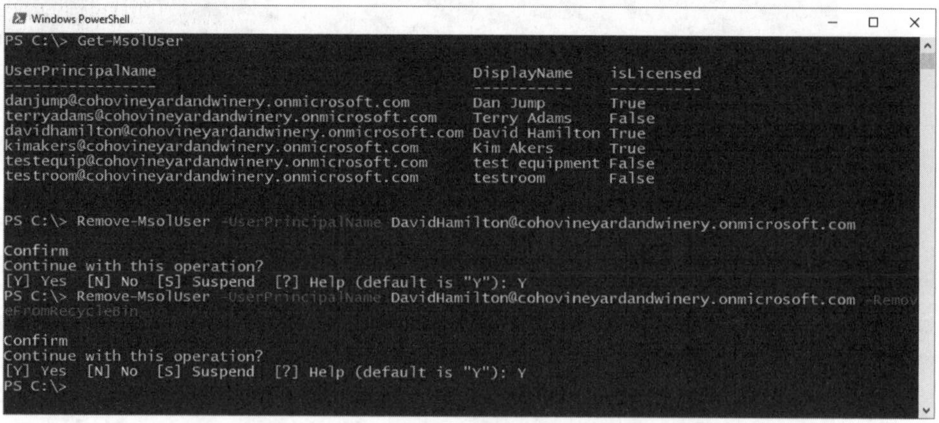

Figure 11-8 Removing a user from Azure Active Directory and the Recycle Bin

Contacts

Contacts are objects that you can create to represent mail-enabled external recipients. External recipients can be on-premises mailboxes or distribution lists that aren't synchronized to Office 365, third-party email systems, or partner organizations—any object that you want to configure to appear in the global address list.

Contacts can be created from the Office 365 Admin Center with the following process.

1. Navigate to Office 365 Admin Center.

2. From the Home screen, select Users and then select Contacts.

3. On the Contacts page, click + Add A Contact.

4. Type the properties for the new contact and then click Add.

5. Close the New Contact dialog box.

Contacts, like distribution lists and Office 365 groups, are actually created in Exchange Online and then synchronized back into Azure Active Directory. As such, there is no corresponding new contact cmdlet in either the MSOnline or AzureAD PowerShell modules.

Groups

There are many types of groups in Azure AD and Office 365.

- Microsoft Online roles

- Distribution and security groups

- Modern or unified groups

Role groups

You use roles to grant rights to perform certain functions in either the Office 365 Admin Center or other service admin centers. For example, the Global Administrator role grants full administrative access to every object and inside every service admin center in the tenant.

You can manage role memberships from the Office 365 Admin Center by navigating to a user, clicking the Edit button next to Roles, and then selecting a role you want to assign to the user. By selecting Customized Administrator (Figure 11-9), you can select either built-in Office 365 administrator roles or more restrictive roles for individual services or features.

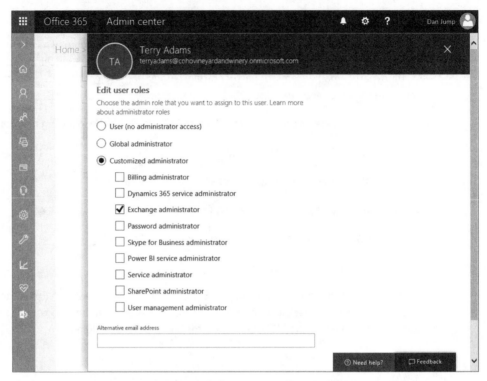

Figure 11-9 Granting a user administrator roles

If you want to manage the user's role membership from Windows PowerShell, you must get a list of roles and role ObjectIds, which you obtain from running Get-MsolRole. See Figure 11-10.

After you find the ObjectId of the role you want to add a member to, you can note it, copy it to the clipboard or Notepad, or save it to a variable.

The next step is to locate the user's ObjectId. You can find that by running:

```
Get-MsolUser -UserPrincipalName user@cohovineyardandwinery.onmicrosoft.com | Select
ObjectId
```

Again, save the value to the clipboard, Notepad, or a variable.

Finally, assign the role to the user and confirm membership. Use this command:

```
Add-MsolRoleMember -RoleObjectId <role_object_ID> -RoleMemberObjectID <user_object_ID>
```

Figure 11-10 Executing Get-MsolRole from Windows PowerShell

In the following example, the object ID for the user Terry Adams is saved to the variable $UserObjectID, and the Object ID of the role to be assigned to the user, SharePoint Service Administrator, is saved as $SharePointRoleObjectID. Review the output in Figure 11-11.

```
$SharePointRoleObjectId = (Get-MsolRole | ? { $_.Name -eq "SharePoint Service Adminis-
trator" }).ObjectId
```

```
$UserObjectID = (Get-MsolUser -UserPrincipalName terryadams@cohovineyardandwinery.onmi-
crosoft.com).ObjectId
```

```
Add-MsolRoleMember -RoleObjectId $SharePointRoleObjectId -RoleMemberObjectId
$UserObjectID
```

```
Get-MsolRoleMember -RoleObjectId $SharePointRoleObjectId
```

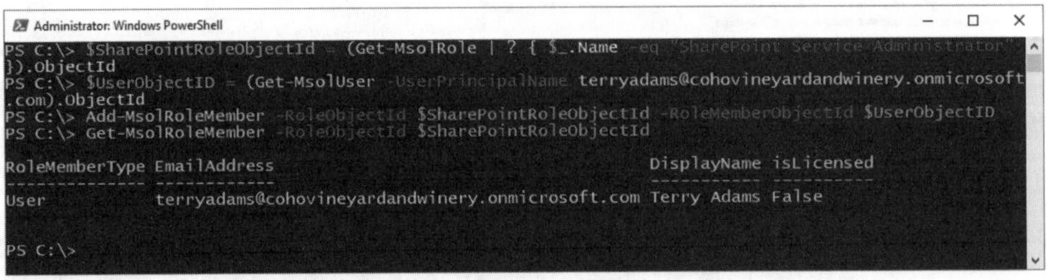

```
Administrator: Windows PowerShell                                          —  □  ×
PS C:\> $SharePointRoleObjectId = (Get-MsolRole | ? { $_.Name -eq "SharePoint Service Administrator"
}).ObjectId
PS C:\> $UserObjectID = (Get-MsolUser -UserPrincipalName terryadams@cohovineyardandwinery.onmicrosoft
.com).ObjectId
PS C:\> Add-MsolRoleMember -RoleObjectId $SharePointRoleObjectId -RoleMemberObjectId $UserObjectID
PS C:\> Get-MsolRoleMember -RoleObjectId $SharePointRoleObjectId

RoleMemberType EmailAddress                                        DisplayName isLicensed
-------------- ------------                                        ----------- ----------
User           terryadams@cohovineyardandwinery.onmicrosoft.com Terry Adams False


PS C:\>
```

Figure 11-11 Assigning a role to a user through Windows PowerShell

Roles are built in to the service and cannot be added or removed.

Security and distribution groups

Security and distribution groups (or distribution lists, as they're sometimes referred to) are group objects that can be used for granting access to resources or delivering messages to multiple users.

Security and distribution groups can be easily managed from the Office 365 Admin Center, as demonstrated in the following example.

1. Navigate to Office 365 Admin Center.

2. From the Home screen, point to Groups and then select Groups.

3. On the Groups page, click + Add A Group.

4. From the Type drop-down list, select the appropriate type of group.

    Office 365 groups, mail-enabled security groups, and distribution lists are provisioned through Exchange Online, and then the underlying group object is synchronized back to Azure Active Directory through the backward sync process. See Figure 11-12.

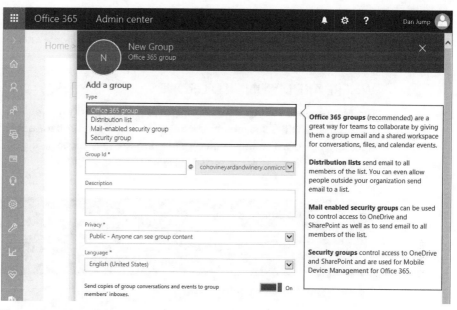

Figure 11-12 The Office 365 New Group dialog box

5. Fill out the appropriate group details.

    If you choose an Office 365 group, a distribution list, or a mail-enabled security group, you can also enable the group to receive messages from Internet users. This sets the RequireSenderAuthenticationEnabled parameter to $false in Exchange Online. For Office 365 groups, you also have options to configure whether the group is public or private, what language the mailbox is in, and whether you want members of the group to receive emails and invites in their mailbox like a traditional distribution or mail-enabled security group. If you want to configure an Office 365 group to receive email from external senders, you have to edit the group after creation.

6. Click Add.

Because Office 365 groups, distribution lists, and mail-enabled security groups are Exchange objects, the only option for creation from the Azure Active Directory module or MSOnline modules is a standard security group. You can create a security group in Azure AD by following this example.

1. Launch a Windows PowerShell window and connect to Azure Active Directory with the Connect-MsolService cmdlet.

2. Use the following cmdlet and parameters to create a new security group with the same options as you selected in the Office 365 Admin Center.

CHAPTER 11

```
New-MsolGroup -DisplayName "Coho Marketing Security Group" -Description "Marketing
Security Group" -ManagedBy (Get-MsolUser -userprincipalname kimakers@cohovineyard-
andwinery.onmicrosoft.com).ObjectID
```

WHERE ARE MY UNIFIED GROUPS?

Get-MsolGroup shows you distribution groups or lists, security groups, and unified groups
(also known as Office 365 groups or modern groups). However, because unified groups are
a combination of a distribution group and a mailbox, they appear as distribution lists with
the Get-MsolGroup cmdlet, as shown in Figure 11-13.

Figure 11-13 Get-MsolGroup

Even though they show up as DistributionList in Get-MsolGroup, they do not show up as
distribution lists when using the companion Get-DistributionList in Exchange Online. You
must use the Get-UnifiedGroup cmdlet, which is covered later in this chapter.

Exchange Online

As is mentioned elsewhere in this book, Exchange Online is the messaging service that's built
on Azure Active Directory. You can administer it through both the Office 365 Admin Center
(under Admin Centers | Exchange) and Windows PowerShell. To connect to Exchange Online by
Windows PowerShell, you only need to import the cmdlets from Exchange Online into your current session. See Figure 11-14.

```
$Credential = Get-Credential

$ExchangeSession = New-PSSession -ConfigurationName Microsoft.Exchange -ConnectionUri
https://outlook.office365.com/powershell-liveid -Authentication Basic -AllowRedirection
-Credential $Credential
```

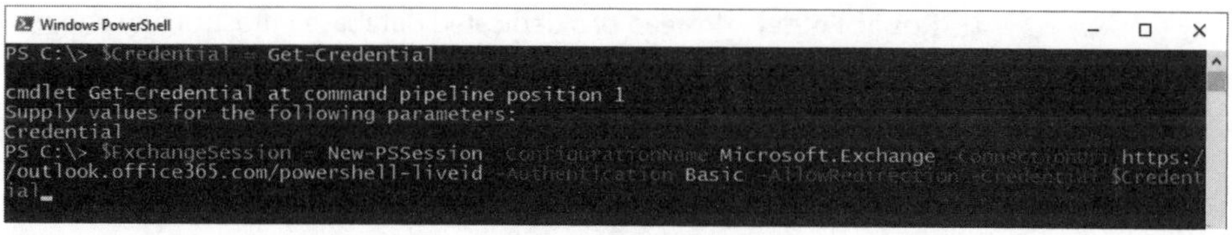

Figure 11-14 Connecting to Exchange Online PowerShell endpoint

Object types

Exchange Online has several types of objects, many of which overlap the objects that you can create or manipulate with Azure Active Directory and MSOnline. The types of objects in Exchange Online include:

- **Mailboxes**   In Exchange terminology, a mailbox is a recipient data storage object attached to an Active Directory security principal. In terms of Office 365 and Exchange Online, it's a tenant-level data storage container attached to an Azure Active Directory user object.

  - **Regular**   A regular mailbox is a normal mailbox attached to a security principal.

  - **Shared**   A shared mailbox is a mailbox that has been configured as a resource. A resource mailbox typically has a disabled logon security principal and isn't logged on to explicitly (with a user name and password). Shared mailboxes in Office 365 don't require licenses. Without a license, a shared mailbox cannot be logged on to with a user name or password or added to an ActiveSync profile. Shared mailboxes, from a resource perspective, cannot have the calendar processing parameters AddNewRequestsTentatively, ProcessExternalMeetingMessages, or ResourceDelegates configured.

  - **Room**   A room mailbox is a resource mailbox with specific recipient attributes that designate it as a conference room. The calendar processing agent is enabled in room mailboxes. You can configure room mailboxes with additional details such as ResourceCapacity to indicate the size of the room.

  - **Equipment**   An equipment mailbox is a resource mailbox with specific attributes that designate it as a type of equipment; it might be used for anything that a user can check out or reserve, such as a laptop, media station, projector, conference line, or car. Calendar processing can be applied to equipment mailboxes.

  - **Group**   A group mailbox is a special type of mailbox containing the storage for a unified group.

  - **Inactive**   An inactive mailbox is a mailbox that has been put on hold prior to removal of its license. Inactive mailboxes are used for preserving content of deleted mailboxes.

CHAPTER 11

- **Public Folder** Instead of a dedicated database infrastructure and model from previous versions of Exchange, Microsoft designed modern public folders to store the public folder hierarchy and data inside of specially designated mailboxes. This facilitates the use of a single resiliency method (Database Availability Groups) for all storage in Exchange.

- **Site** A site mailbox is the combination of a SharePoint site membership, an Exchange mailbox for email messages, and a SharePoint site for documents.

   The Site Mailbox feature was deprecated as of March 2017. You can no longer provision new site mailboxes, but existing site mailboxes will continue to function. Office 365 tenants created after March 2017 do not have access to the site mailbox feature. For more information about the transition plan for site mailboxes to Office 365 groups, visit *https://support.office.com/en-us/article/Prepare-for-using-site -mailboxes-in-Office-365-6381daa5-3d98-4629-972d-d19e1dc48c1b.*

- **Mail-Enabled Users** A mail-enabled user has the features of a contact overlaid with an Active Directory (or Azure Active Directory) security principal. In the context of Exchange Online, mail-enabled users (or mail users) are typically used to represent Exchange on-premises mailboxes in a hybrid configuration. Mail users have the ability to log on to an Office 365 tenant and consume other services.

- **Contacts** As mentioned previously, a contact is an object that represents a recipient in an address book. From an Exchange Online perspective, a contact is a mail object that represents a recipient not present in the Office 365 global address list, such as a mailbox or distribution list in an external organization or in an on-premises solution that doesn't have recipients synchronized to the tenant.

- **Groups** A group is a collection of objects, such as users, contacts, or other groups. There are several types of groups in Exchange Online.

   - **Distribution** A distribution group is the simplest form of list, containing mail-enabled recipients. You can configure all distribution lists to accept or reject mail from Internet senders (by the RequireSenderAuthenticationEnabled parameter).

   - **Mail-Enabled Security** Mail-enabled security groups are distribution lists that can also be used to secure resources such as SharePoint online sites.

   - **Unified** Unified groups (also known as Office 365 groups or modern groups) are the combination of a mailbox (a group mailbox, as listed previously) and a distri-bution list. Unified groups have distribution list–like features that enable users to receive a message in their inboxes and preserve a copy of the message in the group mailbox for later viewing.

- **Room Lists**   A room list is a special type of distribution group made up of room mailboxes and is useful for helping users find an available conference or meeting room from a group of rooms.

- **Dynamic Distribution**   The membership of a dynamic distribution group is calculated each time a message is delivered to it.

Managing the objects

Just as you can manage directory objects through both the admin centers and Azure AD PowerShell, you can also manage Exchange-specific objects both ways.

Mailboxes

As discussed previously in this chapter, users are the fundamental principal objects in Azure Active Directory. A mailbox is the primary recipient object type in Office 365 and Exchange Online. The main cmdlets for creating, managing, and deleting mailboxes are:

- New-Mailbox

- Set-Mailbox

- Remove-Mailbox

In these next two examples, you see a new mailbox created in both the Office 365 Admin Center and in Windows PowerShell. The first is from the admin center.

These steps are identical to those to create an Azure Active Directory user from the Office 365 Admin Center earlier, with one minor change—you must select a license that includes a service plan for Exchange Online.

Here are the steps.

1. On the Home screen, click + Add A User or point to Users and select Active Users.

2. Fill out the user details. Optionally, specify a password (one is randomly generated if you don't select the option) and whether you want to assign any administrative roles.

3. Expand Product Licenses and then select a license that includes an Exchange Online service plan. You can enable a top-level license (which enables all service plans and features) or expand a license and select only Exchange Online, as shown in Figure 11-15.

CHAPTER 11

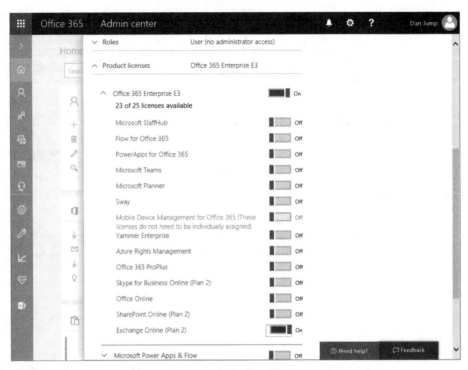

Figure 11-15 Assigning a product license as part of creating a new user

4.   Click Add.

5.   If you would like to send information about the new user and the user's password to the administrator, click Send Email And Close. Otherwise, clear the Send Password In Email check box and click Close.

Although user mailboxes require a license, shared and resource mailboxes do not. You can create these mailboxes through the Office 365 Admin Center (Groups | Shared Mailboxes | Add A Mailbox for shared mailboxes or Resources | Rooms & Equipment | Add for room and equipment mailboxes), the Exchange Admin Center (Recipients | Resources | + | Room Mailbox or Equipment Mailbox for room and equipment mailboxes or Recipients | Shared | + for shared mailboxes), or Windows PowerShell (using New-Mailbox -Type [room | shared | equipment]) for the appropriate mailbox type.

When creating a room, equipment, or shared mailbox through either one of the admin centers or Windows PowerShell, a disabled Azure Active Directory user account is created as well for the mailbox.

You can also remove a mailbox from either the Office 365 Admin Center or Exchange Admin Center or through a remote Exchange Online session by running the Remove-Mailbox cmdlet.

In Exchange Online (as opposed to Azure Active Directory), if you remove a mailbox, the deletion flows through the backward synchronization process to Azure Active Directory, and the associated user account will be moved to the Recycle Bin.

When this happens, the user account's UserPrincipalName is renamed ExRemoved-<*guid*>@ *tenant*.onmicrosoft.com, as shown in Figure 11-16.

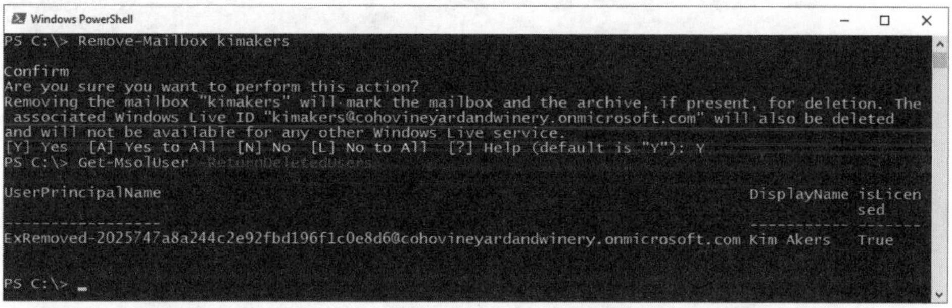

Figure 11-16 Mailbox removed using Windows PowerShell with the Remove-Mailbox cmdlet

INSIDE OUT

Recovering a deleted mailbox

It's a fact of IT administration—at some point, human error happens and a user account is mistakenly deleted. When that happens in an Office 365 environment, how do you recover the account and mailbox?

In the example shown in Figure 11-17, user Kim Akers has been deleted through a remote Windows PowerShell session, although it also could have happened through an automated process or from the admin center.

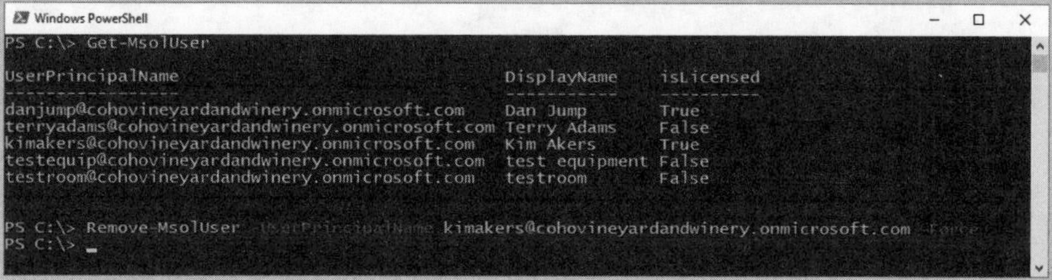

Figure 11-17 User removed in Windows PowerShell

After the user has been deleted, you can confirm that the user is in the Azure Active Directory Recycle Bin and the mailbox is in a SoftDeleted state by using the Windows PowerShell commands Get-MsolUser -ReturnDeletedUsers and Get-Mailbox -SoftDeletedMailbox, as shown in Figure 11-18.

Figure 11-18 Confirming that user and mailbox are deleted

The steps to recover are straightforward, from either the admin center or Windows PowerShell. From the admin center, follow these steps.

1.   Point to Users and then select Deleted Users. See Figure 11-19.

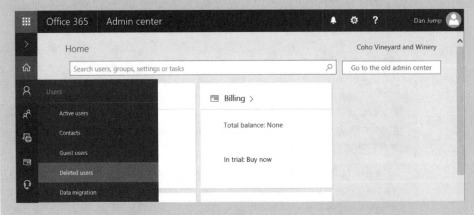

Figure 11-19 Office 365 Admin Center showing the Deleted Users option

2.   Select the user and click Restore.

3.   When prompted, select either Auto-Generate Password or Let Me Create The Password and click Restore. See Figure 11-20.

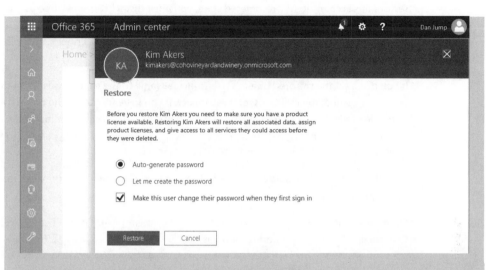

Figure 11-20 Restoring a deleted user

4. If you chose to have the new password auto-generated, record the new password. If you want to email the new password to the administrator, click Send Email And Close. Otherwise, clear the Send Password In Email check box and then click Close.

5. Click Close.

After a short period, the user should be visible in Users | Active Users. You might find that you need to refresh the webpage.

The restore process is similarly easy from Windows PowerShell, as shown in Figure 11-21, using the Restore-MsolUser command.

Figure 11-21 Using Restore-MsolUser to recover a user account and mailbox

If, however, you removed a user with an Exchange mailbox from the Exchange Admin Center, the user account is renamed to ExRemoved-*<guid>*@*tenant*.onmicrosoft.com. To restore this account to its pre-deleted state, you must restore it from Windows PowerShell, using the Restore-MsolUser cmdlet with the NewUserPrincipalName parameter (specifying the original UserPrincipalName as its argument), or reset the UserPrincipalName after the restore has completed.

If you don't set the restored object's UserPrincipalName to the value it was when the mailbox was attached, the mailbox won't reconnect. If you have forgotten the original address of the deleted mailbox, you can retrieve it by running the following command:

```
Get-Mailbox -SoftDeletedMailbox | Select DisplayName,PrimarySmtpAddress,UserPrincipal
Name,WindowsEmailAddress,MicrosfotOnlineServicesID
```

Depending on your configuration, one of those values will contain the previous mailbox identity of the user.

For more advanced account recovery techniques involving AAD Connect, please refer to Chapter 4, "Directory Synchronization Basics."

You can also create a user mailbox by using Windows PowerShell.

1. Launch a Windows PowerShell window and connect to Azure Active Directory with the Connect-MsolService cmdlet.

2. Use the following cmdlet and parameters to create a new mailbox-enabled user with the same options you selected in the admin center (Exchange Online only as part of the Enterprise E3 license).

```
[array]$DisabledPlans = @()

$Sku = (Get-MsolAccountSku | ? { $_.AccountSkuId -like "*ENTERPRISEPACK*"}).
AccountSkuId

[array]$ServicePlans = (Get-MsolAccountSku | ? { $_.AccountSkuId -eq $sku
}).ServiceStatus

[array]$EnabledPlans = @('EXCHANGE_S_ENTERPRISE')

 [regex]$EnabledPlansRegex = '(?i)^(' + (($EnabledPlans |foreach
{[regex]::escape($_)}) -join "|") + ')$'

 Foreach ($Plan in $ServicePlans)

 {

$item = $Plan.ServicePlan.ServiceName

If ($item -notmatch $EnabledPlansRegEx)

{$DisabledPlans += $Plan.ServicePlan.ServiceName}
```

```
}

$LicenseOptions = New-MsolLicenseOptions -AccountSkuId $Sku -DisabledPlans
$DisabledPlans

New-MsolUser -UserPrincipalName DavidHamilton@cohovineyardandwinery.onmicrosoft.
com -FirstName David -LastName Hamilton -DisplayName "David Hamilton" -UsageLoca-
tion US -LicenseAssignment cohovineyardandwinery:ENTERPRISEPACK -LicenseOptions
$LicenseOptions
```

The Get-Mailbox cmdlet returns data about mailboxes in your Exchange Online tenant. You can specify a number of parameters to return different sets of mailboxes.

- **IncludeInactiveMailboxes**   When using this parameter, Get-Mailbox returns mailboxes for deleted users that have had LitigationHold set on them along with active mailboxes.

- **InactiveMailboxesOnly**   As the name implies, this parameter causes Get-Mailbox to return only inactive mailboxes. Active mailboxes are not displayed in the output.

- **PublicFolder**   The PublicFolder parameter causes Get-Mailbox to return only the public folders that were created as part of the public folder topology (either new in Office 365 or migrated from an on-premises environment).

- **GroupMailbox**   With the GroupMailbox parameter, Get-Mailbox shows the mailbox storage used for Office 365 groups (also known as unified or modern groups).

- **SoftDeletedMailbox**   Soft-deleted mailboxes are mailboxes that have been disconnected from a deleted user account. A soft-deleted mailbox can be reconnected to a user account by restoring or creating a user with the same mailbox identity as the deleted soft-deleted mailbox.

You can run Set-Mailbox commands against all mailbox types (user and resource) to configure or update various settings, such as mailbox quotas, regional configurations, proxy addresses, and names. In synchronized environments, however, a number of attributes are managed in the on-premises directory. If you attempt to manage attributes that are synchronized from the on-premises environment, you receive an error and guidance to update the attribute in Active Directory.

For more information on customizing Office 365 licensing, see Chapter 5, "Installing Azure AD Connect," and *https://blogs.technet.microsoft.com/undocumentedfeatures/2016/06/21 /office-365-license-assignment*.

Mail-enabled users

A mail-enabled user (or mailuser) is a user account in Azure Active Directory that has mail properties applied to it so that it shows up in the Exchange global address list.

CHAPTER 11

A mail-enabled user can be created or managed from the Exchange Admin Center or Windows PowerShell.

To create a mail-enabled user in the Exchange Admin Center, follow these steps.

1. Launch the Exchange Admin Center.

2. Navigate to Recipients | Contacts.

3. Click the + (plus) sign and then select Mail User. See Figure 11-22.

Figure 11-22 Exchange Admin Center Mail User option

4. Fill out the user details, as shown in Figure 11-23. Because this is a security principal, it requires a password (which enables the user to log on to the Office 365 portal and access any applications for which they might be licensed). Click Save to create the new mail user.

Figure 11-23 New Mail User dialog box

5. If necessary, refresh the page to see the newly created mail user.

From Windows PowerShell, the creation of a new mail-enabled user is accomplished by running New-MailUser, as shown in Figure 11-24, after you import the remote Exchange Online session.

```
New-MailUser -FirstName Sanjay -LastName Patel -Alias sanjaypatel -ExternalEmailAddress
sanjaypatel@cohovineyardandwinery.com -DisplayName "Sanjay Patel" -Name "Sanjay Patel"
-Password (Get-Credential).Password -MicrosoftOnlineServicesID sanjaypatel@cohovineyard-
andwinery.onmicrosoft.com
```

Figure 11-24 Creating a new mail-enabled user with the New-MailUser cmdlet

Contacts

Contacts are mail-enabled objects that show up in the global address list. You can create contacts from the Office 365 Admin Center (mentioned earlier in this chapter), through the Exchange Admin Center, or through Windows PowerShell.

To create contacts through the Office 365 Admin Center, follow these steps.

1. Navigate to Office 365 Admin Center.

2. From the Home screen, point to Users and then select Contacts.

3. On the Contacts page, click + Add A Contact.

4. Enter the details for the new contact. Click Add.

5. Close the New Contact dialog box.

Creating and managing a contact from a remote Exchange Online PowerShell session requires only a single line of code. See Figure 11-25.

```
New-MailContact -FirstName David -LastName Pelton -Name DavidPelton -DisplayName "David
Pelton" -Alias davidpelton -ExternalEmailAddress davidpelton@cohovineyardandwinery.com
```

Figure 11-25 Using Exchange Online PowerShell to create a new mail contact

Groups

Exchange Online has many available types of groups, depending on the needs of the organization. Distribution lists, for example, can be managed from the Office 365 Admin Center, Exchange Admin Center, or Windows PowerShell.

Security and distribution groups can be managed easily from the Office 365 Admin Center, as demonstrated in the following example.

1. Navigate to Office 365 Admin Center.

2. From the Home screen, point to Groups and then select Groups.

3. On the Groups page, click + Add A Group.

4. From the Type drop-down list, select the appropriate type of group (Security Group or Distribution List).

5. Fill out the appropriate group details.

   If you choose an Office 365 group, a distribution list, or a mail-enabled security group, you can also enable the group to receive messages from Internet users. This sets the RequireSenderAuthenticationEnabled parameter to $false in Exchange Online. For Office 365 groups, you also have options to configure if the group is public or private, mailbox language, and whether you want members of the group to receive email and invites in their mailbox like a traditional distribution or mail-enabled security group. If you want to configure an Office 365 group to receive email from external sources, you have to edit the group after creation.

6. Click Add.

Manage groups from the Exchange Admin Center by following these steps.

1. Launch Exchange Admin Center.

2. Navigate to Recipients | Groups.

3. Select the + and then select the type of group to create. See Figure 11-26.

Figure 11-26 New group in the Exchange Admin Center

4. Select a group type.

   If you select an Office 365 group, a dialog box appears similar to the following, shown in Figure 11-27.

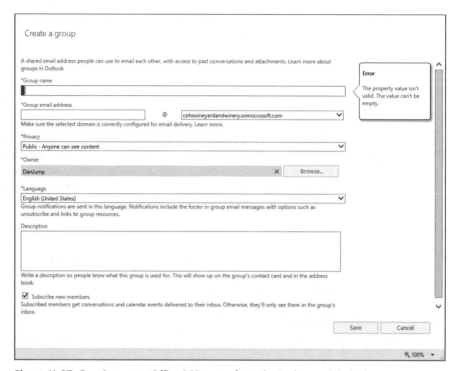

Figure 11-27 Creating a new Office 365 group from the Exchange Admin Center

Although the Office 365 New Group dialog box in the Office 365 Admin Center enables you to configure the group to allow anonymous senders from outside the organization in setup, you must configure that afterward, when adding an Office 365 group in the Exchange Admin Center.

If you select a distribution group, a very similar dialog box appears, except it has a link, to create a standard distribution group if you would rather do that.

If you select Security Group, the New Security Group dialog box appears, as shown in Figure 11-28.

Figure 11-28 New Security Group dialog box

If you select Dynamic Distribution Group, you see the dialog box shown in Figure 11-29, which enables you to select criteria for creating and evaluating the group.

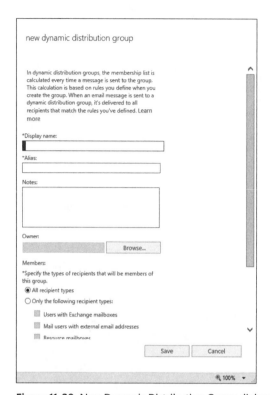

Figure 11-29 New Dynamic Distribution Group dialog box

5.   Fill out the appropriate details and click Save.

Because there are a few types of distribution groups in Office 365, there are slightly different cmdlets to configure them all from an Exchange Online PowerShell session.

To create a standard distribution list, use the following command.

```
New-DistributionGroup -Name Coho-Marketing-DL -DisplayName "Coho Marketing DL" -Require-
SenderAuthenticationEnabled $false -PrimarySmtpAddress cohomarketing@cohovineyardandwin-
ery.onmicrosoft.com -alias cohomarketingdl
```

A room list is a special distribution list that is designed to contain room mailboxes. Room lists help users search for available rooms across the entire group and appear in Room Finder in Microsoft Outlook. Room lists can only be created from Windows PowerShell. Creating a room list is exactly the same as a normal distribution list, except it also includes the RoomList parameter, as shown in Figure 11-30.

```
New-DistributionGroup -Name Coho-MeetingRooms -DisplayName "Coho MeetingRooms" -Require-
SenderAuthenticationEnabled $true -PrimarySmtpAddress cohomeeting@cohovineyardandwinery.
onmicrosoft.com -alias cohomeeting -RoomList
```

CHAPTER 11

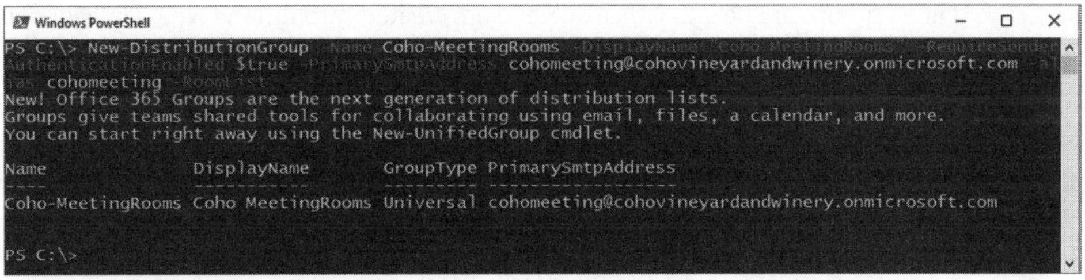

Figure 11-30 Creating a new room list with the New-DistributionGroup cmdlet

A mail-enabled security group is a type of distribution group that can be used to grant permissions to resources. The syntax is again very similar to creating a distribution group, except it uses the Type parameter with a value of Security, as shown in Figure 11-31.

```
New-DistributionGroup -Name Coho-SalesSecurity -DisplayName "Coho Sales Security Group"
-RequireSenderAuthenticationEnabled $true -PrimarySmtpAddress cohosalessecurity@
cohovineyardandwinery.onmicrosoft.com -alias cohosalessecurity -Type Security
```

Figure 11-31 Creating a mail-enabled security group with the New-DistributionGroup cmdlet

All the distribution groups based on the New-DistributionGroup cmdlet can be viewed, modified, or removed using these additional cmdlets.

- Get-DistributionGroup

- Set-DistributionGroup

- Remove-DistributionGroup

- Get-DistributionGroupMember

- Add-DistributionGroupMember

- Remove-DistributionGroupMember

You can find additional syntax for these cmdlets online at *https://technet.microsoft.com/en-us /library/dn641234(v=exchg.160).aspx*, "Users and groups cmdlets in Exchange Online."

CHAPTER 11

Unified groups are new to Office 365 and are created through the New-UnifiedGroup cmdlet. They're referred to as Office 365 groups in the Office 365 and Exchange admin centers. See Figure 11-32.

```
New-UnifiedGroup -Name "CohoHR-UnifiedGroup" -DisplayName "Coho HR" -PrimarySmtpAd-
dress cohohr@cohovineyardandwinery.onmicrosoft.com -Alias cohohr -AccessType Public
-SubscriptionEnabled
```

Figure 11-32 Creating an Office 365 group

SPECIAL CONSIDERATIONS FOR ALLOWING EXTERNAL MAIL DELIVERY TO OFFICE 365 GROUPS

If you are running Azure Active Directory Connect (AAD Connect) with Group Writeback enabled and have your domain's MX record pointed to the on-premises environment, external senders might receive non-delivery reports (NDRs) when sending to your Office 365 groups, even if you have RequireSenderAuthenticationEnabled set to $false in Office 365, because a constant value of True is configured to flow for the msExchRequireAuthToSendTo attribute to on-premises Active Directory.

When the domain's MX record points on-premises, you must either run Set-UnifiedGroup `<groupname> -RequireSendAuthenticationEnabled $false` in the on-premises environment or deploy a custom out-to-AD AAD Connect rule to set msExchRequireAuthToSendTo to $false.

Unified groups have a unique set of cmdlets available to them.

- Get-UnifiedGroup

- Remove-UnifiedGroup

- Set-UnifiedGroup

- Add-UnifiedGroupLinks

- Get-UnifiedGroupLinks

- Remove-UnifiedGroupLinks

Additional syntax for these cmdlets is online at *https://technet.microsoft.com/en-us/library /dn641234(v=exchg.160).aspx*, "Users and groups cmdlets in Exchange Online."

INSIDE OUT

Controlling the sprawl of Office 365 groups

Although Office 365 groups have a lot of great features, by default, their creation is enabled automatically in all tenants. Depending on your organization's governance policy, this might be undesirable.

You do have some options, however, when it comes to controlling who can do what with them.

You can either disable them outright or restrict their creation to a smaller subset of users by using the following technique (which requires the newer Azure AD Preview module as well as the older MSOnline module, and sessions established to Exchange Online and Azure Active Directory through both Connect-MsolService and Connect-AzureAD).

The following script will:

- Connect to Microsoft Online Service.

- Connect to the Azure Active Directory endpoint.

- Connect to Exchange Online.

- Specify Global Admins as the group that can create unified groups (Office 365 Groups).

- Disable Groups Creation in Outlook Web App.

```
Import-Module AzureADPreview

Import-Module MSOnline

$UserCredential = Get-Credential

$Session = New-PSSession -ConfigurationName Microsoft.Exchange -ConnectionUri
https://outlook.office365.com/powershell-liveid/ -Credential $UserCredential -Authen-
tication Basic -AllowRedirection

Import-PSSession $Session

Connect-AzureAD -Credential $UserCredential

Connect-MsolService -Credential $UserCredential

$GlobalAdmins = Get-MsolRole -RoleName "Company Administrator"

$GlobalAdminsObjectID = $GlobalAdmins.ObjectId.ToString()
```

```
$template = Get-AzureADDirectorySettingTemplate | where-object {$_.DisplayName -eq
"Group.Unified"}

$setting = $template.CreateDirectorySetting()

$setting["EnableGroupCreation"] = "false"

$setting["GroupCreationAllowedGroupId"] = $GlobalAdminsObjectID

New-AzureADDirectorySetting -DirectorySetting $setting

Get-OwaMailboxPolicy | ? { $_.IsDefault -eq $true } | Set-OwaMailboxPolicy -GroupCre-
ationEnabled $false
```

Several services use Office 365 groups, such as Exchange Online, Skype Teams, and Planner. Disabling or restricting Office 365 Groups creation affects those services that depend on the groups. Disabling Office 365 Groups creation has no effect on existing groups.

The membership for dynamic distribution groups is evaluated during delivery. By using Windows PowerShell, you can use filters and attributes to specify which members to include.

```
New-DynamicDistributionGroup -Name 'Coho Wine Club Administartors' -Alias 'cohowine'
-IncludedRecipients 'MailboxUsers' -ConditionalDepartment @('Wine Club')
```

After a dynamic distribution group is created, you can use the following cmdlets to view, update, or remove the group.

- Get-DynamicDistributionGroup

- Set-DynamicDistributionGroup

- Remove-DynamicDistributionGroup

Additional syntax for these cmdlets is online at *https://technet.microsoft.com/en-us/library /dn641234(v=exchg.160).aspx*, "Users and groups cmdlets in Exchange Online."

Summary

This chapter discussed the various object types in Office 365 and how to manage them. There are many types of objects (users, groups, contacts), and most of them have dozens of proper- ties that are used to define them further. Some properties are only manageable through certain interfaces, so as you gain more experience in managing Office 365, you'll know which cmdlets or user interface to use by which types of properties you need to modify.

Mailbox Migration Types

Chapter 10, "Preparing an On-Premises Environment to Connect to Exchange Online," discussed the foundation for Exchange Online tenants and covered service descriptions, domain and organization configuration, mail routing, and basic hybrid concepts. Chapter 11, "Understanding the Office 365 Resource Types," covered the key Exchange Online Recipient types. This chapter covers the three main types of migration available to Office 365 Exchange Online customers: cutover, staged, and express. Exchange full hybrid configuration and migrations are covered in Chapter 13, "Exchange Online Hybrid."

Cutover, staged, and IMAP migration types haven't changed much in many years, except for a newer user interface a few years ago, and migration batch commands to help manage large groups. IMAP migration is not covered because this chapter is focusing on the primary methods used to migrate to Exchange Online, and IMAP migration is limited to mail only. You can find a guide for IMAP migrations at *https://support.office.com/en-us/article/Migrate-other-types-of-IMAP-mailboxes-to-Office-365-58890ccd-ce5e-4d94-be75-560a3b70a706?ui=en-US&rs=en-US&ad=US*.

THE OFFICE 365 PST IMPORT SERVICE

You can also use the Office 365 PST Import Service for migrations; go to *https://support.office.com/en-us/article/FAQ-about-importing-PST-files-to-Office-365-2fe71b05-f5a2-4182-ade7-4dc5cabdfd51?ui=en-US&rs=en-US&ad=US* for more information. Due to the challenges of collecting and ensuring that PST files aren't corrupted, this method is normally not used as a first choice for a migration; however, it is commonly used to inject PST archives or extracts from other archived systems.

Migration decision process and key concepts

A key decision point for mailbox migrations is which option to choose to have a balance between the speed of using Office 365 as a service and user satisfaction due to mailbox resynchronization issues. To help illustrate the decision process, see Table 12.1.

Table 12.1 Migration options based on Exchange versions and coexistence state in the customer topology

Exchange Version	Cutover	Staged	Express, Minimal, or Full Hybrid
Exchange Server 2003 Exchange Server 2007	Available if fewer than 2000 users	Available, recommended if not deploying a newer version of Exchange	Not available
Exchange Server 2003 Exchange Server 2007 Exchange2010	Available, not recommended	Not available	Available, recommended
Exchange Server 2007 Exchange 2010 Exchange 2013	Available, not recommended	Not available	Available, recommended
Exchange 2010 Exchange2013 Exchange2016	Available, not recommended	Not available	Available, recommended

There are three key recommendations to understand.

- **Available, recommended**   This version of Exchange and the migration options work and are recommended as the solution. Caveats such as user count limitations might be listed.

- **Available, not recommended**   This version of Exchange and the migration options would work but result in poor user experience and are therefore not recommended.

- **Not available**   This option is blocked by the migration tool set or does not work.

Each migration type explains the considerations regarding the limitations of that migration type, usually related to the Microsoft Outlook resynchronization Offline Storage Folder (OST) process, new Outlook profile configuration, or lack of data migration in an IMAP case when it is mail only.

One of the key concepts after considering the migration method is how the migration will be managed. The two methods available are browser-based access, using the Office 365 Admin Center and the Exchange Admin Center, or using Windows PowerShell to connect to Exchange

Online. (The two ways to connect to Exchange Online follow.) The older method does not enable users who have multifactor authentication configured to function properly; the newer connection option is specifically designed to use the Azure Active Directory Authentication Library (ADAL) to connect and use multifactor authentication.

Each migration method can be executed either through a web browser using the Exchange Admin Center or by using Windows PowerShell. The following commands are referred to and reused in each of the subsequent Windows PowerShell migration method sections. Windows PowerShell has two methods of connecting to Exchange Online, one without multifactor authentication and one with multifactor authentication.

Connecting to Exchange Online with Windows PowerShell uses basic authentication if you aren't using multifactor authentication. For minimum operating system and .NET requirements, refer to *https://technet.microsoft.com/en-us/library/jj984289(v=exchg.160).aspx*.

Launch Windows PowerShell as administrator and type the following commands:

```
$Credentials = Get-Credential

$Session = New-PSSession -ConfigurationName Microsoft.Exchange -ConnectionUri https://
outlook.office365.com/powershell-liveid/ -Credential $UserCredential -Authentication
Basic -AllowRedirection

Import-PSSession $Session
```

When prompted in the Windows PowerShell Credential Request dialog box, type the user principal name to save the credentials for the connection (for example, *admin@contoso.onmicrosoft.com*) in the user name box and then type the appropriate password.

To close the session properly, use Remove-PSSession:

```
Remove-PSSession $Session
```

For minimum operating system and .NET requirements when connecting to Exchange Online with Windows PowerShell and multifactor authentication, refer to *https://technet.microsoft.com/en-us/library/mt775114(v=exchg.160).aspx*.

To install the Microsoft Exchange Online PowerShell module that supports multifactor authentication, follow these steps.

1. Launch a browser and connect to portal.office.com.

2. Navigate to the Exchange Admin Center.

3. On the left side, select Hybrid.

4. Below The Exchange Online PowerShell Module Supports Multi-Factor Authentication, click Configure to download the specific module that contains the proper authentication libraries that support multifactor authentication. Download and then install the module.

5. After this module is downloaded and installed, launch the module from the Start menu by navigating to Microsoft Corporation | Microsoft Exchange Online PowerShell Module.

    This launches a Windows PowerShell module with the multifactor libraries for Exchange Online PowerShell ready to connect using multifactor authentication.

6. To connect to Exchange Online, use the following command.

    ```
    Connect-EXOPSSession -UserPrincipalName admin@contoso.onmicrosoft.com
    ```

7. To close the session properly, use Remove-PSSession.

    ```
    Remove-PSSession $Session
    ```

When the connection starts, the Microsoft Exchange Online PowerShell dialog box launches with the user name that was provided in the User Principal Name string of the Connect-EXOPSession command. Type the password for that account. If multifactor authentication (MFA) is enforced on the account, the second factor of authentication by authentication application prompts for permission, for a series of digits as a verification code sent to an email account, or as a text message to a mobile phone. After this second factor of authentication is verified, the Windows PowerShell connection is complete.

The second key concept to understand while using the built-in Exchange Online migration tools is the concept of migration endpoints. Migration endpoints are a group of settings that are configured either before or during the start of the migration process. They can be configured by using a browser or with Exchange Online PowerShell. Each migration option is discussed later in this chapter, which covers how to create the Windows PowerShell endpoints specific to their migration type if they aren't created automatically. Two of the settings that can be tuned to increase migration velocity are MaxConcurrentMigrations and MaxConcurrentIncrementalSyncs. The definitions of these parameters appear as follows.

- "MaxConcurrentMigrations parameter specifies the maximum number of mailboxes that will be migrated for this endpoint at a specified time."

- "The MaxConcurrentIncrementalSyncs parameter specifies the maximum number of incremental syncs allowed for this endpoint at a specified time. This value must be less or equal to MaxConcurrentMigrations parameter."

Currently, the MaxConcurrentMigrations per migration type per tenant is limited to 300 connections. This means 300 Remote, 300 Outlook Anywhere, and 300 IMAP MaxConcurrentMigrations connections are available in a single tenant. Most customers do not have a mixed set of endpoint types, but it is possible. When configured through the

Office 365 Admin portal or the Exchange Admin Center, the normal default settings are 20 for MaxConcurrentMigrations and 10 for MaxConcurrentIncrementalSyncs, for example, when using express migration. For smaller customers, these numbers normally work out well and provide a balance between migration speeds and the amount of traffic on the on-premises network or environment. These numbers can be modified to increase concurrency, through either the Exchange Admin Center or Exchange Online PowerShell; however, performance should be carefully monitored so that the existing on-premises environment is not compromised. Be careful with the MaxConcurrentIncrementalSyncs parameter; if that number is too close or matches MaxConcurrentMigrations, the source environment and network will likely have performance-related issues. The maximum of 300 per type of connection does provide configuration flexibility. For example, if a European endpoint and a U.S. endpoint were needed for migrations, each endpoint could have 150 connections.

Cutover Exchange migrations

The cutover migration process is designed for customers with the following criteria.

- Up to a maximum of 2000 users

- Have not deployed Azure AD Connect for directory synchronization

- Are using Microsoft Exchange 2003 or Exchange 2007 without later versions of Exchange in their environments

Although cutover migrations can also be used for later versions of Exchange (Exchange 2010, Exchange 2013, and Exchange 2016), the newer express hybrid option, covered later in the "Express Migrations" section, offers the user and administrator a much better experience and is highly recommended over cutover migration due to the limitations. If the customer has deployed Azure Active Directory Connect (AAD Connect) and synchronized the directory at least once, cutover migration will be blocked in the Exchange Admin Center as a migration option. The customer then must choose a staged migration if Exchange Server 2003 or Exchange Server 2007 is the source; the best choice would be to use Exchange Express or full hybrid Exchange migration with Exchange 2010 and later versions.

Cutover Exchange migrations can be achieved by two methods; one is through the Exchange Admin Center (EAC), and the second is through Windows PowerShell when connected to Exchange Online. The key limitations and considerations of Exchange cutover migrations are that:

- You must have fewer than 2000 users for Exchange Server 2003, Exchange Server 2007, Exchange 2010, Exchange 2103, and Exchange 2016, although better methods are available for Exchange 2010 and later (see the "Express Migrations" section).

- All domains must be registered in Office 365.

- Directory synchronization by AAD Connect must be disabled. If this is enabled by accident, it can be disabled but is a significant amount of work for the customer. Explore staged migration if AAD Connect has been enabled.

- The Offline Storage Folder (OST) signature is not preserved. This means the entire mailbox must be downloaded post-migration.

- Administrators need to provide users with passwords to their mailboxes post-migration.

- Client-side rules and customizations are not migrated. Outlook profiles need to be re-created and are not updated.

- Additional objects or scenarios not migrated are security groups, dynamic distribution lists, system mailboxes, Dumpster, send-as permissions, and messages larger than 150 MB.

- The account performing the migration must have, at minimum, Receive-As permission to the mailbox; full access to the mailbox is preferred.

Cutover Exchange migration requirements

The requirements for performing a cutover migration are as follows and apply to both the Exchange Admin Center and Windows PowerShell methods.

- You must have administrative access to Office 365, global administrator account. This account enables the administrator to perform the license process and migration process.

- Outlook Anywhere must be configured and publicly accessible with a third-party SSL certificate. Depending on the source version of Exchange and what is already accessible on the Internet, some additional work might be needed for the cutover endpoint process to function.

- You must add and verify domains in Office 365. For in-depth information about adding domains, (see Chapter 2, "Preparing Your Environment for the Cloud."

- Prepare for Mail Exchange (MX) and Autodiscover cutover when migration is complete.

- Disable Unified Messaging on source mailboxes.

- Pre-stage security groups if the desire is to have mail-enabled security groups; otherwise, the default is to have distribution groups.

Cutover using Exchange Admin Center (EAC)

A global administrator logged on to the customer tenant performs the following steps by using the Edge or Internet Explorer browser.

1. Launch *https://portal.office.com* and log on with the global administrator account. Select the Admin tile from the Office 365 app launcher.

2. Navigate to the Exchange Admin Center, using the Admin Centers shortcut in the lower left pane of the Office 365 portal.

3. In the Exchange Admin Center, select Recipients | Migration.

4. Click + and choose Migrate To Exchange Online, as shown in Figure 12-1.

    This launches the New Migration Batch Wizard.

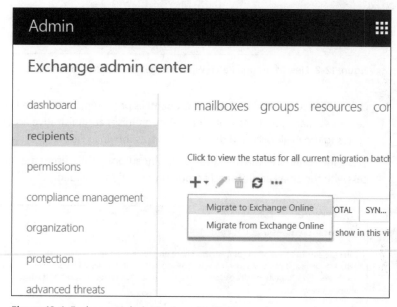

Figure 12-1 Exchange Admin Center migration console

5. Select Cutover Migration and click Next, as shown in Figure 12-2.

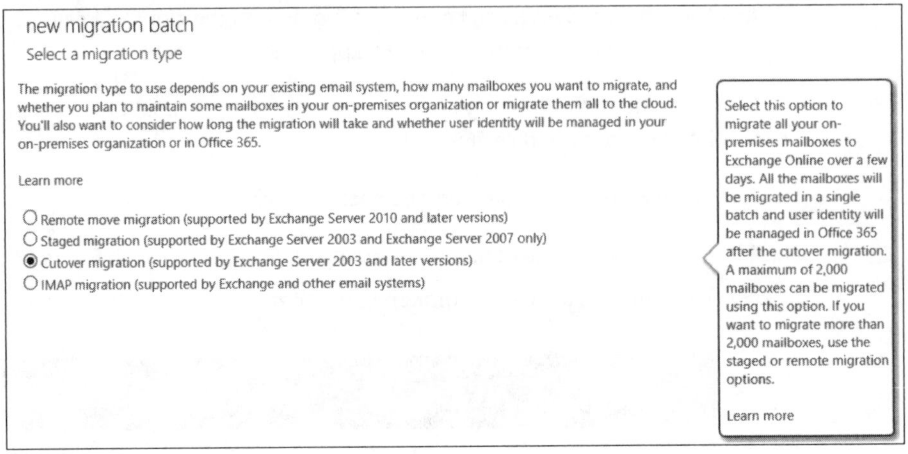

new migration batch

Select a migration type

The migration type to use depends on your existing email system, how many mailboxes you want to migrate, and whether you plan to maintain some mailboxes in your on-premises organization or migrate them all to the cloud. You'll also want to consider how long the migration will take and whether user identity will be managed in your on-premises organization or in Office 365.

Learn more

○ Remote move migration (supported by Exchange Server 2010 and later versions)
○ Staged migration (supported by Exchange Server 2003 and Exchange Server 2007 only)
◉ Cutover migration (supported by Exchange Server 2003 and later versions)
○ IMAP migration (supported by Exchange and other email systems)

Select this option to migrate all your on-premises mailboxes to Exchange Online over a few days. All the mailboxes will be migrated in a single batch and user identity will be managed in Office 365 after the cutover migration. A maximum of 2,000 mailboxes can be migrated using this option. If you want to migrate more than 2,000 mailboxes, use the staged or remote migration options.

Learn more

Figure 12-2 New Migration Batch Wizard page, Cutover Migration selected

6. On the Enter On-Premises Account Credentials page, type in the email address, domain name\user name, and password for the on-premises administrative account that has access to the mailboxes and then click Next, as shown in Figure 12-3.

This page configures the migration endpoint automatically, using the Autodiscover process with the email address and account information provided.

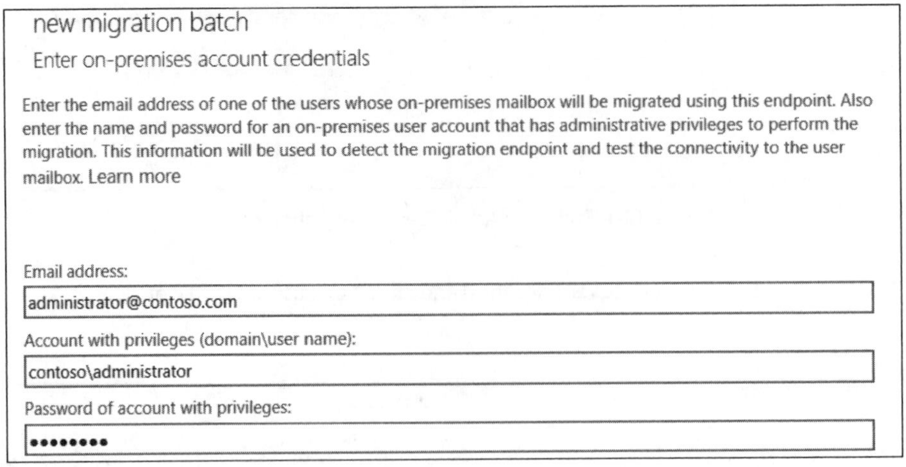

new migration batch

Enter on-premises account credentials

Enter the email address of one of the users whose on-premises mailbox will be migrated using this endpoint. Also enter the name and password for an on-premises user account that has administrative privileges to perform the migration. This information will be used to detect the migration endpoint and test the connectivity to the user mailbox. Learn more

Email address:
administrator@contoso.com

Account with privileges (domain\user name):
contoso\administrator

Password of account with privileges:
••••••••

Figure 12-3 The Enter On-Premises Account Credentials page

7. If the automatic configuration fails, see the example and troubleshooting section shown in Figure 12-4.

Automatic configuration uses the email address, privileged domain account, and password of the account in an attempt to detect the Outlook Anywhere configuration automatically and create a migration endpoint. Normally when automatic configuration fails, it is due to an Autodiscover lookup or the Outlook Anywhere configuration. Use the Troubleshooting tip for additional assistance.

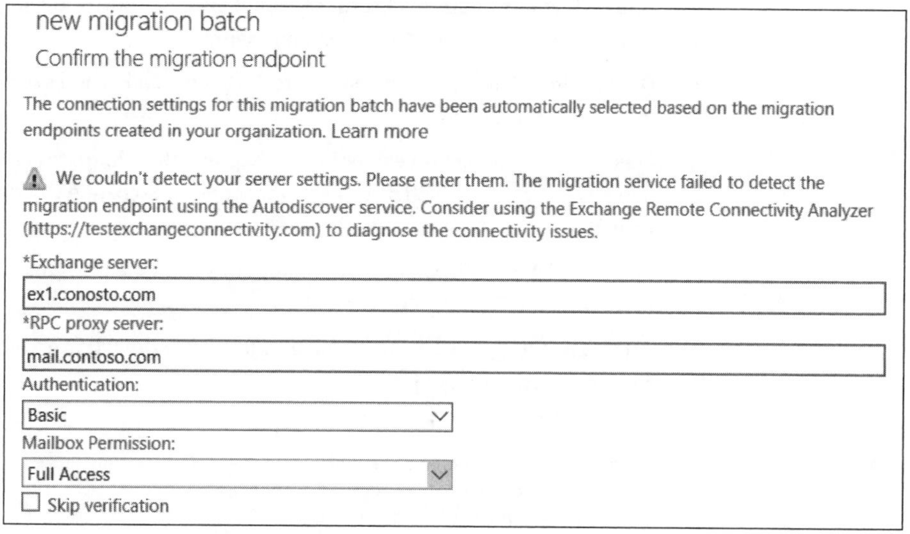

new migration batch

Confirm the migration endpoint

The connection settings for this migration batch have been automatically selected based on the migration endpoints created in your organization. Learn more

⚠ We couldn't detect your server settings. Please enter them. The migration service failed to detect the migration endpoint using the Autodiscover service. Consider using the Exchange Remote Connectivity Analyzer (https://testexchangeconnectivity.com) to diagnose the connectivity issues.

*Exchange server:

ex1.conosto.com

*RPC proxy server:

mail.contoso.com

Authentication:

Basic   ∨

Mailbox Permission:

Full Access   ∨

☐ Skip verification

Figure 12-4 New Migration Batch page with failed automatic endpoint creation

TROUBLESHOOTING

Connectivity for migration endpoints

Use the Microsoft Remote Connectivity Analyzer to troubleshoot configuration or connectivity issues between Exchange Online and Exchange on-premises. The Exchange on-premises administrator credentials are used in this troubleshooting process.

1. Use the Microsoft Remote Connectivity Analyzer at *https://testconnectivity .microsoft.com/* to verify Outlook connectivity. On the Exchange Server tab, in the Microsoft Office Outlook Connectivity Tests section, choose Outlook Connectivity, click Next, and follow the directions.

    A successful test provides you with the necessary information to fill in the Exchange Server, RPC Proxy Server, and Authentication boxes. The Exchange administrator must determine the mailbox permissions.

2. In the Exchange Server box, type the fully qualified domain name (FQDN) for the on-premises Exchange server.

CHAPTER 12

This is the host name for your mailbox server, for example, EXCH-SRV-01.corp. contoso.com.

3. In the RPC Proxy Server box, type the FQDN for the RPC proxy server for Outlook Anywhere.

   Typically, the proxy server address is the same as the address of your Outlook Web App URL. For example, mail.contoso.com is also the URL for the proxy server that Outlook uses to connect to an Exchange server.

4. Use Windows PowerShell to connect to Exchange Online and execute the test migration end sequence.

   Please review the section earlier in the chapter, titled "Migration Decision Process and Key Concepts," which discusses connecting to Exchange Online with Windows PowerShell.

   This is useful only if you know your endpoints from the previous step or can pull them from the Exchange server.

5. After connecting to Exchange Online by using Windows PowerShell, run the following two commands.

   ```
   $Credentials = Get-Credential

   Test-MigrationServerAvailability -ExchangeOutlookAnywhere -ExchangeServer
   EXCH-SRV-01.corp.contoso.com -Credentials $Credentials -RPCProxyServer mail.
   contoso.com -Authentication NTLM
   ```

   The first command captures the domain\username of the mailbox account that is being tested. Use your server-specific names in the RPC proxy server and Exchange server parameters. The second command uses those credentials to execute the test with the specified endpoints.

   If the command completes successfully, no further action is needed, and those parameters can be used in creating the migration endpoint. If the connection fails, consider additional Outlook Anywhere configuration and troubleshooting steps.

8. If automatic configuration is successful, confirm the automatically detected settings for the migration endpoint and click Next. See the successful automatically configured batch in Figure 12-5.

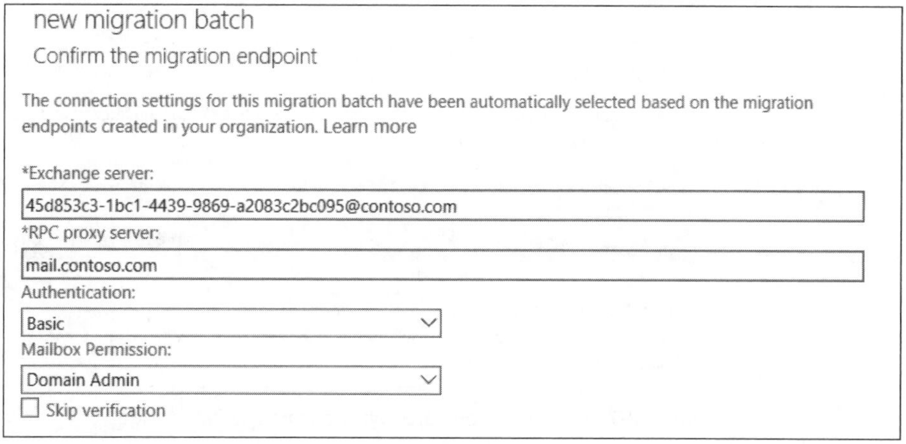

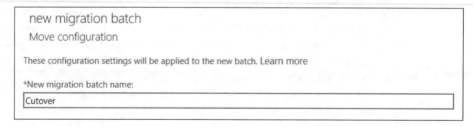

Figure 12-5 New Migration Batch Wizard Confirm The Migration Endpoint page

NOTE

The Exchange Server box in Figure 12-5 varies, depending on the source version of the Exchange server. The example in 12-5 is from an Exchange 2013 or Exchange 2016 source. Exchange Server 2003, Exchange Server 2007, and Exchange 2010 would have a server name such as Ex01.contoso.com.

9. On the Move Configuration page, name the migration batch **Cutover** and then click Next, as shown in Figure 12-6.

---

new migration batch

Move configuration

These configuration settings will be applied to the new batch. Learn more

*New migration batch name:

Cutover

Figure 12-6 New Migration Batch Wizard Move Configuration page

Configure report by clicking the Browse button and selecting one or more mailboxes or by typing their SMTP addresses in the Check Name box and clicking OK. Choose either to start the batch manually or allow it to start automatically. Click New to create the batch. See Figure 12-7.

CHAPTER 12

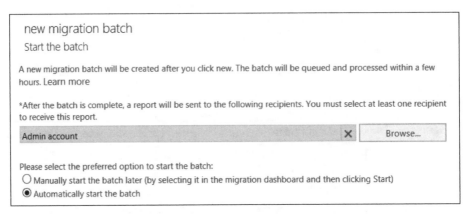

Figure 12-7 New Migration Batch Wizard Start The Batch page

After clicking the New button and creating the cutover batch, the default migration page opens in the Exchange Admin Center, on the migration monitoring page. This is the main page where you monitor the cutover progress. You can select the batch to get more information about the process of the users, and each column in the table provides insight into the total number of objects in the cutover migration: number synchronized so far; how many are finalized (completed); and how many objects failed. You can also view additional logging information, as shown in Figure 12-8.

As the cutover process starts and progresses, the numbers increment in the migration console. If additional information is needed about an object-level failure, the View Details hyperlink in the right pane of the migration console can open another window to review the individual object level success or failure. In Figure 12-9, this migration had permissions issues during the cutover process. In this instance, the administrator performing the migration did not have the proper permission to the source mailboxes. The other object types, such as groups and contacts, although referenced as mailboxes, were migrated and synchronized successfully, as shown in the Finalized column, 15 in all; the Failed column shows that 13 user mailboxes failed to start the synchronization process. To fix this issue, add full mailbox access permissions to the mailboxes that failed, stop the batch, and then restart it.

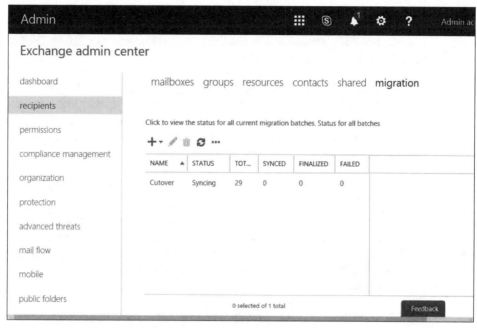

Figure 12-8 Exchange Admin Center migration monitoring view

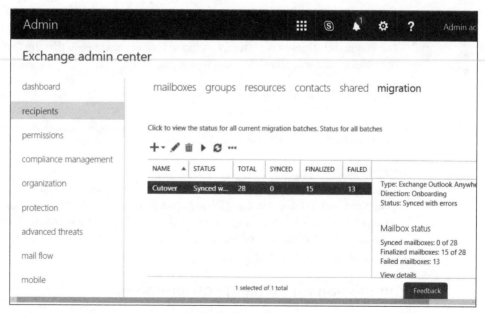

Figure 12-9 Exchange Admin Center migration status with failures

CHAPTER 12

Completing the cutover migration process

After the mailbox permissions were fixed, the batch completed successfully. The post-migration steps for a cutover migration are as follows.

1. Change the MX (Mail Exchanger) Record in the customer's public DNS to refer to Exchange Online as the domain's new email endpoint. Validate that mail flow is working, check message headers on received mail, and optionally click the Message Header Analyzer tab on the Microsoft Remote Connectivity Analyzer webpage at *https://testconnectivity.microsoft.com/*.

2. Change the DNS entries for the on-premises Autodiscover endpoint to refer to the Office 365 Autodiscover endpoint.

    This normally requires an internal and external DNS name change. For example, Autodiscover.contoso.com would have a CNAME record in DNS pointing to Autodiscover.outlook.com in both internal and external DNS, removing the existing records and creating the CNAME record to complete the Autodiscover migration process to point to Office 365.

3. Remove the internal service connection point (SCP) in Exchange (required for Exchange Server 2007 and later). Use the Exchange Management Shell to run the following command.

    ```
    Get-ClientAccessServer | Set-ClientAccessServer -autodiscoverserviceinternaluri
    $null
    ```

    This command removes the internal endpoint for Autodiscover so that the Outlook client uses DNS to find the Office 365 Autodiscover endpoint.

4. Assign the appropriate Office 365 licenses to the migrated users; an Exchange Online license is the minimum required.

5. Re-create user profiles for Outlook and provide passwords for the Office 365 users.

6. Delete the migration batch.

    Although this can occur earlier in the sequence, as some cutover documentation states, it does not hurt to leave it in place while Autodiscover records and MX records are being changed, users are being licensed, and new Outlook profiles are being created. Waiting to delete the batch enables the administrator to ensure that everything post-migration is functional prior to removing the batch.

Decommissioning Exchange on-premises

Normally when a cutover migration is performed, the Exchange server can be decommissioned after all user profiles have been successfully pointed to Office 365, Autodiscover is pointed to

Office 365, and mail flow is pointing to Office 365. In a cutover scenario, there is no need for AAD Connect for directory synchronization; it is blocked if directory synchronization is enabled in the tenant. If a customer is 100% sure they will never need AAD Connect for directory synchronization and will manage all the new Exchange Online mailboxes and Office 365 users in the cloud, decommissioning can occur at any time. More information about how and when to decommission is in the Microsoft TechNet article at *https://technet.microsoft.com/en-us/library /dn931280(v=exchg.150).aspx.*

Cutover Exchange migration summary

Cutover Exchange migrations are one of the fastest methods to bring users onboard when the user count is under 2000 users. Remember that there are key limitations in the methodology that might cause user dissatisfaction, such as the need for a separate user name and password, re-creation of the Outlook profile, and resynchronization of all their mail to their local computer.

Staged Exchange migrations

The staged migration process is designed for customers who are only using Exchange Server 2003 and Exchange Server 2007. It is unavailable in later versions of Exchange. Staged migration does not have a maximum user count restriction; however, due to some of the limitations, discussed in sections later in this chapter, many customers choose to add newer versions of Exchange to the environment to coexist with and take advantage of the Exchange hybrid topologies and technology.

Staged Exchange migrations can be achieved by two methods; one is through the Exchange Admin Center (EAC), and the other is by using Windows PowerShell when connected to Exchange Online. The following is a list of the key limitations and considerations of staged Exchange migrations; some are the same limitations as those in a cutover migration due to the use of an Outlook Anywhere migration endpoint.

- This kind of migration is applicable for Exchange Server 2003 and Exchange Server 2007 only and will not work for any other version of Exchange.

- Directory Synchronization must be enabled, which you can accomplish by using AAD Connect.

- All domains must be registered in Office 365.

- The offline Outlook data file (.OST) signature is not preserved; the entire mailbox must be downloaded again post-migration because the Exchange GUID is not preserved on the user account object due to the migration process that staged migrations use.

- Client-side rules and customizations are not migrated; Outlook profiles need to be re-created and are not updated.

- Additional items not migrated are: Out of Office configuration, security groups, dynamic distribution lists, system mailboxes, Dumpster, send-as permissions, and messages larger than 150 MB.

- The account performing the migration must have, at minimum, Receive-As permission to the mailbox; full access to the mailbox is preferred. This should be a secured account to ensure data privacy because these permissions allow the account to read the email of the source mailbox.

- Additional post-migration scripts must be run to remove the mailbox object and convert it to a migrated, mail-enabled user object for best experience.

Staged Exchange migration requirements

The requirements for performing a staged migration are as follows and apply to both Exchange Admin Center and Windows PowerShell methods.

- Administrative access to the Office 365, global administrator account is required for the administrator to perform the license process and migration process.

- Outlook Anywhere must be configured and publicly accessible with a third-party SSL certificate.

- Domains in Office 365 must be added and verified. See Chapter 2.

- Mail Exchange (MX) and Autodiscover cutover must be prepared for when all staged migrations are complete.

- Unified Messaging on source mailboxes must be disabled.

- Outlook Anywhere must be configured properly. (You can use Microsoft Connectivity Analyzer, Exchange Server, Microsoft Office Outlook Connectivity Tests, or Outlook Connectivity at *https://testconnectivity.microsoft.com/* to validate this.)

- A migration .csv file must be created for user migration with a maximum of 2000 rows, including header row. If you have more than 2000 users, multiple CSV files will be needed. For more information, see *https://support.office.com/en-us/article/CSV-files-for-Mailbox -migration-b79fb81d-d6f4-4385-867e-7bdd0238366e?ui=en-US&rs=en-US&ad=US.*

  The following is a managed domain example for a migration.csv file. The first line is the required header.

  ```
  EmailAddress,Password,ForceChangePassword
  pilarp@contoso.com,Pa$$w0rd,False
  tobyn@contoso.com,Pa$$w0rd,False
  briant@contoso.com,Pa$$w0rd,False
  ```

The following is a federated domain example for a migration.csv file. The first line is the required header.

```
EmailAddress,Password,ForceChangePassword
pilarp@contoso.com,,
tobyn@contoso.com,,
briant@contoso.com,,
```

NOTE

If the domain of the user is a federated domain and you forget to leave the password options blank, this error appears:

Error: MigrationProvisioningPermanentException: You cannot set a Password or the ResetPasswordOnNextLogon property for a federated account. Please use your on-premises tools for these operations. In the case of a federated domain, leave those two fields blank. Ensure to pay attention when saving the CSV file, the encoding format is important. If using non-ASCII or special characters when saving the file, use UTF-8 encoding.

Staged Exchange migration using Exchange Admin Center (EAC)

You perform the following steps as a global administrator, logged on to the customer tenant in Office 365, using the Edge or Internet Explorer browser. These steps assume that the customer has completed AAD Connect to synchronize Active Directory, Office 365 domain registration, and migration spreadsheet prerequisites.

1. Launch *https://portal.office.com* and log on with the global administrator account. Select the Admin tile from the Office 365 app launcher.

2. Navigate to the Exchange Admin Center by using the Admin Center shortcut in the lower left pane of the Office 365 portal.

3. In the Exchange Admin Center, select Recipients | Migration.

4. Click the New icon (plus sign) and choose Migrate To Exchange Online to launch the New Migration Batch Wizard.

5. Select Staged Migration, as shown in Figure 12-10, and then click Next.

new migration batch

Select a migration type

The migration type to use depends on your existing email system, how many mailboxes you want to migrate, and whether you plan to maintain some mailboxes in your on-premises organization or migrate them all to the cloud. You'll also want to consider how long the migration will take and whether user identity will be managed in your on-premises organization or in Office 365.

Learn more

○ Remote move migration (supported by Exchange Server 2010 and later versions)
◉ Staged migration (supported by Exchange Server 2003 and Exchange Server 2007 only)
◌ Cutover migration (supported by Exchange Server 2003 and later versions)
○ IMAP migration (supported by Exchange and other email systems)

Figure 12-10 New Migration Batch Wizard Select A Migration Type page

NOTE

The Cutover Migration button is dimmed and unavailable because AAD Connect and Directory Synchronization have been enabled in the tenant, and users have been synchronized, which prevents you from performing a cutover migration.

6. On the Select The Users page, click the Browse button and select the location of the saved CSV file that you created for this user migration batch. See Figure 12-11. If more than the standard three columns are in the CSV file, select the Allow Unknown Columns In The CSV File check box. If the wrong CSV file is selected, click Change to display the Open dialog box to select the correct file. Click Next.

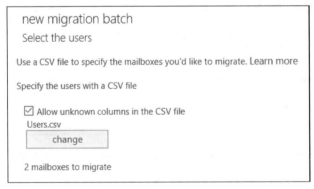

new migration batch

Select the users

Use a CSV file to specify the mailboxes you'd like to migrate. Learn more

Specify the users with a CSV file

☑ Allow unknown columns in the CSV file
Users.csv

| change |

2 mailboxes to migrate

Figure 12-11 Staged migration, New Migration Batch Wizard Select The Users page

7. Type in the email address, domain name\user name, and password for the on-premises administrative account that has access to the mailboxes and click Next, as shown in Figure 12-12.

The service is detecting the settings automatically for Outlook Anywhere to create the migration endpoint in the tenant.

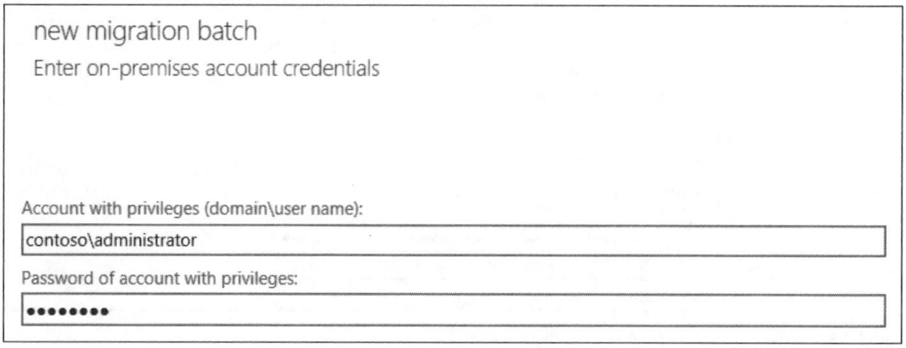

new migration batch

Enter on-premises account credentials

Account with privileges (domain\user name):

contoso\administrator

Password of account with privileges:

••••••••

Figure 12-12 Staged migration, New Migration Batch Wizard Enter On-Premises Account Credentials page

8. If the automatic configuration fails for domain name\user name and password, additional pages appear with text boxes for email address, domain\username, and password. Complete the three boxes and select Next, as shown in Figure 12-13.

   If the server settings cannot be detected, the following four boxes must be filled out to create the Outlook Anywhere migration endpoint: Exchange Server, RPC Proxy Server, Authentication, and Mailbox Permission. The first three settings can be validated by using the Outlook Connectivity test as mentioned in the Troubleshooting sidebar in the "Cutover Using Exchange Admin Center (EAC)" section earlier in this chapter. The Exchange or Active Directory administrator determines and communicates the mailbox permission level.

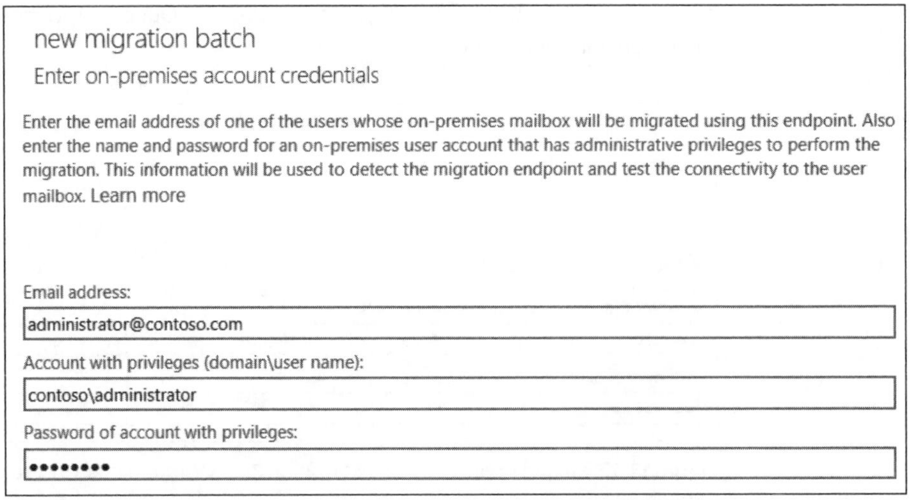

new migration batch

Enter on-premises account credentials

Enter the email address of one of the users whose on-premises mailbox will be migrated using this endpoint. Also enter the name and password for an on-premises user account that has administrative privileges to perform the migration. This information will be used to detect the migration endpoint and test the connectivity to the user mailbox. Learn more

Email address:

administrator@contoso.com

Account with privileges (domain\user name):

contoso\administrator

Password of account with privileges:

••••••••

Figure 12-13 Staged migration, New Migration Batch, Enter On-Premises Account Credentials page

Figure 12-14 shows that the migration endpoint could not be automatically detected.

If automatic detection is successful, the automatically detected configuration appears, as shown in Figure 12-15, and you do not need to enter the information manually. If the configuration wasn't detected, the administrator must fill out all four sections manually and configure the endpoint again.

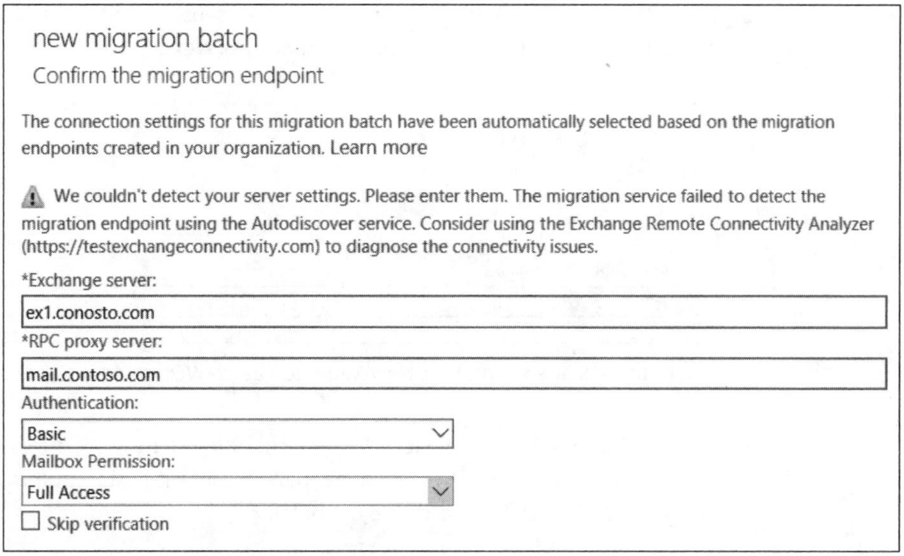

Figure 12-14 Staged migration, New Migration Batch Wizard Confirm The Migration Endpoint page showing that automatic detection failed

9. If automatic configuration is successful, confirm the automatically detected settings for the new Outlook Anywhere staged migration endpoint and click Next, as shown in Figure 2-15.

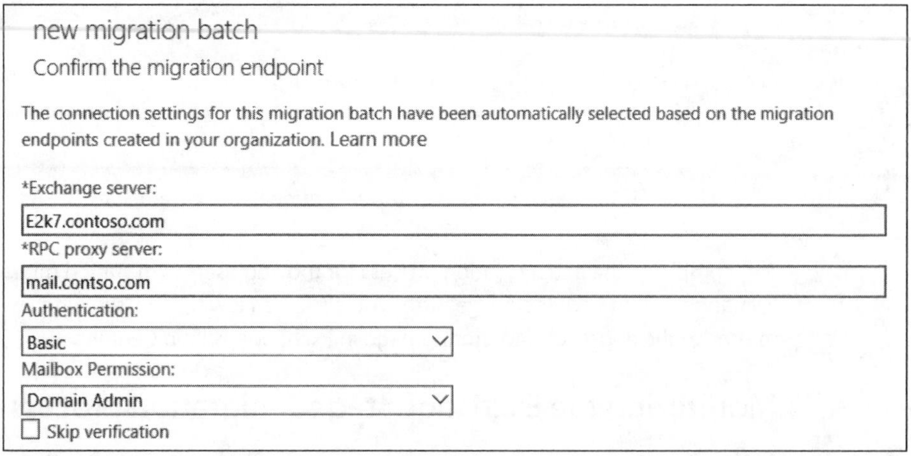

Figure 12-15 Staged migration, New Migration Batch Wizard Confirm The Migration Endpoint page, automatic detection success

10. Name the migration batch any name that makes sense to you in the New Migration Batch Name text box, as shown in Figure 12-16, and click Next.

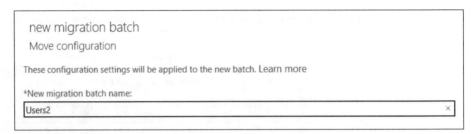

Figure 12-16 Staged migration, New Migration Batch Wizard Move Configuration page

11. Decide which notification mailbox to alert, click Browse to select the user from the list, and choose either to start the batch manually or allow it to start automatically, as shown in Figure 12-17. Click New to create the batch.

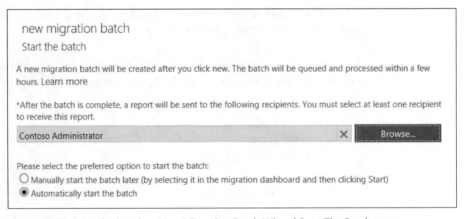

Figure 12-17 Staged migration, New Migration Batch Wizard Start The Batch page

This completes the batch creation process for moving users with staged migration in the Exchange Admin Center console. After you click the New button, the batch wizard process returns to the migration monitoring page in Exchange Admin Center.

Monitoring the Exchange staged migration process

Figure 12-18 shows a staged migration in process and where to monitor that information during the time the mailboxes synchronize to Exchange Online.

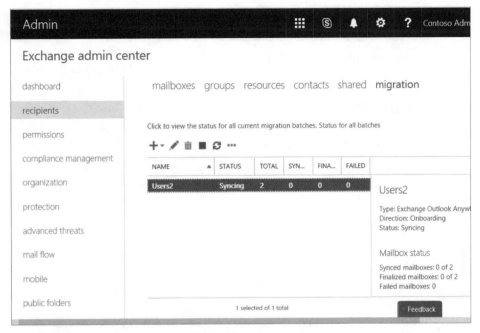

Figure 12-18 Staged Exchange migration dashboard monitoring

Figure 12-19 shows the migration Notifications fly-out, which the Office 365 Exchange Admin Center uses to notify the user of major events, in this case, a migration batch in progress and when it started.

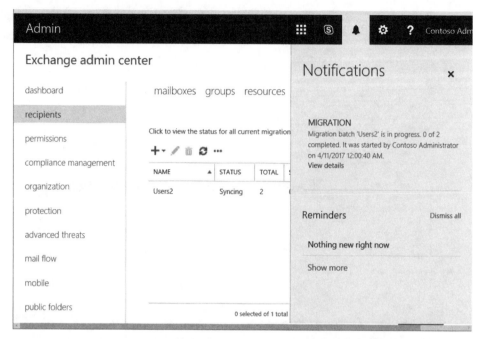

Figure 12-19 Staged Exchange migration Exchange Admin Center notification

Completing the staged Exchange migration process

During a staged migration, the administrator continues to use the batch process to migrate the users by a CSV file. After the batch of users has been processed, it can be deleted. Use the following steps after the user's mailbox has been fully synchronized. Steps 1 through 4 are repeated until all users have been migrated.

1. Validate that the user sync status is complete in the migration dashboard. Delete the batch after ensuring that the status of all the users shows them synced.

2. Convert the migrated user mailbox to a mail-enabled user account.

   Scripts are available to do this for Exchange Server 2003 and Exchange Server 2007. The primary reasons for doing this are so the users who haven't been migrated can still send mail to the migrated user and have it route properly and, when mailbox profiles are re-created for the migrated user, the mail-enabled user object redirects the migrated user to Office 365 by Autodiscover instead of logging on to their old mailbox, which was synchronized to Office 365 by staged migration.

NOTE

Exchange Server 2003 and Exchange Server 2007 post-migration conversion scripts are located at these URL locations:

- *https://support.office.com/en-us/article/Convert-Exchange-2003-mailboxes-to -mailenabled-users-5296a30b-00cb-44be-8855-ed9d14d93e17*

- *https://support.office.com/en-us/article/Convert-Exchange-2007-mailboxes-to -mailenabled-users-a1f79f3c-4967-4a15-8b3a-f4933aac0c34*

3. Assign the appropriate Office 365 licenses to the migrated users; an Exchange Online license is the minimum required.

4. Re-create user profiles for Outlook and provide passwords if applicable for the Office 365 users.

   This step is performed only once.

5. After all user objects have been migrated to Office 365, repoint on-premises Autodiscover DNS records to Office 365.

   This normally requires an internal and external DNS name change. For example: Auto-discover.contoso.com would have a CNAME record in DNS, pointing to Autodiscover. outlook.com.

6. After all user objects have been migrated to Office 365, remove the internal SCP point in Exchange if you are using Exchange 2007 or later. Use the Exchange Management Shell to run the following command.

```
Get-ClientAccessServer | Set-ClientAccessServer -autodiscoverserviceinternaluri
$null
```

   This step is performed only once.

NOTE

This command removes the internal endpoint for Autodiscover. This way, the Outlook client now uses DNS to find the Office 365 Autodiscover endpoint.

7. Repoint the MX and SPF records to Exchange Online Protection.

   This is an optional customer choice and can be done prior to the migration, during the migration, or at the end of migration. Planning is required.

Decommissioning Exchange on-premises

A staged migration requires AAD Connect directory synchronization. To manage Exchange attributes when the source of authority is on-premises Active Directory, the recommended practice is to maintain a single on-premises Exchange server to manage those attributes on-premises by using either the Exchange Admin Center or Exchange Management Shell. Prior to removing the older versions of Exchange, consider introducing the latest version that is compatible with the oldest version in the environment for management purposes. For example, Exchange Server 2003 environments can have an Exchange 2010 server added to the environment. After all of the Exchange Server 2003 environment has been decommissioned, the customer can then add Exchange 2016 to the environment and remove Exchange 2010, maintaining the latest version of Exchange for attribute management. More information about how and when to decommission is in the Microsoft TechNet article at *https://technet.microsoft.com/en-us/library /dn931280(v=exchg.150).aspx.*

Staged Exchange migrations work only for Exchange Server 2003 and Exchange Server 2007, and Microsoft no longer supports either of them. Customers will have a much better experience in the migration process if they forgo the use of staged migration and install a later version of Exchange—Exchange 2010 or newer—in the environment and then use express migration. Remember that there are key limitations in the methodology that might cause user dissatisfaction, such as requiring a separate user name and password, re-creation of the Outlook profile, and resynchronization of all users' mail to their local computer.

Express migrations

Express migration provides customers who are using Exchange 2010 and later the best migration scenario. From a user and administrative perspective, this is the best scenario due to the advanced feature set, using the Mailbox Replication Service (MRS or MRS Proxy). In this topology, either Exchange Server 2003 or Exchange Server 2007 would need to be configured to coexist with Exchange 2010, or Exchange Server 2007 could also be configured with Exchange 2010 and Exchange 2013 in a coexistence topology to support migrations from the older source environments. Express is a newer configuration option that is part of the Office 365 Hybrid Configuration Wizard that was released in 2016. This new feature helps smaller customers who do not want to deal with the limitations of cutover or staged migrations but want to move quickly to Office 365 while maintaining the best Outlook user experience. It takes advantage of a combination of AAD Connect in express configuration and Office 365 hybrid configuration in minimum mode.

The benefits of the express migration method are as follows.

- The Active Directory user and a hash of their password synchronize to Azure Active Directory. For more details about how that functions, see Chapter 5, "Installing Azure AD Connect."

- Outlook users do not have to re-create Outlook profiles or synchronize a new offline storage file (OST file).

- Mail flow is not interrupted; it continues to function during and after migration, without the need to configure MX records and Exchange Online protection.

- Downtime for users is minimized.

Express migration requirements

The new express migration option is a wizard-driven configuration toolset that has a specific set of requirements. These requirements set up a single server or group of servers to serve as a rapid onboarding system and process instead of the lengthier full hybrid option that is covered in Chapter 13, "Office 365 Hybrid Configuration Wizard."

- You must plan to migrate to Exchange Online in a rapid time frame with minimal coexistence.

- You must plan to synchronize the users and their password (hash) one time only and not deploy AAD Connect permanently.

- You must have at least one on-premises Exchange 2010, Exchange 2013, or Exchange 2016 server.

- If Exchange Server 2003 is installed, you must install Exchange 2010 to use it with express migration.

- If Exchange Server 2007 is installed, you must install either Exchange 2010 or Exchange 2013 and use it with express migration.

- TCP port 443 must be open and routable from the Internet to the Exchange server.

- You must have a third-party certificate for SSL connection with the fully qualified domain name that is installed and configured on the Exchange server. The name on the certificate can be the subject name or the one in the subject alternative name field. Alternatively, you can use a domain wildcard certificate. For more information about certificates, review the article at *https://technet.microsoft.com/en-us/library/hh563848(v=exchg.150).aspx*.

- You must have an external DNS address record matching the fully qualified domain name and certificate of the Exchange server.

- You must have an external Exchange Web Services (EWS) URL configured and matching the fully qualified domain name on the certificate and the external DNS address record, known as a DNS A record.

- You must have an Office 365 global administrator account.

CHAPTER 12

- You must have an Exchange on-premises account with organizational management rights.

- Any domain to be migrated to Office 365 must already be added to the portal. For details, see Chapter 2.

- You must have an Internet browser capable of managing Office 365.

Express migration limitations

Express migration has some limitations, most of which are built into the migration dashboard to enforce completion of certain tasks such as licensing a user mailbox prior to migration or only supporting a single migration endpoint at a time.

- Users must be licensed prior to using the Data Migration dashboard for migration. Shared, room, or equipment mailboxes do not need licenses to migrate.

- A single migration endpoint is currently the only supported option; if multiple endpoints are needed, use the more advanced option discussed in Chapter 13.

- Batches currently do not run in parallel. If a batch is started, it must complete prior to starting the next batch. If parallel batches are needed, see Chapter 13.

- The same limitations of a full hybrid MRS migration apply; specifically, non-inherited permissions do not migrate and should be captured and re-applied.

Installing and configuring express migration

To start the express migration process, the easiest method is to log on to the Exchange server and navigate to *https://portal.office.com*; any domain-joined, Windows-based computer will work if that isn't possible. Sign in to the portal with global administrator account credentials.

1. In the Office 365 Admin Center, shown in Figure 12-20, select Users | Data Migration to open the Migration page. Select Exchange.

   Clicking Exchange launches the first run experience for the Office 365 Hybrid Configuration Wizard.

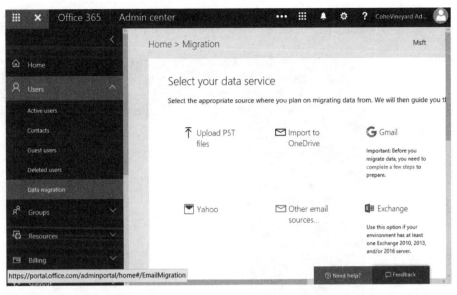

Figure 12-20 Data Migration, Exchange option

2. Click Download Application, as shown in Figure 12-21, and then click Run when prompted. After clicking Run, the Office 365 Hybrid Configuration Wizard prepares to install.

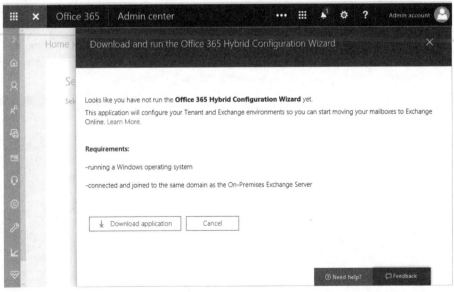

Figure 12-21 Download And Run The Office 365 Hybrid Configuration Wizard fly-out

You can also launch the hybrid wizard by clicking the settings box on the migration dash-board page and then selecting Run Hybrid Wizard, as shown in Figure 12-22.

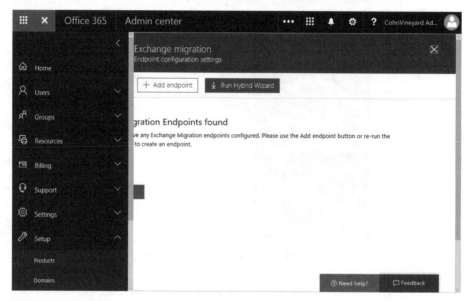

Figure 12-22 Exchange Migration Endpoint Configuration Settings page

3. When prompted, click Install, as shown in Figure 12-23.

The install process pulls the source files from a Microsoft Azure blob data storage loca-tion. Depending on the operating system version of your computer and User Account Control (UAC) configuration, when the install completes, you might need to click Run in the UAC Open File – Security Warning dialog box.

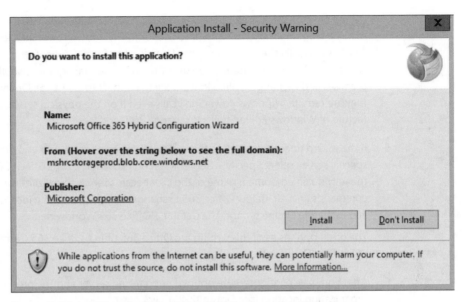

Figure 12-23 Installing the Office 365 Hybrid Configuration Wizard

The Office 365 Hybrid Configuration Wizard (see Figure 12-24) provides a built-in help option in the What Does This Application Do? hyperlink. It also provides Exchange system information, account information, and tenant information.

4. Click Next to start the configuration process.

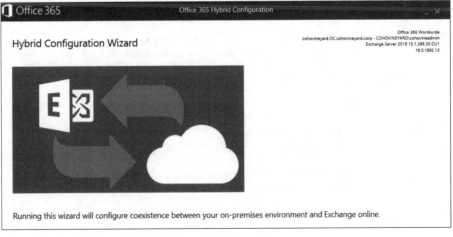

Figure 12-24 Office 365 Hybrid Configuration Wizard, first page

On the on-premises Exchange server organization configuration page, the wizard determines the optimal Exchange server to use for the Windows PowerShell execution process, which is normally the server the wizard is being run from if it meets the Client Access Server role criteria. The application uses the Exchange Management Shell to connect on-premises and Exchange Online PowerShell to connect to Exchange Online. In both cases, they are remote Windows PowerShell calls even if on the physical server due to the architecture of Windows PowerShell in Exchange 2010 and later.

5. If the wizard doesn't determine the optimal Exchange server, or if you prefer to use a specific server, select Specify A Server Running Exchange 2010, 2013 Or 2016 and type in the fully qualified domain name of the client access server the wizard will use to run the commands against. Below Office 365 Exchange Online, specify the location of the Office 365 Exchange Online tenant. The default is Office 365 Worldwide.

   The other options as of this writing are Office 365 China, Office 365 Germany, and Office 365 vNext (Dedicated).

6. After you have configured the optimal or preferred server and the proper Office 365 organization location (see Figure 12-25), click Next.

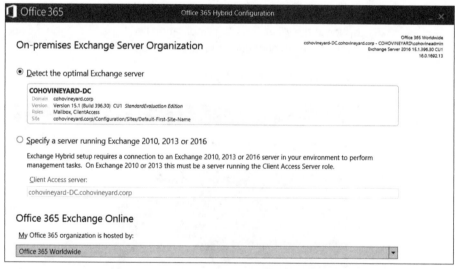

Figure 12-25 Office 365 Hybrid Configuration Wizard, On-Premises Exchange Server and Exchange Online selection

INSIDE OUT

Give feedback and rating in the Office 365 Hybrid Configuration Wizard

Microsoft is listening to its customer feedback. The Office 365 Hybrid Configuration Wizard has a direct feedback mechanism by which you can rate almost every page with between one and four stars, provide written feedback, and optionally supply an email address and a screenshot of the wizard page. Click Give Feedback in the lower left corner of the wizard and fill out the form.

For the Office 365 Hybrid Configuration Wizard to run, two accounts are required. One is an on-premises Exchange account, which is auto-detected when the Use Current Windows Credentials check box is selected, as shown in Figure 12-26, or you can override this option by clearing the check box and specifying an account, using a domain\username format and the account password. Clicking the Sign-In button below Office 365 Exchange Online Account enables you to provide the second required account, which is the Office 365 global administrator user name and password, as shown in Figure 12-27.

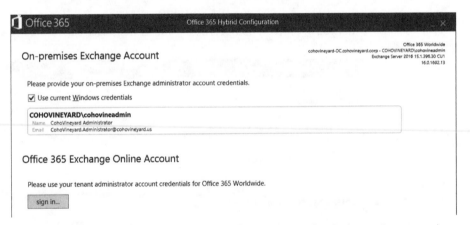

Figure 12-26 Office 365 Hybrid Configuration Wizard, On-Premises Exchange Account and Office 365 Exchange Online Account

7. As shown in Figure 12-27, type in the global administrator username and password specific to your tenant and click Sign In.

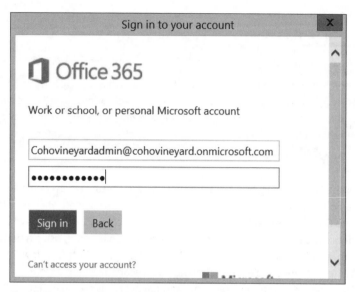

Figure 12-27 Sign in to the Office 365 Exchange Online Account

8. After you have typed both sets of credentials, click Next. See Figure 12-28.

Figure 12-28 Office 365 Hybrid Configuration Wizard, On-Premises Exchange Account and Office 365 Exchange Online Account completed

The Office 365 Hybrid Configuration Wizard now tests Windows PowerShell connectivity to the on-premises Exchange server and Office 365, using the credentials you provided on the previous page. If successful, information from both the on-premises and online environments are gathered for logging use as well as for decisions to be made later in the wizard.

INSIDE OUT

Stop. Read this. Hybrid features selection

Hybrid Features is one of those pages in the Office 365 Hybrid Configuration Wizard on which you come to an important decision point. Which do I pick: Minimal Hybrid Configuration (Recommended) or Full Hybrid Configuration? If you select Minimal and complete the wizard, the next time you run the wizard, you can select Minimal Hybrid again or upgrade to Full Hybrid Configuration. If you select Full Hybrid Configuration and complete the configuration, covered in detail in Chapter 13, the next time you run the wizard, this page to select a Hybrid Features type does not appear. Express migration is an optional component of Minimal Hybrid Configuration.

Express migration is part of the Minimal Hybrid Configuration process.

9. Select Minimal Hybrid Configuration, as shown in Figure 12-29, and click Next.

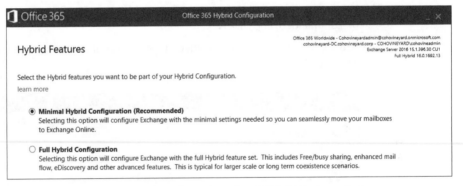

Figure 12-29 Office 365 Hybrid Configuration Wizard, Hybrid Features choice

The Ready For Update page, shown in Figure 12-30, runs the commands against the on-premises Exchange server and Exchange Online.

10. Click Update and let it configure.

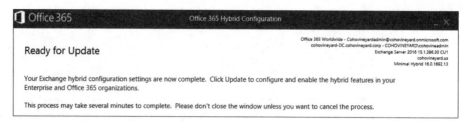

Figure 12-30 Office 365 Hybrid Configuration Wizard, Ready For Update page

During the configuration process, the green bar progresses, with the various tasks, phases, and commands changing as the process runs through the on-premises and online Power-Shell cmdlets. If you click the Stop button, you stop the configuration process but do not roll back any changes that the wizard has already completed.

The User Provisioning options page, shown in Figure 12-31, only appears when you select Minimal Configuration and users have not been synchronized to Azure Active Directory through AAD Connect.

11. Use express migration to select Synchronize My Users And Password One Time (Recommended) and click Next.

AzureADConnect.msi is downloaded in the background, and the installation process of Azure AD Connect starts.

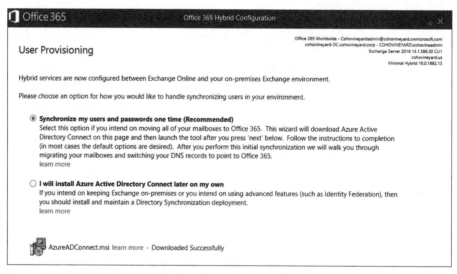

Figure 12-31 Office 365 Hybrid Configuration Wizard, configuration in progress

Azure AD Connect installs and enables the administrator to choose an express or custom install. Both options are covered in detail in Chapter 5. Because this is an express migration, choosing Express is recommended while installing and configuring Azure AD Connect.

12. At the prompt, indicate whether the install succeeded or failed. If it failed, you can retry it. If it succeeded, click Next to start the user synchronization process from the local Active Directory to Azure Active Directory. See Figure 12-32.

Depending on the size of Active Directory, this might take some time.

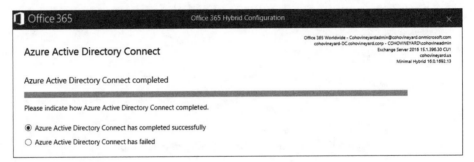

Figure 12-32 Office 365 Hybrid Configuration Wizard, Azure Active Directory Connect completion status page

13. When the Synchronizing Users page is finished, which might take some time, depending on the total number of users in Active Directory, click Next to proceed to the final page.

14. Rate the experience, provide feedback, and include your email address, if so desired, as shown in Figure 12-33. Click Close.

CHAPTER 12

Figure 12-33 Office 365 Hybrid Configuration complete

Figure 12-33 shows that the Office 365 hybrid configuration is complete and successful. The mailbox migration process can begin. See Figure 12-34 for a user's account that is ready to be migrated.

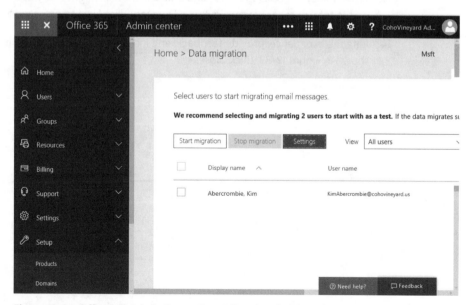

Figure 12-34 Office 365 Admin Center Data Migration dashboard

15. Navigate to the Data Migration dashboard in the Users section of the Office 365 Admin Center.

This Data Migration page is where migrations are managed during express migration. Users must be licensed to be migrated. See Chapter 8, "Inside the Security & Compliance Center: Data Classification, Loss Prevention, Governance, and Discovery," for more details about licensing users. A status column, which indicates whether the user needs a license, appears on the right side of the migration dashboard. If the mailbox type is a shared, room, or equipment mailbox, it normally doesn't need a license and shows a status of Not Started. If the user has been licensed and successfully migrated, the status shows In Cloud. If the user status shows License Required, this user needs at least an Exchange Online license to start the migration process.

16. When the user licensing is complete, select the check box next to the user to add the user to the batch. After the users for this batch are selected, click the Start Migration button.

Only one batch of users is possible while using this Data Migration dashboard at the time of this writing.

In-depth details of the user migration process are not available in the Data Migration dashboard. Using the Refresh button in the browser forces the status to be updated if there is a change; otherwise, it refreshes as the updates are received during the move request process. The normal process starts with Validating, ensuring that it can use the migration endpoint; when it proceeds to Syncing, it starts the process of migrating the mailbox data, progressing finally to Completed. If the user data fails to migrate, it is marked as Failed, and additional details become available. The user has to have logged on to their Exchange on-premises mailbox at least once to ensure that the mailbox initializes properly, or the migration will fail. When the failed issue is resolved, you can select the user and click Start Migration to start the process again.

INSIDE OUT

Express migration: msExchMailboxGuid is the key

The magic behind express migration is using AAD Connect to synchronize the on-premises Exchange mailbox to Azure Active Directory and Office 365 with a key object property that makes this process work. The key property is the msExchMailboxGuid. This is the globally unique identifier for each user's Exchange mailbox. During the one-time synchronization, using AAD Connect in Express configuration during express migration, the user object is synchronized as a mail-enabled user object with that user's msExchMailboxGuid. This sets the user up so they can be licensed, and because that property is present on the mail-enabled user, it won't create a mailbox and will be a ready target for the mailbox migration process using MRS Proxy (the Mailbox Replication Service), which is enabled during Express and Minimal Hybrid configuration.

CHAPTER 12

Express migration summary

Express migration is the best method for smaller customers to use to migrate from Exchange 2010, Exchange 2013, and Exchange 2016. Exchange Server 2003 and Exchange Server 2007 customers need to decide whether the effort to install a compatible version of Exchange and configure it for express migration is worth the time, cost, and effort to obtain the best user migration experience. The dashboard migration process is new and will evolve and get better to support more complex scenarios in the future.

Migration performance

Migration performance involves a multitude of factors that affect the speed with which onboarding to the Office 365 service can be achieved. The size, number of items, and attachment size are factors to consider while testing the onboarding process. The currently available network bandwidth that the migration connection will use, as well as the network latency between the data center and Office 365, is an important factor. Many migrations start after normal working hours or at the end of a work week, when the weekend time can be used for the bulk of the data synchronization process. The type of migration might also have different and important factors that affect speed, such as the three types of throttling Office 365 uses to protect the overall performance of the system: user throttling, migration-service throttling, and resource health–based throttling. The migration administrator can control only some of these parameters.

User throttling does not affect any of the migration types discussed in this chapter; it only affects third-party migration utilities using a single account to perform MAPI migrations or a user manually uploading their own PST file. If a third-party vendor is using a single account for migrations with a protocol such as Exchange Web Services, it is recommended to explore application impersonation configuration. Even then, multiple accounts with impersonation might allow better scalability of the solution.

Migration-service throttling is governed by the concurrency values discussed earlier in this chapter, MaxConcurrentMigrations and MaxConcurrentIncrementalSyncs. This enables the administrator performing the migration to tune the number of migrations as well as the number of daily incremental syncs that occur. These numbers should be tuned and modified with caution; to ensure that the source environment can handle the configuration, start small and increment the MaxConcurrentMigrations value. Incrementing the MaxConcurrentIncrementalSyncs number to match MaxConcurrentMigrations or setting it too close to the MaxConcurrentMigrations number is not recommended. Normal ratios that have been observed are 2:1, with as much as a 5:1 difference, meaning MaxConcurrentMigrations 100 to MaxConcurrentIncrementalSyncs 20. Note that these are observed settings that worked in specific customer instances; testing and validating your own is recommended.

Office 365 resource health–based throttling is how the Office 365 service protects itself when there is a service availability issue. Normally, it manifests by queueing migrations. This can also be traced to the service health dashboard in the Office 365 Admin Center where service incidents are reported. Migration speed varies from many factors as well. The source, the data injection method, the protocol involved, and speeds as low as .1 GB per hour or up to 14 GB per hour with 20 mailboxes concurrently migrating have been tested in the past. A key performance metric many forget about during a migration is how healthy the system was prior to starting the migration. Did the migration methodology tip the performance scales far enough to cause a performance issue? Is the firewall performing intrusion detection during the mailbox migration moves and throttling the request from Office 365?

INSIDE OUT

Office 365 migration performance

This chapter discussed many possible issues and options concerning Office 365 migration performance. Microsoft has published an article that has deeper detail and recommendations along with some charts to explain some options. For further information, please review the article at *https://support.office.com/en-us/article/Office-365-migration -performance-and-best-practices-d9acb371-fd6c-4c14-aa8e-db5cbe39aa57?ui=en -US&rs=en-US&ad=US*.

Summary

This chapter covered which migration method is applicable to the source environment; key planning and configuration concepts; the three migration methods that are options for many customers who are not interested in a full hybrid migration and configuration; and how to complete these migrations when using the Exchange Admin Center, Windows PowerShell, or the new Data Migration dashboard using the latest express migration option provided by a combination of Azure Active Directory Connect and the Minimal HyConfiguration Wizard. The chapter ended by briefly discussing key performance concerns to watch for during migrations.

Exchange Online hybrid

Most organizations that have been managing on-premises infrastructure and want to move to software-as-a-service offerings (such as Exchange Online) won't be able to pivot and begin using online services immediately. They need to understand the features and capabilities, test the resiliency and features, and plan for coexistence, migration, and user experiences.

Deploying Exchange Online in a hybrid configuration enables you to test the features of Office 365 as well as provide a path to migrate your data and configurations online at a pace that meets your organization's requirements.

This chapter covers architecture and planning for Exchange Online hybrid configurations, enabling the on-premises and cloud infrastructures, migrating mailboxes between the platforms, public folder coexistence and migration, and management.

This chapter is broken down into seven topics.

- Overview of Exchange Online hybrid features

- Planning

- Office 365 Hybrid Configuration Wizard

- Moving mailboxes to or from Exchange Online

- Public folders

- Mailbox provisioning

- Decommissioning the hybrid environment

Overview of Exchange Online hybrid features

Although the overall architecture of an organization's Exchange on-premises and Exchange Online deployment varies based on technical, security, or business constraints, each organization must identify the components and features it will be using.

Configuring a hybrid environment enables your organization to take advantage of several features, such as the following.

- Secure mail flow between on-premises and cloud environments with a shared namespace

- A unified global address list (GAL) for both on-premises and cloud users

- Free/busy and calendar sharing

- A single Outlook Web Access URL

- Ability to move mailboxes between on-premises and online environments

- Centralized mailbox management and provisioning from the on-premises environment

- Cross-premises mailbox search, MailTips, and message tracking

- Cloud-based archiving for both on-premises and cloud mailboxes

From an architectural perspective, implementing an Exchange Online hybrid configuration is similar to a multi-forest Exchange organization with identity synchronization, permissions delegation, and mail routing concerns. For services to work across environments, you must allow network connectivity between Exchange Online and your organization, manage identity, and provide a way for users to resolve resources in either environment.

The Office 365 Hybrid Configuration Wizard, formerly known as the Exchange Hybrid Configuration Wizard, is an organization-wide Exchange configuration toolset.

The Hybrid Configuration Wizard runs a series of Windows PowerShell commands against both the on-premises Exchange Server configuration and the Office 365 Exchange Online tenant. The Hybrid Configuration Wizard configures organization-level and server-level parameters to support the rich coexistence topology with two key protocols, HTTPS and SMTP, to build the bridge between one or more on-premises Exchange organizations and Exchange Online.

Although many people refer to the server(s) that the Hybrid Configuration Wizard has been run against as "the hybrid servers," there isn't a role for a hybrid server during the Exchange installation process. You can run the Hybrid Configuration Wizard on any server with the appropriate connectivity in the organization, and it can enable or disable the participation of other servers in the hybrid configuration. Only servers with an enabled transport role appear selectable in the Hybrid Configuration Wizard. This role name differs by version: Hub Transport role in Exchange 2010, Client Access Server (CAS) and Mailbox role in Exchange 2013, and Mailbox role in Exchange 2016.

INSIDE OUT
Client access server roles and the Hybrid Configuration Wizard

In previous versions of the Hybrid Configuration Wizard, it was possible to choose which servers participated in the hybrid configuration for transport and mailbox migration functions. When a server was selected for a client access role, the MRSProxy service was enabled on the selected servers for performing mailbox migrations. In very large organizations, the enumeration of client access servers could take hours and led to timeouts and failures during configuration.

The Hybrid Configuration Wizard now enables MRSProxy for all eligible client access servers in the organization automatically. The ExternalUrl property on eligible client access servers is populated (Get-WebServicesVirtualDirectory). If an organization has only a single CAS and the ExternalUrl property is null, the Hybrid Configuration Wizard returns a warning. If an organization has more than one CAS and the ExternalUrl property on at least one of them is defined, MRSProxy is silently enabled on that server.

Outbound traffic (HTTPS for connections to Exchange Online and HTTP for certificate revocation list checking) must be allowed for every server with the Client Access Server role in Exchange 2010, Client Access Server and Mailbox role in Exchange 2013, and Mailbox role in Exchange 2016. Inbound HTTPS routing for Autodiscover and mailbox migration requests can be directed to specific servers as a function of DNS and load-balancing configuration.

The most critical planning topics are Autodiscover, free/busy, mail flow and transport, public folders, and cross-premises access.

Planning

Prior to implementing a hybrid configuration, ensure that your environment meets all the basic requirements and notify your network team for any changes that might need to be made. In addition, some organizations have strict requirements around configuring endpoints for access to the Internet, so you might also need to work with your organization's security team to ensure that your deployment meets both the operational and security requirements of the business.

General

One of the most often overlooked planning steps in an Exchange Online hybrid configuration is making sure your environment meets the prerequisites. Please refer to Chapter 10, "Preparing an On-Premises Environment to Connect to Exchange Online," for details on minimum software versions as well as other important server and networking prerequisites.

Autodiscover

Clients use the Autodiscover service to locate mailboxes. Clients can be users or servers querying on their behalf. The best practice for Exchange deployments is to update the Autodiscover configuration to point to the newest version of Exchange to enable the newest feature set and ensure the widest compatibility. When designing a hybrid solution, the best-practice recommendation is no different. If you are deploying a newer version of Exchange into your environment than currently exists, it is recommended to update Autodiscover to use the newer version of Exchange.

For more information about Autodiscover, see Chapter 10.

Azure Active Directory Connect

To synchronize mailboxes as mail-enabled users to Office 365 as well as perform necessary writeback of Exchange hybrid permissions, you must install and configure Azure Active Directory Connect (Azure AD Connect or AAD Connect).

For information about how to deploy and configure AAD Connect, please review Chapter 4, "Directory Synchronization Basics," and Chapter 5, "Installing Azure AD Connect." For additional information about configuring permissions delegation for Azure AD Connect scenarios, see *https://gallery.technet.microsoft.com/AD-Advanced-Permissions-49723f74*.

Cross-premises access and delegation

Cross-premises access is the ability to continue to access a mailbox as an additional resource after it has been moved to Exchange Online. Currently, only the Full Access mailbox permission is supported for a migrated mailbox when an on-premises mailbox accesses it.

Other permissions, such as Send As, Receive As, or Send on Behalf Of, are not supported in a cross-premises scenario. Delegation using the Microsoft Outlook client is also not supported cross-premises. Office 365 Dedicated and International Traffic in Arms (ITAR) (vNext) environments are the exception to this because they support additional functionality more closely aligned with an Exchange resource forest model.

When mailboxes are moved to Exchange Online, most permissions and delegation of those mailboxes are moved as well. Careful analysis of who to move with whom is required so certain things don't break such as cross-premises access or delegation. For instance, if you move an executive to Office 365 Exchange Online and do not move the executive's assistant, and the executive's assistant has delegated calendar rights to the executive's calendar, that breaks their connection temporarily. For that reason, they should be in the same migration batch and migrated together.

INSIDE OUT

Permissions migrations

Mailbox permissions are typically translated to Office 365 during properly batched hybrid MRS moves. However, there are still scenarios in which permissions must be audited on-premises and re-applied after migration. Permissions auditing and reapplication are required when using third-party migration tools or when using non-inherited permissions such as when granting Send As to a distribution group.

In these instances, it's best to back up permissions before migrations start and then reapply them if necessary post migration. You can use the community-provided script in the Tech-Net Gallery at *https://gallery.technet.microsoft.com/scriptcenter/Migrate-Mailbox -Permissions-2f262f8b* to back up and reapply permissions.

DNS

Successful configuration of an Exchange Online hybrid environment requires adding records to your organization's external DNS. All domains to be shared between Exchange Online and Exchange on-premises must be verified in the Office 365 tenant, which is accomplished by a DNS TXT record. In addition, federation also requires external DNS records to prove domain ownership.

Email address policies and proxy addresses

The Exchange hybrid configuration process updates the email address policies of domains that are selected to be shared between the on-premises and online environments. After the email address policy update, users configured to inherit email address policies are updated.

Because updating proxy addresses can have a large impact on your address book (and, subsequently, offline address book downloads), you might want to perform the email address policy and proxy address templates manually. If the Hybrid Configuration Wizard detects that the policies have been updated, that step of the process will be skipped.

Email address policies can be updated manually (the default format is *<alias>@<tenant>.mail. onmicrosoft.com*) or by using a script (*https://gallery.technet.microsoft.com/Bulk-or-Selectively -Update-be06b784*). Proxy address can also be updated manually, using a script (*https://gallery.technet.microsoft.com/Add-Office-365-Tenant-93391e4c*) or by adding a rule to AAD Connect (*https://gallery.technet.microsoft.com/Create-an-AAD -Connect-Rule-45ea6591*).

Exchange Server Deployment Assistant

The Microsoft Exchange Server Deployment Assistant is a web-based tool that you can use to build a roadmap or checklist of tasks to complete for a number of Exchange server configurations, including hybrid, based on your organization's existing topology and business requirements. It asks several questions about your current infrastructure and then prescribes a set of general steps to follow to complete the configuration. You can find the Microsoft Exchange Server Deployment Assistant at *http://aka.ms/exdeploy*.

Exchange server versions

A hybrid configuration can be performed with on-premises Exchange servers from 2003 and later. However, there are certain coexistence requirements, based on your deployed version of Exchange. See Table 13-1 for a version support matrix.

Table 13-1 Supported Exchange Server versions

Minimum Exchange Version	Minimum Hybrid Configuration Version Based on Exchange Coexistence
Exchange 2003	Exchange 2010 coexistence required. Exchange 2013 or Exchange 2016 are not options because they cannot be installed in a forest with Exchange 2003 present.
Exchange 2007	Exchange 2010 coexistence or Exchange 2013 if OAuth is required. Exchange 2016 is not an option.
Exchange 2003 and Exchange 2007	Exchange 2010 coexistence required. Exchange 2013 and Exchange 2016 are not options because they cannot be installed in a forest with Exchange 2003 present.
Exchange 2007 with Exchange 2010	No additional version requirements unless OAuth is required. If OAuth is necessary, deployment with Exchange 2013 is required. Exchange 2016 is not an option because it cannot be installed in a forest with Exchange 2007 present.
Exchange 2010	No additional version requirements unless OAuth is required. If OAuth is necessary, deployment with Exchange 2013 or Exchange 2016 is required.
Exchange 2013	No version requirement, Use existing topology.
Exchange 2016	No version requirement, Use existing topology.

Free/busy and hybrid authentication

Free/busy is the ability to check calendar availability for one or more users or resources. Free/busy endpoints are located through the availability service, looking by default for the Autodiscover endpoint. For more information about the Autodiscover service, refer to Chapter 10.

Depending on the versions of Exchange in the environment, the Hybrid Configuration Wizard might allow the configuration of two methods of free/busy lookup: OAuth (Open Authorization) and DAuth (Delegated Authentication).

Delegated authentication occurs when a network service accepts a request from a user, obtains a token to act on behalf of that user, and then initiates a new connection to a second network service on behalf of the user. OAuth is an authorization mechanism whereby a third-party application or service accesses a user's data without the user providing credentials.

Exchange 2010 uses DAuth to facilitate the server-to-server communication required for free/busy lookups. Environments that include only Exchange 2013 or later can use OAuth in addition to DAuth to provide authentication for additional features. Table 13-2 explains which authentication configurations are available, configured as part of the Hybrid Configuration Wizard, and which require additional configuration.

Table 13-2 Hybrid configuration DAuth and OAuth options

Versions	DAuth	OAuth
Exchange Server 2003/2007/2010	Part of Hybrid Configuration Wizard Configuration	Not available
Exchange Server 2007/2010/2013	Part of Hybrid Configuration Wizard Configuration	Manual configuration
Exchange Server 2010/2013/2016	Part of Hybrid Configuration Wizard Configuration	Manual configuration
Exchange Server 2013/2016	Part of Hybrid Configuration Wizard Configuration	Part of Hybrid Configuration Wizard Configuration
Exchange Server 2013	Part of Hybrid Configuration Wizard Configuration	Part of Hybrid Configuration Wizard Configuration
Exchange Server 2016	Part of Hybrid Configuration Wizard Configuration	Part of Hybrid Configuration Wizard Configuration

INSIDE OUT

Manual OAuth configuration

OAuth configuration is required if advanced features such as Messaging Records Management (MRM), In-Place eDiscovery, and cross-premises archiving are required. You can learn about the process to enable OAuth by following the steps located at *https://technet .microsoft.com/en-us/library/dn594521(v=exchg.150).aspx,* "Configure OAuth Authentication Between Exchange and Exchange Online Organizations." This configuration process requires Windows PowerShell and the ability to connect to Exchange on-premises, Exchange Online, and Azure Active Directory.

If you have already configured OAuth and are experiencing issues or want to learn about potential problems you might encounter, you can review the information at *https://blogs .technet.microsoft.com/exovoice/2016/02/12/OAuth-troubleshooting.* For an in-depth look at the hybrid authentication flow, see *https://blogs.technet.microsoft.com/exchange/2017 /05/24/deep-dive-how-hybrid-authentication-really-works.*

As Table 13-2 shows, DAuth is always configured. This means the administrator must configure at least one federated domain proof prior to running the Hybrid Configuration Wizard or during the Hybrid Configuration Wizard process. If you do not create a federated trust prior and add a domain proof, it will be done as part of the Hybrid Configuration Wizard process. Configuring a domain proof (either before or during the Hybrid Configuration Wizard) requires the ability to add an external DNS text record.

The Azure Active Directory Authentication Service is a trust broker between two federated Exchange organizations. Configuration of the federation trust is required to enable sharing free/busy information. Because each organization's federation trust is configured with the Azure Active Directory Authentication Service, it can be used to enable federated sharing with other organizations, using Exchange on-premises or Exchange Online.

Organization relationships contain the parameters for free/busy in Exchange on-premises and Exchange Online; specify which domains are part of the configuration as well as the target endpoint to resolve the free/busy query.

When planning free/busy for your organization, you must ensure that you enable network access to the endpoints for free/busy lookup. Your organization might require exchanging availability information with other organizations as well, and those can be managed with additional organization relationships. If you are attempting to federate with an organization that is already in Exchange Online, you must configure additional organization relationships to create a mesh topology. Architecture of a hybrid mesh can be found on the Exchange Team Blog at *https://blogs.technet.microsoft.com/exchange/2016/10/17/the-hybrid-mesh.*

Message sizes

The Mailbox Replication Service migration method enables you to migrate individual messages up to 150 MB. If you will be migrating mail with third-party tools or have items larger than 150 MB, review the number of messages exceeding the threshold. You can use the Exchange Large Item Compliance script to assist in this process. Go to *https://gallery.technet.microsoft.com /office/PowerShell-Script-Office-54d367ea.*

Mail transport

Planning for mail transport is an essential part of the overall hybrid deployment process. By default, the hybrid configuration enables secure mail between on-premises and cloud environments by creating inbound and outbound connectors in Exchange Online and either creating new or modifying existing connectors in your Exchange on-premises environment. Mail originating from the Internet is delivered to the host listed in your organization's MX record (whether the record points to your on-premises environment or to Exchange Online), and then Exchange continues to route the mail to its final destination, relaying over the hybrid mail flow connectors to reach recipients in the connected environments.

Mail originating in Office 365 and Exchange Online is routed, by default, out to the MX hosts for recipient organizations. Mail originating on-premises continues to egress through the existing configuration. This configuration is suitable for most organizations, but you might have other requirements, depending on your business or security posture.

If your organizations have Exchange Server 2013 or Exchange Server 2016 edge transport servers, they can be configured during the hybrid configuration, if desired, although they add complexity to the overall solution. If you plan to use Exchange Server 2010 edge transport servers, they will require manual configuration. You can find specific instructions for Exchange Server 2010 edge transport servers in the Exchange Server Deployment Assistant (*http://aka.ms /exdeploy*).

Centralized mail transport (CMT) is a mail routing architecture that routes all outbound mail from Office 365 through the on-premises environment. Centralized mail transport (also commonly referred to as central mail flow or centralized mail) is frequently used when organizations are required to apply additional processing to outbound mail. Such requirements might include the following.

- On-premises data loss prevention (DLP) systems

- On-premises encryption gateways

The physical and logical network requirements for either standard or centralized mail transport are the same (both requiring inbound and outbound port 25 between your transport servers and Exchange Online Protection). If centralized mail transport is enabled, but a specific domain needs a different path, a criteria-based routing rule must be configured separately.

Interruption of the SMTP/TLS mail flow between Exchange Online and the Exchange on-premises systems with a third-party appliance is not supported. Breaking the TLS handshake results in the messages being seen as "out of organization" and might prevent name resolution of user email addresses when displayed in Outlook or cause automatic resource booking requests to fail.

If your organization will be configuring a hybrid environment by using Exchange Server 2010 hub transport servers and they are behind a network address translation device, you might need to plan to modify the Office 365 receive connector on each hub/transport server to include the IP address of the device performing the translation.

Networking

Configuring a hybrid Exchange Online environment has the following network requirements.

- Exchange on-premises servers that will be configured for mail transport must have inbound and outbound access on port 25 to Exchange Online Protection (*http://aka.ms /o365endpoints*) with no pre-authentication, Secure Sockets Layer (SSL) offloading, or packet inspection.

- Exchange on-premises servers with the Client Access Server role must be accessible (at a minimum) from Exchange Online over port 443 to resolve Autodiscover requests for free/busy and to perform mailbox moves.

Public folders

Many organizations have deployed public folders on-premises. If your organization has deployed them on-premises and needs to maintain them, plan for hybrid connectivity to public folders and, potentially, a migration to Exchange Online modern public folders. Both hybrid coexistence and migration are covered later in this chapter.

Public folders can be enabled in a hybrid fashion (so that cloud users can access on-premises public folders). This can be configured immediately to provide continued access to the public folder data throughout the course of a migration. It is recommended to migrate public folders last.

Hybrid public folder configuration is relatively straightforward and requires a working organization relationship. Hybrid public folders rely on the organization relationship created during the Hybrid Configuration Wizard.

Office 365 Hybrid Configuration Wizard

The Office 365 Hybrid Configuration Wizard is a tool that configures one or more on-premises organizations to connect to Office 365. It simplifies the process of configuring federation and secure mail flow and enabling your on-premises environment for mailbox migrations.

In September 2015, the product group released the third version of the Hybrid Configuration Wizard, rebranding it the Office 365 Hybrid Configuration Wizard. The new Office 365 Hybrid Configuration Wizard is now hosted in the Office 365 service, and the most recent configuration updates are downloaded and used each time the wizard is run.

Overview

The Office 365 Hybrid Configuration Wizard itself has been improved in many ways.

- **Version-agnostic hybrid experience**   Prior to this release, the hybrid configuration experience depended on the specific Exchange Server version, service pack, cumulative update, or rollup. By hosting the engine in the service, the latest version and features are applied to the configuration automatically. The new wizard is no longer tied to the Exchange update release cycle, so updates based on best practices and user feedback can be integrated with the process more quickly. You can open the Hybrid Configuration Wizard from the Exchange Admin Center or by going directly to *http://aka.ms /hybridwizard*.

- **Early access for First Release customers**   Another benefit of a stand-alone, web-based distribution method is the ability to pilot specific versions as needed. The First Release version is available at *http://aka.ms/taphcw*.

- **Enhanced error handling and logging**   Logging detail has been updated and is easier to understand. The wizard now has more information per phase and task, error codes that map to specific errors, a specific error-handling option code (HCW8****), and access to log files in *%appdata%\Microsoft\ExchangeHybridConfiguration* by using a shortcut. Diagnostic information can be accessed by pressing F12 during the wizard. This F12 function also enables launching dedicated Windows PowerShell consoles connected to both Exchange on-premises and Exchange Online, each with a different color background to make it easier to differentiate between the two environments.

- **Telemetry**   By default, every execution of the Hybrid Configuration Wizard uploads the logs for analysis. This can be disabled using a registry key if required. This provides the team invaluable insight into the running of the configuration wizard and helps the team diagnose and fix issues faster than ever before.

The Hybrid Configuration Wizard enables the following features over HTTPS for coexistence.

- Free/busy between the two (or more) Exchange organizations by using OAuth and Intra-Organization connectors or the Azure Active Directory authentication service.

- Mailbox migrations using the Mailbox Replication Service Proxy (MRSProxy). MRS-based mailbox moves, in conjunction with the synchronization of the Exchange Mailbox GUID by AAD Connect, preserves the user's Outlook Offline Storage (OST) file and allows for automatic profile configuration post-migration. This feature also provides offboarding from Office 365 if needed.

- MailTips to display important informative messages (such as data loss prevention–related tips or out-of-office messages) during message composition.

- Cross-premises E-discovery search, Exchange Online Archiving and Messaging Records Management policy cross premises, using OAuth configuration.

- Outlook Web Access redirection to Office 365 from on-premises Outlook Web Access, using organization relationship settings.

The Hybrid Configuration Wizard enables secure SMTP mail flow, using one of the following methods (depending on the versions of the Exchange servers involved in hybrid transport).

- TLS-secured transport between Exchange Server 2013 or Exchange Server 2016 and Exchange Online, using certificates.

- TLS-secured transport between Exchange Server 2010 and Exchange Online, using remote domains and remote IP address ranges, and certificates.

The Hybrid Configuration Wizard also enables these features regardless of Exchange version.

- Message tracking, which records messages to and from the on-premises and online Exchange organizations.

- Accepted domains/remote domains and email address policies configured to support hybrid mail flow by using tenant.mail.onmicrosoft.com.

INSIDE OUT

Hybrid Configuration engine

The Hybrid Configuration engine is the component that runs the actual configuration. A number of server, domain, and organization-level changes are performed in both the Exchange on-premises and Exchange Online environments.

The components that the Hybrid Configuration engine modifies are detailed in Table 13-3.

Table 13-3 Hybrid Configuration engine architecture

On-premises Exchange Organization			Exchange Online Organization	
Exchange Server	Domain	Organization	Domain	Organization
Mailbox Replication Service Proxy	Accepted domains	Exchange federation trust	Accepted domains	Exchange federation trust
Certificates	Remote domains	Organization relationship	Remote domains	Organization relationship
Exchange Web Services virtual directories	Email address policies	Availability address space		Inbound and outbound connector
Receive connector		Send connector		Migration endpoint
		OAuth configuration		OAuth configuration

When you run the Hybrid Configuration Wizard, the engine runs through the following task sequence.

1. The wizard runs Get-HybridConfiguration cmdlet, starting the process.

2. The hybrid configuration engine examines the stored desired state from the hybrid configuration object, stored in Active Directory. If the Hybrid Configuration Wizard has not been run before, the values are null. If the wizard has been run before, values retrieved from the hybrid configuration object are populated.

3. Changes made during the navigation of the wizard are stored in memory as the new desired state configuration.

4. The hybrid configuration engine runs a discovery process against the on-premises Exchange organization, checking the current topology and configuration.

5. The hybrid configuration engine runs a discovery process against the Exchange Online organization, checking the current topology and configuration.

6. The current state and new desired state are compared, and any differences are applied using Set-HybridConfiguration. The engine runs the specific tasks to establish the new desired state.

During the progress of the wizard, no changes are made to the system. If you cancel the wizard before clicking Update, no changes will be made. After the updates have been set in the configuration object and you have clicked the Update button, the desired state configuration is applied. If the desired state matches the existing state, no changes occur.

Prerequisites

The minimum architecture required to use the Office 365 Hybrid Configuration Wizard varies by Exchange version.

- Exchange 2016 requires a mailbox server role because the roles have been combined in the most recent Exchange version.

- Exchange 2013 requires the client access and mailbox server roles; although they can be split between separate servers, deploying them on the same server is recommended.

- Exchange 2010 requires the Client Access Server role and the Hub Transport role. The mailbox server role is required if the Exchange 2010 environment is coexisting with an Exchange 2003 environment.

The Hybrid Configuration Wizard also requires an Office 365 global admin account as well as an account that has been granted the Exchange Organization Management role.

There is no sizing guide for Office 365 Hybrid Configuration Wizard, because it is simply a tool to configure features already in use in your organization and extends your organization to the cloud. Use the Microsoft Exchange Server Role Requirements calculator located at *http://aka .ms/exchangecalc*. Calculate using the existing or projected maximum number of users in the organization and follow the published calculator guidance.

You can find more information about the release announcement of the updated Office 365 Hybrid Configuration Wizard at *https://blogs.technet.microsoft.com/exchange/2015/09/04 /introducing-the-microsoft-office-365-hybrid-configuration-wizard/*.

INSIDE OUT
Exchange management servers

When migrating from a third-party mail platform, most organizations don't have an on-premises Exchange server. Some organizations haven't even deployed Active Directory but might deploy it so they can synchronize with Azure Active Directory and provision Exchange Online mailboxes. If you have a greenfield environment or an environment that has never had Exchange, you can use *https://gallery.technet.microsoft.com/Configure -Exchange-2013-as-bae517b8* to help configure the default attributes for deploying Exchange in your environment prior to running the Hybrid Configuration Wizard.

The only supported method to manage the Active Directory attributes for users synchronized through AAD Connect is to use the Exchange Admin Center or Exchange Management Shell with an on-premises Exchange Server. Remote mailbox provisioning and MRS mailbox moves between cloud and on-premises use the targetAddress attribute to determine mailbox location. Outlook for on-premises mailbox users follows the targetAddress attribute to follow to Office 365. The Hybrid Configuration Wizard configures email address policies for all domains included in the hybrid domain selection and updates the proxy addresses for all users with EmailAddressPolicyEnabled set to True with a proxy address of *<alias@tenant.mail.onmicrosoft.com>*.

Many organizations migrating from third-party mail systems might not require a full hybrid configuration and can use the express hybrid migration option as mentioned in Chapter 12, "Mailbox Migration Types." Express hybrid configures the addressing components for the Exchange organization such as email address policy and accepted domains and enables the MRS proxy. Regardless of the type of hybrid configuration being deployed, the on-premises environment still requires a supported version of Exchange Server.

Installing the Office 365 Hybrid Configuration Wizard

As previously mentioned, the Office 365 Hybrid Configuration Wizard is a stand-alone tool that has components downloaded on the server from where it is run. Because the tool checks for updates each time it is launched, the server requires Internet access to complete the configuration.

1. Log on to an Exchange server in your organization. It does not have to be one that will be included in the hybrid configuration.

2. Launch the Hybrid Configuration Wizard through one of the three methods.

3. For any version of Exchange, open a browser and navigate to *http://aka.ms/hybridwizard*.

4. For Exchange Server 2013 or Exchange Server 2016, launch the Exchange Admin Center, navigate to the hybrid node, and click Configure.

5. For any version of Exchange, log on to the Office 365 Admin Center, navigate to the Exchange Admin Center, select the hybrid node, and then click the Configure button located under the Exchange Hybrid Deployment text, as shown in Figure 13-1.

Figure 13-1 Exchange hybrid setup page

6.   After launching the process and after the application has downloaded, click the Install
button shown in Figure 13-2. If you've already installed the Hybrid Configuration Wizard
before, you can launch it by clicking the desktop shortcut. If a newer version exists, you
are prompted to update. Click Yes.

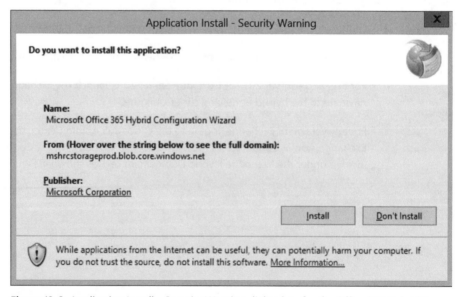

Figure 13-2 Application Install – Security Warning dialog box for the Office 365 Hybrid Configuration Wizard

The wizard launches automatically.

7. Click Cancel to close the wizard.

Running the Office 365 Hybrid Configuration Wizard

Before starting the configuration, review the configuration settings described in Table 13-4 to understand which configuration option (Minimal, Express, Full) configures the features necessary for your environment.

Table 13-4 Office 365 Hybrid Configuration Wizard selection options

Hybrid Features	Minimal	Express	Full
E-mail Address Policy and Domain Configuration	Yes	Yes	Yes
Send and Receive Connector Configuration	No	No	Yes
OAuth Configuration	No	No	Yes (Exchange version–dependent)
Federation Trust and Organization Relationship	No	No	Yes
MRS Endpoint Configuration	Yes	Yes	Yes
AAD Connect in Express Configuration	No	Yes	No

INSIDE OUT

Configuring the Exchange federation trust before the Hybrid Configuration Wizard

During the Hybrid Configuration Wizard, you are asked to configure DNS records to prove ownership of your domains for the federation trust. Depending on your organization's change control process or your access to external DNS, you might choose to configure those records prior to the actual Hybrid Configuration Wizard. Otherwise, you must wait to complete the Hybrid Configuration Wizard until those records (proofs) have been added to DNS.

If the federation trust has already been completed, the Enable Federation Trust page is suppressed in the Hybrid Configuration Wizard, and a Hybrid Domains selection page appears, displaying the list of accepted on-premises domains that are verified in the Office 365 tenant.

To enable the federation trust prior to running the Hybrid Configuration Wizard, follow these steps.

1. Launch the Exchange Management Shell and then run the following commands to create a self-signed certificate, create the federation trust, and generate domain proof values for all of the organization's accepted domains.

```
$ski = [System.Guid]::NewGuid().ToString("N")
```

```
New-ExchangeCertificate -FriendlyName "Exchange Federated Delegation"
-DomainName $env:USERDNSDOMAIN -Services Federation -KeySize 2048
-PrivateKeyExportable $true -SubjectKeyIdentifier $ski
```

```
Get-ExchangeCertificate | ?{$_.friendlyname -eq "Exchange Federated
Delegation"} | New-FederationTrust -Name "Microsoft Federation Gateway"
```

```
Get-AcceptedDomain | % { Get-FederatedDomainProof -DomainName $_.DomainName.
ToString() | Select DomainName,Proof } | FL
```

2. For each domain entry, create a TXT record containing that value of the associated proof.

3. After DNS proofs have been created, you can run the wizard again to complete the federation configuration or use Set-FederatedOrganizationIdentifier. To use Set-FederatedOrganizationIdentifier, select the primary domain for your organization for the AccountNameSpace parameter or use the command as displayed to select the first domain that appears in Get-AcceptedDomain:

```
Set-FederatedOrganizationIdentifier -DelegationFederationTrust "Microsoft
Federation Gateway" -AccountNamespace (Get-AcceptedDomain)[0].DomainName.
ToString() -Enabled $True
```

4. Use Add-FederatedDomain to add the domains to the federation trust. You can specify your domains individually with the -DomainName parameter, or you can use the following command example to add all your accepted domains.

```
Get-AcceptedDomain | % { Add-FederatedDomain -DomainName $_.DomainName.
ToString() }
```

After you have decided which options to select for the Hybrid Configuration Wizard, double-click Microsoft Office 365 Configuration Wizard on the Exchange Server desktop to begin the configuration process. Follow these steps to complete the wizard.

1. On the Office 365 Hybrid Configuration Wizard launch page, which provides a built-in help option in the lower left corner, indicated by the hyperlink, What Does This Application Do? as shown in Figure 13-3, click Next.

Figure 13-3 Office 365 Hybrid Configuration Wizard launch page

On the On-Premises Exchange Server Organization configuration page, shown in Figure 13-4, the wizard determines the optimal Exchange server to use for the configuration process.

2. If you prefer to use a specific server, select the Specify A Server Running Exchange 2010, 2013, Or 2016 button and then enter the fully qualified domain name of a Client Access Server.

Figure 13-4 Selecting the on-premises Exchange server

3.   From the Office 365 Exchange Online drop-down menu, select the appropriate Office 365 hosting organization. For most organizations, this is Office 365 Worldwide. Other options include Office 365, Office 365 Germany, and Office 365 vNext (Dedicated). Click Next.

For the Hybrid Configuration Wizard to complete successfully, credentials for both the Exchange on-premises and Exchange Online environments must be supplied, as shown in Figure 13-5. If the Use Current Windows check box is selected, the currently logged-on account will be used to connect to Exchange on-premises. The account must be an organization administrator to complete the on-premises configuration and must be a local administrator on each server that will be configured.

Figure 13-5 Office 365 Hybrid Configuration Wizard account selection

4.   Click the Sign In button under Office 365 Exchange Online Account, as shown in Figure 13-5. Enter an Office 365 Global Admin account credential. See Figure 13-6.

CHAPTER 13

Figure 13-6 Office 365 Exchange Online Account credential prompt

5. After both sets of credentials have been entered as shown in Figure 13-7, click Next.

Figure 13-7 Office 365 Hybrid Configuration Wizard saved credentials

On the Gathering Configuration Information page, the Office 365 Hybrid Configuration Wizard tests Windows PowerShell connectivity by using the provided credentials. If successful, information for both the on-premises and online environment are collected, as shown in Figure 13-8.

6. Click Next.

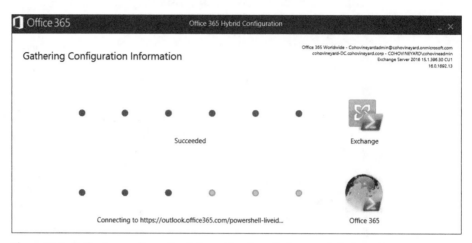

Figure 13-8 Gathering configuration information from Exchange environments

7. On the Hybrid Features page, select the Full Hybrid Configuration button (shown in Figure 13-9) and click Next.

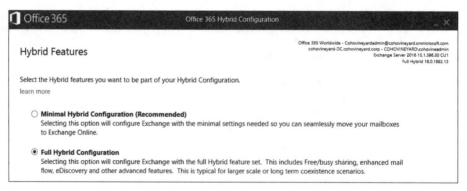

Figure 13-9 Hybrid features selection

8. On the Federation Trust page, click Enable and then click Next, as shown in Figure 13-10. This page is shown only if there is no existing federation trust.

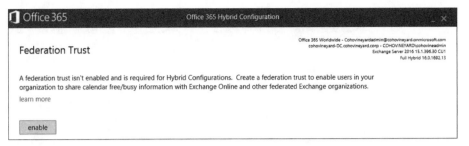

Figure 13-10 Federation Trust page

9. Depending on your environment configuration, choose the option that relates to one of three scenarios on the Hybrid Domains page.

    a. **No hybrid domains**   To complete the Hybrid Configuration Wizard successfully, the wizard must detect at least one common domain configured in both the Exchange on-premises and Exchange Online environments. If no common domains are configured, you receive the error shown in Figure 13-11. The only course of action is to close the wizard, verify a domain in Office 365 that matches a domain in your on-premises Exchange environment (or add an accepted domain in your Exchange environment that matches a verified domain in Office 365), and restart the wizard.

Figure 13-11 Office 365 Hybrid Domains selection with no shared domains

    b. **A single shared domain**   If the Hybrid Configuration Wizard detects a single shared domain in common between Office 365 and the Exchange on-premises environment, it skips to the Domain Ownership page to obtain the text record for the federated domain proof. If the domain proofs were already generated and verified, the wizard skips to the Mail Transport page.

    c. **Multiple shared domains**   If the Hybrid Configuration Wizard detects more than one shared domain in common between Office 365 and the Exchange on-premises environment, the page shown in Figure 13-12 appears. Select each domain that you want to include in the hybrid configuration. Each domain selected can also have an Autodiscover configuration set to either True or False. Configure the settings to True for each domain that has an external Autodiscover record that responds to queries.

Figure 13-12 Hybrid Domains page with multiple shared domains

10. Select all domains that will handle mail flow or free/busy requests between Exchange Online and Exchange on-premises. See Figure 13-13. Click Next.

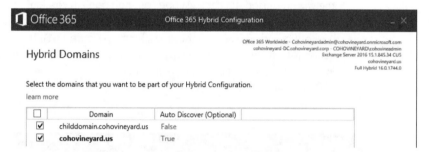

Figure 13-13 Hybrid Configuration Wizard with multiple shared domains selected

If federated domain proofs have not been completed previously, the Domain Ownership page appears (Figure 13-14). Each domain to be included in the hybrid configuration has a value in the Token column that needs to be added as a TXT record in the domain's external DNS.

Figure 13-14 Domain Ownership page

11. After you have created the external TXT records to verify ownership, select the I Have Created A TXT Record For Each Token In DNS check box and click Verify Domain Ownership (see Figure 13-15).

Federated domain proofs need to be completed only once per accepted domain. If you rerun the Hybrid Configuration Wizard, you will not need to verify additional proofs unless you add more domains.

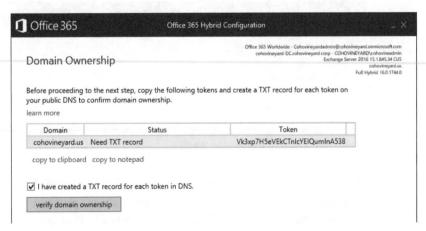

Figure 13-15 Office 365 Domain Ownership page, text record complete

TROUBLESHOOTING

Domain verification failed

If you attempt to verify domain ownership too soon after adding the TXT records to external DNS, you might receive the following error.

It appears that your TXT record is either not yet replicated or is missing from external DNS. Please verify the record is correct in your public DNS and allow for enough time for the record to replicate. NOTE: Use caution in attempting to verify too quickly or too many times as the result could be that subsequent domain queries might be temporarily disabled.

This message indicates that the Hybrid Configuration Wizard was unable to verify the TXT record for one or more domains. The Domain Ownership page shows you which domains failed verification. Use an external DNS lookup tool to verify that the token displayed on the Domain Ownership page matches what is returned by a DNS query. Failing domain verification repeatedly locks the process for up to 24 hours.

When the domain verification process is complete, the wizard adds the domains to the federation, as shown in Figure 13-16.

12. Click Next.

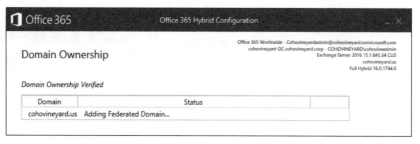

Figure 13-16 Adding a federated domain

13. On the Hybrid Configuration page, choose the servers to configure for mail transport.

By default, the Configure My Client Access And Mailbox Servers For Secure Mail Transport (Typical) button is selected. In Figure 13-17, the Advanced button has been selected to show the Enable Centralized Mail Transport option.

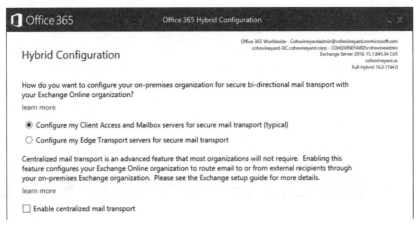

Figure 13-17 Hybrid Configuration page

INSIDE OUT

Edge transport servers

If your configuration requires the use of edge transport servers, keep these important things in mind.

- Although you can select edge transport servers in the Hybrid Configuration Wizard, one additional step still must be performed on each edge transport server after the wizard has completed. From the Exchange Management Shell on each edge transport server, run the following command:

```
Set-ReceiveConnector -Identity "Edge\Default Internal Receive Connector" -Tls-
DomainCapabilities mail.protection.outlook.com:AcceptOOrgProtocol -FQDN <Edge
Server FQDN>
```

- Hybrid configurations with edge transport servers require Edge Transport Server Sync to be configured. For more information about Edge Transport Server Sync, see *https://technet.microsoft.com/en-us/library/aa997438(v=exchg.160).aspx.*

- The edge transport server certificate must be exported from the edge servers and imported into the machine certificate store of a reference Exchange server. When importing the certificate and configuring SMTP, ensure that you select No when prompted to overwrite the default self-signed certificate. After selecting Edge Transport Configuration in the Hybrid Configuration Wizard, it prompts you to select the reference server where the Edge certificate has been imported.

14. On the Receive Connector Configuration page, select which servers will be configured to receive mail from Exchange Online.

If you select servers running Exchange Server 2013 or Exchange Server 2016, the Hybrid Configuration Wizard modifies the default receive connector to support hybrid mail transport. If you select servers running Exchange Server 2010, the Hybrid Configuration Wizard creates a new receive connector. Figure 13-18 shows an Exchange 2016 server selected.

15. After selecting servers, click Next.

Figure 13-18 Receive Connector Configuration page

The servers selected must be able to receive mail from the Exchange Online Protection IP address ranges. For more information about the Exchange Online Protection endpoints, see *http://aka.ms/o365endpoints*.

16. On the Send Connector Configuration page, select one or more servers to be used to host the send connector to Exchange Online. If you are configuring Exchange Server 2013 or Exchange Server 2016, the server must be configured with the Mailbox role. If you are configuring Exchange Server 2010, the server must have the Hub Transport role. See Figure 13-19.

Figure 13-19 Send Connector Configuration page

The servers selected must be able to connect on port 25 to the Exchange Online Protection IP address ranges and will be responsible for relaying mail to the *tenant.mail.onmicrosoft.com* address space. For more information about the Exchange Online Protection endpoints, see *http://aka.ms/o365endpoints*.

17. On the Transport Certificate page, select the third-party certificate that will secure mail (Figure 13-20) and click Next.

This certificate must be installed on all servers that will be involved in mail transport to or from Exchange Online.

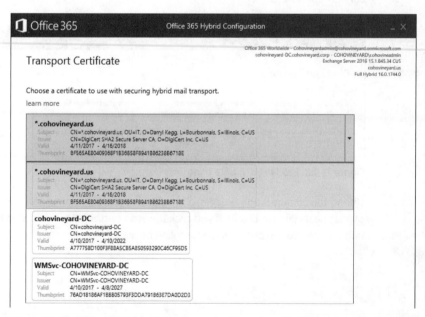

Figure 13-20 Office 365 Hybrid Configuration, Transport Certificate page

18. On the Organization FQDN page (shown in Figure 13-21), enter the fully qualified name for the on-premises mail hosts that will be sending to Exchange Online. The name entered must match a name in either the Subject or Subject Alternative Name field on the transport certificate. If you selected a wildcard certificate, enter a name valid for the certificate domain. The name entered must be resolvable on the Internet. Click Next when finished.

Figure 13-21 Organization FQDN page

19. On the Ready For Update page, click Update.

The Office 365 Hybrid Configuration Wizard, shown in Figure 13-22, runs the necessary configuration steps.

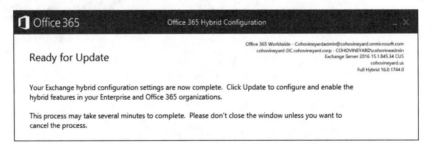

Figure 13-22 Ready For Update page

During the configuration process, a progress meter and information about the current task appears (Figure 13-23). If you click the Stop button, the wizard stops the configuration process, but no changes will be rolled back.

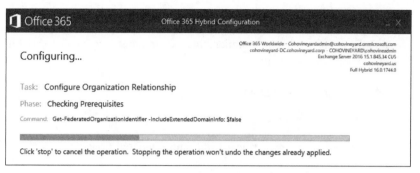

Figure 13-23 Hybrid Configuration Wizard processing changes

After the Office 365 Hybrid Configuration has completed, a final screen appears so you can rate the experience and provide feedback if desired.

20. Click Close to complete the wizard. See Figure 13-24.

Figure 13-24 Congratulations page

When the Hybrid Configuration Wizard has completed successfully, you are ready to route mail between your on-premises and cloud environments, migrate mailboxes, and configure public folders.

Rerunning the Hybrid Configuration Wizard

After the initial hybrid configuration, there are four instances when the Hybrid Configuration Wizard needs to be run again.

- Adding or removing transport servers

- Adding or removing hybrid domains

- Changing between standard and centralized mail flow

- Updating the transport certificate

The Hybrid Configuration Wizard does not need to be run after updates, roll-ups, or cumulative updates are applied, unless otherwise specified in the update.

Moving mailboxes to or from Exchange Online

After the Hybrid Configuration Wizard has completed, your environment should be configured to enable you to move mailboxes between on-premises and cloud environments.

Overview

Mailboxes migrations can be performed using either the Exchange Admin Center or Windows PowerShell. When a mailbox migration is run, the Mailbox Replication Service Proxy (MRSProxy) queues and manages the requests.

For a mailbox to be migrated to Exchange Online, the following criteria must be met.

- The mailbox must be synchronized to Exchange Online as a mail-enabled user.

- The synchronized mail-enabled user must have a value for ExchangeGuid that matches the value of the on-premises mailbox being migrated.

- The synchronized mail-enabled user must have a proxy address with a domain suffix that matches *<tenant>.mail.onmicrosoft.com*.

- The synchronized mail-enabled user must not have any proxy email addresses containing domains not verified in Office 365.

- The mailbox must have Active Directory inheritance enabled.

- The migration endpoint must be accessible by HTTPS from Exchange Online. SSL Offloading is not supported.

Migration endpoints

The Hybrid Configuration Wizard attempts to create a migration endpoint in Exchange Online, named Hybrid Migration Endpoint - <FQDN>, where *<FQDN>* is the external Exchange Web Services (EWS) URL of your on-premises environment. If that was unsuccessful, you can create the endpoint manually by using the following steps.

1. Log on to the Office 365 portal, navigate to the Exchange Admin Center, and click Recipients.

2. On the Recipients page, select Migration. To view existing migration endpoints, click the ellipsis and select Migration Endpoints. See Figure 13-25.

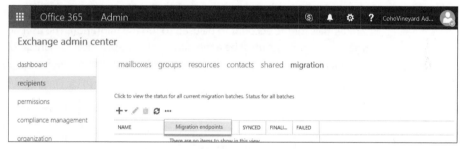

Figure 13-25 Viewing migration endpoints

3. Click the plus sign (+) to add a new migration endpoint, as shown Figure 13-26.

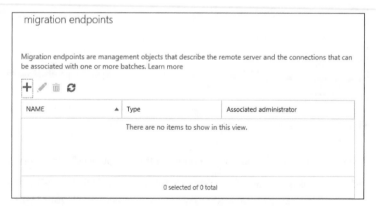

Figure 13-26 Migration Endpoints page

4. On the Select The Migration Endpoint Type page, select the Exchange Remote button (Figure 13-27) and click Next.

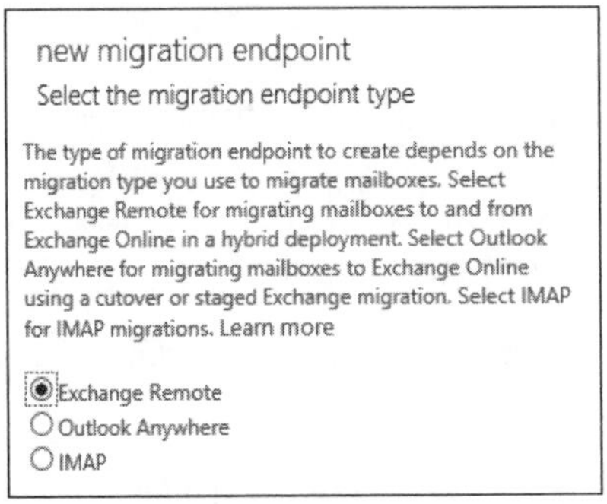

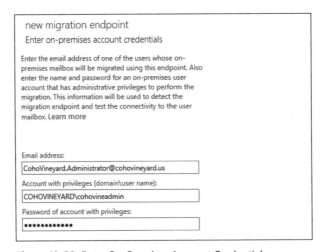

Figure 13-27 Select The Migration Endpoint Type page

5. Type in the email address of an on-premises mailbox that Autodiscover can discover and credentials for the account to be used to run the migration. The user account used for mailbox migrations must be a member of the on-premises Organization Management or Recipient Management Role Based Access Control Group. See Figure 13-28. Click Next.

Figure 13-28 Enter On-Premises Account Credentials page

6. Type in the fully qualified domain name of the remote MRS proxy server.

   Normally, this is the same host name as the external EWS URL or the external-facing Client Access Server with the MRSProxy service enabled. See Figure 13-29.

7. Click Next.

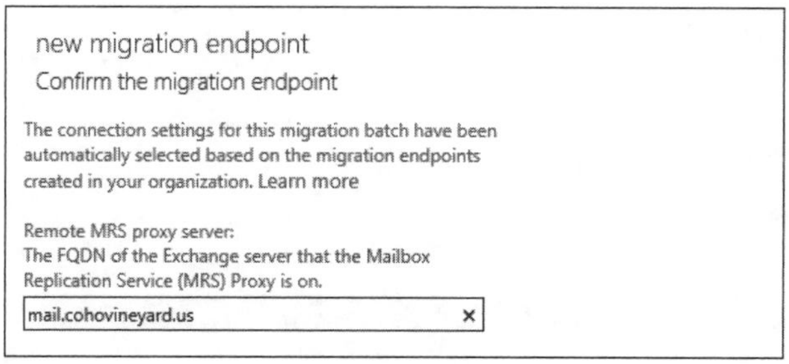

new migration endpoint
Confirm the migration endpoint

The connection settings for this migration batch have been automatically selected based on the migration endpoints created in your organization. Learn more

Remote MRS proxy server:
The FQDN of the Exchange server that the Mailbox Replication Service (MRS) Proxy is on.

mail.cohovineyard.us   ✕

Figure 13-29 Confirm The Migration Endpoint page

8. Enter a migration endpoint name.

    In this example, it is mirroring what the Hybrid Configuration Wizard would call the migration endpoint. The value for Maximum Concurrent Migrations is set to 20 by default and can be increased up to 300. The value for Maximum Concurrent Incremental Syncs is set to 10 by default.

9. Click New to create the migration endpoint, as shown in Figure 13-30.

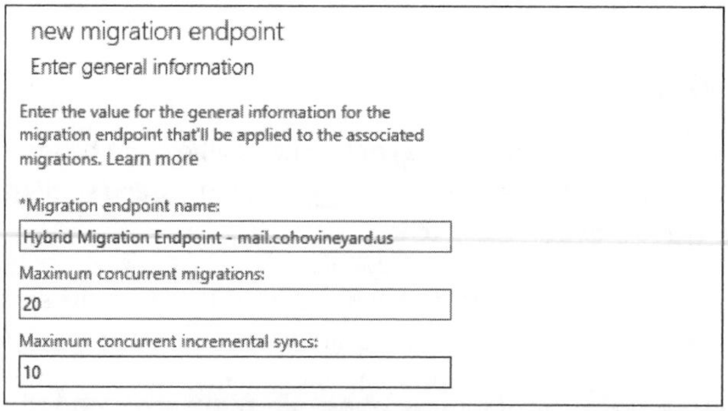

new migration endpoint
Enter general information

Enter the value for the general information for the migration endpoint that'll be applied to the associated migrations. Learn more

*Migration endpoint name:

Hybrid Migration Endpoint - mail.cohovineyard.us

Maximum concurrent migrations:

20

Maximum concurrent incremental syncs:

10

Figure 13-30 General Configuration Information page for migration endpoint

After the migration endpoint has been created, the Migration Endpoints page is updated with the newly created endpoint. See Figure 13-31.

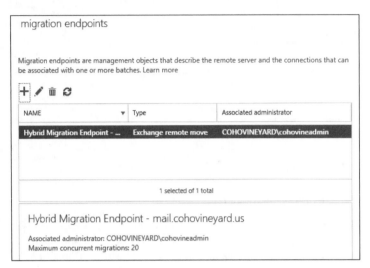

Figure 13-31 New migration endpoint created

At this point, migration batches can be created to move mailboxes to or from the on-premises environment.

Migration batches

Migration batches are configuration objects containing mailboxes to be moved between organizations. A migration batch can contain one or more mailboxes, and settings configured for the batch apply to all mailboxes in the batch.

After a batch is created, a validation process checks the availability of the endpoint and credentials and that the mailboxes included meet the prerequisites. Migration batches that are configured for manual completion are set for automatic incremental synchronizations to keep batches up to date and minimize the time to finalize a migration. Migration batches also include notification and reporting.

After a migration batch has been validated, Exchange Online generates a move request for each mailbox being migrated. Migration batches are the recommended method for migrating mailboxes.

Onboarding

Onboarding is the process of migrating a mailbox to Exchange Online. At the completion of the batch, the on-premises mailbox is migrated to Exchange Online, the on-premises mailbox is disconnected from the user account, and the on-premises mailbox account is converted to a remote mailbox user. The target address for the on-premises account is updated to point to *<tenant>.mail.onmicrosoft.com*.

Creating a batch

Follow these steps to create an onboarding migration batch.

Launch a browser and log on to the Office 365 Admin Center. Navigate to the Exchange Admin Center and then select Recipients | Migration.

Click the plus sign (+) and select Migrate To Exchange Online.

1. Select the Remote Move Migration (Supported By Exchange Server 2010 And Later Versions) button, as shown in Figure 13-32, and click Next.

new migration batch

Select a migration type

The migration type to use depends on your existing email system, how many mailboxes you want to migrate, and whether you plan to maintain some mailboxes in your on-premises organization or migrate them all to the cloud. You'll also want to consider how long the migration will take and whether user identity will be managed in your on-premises organization or in Office 365.

Learn more

- ● Remote move migration (supported by Exchange Server 2010 and later versions)
- ○ Staged migration (supported by Exchange Server 2003 and Exchange Server 2007 only)
- ◉ Cutover migration (supported by Exchange Server 2003 and later versions)
- ○ IMAP migration (supported by Exchange and other email systems)

Select this if you're planning an Exchange hybrid deployment with mailboxes both on-premises and in Exchange Online. If you plan to migrate all mailboxes to Exchange Online over a long period of time, this migration type lets you use hybrid deployment features during migration. After the migration, user identity will still be managed in your on-premises organization. You have to use this type of migration to migrate more than 2,000 Exchange 2010 or Exchange 2013 mailboxes.

Learn more

Figure 13-32 Select A Migration Type page

2. On the Select The Users page, click the plus sign (+) to add mail-enabled users from the global address list, as shown in Figure 13-33. Alternatively, you can upload a comma-separated value (CSV) populated with email addresses. The CSV must have the EmailAddress header.

new migration batch
Select the users

You can either use a CSV file to specify the users you'd like to move, or you can select mailboxes individually. Learn more

◉ Select the users that you want to move

+ −

DISPLAY NAME	▲	EMAIL ADDRESS

○ Specify the users with a CSV file

☐ Allow unknown columns in the CSV file

Browse...

0 mailboxes to migrate

Figure 13-33 Select The Users page

3. Select users from the list and click Add, as shown in Figure 13-34, to add users to the migration batch. If you want to select multiple users, hold down the CTRL key and click each user to highlight each as a selection and then click the Add key. Click OK to close the window.

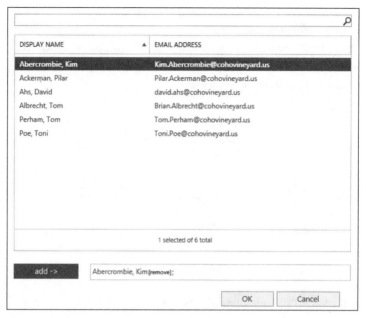

Figure 13-34 Selecting the mail user for migration

4.   Verify the users to migrate and click Next. See Figure 13-35.

Figure 13-35 Users added to migration batch

5. On the Confirm The Migration Endpoint page, select the endpoint that will be used to perform the migrations.

   If multiple endpoints have been configured, a drop-down box becomes available to select a specific migration endpoint for use. If only one exists, the wizard automatically selects the endpoint, as shown in Figure 13-36.

6. Click Next.

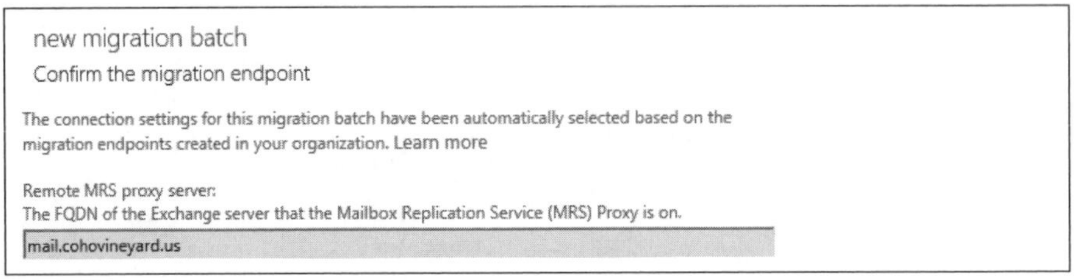

new migration batch
Confirm the migration endpoint

The connection settings for this migration batch have been automatically selected based on the migration endpoints created in your organization. Learn more

Remote MRS proxy server:
The FQDN of the Exchange server that the Mailbox Replication Service (MRS) Proxy is on.

mail.cohovineyard.us

Figure 13-36 Confirm The Migration Endpoint page

7. On the Move Configuration page, type a name for the batch.

8. Select a target delivery domain.

   When moving to Exchange Online, the target delivery domain is the domain ending in *<tenant>.mail.onmicrosoft.com*. A proxy address with this domain suffix will be configured as the target address for the mail user account in the Exchange on-premises environment after the mailbox move is complete.

9. Select an option for any attached Exchange Archive mailboxes.

   The Move The Primary Mailbox And The Archive Mailbox If One Exists button is selected by default.

10. Select a value for the Bad Item Limit, the number of items the migration skips before failing the migration. The default is 10 and can be increased to Unlimited.

11. Select a value for Large Item Limit.

    The maximum size for an individual message migrating to Office 365, including all attachments, is 150 MB. If the limit is set to zero, any large message exceeding 150 MB causes the migration to fail. If Large Item Limit is set to a non-zero number, that number of large messages are skipped before the migration fails. Choosing a non-zero limit results in data loss for the messages exceeding the 150 MB limit.

12. Confirm that all the fields have been populated, as depicted in Figure 13-37. Click Next.

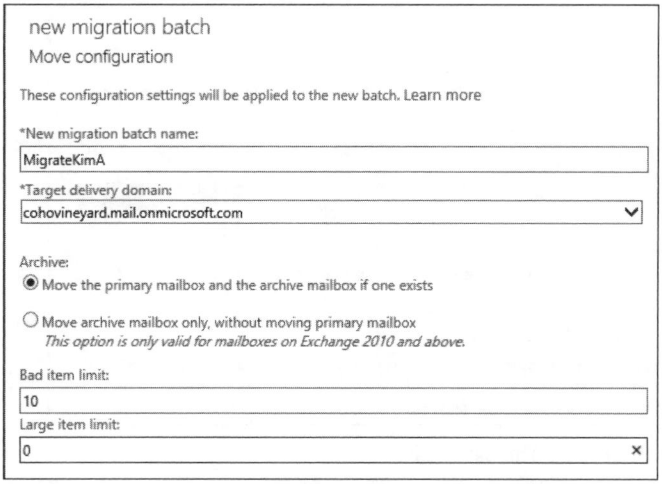

new migration batch
Move configuration

These configuration settings will be applied to the new batch. Learn more

*New migration batch name:

MigrateKimA

*Target delivery domain:

cohovineyard.mail.onmicrosoft.com

Archive:
◉ Move the primary mailbox and the archive mailbox if one exists

○ Move archive mailbox only, without moving primary mailbox
   This option is only valid for mailboxes on Exchange 2010 and above.

Bad item limit:

10

Large item limit:

0

Figure 13-37 Confirm migration options

13. On the Start The Batch page, select a user or distribution list to receive email notifications about the batch.

14. Select a batch start method.

The Automatically Start The Batch button is selected. The batch starts synchronizing immediately.

15. Select a batch completion method.

16. The Manual Complete The Batch (by clicking the Complete This Migration Batch Link on the right pane, after the link becomes active) button is selected by default, as shown in Figure 13-38.

With this option selected, the batch synchronizes all selected mailboxes and leaves the migration process at 95% complete. The migration batch automatically performs an incremental synchronization every 24 hours.

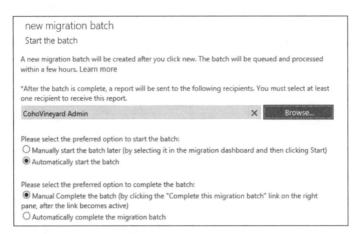

Figure 13-38 Start The Batch page

17. Click New to create the batch and start the synchronization process.

INSIDE OUT

One batch a time

It is important to note that a mailbox can be part of only a single batch. If a mailbox is present in a batch and then added to a second batch, the mailbox in the second batch will fail with the UserDuplicateInOtherBatchException error.

Similar to how a move request must be cleared in an Exchange on-premises environment when moving a mailbox between servers, a mailbox must be removed from one batch (even if it is completed) before it can be added to another batch.

Monitoring a batch

The migration status page shows the status of each batch. The newly created batch is shown in Figure 13-39.

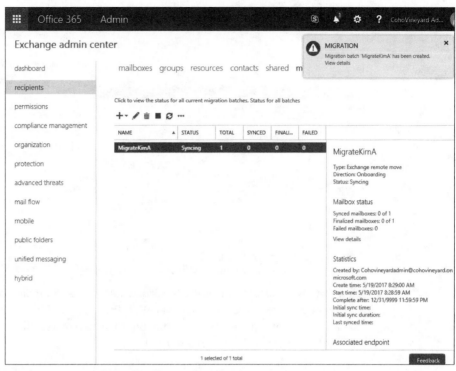

Figure 13-39 Exchange Admin Center migration batch status

If the batch is selected, statistics appear on the right side in a column. Three links in the status page are actionable.

- **Complete The Migration Batch**   For batches that are synchronized, selecting Complete The Migration Batch starts the finalization process.

- **View Details**   Select the View Details link under Mailbox Status to launch a new window with more details on the migration process, including completed mailboxes and errors. See Figure 13-40.

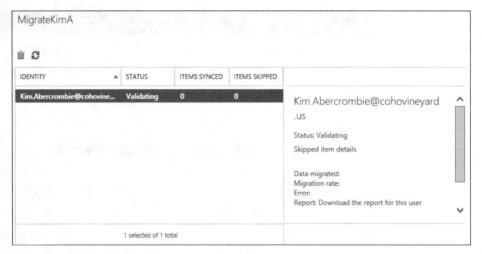

Figure 13-40 Migration details

- **View Details** Select the View Details link under Associated Endpoint to view or edit the endpoint being used for the selected migration. For example, if the credentials for the migration account change after the migration batch was created, they can be changed through the interface shown in Figure 13-41.

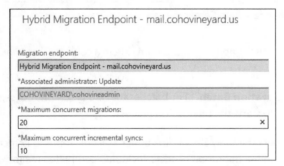

Figure 13-41 Viewing migration endpoint details

Completing a batch

Batches configured for manual completion automatically perform an incremental update every 24 hours after the initial synchronization has been completed.

To complete the migration to Exchange Online, select a batch and click the Complete This Migration Batch link, highlighted in Figure 13-42.

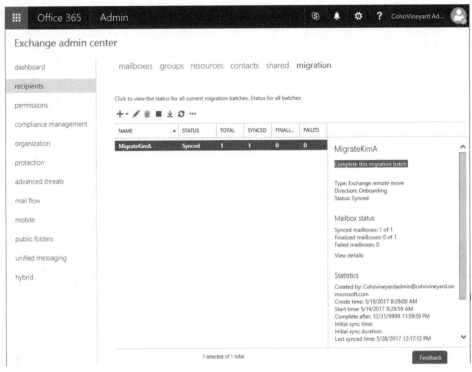

Figure 13-42 Complete This Migration Batch migration status page

When prompted, select Yes to continue the completion process.

The status changes from Synced to Completing and then to Completed. In the background, the mailbox move process is synchronizing the mailbox delta since the last incremental sync. The target Exchange Online mail user is converted to a mailbox, and the on-premises mailbox is converted to a Remote User Mailbox (a special type of mail-enabled user) with the target or external email address set to *alias@<tenant>.mail.onmicrosoft.com*.

After all mailboxes in the batch have completed the migration process, the batch status is updated to Completed, as shown in Figure 13-43.

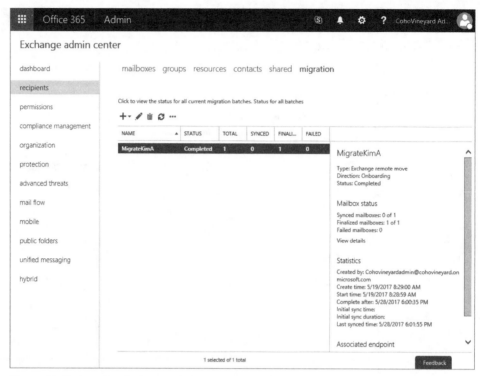

Figure 13-43 Completed migration batch

Completing a user within a batch

If you have configured a migration batch, you might want to complete just a single user to ensure that everything works correctly. You can accomplish this task, though not through the Exchange Admin Center. To complete an individual user in a migration batch, follow these steps.

1.   Connect to Exchange Online PowerShell.

2.   Identify the migration batch with the following command.

```
Get-MigrationBatch | FL Identity,CompleteAfter
```

The data returned should look like the following.

```
Identity:CohoMail
CompleteAfter : 12/31/9999 11:59:59 PM
```

The CompleteAfter date indicates the earliest time that the batch can be completed. Tenants that have been configured for Protocol Agnostic Workflow (PAW) have the CompleteAfter date set for the year 9999. PAW can be confirmed with the following command.

```
Get-MigrationConfig | FL Identity,Features
Identity : cohovineyard.onmicrosoft.com
Features : MultiBatch, PAW
```

If PAW is in the Features list, the tenant is enabled.

3. Update the user's move request.

```
Get-MoveRequest -Identity user@contoso.com | Set-MoveRequest -CompleteAfter (Get-
Date).AddDays(-1)
Resume-MoveRequest -Identity user@contoso.com
```

This changes the complete-after date for the individual user within the batch to the day before the current date and completes the migration for the user without completing the entire batch.

Now that the migration process is complete, the user should be redirected to Exchange Online. When Outlook is launched, it reconfigures the profile to connect to Exchange Online. Mail sent to the user is also redirected to the Exchange Online mailbox.

INSIDE OUT

Protocol Agnostic Workflow

Protocol Agnostic Workflow (PAW) is a new feature in Office 365 tenants, designed to give better management of migration batches. Tenants that have PAW enabled can use the additional benefits for migration batches listed in Table 13-5.

Table 13-5 Protocol Agnostic Workflow

Feature	Pre-PAW (Legacy)	PAW
Start/Stop/Remove	Allowed at only certain times, making it difficult for admins to start, stop, and remove batches.	Allows start, stop, and remove operations at any time for the batch.
Failure retry behavior	Restarts whole batch and all items from the beginning.	Restarts each failed item from the beginning of the step where it left off.
Failure retry management	Must use Start-MigrationBatch to retry failures unless batch has completed, in which case must use Complete-MigrationBatch.	Always use Start-MigrationBatch to retry failures.
Completion options	Automatic or manual.	Automatic, manual, or scheduled.

Feature	Pre-PAW (Legacy)	PAW
Completion semantics	Must choose between "AutoComplete" and "Manual Completion" at the beginning.	Can convert between any completion option at any time before completion has occurred.
User management	Can only remove users with status Synced or Stopped.	Can remove a user from a batch at any time, regardless of status, as well as start, stop, or modify individual users.
Duplicate users	Results in Validation Warnings and zero-sized batches.	Results in two MigrationUser objects (one per batch), only one of which can be active at a time. If the first one was Completed, it processes the second one. Otherwise, it fails the second one with a message indicating that the first one is being processed. That failed user can later be resumed and completed successfully or removed from the batch.
Throttling	Handled by MigrationService, leading to inefficient resource usage. Throttling limit is rarely (if ever) reached, resulting in less than optimal performance.	Handled by MRS, which is already used to handling resource usage (maximized throughput resulting in throttle limit being reached).
Reports	Only initial sync and completion reports.	Initial sync reports, completion reports, and periodic status reports.
Counts	15-minute delay in generating accurate reports.	Real-time reports.

All new tenants are PAW-enabled. To convert a tenant to PAW, all existing ones (new, synced, failed, or completed) must be removed. The PAW enablement process happens automatically as long as there are no existing batches in the tenant.

Offboarding

At some point, it might be necessary to migrate users from Exchange Online to an on-premises Exchange environment. You can complete this migration process, referred to as offboarding, through the Exchange Admin Center or with Exchange Online PowerShell.

The overall process is nearly identical to onboarding and requires you to select a migration endpoint, users to migrate, and target delivery domain (which is generally the primary SMTP address domain). The only additional piece of information required is the on-premises target database name.

When offboarding a mailbox, the same requirements must be met as for onboarding (such as valid proxy addresses and an ExchangeGuid). There is also the additional consideration of archive mailboxes. If you are offboarding to an Exchange Server 2007 or Exchange Server 2010 environment, you must migrate the content to the primary mailbox first, disable the archive, and then migrate.

Depending on how a cloud mailbox was enabled, the on-premises remote mailbox might also be missing the ExchangeGuid. For mailboxes that were moved to Exchange Online from an on-premises environment, the ExchangeGuid property will be populated. However, for mailboxes created online, using the New-RemoteMailbox or Enable-RemoteMailbox commands, the on-premises account will not have a valid ExchangeGuid. To check a remote mailbox for the presence of the ExchangeGuid, follow these steps.

1. Connect to the Exchange Management Shell.

2. Run `Get-RemoteMailbox user@domain.com | FL Name,ExchangeGuid` to view the user's ExchangeGuid property.

   ```
   Get-RemoteMailbox lzhang | FL Name,ExchangeGuid
   Name        : Larry Zhang
   ExchangeGuid : 00000000-0000-0000-0000-000000000000
   ```

The ExchangeGuid property has all zeros for the value. This is normal for mailboxes provisioned using New-RemoteMailbox or Enable-RemoteMailbox commands. To update the ExchangeGuid for a user, follow these steps.

1. Connect to Exchange Online PowerShell.

2. Run `Get-Mailbox user@contoso.com | FL Name,ExchangeGuid` to display the mailbox's ExchangeGuid.

3. Copy the ExchangeGuid.

4. Launch the Exchange Management Shell on-premises and run the following command.

```
Set-RemoteMailbox -identity user@contoso.com -ExchangeGuid <ExchangeGuid value
copied in step 3>
```

After the ExchangeGuid is synchronized, you can offboard the mailbox.

To complete the offboarding, specify an Exchange mailbox database in the on-premises environment to where the offboarded mailbox will be migrated. Depending on the version of the
target Exchange environment, you might need to specify the database as a single name (such
as MBXDB01) for destinations in Exchange Server 2010 or later, or in SERVER\DATABASE format
(CONTOSOSERVER\MBXDB02) for Exchange Server 2003 or Exchange Server 2007 destinations.

You can also use the mailbox database GUID to identity the target database. To obtain a list of
database GUIDs, run `Get-MailboxDatabase -IncludePre | FT Name,Guid`.

To create the migration batch for offboarding, you can use the Exchange Admin Center (selecting Migrate From Exchange Online on the migration page) and select the users and endpoint
details or use Windows PowerShell, as shown in the following example.

1. Create a CSV with the header EmailAddress and enter the email addresses of the users to
    offboard, one per line, and save to a temp folder (such as C:\Temp\Offboard.csv).

2. Connect to Exchange Online PowerShell.

3. Run the following command.

    ```
    New-MigrationBatch -Name Offboard -CSVData ([System.IO.File]::ReadAllBytes("C:\
    Temp\Offboard.csv")) -TargetEndpoint ((Get-MigrationEndPoint)[0]) -TargetDelivery-
    Domain <PrimarySMTPDomain> -TargetDatabase MBX1 -AutoStart -AutoComplete -Notifi-
    cationEmails adminuser@contoso.com
    ```

Troubleshooting

Mailbox moves might fail for a number of reasons, including network timeouts, inaccessible
databases, insufficient permissions, invalid proxy addresses, or missing Exchange GUIDs. For any
migrations that fail, you can export the underlying move request and use the MRS Explorer tool
(*https://gallery.technet.microsoft.com/office/MRS-Explorer-for-Exchange-b55c0c67*) to examine
the error. Some of the more common errors (and resolutions) follow.

- **You Can't Use The Domain Because It's Not An Accepted Domain For Your
  Organization**

  This error occurs because a proxy address on the source mailbox doesn't match an
  accepted domain in the target environment. This frequently happens if you have removed
  accepted domains in your on-premises environment without updating the proxy address
  for the users, or if you have not added and verified all on-premises accepted domains in
  the Exchange Online environment.

You can use the following script to identify proxy addresses that are causing this error.

```
$Users = (Get-MigrationUser -Status Failed | ? { $_.ErrorSummary -match "not an
accepted domain" }).Identity

[regex]$AcceptedDomainsRegex = '(?i)(' + (($Domains |foreach
{[regex]::escape($_)}) -join "|@") + ')$'

Foreach ($user in $users)
    {
    Write-host processing $user
    $obj = Get-MailUser $user
    for ($i=($obj.EmailAddresses.count)-1; $i -ge 0; $i--)
        {
        $address = $obj.EmailAddresses[$i]
        if ($address -notlike "*@*")
            {
            Continue
            }
        if ($address -inotlike "*x500:*" -and $address -like "*@*" -and $address
-notmatch $AcceptedDomainsRegex)
                { Write-Host -ForegroundColor Red "     Address $($address)
doesn't match" }
            else { }
        }
    Write-host "-----------"
    }
```

Review the output and then add the necessary domains to the Office 365 tenant or remove the offending proxy addresses from the on-premises users and retry the migration.

- **Target Mailbox Doesn't Have An SMTP Proxy Matching <*tenant*>.mail.onmicro-soft.com**

  During an Exchange mailbox migration, the source mailbox's targetAddress attribute is configured to point to an email address in the new Exchange environment. The Hybrid Configuration Wizard configures an email address template for all email address policies that contain domains selected on the Hybrid Domains page of the wizard. The email addresses are applied during the next email address policy update cycle.

  However, if you have mailboxes with the EmailAddressPolicyEnabled attribute set to False, those mailboxes will never receive the updated proxy address from the email address template. Without a valid proxy address matching the Exchange Online routing domain, MRS cannot configure the targetAddress value for the source account.

  To resolve this error, add a proxy address for the mailbox in the format of <*alias*>@<*tenant*>.*mail.onmicrosoft.com*. You can use a script, such as the one located at *https://gallery.technet.microsoft.com/Add-Office-365-Tenant-93391e4c/file/145326/4 /Add-TenantProxyAddress.ps1*, to help automate this task.

- **Insufficient Access Rights To Perform The Operation (INSUFF_ACCESS_RIGHTS)**

  This error frequently occurs when Active Directory inheritance has been disabled for the mailbox account being migrated.

  The two primary sources of permissions inheritance problems are the following.

  - A security policy for least-privilege access to sensitive accounts
  - adminSDHolder and SDProp

  Exchange depends on the presence of a certain set of permissions for the migration account to update the attributes of the migrated user. If permissions inheritance has been disabled, the permissions for the Exchange Server groups will not be applied to the mailbox.

  To resolve this error, verify that Active Directory object security inheritance is enabled on all mailboxes being migrated. You can use a script, such as the one located at *https://gallery.technet.microsoft.com/Find-and-Fix-Broken-Object-5ae18ab1*, to identify and resolve accounts with disabled inheritance.

- **The User Object Does Not Have A Valid ExchangeGUID Property And Cannot Be Migrated**

  As previously mentioned, for a mailbox migration to be successful, the ExchangeGuid (msExchMailboxGuid, when viewed from Active Directory) property of the source user mailbox and target mail-enabled user must be populated with the same value.

  If the ExchangeGuid property of the target mail-enabled user in Exchange Online is not synchronized, remove the user from Azure AD and re-synchronize the user account with the following steps.

  a. Connect to Azure AD PowerShell by using the Connect-MsolService cmdlet.

  b. Remove the user object from Azure AD and the Azure AD recycle bin:

  ```
  Remove-MsolUser -UserPrincipalName <user@domain.com> -Force
  Remove-MsolUser -UserPrincipalName <user@domain.com> -RemoveFromRecycleBin
  -Force
  ```

  c. Wait for AAD Connect to run a delta synchronization (or run a manual delta synchronization task).

- **A Recipient Wasn't Found For user@domain.com On The Target**

  No mail-enabled user in Exchange Online matches a mailbox in the migration batch. This usually happens because an address specified in a CSV file was typed incorrectly. Verify that all mailboxes in the CSV file for migration have a matching recipient object in the Office 365 tenant.

- **This Mailbox Exceeded The Maximum Number Of Corrupted Items That Were Specified For This Move Request**

  If the mailbox being migrated has more bad items or large items than either the BadItem-Limit or LargeItemLimit thresholds, the migration generates this error. There are two ways to resolve the error.

    - Remove the corrupt or large items from the source mailbox.

    - Increase the BadItemLimit and LargeItemLimit parameters for the move request by using Set-MoveRequest -BadItemLimit <number> -LargeItemLimit <number> -AcceptLargeDataLoss

- **Target User Already Has A Primary Mailbox**

  This error occurs when a user is included in a migration batch that has already been migrated. Remove the user from the migration batch.

- **Mailbox Is Already Being Moved To *<databasename>***

  This error can happen if a move request is created manually using the New-MoveRequest cmdlet prior to the mailbox's inclusion in a batch. Either remove the existing move request or remove the user from the migration batch.

- **The Request Channel Timed Out While Waiting For A Reply**

  This error is frequently caused by an incorrect load-balancer configuration or another device interrupting the MRSProxy traffic (such as an intrusion detection/intrusion prevention appliance or an SSL offloading configuration). Ensure that Exchange Online can reach the on-premises Exchange server environment without any packet-inspecting devices acting as intermediaries.

Public folders

In a hybrid Exchange deployment, public folders can exist either on-premises or in-cloud. They can only exist in one place at a time, so it's important to plan where they will be, based on your user mailbox locations and Exchange versions.

Typically, the recommended migration plan is to move public folders to Office 365 after all the mailboxes have been moved to Exchange Online.

Hybrid public folders

There are two types of hybrid public folder implementations—those in which the public folders exist on-premises and those in which the public folders exist online. Use the information in Table 13-6 to determine what options are available, based on your public folder and user mailbox locations.

Table 13-6 Hybrid public folder topologies

Public folder location	On-premises Exchange 2007 or Exchange 2010 mailbox	On-premises Exchange 2013 mailbox	Exchange Online mailbox
Exchange 2003	Not Supported	Not Supported	Not Supported
Exchange 2007 or Exchange 2010	N/A	N/A	Supported
Exchange 2013	N/A	N/A	Supported
Exchange Online	Not Supported	Supported	N/A

OUTLOOK VERSIONS AND FEATURE AVAILABILITY

It's not uncommon, especially in large organizations, for multiple versions of desktop software to be installed. Multiple versions of desktop Outlook clients, Exchange on-premises server versions, and the introduction of Exchange Online can lead to unexpected issues. To minimize connectivity issues and maximize feature availability, be advised of the following.

- Outlook 2016 cannot access public folders hosted on Exchange 2007 or earlier. If you have users with Outlook 2016, either move your on-premises public folders to Exchange 2010 or newer, or downgrade your Outlook clients to 2013 or earlier.

- Outlook 2007 or 2010 clients must be updated to the November 2012 public update to access cross-premises public folders.

- Outlook for Mac and Outlook for Mac for Office 365 are not supported for cross-premises public folder access. Outlook for Mac clients can only access public folders hosted in the same location as the user mailbox.

On-premises public folders

Hybrid public folder deployments in which the public folders are on-premises are the most common coexistence or migration strategy. In this case, you might be migrating your users and data to Office 365 and need to provide access to on-premises public folders for users whose mailboxes have already been moved.

This is the simplest deployment, because the requirements are the easiest to meet and the configuration steps can be minimal, depending on your on-premises environment. The prerequisites are as follows.

- Your on-premises Exchange environment is accessible through the Internet.

- Autodiscover is configured properly and points to an on-premises endpoint. Hybrid public folders in Exchange Online use Autodiscover to locate on-premises public folders.

- Outlook Anywhere has been configured on your Exchange servers.

- You have the correct permissions or role group memberships.

  - For Exchange Online, you are a member of the Organization Management role group.

  - For Exchange 2010, you are a member of the Organization Management or Server Management role-based access control (RBAC) role groups.

  - For Exchange 2007, you have been assigned the Exchange Organization Administrator or Exchange Server Administrator roles as well as the Public Folder Administrator role. You are also a member of the local Administrators group on the Exchange server hosting the public folder database.

- For Exchange 2007, if your server is running Windows Server 2008 x64 or Windows Server 2003 x64, you have upgraded to Windows PowerShell 2.0 and WinRM 2.0.

- All Exchange Online users attempting to access on-premises public folders are represented by an on-premises mail-enabled user object.

- You have downloaded the public folder sync scripts from *https://www.microsoft.com /en-us/download/details.aspx?id=46381* and saved them to a folder on one of the public folder servers, such as C:\PFScripts.

Exchange 2007

When configuring prerequisites for hybrid public folders or public folder migrations for Exchange 2007, you only need to create a mailbox database and a mailbox and then update the organization configuration in Exchange Online to point to the new mailbox.

1. Create an empty mailbox database on each public folder server. This mailbox database will be used for the public folder proxy mailbox you create. No other mailboxes should be placed on this database.

    ```
    New-MailboxDatabase -StorageGroup "<PFServerName\StorageGroup>" -Name
    <NewPFDatabaseName>
    ```

2. On each public folder server, add a mailbox in the database created in the previous step.

    ```
    New-Mailbox -Name <PFMailbox1> -Database <NewPFDatabaseName>
    Set-Mailbox -Identity <PFMailbox1> -HiddenFromAddressListsEnabled $true
    ```

3. Launch a Windows PowerShell session and change to the folder containing the public folder sync scripts.

4. Run the following command daily to synchronize the mail-enabled public folders to Exchange Online, using your Office 365 credentials when prompted.

```
Sync-MailPublicFolders.ps1 -Credential (Get-Credential) -CsvSummaryFile:sync_sum-
mary.csv
```

5. Connect to Exchange Online PowerShell and run the following command, specifying all the public folder mailboxes created in step 1 for the RemotePublicFolderMailboxes parameter.

```
Set-OrganizationConfig -PublicFoldersEnabled Remote -RemotePublicFolderMailboxes
PFMailbox1,PFMailbox2,PFMailbox3
```

Exchange 2010

The prerequisites for configuring hybrid public folders or public folder migrations for Exchange 2010 are a little more involved, requiring everything that Exchange 2007 does, as well as configuration of the Client Access Server role on public folder servers.

1. Install and configure the Client Access Server role on all mailbox servers that have a public folder database.

   The public folder servers do not have to be part of a client access load balancing, but they do need the Microsoft Exchange RpcClientAccess service to be running.

2. Create an empty mailbox database on each public folder server and exclude it from the mailbox provisioning load balancer.

   This mailbox database will be used for the public folder proxy mailbox you create. No other mailboxes should be placed on this database.

   ```
   New-MailboxDatabase -Server <PFServerName> -Name <NewPFDatabaseName> -IsExcluded-
   FromProvisioning $true
   ```

3. On each public folder server, add a mailbox in the database created in the previous step.

   ```
   New-Mailbox -Name <PFMailbox1> -Database <NewPFDatabasename>
   Set-Mailbox -Identity <PFMailbox1> -HiddenFromAddressListsEnabled $true
   ```

4. On each public folder server, enable Autodiscover to return the public folder mailboxes.

   ```
   Set-MailboxDatabase <NewPFDatabaseName> -RPCClientAccessServer <PFServerName>
   ```

5. Launch a Windows PowerShell session and change to the folder containing the public folder sync scripts.

6. Run the following command daily to synchronize the mail-enabled public folders to Exchange Online, using your Office 365 credentials when prompted.

   ```
   Sync-MailPublicFolders.ps1 -Credential (Get-Credential) -CsvSummaryFile:sync_sum-
   mary.csv
   ```

7. Connect to Exchange Online PowerShell and run the following command, specifying all the public folder mailboxes created in step 1 for the RemotePublicFolderMailboxes parameter.

    ```
    Set-OrganizationConfig -PublicFoldersEnabled Remote -RemotePublicFolderMailboxes
    PFMailbox1,PFMailbox2,PFMailbox3
    ```

Exchange 2013 and Exchange 2016

Due to the consolidation of server roles for Exchange 2013 and Exchange 2016, the Client Access Server role is already present on any servers on which mailboxes or public folders are deployed. Exchange 2013 and Exchange 2016 use modern public folders (where the public folder data is stored in public folder mailboxes), so the steps to create separate public folder mailboxes are unnecessary. You only need to configure Exchange Online with the on-premises public folder mailbox names.

1. Get a list of all on-premises public folder mailboxes from Exchange Management Shell.

    ```
    Get-Mailbox -PublicFolder | Select Alias
    ```

2. Launch a Windows PowerShell session and change to the folder containing the public folder sync scripts.

3. Run the following command daily to synchronize the mail-enabled public folders to Exchange Online, using your Office 365 credentials when prompted.

    ```
    Sync-MailPublicFolders.ps1 -Credential (Get-Credential) -CsvSummaryFile:sync_sum-
    mary.csv
    ```

4. Connect to Exchange Online PowerShell and run the following command, specifying all the public folder mailboxes obtained in step 1 for the RemotePublicFolderMailboxes parameter.

    ```
    Set-OrganizationConfig -PublicFoldersEnabled Remote -RemotePublicFolderMailboxes
    PFMailbox1,PFMailbox2,PFMailbox3
    ```

Online public folders

In this type of hybrid configuration, your mailbox users are on-premises, and your public folders are online. You might have already migrated your public folders to Exchange Online, or you might have created and begun using new public folders in Exchange Online. In either case, you need to synchronize contacts for the mail-enabled public folders to your on-premises environment so they are available as mail recipients. The prerequisites are as follows.

- All user mailboxes are hosted on Exchange 2013.

- Autodiscover is configured properly and points to an on-premises endpoint.

- Outlook Anywhere has been configured on your Exchange servers.

- You have downloaded the public folder sync scripts from *https://www.microsoft.com /en-us/download/details.aspx?id=52037* and saved them to a folder on one of the Exchange servers, such as C:\PFScripts.

To configure Exchange Online public folders, follow these steps.

1. Launch a Windows PowerShell session and change to the folder containing the public folder sync scripts.

2. Run the following command daily to sync mail-enabled public folders from Exchange Online to your on-premises Active Directory.

   ```
   Sync-MailPublicFoldersCloudToOnprem.ps1 -Credential (Get-Credential)
   ```

3. Run the following command daily to sync public folder mailboxes from Exchange Online to your on-premises Active Directory.

   ```
   Import-PublicFolderMailboxes.ps1 -Credential (Get-Credential)
   ```

4. From the on-premises Exchange Management Shell, run the following command to enable access to Exchange Online public folders.

   ```
   Set-OrganizationConfig -PublicFoldersEnabled Remote
   ```

Public folder migration

Public folders can be migrated from Exchange 2007, Exchange 2010, Exchange 2013, or Exchange 2016 to Office 365 or Exchange Online. The following are the general prerequisites to do this.

- Your on-premises Exchange environment is accessible through the Internet.

- Autodiscover is configured properly and points to an on-premises endpoint. Hybrid public folders in Exchange Online uses Autodiscover to locate on-premises public folders.

- Outlook Anywhere has been configured on your Exchange servers.

- You have the correct permissions or role group memberships.

  - For Exchange Online, you are a member of the Organization Management role group.

  - For Exchange 2007, you have been assigned the Exchange Organization Administrator role or Exchange Server Administrator role as well as the Public Folder Administrator role. You are also a member of the local Administrators group on the Exchange server hosting the public folder database.

- For Exchange 2010, Exchange 2013, and Exchange 2016, you are a member of the Organization Management or Server Management role-based access control (RBAC) role groups.

- You have checked your public folders for invalid names by using IDFix for Public Folders, available at *https://gallery.technet.microsoft.com/IDFix-for-Public-Folders-341522d6*.

- SMTP addresses and aliases for mail-enabled public folders are unique across your organization.

- There are no orphaned public folder mail objects in the Microsoft Exchange System Objects container in Active Directory.

- You have checked your public folders for size. If you have any individual folders greater than 2 GB, consider deleting some content, migrating some content to another folder, or increasing the public folder quota size.

- You don't have more than 10,000 subfolders in any particular folder, because this can cause the migration to fail. This is typically only an issue in the DUMPSTER_ROOT folder. To see whether this could affect you, run the following command from the on-premises Exchange Management Shell.

```
(Get-PublicFolder -GetChildren "\NON_IPM_SUBTREE\DUMPSTER_ROOT").Count
```

- You have verified that your servers meet the minimum software requirements.

  - For Exchange 2007, your servers are running Service Pack 3 with RollUp 15 or later.
  - For Exchange 2007, if your server is running Windows Server 2008 x64 or Windows Server 2003 x64, you have upgraded to Windows PowerShell 2.0 and WinRM 2.0.
  - For Exchange 2010, your servers are running Service Pack 3 with RollUp 8 or later.
  - For Exchange 2013, you have deployed Cumulative Update 15 or later.

Exchange 2007 or Exchange 2010

Before you begin migrating, you must ensure that your environment meets the prerequisites and that you have completed the planning exercises necessary.

In addition to the general prerequisites, there are some version-specific prerequisites as well.

- You have downloaded the scripts and supporting files from *https://www.microsoft.com /en-us/download/details.aspx?id=38407* and saved them to a folder on one of your Exchange servers in a directory such as C:\PFScripts.

- You have downloaded the public folder sync scripts from *https://www.microsoft.com /en-us/download/details.aspx?id=46381* and saved them to a folder on one of the public folder servers, such as C:\PFScripts.

To migrate public folders, follow these steps.

1. If you are using Azure AD Connect to synchronize your directories, ensure that you are not synchronizing Exchange mail public folders, because that causes the migration to fail. If you are not using AAD Connect, you can skip this step.

   a. On the server running AAD Connect, launch the Azure AD Connect Setup Wizard.

   b. Click Configure.

   c. Click Customize Synchronization Options and then click Next.

   d. On the Connect To Azure AD page, enter your Office 365 credentials and click Next.

   e. On the Connect Your Directories page, click Next.

   f. On the Domain And OU Filtering page, click Next.

   g. On the Optional Features page, ensure that the check box for Exchange Mail Public Folders is cleared. If it is selected, clear it and click Next. Otherwise, you can cancel the wizard and exit it.

   h. If Group Writeback was selected, click Next on the Writeback page.

   i. On the Ready To Configure page, click Configure.

   j. Click Exit.

      If you had to clear the Exchange Mail Public Folders check box on the Optional Features page, you must run a full import and synchronization because the wizard removes six synchronization rules and clears the public folder object type in the connector properties.

2. On the older Exchange server you have downloaded the public folder scripts to, launch a Windows PowerShell session, change to the directory containing the downloaded public folder scripts, and connect to Exchange Online:

   ```
   $Session = New-PSSession -ConfigurationName Mircrosoft.Exchange -ConnectionUri
   https://outlook.office365.com/powershell-liveid -Authentication Basic -AllowRedi-
   rection -Credential (Get-Credential)

   Import-PSSession $Session
   ```

3. On the older Exchange server you have downloaded the public folder scripts to, launch an Exchange Management Shell session and change to the directory containing the downloaded public folder scripts.

4. Check for existing public folder migrations in both Exchange Online and Exchange on-premises management shells and check to make sure all entries are returned as False.

```
Get-OrganizationConfig | FL Public*Migration*
```

The screen output should look similar to the following.

```
PublicFoldersLockedForMigration         : False
PublicFolderMigrationComplete           : False
PublicFolderMailboxesMigrationComplete : False
```

If any of the preceding conditions are true, a public folder migration has been started or completed or is underway.

5. If you are certain that no public folder migrations have occurred or are in progress, you can set the values to false with the following command.

```
Set-OrganizationConfig -PublicFoldersLockedforMigration:$false -PublicFolderMigrat
ionComplete:$false
```

6. Check to ensure that no public folder mailboxes have been created in Exchange Online. If they have, remove them with the following commands from your Exchange Online PowerShell session.

```
Get-PublicFolderMigrationRequest | Remove-PublicFolderMigrationRequest
-Confirm:$False

$PFMigrationBatch = Get-MigrationBatch | ? { $_.MigrationType.ToString() -eq "Pub-
lic Folder" }

$PFMigrationBatch | Remove-MigrationBatch -Confirm:$False

Get-MailPublicFolder | where {$_.EntryId -ne $null}| Disable-MailPublicFolder
-Confirm:$false

Get-PublicFolder -GetChildren \ | Remove-PublicFolder -Recurse -Confirm:$false

$hierarchyMailboxGuid = $(Get-OrganizationConfig).RootPublicFolderMailbox.
HierarchyMailboxGuid

Get-Mailbox -PublicFolder:$true | Where-Object {$_.ExchangeGuid -ne $hierarchy-
MailboxGuid} | Remove-Mailbox -PublicFolder -Confirm:$false

Get-Mailbox -PublicFolder:$true | Where-Object {$_.ExchangeGuid -eq $hierarchy-
MailboxGuid} | Remove-Mailbox -PublicFolder -Confirm:$false
```

7. Check the public folder quota sizes by using the following command from your Exchange Online PowerShell session.

```
Get-OrganizationConfig | fl *quot*
```

The default output will show:

```
DefaultPublicFolderIssueWarningQuota : 1.7 GB (1,825,361,920 bytes)
DefaultPublicFolderProhibitPostQuota : 2 GB (2,147,483,648 bytes)
```

8. If you have public folders larger than 2 GB, adjust this. For example, this command can be run in the Exchange Online PowerShell session to set the public folder warning quota to 9.5 GB and the hard quota to 10 GB.

```
Set-OrganizationConfig -DefaultPublicFolderIssueWarningQuota 9.5GB -DefaultPublic-
FolderProhibitPostQuota 10GB
```

9. Capture public folder statistics and permissions by using the following commands from the on-premises Exchange Management Shell.

```
Get-PublicFolder -Recurse -ResultSize Unlimited | Export-Clixml .\LegacyPFStruc-
ture.xml
```

```
Get-PublicFolder -Recurse -ResultSize Unlimited | Get-PublicFolderStatistics |
Export-Clixml .\LegacyPFStatisticsRecurse.xml
```

```
Get-PublicFolder -Recurse -ResultSize Unlimited | Get-PublicFolderClientPermission
| Select-Object Identity,User -ExpandProperty AccessRights | Export-Clixml .\Leg-
acyPFPerms.xml
```

10. From your on-premises Exchange Management Shell, create an accepted domain to be used to route mail for mail-enabled public folders. The DomainName parameter is a well-known ID, so be sure to create it as specified, replacing *<tenant>*.onmicrosoft.com with your Office 365 tenant ID.

```
New-AcceptedDomain -Name "PublicFolderDestination_78c0b207_5ad2_4fee_8cb9_
f373175b3f99" -DomainName <tenant>.onmicrosoft.com -DomainType InternalRelay
```

11. Run a final check to ensure that you don't have any public folders with forward slashes or backslashes.

   a. For Exchange 2007, run this command from the Exchange Management Shell.

   ```
   Get-PublicFolderDatabase | % { Get-PublicFolderStatistics -Server $_.Server
   | ? { ($_.Name -like "*\*") -or ($_.Name -like "*/*")} | FL Name,Identity
   ```

   b. For Exchange 2010, run this command from the Exchange Management Shell.

   ```
   Get-PublicFolderStatistics -ResultSize Unlimited | ? { ($_.Name -like "*\*")
   -or ($_.Name -like "*/*")} | FL Name,Identity
   ```

12. Back up the Send-As permissions. From the Exchange Management Shell, run the following command.

```
Get-MailPublicFolder -ResultSize Unlimited | Get-ADPermission | ? {($_.Extended-
Rights -Like "Send-As") -and ($_.IsInherited -eq $False) -and -not ($_.User -like
"*S-1-5-21-*")} | Select Identity,User | Export-Csv Send_As.csv -NoTypeInformation
```

13. Back up the Send-On-Behalf permission. From the Exchange Management Shell, run the following script.

```
Get-MailPublicFolder | Select Alias,PrimarySmtpAddress,@
{N="GrantSendOnBehalfTo";E={$_.GrantSendOnBehalfTo -join "|"}} | Export-Csv Grant-
SendOnBehalfTo.csv -NoTypeInformation

$File = Import-Csv .\GrantSendOnBehalfTo.csv
$Data = @()
Foreach ($line in $File)
    {
    If ($line.GrantSendOnBehalfTo)
        {
        Write-Host -ForegroundColor Green "Processing Public Folder $($line.
Alias)"
        [array]$LineRecipients = $line.GrantSendOnBehalfTo.Split("|")
        Foreach ($Recipient in $LineRecipients)
            {
            Write-Host -ForegroundColor DarkGreen "      $($Recipient)"
            $GrantSendOnBehalfTo = (Get-Recipient $Recipient).PrimarySmtpAddress
            $LineData = New-Object PSCustomObject
            $LineData | Add-Member -Type NoteProperty -Name Alias -Value $line.
Alias
            $LineData | Add-Member -Type NoteProperty -Name PrimarySmtpAddress
-Value $line.PrimarySmtpAddress
            $LineData | Add-Member -Type NoteProperty -Name GrantSendOnBehalfTo
-Value $GrantSendOnBehalfTo
                $Data += $LineData
                }
            }
    }
$Data | Export-Csv .\GrantSendOnBehalfTo-Resolved.csv -NoTypeInformation
```

14. Run the Export-PublicFolderStatistics.ps1 script from the Exchange Management Shell.

```
.\Export-PublicFolderStatistics.ps1 C:\PFScripts\PFStatistics.csv <PFServerName>
```

MAXIMUM PUBLIC FOLDERS RETURNED

If you have more than 10,000 public folders, you probably want to modify the Export-PublicFolderStatistics.ps1 script. Look for the *$index%10000* string and update it to *$index%100000* (or a number higher than your existing public folder count), as shown in Figure 13-44.

```
152    if ($publicFolderIdentity -ne "")
153    {
154        #if(($index%10000) -eq 0)
155        if(($index%100000) -eq 0)
156        {
157            Write-Host "[$($(Get-Date).ToString())]" ($PublicFolderStatistics_LocalizedStrings.ProcessedFolders -f $index);
158        }
159
160        # Create a folder object to be exported to a CSV
161        $newFolderObject = New-Object PSObject -Property @{FolderName = $publicFolderIdentity; FolderSize = $folderSize}
162        $retvalue = $script:ExportFolders.Add($newFolderObject);
163        $index++;
```

Figure 13-44 Updating code for public folder count

15. Run the public folder mapping generator.

The mapping generator reads the CSV created in the previous step and assigns branches of the public folder tree to individual public folder mailboxes based on the size of the public argument you give it. The syntax is:

```
.\PublicFolderToMailboxMapGenerator.ps1 <size> <Name of CSV from previous step>
<output map file>
```

For example, if you want to divide the public folder content into 10 GB mailboxes, use the previously generated PFStatistics.csv file and set the output to PFMapFile.csv.

```
.\PublicFolderToMailboxMapGenerator.ps1 10000000000 PFStatistics.csv PFMapFile.csv
```

You should receive output that looks similar to the following.

```
[4/8/2017 4:02:22 AM] Reading public folder list...
[4/8/2017 4:02:22 AM] Loading folder hierarchy...
[4/8/2017 4:02:24 AM] Allocating folders to mailboxes...
[4/8/2017 4:02:24 AM] Trying to accomodate folders with their parent...
[4/8/2017 4:02:24 AM] Exporting folder mapping...
```

RIGHT-SIZING THE MAPPING GENERATOR OUTPUT

The public folder map file output is a list of target public folder mailboxes and which branch of the public folder tree is the first one in the public folder mailbox. The public folder mapping generator processes the public folder statistics output and distributes the public folder branches among the public folder mailboxes by using the specified target public folder mailbox size.

Because the output is readable, you can edit it and make adjustments based on your working knowledge of the public folder hierarchy, how you might expect data to grow, or how active a particular folder or branch might be. See Figure 13-45.

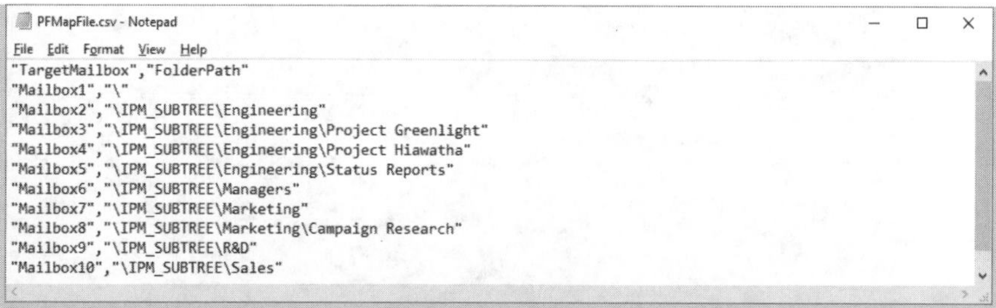

Figure 13-45 Public folder mapping generator output

After you have completed the mapping file, you create public folder mailboxes in Exchange Online based on the mapping file.

16. Switch to the Windows PowerShell window connected to Exchange Online and then use the Create-PublicFolderMailboxesForMigration.ps1 script to complete this task.

```
.\Create-PublicFolderMailboxesForMigration.ps1 -FolderMappingCsv C:\PFScripts\
PFMapFile.csv -EstimatedNumberOfConcurrentUsers 40000
```

ESTIMATING THE NUMBER OF USERS

Public folder design is as much art as it is science. In addition to the public folder limits (1,000,000 public folders, 1,000 public folder mailboxes, and 100 GB per public folder mailbox), you also have to plan for the number of active users in your organization who will be using public folders. To keep contention low, you want no more than 2,000 users per public folder mailbox.

Depending on how many users you have, the Create-PublicFolderMailboxesForMigration.ps1 script might generate more public folder mailboxes than the mapping generator tool said you needed. The Create-PublicFolderMailboxesForMigration.ps1 script creates one mailbox for every 2,000 users, and if that comes to a greater number of mailboxes than the mapping generator recommended, you are prompted to acknowledge the update. After it has completed, you see an output similar to Figure 13-46. If you were prompted to create more mailboxes, you see them named AutoSplit_GUID, and the IsMigrationTarget property is set to False for those mailboxes.

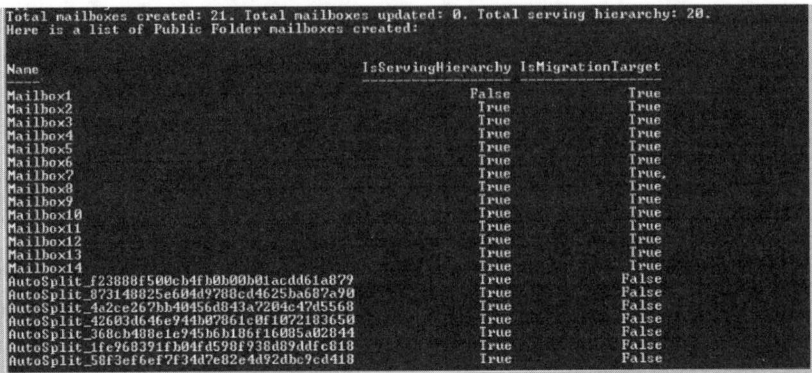

Figure 13-46 Create-PublicFolderMailboxesForMigration.ps1 output

17. Launch a new Windows PowerShell prompt and run .\Sync-MailPublicFolders.ps1 to sync the mail objects to Exchange Online. Don't run this from the Exchange Management Shell *or* the existing Windows PowerShell prompt connected to Exchange Online. After the sync has run, you can close this Windows PowerShell window.

```
.\Sync-MailPublicFolders.ps1 –Credential (Get-Credential)
-CsvSummaryFile:SyncOutput.csv
```

18. Review the output in the CSV Summary File for errors.

    These errors must be resolved prior to migration.

19. In your Exchange Management Console window, ensure that you are in the C:\PFScripts directory and then run the following commands.

```
(Get-Mailbox <admin user>).legacyExchangeDN | Out-File .\MailboxLegacyExchangeDN.
txt

(Get-ExchangeServer <public folder server>).ExchangeLegacyDN | Out-File .\Server-
ExchangeLegacyDN.txt

$OAEndpoint = ((Get-ExchangeServer | ? { $_.ServerRole -match "ClientAccess"})
[0]|Get-OutlookAnywhere).ExternalHostName

$OAEndpoint | Out-File .\OAEndpoint.txt
```

OUTLOOK ANYWHERE ENDPOINT SELECTION

If your organization has more than one Outlook Anywhere endpoint or you have configured the TargetAutoDiscoverEpr in your Office 365 tenant, use that value instead. This value is used for creating the migration endpoint, so if it is not the endpoint that you are using for mailbox migrations, your public folder migrations might fail.

> **For example, in your Office 365 tenant, you can run:**
>
> ```
> Get-OrganizationRelationship | FL TargetAutoDiscoverEpr
> ```
>
> **The output by default is null, but if you have configured it, it will look something like this:**
>
> ```
> TargetAutodiscoverEpr : https://hybrid.domain.com/autodiscover/autodiscover.svc/
> WSSecurity
> ```
>
> **Use the endpoint hostname (hybrid.domain.com, in this example) instead in the Exchange Management Shell window.**
>
> ```
> $OAEndPoint = "hybrid.domain.com"
> $OAEndPoint | Out-File .\OAEndPoint.txt
> ```

20. Switch to the Windows PowerShell window connected to Exchange Online and ensure that you are in the C:\PFScripts directory, because that is where the output of the previous step's commands was saved. Run these commands in the Exchange Online PowerShell window:

```
cd \PFScripts
$OAEndopint = gc .\OAEndpoint.txt
$MailboxLegacyExchangeDN = gc .\MailboxLegacyExchangeDN.txt
$ServerExchangeLegacyDN = gc .\ServerExchangeLegacyDN.txt
$Credential = Get-Credential <domain\admin user>
```

The credential specified in the $Credential variable must be an on-premises administrator account in DOMAIN\Username format. If it is not in that format, the endpoint creation will fail with an authentication error.

21. Create the public folder migration endpoint in Exchange Online. From the Exchange Online PowerShell window, run the following command.

```
$PFEndpoint = New-MigrationEndpoint -PublicFolder -Name PublicFolderEndPoint
-RpcProxyServer $OAEndPoint -Credentials $Credential -SourceMailboxLegacyDN $Mail-
boxLegacyExchangeDN -PublicFolderDatabaseServerLegacyDN $ServerExchangeLegacyDN
-Authentication Basic
```

22. Create the public folder migration batch.

```
New-MigrationBatch -Name PublicFolderMigration -CSVData (Get-Content .\PFMap-
File.csv -Encoding Byte) -SourceEndpoint $PFEndpoint.Identity -NotificationEmails
<emailaddress>
```

23. To begin the migration, run the following command.

```
Start-MigrationBatch -Identity PublicFolderMigration
```

24. To check on the status of the migration, you can run:

```
Get-Migrationuser -BatchID PublicFolderMigration | Get-MigrationUserStatistics |
Select Identity,Status,SyncedItemCount,SkippedItemCount,BytesTransferred,Percentag
eComplete
```

25. After all mailboxes show the Synced status, you can complete the migration batch. To do this, lock the public folders on the source side first. From the on-premises Exchange Management Shell, run the following command.

```
Set-OrganizationConfig -PublicFoldersLockedForMigration $True
```

26. Run the Complete-MigrationBatch command from the Exchange Online PowerShell session to complete the migration.

```
Complete-MigrationBatch -Identity PublicFolderMigration
```

Exchange 2013 or Exchange 2016

Before you begin migrating, you must ensure that your environment meets the prerequisites and that you have completed the planning exercises necessary.

In addition to the general prerequisites, make sure you have downloaded the scripts and supporting files from *https://www.microsoft.com/en-us/download/details.aspx?id=54855* and saved them to a folder on one of your Exchange servers in a directory such as C:\PFScripts.

To migrate public folders, follow these steps.

1. If you are using Azure AD Connect to synchronize your directories, ensure that you are not synchronizing Exchange mail public folders, because that causes the migration to fail. If you are not using AAD Connect, you can skip this step.

   a. On the server running AAD Connect, launch the Azure AD Connect Setup Wizard.

   b. Click Configure.

   c. Click Customize Synchronization Options and then click Next.

   d. On the Connect To Azure AD page, enter your Office 365 credentials and click Next.

   e. On the Connect Your Directories page, click Next.

   f. On the Domain And OU Filtering page, click Next.

   g. On the Optional Features page, ensure that the Exchange Mail Public Folders check box is cleared. If it is selected, clear it and click Next. Otherwise, you can cancel the wizard and exit it.

   h. If Group Writeback was selected, click Next on the Writeback page.

   i. On the Ready To Configure page, click Configure.

   j. Click Exit.

If you had to clear the Exchange Mail Public Folders check box on the Optional Features page, you must run a full import and synchronization because the wizard removes six synchronization rules and clears the public folder object type in the connector properties.

2. On the Exchange server you have downloaded the public folder scripts to, launch a Windows PowerShell session, change to the directory containing the downloaded public folder scripts, and connect to Exchange Online.

```
$Session = New-PSSession -ConfigurationName Mircrosoft.Exchange -ConnectionUri
https://outlook.office365.com/powershell-liveid -Authentication Basic -AllowRedi-
rection -Credential (Get-Credential)

Import-PSSession $Session
```

3. On the Exchange server you have downloaded the public folder scripts to, launch an Exchange Management Shell session and change to the directory containing the downloaded public folder scripts.

4. Check for existing public folder migrations in the Exchange Online PowerShell window and make sure all entries are returned as False. From the Exchange Online PowerShell, run the following commands to clear any existing migration requests.

```
Get-PublicFolderMigrationRequest | Remove-PublicFolderMigrationRequest

Get-MigrationBatch | ?{$_.MigrationType.ToString() -eq "PublicFolder"} |
Remove-MigrationBatch
```

5. Remove any existing public folder mailboxes or public folders that have been created in Exchange Online. If they do exist, you might want to confirm that the data is no longer needed. Existing public folder mailboxes or public folders cause the migration to fail. From the Exchange Online PowerShell window, run the following commands.

```
Get-MailPublicFolder -ResultSize Unlimited | where {$_.EntryId -ne $null}| Dis-
able-MailPublicFolder -Confirm:$false

Get-PublicFolder -GetChildren \ -ResultSize Unlimited | Remove-PublicFolder
-Recurse -Confirm:$false

$hierarchyMailboxGuid = $(Get-OrganizationConfig).RootPublicFolderMailbox.
HierarchyMailboxGuid

Get-Mailbox -PublicFolder | Where-Object {$_.ExchangeGuid -ne $hierarchyMail-
boxGuid} | Remove-Mailbox -PublicFolder -Confirm:$false -Force

Get-Mailbox -PublicFolder | Where-Object {$_.ExchangeGuid -eq $hierarchyMail-
boxGuid} | Remove-Mailbox -PublicFolder -Confirm:$false -Force

Get-Mailbox -PublicFolder -SoftDeletedMailbox | Remove-Mailbox -PublicFolder
-PermanentlyDelete:$true
```

6. Check for any existing public folder migrations in your on-premises environment. You might have previously migrated to Exchange 2013 or 2016, so you must remove those migration requests and artifacts to migrate to Office 365. From the on-premises Exchange Management Shell, run the following command.

```
Get-OrganizationConfig | Format-List PublicFoldersLockedforMigration, Pub-
licFolderMigrationComplete, PublicFolderMailboxesLockedForNewConnections,
PublicFolderMailboxesMigrationComplete
```

If either the PublicFoldersLockedforMigration or PublicFolderMigrationComplete parameters are $true, it means you have migrated older public folders at some point. Make sure any older public folder databases have been decommissioned before you continue.

7. If any of the properties from the preceding command are listed $true, set them to $false by running the following command in the on-premises Exchange Management Shell.

```
Set-OrganizationConfig -PublicFoldersLockedforMigration:$false -PublicFolderMigrat
ionComplete:$false -PublicFolderMailboxesLockedForNewConnections:$false -PublicFol
derMailboxesMigrationComplete:$false
```

8. Run the following commands from the on-premises Exchange Management Shell to capture information about the current public folder structure.

```
Get-PublicFolder -Recurse -ResultSize Unlimited | Export-CliXML OnPrem_PFStruc-
ture.xml
```

```
Get-PublicFolderStatistics -ResultSize Unlimited | Export-CliXML OnPrem_PFStatis-
tics.xml
```

```
Get-PublicFolder -Recurse -ResultSize Unlimited | Get-PublicFolderClientPermission
| Select-Object Identity,User -ExpandProperty AccessRights | Export-CliXML OnPrem_
PFPerms.xml
```

```
Get-MailPublicFolder -ResultSize Unlimited | Export-CliXML OnPrem_MEPF.xml
```

9. Run the following command from the on-premises Exchange Management Shell to capture Send-As permissions.

```
Get-MailPublicFolder -ResultSize Unlimited | Get-ADPermission | ? {($_.Extended-
Rights -Like "Send-As") -and ($_.IsInherited -eq $False) -and -not ($_.User -like
"*S-1-5-21-*")} | Select Identity,User | Export-Csv Send_As.csv -NoTypeInformation
```

10. Run the following script from the on-premises Exchange Management Shell to capture Send-On-Behalf permissions.

```
Get-MailPublicFolder | Select Alias,PrimarySmtpAddress,@
{N="GrantSendOnBehalfTo";E={$_.GrantSendOnBehalfTo -join "|"}} | Export-Csv Grant-
SendOnBehalfTo.csv -NoTypeInformation
```

```
$File = Import-Csv .\GrantSendOnBehalfTo.csv
$Data = @()
```

```
Foreach ($line in $File)
    {
    If ($line.GrantSendOnBehalfTo)
        {
        Write-Host -ForegroundColor Green "Processing Public Folder $($line.
Alias)"
        [array]$LineRecipients = $line.GrantSendOnBehalfTo.Split("|")
        Foreach ($Recipient in $LineRecipients)
            {
            Write-Host -ForegroundColor DarkGreen "    $($Recipient)"
            $GrantSendOnBehalfTo = (Get-Recipient $Recipient).PrimarySmtpAddress
            $LineData = New-Object PSCustomObject
            $LineData | Add-Member -Type NoteProperty -Name Alias -Value $line.
Alias
            $LineData | Add-Member -Type NoteProperty -Name PrimarySmtpAddress
-Value $line.PrimarySmtpAddress
            $LineData | Add-Member -Type NoteProperty -Name GrantSendOnBehalfTo
-Value $GrantSendOnBehalfTo
            $Data += $LineData
            }
        }
    }
$Data | Export-Csv .\GrantSendOnBehalfTo-Resolved.csv -NoTypeInformation
```

11. From the on-premises Exchange Management Shell, run the Export-ModernPublicFolderStatistics.ps1 script to create the initial statistics data you will use for the public folder mapping generator.

```
.\Export-ModernPublicFolderStatistics.pf1 PFStatistics.csv
```

12. From the on-premises Exchange Management Shell, run the ModernPublicFolderToMailboxMapGenerator.ps1 script to create the CSV file that maps public folder branches into individual public folder mailboxes.

   - The MailboxSize parameter specifies the maximum size each public folder mailbox should be.

   - The MailboxRecoverableItemsSize parameter is the recoverable items quota for Exchange Online mailboxes.

   - The ImportFile parameter specifies the public folder statistics file created in the previous step.

   - The ExportFile parameter specifies the output file that will contain the public folder top-level branch-to-public folder mailbox mapping.

```
.\ModernPublicFolderToMailboxMapGenerator.ps1 -MailboxSize 25GB -MailboxRecover-
ableItemsSize 1GB -ImportFile .\PFStatistics.csv -ExportFile PFmap.csv
```

13. From the Exchange Online PowerShell window, run the following commands to create the public folder mailboxes.

```
$mappings = Import-Csv PFMap.csv
$primaryMailboxName = ($mappings | Where-Object FolderPath -eq "\" ).TargetMailbox

New-Mailbox -HoldForMigration:$true -PublicFolder -IsExcludedFromServingHierarchy:
$false $primaryMailboxName

($mappings | Where-Object TargetMailbox -ne $primaryMailboxName).TargetMailbox |
Sort-Object -unique | ForEach-Object { New-Mailbox -PublicFolder -IsExcludedFromSe
rvingHierarchy:$false $_ }
```

14. From the on-premises Exchange Management Shell, run the following script and enter your Office 365 credential when prompted.

```
.\Sync-ModernMailPublicFolders.ps1 -Credential (Get-Credential)
-CsvSummaryFile:sync_summary.csv
```

15. From the on-premises Exchange Management Shell, run the following commands.

```
(Get-Mailbox <admin user>).legacyExchangeDN | Out-File .\MailboxLegacyExchangeDN.
txt

(Get-ExchangeServer <public folder server>).ExchangeLegacyDN | Out-File .\Server-
ExchangeLegacyDN.txt

$OAEndpoint = (Get-ExchangeServer).[0].ExternalHostNameHostnameString

$OAEndpoint | Out-File .\OAEndpoint.txt
```

16. Switch to the Windows PowerShell window connected to Exchange Online and ensure that you are in the C:\PFScripts directory, because that is where the output of the previous step's commands was saved. Run these commands in the Exchange Online PowerShell window:

```
cd \PFScripts
$OAEndopint = gc .\OAEndpoint.txt
$MailboxLegacyExchangeDN = gc .\MailboxLegacyExchangeDN.txt
$ServerExchangeLegacyDN = gc .\ServerExchangeLegacyDN.txt
$Credential = Get-Credential <domain\admin user>
```

The credential specified in the $Credential variable must be an on-premises administrator account in DOMAIN\Username format. If it is not in that format, the endpoint creation will fail with an authentication error.

17. Create the public folder migration endpoint in Exchange Online. From the Exchange Online PowerShell window, run the following command.

```
$PFEndpoint = New-MigrationEndpoint -PublicFolder -Name PublicFolderEndPoint
-RpcProxyServer $OAEndPoint -Credentials $Credential -SourceMailboxLegacyDN $Mail-
boxLegacyExchangeDN -PublicFolderDatabaseServerLegacyDN $ServerExchangeLegacyDN
-Authentication Basic
```

18. Create the public folder migration batch.

```
New-MigrationBatch -Name PublicFolderMigration -CSVData (Get-Content .\PFMap-
File.csv -Encoding Byte) -SourceEndpoint $PFEndpoint.Identity -NotificationEmails
<emailaddress>
```

19. To begin the migration, run the following command.

```
Start-MigrationBatch -Identity PublicFolderMigration
```

20. To check on the status of the migration, you can run:

```
Get-Migrationuser -BatchID PublicFolderMigration | Get-MigrationUserStatistics |
Select Identity,Status,SyncedItemCount,SkippedItemCount,BytesTransferred,Percentag
eComplete
```

21. After all mailboxes show the Synced status, you can complete the migration batch. To do this, lock the public folders on the source side first. From the on-premises Exchange Management Shell, run the following command.

```
Set-OrganizationConfig -PublicFoldersLockedForNewConnections $True
```

TROUBLESHOOTING

PublicFoldersLockedForNewConnections

If you cannot access the PublicFoldersLockedForNewConnections parameter, it could be that you did not prepare Active Directory during the Cumulative Update installation. From the Exchange Cumulative Update download, launch an elevated command prompt and run the following command.

```
Setup.exe /PrepareSchema /IAcceptExchangeServerLicenseTerms
```

22. After the PublicFoldersLockedForNewConnections parameter has replicated, run the following command from the Exchange Online PowerShell window.

```
Compete-MigrationBatch -Identity PublicFolderMigration
```

Post-migration configuration

After migrations have completed, you might need to reapply permissions, configure the location of public folders in both the Exchange cloud and on-premises organizations, and update the mail routing configuration.

Exchange Online public folder location

Update the organization settings to use Exchange Online as the public folder source.

From an Exchange Online PowerShell session, run the following commands.

```
Set-OrganizationConfig -PublicFoldersEnabled Local -RemotePublicFolderMailboxes $null
Get-Mailbox -PublicFolder | Set-Mailbox -PublicFolder -IsExcludedFromServingHierarchy
$false
Set-Mailbox -Identity <test user> -DefaultPublicFolderMailbox <public folder mail-
box1>
```

After waiting for a few minutes, log on to Outlook at the user specified in the -Identity parameter and access the public folders.

Exchange Online mail-enabled public folder routing

Depending on how the on-premises organization is configured and where the organization's
MX record is configured, you might need to perform one or more mail routing configurations.

If your MX record is pointed to Office 365, disable Directory-Based Edge Blocking (DBEB)
so that mail-enabled public folders can receive Internet mail. From the Exchange Online
PowerShell window, run the following command to disable DBEB.

```
Set-AcceptedDomain -Identity <domain.com> -DomainType InternalRelay
```

Exchange Online mail-enabled public folder external email address

If your on-premises public folders were migrated from Exchange 2013 or Exchange 2016, run
the following script to update the on-premises mail-enabled public folder objects with the
appropriate Exchange Online object. From the on-premises Exchange Management Shell, run
the following script from the C:\PFScripts directory.

```
.\SetMailPublicFolderExternalAddress.ps1 -ExecutionSummaryFile:mepf_summary.csv
```

Exchange on-premises mail routing domain

If your MX record points to an on-premises gateway, or on-premises systems send mail to mail-
enabled public folders in Exchange Online, you might need to configure the on-premises Office
365 connector to route messages for mail-enabled public folders over the Office 365 hybrid
transport connector. This step might not be necessary if you have disabled DBEB in Exchange
Online.

Modify the properties for the on-premises Outbound To Office 365 connector and add the
<tenant>.onmicrosoft.com domain that was created as part of the public folder migration
process.

Exchange on-premises public folder migration complete

Set the PublicFolderMigration property to true. From the on-premises Exchange Management
Shell, run the following command.

```
Set-OrganizationConfig -PublicFolderMigrationComplete $True
```

Apply Send-As permissions

From the Exchange Online PowerShell session, change to the C:\PFScripts directory containing
the exported Send-As permissions file (SendAs.csv) created during the migration process and
run the following script.

```
$SendAs = Import-Csv .\SendAs.csv
$i=1
foreach ($obj in $SendAs)
    {
    write-host "$($i)/$($SendAs.Count) adding $($obj.User) to $($obj.Identity)"
    Add-RecipientPermission -Identity $obj.Identity.Split("/")[2] -Trustee $obj.User.
Split("\")[1] -AccessRights SendAs -confirm:$false; $i++
    }
```

Apply Grant-Send-On-Behalf-To permissions

From the Exchange Online PowerShell session, change to the C:\PFScripts directory containing
the exported Send-On-Behalf permissions file (GrantSendOnBehalfTo-Resolved.csv) created
during the migration process and run the following script.

```
$GrantSendOnBehalfTo = Import-Csv .\GrantSendOnBehalfTo-Resolved.csv
$i=1
Foreach ($obj in $GrantSendOnBehalfTo)
    {
    Write-host "$($i)/$($grantsendonbehalfto.count) Granting $($obj.GrantSendOnBehalfTo)
Send-On-Behalf to folder $($obj.PrimarySmtpAddress)"
    Set-MailPublicFolder -Identity $obj.PrimarySmtpAddress -GrantSendOnBehalfTo $obj.
GrantSendOnBehalfTo
    $i++
    }
```

Troubleshooting

While migrating public folders, you might run into a number of kinds of errors, especially if your
organization has a long history of public folders. Here are common errors you might encounter
during migrations and how to resolve them.

- **Active Directory Operation Failed. The Object Already Exists.**

  Error text: 4/12/2017 6:11:16 PM,1a3a8d9e-0eb6-4b8a-bf00-a305f5229c2e,Update,"Active
  Directory operation failed on CY1PR14A001DC04.NAMPR13A001.PROD.OUTLOOK.COM.
  The object 'CN=FolderName,OU=tenant.onmicrosoft.com,OU=Microsoft Exchange
  Hosted Organizations,DC=NAMPR13A001,DC=PROD,DC=OUTLOOK,DC=COM' already
  exists.","Set-EXOMailPublicFolder -OnPremisesObjectId:""ae9563f4-1056-44c1-846a-
  c948c771720b"" -HiddenFromAddressListsEnabled:""False"" -ExternalEmailAddress:""Fo
  lderName@domain.com"" -Alias:""FolderName"" -EmailAddresses:@(""X400:C=US;A=
  ;P=ORG;O=Exchange;S=FolderName;"","""SMTP: FolderName@domain.com""","x500:/

O=ORG/OU=EXCHANGE/CN=RECIPIENTS/CN=FOLDERNAMEC89080BC4725C2AEEDFB 74A5292C16AE6F7CEE"","""smtp: FolderName@tenant.onmicrosoft.com""") -Name:""Folder Name"" -Identity:""CN=Folder Name,OU=tenant.onmicrosoft.com,OU=Microsoft Exchange Hosted Organizations,DC=NAMPR14A001,DC=PROD,DC=OUTLOOK,DC= COM"" -ErrorAction:""Stop"" -WindowsEmailAddress:""FolderName@domain.com"" -DisplayName:""Folder Name"""

Cause: This error appears in the CSVSummaryFile that Sync-MailPublicFolders.ps1 generates. It means there is a mail-enabled public folder and another mail-enabled public folder, mail-enabled group, contact, or user with one or more of the same values.

Resolution: You can use the following command in the on-premises Exchange Management Shell to locate it, replacing "Folder Name" with the value referenced in the error message:

```
Get-Recipient -anr "Folder Name"
```

- **Exceeded Maximum Number Of Corrupted Items**

    Error text: Error: This mailbox exceeded the maximum number of corrupted items that were specified for this move request.

    Cause: The number of corrupt or unreadable source items exceeded the BadItemLimit threshold.

    Resolution: Remove corrupt items in the source public folder(s) or increase the error threshold. Increasing the error threshold is the simpler solution (and the result is the same).

    ```
    Set-MigrationBatch -BadItemLimit 10000
    ```

- **Subscription Couldn't Be Loaded**

    Error text: WARNING: The subscription for the migration user <Mailbox> couldn't be loaded. The following error was encountered: A subscription wasn't found for this user.

    Cause: Transient error retrieving mailbox information from Office 365.

    Resolution: Non-fatal. This error usually resolves itself.

- **Make Sure Public Folder Access Is Locked**

    Error text: Before finalizing the migration, it is necessary to lock down public folders on the legacy Exchange server (downtime required). Make sure public folder access is locked on the legacy Exchange server and then try to complete the batch again.

    Cause: When running `Complete-MigrationBatch`, you might receive this error if you haven't updated the organization configuration to lock the public folders or have not waited long enough for the change to replicate.

Resolution: Wait for the `Set-OrganizationConfig` command to replicate. If you have not run it, run the following command in the on-premises Exchange Management Shell and wait 15 minutes before attempting to complete the migration.

```
Set-OrganizationConfig -PublicFoldersLockedForMigration $True
```

- **No Such Request Exists**

Error text: Couldn't find a request that matches the information provided. Reason: No such request exists.

Cause: Transient error when running Get-MigrationUser *<mailbox>* on a failed public folder mailbox. This error can happen during a database failover or while the mailbox request is being restarted.

Resolution: This error will resolve itself.

- **Public Folder "/Path" Could Not Be Mail-Enabled**

Error text: Public folder "/Path/To/Public Folder" could not be mail-enabled. This error message is displayed when reviewing the Get-MigrationUserStatistics report for a failed mailbox.

Cause: The mail-enabled public folder is missing required attributes.

Resolution: Launch the public folder administration tool and navigate to the public folder path specified in the error. Mail-disable the folder. Mail-enable the folder again, run Sync-MailPublicFolders.ps1 again, and restart the migration batch.

- **Public Folders Could Not Be Mail-Enabled**

Error text: Error: There are 30 Public Folders that could not be mail-enabled. Please, check the migration report starting at 4/9/2017 8:13:15 PM for additional details. This may indicate that mail public folder objects in Exchange Online are out of sync with your Exchange deployment. You may need to rerun the script Sync-MailPublicFolders.ps1 on your source Exchange server to update mail-enabled public folder objects in Exchange Online Active Directory.

Cause: The Microsoft Exchange System Objects container in Active Directory contains orphaned objects (objects without a parent path).

Solution: From the on-premises Exchange Management Shell, run the following script.

```
$resultsarray = @()
$mailpub = Get-MailPublicFolder -ResultSize unlimited
foreach ($folder in $mailpub) {
    $email       = $folder.primarysmtpaddress.local + "@" + $folder.primarysmtpad-
dress.domain
    $pubfolder   = Get-PublicFolder -Identity $folder.identity
    $folderpath  = $pubfolder.parentpath + "\" + $pubfolder.name
    # Create a new object for the purpose of exporting as a CSV
```

```
$pubObject = new-object PSObject
$pubObject | add-member -membertype NoteProperty -name "Email" -Value $email
$pubObject | add-member -membertype NoteProperty -name "FolderPath" -Value $fol-
derpath
  # Append this iteration of our for loop to our results array.
  $resultsarray += $pubObject
}

$resultsarray | export-csv -Path .\mail-enabled-public-folders.csv -NoType

$NoPublicFolderPath = Import-Csv C:\Temp\mail-enabled-public-folders.csv | ? {
$_.Parentpath -eq "" } | Export-Csv .\NoFolderPath.csv -NoType
```

Launch Active Directory Users And Computers, enable View Advanced Features, and navigate to the Microsoft Exchange System Objects container. Review the NoFolderPath. csv and remove the corresponding items in the Microsoft Exchange System Objects container. Run Sync-MailPublicFolders.ps1 again and then restart the migration batch.

Mailbox provisioning

When the hybrid configuration is complete, new mailboxes can be provisioned directly in Exchange Online from the Exchange Management Shell. These new mailboxes are provisioned as *remote mailboxes*. The remote mailbox is a special type of mail-enabled user. In Exchange Server 2010, the objects are referred to as *remote mailboxes*. In Exchange Server 2013 and Exchange Server 2016, the display name has changed to Office 365 Mailbox.

The following steps illustrate how to create a new user and remote mailbox in one step or enable an existing user as a remote mailbox with Exchange Management Shell. In either case, after the next AAD Sync cycle is run, a temporary 30-day mailbox is created. The mailbox then must be licensed in Office 365 to make it a fully functional mailbox.

1. Launch a browser and connect to the Exchange Admin Center for the on-premises Exchange organization.

2. Navigate to Recipients | Mailboxes.

3. Click the plus sign (+) and select Office 365 mailbox, as shown in Figure 13-47.

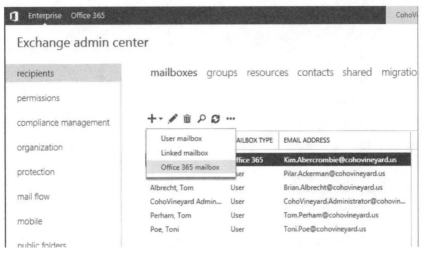

Figure 13-47 Creating a new Office 365 mailbox

4. Fill out the new Office 365 Mailbox page with the required attributes as shown in Figure 13-48.

The email address policy that the Hybrid Configuration Wizard updated creates the proper proxy address for the remote mailbox and sets its remote routing address to the Exchange Online organization.

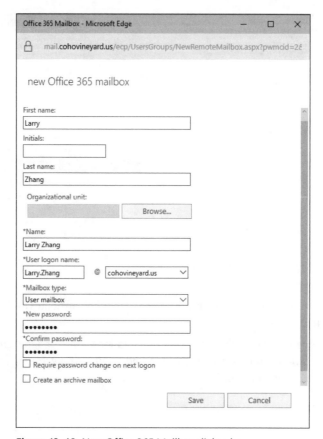

Figure 13-48 New Office 365 Mailbox dialog box

5. Click Save.

The Exchange Admin Center shows the newly created Active Directory user account with an Office 365 mailbox. See Figure 13-49.

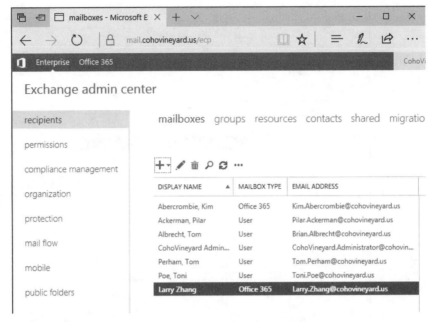

Figure 13-49 Recipients page showing new Office 365 mailbox

6. Double-click the newly created user and select the Email Address tab as shown in
    Figure 13-50. View the email address details, including the remote routing address. Click
    Cancel.

Figure 13-50 User email address properties

Decommissioning the hybrid environment

After all migrations have been completed, depending on the mail flow configuration, many existing Exchange servers can be decommissioned.

Unless your organization is completely removing AAD Connect and moving to a cloud-only identity management scenario, it is strongly recommended to keep a minimum of one Exchange server on-premises for attribute management and mailbox provisioning. Additional servers might be required for fault tolerance and disaster recovery or if mail flow is still occurring from on-premises systems through the Exchange servers for secure mail flow to Exchange Online.

If you decide that you want to remove your entire Exchange environment, including the hybrid components, you must remove or disable the following items.

- Inbound and outbound hybrid connectors in Exchange Online

- The O365 to On-Premises Organization Relationship in Office 365

- Intra-Organization connectors if OAuth has been configured

- Hybrid configuration object

For more information about decommissioning scenarios, please see *https://technet.microsoft .com/en-us/library/dn931280(v=exchg.150).aspx*, "How and when to decommission your on-premises Exchange servers in a hybrid deployment."

Summary

This chapter discussed the planning and configuration aspects of an Exchange hybrid environment, including Autodiscover, free/busy, name resolution, networking, transport, and public folders, as well as migration tasks to and from the Exchange Online environment.

The configuration of an Exchange Online hybrid environment enables your organization to transition seamlessly from a current or older on-premises environment to Office 365 while maintaining mail flow and operational management capabilities. Hybrid configurations might also provide value for organizations migrating from non-Exchange systems to Office 365 by enabling secure mail transport and integrated provisioning with Active Directory.

CHAPTER 13

Managing Exchange Online

Whether you have performed a greenfield deployment to Exchange Online, started or completed a migration (or are somewhere in between), at some point, you'll need to administer the environment.

This chapter is divided into sections based on the areas you typically need to manage:

- Recipients

- Transport services

- Organization settings

- Auditing

- Hybrid configuration

Although many of the settings can be configured inside the Exchange Admin Center, some tasks are quicker to perform or can only be achieved through Windows PowerShell.

Exchange Admin Center

If you are familiar with managing Exchange Server on-premises, the Exchange Admin Center in Office 365, as shown in Figure 14-1, should feel familiar.

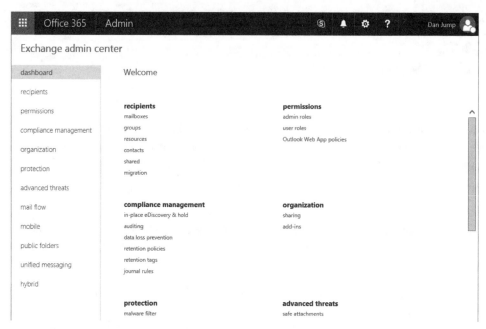

Figure 14-1 Exchange Admin Center in Office 365

The layout of the Exchange Admin Center is very similar to the Exchange Admin Center for Exchange Server, displayed in Figure 14-2, with just a few feature changes.

They both are styled very similarly, with the Office 365 or Exchange Online version of the Admin Center displaying a dashboard (and, optionally, Advanced Threats if your tenant has the appropriate service plans), whereas the on-premises Exchange Server version has menu items for Servers and Tools. Because you are not responsible for the underlying server health in Office 365, there is no need to expose the Servers and Tools options in Office 365.

The admin center available for Exchange Server also has two tabs at the top—Enterprise and Office 365—to enable you to enter credentials and switch back and forth between the two environments inside a single management interface.

For more information on the Exchange Admin Center for Office 365, see Chapter 6, "The Office 365 Portal, Dashboard, and Admin Centers."

Figure 14-2 Exchange Server Admin Center for Exchange Server

Recipient management

Most of the things that you will be administering in Office 365 are recipients of some sort—whether they are mailboxes, mail-enabled users, contacts, or one of the types of distribution groups. For more information on the various types of recipients in Office 365, please see Chapter 11, "Understanding the Office 365 Resource Types."

This next section gives you some ideas about tasks that you can perform against the various recipient types in Office 365.

Mailboxes

User mailboxes can contain mail, folders, calendars, contacts, tasks, and rules, and their management rights can be delegated to others.

Permissions and rights

One of the most common tasks you will perform is manage permissions or rights for a mailbox. Here are some common scenarios.

Grant full-mailbox access

With full mailbox access, the delegate can perform any mailbox management task that the original owner can perform, such as creating or deleting folders or moving messages.

To grant full mailbox access for the mailbox Ayla Kol to the user Dan Jump, you can add the permission through the admin center by navigating to Recipients, selecting a recipient, clicking the Edit (pencil) icon, and then selecting Mailbox Delegation, as shown in Figure 14-3.

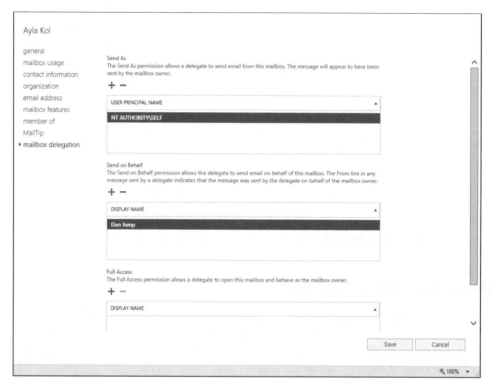

Figure 14-3 Mailbox delegation

Click the plus sign (+) under Full Access, add the user from the picker to whom you wish to grant access, and then click Save.

TROUBLESHOOTING

AutoMapping and that extra mailbox

If you have configured full mailbox access permission for a mailbox in the Exchange Admin Center, your users might report that the mailbox is automatically appearing in their Outlook profile and that they have no way to close or disconnect it.

This happens because the Exchange Admin Center enables AutoMapping when it is used to grant full mailbox access. AutoMapping is an Exchange feature that automatically mounts mailboxes for which a user has full mailbox access. When a mailbox is automatically added, the user has no way to remove it. This can be a useful feature, but many people find it undesirable—especially if they only administer a secondary mailbox occasionally.

To remove an automatically mounted mailbox from an Outlook profile, remove the Full Access permissions entry and re-add it through Windows PowerShell, using this syntax:

```
Remove-MailboxPermission -Identity <mailbox> -User <delegate> -AccessRights
FullAccess
```

```
Add-MailboxPermission -Identity <mailbox> -User <delegate> -AccessRights Ful-
lAccess -InheritanceType None
```

For more information about adding mailbox permissions, see *https://technet.microsoft.com/en-us/library/bb124097(v=exchg.160).aspx*, "Add-MailboxPermission."

Grant Send-On-Behalf or Send-As permission

If your users need to perform activities as another mailbox, such as sending mail, then you must grant them Send-On-Behalf or Send-As permissions. A common scenario is to include sending as a shared mailbox (such as Sales) to mask the sender.

Users access the Send-As and Send-On-Behalf-Of feature in the same way—by exposing the From field in Outlook and then entering the address of the mailbox they're acting as. The difference is in how the recipient sees it. Messages sent on behalf of someone else include both the sender and the original mailbox owner's name in the From line (such as "From Ayla on behalf of Dan"), whereas messages sent using the Send As permission show the mailbox owner as the sender.

Both Send-On-Behalf and Send-As can be granted from the Mailbox Delegation page in the Exchange Admin Center, as shown previously in Figure 14-3, or through Windows PowerShell.

```
Add-RecipientPermission -Identity <mailbox> -GrantSendOnBehalfTo <delegate>
Add-RecipientPermission -Identity <mailbox> -AccessRight SendAs -Trustee <delegate>
```

For more information on managing recipient permissions, see *https://technet.microsoft.com/en-us/library/ff935839(v=exchg.160).aspx*.

Folder permissions

If you configure shared mailboxes to be used as calendars, or want to update calendar permissions for your users, you can use the Add-MailboxFolderPermission or Set-MailboxFolderPermission cmdlets. Although you can use the *MailboxFolderPermission cmdlets to manage the permissions on any folder in the mailbox, the most common usage for it is to manage the calendar. You can specify the folder by using the `<mailbox>:\Folder` syntax.

Table 14-1 lists the individual permissions you can assign.

Table 14-1 Folder permissions

Permission	Description
CreateItems	The user can create items in the specified folder.
CreateSubfolders	The user can create subfolders in the specified folder.
DeleteAllItems	The user can delete all items in the specified folder.
DeleteOwnedItems	The user can only delete items that they created from the specified folder.
EditAllItems	The user can edit all items in the specified folder.
EditOwnedItems	The user can only edit items that they created in the specified folder.
FolderContact	The user is the contact for the specified public folder.
FolderOwner	The user is the owner of the specified folder. The user can view the folder, move the folder, and create subfolders. The user can't read items, edit items, delete items, or create items.
FolderVisible	The user can view the specified folder but can't read or edit items in the specified public folder.
ReadItems	The user can read items in the specified folder.

The permissions are grouped into roles, which can also be assigned using the Add-MailboxFolderPermission or Set-MailboxFolderPermission cmdlet. Table 14-2 lists the roles and their associated permissions.

Table 14-2 Roles and permissions

Role	Permissions
Author	CreateItems, DeleteOwnedItems, EditOwnedItems, FolderVisible, ReadItems
Contributor	CreateItems, FolderVisible
Editor	CreateItems, DeleteAllItems, DeleteOwnedItems, EditAllItems, EditOwnedItems, FolderVisible, ReadItems
None	FolderVisible

Role	Permissions
NonEditingAuthor	CreateItems, FolderVisible, ReadItems
Owner	CreateItems, CreateSubfolders, DeleteAllItems, DeleteOwnedItems, EditAllItems, EditOwnedItems, FolderContact, FolderOwner, FolderVisible, ReadItems
PublishingEditor	CreateItems, CreateSubfolders, DeleteAllItems, DeleteOwnedItems, EditAllItems, EditOwnedItems, FolderVisible, ReadItems
PublishingAuthor	CreateItems, CreateSubfolders, DeleteOwnedItems, EditOwnedItems, FolderVisible, ReadItems
Reviewer	FolderVisible, ReadItems
AvailabilityOnly	View only availability data (only applicable to Calendar folder)
LimitedDetails	View availability data with subject and location (only applicable to Calendar folder)

The following examples illustrate how to manage the permissions.

Grant Ayla Kol the ability to create items on Dan Jump's calendar, using permissions granted in the Author role.

```
Add-MailboxFolderPermission -Identity DanJump:\Calendar -AccessRights Author -User
AylaKol
```

Change the default permission for all calendars from AvailabilityOnly to LimitedDetails.

```
Get-Mailbox -ResultSize Unlimited | % { Set-MailboxFolderPermission -Identity "$($_.
Alias):\Calendar" -User Default -AccessRights LimitedDetails }
```

For more information on folder permissions cmdlets, see *https://technet.microsoft.com/en-us /library/dd298062(v=exchg.160).aspx*, "Add-MailboxFolderPermission."

Email addresses

All the addresses that a mailbox can receive mail as are listed in the EmailAddresses attribute. The name of the underlying attribute in Active Directory (and Azure Active Directory) is proxyAddresses.

If your objects are authored in the cloud, you can modify the EmailAddresses attribute. If they are synchronized from an on-premises environment, you must modify the mail-enabled user object or remote mailbox object from that environment. In either scenario, the syntax is the same—simply replace "mailbox" in the cmdlet with "remotemailbox."

To add a proxy address to a user mailbox, use:

```
Set-Mailbox TerryAdams -EmailAddresses @{add="tadams@cohovineyardandwinery.com"}
```

You can also replace all the proxy addresses by using a different syntax for the -EmailAddresses parameter.

```
Set-Mailbox TerryAdams -EmailAddresses @("SMTP:terryadams@cohovineyardandwinery.com",
"tadams@cohovineyardandwinery.com", "terrya@cohovineyardandwinery.com")
```

INSIDE OUT
Using SMTP and smtp

When working with the EmailAddresses parameter in the second example, you have the opportunity to specify the primary SMTP address, using the SMTP: prefix. The uppercase SMTP: prefix in the EmailAddresses array designates which address will be primary in the array. If you do not pick one, Set-Mailbox uses the first value in the array as the primary SMTP address.

Automatic calendar processing

When you create shared mailboxes for equipment or conference rooms, you might not be able to enter all the configuration parameters that accurately describe how the resource is to be used. One of those areas might be calendar processing.

Calendar processing controls how the Calendar Attendant or Resource Booking Attendant manages meetings for a given mailbox. For example, you have options to control who is allowed to book a conference room, whether recurring meetings will be accepted, or whether meetings need to be approved by a delegate.

By default, user mailboxes have calendar processing set to AutoUpdate, and resource mailboxes have calendar processing set to AutoAccept.

With calendar automation, requests fall into two classes:

- **In-policy requests**   In-policy requests don't violate any of the resource scheduling options, such as conflicts or duration.

- **Out-of-policy requests**   Out-of-policy requests violate one or more resource scheduling options.

Seven settings work together to form the foundation of booking policies.

AllBookInPolicy   Everyone can automatically reserve a resource with a valid, in-policy meeting request. The default setting is $True.

BookInPolicy   Use this setting to specify a list of users who can automatically book a resource with a valid, in-policy meeting request if AllBookInPolicy is set to $False.

AllRequestInPolicy   Everyone can request to reserve the resource with a valid, in-policy meeting request. The request is routed to the value stored in the mailbox's ResourceDelegates property. The default setting is $false.

RequestInPolicy   Use this setting to specify a list of users who can request to reserve a resource with a valid, in-policy meeting request. The request is routed to the value stored in the mailbox's ResourceDelegates property.

AllRequestOutOfPolicy   Everyone can reserve a resource with a valid, in-policy meeting request. If the meeting request violates the policy defined in the scheduling options, the request can be approved by one of the mailbox's resource delegates, stored in the mailbox's ResourceDelegates property. The default value is $false.

RequestOutOfPolicy   Use this setting to specify a list of users who can automatically reserve a resource with a valid, in-policy meeting request. If the request violates the policy defined in the scheduling options, the request can be approved by one of the mailbox's resource delegates, stored in the ResourceDelegates property.

ResourceDelegates   This setting is for users who can approve or decline meeting requests on behalf of a resource mailbox.

Here are some examples of how you might configure the Room1 conference room.

Enable Room1 to accept meeting requests from people outside the organization. This might be useful if you have a facility with public meeting rooms, such as a library, that you want to allow people who are outside the organization to schedule.

```
Set-CalendarProcessing -Identity Room1 -ProcessExternalMeetingMessages $True
```

Specify additional text to be sent back to a meeting organizer when the resource is booked.

```
Set-CalendarProcessing -Identity Room1 -AddAditionalResponse $True -AdditionalResponse
"Your room has been successfully booked. Please arrive at least 5 minutes prior to your
scheduled meeting."
```

Choose to retain attachments on resource mailboxes. By default, attachments to meeting requests are deleted.

```
Set-CalendarProcessing -Identity Room1 -DeleteAttachments $False
```

Allow only members of the mail-enabled Marketing security group to be able to schedule meetings in Room1.

```
Set-CalendarProcessing -Identity Room1 -BookInPolicy Marketing -AllBookInPolicy $False
```

Allow only members of the mail-enabled Marketing security group to be able to schedule meetings in Room1, but allow members of the mail-enabled security group Sales to be able to schedule a meeting with the delegate's approval. Finally, set Lori Penor as the delegate.

```
Set-CalendarProcessing -Identity Room1 -BookInPolicy Marketing -AllBookInPolicy $False
-RequestInPolicy Sales -ResourceDelegates LoriPenor
```

For more information about the Calendar Attendant and Resource Booking Attendant, please see *https://technet.microsoft.com/en-US/library/ms.exch.eac.EditEquipmentMailbox _ResourceDelegates(EXCHG.150).aspx*, "Set scheduling permissions for an equipment mailbox."

Mail-enabled users

As discussed in Chapter 11, a mail-enabled user is a security principal (an object that has an account and could log on to a system) that has the mail properties of a contact applied to it.

Mail-enabled users can have many of the same properties that a mailbox user can, but it is only a routing entity from the global address list's point of view. The core properties of a mail enabled user are:

- **msExchRecipientDisplayType**   This property is set to 6.

- **msExchRecipientTypeDetails**   This property is set to 128.

- **mail**   This property is set to an email address, either inside or outside of your environment's authoritative domain name space.

- **targetAddress**   This property is set to an email address, typically outside of your environment's authoritative name space.

For example, you can create a mail-enabled user with the following syntax.

```
New-MailUser -Name "Jeff Hay" -FirstName Jeff -LastName Hay -ExternalEmailAddress jef-
fhay@cohovineyard.com -MicrosoftOnlineServicesID jeffhay@cohovineyardandwinery.onmicro-
soft.com
```

The user account would have a primary SMTP address matching the value for ExternalEmailAddress, and you would be able to sign in to the Office 365 service with the password you assigned to it. Because mail-enabled users are security principals and mail recipients, they can be granted management permissions on objects as well as become members of distribution lists.

Contacts

Contacts are designed to give representation only to mail objects inside the global address list. They are recipients and can be made members of distribution groups but cannot be granted management rights or permissions, nor can a contact object be used to log on to Office 365.

Contacts can be created from the Exchange Admin Center or through Windows PowerShell.

```
New-MailContact -FirstName Tanja -LastName Plate -Name "Tanya Plate" -ExternalEmailAd-
dress tanya@tailspintoys.com
```

Distribution groups

Distribution groups are collections of objects designed to make addressing simpler. Office 365 has several kinds of groups. The types of groups, as well as cmdlets used to add and remove members, are discussed in Chapter 11.

Restricting delivery

At some point, you might need to restrict sending to either users or groups. You can set different types of restrictions, including allowing or prohibiting sending to users and groups, or ensure that content goes through review (perhaps by a manager) before being delivered to recipients.

Restrict delivery from outside senders

You can configure both users and distribution groups to accept mail only from internal users. To do this, you can set the RequireSenderAuthenticationEnabled property to $True, as shown in the following examples.

```
Set-Mailbox TerryAdams -RequireSenderAuthentication $True
```

```
Set-DistributionGroup "Quality Control" -RequireSenderAuthentication $True
```

> ### OFFICE 365 GROUPS AND ANONYMOUS SENDERS
>
> Although configuring delivery from anonymous senders can be easily managed using the RequireSenderAuthenticationEnabled property, there is a set of conditions under which it will not work correctly.
>
> - Office 365 Group Writeback is enabled.
> - RequireSenderAuthenticationEnabled is set to False for an Office 365 group.
> - The organization's MX record is configured to point on-premises.

In this scenario, external emails sent to Office 365 Groups are returned to sender with the error, "You do not have permission to send to this recipient." This happens because the RequireSenderAuthenticationEnabled property is set to the constant value TRUE in the AAD Connect rule. To enable sending to Office 365 groups in this scenario, you must modify the msExchRequireAuthToSendTo attribute for the on-premises group object created by the AAD Connect Group Writeback feature.

Restrict delivery to allowed senders

You can also restrict delivery to users or distribution lists to usage by named individuals by using the AcceptMessagesOnlyFrom parameter. The following example configures the All Employees distribution group to allow only Lori Penor to send to it.

```
Set-DistributionGroup "All Employees" -AcceptMessagesOnlyFrom LoriPenor@cohovineyardan-
dwinery.com
```

If you want to grant a group send-to permissions (instead of a user), you can use the AcceptMessagesOnlyFromDLMembers parameter, and, if you want to restrict sending to a user or group by using a combination of named users and group memberships, you can use the AcceptMessagesOnlyFromSendersOrMembers.

> ### NOTE
> The AcceptMessagesOnlyFromSendersOrMembers overwrites the values in AcceptMessagesOnlyFromDLMembers and AcceptMessagesOnlyFrom.

Moderate messages sent to a group

You can also configure moderation for a distribution group. Messages sent to a distribution group are first routed to the listed moderator for approval. You can configure moderation by using the ModerationEnabled and ModeratedBy parameters, as shown in the following example.

```
Set-DistributionGroup "Ask the CEO" -ModerationEnabled $True -ModeratedBy DanJump
```

Require approval for messages sent to a user

You can configure a transport rule to redirect messages to another user (such as a manager) prior to delivery.

To configure a rule redirecting all messages by using the Exchange Admin Center, follow these steps.

1. In the Exchange Admin Center, select Mail Flow | Rules.

2. Click the plus sign (+) and then select Create A New Rule.

3. In the Name box, enter a name for the rule.

4. In the Apply This Rule If drop-down list, select The Recipient Is and then choose a name from the Select Members dialog box.

5. In the Do The Following drop-down list, select Forward The Message For Approval To and then choose a name from the Select Members dialog box.

6. Click Save.

To configure a transport rule to redirect all messages intended for Ayla Kol to Dan Jump for approval, using Windows PowerShell, use the following command.

```
New-TransportRule -SentTo AylaKol -ModerateMessageByUser DanJump -Name 'Moderate Mes-
sages Sent to ''Ayla Kol''' -StopRuleProcessing:$false -Mode 'Enforce' -RuleErrorAction
'Ignore' -SenderAddressLocation 'Header'
```

As with any transport rule, you can add additional conditions and exceptions to meet your requirements.

Transport

For many organizations that move to Office 365, the default mail routing configuration is sufficient. In the default Office 365 mail flow, all outbound mail goes directly to the Internet from Office 365, and inbound mail is received directly from the Internet (if your MX record is pointed to Office 365), from your on-premises environment (if you have on-premises applications or mailboxes delivering through a hybrid environment), or both.

Connectors

Connectors are configuration objects that direct mail flow. In Office 365, connectors go in two directions: inbound (in to Office 365) and outbound (out from Office 365). These map to the on-premises receive (into the Exchange environment) and send (out to other servers or systems) connectors. If you have a hybrid environment, you have inbound and outbound connectors in Office 365 and send and receive connectors in your Exchange on-premises environments.

To manage connectors, you can navigate to the Exchange Admin Center and select Mail Flow | Connectors. By default, Exchange Online has no connectors and routes mail directly to the Internet.

You can control the path that a connector takes or restrict it to handle traffic only for certain domains. Exchange automatically uses the connector with the most specific match. Consider the following configuration.

```
PS C:\> Get-OutboundConnector

Name            RecipientDomains            SmartHosts   Enabled
----            ----------------            ----------   -------
Coho Vineyard   {cohovineyard.com}          {[1.2.3.4]}  True
Marketing       {marketing.cohovineyard.com} {[5.6.7.8]}  True
```

If you sent a message to TerryAdams@marketing.cohovineyard.com, the message would use the connector marketing.cohovineyard.com with the smart host 5.6.7.8, because the email address domain marketing.cohovineyard.com is an exact match for the Marketing connector.

Transport rules

Transport rules are a set of logic that can be applied to messages as they pass through the system to influence which route a message might take or other actions that can happen to a message based on sender, recipient, or contents in the header or message body.

Transport rules are made up of three parts:

- **Conditions** Conditions are settings or properties under which a particular rule is applied. Conditions might specify senders or recipients; sensitive information types; contents in the subject, body, or header; attachments; or other message properties. Conditions are also referred to as predicates in some documentation.

- **Actions** Actions specify which functions are performed on a message. Actions might include forwarding a copy of a message to another recipient, redirecting the message to a new recipient, applying encryption, redirecting the message to a designated connector, or rejecting the message.

- **Exceptions** Exceptions are conditions or properties under which a particular rule is blocked or skipped. For example, you might configure a rule to add recipients to the Cc line if the subject is Sales Order but make an exception if the subject contains the text RE: at the beginning.

You configure transport rules on the Mail Flow page (Figure 14-4) in the Exchange Admin Center or through Windows PowerShell.

To create a rule, click the plus sign (+) and select from the available options, as shown in Figure 14-5. The drop-down list has a number of available rule templates, or you can select Create A New Rule to start with a blank rule.

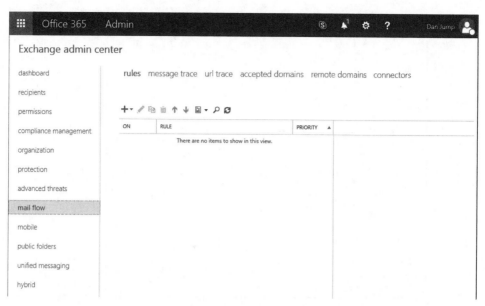

Figure 14-4 Mail flow rules

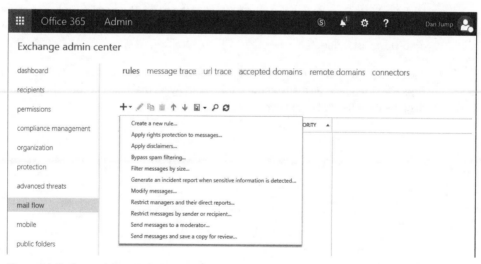

Figure 14-5 Create A New Rule

When you create a new rule, it might seem like there aren't a lot of choices for actions (see Figure 14-6).

CHAPTER 14

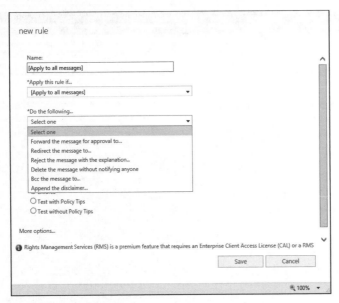

Figure 14-6 New Rule page

Click the More Options link near the bottom of the page. The page refreshes to show the Except If button to specify rule exceptions, and the list of available actions under the Do The Following drop-down list is updated.

You can then create the rule, using all the available predicates and actions. The rule shown in Figure 14-7 redirects all mail intended for Lori to Ayla's mailbox, except if the messages are of the type Read Receipt or are over 2 MB in size.

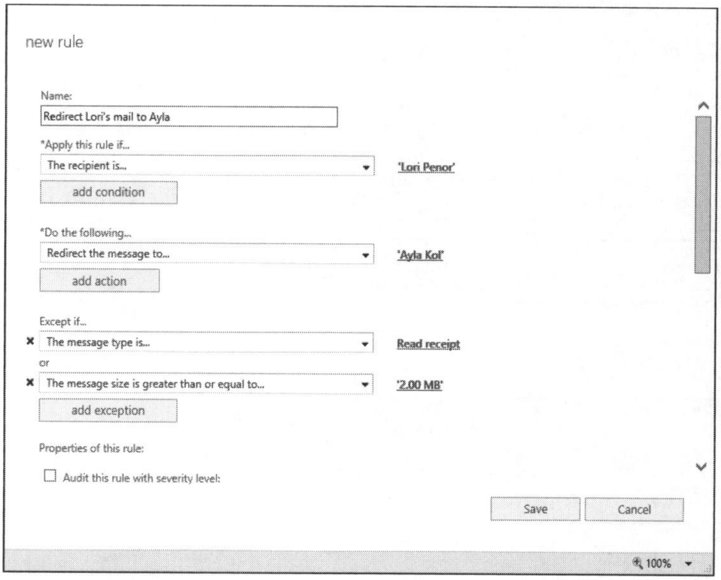

Figure 14-7 Mail redirect rule

You can also create the same rule with Windows PowerShell by using the New-TransportRule cmdlet.

```
New-TransportRule -SentTo LoriPenor@cohovineyardandwinery.onmicrosoft.com -Redirect-
MessageTo AylaKol@cohovineyardandWinery.onmicrosoft.com -ExceptIfMessageTypeMatches
'ReadReceipt' -ExceptIfMessageSizeOver 2MB -Name 'Redirect Lori''s mail to Ayla'
-StopRuleProcessing:$false -SetAuditSeverity 'DoNotAudit' -Mode 'Enforce' -RuleErrorAc-
tion 'Ignore' -SenderAddressLocation 'Header'
```

Attachment blocking

Attachment blocking occurs when your organization might wish to block all attachments or all attachments of a certain type.

In this example, you can block a message with attachments based on type, using a malware filter rule.

On the Mail Flow page, select Protection | Malware Filter and then click the plus sign (+) to add a new filter, as shown in Figure 14-8.

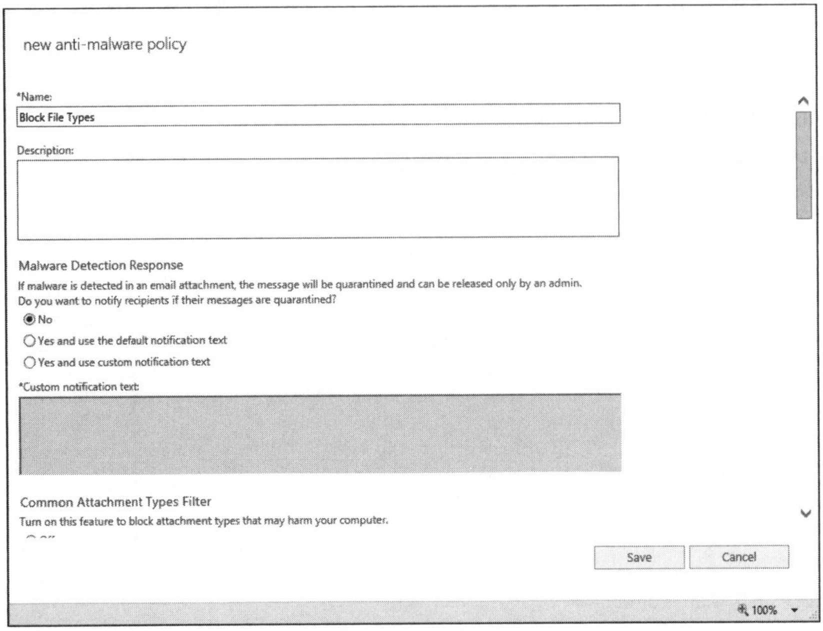

Figure 14-8 New Anti-Malware Policy page

Scroll down to the File Types list box and click the plus sign (+) to add a new file type to the list. You can select from the default file types. Click OK to add the file type, add a condition under Applied To, and then click Save to save the rule.

If you want to add a file type that is not present in the file types list, you must either create the rule in Windows PowerShell, using the New-MalwareFilterPolicy cmdlet, or edit one that you have already created, using the Set-MalwareFilterPolicy cmdlet.

For example, to add the ZIP file type to the malware filter policy created in Figure 14-8, you can run this command:

```
[array]$FileTypes = (Get-MalwareFilterPolicy "Block File Types").FileTypes
$FileTypes += "zip"
Set-MalwareFilterPolicy "Block File Types" -FileTypes $FileTypes
You can then view the malware filter policy to make sure your file type has been added.
Get-MalwareFilterPolicy "Block File Types" | Select -ExpandProperty FileTypes
ace
ani
app
docm
exe
jar
reg
scr
```

```
vbe
vbs
zip
```

To create a policy that blocks all attachments, you can use a transport rule.

1. In the Exchange Admin Center, under Mail Flow, select Rules, click the plus sign (+), and select Create New Rule.

2. In the Name box, specify a name for the rule and then click More Options.

3. Select the Any Attachment Is Greater Than Or Equal To condition and then type a size of 1 KB.

4. Configure an action and click Save.

Although 1 KB will detect most attachments, there might still be some that get through. You can modify the policy in Windows PowerShell by using the `Set-TransportRule` cmdlet:

```
Set-TransportRule <Rule> -AttachmentSizeOver 1B
```

Many senders, however, have images in their email signatures that, depending on the formatting of the message, might be inserted as attachments. This setting renders those undeliverable, so make sure you understand your organization's requirements before configuring this.

Encryption

You can configure Office 365 Message Encryption to enable users to send encrypted messages to users inside or outside the organization. Common scenarios for message encryption might be to enable encryption if certain keywords are detected in the message or subject, or certain sensitive information types are present.

To use encryption, Azure Rights Management Services (RMS) licenses must be applied to users, the Rights Management service must be enabled in your tenant, and you must have created transport rules to apply encryption.

Users who receive an encrypted message are prompted to sign in to the Office 365 encryption portal to view them. From there, users can read and reply to the secure messages.

CHAPTER 14

Activate Azure Rights Management

You can activate Azure Rights Management either from the Office 365 Admin Center or through Windows PowerShell. To enable Azure Rights Management from the Office 365 Admin Center, follow these steps.

1.   Log on to the Office 365 Admin Center with an account that has been assigned the Global Admin role.

2.   Select Settings | Services & Add-Ins and then select Microsoft Azure Information Protection, as shown in Figure 14-9.

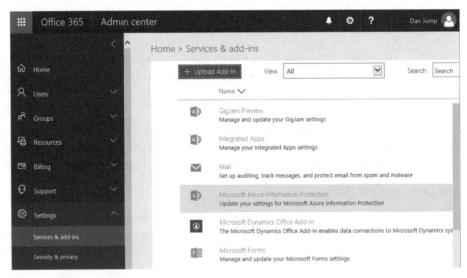

Figure 14-9 Microsoft Azure Information Protection

3.   Click Manage Microsoft Azure Information Protection Settings to open the Rights Management page, shown in Figure 14-10.

Figure 14-10 Rights Management page

4. Click Activate.

5. In the Do You Want To Activate Rights Management dialog box, click Activate.

6. Determine your RMS key sharing location by using the informatioin Table 14-3.

Table 14-3 RMS Online key sharing locations

Tenant Location	RMS Online key sharing location
North America	https://sp-rms.na.aadrm.com/TenantManagement /ServicePartner.svc
European Union	https://sp-rms.eu.aadrm.com/TenantManagement /ServicePartner.svc
Asia	https://sp-rms.ap.aadrm.com/TenantManagement /ServicePartner.svc
South America	https://sp-rms.sa.aadrm.com/TenantManagement /ServicePartner.svc
Office 365 for Government (Government Community Cloud)	https://sp-rms.govus.aadrm.com/TenantManagement /ServicePartner.svc

7. From Exchange Online PowerShell, run the following cmdlet, replacing the value for RMSOnlineKeySharingLocation with the value best suited for your deployment.

```
Set-IRMConfiguration -RMSOnlineKeySharingLocation <RMS Online key sharing location>
```

8. Import the Trusted Publishing Domain from RMS Online by using the following command:

```
Import-RMSTrustedPublishingDomain -RMSOnline -name "RMS Online"
```

9. Enable IRM with the following command:

```
Set-IRMConfiguration -InternalLicensingEnabled $True
```

Create rule to encrypt messages

After Information Rights Management has been enabled and configured in your tenant, you can configure transport rules to apply encryption to messages. To create an Office 365 Message Encryption rule in the Exchange Admin Center that will encrypt messages sent to recipients outside the organization if the subject contains the keyword #encrypt, follow these steps.

1. In the Exchange Admin Center, select Mail Flow | Rules.

2. Click the plus sign (+) | Apply Rights Protection To Messages.

3. In the Name box, enter a name for the rule.

4. In the Apply This Rule If drop-down list, select The Subject Matches and then type **#encrypt**. Click the plus sign (+) and then click OK.

5. In the Do The Following drop-down list, point to Modify The Message Security and then select Apply Office 365 Message Encryption, as shown in Figure 14-11.

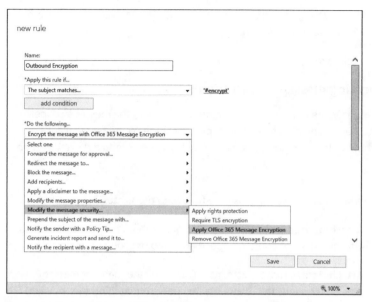

Figure 14-11 Applying an Office 365 Message Encryption rule

6. Click Save.

Create rule to decrypt messages

When a user receives an encrypted message in the Office 365 encryption portal, they can respond to the message there as well. You might want to configure Office 365 to decrypt those messages automatically so your internal users don't have to sign in to the encryption portal to review encrypted messages.

> **NOTE**
>
> You can only decrypt messages that are sent within your organization or that are replies to messages sent from your organization. You cannot automatically decrypt messages that originate outside your organization.

To create a rule to remove Office 365 Message Encryption, follow these steps.

1. In the Exchange Admin Center, navigate to Mail Flow | Rules.

2. Click the plus sign (+) and then select Create A New Rule.

3. In the Apply This Rule If drop-down list, point to The Recipient Is Located and select Inside This Organization.

4. Under Do the Following, point to Modify The Message Security and select Remove Office 365 Message Encryption.

5. Click Save.

Inspecting message attachments

Exchange Online transport rules can not only look at the message properties when determining how to handle them, but can also inspect message content—even if it's buried inside another attachment (for example, a Microsoft Excel workbook inserted in a Word document or inside a ZIP file).

To use these features, you can use the following predicates.

- **AttachmentContainsWords**   This predicate matches messages with supported file type attachments that contain a specified string or group of characters.

- **AttachmentMatchesPatterns**   This predicate matches messages with supported file type attachments that contain a text pattern matching the specified regular expression.

- **AttachmentNameMatchesPatterns**   This predicate matches messages with attachments whose file name contains the characters specified.

- **AttachmentExtensionMatchesWords**   This predicate matches messages with attachments with the specified file name extension.

- **AttachmentSizeOver**   This predicate matches messages with attachments that are greater than or equal to the size specified.

- **AttachmentProcessingLimitExceeded**   This predicate matches messages when an attachment is not inspected by the transport rules agent.

- **AttachmentHasExecutableContent**   This predicate matches messages that contain executable files as attachments.

- **AttachmentIsPasswordProtected**   This predicate matches messages with password-protected attachments.

- **AttachmentPropertyContainsWords**   This predicate matches messages when the specified property of the attached Office document contains specified words.

The predicates are accessed by the Any Attachment menu option under Apply This Rule If, as shown in Figure 14-12.

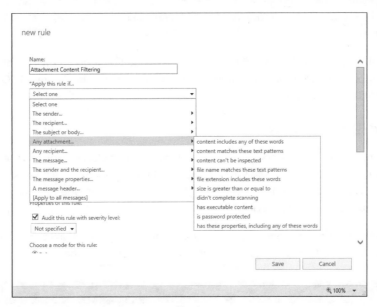

Figure 14-12 Attachment content filtering

For more information about transport rule predicates, see *https://technet.microsoft.com/en-us /library/jj919235(v=exchg.150).aspx*, "Mail flow rule conditions and exceptions (predicates) in Exchange Online." For more information on transport rule actions, see *https://technet.microsoft .com/en-us/library/jj919237(v=exchg.150).aspx*, "Mail flow rule actions in Exchange Online."

Central mail transport

Your organization has more complex requirements, such as an on-premises data loss prevention (DLP) infrastructure or an on-premises encryption gateway, you might find that you need to configure your outbound mail from Office 365 to route through your on-premises environment. Central Mail Transport (also referred to as Central Mail Flow in some documentation) routes all outbound mail to the on-premises environment through the hybrid mail connector for further processing.

> **CAUTION!**
>
> If you want to use Central Mail Transport but still route mail back out to Office 365 for egress through Exchange Online Protection, you must create a transport rule to insert an X-header in your message when you leave your on-premises environment. You can then

> create an additional transport rule in Exchange Online to check for that header and pro-
> cess the message differently. This is important—otherwise, you'll end up in a loop with
> Exchange Online following Central Mail Transport to deliver mail on-premises, and then
> Exchange On-Premises forwarding mail to Exchange Online.

You can enable Central Mail Transport by running the Hybrid Configuration Wizard on your
on-premises Exchange Server and selecting the options as described in Chapter 13, "Office 365
Hybrid Configuration Wizard."

Manage IP filtering lists

If you want to ensure that messages from a trusted source aren't blocked, you can use the connection filter policy to create an Allow list. Conversely, if there are sources that you know you
don't trust or want to block from delivering mail to your organization, you can modify the connection filter policy to create a block list.

To configure settings for the connection filter policy, navigate to Protection | Connection Filter
inside the Exchange Admin Center, as shown in Figure 14-13, and click the pencil icon.

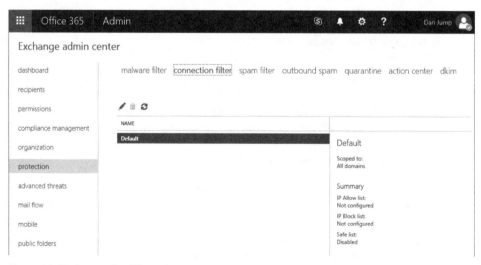

Figure 14-13 Connection Filter tab

You can add IP addresses and classless inter-domain routing (CIDR) blocks to either the Allowed
IP Address or Blocked IP Address list boxes, as shown in Figure 14-14.

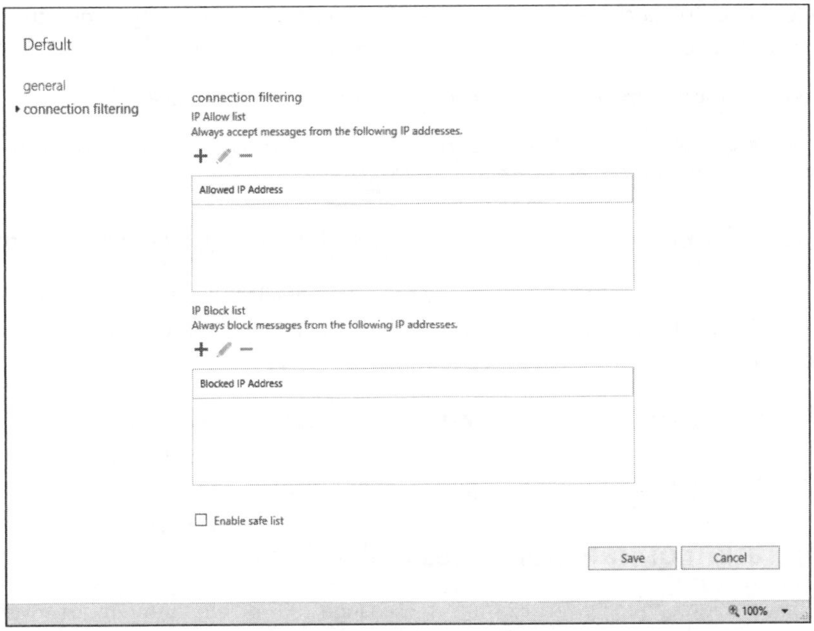

Figure 14-14 Allow and block list management

Selecting the Enable Safe List check box also whitelists connections from a trusted sender list that Microsoft provides.

Message trace

As part of administration duties, you might need to find out what happened to an email message. You can do this by performing a message trace in the Exchange Admin Center.

To perform a message trace, you can navigate to Mail Flow | Message Trace in the Exchange Admin Center.

You can create a message trace using date ranges or delivery status as well as search for individual message IDs (obtained from the message header) and filter by sender or recipient.

Message tracing is also available from Exchange Online PowerShell, using the Get-MessageTrace cmdlet. You can filter your search based on starting and ending dates (starting as the earlier of the two dates), sender, recipient, subject, and status.

Running a message trace in Windows PowerShell also gives you more flexibility in creating queries (such as structuring for multiple senders or to see communication between two users).

CHAPTER 14

For example, to search for all messages sent between Dan Jump and Ayla Kol in the past seven days, you can use this command:

```
$Users = @('DanJump@cohovineyard.com','AylaKol@cohovineyard.com')

Get-MessageTrace -SenderAddress $Users -RecipientAddress $Users -StartDate (Get-Date).
AddDays(-7) -EndDate (Get-Date)
```

Migration of transport settings between Office 365 tenants

At some point in the future, your organization might need to divest a business unit to a new Office 365 tenant. You can export and copy your existing transport settings between organizations.

You can use the script at *https://gallery.technet.microsoft.com/Migrate-EOP-Settings-9d480325* to help you migrate all mail routing configuration parameters between tenants, including malware filter policies, connection filter policies, transport rules, and connectors.

Migration of transport rules collections

If you are migrating to Office 365 from an Exchange 2007 or later on-premises environment, you can export your transport rules and import them into Office 365, using the Export-TransportRuleCollection and Import-TransportRuleCollection cmdlets. Transport rules can also be migrated between Office 365 tenants by using the same procedure.

Export transport rules

Exporting transport rules is a straightforward task. From the Exchange Management Shell, run the following script:

```
$file = Export-TransportRuleCollection
Set-Content -Path "C:\temp\Rules.xml" -Value $file.FileData -Encoding Byte
```
The transport rules are exported to the Rules.xml file.

Import transport rules

Importing transport rules is also a straightforward task. After connecting to Exchange Online through remote PowerShell, you can run the following script to import the rules exported in the previous step.

```
[Byte[]]$Data = Get-Content -Path "C:\temp\Rules.xml" -Encoding Byte -ReadCount 0
Import-TransportRuleCollection -FileData $Data
```

INSIDE OUT
Transport rules collections

The format for the exported rules has changed a few times between versions of Exchange Server. Rules collections from 2007 and 2010 are a structured XML format with nodes for each parameter and value:

```
<rule name="Transport Rule">
    <fork>
            <ConditionParameter1 value="value"/>
    </fork>
    <Condition>
            <and>
                    <true />
                    <ConditionParameter2 property="">
                            <value>Value</value>
                    </ConditionParamete2r>
            </and>
    </Condition>
    <Action name="Action">
            <argument value="Value" />
    </Action>
</rule>
```

However, rules for Exchange Server 2013, Exchange Server 2016, and Exchange Online are formatted differently, with the entire rule and all of its parameters exported as a New-TransportRule command:

```
<rule name="Transport Rule" id="224623e8-1a02-4c09-aa6f-83937c84dd4a"
format="cmdlet">
<version requiredMinVersion="15.0.3.0">
<commandBlock><![CDATA[New-TransportRule -Name 'Transport Rule -Comments ''
-Mode Enforce -ConditionParameter1 'Value' -ConditionParameter2 'Value' -Action
'value']]></commandBlock>
            </version>
    </rule>
```

You cannot import rules from Exchange 2007 or Exchange 2010 directly into Exchange Online. You must import them to an Exchange Server 2013 server first and then run Export-TransportRuleCollection against that server.

One advantage of running Export-TransportRuleCollection from an Exchange Server 2013 or Exchange Server 2016 environment is that if you view the XML file, you can extract the command in the <commandBlock> tag and use it to import rules selectively or see what is created if you import the entire collection.

> Importing a transport rule collection overwrites any rules in the destination environment, so you should back up your destination environment prior to running Import-TransportRuleCollection in case you need to back out your changes.

DKIM

Domain Keys Identified Mail, or DKIM, is an authentication process that relies on DNS records and signing of messages to indicate that messages originated from users inside your organization. You can view or configure DKIM settings for your organization by navigating to Protection | DKIM.

You can learn more about DKIM configuration in Chapter 7, "Inside the Security & Compliance Center: Alerting, Threat Management, and Reporting."

Spam and malware filtering

Aside from recipient management tasks, managing your organization's malware and spam settings will most likely be the next most common administrative task. In Exchange Online, malware and spam are separate items—malware is reserved to describe content that performs adverse actions in your environment (such as a virus), whereas spam is generally recognized as unwanted email (such as unsolicited bulk email).

Malware filter

The malware filter is normally configured to manage the flow of messages with attached executable content. However, under the Transport Rules | Attachment Blocking topic earlier in this chapter, the malware filter was configured to block attachments based on file extension.

You can create multiple malware filters for your organization, applying different settings and parameters to different types of content or different groups of users. To configure the malware filter, navigate to Protection | Malware Filter, as shown in Figure 14-15.

You can customize a malware filter policy to respond with custom text, block certain attachment types, and notify internal or external senders about email disposition as well as notify an administrator. You must configure a malware filtering policy to apply to a group of users, as shown in Figure 14-16. You can configure the scope based on user, domain, or distribution group.

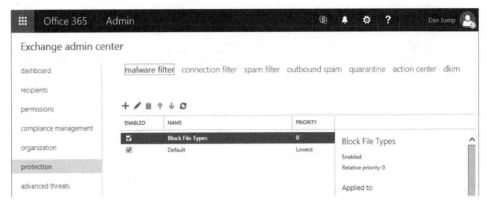

Figure 14-15 Malware Filter page

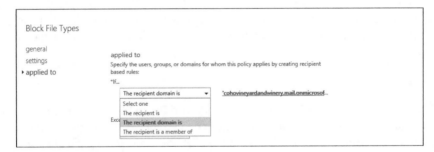

Figure 14-16 Malware filter scope settings

The default malware filter applies to all users in the organization.

Spam filter

Similar to the malware filter policies, you can configure multiple spam filter policies for your organization. To configure a spam filter policy, navigate to Protection | Spam Filter in the Exchange Admin Center. Select the pencil icon to edit an existing policy, as shown in Figure 14-17, or the plus sign (+) to create a new policy.

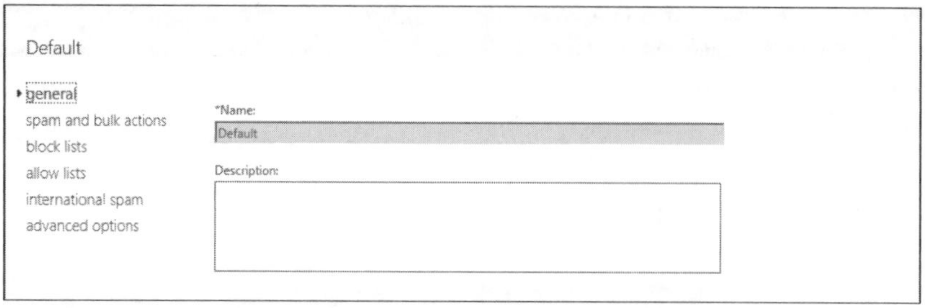

Figure 14-17 Edit spam filter policy

Under Spam And Bulk Actions, you can set the spam disposition for messages meeting a specific spam confidence level (SCL). By default, spam messages are sent to the user's Junk Email folder. You can configure the action to Delete Message or Quarantine Message. If you select Quarantine Message, you can configure Retain Spam For (Days), after which it will be automatically deleted. If you select the Quarantine Message action, messages will show up in quarantine in the Exchange Admin Center and can be released by an administrator or by the user.

On the Block and Allow list pages, you can configure whitelisting or blocking of senders and domains.

By using the International Spam settings, as shown in Figure 14-18, you can configure filtering for messages from certain countries or regions or messages written in certain languages. If, for example, your organization receives a high level of financial-related spam or phishing attempts from certain parts of the world or your organization is prohibited from procuring services in certain regions, you can enter those country codes on this page.

There are also a number of advanced settings that you can adjust to fit the needs of your organization. The settings on the Advanced Options page can be used either to increase the spam score for a message or mark it as spam outright (depending on the individual parameter configured).

The default spam filter applies to all users in the organization.

For more information about the spam filter settings, see *https://technet.microsoft.com/en-us /library/jj200684(v=exchg.150).aspx*, "Configure your spam filter policies."

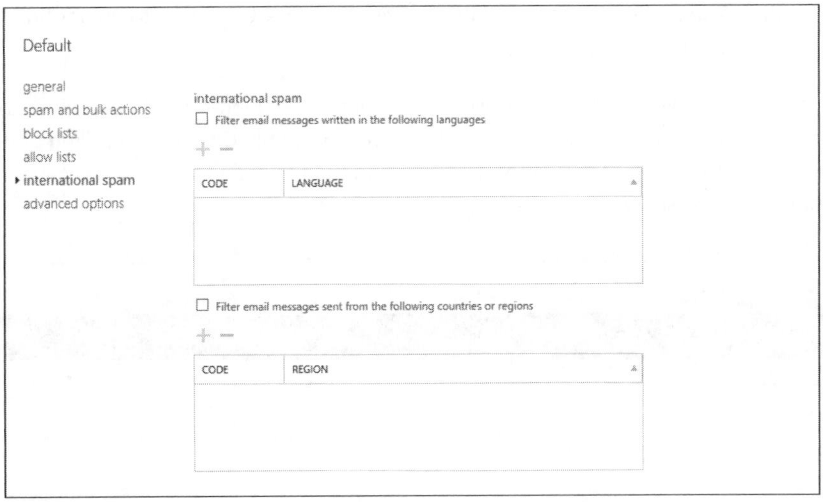

Figure 14-18 International spam settings

Outbound spam

Outbound spam filtering is enabled automatically for all Office 365 and Exchange Online subscribers. Although the overall settings aren't visible or configurable, you can configure notification settings to inform administrators or senders when messages are suspicious or blocked.

To configure outbound spam filtering notifications, navigate to Protection | Outbound Spam in the Exchange Admin Center. Select the pencil icon to edit the Default policy as shown in Figure 14-19.

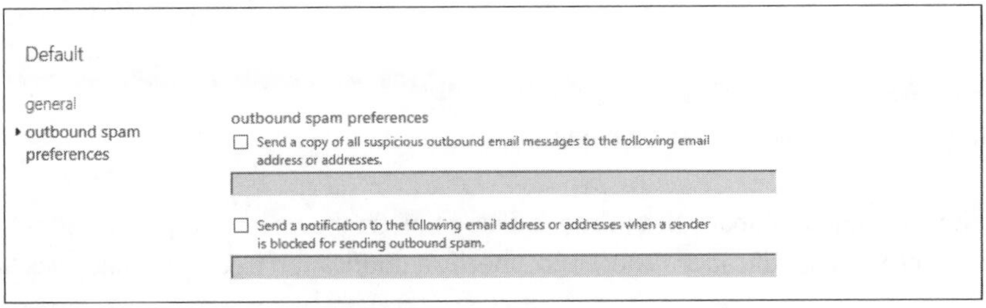

Figure 14-19 Outbound spam notification settings

Quarantine

The spam quarantine holds messages deemed to be spam by the service. By default, messages flagged as spam are delivered to the user's Junk Email folder. To quarantine messages, you have to configure spam filter or content filter policies to deliver messages to quarantine instead of to the user's Junk Email folder.

If you configure your spam filter policy to deliver mail to quarantine, you might want to enable the user quarantine. You can do this in the Exchange Admin Center by scrolling down in the spam filter policy with the quarantine action and then selecting Configure End-User Spam Notifications, as shown in Figure 14-20.

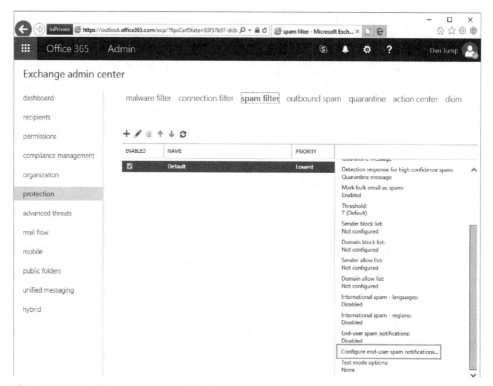

Figure 14-20 Enabling user spam notifications

In the Edit End-User Spam Notifications dialog box, as shown in Figure 14-21, select the Enable End-User Spam Notifications check box, specify a notification frequency, and click Save.

Default

☑ Enable end-user spam notifications

Send end-user spam notifications every (days):

3

Notification language:

Default	⌄

Figure 14-21 Editing user spam notifications

You can also enable the user quarantine by using the Set-HostedContentFilterPolicy cmdlet. For example, to enable the user quarantine setting for the Default spam filter, you can use this command:

```
Set-HostedContentFilterPolicy -Identity Default -EnableEndUserSpamNotifications $True
```

Users can access their quarantined messages by following the link in the spam notification email or by navigating to *https://admin.protection.outlook.com/quarantine*. The user quarantine is simple to use and includes the ability to search, view the details of a message, and release messages to the mailbox. See Figure 14-22. The interface for the user quarantine is identical to the administrator quarantine—the difference is only that the user sees only their own messages.

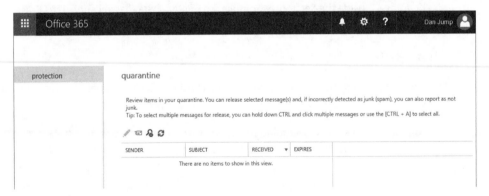

Figure 14-22 User quarantine interface

Blocked accounts

If a user repeatedly sends messages that are classified as spam, they will be blocked from sending any more messages. Users who have been blocked from sending receive non-delivery reports (NDRs) for messages they attempt to send and need to be unblocked.

You can configure the Outbound Spam settings to notify an administrator when an account is blocked.

To unblock an account, navigate to Protection | Action Center, search for the user, and then click Unblock Account in the description pane.

Compliance and reporting

Because organizations are under increasing threats (both internal and external), regulation and accountability requirements and the need for compliance and auditing becomes more important than ever. Exchange Online (and Office 365) provides a suite of tools and capabilities designed to help your organization meet those requirements.

eDiscovery and hold

In-place hold and eDiscovery features have been part of Exchange for several years. As organizations' business requirements have grown, the per-application tools for eDiscovery and legal holds have grown as well. Although holds and searches can still be performed in the Exchange Admin Center, those features are being deprecated in favor of more comprehensive tools available in the Office 365 Security & Compliance Center.

For more information on eDiscovery and holds in the Security & Compliance Center, see Chapter 8, "Inside the Security & Compliance Center: Data Classification, Loss Prevention, Governance, and Discovery."

Auditing

The auditing reports available in the Exchange Admin Center (Figure 14-23) can be used to provide valuable insight into how your data is being accessed.

You must enable mailbox logging before the Non-Owner Mailbox Access Report will return any data. In addition, for the admin audit log to return results, you must enable admin audit logging.

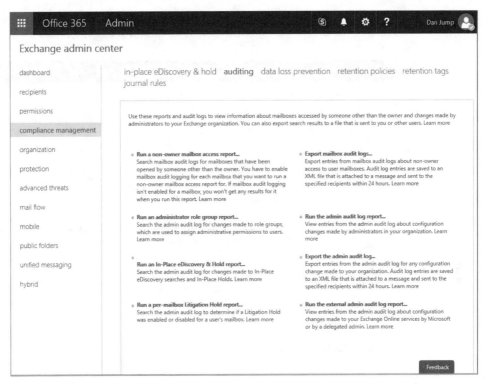

Figure 14-23 Audit reports

To enable mailbox auditing on all mailboxes, use the following command.

```
Get-Mailbox -ResultSize Unlimited | Set-Mailbox -AuditEnabled $True
```

You can enable admin audit logging for all services in Office 365 by using the Security & Compliance Center. For more information on globally enabling audit logging, see Chapter 8.

Data loss prevention

Data loss prevention (DLP) enables you to create policies to help manage the flow of sensitive data or data meeting certain policy requirements. Although you can still configure the features in the Exchange Online Admin Center, you can create more comprehensive policies in the Security & Compliance Center.

The exception to this is Document Fingerprinting. Document Fingerprinting enables you to use a document as a template to detect sensitive data. To create a document fingerprint DLP Policy rule, follow these steps.

1. In the Exchange Admin Center, navigate to Compliance Management | Data Loss Prevention and click Manage Document Fingerprints. See Figure 14-24.

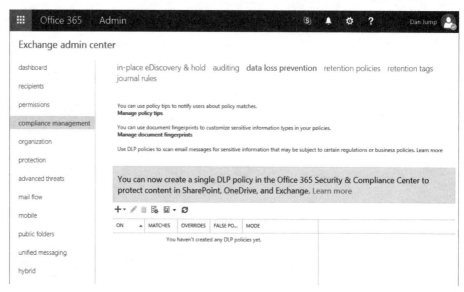

Figure 14-24 Data Loss Prevention page

2. On the Document Fingerprints page, click the plus sign (+) to upload a document to use as a fingerprint or template. See Figure 14-25.

Figure 14-25 Document Fingerprints page

3. Click Close.

4. Click the plus sign (+) and select New Custom DLP Policy, as shown in Figure 14-26.

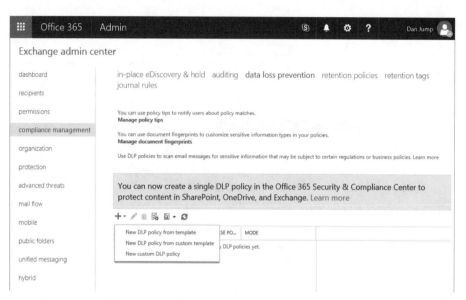

Figure 14-26 New Custom DLP Policy

5.   Type details for the policy and click Save. See Figure 14-27.

Figure 14-27 New Custom DLP Policy page

6.   With the new policy selected, click the pencil icon to edit the policy.

7. Select Rules, click the plus sign (+), and then select an action that most closely matches your requirement. See Figure 14-28.

Figure 14-28 Edit DLP Policy page

8. Select Sensitive Information Types, as shown in Figure 14-29.

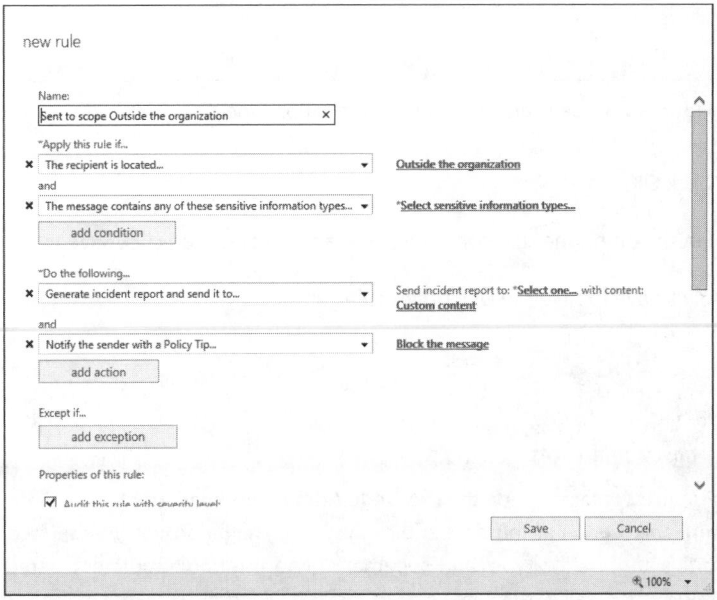

Figure 14-29 New Rule page

9. On the Contains Any Of These Sensitive Information Types page, click the plus sign (+) and select the custom sensitive information type containing the document fingerprint, as shown in Figure 14-30.

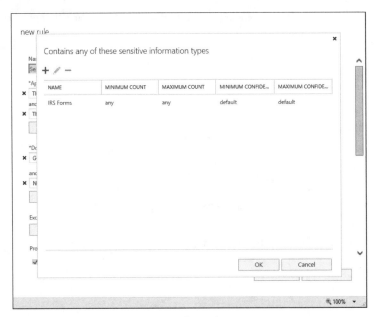

Figure 14-30 Selecting a sensitive information type

10. Click OK.

11. Finish editing the rule conditions and actions and then click Save.

12. Click Save to save the DLP policy rule.

INSIDE OUT

DLP policy differences

DLP policies created inside the Exchange Admin Center are not visible in the Security & Compliance Center at this time and cannot be managed from that interface. In addition, sensitive information types and document fingerprinting templates created in the Exchange Admin Center are not available for use inside a DLP policy created in the Security & Compliance Center.

Both sets of policies are visible from Windows PowerShell, albeit using different commands. To view policies created in the Security & Compliance Center, use the Get-DlpCompliancePolicy cmdlet. To view policies created in the Exchange Admin Center, use the Get-DlpPolicy cmdlet.

For more information about creating DLP policies, see Chapter 8.

Retention policies and tags

In Office 365, there are two types of retention policies—retention policies created and managed inside the Security & Compliance Center, which can cover Exchange, Microsoft SharePoint, Microsoft OneDrive, and Skype, and retention policies and retention tags created and managed in Exchange Online. Although the retention policies and retention tags in Exchange Online are used to manage information inside the mailbox, they work a little differently than the policies in the Security & Compliance Center.

Office 365 and Exchange Online, by default, have a retention tag that moves content to an online archive after two years. This default policy is applied to all users, but only takes effect if the user has had an online archive enabled. To enable the archive for a user, edit the user properties under Recipients | Mailboxes or use the following cmdlet to enable the archive.

```
Set-Mailbox -Identity <user> -EnableArchive
```

To manage a retention policy that automatically moves messages to the online archive, follow these steps.

1. In the Exchange Admin Center, navigate to Compliance Management | Retention Tags.

2. Select the Default 2 Year Move To Archive retention tag and click the pencil icon.

3. Update the Name and the Retention Period parameters to match your requirements and click Save. See Figure 14-31.

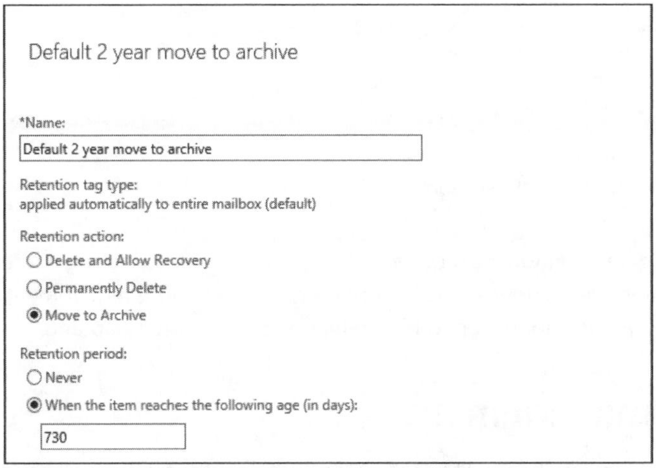

Figure 14-31 Retention tag settings

Moving forward, it is recommended that you use the retention policies inside the Security & Compliance Center to manage the preservation of data and, if necessary, use Exchange retention policies and retention tags inside the Exchange Admin Center to move content to archive mailboxes. For more information about overall Office 365 retention policies, see Chapter 8.

Journaling

Journaling is a feature that stores all copies of messages sent and received in an organization. Some organizations refer to this as an archive or a journal archive. Although Exchange Online can send journal messages to an external journaling destination, it is against the service agreement to use an Exchange Online mailbox as a journal destination.

Journal rules can be applied to all users and all messages inbound and outbound and all internal messages or external messages. To configure one or more journal rules, navigate to Compliance Management | Journal Rules in the Exchange Admin Center and click the plus sign (+).

Configure the journal rule parameters, as shown in Figure 14-32, and click Save.

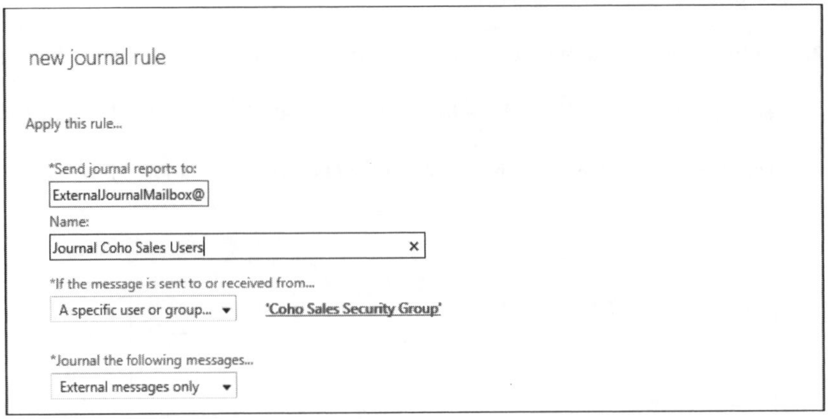

Figure 14-32 New Journal Rule page

If long-term data retention is a requirement in your organization, using a retention policy configured through the Security & Compliance Center to meet your requirement is recommended. For more information about configuring retention policies, see Chapter 8.

Organization management

At some point, you might need to configure calendar sharing with another organization. This other organization might use Office 365, Exchange on-premises, or a hybrid scenario in which users might exist in either location.

Organization relationships, sharing policies, and Availability address spaces all play a part in how Exchange Online locates resources in your own or other Exchange organizations.

Organization relationships

An organization relationship is the container object used to configure a sharing relationship with an external organization. The organization relationship object describes the other organization's domains with which you'll be sharing, what level of calendar and free/busy information sharing you'll grant, and what remote endpoints the relationship will use to connect to the other organization.

To manage organization relationships, navigate to Organization in the Exchange Admin Center, as shown in Figure 14-33, and select Sharing.

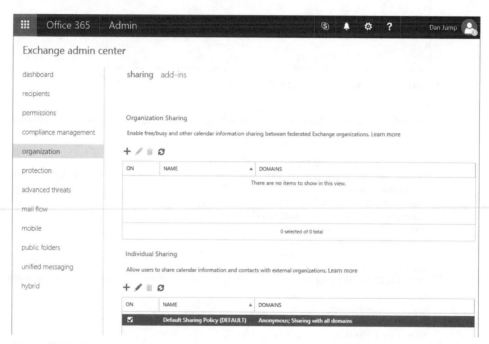

Figure 14-33 Organization management

Click the plus sign (+) in the Organization Sharing area to create a new organization relationship.

See Figure 14-34 for an example of creating a new organization relationship.

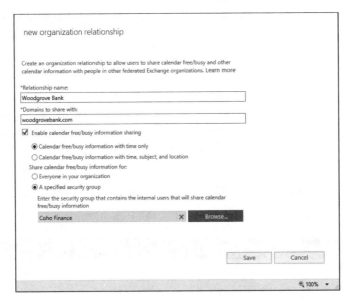

Figure 14-34 New Organization Relationship page

To verify the organization relationship settings, you can use the Get-OrganizationRelationship cmdlet.

```
PS C:\> Get-OrganizationRelationship | FL
DomainNames              : {woodgrovebank.com, woodgrovebank.mail.onmicrosoft.com, wood-
grovebank.onmicrosoft.com}
FreeBusyAccessEnabled : True
FreeBusyAccessLevel   : AvailabilityOnly
FreeBusyAccessScope   : Coho Finance
MailboxMoveEnabled    : False
MailboxMoveDirection  : None
DeliveryReportEnabled : False
MailTipsAccessEnabled : False
MailTipsAccessLevel   : None
MailTipsAccessScope   :
PhotosEnabled         : False
TargetApplicationUri  : outlook.com
TargetSharingEpr      :
TargetOwaURL          :
TargetAutodiscoverEpr : https://autodiscover-s.outlook.com/autodiscover/autodiscover.
svc/WSSecurity
OrganizationContact   :
Enabled               : True
ArchiveAccessEnabled  : False
AdminDisplayName      :
ExchangeVersion       : 0.10 (14.0.100.0)
Name                  : Woodgrove Bank
DistinguishedName     : CN=Cohovineyard,CN=Federation,CN=Configuration,CN=cohovineyardan
```

```
dwinery.onmicrosoft.com,CN=ConfigurationUnits,DC=NAMPR14A003,DC=PROD,DC=OUTLOOK,DC=COM
Identity              : Woodgrove Bank
Guid                  : 29065b56-cf6a-4da7-aabc-fb1a3a6a08c7
ObjectCategory        : NAMPR14A003.PROD.OUTLOOK.COM/Configuration/Schema/ms-Exch-Fed-
Sharing-Relationship
ObjectClass           : {top, msExchFedSharingRelationship}
Id                    : WoodgroveBank
IsValid               : True
ObjectState           : Changed
```

The output shows the settings that were automatically configured, with the exception of FreeBusyAccessScope, which was restricted to the Coho Finance group of users.

TROUBLESHOOTING

When you need settings other than the default ones

There are times when the remote organization has other settings configured than the defaults that the New-OrganizationRelationship cmdlet is designed to locate automatically. The remote organization could also have restricted external access to its environment or have another endpoint that it wants to use for federated sharing requests. When any of those is the case, you can create the organization relationship manually in Windows PowerShell by using the TargetApplicationUri, TargetAutodiscoverEpr, and TargetSharingEpr parameters.

TargetApplicationUri

The TargetApplicationUri parameter specifies the target Uniform Resource Identifier of the external organization. The parameter is specified by Exchange when requesting a delegated token for the external organization. This is typically the top-level Outlook Web App URL of the organization. For retrieving free/busy information from an Office 365 organization, this is setting outlook.com as the target. If the organization's Outlook Web App server URL is *https://mail.cohovineyard.com, then the TargetApplicationUri would be mail.cohovineyard.com*.

To update the TargetApplicationUri to use the Outlook Web App server at *https://mail.cohovineyard.com*, you would use the following command:

```
Set-OrganizationRelationship -Identity <Identity> -TargetApplicationUri mail.cohovine-
yard.com
```

TargetAutodiscoverEpr

The TargetAutodiscoverEpr parameter specifies the Autodiscover URL of Exchange Web Services for the external organization. For example, if the external organization's external Autodiscover service points to autodiscover.cohovineyard.com, the URL would most likely be *https://autodiscover.cohovineyard.com/autodiscover/autodiscover.svc/wssecurity*. Exchange uses the Autodiscover service to detect the correct Client Access server endpoint automatically for external requests. Hybrid public folder coexistence uses the setting in this parameter to locate the on-premises Exchange environment.

To update the TargetAutodiscoverEpr to point to the Autodiscover service located on *https://ex2016.cohovineyard.com*, you would run this command:

```
Set-OrganizationRelationship -Identity <Identity> -TargetAutodiscoverEpr https://ex2016.
cohovineyard.com/autodiscover/autodiscover.svc/wssecurity
```

TargetOwaURL

The TargetOwaURL parameter specifies the Office Outlook Web App URL of the external organization. It is used for Outlook Web App redirection in a cross-premise Exchange scenario. Configuring this attribute enables users in the organization to use their current Outlook Web App URL to access Outlook Web App in the external organization.

TargetSharingEpr

The TargetSharingEpr parameter specifies the URL of the target Exchange Web Services for the external organization. If the TargetSharingEpr parameter is used, it takes precedence over the TargetAutodiscoverEpr parameter information to locate the Client Access server. In Exchange Hybrid scenarios, this might need to be updated if the URL specified in TargetAutoDiscoverEpr points to a version of Exchange Server prior to Exchange Server 2010 SP3.

To update TargetSharingEpr to use the server located at *https://hybrid.cohovineyard.com*, use the following command:

```
Set-OrganizationRelationship -Identity <Identity> -TargetSharingEpr https://hybrid.
cohovineyard.com/EWS/Exchange.asmx
```

Sharing policies

Although organization relationships govern the sharing between federated Exchange organizations, sharing policies can be used to provide sharing capabilities on a mailbox-level basis to external users in external Office 365 or Exchange on-premises environments. If the external users aren't in an Exchange-based organization, sharing policies allow the sharing of calendar information through the use of Internet Calendar Publishing.

To create a sharing policy from the Exchange Admin Center, navigate to Organization | Sharing and click the plus sign (+) in the Individual Sharing area.

After naming the policy, click the plus sign (+) to define the sharing rules. See Figure 14-35 for an example of available options.

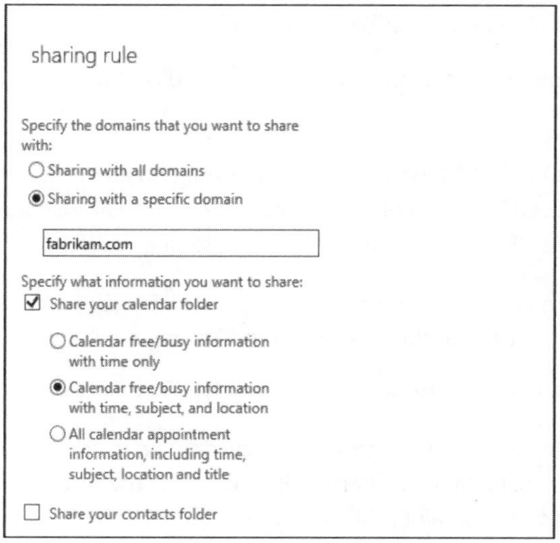

Figure 14-35 Sharing rule configuration

Hybrid management

In hybrid coexistence environments, you must perform several administrative tasks—such as creating new users and adding or removing domains that your organization uses for email routing.

Provisioning remote mailboxes

As you enter the daily routine of Office 365 and Exchange Online administration, you will undoubtedly need to create mailboxes. Using the Exchange Admin Center from your on-premises Exchange Server, you can create a new Active Directory account and enable it as an Exchange Online mailbox or add a mailbox to an existing Active Directory user.

You can also use either the Enable-RemoteMailbox cmdlet to provision the Exchange attributes on an existing Active Directory user account or the New-RemoteMailbox cmdlet to create a new Active Directory User and enable it as a mailbox in Office 365.

After the mailbox attributes have been provisioned, AAD Connect synchronizes the attributes to Office 365, triggering a mailbox creation. For more information about provisioning remote mailboxes, see Chapter 13.

Updating domains in a hybrid configuration

In the event that you need to add or remove domains in your hybrid configuration, you can follow this simple process.

1. Add the domain to your Office 365 tenant. For more information about adding and verifying a domain in your Office 365 tenant, see Chapter 1, "Office 365 Deployment Milestones," and Chapter 2, "Preparing Your Environment for the Cloud."

2. Configure the domain as an accepted domain in your on-premises Exchange Server environment. To do this, you can run the New-AcceptedDomain cmdlet:

```
New-AcceptedDomain -DomainName newdomain.com -DomainType Authoritative
```

3. Run the Hybrid Configuration Wizard and select the new domain to add. This generates a DNS TXT record that you must add to yoexternal DNS. To create the record ahead of time, you can use the Get-FederatedDomainProof cmdlet:

```
Get-FederatedDomainProof -DomainName newdomain.com
```

4. Add the DNS record to the external DNSto the Hybrid Configuration Wizard, select the I Have Created A TXT Record For Each Token In DNS check box and click Verify Domain Ownership.

5. Complete the Hybrid Configuration Wizard. For more information about completing the Hybrid Configuration Wizard, see Chapter 13.

Summary

This chapter discussed management tasks that cover a wide variety of areas, including recipients, transport, and the organization as well as some general hybrid management tasks.

PART V
Skype for Business Online

Skype for Business Online Concepts and Planning

This chapter looks at the basic concepts of Skype for Business Online, including the features it supports, the fundamental requirements to implement it, the protocols involved, and the clients you can deploy to your users for them to get online.

What is Skype for Business Online?

Skype for Business Online (SBO) is one of the key services in Office 365. It offers secure instant messaging, peer-to-peer audio and video conferencing, and presentation-sharing capabilities and enables you to provide your users secure communications and collaboration capabilities on any computer, tablet, or mobile phone. Whether you are at your desk or on the road, SBO enables you to communicate with your colleagues, attend meetings, share your entire desktop or just one application, or present Microsoft PowerPoint decks to one or many people quickly and easily. As an administrator, you can control which services you want your users to have and extend your connectivity to partners or even to your customers over the Skype consumer platform.

Features

SBO has several built-in features and capabilities that work across all client software applications. These include the following.

- Instant messaging

- Presence information incorporated across the Office 365 platform

- Peer-to-peer Voice over IP (VoIP) audio communications

- Peer-to-peer video communications

- Peer-to-peer file transfers

- Web conferencing, including text, audio, video, and presentation sharing

- Federated connectivity with other Session Initiation Protocol (SIP)–based systems and the consumer Skype network

- Software development kits (SDKs) for developing client applications

- Optional integration with PSTN for dial-in conferencing and full telephony features

- Clients available for Windows and Mac, Android, iOS, Windows Phone, and web clients

Here are more details about each of these features.

Instant messaging

SBO clients can use text, emoticons, and GIFs to communicate, using instant messaging. The full Windows and Mac clients have full control over fonts and formatting. Instant messaging provides real-time communications and is an excellent choice for when you are multitasking or need to ask a question that is either less formal in nature or more time-sensitive than an email. Instant messaging is also very tolerant of latency and poor network connectivity, and SBO works very well over in-flight Internet connectivity, edge cellular networks, and satellite links.

Presence

SBO provides presence indications within the application and integrates with both Exchange Online and SharePoint Online. Presence uses colored icons, commonly called jelly beans, to indicate whether another user is available, away, busy, or offline. With presence, you can see at a glance whether a colleague is available to chat, and you can launch chats right out of email or from Microsoft SharePoint sites. See Figure 15-1 for a list of the default presence indicators.

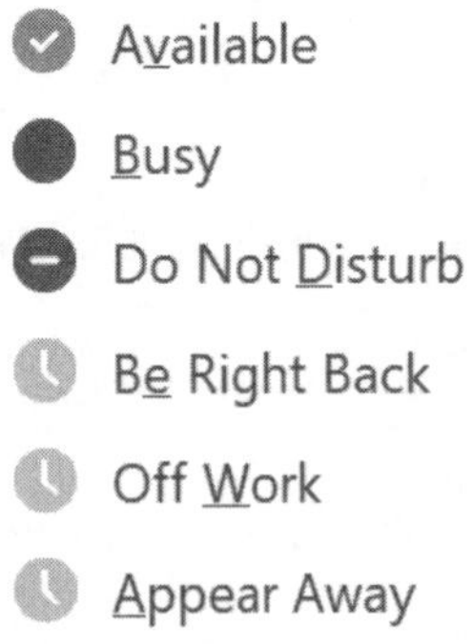

Available

Busy

Do Not Disturb

Be Right Back

Off Work

Appear Away

Figure 15-1 Skype for Business Online presence indicators

Peer-to-peer Voice over IP audio communications

Because it uses VoIP, SBO gives you the ability to conduct voice calls with others, using either your computer's built-in microphone and speakers or external hardware. Voice chats can be one to one or involve multiple participants and, if policy permits, be recorded by a participant for later playback.

Peer-to-peer video communications

As long as you have a webcam, SBO can take voice chats to the next level with video. Again, whether one to one or many, you can conduct video calls with others over the network to provide more interaction or to show someone something specific, and video calls can also be recorded for later playback if policy permits.

Peer-to-peer file transfers

Users can also use SBO to transfer files to one another. This can be disabled by policy if compliance needs require it, but when enabled, it provides a very fast and easy way for users to perform ad hoc file transfers without having to set up any infrastructure or send links to their OneDrive for Business. These can be small text files or multi-gigabyte virtual hard drive images or anything in between. The sender can either drag and drop a file to the chat window or browse their file system, and the receiver will find the file transfer in their My Received Files folder in their profile.

Web conferencing including text, audio, video, and presentation sharing

SBO also enables you to share content with others. Whether it's a user sharing their desktop with the help desk, a manager sharing the latest Microsoft Excel workbook with their team, or a presenter sharing a PowerPoint deck with their audience, content sharing enables users to engage by using a live presentation of whatever content you need to share. Presenters can share an entire desktop or only a single window and can pause or stop sharing at any time. This is an excellent way to deliver presentations or training or simply to demonstrate something to a remote user. Any client can join web conferences, and users without an installed SBO client can participate using only a web browser.

Federated connectivity with other SIP-based systems and the consumer Skype network

One of the most useful features of SBO is that it can interoperate with other systems. Although you can control this as the admin, if your corporate policy permits it, you can establish federation with other Skype for Business and Skype for Business Online organizations and the consumer Skype network. That way, your users can easily communicate with customers, partners, and vendors to provide a fully interactive experience with them. You can configure your SBO organization to be fully open or to federate only with the specific organizations that you choose, and you can grant or deny permission to communicate with external parties on a per-user basis if need be. As an example, you might want to permit connectivity to the consumer Skype system, but only for customer service and human resources users to interact with customers and job candidates. You can easily configure this or any other mix of capabilities to meet your company's needs.

SDKs for developing client applications

SDKs are designed to help developers extend Skype for Business and Skype for Business Online capabilities across both desktop and mobile apps. There are Web SDKs that support instant messaging and presence (IM&P), audio and video, a user representational state transfer (REST) application programming interface (API) that provides IM&P, Desktop APIs for developers to build their own clients, and the Unified Communications Managed API that developers can use to incorporate both hardware and software into SBO. You can learn more about these at *https://dev.office.com/skype/sdks*.

Optional integration with PSTN for dial-in conferencing and full telephony features

With the right licenses, Skype for Business Online offers PSTN conferencing and telephony capabilities, enabling customers to use SBO for their full telephone solution. Cloud PBX lets you provide direct-dial telephone numbers, call groups, call parking and forwarding, voicemail, and more. Calling plans are available that can include toll-free dial-in numbers for conferencing, enabling you to provide your users with a complete telephone solution that works with both soft phones and VoIP hardware phones.

Clients available for Windows and Mac, Android, iOS, Windows Phone, and web clients

There are Skype for Business clients for both the Windows and Mac platforms as well as all three major mobile platforms. Users can also take advantage of many of the SBO features by using only a web browser, and third-party and open-source options are also available.

Differences with on-premises

Skype for Business Online is powered by Office 365. Although almost all the features and capabilities of on-premises functions are available online, the online version does require you to have the latest version of the client software, whereas on-premises can support older client versions. On-premises also supports persistent chat rooms, which are not available in SBO. Finally, there is more integration and compatibility with various conference-room systems when using on-premises than there is with online.

Skype for Business Online only works with other SIP products at this time, although a number of gateways are available that can enable Skype on-premises to integrate with other messaging systems, such as those based on the Extensible Messaging and Presence Protocol (XMPP) or Sametime protocol.

If your business does not have an existing SIP-based conferencing and instant messaging solution, SBO is the obvious choice, but if you have an existing investment in conferencing hardware such as speaker phones and telepresence, you might find that older hardware can work with on-premises, but you will need to upgrade to go to online.

Both Skype for Business and Skype for Business Online evolved from a long line of Microsoft products, including Windows Messenger, Live Communications Server, Office Communications Server, and then Microsoft Lync and, finally, Skype for Business.

Differences from consumer Skype

Although both Skype for Business Online and the consumer Skype product are from Microsoft and can interoperate, they are completely different solutions. They do not share any infrastructure, use separate code bases, and should not be confused with one another. The consumer Skype platform was acquired by Microsoft in 2012 and is free to use for many features, with additional ones at a cost. Users create and manage their own accounts and can interact with any other Skype user they wish to, with the full set of features in the consumer product. Skype for Business Online is available as part of an Office 365 subscription, is managed by a company's administrators, and can be configured to remove features or lock down aspects that a company wishes to control. You control access to SBO as the administrator assigning licenses to your users for the features you wish them to use.

Understanding the protocols

SBO uses many protocols, depending on workload and network conditions. It also uses several ports and both TCP and UDP, depending on what the client is trying to do. Do not assume that everything will work fine if you only open outbound connections to TCP 443. SBO clients can fall back to that when other ports are blocked, but that affects performance severely. You will not need to make any configuration as an administrator related to any of these protocols, but it is helpful to understand them, especially when you need to troubleshoot connections. Take a look at the protocols SBO and clients use.

Session Initiation Protocol

SIP is probably the hardest working protocol in the Skype for Business Online service. It's responsible for signaling, establishing multimedia communication sessions, and instant messaging. It doesn't work alone, but as the most important protocol within SBO, it's the one to which you pay the most attention.

SIP stands for Session Initiation Protocol, and the name does indicate the protocol's main purpose. It is an Internet Engineering Taskforce (IETF) standard Internet protocol first defined by RFC 2543, currently defined by RFC 3261 (*https://tools.ietf.org/html/rfc3261*) and numerous updates or enhancements. Numerous systems, supporting the same types of services as SBO, use it. These systems might have varying degrees of compatibility.

Although it does perform work on its own, it also helps all the other protocols by establishing the session(s) necessary for them to operate. It sets up and terminates all the sessions between endpoints and can carry data to support voice, video, instant messaging, and presence.

The most important aspect of SIP, as far as administering SBO is concerned, has to do with addressing. A SIP namespace is a DNS zone associated with an organization using a SIP-based messaging platform. Within that namespace are some DNS records to help clients identify the network address of endpoints and to help other organizations' systems establish federation so that users in both organizations can all communicate with one another. Users have SIP addresses, or Uniform Resource Identifiers (URIs), that define their address within a SIP system. These SIP addresses take the form of username@SIPdomain and most closely resemble an SMTP address. More about that follows in this chapter.

Interactive Connectivity Establishment

Another IETF protocol, Interactive Connectivity Establishment (ICE), is defined in RFC 5245 (*https://tools.ietf.org/html/rfc5245*). Its purpose is to help two systems identify the optimum path to communicate with one another. If two clients are on the same network, have no firewall or other network access control list (ACL) between them to block communications, and have no device performing network address translation (NAT), then they can establish a direct, peer-to-peer connection between them for voice, video, and instant messaging. SBO uses ICE to determine whether peer-to-peer communication is possible for voice, video, and file transfer. However, you will see that instant messaging and presence traffic always passes between client and server in SBO. ICE uses both STUN and TURN, explanations of which follow, to find the best path for communications.

Session Traversal Utilities for NAT

The protocol formerly known as Simple Traversal of UDP through NAT provides a standard set of approaches to enable applications to discover and work with NAT devices. It is defined by RFC 5389 (https://tools.ietf.org/html/rfc5389). When SBO clients can make direct connections with one another, they will, but they first have to find one another. SIP registration uses Session Traversal Utilities for NAT (STUN) to identify the public network address that traffic exiting the client network is translated to and then to register that with the SBO service.

Traversal Using Relay around NAT

Traversal Using Relays around NAT (TURN) defines several extensions to STUN and enables communications when two hosts cannot communicate directly with one another by using a relay system that both can reach independently. In SBO, audio, video, presentation sharing, and file transfer all travel directly from one client to another over the network when possible, but if they cannot, TURN enables this communication to take place by establishing a relay through the SBO service. TURN is defined in RFC 5766 (*https://tools.ietf.org/html/rfc5766*).

SIP addresses

Every user of Skype for Business Online must have a SIP address. This address is the unique identifier that enables one user to contact another. SIP addresses are in the format of username@SIPdomain, where the SIPdomain is a unique, registered DNS namespace with the appropriate DNS records. When clients start the SBO client, it uses that SIP address to find the appropriate endpoints for the service and register the client connection with the service. Users can inform their clients, customers, colleagues, and others of their SIP address to facilitate communications over SBO if desired. Every user of SBO has one, and only one, SIP address. Unlike email, there are no SIP aliases.

proxyAddresses

A user's SIP address is stored in the Exchange proxyAddresses attribute in Azure Active Directory. If you have synchronized your on-premises Active Directory with your Office 365 tenant, and you have extended your on-premises schema for Exchange, the user's SIP address is mastered in your Active Directory. If not, you can set it directly in Office 365. However, if your Active Directory has been extended for Exchange and is synchronizing to Azure Active Directory, but a user does not have a SIP address in their proxyAddresses attribute, Skype for Business Online sets the user's SIP address to match the User Principal Name in Azure AD. See Figure 15-2 for an example of the proxyAddresses attribute for a user.

Figure 15-2 The proxyAddresses attribute in Active Directory

Ideally, you extend your on-premises Active Directory schema for Exchange, even if you are not using Exchange on-premises, and you control the SIP Address locally in Active Directory.

msRTCSIP-* attributes

If you had one of the older communications systems in your environment, such as Office Communications Server, you have several attributes in your Active Directory that start with MS-RTC*. If they are blank, they can be ignored, but if some of them are populated, they can have interesting effects on your users' SBO experience. The first is the msRTCSIP-PrimaryUser-rAddress attribute. This attribute in your on-premises Active Directory stores the SIP address for a user in older platforms and is synchronized to Azure AD. If it is blank, nothing is synchronized and no harm is caused, but if it is populated, it must match the SIP address in the proxyAddresses attribute, or it will prevent the user from successfully using SBO.

The second is msRTCSIP-UserEnabled. If blank or set to True, a user can use SBO if they have a license, but if set to False, it prevents a user from using SBO even if you have given them a license.

The third is msRTCSIP-OptionFlags. These values are also synchronized from on-premises Active Directory to Azure AD and can prevent certain SBO features from being available to users. It is not the intended way to permit or deny users' access to SBO features, so it should be blanked if any data exists.

There are others, but these three are the ones you should check when using SBO. Check your users to see whether these attributes, and the others, are populated. If they are, and you no longer have any on-premises SIP system that might be using them, consider blanking them out for all users before you start to deploy SBO. You should test this for several users to ensure that there are no unforeseen consequences. Otherwise, compare the msRTCSIP-PrimaryUserAddress to the SIP address in proxyAddresses for every user to ensure that they match, and make sure no user has msRTCSIP-UserEnabled set to False.

SMTP, UPN, and SIP

Although a userObject exists in Azure AD and usually has a one-to-one relationship with an actual person, there are three attributes that all identify the user. The User Principal Name (UPN), the primary SMTP address, and the SIP address all work together to enable users to access Office 365 services and for those services to interoperate. Although there is no technical reason for all three to match for the service to work, you absolutely want them all to match to ensure ease of use and the best user experience and to reduce calls to the help desk from users.

If at all possible, ensure that your SIP namespace is the same as your SMTP namespace and that users' primary SMTP address matches their SIP address. This both makes it simple for your users to communicate with others on different systems and enables presence within Microsoft Outlook and SharePoint Online to work automatically. Users should know what their email address is, and when both UPN and SIP match, it is easier for users to know what to enter in a specific client or prompt because the values are the same no matter which attribute is actually required. The answer to the question, "What do I put in here," is always "Your email address."

Authentication always requires the UPN. Exchange Online Autodiscover requires the user to authenticate and uses the primary SMTP address to discover the user's mailbox and configure the email client. Skype for Business Online also requires users to authenticate but then uses the SIP address to discover the appropriate SIP endpoint to connect to. However, Outlook and Outlook Web App, SharePoint Online, the Office apps, and Skype for Business clients all need to talk to the other services to provide users with the best experience.

Presence relies on Skype for Business Online. When Outlook wants to display presence for someone in the Outlook client, such as when they have sent an email or are copied on it, it relies on the SBO client to use the SMTP address of that recipient to query presence for that user by assuming that that is also the user's SIP address. If it is, presence works. If it is not, the only way presence works is if the client has a contact object that maps the primary SMTP address to the SIP address. The same thing happens in SharePoint Online. Users who have uploaded or modified documents in SharePoint Online, or who have a document open, appear by their display-Name but are identified in the service by their SMTP address. When your SBO client attempts to query for presence, it uses the SMTP address as if it is also the SIP address.

CHAPTER 15

The Skype for Business client can also pull your Exchange calendar information to update your presence automatically for meetings and to enable you to launch Skype meetings without having to log on to your email or even switch to Outlook. It uses your SIP address to connect to your Exchange or Exchange Online mailbox. If they match, this rich presence capability works.

Finally, in all cases, because the clients require authentication, they might prompt users to authenticate as well as enter values for what the client is trying to connect. Because the various prompts do not clearly indicate what value they need, UPN or SIP or SMTP, users can easily become confused trying to determine what value they should use for a specific prompt. When all values match, there is no confusion, and the number of prompts might also be reduced.

If you have multiple DNS names to support different business units or brands, that is fine. You can have up to 900 in a single Office 365 tenant. If users move from one brand to another and need to start using a new primary SMTP address, update their UPN and SIP to keep them consistent.

NOTE

Several customers' security teams might object to setting UPN, primary SMTP address, and SIP address to the same value because it is easier for an attacker to determine what a user's logon is. Although that is true to an extent, unless you are assigning truly random strings to all users for their UPN, odds are very good that an attacker can guess or phish one user's UPN and, from that, infer others'. By setting these values to match, you provide the best user experience and the greatest compatibility with third-party clients, some of which don't support mismatches between UPN and the other two values. You should also be using multifactor authentication to strengthen your security further, because even with a random UPN and strong password, users give up those credentials by falling for phishing attacks on a daily basis.

At one customer I worked with, where its security team insisted that they do not match UPN to primary SMTP or SIP, greater than 25% of calls to their help desk following their SBO deployment were because users just couldn't remember what to enter when prompted. Ultimately, they went back and set users' UPNs to match.

Network requirements

Skype for Business Online has more exacting requirements on the network than either Exchange Online or SharePoint Online. In addition to the various DNS records you have to create, the multiple protocols you need to permit, and the latency thresholds you need to monitor, you will find that SBO is a first indicator of any network issues. Do not underestimate the importance of ensuring that your network meets all the requirements for SBO so that your users enjoy the optimum SBO experience.

DNS records

It shouldn't surprise you that Skype for Business Online depends heavily on DNS for it to function. You must set up two CNAME and two SRV records for each DNS namespace you plan to use. No matter what domain(s) you are using, the same four records are required, and you should add them to both internal and external DNS.

The two CNAME records help clients find the SIP and discovery endpoints for the service. The first SRV record identifies the SIP endpoint; the second is used for federation. Whether you plan to use federation or not, you must deploy all four records if you want all Skype for Business Online clients, including the web browser, to work properly.

To confirm what you should add to your DNS, follow these steps.

1. Using a global admin account, log on to the administrative portal.

2. On the left side, navigate to Setup | Domains.

3. Select the domain you want to use.

   If you have not verified the domain yet, you must do so before displaying the DNS records, but if you completed the domain verification and set the domain purpose for Skype for Business Online, you should see something like Figure 15-3 about half-way down the domain management page.

Type	Priority	Host name	Points to address or value	TTL
CNAME	-	sip	sipdir.online.lync.com	1 Hour
CNAME	-	lyncdiscover	webdir.online.lync.com	1 Hour

Type	Service	Protocol	Port	Weight	Priority	TTL	Name	Target
SRV	_sip	_tls	443	1	100	1 Hour	@	sipdir.online.lync.com
SRV	_sipfederationtls	_tcp	5061	1	100	1 Hour	@	sipfed.online.lync.com

Figure 15-3 Skype for Business DNS records

When it's time to deploy Skype for Business Online for your domain, ensure that these records are in both internal and external DNS before you attempt to use SBO. Chapter 16, "Deploying Skype for Business Online," goes into more detail on this.

INSIDE OUT

When clients can't connect or the Outlook Web Access app won't work

Some of the most common mistakes admins make when it comes to Skype for Business Online have to do with DNS records. Missing or incomplete records, or putting the records into your external DNS but not into your internal DNS, can lead to client connectivity problems, the inability of the web browser–based component in Outlook Web App to function, or the inability of federated partners to connect with your SBO service. Remember that you need to use a DNS namespace that is split for authentication and has different records for the internal and the external Secure Token Service (STS.) However, you still need the external-only records in the internal zone for SBO to work. Some hosted DNS service providers don't support SRV records, at least not through whatever web browser interface or CPanel front end was provided to customers. If your DNS provider cannot support SRV records, and you want to use Skype for Business Online, get a new provider! Office 365 can host your DNS for you, or you can set up your own servers.

Ports and protocols

Microsoft maintains a list of the Office 365 URLs and IP address ranges at *https://support .office.com/en-us/article/Office-365-URLs-and-IP-address-ranges-8548a211-3fe7-47cb -abb1-355ea5aa88a2?ui=en-US&rs=en-US&ad=US*, which you can also find at *http://aka.ms /ipaddrs*. Bookmark this site and subscribe to the RSS feed so you are aware of any changes. On this page, all the various network addresses and FQDNs Office 365 uses are documented, as are the required specific ports and protocols. For all the services other than Skype for Business Online, that's TCP 80 and TCP 443. With SBO, there are many more; permit them all if you want to have the best experience with SBO. Fortunately, when you are using SBO, you only need to permit your clients to initiate *outbound* connections to the service. There is no inbound, so your security teams and firewall admins should not object too strenuously to this. All connectivity to SBO services is encrypted, so you will see HTTP traffic associated with certificate validation. Always check the documentation at *http://aka.ms/ipaddrs* for the most current requirements. See Table 15-1 for current SBO requirements.

Table 15-1 Skype for Business ports and protocols

Protocol	Port	Reason
TCP	80	CRL/OCSP checks and CDN content
TCP	443	SIP, PSOM, HTTPS downloads, Call Quality Dashboard, Outlook Web App integration, Quick ips, federation with Skype consumer, and contact picture retrieval; also the fallback when other ports are blocked

Protocol	Port	Reason
UDP	3478–3481	Audio, video, and desktop sharing
TCP	5223	This is only required for older push notifications for the Lync mobile 2010 client for iOS.
TCP and UDP	50000–59999	Audio, video, and desktop sharing (optional)

TCP versus UDP

It's very important for you to ensure that all the required connectivity is permitted in your environment. If any of the required outbound connectivity is blocked, you will drastically reduce the overall performance of SBO for your users and be in an unsupported configuration. The single most common cause of complaints about SBO performance is caused by not permitting the outbound UDP traffic.

TCP is a reliable, session-oriented transport protocol that ensures data delivery. It's meant for applications that require all of the data to be delivered and when reliability is more important than both speed and efficiency. Sessions are established, packets are acknowledged, lost packets are retransmitted, out-of-order packets are held until they can be reassembled in order, and, when done, sessions are torn down. Use TCP for messages that you need to ensure are received, or for file transfers.

UDP is a connectionless transport protocol. It focuses on speed and low overhead; lost packets can be ignored and delivery order is not as important. You use UDP for queries that generate answers or when you are streaming data and any individual lost packets won't matter.

Instant messaging and presence (IM&P), signaling, and data downloads all use TCP to ensure reliable message delivery. Those messages are both very small and very tolerant of latency. It's very common to use Skype for Business Online when on an airplane to communicate with colleagues. Even when GoGo is satellite-based and latency is measured in seconds, IM&P works great over TCP 443.

However, audio, video, and desktop sharing all use streaming protocols to convey data. These are all more concerned with ensuring that the stream of data is delivered consistently without delay than with complete reliability. If a UDP datagram is lost or delivered out of order, it's simply dropped. Most people won't even notice this when listening to audio or viewing video, because the amount of data in that one lost datagram is insignificant. Audio, video, and desktop sharing are all very latency-sensitive. Anything that slows down the connection from client to service reduces performance, but because any single datagram is just a small sample of the audio or video stream, its loss will probably not even be noticed as long as the stream is uninterrupted.

CHAPTER 15

When you force Skype for Business clients to use TCP 443 for everything, such as when your firewall admin doesn't want to open those ports, or your security team wants to put everything through the proxy, any packet that is lost requires the entire stream to stop and wait for retransmission. That can take seconds to happen and results in many audio as well as video problems. You have probably been on a VoIP call when you heard buzzing or chirps, or someone on the call sounds like a bad text-to-speech engine. You have probably also been viewing a video share when the screen freezes, or the slides stop advancing, or you lose the presentation entirely and have to rejoin. All these issues and more can occur when a client cannot make connection over the UDP port ranges. Make sure that the firewall permits clients to make connections over the UDP ranges before you deploy Skype for Business Online to your users. In pilot, you might not notice as many issues because fewer users are online, but after you deploy to production, it will quickly become apparent if UDP is blocked.

The bottom line is simple. You must permit all the documented connectivity required to deliver proper performance.

Latency

Latency refers to any delay on a network. Low-latency networks usually have only small delays between a client requesting something and the server responding. High-latency networks have larger delays. Many things can contribute to high latency. Some are within your control; others might fall to your ISP. Although all applications benefit from the lowest latency possible, Skype for Business Online is one of the most latency-sensitive applications you have to support. For IM&P, latency is not really a problem, as mentioned, but for voice and video, you want to do everything you can to reduce latency. You want the latency between your clients and the service to be under 100 milliseconds. Under 50 is better and the target to shoot for. Although you cannot increase the speed of light, there are several things you can do to minimize latency.

- Keep DNS services local to the clients.

- Make sure those DNS servers can resolve Internet names directly rather than having to forward queries to remote DNS servers for resolution.

- Provide local Internet egress for your users in each key location.

- Do not proxy SBO traffic.

- Make sure your ISP peers with Microsoft to provide the optimum network path from your egress point to the service. See *http://www.microsoft.com/peering* for more information and ask your ISP to request peering with Microsoft if it is not already doing so.

- Do not force Skype traffic for virtual private network (VPN) users to route over the VPN. Use split-tunneling to ensure the fastest connection to the service.

NOTE

Although several ISPs do peer with Microsoft, and in multiple locations, the path between your egress point and ingress to the Microsoft Office 365 network might not be optimum. Check from all your key locations to confirm that the route is as short as possible. Tools such as tracert can help you check the path, but you might need to engage your ISP's technical support to confirm that it is peering optimally. As a general rule, you should be able to get onto the Microsoft network in less than 50 milliseconds from most locations in the world. If you cannot (and you are not using satellite or dial-up) there is room for improvement. Finding where the latency occurs is the first step. You can download PsPing from *https://live.sysinternals.com/* and use it to test latency.

Planning connectivity

Skype for Business Online depends more on network connectivity than any other Office 365 service. SBO can provide you and your users with an excellent experience for audio and video when the network is good, but any problems with the network can lead to a very poor experience. SBO is often the first indicator of network issues because it is the first application to suffer if the network is not healthy.

SBO clients can provide great performance over wireless networks when those networks are configured properly, but will suffer from terrible performance when they are not. If you just bought and connected several access points, set a Service Set Identifier (SSID), and called it done, expect to have Skype audio and video problems related to your Wi-Fi network, but if you had a site survey performed, scaled your Wi-Fi network for both user and bandwidth demands, and made sure your access points are optimized for real-time communications needs, your users should see just as good performance on Wi-Fi as on wired.

SBO can also be bandwidth intensive when using it for audio, video, and presentation sharing. Although peer-to-peer communications only use your LAN or WAN bandwidth, any session that involves three or more participants requires client–server communications. Audio uses between 64 and 80 kbps per channel, so a three-way audio call uses between 192 and 240 kbps. A larger meeting, with 20 users, consumes between 1.2 and 1.6 Mbps. Now consider the same meetings with video. If each user has HD-capable hardware, the three-person call could peak at 12 Mbps, whereas the 20-user video call could use 80 Mbps. You will want to use the Skype for Business Online Client Bandwidth calculator, available at *https://www.microsoft.com/en-us /download/details.aspx?id=19011*.

Considerations with proxies

As a general rule, you should not use a proxy server with Skype for Business at all. Proxies add latency to all traffic, even when they are configured with whitelists to permit traffic to connect without inspection. Those that attempt to do any kind of inspection introduce even more latency. Because all SBO traffic is encrypted, a proxy can do little unless you enable Transport Layer Security (TLS) inspection so that the proxy terminates the TLS connection, inspects the traffic, and then re-encrypts the connection. As you can imagine, that adds even more latency to your SBO traffic and might cause so much latency that you are over the 50-millisecond target before your traffic has even left your network. Unless your proxy is a Socket Secure (SOCKS) proxy, to put Skype traffic through a proxy requires it all to go over TCP 443, which, as mentioned, can make client performance much worse. Add to all of those considerations that most proxy solutions don't have parsers that do anything with SIP, and you wind up with a very expensive latency engine.

If you really must proxy all traffic, and you are willing to accept that doing so might deteriorate audio and video performance, be aware that the Skype for Business client will attempt to make direct connections for all SIP traffic, and only when that fails or times out will it attempt to use any configured proxy. If your firewall sends RST ACK packets, the client will realize very quickly that it cannot connect directly, but because most firewalls are configured to drop traffic silently, this can add several seconds to the establishment of any SIP session. You really want to permit that traffic to go directly.

If you cannot, visit *https://support.microsoft.com/en-us/help/3207112/skype-for-business -should-use-proxy-server-to-sign-in-instead-of-tryin* to deploy the registry key that tells Skype for Business not to bother trying direct and, instead, go straight to using the proxy. Here is what you need to do.

1.   Ensure that the client is fully updated.

2.   Exit the Skype for Business client by choosing File | Exit.

3.   Launch the Registry Editor.

4.   Find the key HKEY_CURRENT_USER\Software\Microsoft\UCCPlatform\Lync.

5.   Create a new DWORD in this key named **EnableDetectProxyForAllConnections**.

6.   Set the value to 1.

7.   Restart the Skype for Business client.

Optimizing connectivity

Microsoft offers an entire deliverable called the Network Performance Assessment, which you can use to confirm that your network is sufficient for consuming SBO or to identify where it isn't. Consider carefully whether you want to take advantage of that or perform your own assessment before deploying SBO to your users. The key things to assess include the following.

Table 15-2 Skype for Business Online target values for network tolerances

Metric	Target value
Latency between client and service	< 50 milliseconds
Round-trip Time	< 100 milliseconds
Burst packet loss	< 10% measured during any 200-millisecond interval
Packet loss	< 1% during any 15-second interval
Packet inter-arrival Jitter	< 30 milliseconds during any 15-second interval
Packet reorder	< 0.05% out-of-order packet arrival

Work with your network team, your security team, and your ISP together to ensure that you have the best connectivity to Office 365.

Troubleshooting connectivity

The end-to-end path ultimately determines whether SBO performs well or poorly. There are several tools you can use to assess your network and the quality of your connection to Office 365 for SBO before you deploy your first user.

Skype for Business Network Assessment Tool

The Skype for Business Network Assessment Tool can evaluate the path between your client and the SBO service. It's a command-line tool you can download from *https://www.microsoft.com /en-us/download/details.aspx?id=53885* and run on various workstations to assess the network conditions between client and service. It uses an audio file to place an audio call from the client to the closest SBO edge point and measures latency, round-trip time (RTT), jitter, loss, and packet reorder. You can edit the configuration file to run multiple consecutive tests over time and aggregate the results. To check your network, do the following.

1. Download the tool from *https://www.microsoft.com/en-us/download/details .aspx?id=53885*.

2. Expand the zip file to your directory of choice.

3. To run multiple tests over time, use Notepad or another text editor to edit the NetworkAssessmentTool.exe.config file.

4. Edit line 21 to set the number of tests you wish to run and edit line 24 to set the delay between each test you wish to run. In the following example, the test will run 36 times, pausing 5 minutes (300 seconds) between each test. This equates to a three-hour span with a 5-minute sample.

```xml
<?xml version="1.0" encoding="utf-8" ?>
<configuration>
    <startup>
        <supportedRuntime version="v4.0" sku=".NETFramework,Version=v4.5" />
    </startup>
    <appSettings>
      <add key="Relay.IP" value="13.107.8.2"/>

      <!-- At least one of the following two protocols must be configured   -->
      <!-- Configure only one if testing only one protocol                  -->
      <!-- If both are configured, UDP will be preferred if it is available -->
      <add key="Relay.UDPPort" value="3478"/>
      <add key="Relay.TCPPort" value="443"/>

      <!-- WMAFilePath configures the WMA file to be streamed
-->
      <!-- WMAOutputFilePath contains the received audio (for the duration of the
call). -->
      <!-- If WMAOutputFilePath already exists, the existing file will be over-
written.   -->
      <add key="WMAFilePath" value="Tone.wma"/>
      <add key="WMAOutputFilePath" value="ReceivedAudioFile.wma"/>

      <add key="NumIterations" value="36"/>
      <add key="ResultsFilePath" value="results.tsv"/>
      <add key="Delimiter" value=" "/>
      <add key="IntervalInSeconds" value="300"/>
    </appSettings>
</configuration>
```

5. Save the file.

6. Open a .cmd prompt in the working directory where you extracted the zip file and run the NetworkAssessmentTool.exe [enter] command.

7. When the tool completes, run the ResultsAnalyzer.exe results.tsv [enter] command. You should see results like those shown in Figure 15-4.

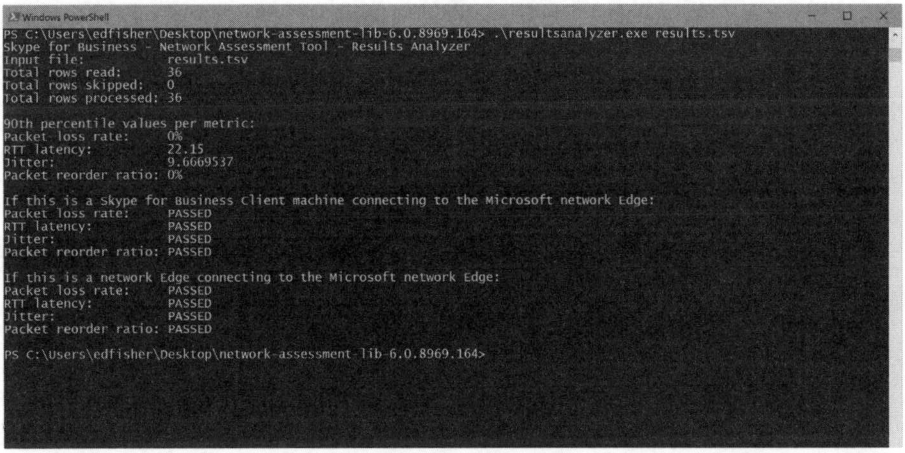

Figure 15-4 An example analysis of the Network Assessment Tool, showing that all tests passed

Figure 15-4 shows that all tests passed, with an average packet loss rate of 0%, an RTT latency of 22.15 milliseconds, jitter of ~9.67 milliseconds, and a packet reorder ratio of 0%. Note that it provides these results for both client to edge and edge to edge. If you try this from a client and it fails, move your test machine to the edge and test again. If it succeeds there, you have issues to address within your network. If it still fails, you need to engage your ISP to determine where the problem is.

Fast Track Network Analysis

You can perform more detailed testing with the Fast Track Network Analysis tool. This is an online test you can use with a web browser as long as you have Java installed. It does require you to have a tenant already set up, but you do not have to have the SBO client installed or use a licensed user account. This tool tests your connectivity to confirm that outbound TCP and UDP ports are permitted; that the route and bandwidth are available; and that you have the quality of the connection to support VoIP, the capacity, the round-trip time, and the packet loss. Results are provided in a graphical view. Here's how to use it.

1. Open a web browser and go to *http://na1-fasttrack.cloudapp.net/o365nwtest*.

2. Run the Java app when prompted to.

3. Type the name of your Office 365 tenant and click OK.

   That is, the tenantname.onmicrosoft.com name, not your SIP namespace or company domain.

   Several tests run, including some for both Exchange Online and SharePoint Online.

4. Check each to confirm that all tests pass. If any show a fail, investigate and resolve the issues before you deploy the service to any users. See Figure 15-5.

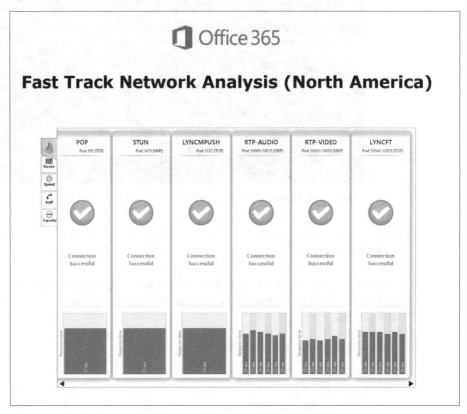

Figure 15-5 The Fast Track Network Analysis tool showing all SBO ports open

There are more tools you can use to troubleshoot Skype for Business Online performance; Chapter 16 discusses those.

Network flows

Skype for Business Online uses both client–server and peer-to-peer connections, depending on the number of users and the scenario. Understanding the differences and when which is used can help you plan for sufficient capacity and troubleshoot issues if they arise.

Client–server

Most of the network traffic you see when using Skype for Business Online is client–server. Clients on your network initiate outbound connections to the Skype for Business servers in

Office 365, using your Internet connection to reach the service. This includes registration, session setup, instant messaging, and presence and often includes audio, video, and desktop sharing. Whenever more than two clients are involved in audio/video/desktop sharing, or when two cannot make a direct IP connection to one another, that traffic goes client–server. When sizing your Internet connection and setting up your firewall for network address translation, keep this in mind.

Peer-to-peer

But when two (and only two) clients can make a direct IP connection to one another, are not blocked by any network filter or host-based firewall, and no NAT is between them, audio, video, and desktop sharing occurs over a peer-to-peer connection across your LAN or WAN. The session setup is still performed client–server, and presence updates are too, but one-on-one communications won't use your Internet connection unless it has to, which helps conserve bandwidth and reduces outbound connections. Make sure any firewalls between locations permit the same UDP port ranges internally and that any client firewall is configured to permit the Skype client to make and receive connections from the internal network.

Licensing and client types

Skype for Business Online users have a number of options for connecting to and using the service. There are full-featured rich clients for their computers, mobile clients for their phones/tablets, and even some capabilities accessible through a web browser. As an admin, you have a number of options for licensing your users, based on what features and capabilities you want to provide. Because you must assign licenses before clients can use SBO no matter what client software is involved, the license and feature mix is discussed next.

Licenses and features

You can purchase several licenses to use Skype for Business Online. You want to make sure the license you choose includes the features you need to support for your users, including the client software you will deploy.

Skype for Business Online in E1, E3, and E5

Many customers obtain Skype for Business Online as part of a larger suite purchase of Office 365 services. In both the E1 and E3 suites, SBO includes the following features.

- Instant messaging
- Presence
- Audio, video, and desktop sharing

- Host meetings for up to 250 users

- Host meetings for up to 10000 users with Skype Meeting Broadcast

Compatible hardware and client software are required for all functions to work completely.

In the E5 suite, SBO also provides for the following.

- Make, receive, and transfer calls across a wide range of devices with Cloud PBX.

- Make domestic or international calls from current or new phone numbers with add-on PSTN calling.

- Create meetings with a dial-in number that attendees can join by telephone with PSTN conferencing.

Skype for Business Online for smaller businesses

Both the Office 365 Business Essentials and Business Premium licenses come with Skype for Business Online, with almost all of the same features as in the E1 and E3 enterprise suites.

- Instant messaging

- Presence

- Audio, video, and desktop sharing

- Host meetings for up to 250 users

The only thing missing is the 10,000 attendee Skype Meeting Broadcast feature.

Stand-alone Skype for Business Online

Skype for Business Online can also be purchased separately. Two plans are available. Plan 1 includes IM&P and PC-to-PC audio and video calling. Plan 2 includes online meetings of up to 250 attendees in Skype for Business Online and up to 10,000 attendees, using Skype Meeting Broadcast.

Client software

To use Skype for Business Online, users must have client software of some type. The SBO clients for mobile devices and tablets can be downloaded for free from the various app stores such as iTunes, Google Play, and the Windows Store. The Outlook Web Access capabilities for IM&P are available to any user on a supported web browser and with the appropriate license. The full rich client, which has to be installed on PCs, is included only with the E3 and E5 plans. E1 and SBO Plan 1 and Plan 2 users users can download the free client, but it is not full-featured.

Skype for Business full client

The full version of the Skype for Business client is software that is included with the various Office perpetual suites, Office ProPlus, or with the SBO Plan 2 license. You can download it from the Office 365 portal or install it with the Office or Office ProPlus suite. The full Skype client supports all the features and capabilities of Skype for Business Online as long as you have licensed the user appropriately.

Skype for Business basic client

The Skype for Business basic client can be downloaded from the Office 365 portal or separately from *https://products.office.com/en-us/skype-for-business/download-app?tab=tabs-3*. Although almost all features of SBO work with this client, the following features are not available when using the basic client, even when a user is properly licensed for them.

- Manage team call settings

- Manage delegates

- Make calls on behalf of another contact (manager/delegate scenario)

- Handle another's calls if configured as a delegate

- Manage a high volume of calls

- Initiate a call to a Response Group

- Call park

- Group call pickup

Lync

If you have users with older versions of the Lync client installed, they will work with Skype for Business Online. However, not all features work, and you should expect the overall experience to be less than when using the current Skype client. You definitely want your users to be on the latest, current, and fully supported client software when using Office 365, whether older versions could work or not. See *https://technet.microsoft.com/en-us/library/dn933896.aspx* for a comparison.

Outlook Web App client

Users can access Skype for Business Online in Outlook Web App. Skype for Business Online IM&P is integrated right into the Outlook Web App client. To use it, in addition to being properly licensed, your users must have mailboxes in Exchange Online already. Then, they can just click the Skype for Business Online icon in the top toolbar, as Figure 15-6 shows.

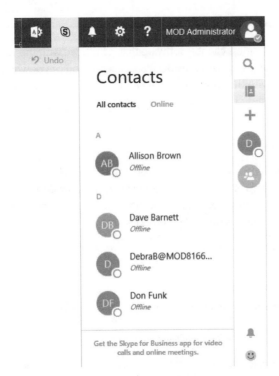

Figure 15-6 Skype for Business Online in Outlook Web App

Skype Meetings app

Users can attend Skype for Business Online meetings by using only their web browser. They can view content and participate in audio discussions by using their Internet connection and a supported browser by installing a browser plug-in. When users are invited to a meeting and click the hyperlink to join an online meeting, they are prompted to install the plug-in if they have not installed the Skype for Business client, as Figure 15-7 shows. As long as they have administrative rights on their workstation, they can install the app and join meetings.

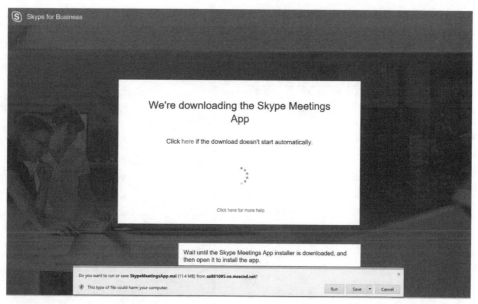

Figure 15-7 Prompt to install the Skype Meetings app after clicking the Join Now link in a meeting invite

Mobile clients

Skype for Business clients are available for iOS, Android, and Windows Mobile, available for download from their respective app stores. These apps provide significant functionality in Skype for Business Online, including IM&P, audio and video over Wi-Fi or cellular networks, and integration with Exchange Online to see upcoming meetings, view your contact list, and even place VoIP calls. You can also attend meetings and view presentations while on your mobile device or start up ad hoc meetings.

Users must download and install the Skype for Business mobile app themselves. Microsoft does not make the installers available separately, so if you are using Mobile Device Management (MDM) to push software to your users' mobile devices, you will have to open things up.

INSIDE OUT

Keep your eye on bandwidth

Video and meeting content both can use a lot of bandwidth, so by default, the Skype mobile client requires you to be on Wi-Fi before it will work with video or display content someone is sharing. You can still participate in a meeting with others who are on video or sharing their desktop, an app, or a deck, but you won't be able to see that content. If you have an unlimited bandwidth plan or are willing to use cellular bandwidth for the content, you can enable that by turning off the requirement to be on Wi-Fi. To do that, open the Settings page, scroll down to Require Wi-Fi For, and turn off both Video and Meeting Content. See Figure 15-8.

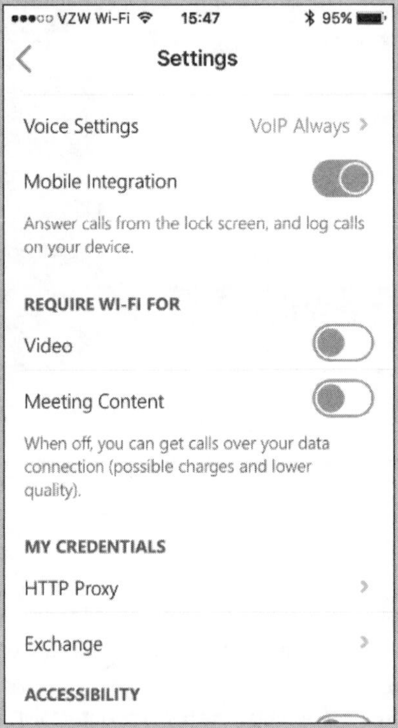

Figure 15-8 Skype for Business iOS client settings

Third-party clients

Although unsupported, open-source instant messaging clients can be used with Skype for Business Online for IM&P. They might require additional third-party plug-ins to work with SBO, and you won't get voice or video, but they do work well for IM&P. Just be aware that future changes to the service might require future updates to the plug-in, but if you use Linux regularly and still want to be online when needed, it's a workable solution even if it's not officially supported.

Skype policies

Policies enable administrators to configure certain settings for their users within the service. These can include disabling actions such as saving Conversation History, limiting the maximum bandwidth available for video calls, or blocking file transfers. Many of these same things can be controlled by using Group Policy objects (GPOs), and if all your Skype for Business Online clients are using domain-joined Windows machines, you can certainly use GPOs to manage their experience. However, with mobile devices and BYODs, you might find that using Skype Policies is the more effective way to ensure that all clients are covered consistently. Take a look at the types of policies that are available to you.

Types of policies

Skype for Business Online offers several types of policies. There are four main types that you will want to focus on, which include:

- Client policies
- Conferencing policies
- External access policies
- Voice policies

As you can imagine, each of these four policy types controls with specific settings. Skype for Business Online includes several pre-configured policies, and as an administrator you can create your own custom policies if one of the included ones does not meet your needs.

Use client policies to enable or disable specific client features, such as file transfer, whether a user can be signed in but appear offline, or saving instant messages (IMs) to their Conversation History. Many of these settings come into play with human resources, regulatory, or compliance concerns.

Use conferencing policies to set limits or features in online conferences, such as the maximum number of attendees, maximum bandwidth for each audio or video stream, or allowing recording. You can use these policies to control or restrict conferences, reduce the overall impact on the network, or ensure that highly confidential meetings are not recorded.

External access policies control what a user can or cannot do with external parties. You might enable external federation but not allow certain users to communicate with external users, or disable certain people's ability to communicate with consumer Skype users. Perhaps you want to permit IM&P but not audio and video. You use these policies when you have to permit external federation for some users but not others or otherwise restrict external communications.

CHAPTER 15

Finally, customers use voice policies with Cloud PBX connectivity to the public telephone system and voicemail to control features such as call forwarding, call transfers, and simultaneous ringing.

The easiest way to work with Skype for Business Online policies is with Windows PowerShell. Here are the additional steps to take to start using Windows PowerShell to work with SBO after you have already set up your computer to work with Office 365, using remote PowerShell.

1. Download and install the Skype for Business Online PowerShell module from *http://go.microsoft.com/fwlink/?LinkId=294688*.

2. Run the SkypeOnlinePowershell.exe file to install the module.

3. Accept the license agreement and complete the installation.

4. Open a Windows PowerShell session on your computer. It does not need to be an administrative shell.

5. Run the following commands, in order, providing your administrative credentials where appropriate.

   ```
   Import-Module SkypeOnlineConnector

   $credential = Get-Credential

   $session = New-CsOnlineSession -Credential $credential -Verbose

   Import-PSSession $session
   ```

If all goes well, you will be connected to your Skype for Business Online tenant. See Figure 15-9.

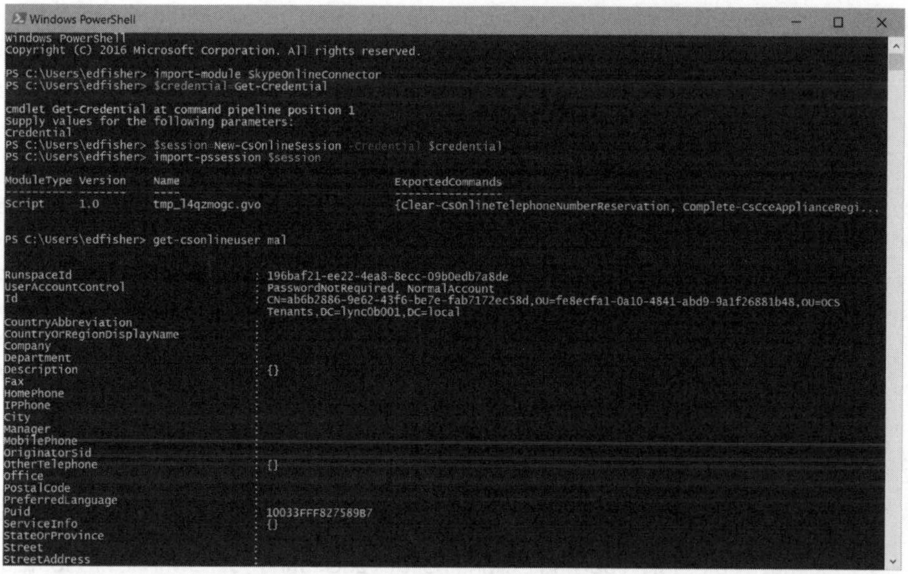

Figure 15-9 Skype for Business Online remote PowerShell session

Finding the settings that work for your organization

As an admin, you might want to determine what policies are available to you and which settings you can change. Take a moment to confirm what your company needs. Work with management, human resources, legal, and the business to identify what might need to be turned off or disabled.

By default, Skype for Business Online provides full functionality to all users for everything you as an admin enable in the tenant. External federation is not on, but if you turn it on, then all users can take advantage of it. The same holds true for Public Internet Connectivity with Skype Consumer. Turn things off only if you must or if you want to control the deployment by rolling things out slowly.

You can list all the policies that are available or review the settings in the portal with the team members who will be involved in deciding which settings are required. Consider what user impact or business functionality might be lost by disabling something and make sure that it's really necessary to do that. One very common thing some customers want to do is disable saving Instant Messaging history. By default, when users have both Outlook and Skype for Business installed, instant messages are saved to the Conversation History folder. This is an incredibly useful feature, because often links to URLs, names of people to contact, or other information is shared over IM. Being able to go back to that keeps you from having to ask the same question again and again, but because it is in email, it could be subject to discovery, and many companies are concerned that the more informal communications within instant messaging might present a risk if they become the subject of a discovery motion. You could spend more time on training your users to treat IM the same as email from that perspective rather than disabling saving IM history, but each business will approach this according to its needs.

Before you set policies for users, consider whether the graphical user interface (GUI) can be used to apply all the settings you require. By using Windows PowerShell, you can set a policy that matches what you can set through the GUI, but you can also control many more of the settings. If you can apply policy consistently to users with Windows PowerShell, this is not an issue, but if some of your administrative users use only the GUI, but others use Windows PowerShell, you might have users with different experiences, depending on whether they were configured through web browser or script. After you start to configure users with Windows PowerShell, it is best to use only Windows PowerShell from that point forward if any setting you need to apply is not available in the GUI. Either help those graphically inclined admins learn how to run basic Windows PowerShell commands, or take care of applying policy yourself.

Finally, refer to Zoran Cvetkovic's blog post at *https://techcommunity.microsoft.com/t5/Skype -for-Business-Blog/Custom-Policies-in-Skype-for-Business-Online/ba-p/60096* before you spend too much time either applying existing policies or creating your own. He has some great tips for ensuring that policy setting remains manageable.

> **NOTE**
>
> Skype for Business Online includes many built-in policies, but not all of them might be relevant to you nor, depending on your licensing or the regulations in the country your users are assigned as their location, might one or more of the included policies be available to you. When listing the policies by using Windows PowerShell, you can either use the modifier "-Include All" to see all the policies in your tenant, or you can use "-ApplicableTo" and specify the SIP or UPN of a user in the location of interest to see what policies are relevant. That is especially useful if you have more than one license type or if you have users in multiple countries.

Authentication

It's very important to understand how authentication in Skype for Business Online works, especially if you plan to restrict access based on network location. Skype for Business Online does not work the same way as the other services do when it comes to using tokens for authentication, access, and refresh.

The initial authentication method you choose for your users (federated authentication to your on-premises IdP, password hash sync, cloud accounts) will be the same as for Exchange Online, SharePoint Online, and so on, with the same requirements for multifactor authentication, conditional access, and so on. Skype for Business Online supports Modern Authentication, just as modern versions of Outlook, the other Office apps, and current browsers do. Assume that you are using Active Directory, have implemented Azure ADConnect, and set up federation between Office 365 and your on-premises Active Directory Federation Services (AD FS) farm. When a user wants to connect to SBO for the first time, here is what happens.

1. The client gets an authentication token from the on-premises identity provider.

2. The client exchanges the authentication token (after verification) for an access token from the Microsoft Federation gateway and is directed to the Skype for Business Online service.

The client presents the access token and is given a Client Access Certificate (CAC.) This certificate, which has an eight-hour lifetime, is then used to connect to the Skype for Business Online service. That certificate looks like the one in Figure 15-10.

Figure 15-10 A client authentication certificate for Skype for Business Online

CHAPTER 15

That is where things become very different from the other services. There is no concept of a refresh token. If the user's session ends, and they reconnect before the certificate expires, they can reconnect without having to go through any additional authentication. That means any network restrictions, which limit how you can get that initial authentication token, do not come into play. If a user on their laptop authenticates to Skype for Business Online while on the corporate network, and then goes home and launches Skype again, they can reconnect to SBO even if you have set up Client Access Policies on AD FS that would prevent them from authenticating unless they were on the corporate network.

Because the user authenticated to your AD FS (and if you disable a user, reset their password, or remove their license, it will not immediately disconnect them from SBO), you hope the eight-hour lifetime of the certificate will not present too great a problem. The eight-hour lifetime for the CAC is not configurable.

Skype clients also need to authenticate to Exchange or Exchange Online to obtain your calendar information. The Skype client might prompt you for username and password, because this uses EWS and, in Exchange Online, that only uses older Active Authentication. This is just another reason for you to ensure that your users' User Principal Name, primary SMTP address, and SIP address all match. When they do not, the prompts can become very confusing to users, and they can easily enter the wrong value when prompted.

What about Teams?

Microsoft Teams is the latest addition to the suite of products in Office 365 and is included with E1 and E3 licenses. It is a hub for teamwork, providing a single application through which teams can work together on projects; share information; collaborate; and conference using IM, audio, and video. It combines the best features of Skype for Business Online, SharePoint Online, and Microsoft OneNote, and it might be the future of collaboration and teamwork. Although there is a lot going on with Teams, this section focuses only on the potential overlap between Teams and SBO.

Comparing Skype for Business Online and Teams

There is some overlap between Skype for Business Online and Microsoft Teams. Some of your users might use only one or the other, but most will use both as appropriate. Each has its own features that the other lacks, and the good news is that you can run both on the same machine at the same time with minimal CPU or RAM usage.

How they are the same

The audio, video, and presentation sharing that Microsoft Teams provides is built on the next generation of Skype for Business technology. The ports and protocols are the same, the endpoints share many of the same namespaces and IP address ranges, and your users can interact directly with one another, whether they are using the Skype for Business Online client or the Microsoft Teams client. Much like SBO, there are mobile clients for all three major platforms as well as a web browser–based client for IM&P. You can schedule meetings in both and work collaboratively with others.

How they are different

Skype for Business Online offers full administration with policies, saves conversation history if desired, can federate with external SIP systems or with consumer Skype, and provides more mature reporting and troubleshooting capabilities. Teams lacks these things, although conversations within Teams are saved in the channel where they took place. Authorized users gain access to that history in Teams, but not through Outlook, and at the time of this writing, that content was not accessible through compliance searches.

However, Teams also offers the long-sought persistent chat room capabilities, which Skype for Business has but Skype for Business Online does not; it also integrates SharePoint Online and Office 365 Groups directly. Teams also has a rich and growing set of add-ins that you can add to a Team channel, including Office web apps, bots, surveys, and third-party apps. See Figure 15-11.

CHAPTER 15

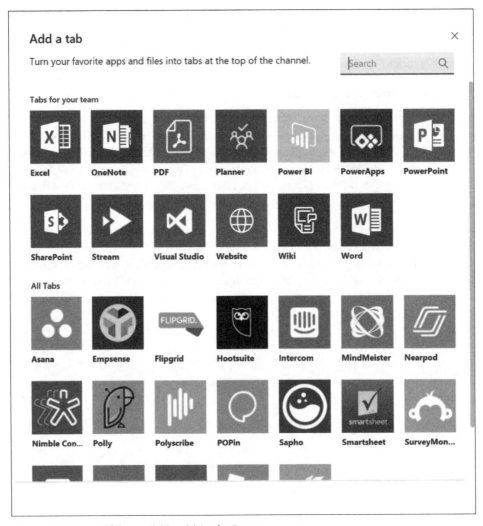

Figure 15-11 Some of the available add-ins for Teams

A growing list of Microsoft and third-party connectors also enables you to use Teams with your other key business applications and processes, some of which appear in Figure 15-12.

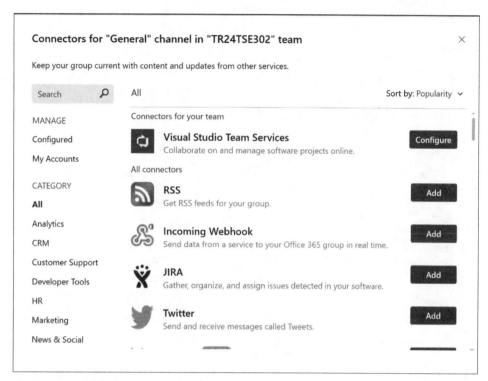

Figure 15-12 Some of the most popular Teams connectors

When should you use which?

That's an easy question to ask but a more difficult question to answer. Skype for Business Online and Microsoft Teams are complementary in the enterprise and might even be so with individual users. You and your users can use one or the other or both as your work needs dictate. You might choose to use Teams for working with internal projects but use SBO for communications with others in the organization as well as with external customers or partners. The beauty of this approach is that you can work the way that works for you.

Summary

In this chapter, you learned the basic concepts of Skype for Business Online, including the features it supports, the fundamental requirements to implement it, the protocols involved, and the clients you can deploy to your users for them to get online. You learned about the options you can set for your users, how to connect to and manage the service through Windows PowerShell, and the importance of ensuring that your network is ready to support SBO. In the next chapter, you put this knowledge to use to deploy and manage the service for your users.

Deploying and administering Skype for Business Online

In this chapter, you learn how to deploy Skype for Business Online (SBO) as well as how to administer it. If you jumped ahead to this chapter, please review Chapter 15, "Skype for Business Online Concepts and Implementation," first, because many of the concepts you need to understand in this chapter are reviewed in that one. SBO, set up and configured, does not require nearly as much administration as Exchange Online or SharePoint Online, but that doesn't mean you just want to deploy it and see what happens. Ensuring that you have set up your service and configured your clients properly is the best way to ensure that you get the most out of SBO.

Configuring Skype for Business Online

Start with what you need to administer SBO. There is no role-based access control (RBAC) or delegated administration in SBO. If you are a global administrator in the tenant, or if you have been configured in customized administration as a Skype for Business administrator, then you can administer SBO.

To grant someone the specific workload administrator capabilities for SBO, use the Office 365 Admin Center portal as follows.

1. Log on to *https://portal.office.com*, using a Global Admin account.

2. Browse to the Office 365 Admin Center | Users | Active Users.

3. Click the user you wish to make an SBO administrator.

4. Click the Edit link in the Roles section.

5. Click the button next to Customized Administrator.

6. Click the check box next to Skype For Business Administrator, as shown in Figure 16-1, and then click Save.

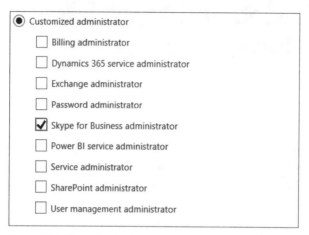

Figure 16-1 Skype for Business customized administrator role

You can also use Windows PowerShell to view the membership of these administrator groups and add members to them. When you are connected to your tenant, run the `Get-MsolRole` command to view all the available administrative roles in your tenant (Figure 16-2). Note the highlighted line.

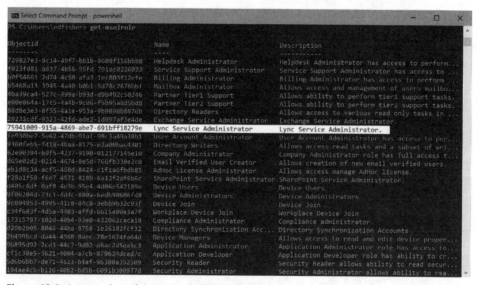

Figure 16-2 A screenshot of the output of Get-MsolRole

Remember that Skype for Business evolved from Lync, and the internal naming still reflects that. You can view everyone who is a Lync service administrator by running the

`Get-MsolRoleMember -RoleObjectID 75941009-915a-4869-abe7-691bff18279e | fl`
command. The ObjectID in your tenant should be the same as any other, but verify it with the
`Get-MsolRole` cmdlet to be sure. As shown in Figure 16-3, there are two members in the SBO
Admins group, Allison Brown and Don Funk.

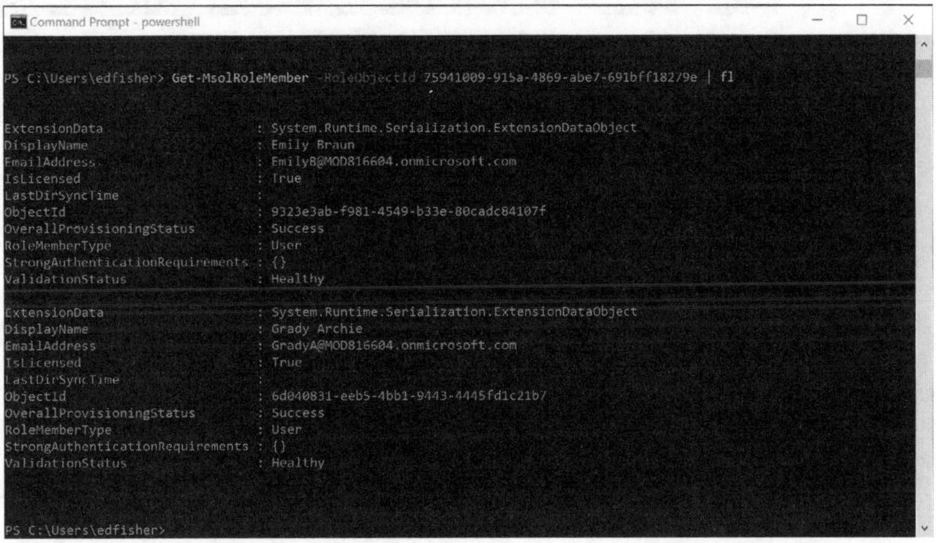

Figure 16-3 Get-MsolRoleMember output

Remember that members of the tenant Global Admins group have SBO administrative rights,
even though they won't show up as members of the Lync Service Administrator group.

When you have the appropriate rights, you're ready to start configuring SBO for your users.
Most of what you do you do only once as a part of your initial configuration. Needs might
change and require you to make adjustments, or you might want to start rolling out features
slowly, but barring changes, the settings you make generally apply to all users in the tenant
and are the settings you use going forward. You can use the Skype Admin portal or Windows
PowerShell to administer SBO.

The dashboard

To open the Skype Admin Center, log on to the Office 365 Admin Center portal and navigate to
the Skype Admin center. Here's how to get there.

1.   Log on to *https://portal.office.com/* by using either a Global Admin account or that of a
     member of the Skype for Business administrator role.

2.   Click the Admin tile.

3. Use the navigation on the left side of the portal to select Admin Centers and click Skype For Business to open the Skype For Business Admin Center dashboard, as shown in Figure 16-4.

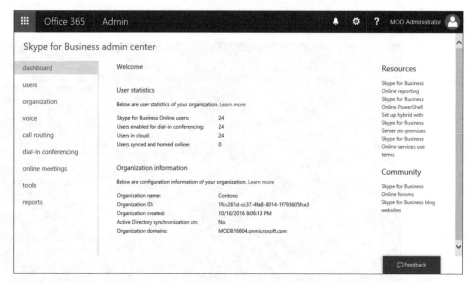

Figure 16-4 Skype for Business Admin Center

From here, you can see an overview of your tenant and navigate to the various areas for configuring SBO. The dashboard shows you how many users you have licensed for SBO and enabled for dial-in conferencing and how many are cloud users or synced from your on-premises Active Directory. You can also see your organization name, organization ID, creation date, whether sync is enabled from on-premises, and your organization domains, which are configured for Session Initiation Protocol (SIP). From here, the chapter examines each of the areas to configure in the portal.

Users

The Users section lists all the users in your tenant who have been licensed for Skype for Business Online. Remember, that is done in the tenant admin center by a Global Admin or a User Account administrator. To appear in this section, a user must be licensed, and they must have no settings that might prevent them from syncing to SBO.

NOTE

If you have licensed a user for SBO but they do not appear in the Users section of the SBO admin center, check to make sure there are no issues in Active Directory that would block them from being synchronized to SBO. In your on-premises Active Directory, make sure that the msRTCSIP-* attributes are all blank or, if they are not, that msRTCSIP-User-Enabled is blank or set to True, and the value in msRTCSIP-PrimaryUserAddress matches the value for the SIP address in the proxyAddresses attribute.

You probably won't spend a lot of time administering users in the Users section. If you find that you need to do this, consider what you are doing and why. In the Users section, you can edit the individual details for one or more users, but you should probably either be making those settings globally for your organization or assigning policies to users through Windows PowerShell. If you do need to manage settings for one or more users, and want to use the GUI, select them in the portal and then click the Edit button. Here is what you can do in the Users section.

General

Under the General settings for a user, you can control audio and video settings, disable their ability to record conversations and meetings, and disable data transfers. Figure 16-5 shows the settings for a user whose default values have not been changed.

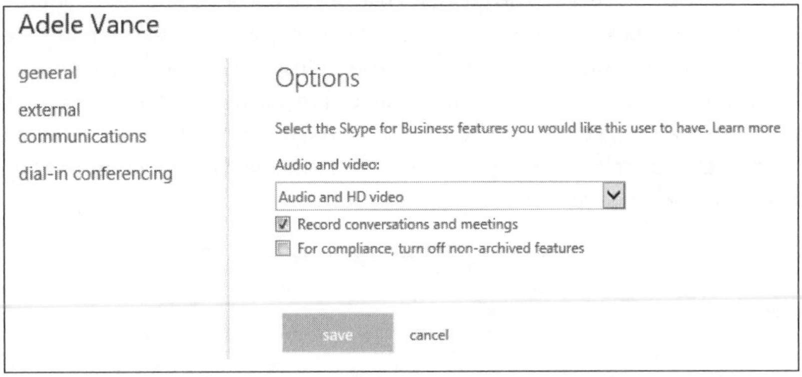

Adele Vance

general

external
communications

dial-in conferencing

Options

Select the Skype for Business features you would like this user to have. Learn more

Audio and video:

| Audio and HD video | ∨ |

☑ Record conversations and meetings

☐ For compliance, turn off non-archived features

save   cancel

Figure 16-5 General user settings

The first setting is Audio And Video, as shown in Figure 16-6. You can select the following options from the drop-down menu.

None
Audio only
Audio and video
Audio and HD video

Figure 16-6 A screenshot of the audio and video options

Audio And HD Video is the default setting, which enables users to use both audio for voice and video for conferencing up to the full bandwidth their hardware and network connection can support. That can use up to 200 Kbps for audio and up to 50,000 Kbps for video. HD video shouldn't consume more than 4096 Kbps per feed, but a conference with several users, all of whom have HD cameras, can use a lot more. Audio And Video still permits both but limits the video bandwidth consumed to a maximum of 1000 Kbps. Audio Only enables audio but disables video, whereas None disables both.

Record Conversations And Meetings is enabled by default. Clear that check box if you don't want to permit a user to record conversations or meetings.

For Compliance, Turn Off Non-Archived Features is off by default. That means that users can use SBO to transfer files over instant messaging (IM) and share OneNote pages and annotations to Microsoft PowerPoint decks. Because these methods of file transfer are not logged or archived, you might need to disable them if your organization must track all data transfers.

External communications

External communications enables users to communicate with others outside of your organization, assuming you have configured your SBO tenant to allow this. At the tenant level, this is off by default, so you don't have to do anything here if you are not going to configure connectivity to external systems, but if you do want to permit your organization to communicate with other SIP systems, including consumer Skype, yet prevent a user from doing so, this is where you configure those exceptions. By default, all users can communicate with external Skype for Business users and external Skype users after you configure the tenant to permit this. Figure 16-7 shows the options set to permit external federation with both other Skype for Business organizations and the consumer Skype service.

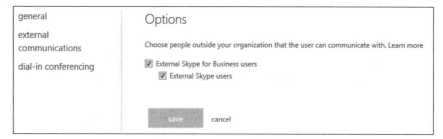

Figure 16-7 A screenshot of the options for external communications

Again, you need to clear those check boxes only if you have permitted external connectivity at the tenant level but want to block a specific user from being able to use that. If it's permitted here (which is the default) but you have not explicitly enabled external connectivity for the tenant, they cannot communicate with other organizations or consumers.

Dial-in conferencing

If you have E5 licenses or subscribe to the SBO Dial-in Conferencing Service separately, you can configure the dial-in conferencing provider and toll and toll-free numbers, reset a user's PIN, and allow or block anonymous callers in meetings. Figure 16-8 shows these settings.

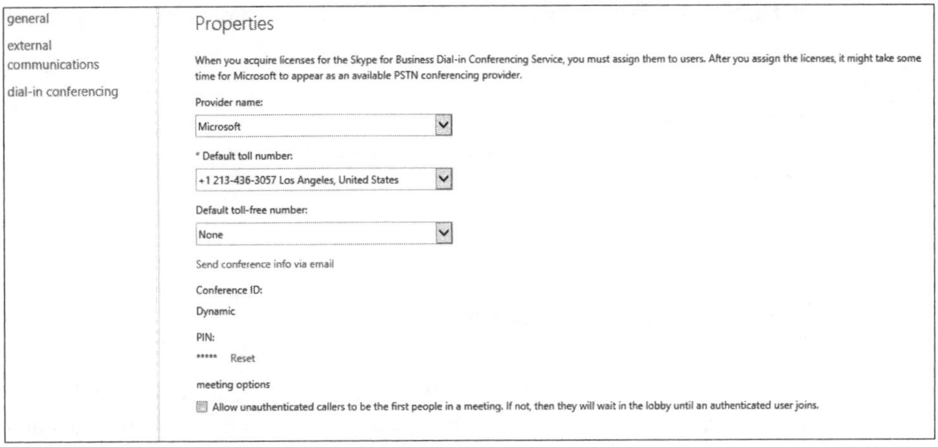

Figure 16-8 Dial-In Conferencing properties

You have a choice of conferencing providers. If you choose one other than Microsoft, you need to have established service with that provider because that is separate from Skype for Business Online. With Microsoft as your provider, several toll numbers are available across various countries. You can establish a toll-free number for people to dial into, but that incurs additional cost.

Note that the default is not to allow unauthenticated callers to enter a meeting. Unless you select that box, anyone who does not authenticate to SBO, either by using the client or dialing in and using their own PIN, will wait in a lobby until the first authenticated user joins. At that point, all dial-in users are admitted to the call.

You will probably spend the most time here for any user, because this is where you can reset their PIN and generate an email to send them their conference information. This is the same information, minus their PIN, that is appended to any meeting invite they create for an SBO meeting.

Organization

The Organization section includes settings that affect your entire organization. Although specific user settings might prevail, if you haven't made any specific user settings, these apply to all users.

CHAPTER 16

General

The General tab includes settings for Presence and for push notification to mobile phones. By default, all SBO users' presence displays to anyone. The other option is to show presence only for a user's contacts. A user can override this setting with specific settings in the SBO client, but this controls the default behaviors for your tenant if your user does nothing. Figure 16-9 shows the default settings. Remember that users can override what presence information is displayed in their client.

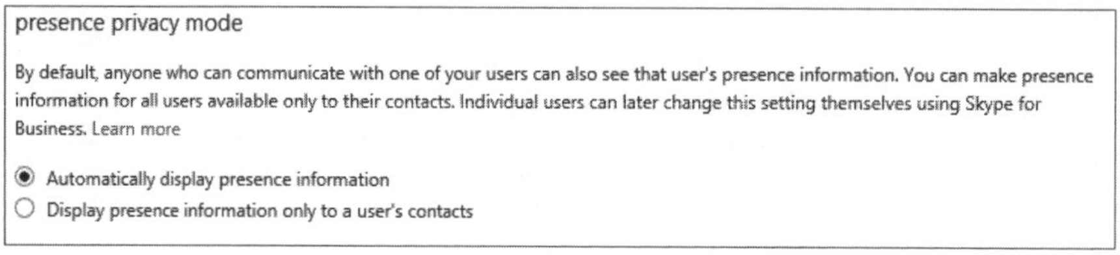

presence privacy mode

By default, anyone who can communicate with one of your users can also see that user's presence information. You can make presence information for all users available only to their contacts. Individual users can later change this setting themselves using Skype for Business. Learn more

◉ Automatically display presence information
○ Display presence information only to a user's contacts

Figure 16-9 Presence Privacy Mode settings

Mobile phone notifications controls whether to use push notifications to mobile clients for incoming IMs, voice mail messages, and missed calls and chats. There are two options, both of which are on by default. The first is to use the Microsoft Push Notification Service, and the second is to use the Apple Push Notification Service. If you leave these on, users can enable or disable notifications on their mobile device, but if you turn them off, they are not available for users at all. Figure 16-10 shows both notification types enabled, which is the default.

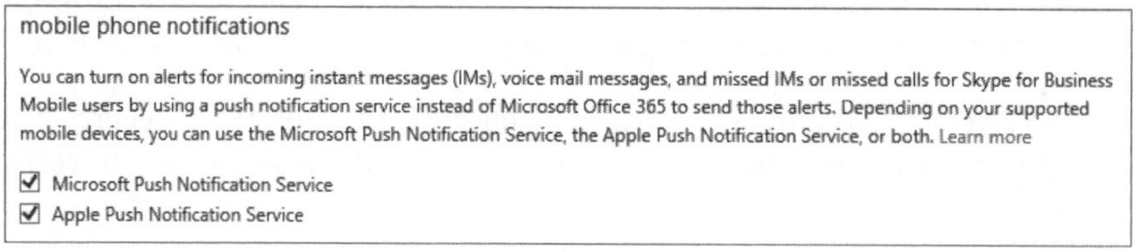

mobile phone notifications

You can turn on alerts for incoming instant messages (IMs), voice mail messages, and missed IMs or missed calls for Skype for Business Mobile users by using a push notification service instead of Microsoft Office 365 to send those alerts. Depending on your supported mobile devices, you can use the Microsoft Push Notification Service, the Apple Push Notification Service, or both. Learn more

☑ Microsoft Push Notification Service
☑ Apple Push Notification Service

Figure 16-10 Mobile Phone Notifications

External communications

External communications includes important settings for you to consider. These options should be set before the first user is enabled for SBO. By default, SBO is a closed system. Users within the tenant can communicate with one another, but no external parties are accessible. However, if you want your users to be able to communicate over IM, voice, and/or video, and to see presence for users in another organization, you can set up Skype federation. You can also set up federation with the Skype consumer service so your users can communicate with users of that public system. This can be very useful for customer service, human resources (HR) functions, and enabling your users to stay in touch with friends and family.

Some organizations might be very open to federation, whereas others might want to control it more tightly or even prevent it completely. Settings here affect the entire organization, but you can permit federation and then restrict specific users from using it. What you cannot do is say that a user can communicate with others in SIP domain X but not SIP domain Y, whereas another user is blocked from SIP domain X and can communicate with SIP domain Y. It can take up to 24 hours for changes in this section to propagate fully throughout the system, so you don't want to deploy one setting and then change your mind.

In external access, the default is for it to be Off Completely. With this setting, your SBO tenant is a self-contained island. Your users can communicate using SBO with one another, but with no one outside your organization. If set to On Except For Blocked Domains, your user can communicate with other users in any Skype for Business or Lync system that permits external communications, except for those SIP domains you explicitly block. If set to On Only For Allowed Domains, you explicitly add those domains with which you want to have Skype federation. Figure 16-11 shows the external access settings when set to permit federation.

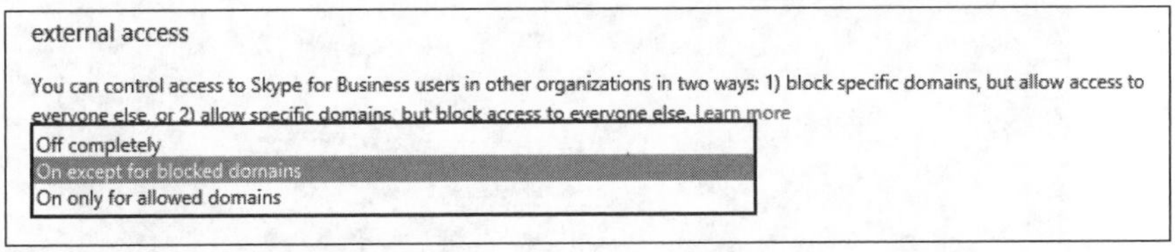

external access

You can control access to Skype for Business users in other organizations in two ways: 1) block specific domains, but allow access to everyone else, or 2) allow specific domains, but block access to everyone else. Learn more

Off completely
On except for blocked domains
On only for allowed domains

Figure 16-11 External Access options

Federation between two SIP organizations, such as two Office 365 tenants or an Office 365 tenant and an on-premises deployment of Skype for Business, is fairly easy to set up, but it does require both SIP organizations to configure the federation. If both organizations use On Except For Blocked Domains, they can communicate, but if one or both of the organizations is using On Only For Allowed Domains, it will have to add the other SIP domain into its allowed list.

TROUBLESHOOTING

When federation doesn't work

Federation between two SIP organizations used to require company A to specify the FQDN of company B's edge and vice versa. Today, SIP federation with SBO requires the use of SRV records in DNS, which is defined in RFC 3263 at *https://tools.ietf.org/html/rfc3263*. SBO does not use FQDNs for itself or to discover federation partners, so if you are trying to federate with another organization and they ask you for your edge FQDN, that is a red flag. To check another company's SIP records to confirm whether it has SRV records in place for SIP federation, use the DNS NSLOOKUP or DIG tools to check for _sipfederationtls._tcp.contoso.com, substituting the SIP domain for contoso.

com. You should see output similar to what is shown in Figure 16-12, which shows both NSLOOKUP and DIG.

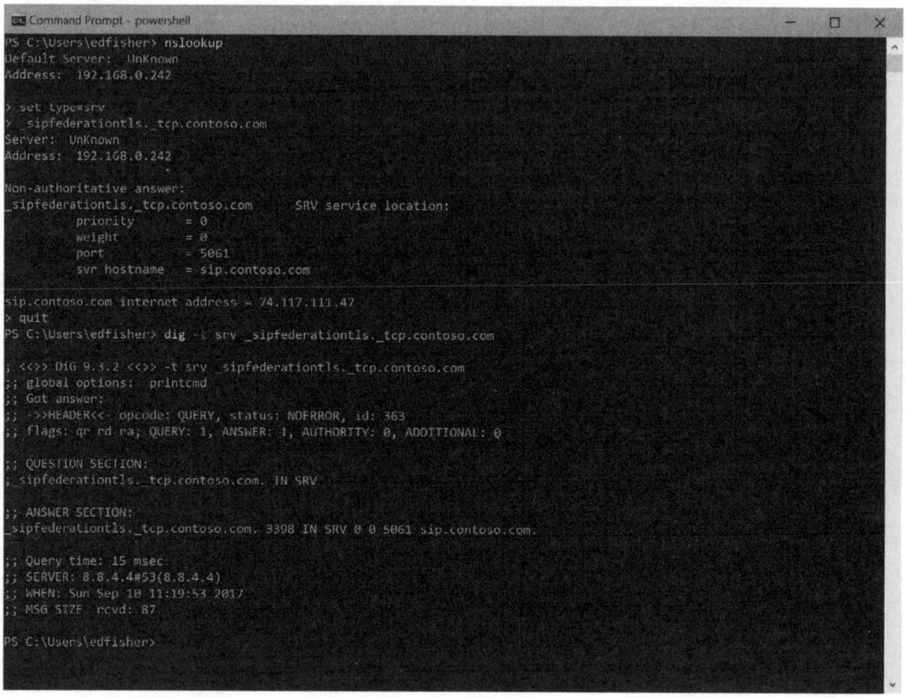

Figure 16-12 SBO DNS records

If you do not get an SRV record for _sipfederationtls, contact your partner organization's admin to confirm that it can use SRV records and ask that admin to implement them into their Internet DNS. Without that record, you cannot federate with them.

Voice

You can configure telephone numbers and other settings in the Voice section if your organization has purchased PSTN services as part of its Office 365 subscription. Customers in the United States can purchase Skype for Business PSTN Domestic Calling or Skype for Business PSTN Domestic and International Calling. Different countries regulate their telephony industries differently, so different options might be available or, in some cases, none at all. If your organization is U.S.-based but has users in different countries, you might not be able to assign some or any of the features for Voice and Call Routing because laws vary from one jurisdiction to another, and it's where the user is based, rather than where the tenant is provisioned, that governs this. Assuming that your tenant is a North American tenant and your company is U.S.-based, and you purchased one of the calling plans, you will see three sections under Voice.

Phone numbers

In the Phone Numbers section, if you have a PSTN Calling license, you can assign specific Direct Inward Dialing (DID) telephone numbers to your users and for services. Users, conference room phones, and individual devices can have their own DIDs, called user numbers, and you can get service numbers for conference bridges.

Voice users

Cloud PBX capabilities enable you to configure voice users for outbound and inbound calling with PSTN connectivity. You might have more users than you have DIDs or users who only need to make outbound calls, or you might want to limit the users who can make calls outside of your organization.

On-premises PSTN

If you have an on-premises connection to the telephone network through a Public Branch Exchange (PBX), you would configure those settings here. This requires you to have configured Skype for Business hybrid connectivity between your Office 365 and your on-premises Skype environments so that cloud users can connect to the telephony network through on-premises hardware (a discussion that is outside the scope of this book).

Call routing

Call Routing, relevant only if you have a dialing plan, enables you to set up both auto-attendants and call queues.

Auto attendants

The Auto-Attendant feature is an automated system that answers the phone, plays a recorded greeting, and then offers callers a menu of choices they can navigate to reach a particular person, department, or other options. You probably have encountered one when calling a company and then promptly held down the zero button on your phone to connect to a person. If you have one or more DIDs, you can create an auto-attendant by clicking the Add New button. Here's how you can set this up.

1. As a global admin or SBO admin, log on to the admin portal and navigate to the Skype for Business Admin Center | Call Routing | Auto Attendants.

2. Click the plus sign (+) Add New link.

3. On the General Info page, give your auto-attendant a name, select the phone number to use, the time zone this number should be in, the language, whether to use speech recognition so callers can speak their desired selection rather than pressing the number

CHAPTER 16

on their keypad, and then whether pressing 0 for an operator should route the call to a specific user or to a call queue, as shown in Figure 16-13.

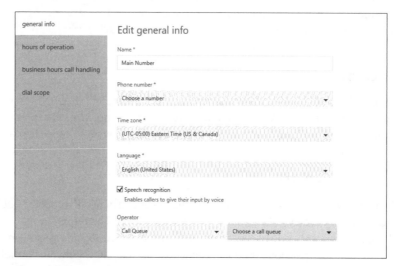

Figure 16-13 Attendant options

4. On the Select Hours Of Operation page, select whether this auto-attendant should function 24/7 or only during specific times, such as office hours or after hours, as shown in Figure 16-14.

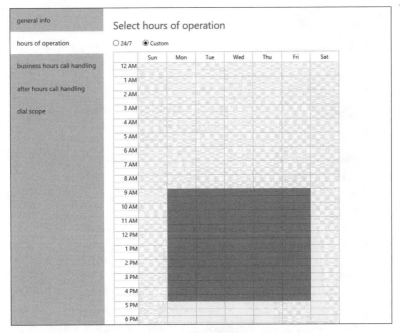

Figure 16-14 Select Hours Of Operation page

In Business Hours Call Handling (which means during the time you selected in the previous menu, including 24/7), you can build out a menu. You have the option of using text to speech or of uploading an audio file for the company greeting, and you can add up to nine menu choices for where to route a call. These can be to individual users, to call queues, or to other auto-attendants if you need another level of menu options. You can set this as shown in Figure 16-15.

CHAPTER 16

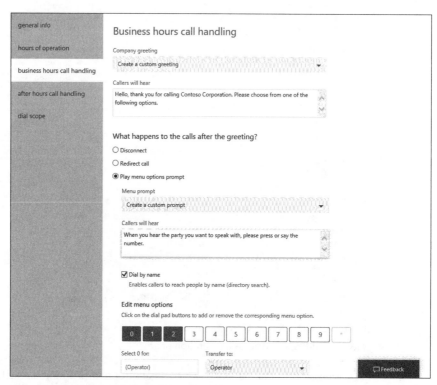

Figure 16-15 Business Hours Call Handling

5. On the After Hours Call Handling page, set options for what happens to calls that come in outside of business hours.

   Figure 16-16 shows how to upload a prerecorded message in MP3, wave (WAV), or Windows Media Audio (WMA) and then how to disconnect the call.

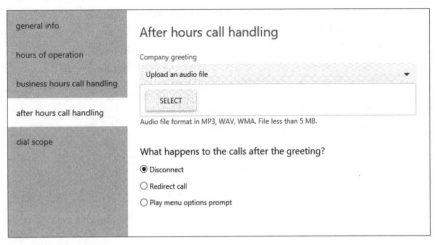

Figure 16-16 After Hours Call Handling options

6. Finally, in Dial Scope, configure which users to include or exclude in Dial By Name (Directory Search).

   By default, this includes all users enabled for telephony, as shown in Figure 16-17.

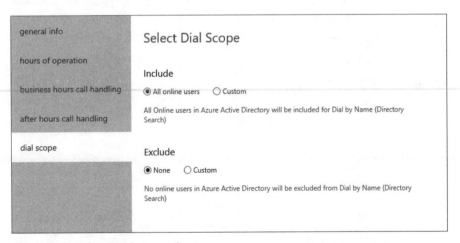

Figure 16-17 Select Dial Scope options

Call queues

Call queues enable multiple callers to dial in to a single number to reach any one of a group of people. You might use a queue for your help desk, customer service, or any other department with a high volume of incoming calls, when the next available person should be able to address the caller's needs. To create a call queue, select the Call Queues tab and fill out the appropriate options. Note that in a call queue, there is no text to speech, so you must upload an audio file for the greeting. You can also upload a file for Music On Hold and set values for the maximum number of callers in the queue, the maximum amount of time callers can wait before being forwarded or disconnected, and what to do if the maximums are reached, such as forwarding to a voicemail. Figure 16-18 shows these options.

Figure 16-18 Call Queue options

Dial-in conferencing

The next section of the SBO admin portal is Dial-In Conferencing. If you did not purchase E5 licenses or the optional Skype for Business Dial-in Conferencing add-on licenses, you won't use anything in this section, but if you did, this is the section where you can determine information for your organization and set specific values.

Microsoft Bridge

The Microsoft Bridge section displays the telephone numbers activated for your service in each country that is available. It also shows you the primary language and enables you to set a default. In Figure 16-19, Chicago is selected, and you can click the Set As Default link on the right if that is the number you want to use for your default. Just above that, Los Angeles is currently the default.

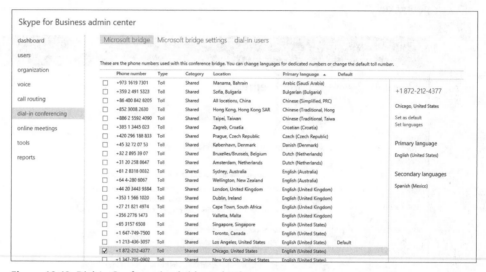

Figure 16-19 Dial-In Conferencing bridge selection

At the bottom of this page, a link to configure third-party audio conferencing providers appears, as shown in Figure 16-20.

Figure 16-20 Additional conferencing options

If you already have a conferencing provider, you can use the Click Here link to import and export your user settings from another provider. Remember that this requires you to have conferencing services from that provider, which will include additional charges.

Microsoft bridge settings

Use the Microsoft Bridge Settings tab to configure the meeting join experience as well as the minimum PIN length for users to log on to their conference bridge. By default, notifications are turned off in all meetings. Meeting owners can turn that on for their meeting and, if they do, this setting determines whether an announcement or a tone is played when someone enters or exits a meeting. With Names Or Phone Numbers selected, you can prompt users to record their name before joining. As an alternative, you can choose a simple tone to be played, although this feature is in preview and might not be available yet in your tenant. Figure 16-21 shows the options to enable notifications and to prompt users to record their name and then to press the pound key.

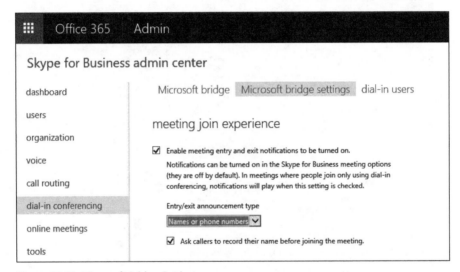

Figure 16-21 Microsoft Bridge Settings page

Each dial-in conferencing user has a PIN that identifies them to the system when they dial in from a landline or mobile phone rather than using the SBO client. In the Security section, you set the PIN length. The default is 5 characters, shown in Figure 16-22.

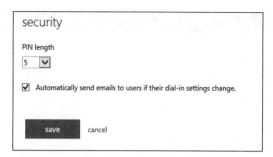

Figure 16-22 A screenshot of the Security settings

Dial-in users

The last section for Dial-In Conferencing is the Dial-In Users section. This shows your users, the default toll and (optionally) toll-free numbers assigned to them, and their conference ID. If you select a user and then click the Edit button, you see the same interface as you would if you went through Users and then selected the Dial-In Conferencing settings for that user, as shown previously in Figure 16-19.

Online meetings

You can use the Online Meetings page to set up options for online meetings and include your company-specific branding, disclaimers, and links. You also configure Skype Meeting Broadcast settings here.

Meeting invitation

Meeting invitations can be branded to make them more identifiable and to customize other details. You can include the company logo by providing a link to a graphic file hosted on one of your servers. You can also include custom links to Help and Legal Disclaimer pages you host on a web server. Figure 16-23 shows these options.

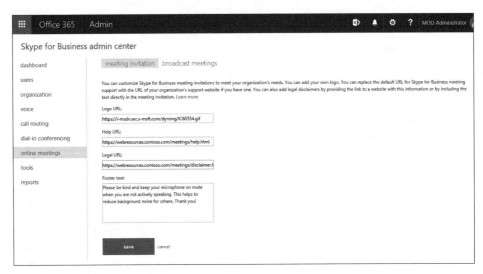

Figure 16-23 Meeting Invitation options

Completing the information shown in Figure 16-23 creates a meeting invite that looks like the one in Figure 16-24.

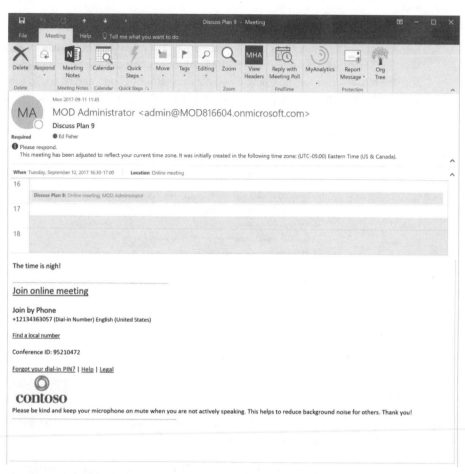

Figure 16-24 Microsoft Outlook meeting invitation

INSIDE OUT

Storing logo, help, and disclaimer files

You want to make sure that the logo, help, and disclaimer files are stored on a web server that is accessible using anonymous connections; otherwise, they will not appear for users who are not part of your organization or who otherwise cannot authenticate. SharePoint Online is not the best choice for storing these files because it typically requires authentication. Instead, use your corporate web server that hosts your public-facing website so you know these files can be accessed by anyone invited to a meeting.

Broadcast meetings

Remember that SBO meetings have a maximum of 250 attendees, but Skype for Business Meeting Broadcast can support up to 10,000 attendees. You can use broadcast meetings to support town hall–type meetings, public webinars, investor briefings, and so on. To use Skype for Business Meeting Broadcast, you have to enable it and configure a few settings. Figure 16-25 shows this setup.

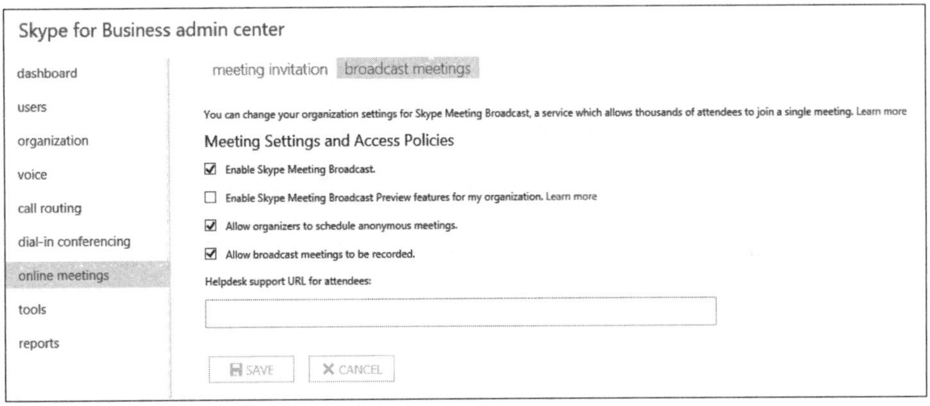

Figure 16-25 Broadcast Meetings settings

Tools

The Tools page includes links to several online tools to help SBO administrators manage or troubleshoot potential issues with SBO.

Troubleshooting Skype for Business Online sign-in for administrators

The Troubleshooting tool is a shortcut to *https://support.microsoft.com/en-us/help/2541980 /how-to-troubleshoot-sign-in-issues-in-skype-for-business-online*, providing tips for troubleshooting sign-in issues, including verifying credentials and network connectivity.

Skype for Business Connectivity Analyzer tool

The Connectivity Analyzer tool links to an older Lync Connectivity Analyzer tool for Lync Server 2013 that has been deprecated. Expect to see this link removed soon.

Microsoft Remote Connectivity Analyzer

You can use the Remote Connectivity Analyzer tool to diagnose logon and Autodiscover issues.

Setting up Skype for Business Online external communications

This tool simply links to the page that shows you how to enable external federation to other SBO organizations as well as to consumer Skype.

Skype for Business Online Call Quality dashboard

The Call Quality dashboard (CQD) provides great information to help you diagnose call quality issues. You can diagnose trouble users might be having that are associated with latency, packet loss, the use of TCP, poor Wi-Fi connectivity, using older clients, poor hardware, and more. See Figure 16-26.

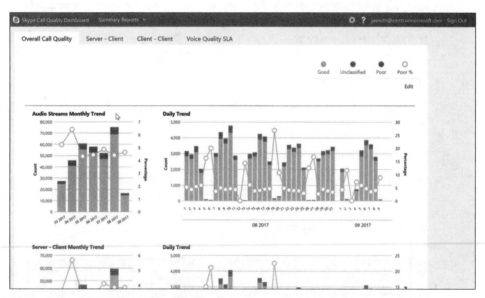

Figure 16-26 Call Quality dashboard

Skype for Business Call Analytics (Preview)

Use Call Analytics, currently in preview mode, to search for specific users and view the quality details of their calls and meetings over the past seven days. You can use this to correlate reports of quality issues against actual metrics and troubleshoot issues. This feature is extremely helpful when someone complains about a specific call. Where the CQD gives you aggregate details, Call Analytics focuses on a specific user's exact call to determine what was wrong.

> ## NOTE
>
> Remember the Skype for Business Network Assessment Tool discussed in Chapter 15? That's another great tool that you might use both to assess your readiness to deploy SBO and to troubleshoot issues that might come up after deployment. The download link for

that is *https://www.microsoft.com/en-us/download/details.aspx?id=53885*, and steps for how to run it are included in the documentation that comes with the tool as well as in Chapter 15.

Reports

The Reports section contains three reports specific to SBO.

PSTN usage details

If you have a dial plan, this is the call details record for your tenant. It reports the user location, user ID, phone number, caller ID, call type, whether it was a domestic or international call, the destination number dialed, the number type, the start time, the duration, the charge, the currency, and the capability of each call. You can use this to check user activity or reconcile your bill. It can also be exported to Microsoft Excel for further analysis, internal chargebacks, and so on.

Users Blocked report

The Users Blocked report shows you which numbers users have blocked, including the time and any supplied reason for the block.

Session Details (preview)

The Session Details report enables you to examine specific time frames for specific users. You can see whether it was an audio or a video call, the start and end times, and the client versions for each participant as well as the Conference URL if it was a meeting rather than a direct call. A sample is shown in Figure 16-27.

Media Types Descript	Start Time	End Time	From Uri	To Uri	From Client Version	To Client Version	Conference Url
[Audio]	9/10/2017 11:39 AM	9/10/2017 11:45 AM	connie...	edfisher@...	UCCAPI/16.0.8326.... OC/16.0.8326.2096 (Skype for Business)	UCCAPI/16.0.8201.... OC/16.0.8201.2171 (Skype for Business)	

Figure 16-27 Session Details report

NOTE

There is one more report that you might want to review related to SBO, but it's not in the SBO Admin Center but, rather, in the Office 365 Admin Center. You can view active usage for your SBO users this way.

1.   Log on to the admin portal, using your Global Admin account.

2. Click Reports | Usage.

3. Click the Skype For Business Activity report.

This report can show you over 7-, 30-, 90-, and 180-day intervals of your users' calls, including their last SBO activity and activity sorted by peer-to-peer, organized conferences, and participated-in conferences. You can also export this report to a CSV file.

Inside Windows PowerShell

The Skype for Business Online Admin Center is where most of your administrative work takes place, assuming you will use the default settings provided in SBO. If you want to customize certain policies or restrict your users from certain capabilities, Windows PowerShell is how to do it. You can download and install the Skype for Business Online PowerShell module on your computer; it uses the same setup as you have already performed for managing Exchange and Azure Active Directory through Windows PowerShell. To manage SBO by using Windows PowerShell, follow these steps.

1. Make sure your administrative workstation is running at least Windows PowerShell version 3.0 and that the Microsoft Online Services Sign-in Assistant is installed.

2. Download the Skype for Business Online Module. At the time of this writing, that is version 7.0.1045.0, and you can download it from *http://www.microsoft.com/en-us /download/details.aspx?id=39366*.

3. Double-click the Download link to install the module.

4. After the module is installed, open Windows PowerShell.

5. Enter the following command to store your global admin or SBO credentials.

    ```
    $credential=Get-Credential
    ```

    A credential dialog box appears; type your UPN and password.

6. Type the following command to create a new session to SBO.

    ```
    $session=New-CsOnlineSession -credential $credential -verbose
    ```

    Text confirming the domain, which is derived from your UPN, and the endpoint for your SBO tenant appears.

7. Type the following command to import the SBO session to your current session.

    ```
    Import-PSSession $session
    ```

CHAPTER 16

> **NOTE**
>
> If you intend to use Windows PowerShell to administer Office 365 often, and you prob-
> ably will, you really don't want to be setting up new Windows PowerShell sessions by
> hand every time. There are many ways to automate this process and to import all the
> modules and connect to all the services, Azure Active Directory, Exchange Online, Share-
> Point Online, Skype for Business Online, Azure RMS, and the Security & Compliance Cen-
> ter, all at once. I use the O365_Logon module that Mike O'Neill created and published
> at *https://blogs.technet.microsoft.com/mconeill/2015/11/30/o365_logon-module/*. With
> that, I type one cmdlet in Windows PowerShell, connect-o365, and I am quickly con-
> nected to all of the services' PowerShell interfaces.

There is a significant amount of documentation online for managing SBO by using Windows
PowerShell. You can find detailed information in "Using Windows PowerShell to manage Skype
for Business Online" at *https://technet.microsoft.com/library/dn362831.aspx*. The following sections in this chapter focus on what you might actually need to do when getting SBO set up for
your users if the default settings are not to your liking. You can apply these policies to some or
all of your users, modify settings in them, or create your own. It's safer if you create your own
rather than modifying an existing policy, because you might want to fall back to the manufac-
turer's settings, so consider that if none of the included policies meets your needs. As an alternative, export the settings to a text file before you make changes so you can set things back if
you need to.

There are two challenges in modifying and applying policies with Windows PowerShell. The first
is that many settings are exposed through Windows PowerShell that are not exposed through
the GUI. If different groups of admins are provisioning users, make sure that policies are applied
to SBO users consistently. Make sure your workflow includes steps for someone to apply any
settings or policies that require Windows PowerShell, or script the provisioning so that even
those admins who are only comfortable using the GUI can easily apply policies that require
Windows PowerShell. The second challenge is that in many cases, policies you wish to apply are
not the default. So again, ensure that your workflow includes steps to ensure that the appropriate policies are applied for each of your SBO users before they log on to the service for the first
time.

Client policy

Client policies control a number of settings related to how the SBO client works and what functionality is available or restricted for a user, including such things that, if left to default, might
go against your organization's security or retention policies. Although many client policies are
included with SBO, and many settings are contained within them, this chapter focuses on the
things customers who want to be a little more circumspect than the default client policy allows
most commonly request.

The ClientPolicyDefault client policy is what users get initially. You can view the settings for this policy by using the cmdlet

```
Get-CsClientPolicy -identity ClientPolicyDefault | fl
```

From that command, the defaults are as follows.

```
Identity                                    : Tag:ClientPolicyDefault
PolicyEntry                                 : {Name=OnlineFeedbackUrl;Value=http://aka.
ms/skypefeedback,

                                              Name=SendFeedbackUrl;Value= , Name=EnableT
raceRouteReporting;Value=TRUE,

                                              Name=PrefetchConfInfo;Value=TRUE...}

Description                                 :
AddressBookAvailability                     : WebSearchOnly
AttendantSafeTransfer                       :
AutoDiscoveryRetryInterval                  :
BlockConversationFromFederatedContacts      :
CalendarStatePublicationInterval            :
ConferenceIMIdleTimeout                     :
CustomizedHelpUrl                           : http://go.microsoft.com/
fwlink/?LinkId=389737
CustomLinkInErrorMessages                   :
CustomStateUrl                              :
DGRefreshInterval                           :
DisableCalendarPresence                     :
DisableContactCardOrganizationTab           :
DisableEmailComparisonCheck                 :
DisableEmoticons                            :
DisableFeedsTab                             :
DisableFederatedPromptDisplayName           :
DisableFreeBusyInfo                         :
DisableHandsetOnLockedMachine               :
DisableMeetingSubjectAndLocation            :
DisableHtmlIm                               :
DisableInkIM                                :
DisableOneNote12Integration                 :
DisableOnlineContextualSearch               :
DisablePhonePresence                        :
DisablePICPromptDisplayName                 :
DisablePoorDeviceWarnings                   :
DisablePoorNetworkWarnings                  :
DisablePresenceNote                         :
DisableRTFIM                                :
DisableSavingIM                             :
DisplayPhoto                                : AllPhotos
EnableAppearOffline                         :
EnableCallLogAutoArchiving                  :
EnableClientAutoPopulateWithTeam            : True
EnableClientMusicOnHold                     : False
EnableConversationWindowTabs                :
EnableEnterpriseCustomizedHelp              : True
```

```
EnableEventLogging                                 :
EnableExchangeContactSync                          : True
EnableExchangeDelegateSync                         : True
EnableExchangeContactsFolder                       : True
EnableFullScreenVideo                              :
EnableHighPerformanceConferencingAppSharing        : False
EnableHotdesking                                   :
EnableIMAutoArchiving                              :
EnableMediaRedirection                             :
EnableMeetingEngagement                            : False
EnableNotificationForNewSubscribers                :
EnableServerConversationHistory                    : True
EnableSkypeUI                                      :
EnableSQMData                                      :
EnableTracing                                      :
EnableURL                                          :
EnableUnencryptedFileTransfer                      :
EnableVOIPCallDefault                              : False
ExcludedContactFolders                             :
HotdeskingTimeout                                  : 00:05:00
IMWarning                                          :
MAPIPollInterval                                   :
MaximumDGsAllowedInContactList                     : 10
MaximumNumberOfContacts                            :
MaxPhotoSizeKB                                     : 30
MusicOnHoldAudioFile                               :
P2PAppSharingEncryption                            : Supported
EnableHighPerformanceP2PAppSharing                 : False
PlayAbbreviatedDialTone                            :
RequireContentPin                                  : RequiredOutsideScheduledMeeting
SearchPrefixFlags                                  :
ShowRecentContacts                                 : True
ShowManagePrivacyRelationships                     : False
ShowSharepointPhotoEditLink                        : False
SPSearchInternalURL                                :
SPSearchExternalURL                                :
SPSearchCenterInternalURL                          :
SPSearchCenterExternalURL                          :
TabURL                                             :
TracingLevel                                       : Light
TelemetryTier                                      : Tier3
PublicationBatchDelay                              : 0
EnableViewBasedSubscriptionMode                    : False
WebServicePollInterval                             :
HelpEnvironment                                    : Office365
RateMyCallDisplayPercentage                        : 10
RateMyCallAllowCustomUserFeedback                  : False
IMLatencySpinnerDelay                              : 1500
IMLatencyErrorThreshold                            : 1500
SupportModernFilePicker                            : False
EnableOnlineFeedback                               : False
EnableOnlineFeedbackScreenshots                    :
```

Sometimes, customers want to restrict certain settings in SBO to reduce what they see as risk or to limit the sort of information that can be exposed through eDiscovery. Several organizations believe that instant messaging conversations, being less formal than email, might contain certain wording or information that a company would not like to be exposed outside, so conversation history is a feature these companies choose to disable. Some information security departments might want to prevent users from sending links through instant messages, especially if they must allow external federation and public connectivity to consumer Skype. In some situations, companies want to disable emoticons because they are considered unprofessional.

You can use one of the included policies, such as ClientPolicyNoSaveIMNoArchivingNoIMURL, or create your own policy and apply it to your users. An example policy that you might create to restrict all of the features mentioned in the preceding command could be created in Windows PowerShell as follows.

```
New-CsClientpolicy -identity "Restrictive" -DisableEmoticons:$true
-DisablePresenceNote:$true -DisableSavingIM:$true -EnableServerConversationHistory:$fa
lse -EnableURL:$false
```

Then, to apply that policy to all users, you would type the following command.

```
Get-CSOnlineUser -ResultSize Unlimited | Grant-CsClientPolicy -PolicyName Restrictive
```

For the best user experience, determine what, if any, restrictions you need to apply to your users before you deploy SBO to them. It's much better to deploy something with limits than to take features away after users experience them. If you are not sure, or if your legal, HR, or security teams have not decided on any restrictions, include them in the pilot and make sure all pilot users understand that some features might not be available after SBO is deployed to production.

Conferencing policy

The conferencing policies in SBO are intended to control what can and cannot be done in SBO meetings. With multiple people attending an SBO meeting, you want to ensure that any restrictions to meet compliance requirements or to prevent anonymous users from joining meetings are in place. SBO meetings often are used to present confidential information, either through screen sharing or by presenting PowerPoint decks. This might mean you want to restrict who can download files from a meeting or even record meetings. SBO meetings might also use significant bandwidth because they can include 1080p video content, so you might want to place upper limits on the bandwidth available.

The default SBO conferencing policy is called *BPOSSModalityAll*. To view what this policy includes, run the following Windows PowerShell command.

```
get-csconferencingpolicy -identity BPOSSAllModality | fl
Identity                              : Tag:BposSAllModality
AllowIPAudio                          : True
```

```
AllowIPVideo                                    : True
AllowMultiView                                  : True
Description                                     :
AllowParticipantControl                         : True
AllowAnnotations                                : True
DisablePowerPointAnnotations                    : False
AllowUserToScheduleMeetingsWithAppSharing       : True
ApplicationSharingMode                          : VideoWithFallback
AllowNonEnterpriseVoiceUsersToDialOut           : False
AllowAnonymousUsersToDialOut                    : False
AllowAnonymousParticipantsInMeetings            : True
AllowFederatedParticipantJoinAsSameEnterprise   : False
AllowExternalUsersToSaveContent                 : True
AllowExternalUserControl                        : True
AllowExternalUsersToRecordMeeting               : False
AllowPolls                                      : True
AllowSharedNotes                                : True
AllowQandA                                      : True
AllowOfficeContent                              : True
EnableDialInConferencing                        : False
EnableAppDesktopSharing                         : Desktop
AllowConferenceRecording                        : True
EnableP2PRecording                              : True
EnableFileTransfer                              : True
EnableP2PFileTransfer                           : True
EnableP2PVideo                                  : True
AllowLargeMeetings                              : False
EnableOnlineMeetingPromptForLyncResources       : False
EnableDataCollaboration                         : True
MaxVideoConferenceResolution                    : VGA
MaxMeetingSize                                  : 250
AudioBitRateKb                                  : 200
VideoBitRateKb                                  : 50000
AppSharingBitRateKb                             : 50000
FileTransferBitRateKb                           : 50000
TotalReceiveVideoBitRateKb                      : 50000
EnableMultiViewJoin                             : True
EnableReliableConferenceDeletion                : True
```

All the features are enabled, and clients can use the maximum bandwidth their hardware can handle when using video. Several conferencing policies are built in to SBO. At the time of this writing, 35 are available to customers with North American tenants and over 200 in total, and you can create your own. As an SBO administrator, review the policies available to you to see whether the default policy is appropriate for your organization, or you need to apply one of the more restrictive policies, or you need to create your own. They all start with the BPOS name, followed by some text that should give you an idea of their purpose. Review the settings and pick the policy that is right for your organization or create your own.

NOTE

As you can tell from the name of the conferencing policies, they have some lineage back to the BPOS days. BPOS stands for Business Productivity Online Services (or Suite) and was the precursor to Office 365. It included Office Communications Online, and some of the settings in this and other policies go all the way back to Office Communications Server (OCS).

When you have chosen a policy, you can apply it to all users in much the same way you applied the client policy.

```
Get-CSOnlineUser -ResultSize Unlimited | Grant-CsConferencingPolicy -PolicyName BposSAllModalityMinVideoBW
```

Mobility policy

The mobility policy you apply to users controls whether they can use the SBO Mobile client and which features are enabled or requirements are in place. The default policy, called the Global policy, permits users to connect to SBO by using their mobile client, to use cellular bandwidth for all functions, to save IM history, and so on. There are four other policies for Mobility. Each is named for the type of policy, Mobility, and their names imply the limitations they put into play.

- MobilityEnableOutsideVoice

- MobilityDisableOutsideVoice

- MobilityEnableOutsideVoiceNoPushNotifications

- MobilityDisableOutsideVoiceNoPushNotifications

The main things you might wish to use mobility policies for are to reduce the bandwidth the Skype for Business client could use by requiring Wi-Fi connectivity for IP video and file sharing. Those settings can be configured by the user, and with the popularity of unlimited bandwidth plans, this is not something you might need to worry about.

Audio/video

You might only want to disable audio and video for users. This is a setting you control directly within the user settings by using the Set-CsUser command. If you simply want to disable audio and video for all your users, you can run the following command.

```
Get-CsOnlineUser -resultsize unlimited | Set-CsUser -AudioVideoDisabled:$false
```

Usage location

It's very important to set Usage Location for users in your tenant correctly. SBO offers VoIP features that might conflict with certain countries' regulations regarding telephony. It is your responsibility to set the correct country for your users to ensure that your company remains in compliance with the laws and regulations in your area. Do not simply set all users' locations as US because you are a company based in the United States. Set the location for where a user is based. Usage Location uses the standard two-letter country code for a country. If you wish to use Windows PowerShell, you can set this for users. If all your users are in the same usage location, this is as simple as the following.

```
Get-MsolUser | Set-MsolUser -UsageLocation US
```

It will take a few moments for that command to sync from Azure Active Directory to Skype for Business Online, so if you do make a change, give it time to forward sync. If you have users in multiple locations, create a CSV file with UPN and UsageLocation and use the Import-Csv cmdlet to read the file and feed the Set-MsolUser command like this.

```
import-csv \file.csv | ForEach-Object {
 Set-MsolUser -UserPrincipalName $_.UserPrincipalName -UsageLocation $_.UsageLocation
 }
```

Piloting Skype for Business Online

It's important for you to pilot SBO. This helps you test any policies or tenant settings you have applied to ensure that you have the required functionality and desired configuration, and to assess your network with real users to ensure that you have the necessary connectivity. For an organization that has no existing SIP solution, such as Lync or Skype on-premises, this is easy. For an organization that has an existing on-premises solution, this can be challenging.

Piloting with no existing solution in place

When you have no existing SIP solution in place, you can deploy SBO at your own pace and test it easily. Ensure that your DNS records are in place (internally and externally if your SIP domain is using split-DNS), configure your tenant to meet your corporate needs, apply any policies, assign the users in the pilot group a license for SBO, and deploy the client to their workstations. You can adjust policies and settings as your user testing identifies the need, with no impact on any production system.

Piloting with an existing solution in place

When you have an existing solution in place, piloting can be more of a challenge. A SIP namespace can only exist in one infrastructure, so unless you choose to deploy Skype hybrid, you cannot really pilot with your production namespace while it is still in use in your existing solution. There are three ways to solve this problem.

- Use the <tenantname>.onmicrosoft.com namespace as the SIP namespace for your pilot.

- Use another DNS namespace that you are not using in your existing solution.

- Create a fake DNS server to host the DNS records and point your clients to this server for DNS during the pilot.

The first option is the easiest and recommended approach. Microsoft already hosts the DNS records you need for the *<tenant>*.onmicrosoft.com namespace, and that namespace is already in your tenant and enabled for SBO. You just need to set your pilot users' SIP URI in the proxy-Addresses attribute to use that domain and sync that to your tenant.

The second option really doesn't offer any advantages over the first and requires you to use another DNS namespace, which might mean you need to purchase a new domain name. It also requires you to set up the DNS records to support SBO and still assign the SIP URI in the proxy-Addresses attribute. There's no advantage to this as far as piloting SBO is concerned.

The third option is the most complex but does enable you to test your production namespace, which might be useful to confirm that a cutover will work successfully. That is the only real advantage to this approach. You need to set up a DNS server that not only hosts an authoritative zone for your DNS namespace but can also resolve any Active Directory or other DNS records for your DNS namespace and any other external records your users need to resolve. Set up the DNS server, add the zone and the necessary records, configure forwarding for Internet name resolution, and then configure the clients you will use in the pilot to use this DNS server instead of your normal production servers. Your pilot users will be able to use your production namespace from the on-premises system but will be cut off from the rest of your users.

Deploying the Skype for Business Client

You need to determine which Skype for Business client software you want your users to use as well as how to deploy it to their workstations. The decision on which client to use comes down to a combination of licensing and features. Office 365 plans that include Skype for Business Online might or might not also include the client software. E3 and higher plans include Office ProPlus, which comes with the Skype for Business 2016 client. E1 plans, as well as stand-alone SBO plans, do not include client software. If you are licensing Office Perpetual, then the version of Office you choose might come with Skype for Business client software, or you might need to download and install the basic client, which is free but does have fewer features.

In short, if you intend to deploy Office ProPlus, you will get the Skype for Business client as part of that install. If you mean to deploy Office Professional 2016, use the Skype for Business 2016 client. If you want to deploy Office Professional 2013, use the Skype for Business 2015 client. If you mean to install Office for Mac, use the Skype for Business on Mac client. If you do not have a license entitlement to the full Skype for Business client, you can use the Skype for Business basic client that is free to use and covers most of the SBO functionality. However, if you want to use the telephone features in SBO, you want to use a full client because the following features do not work with the Skype for Business basic client.

CHAPTER 16

1. Manage team call settings

2. Manage delegates

3. Make calls on behalf of another

4. Handle another's calls

5. Manage a high volume of calls

6. Initiate a response group

7. Park a call

8. Use group call pickup

Refer to *https://technet.microsoft.com/en-us/library/16b14d59-7737-4f9d-aa4d-83765a18ea07*
for the complete list.

During testing and even piloting, manually installing the Skype for Business client software
on your test users' workstations should have been manageable. Smaller organizations might
choose to continue with a manual approach because Skype for Business client software is part
of the Office ProPlus suite. Users licensed for Office ProPlus, and who have administrative rights
on their devices, can log on to the Office 365 portal and install Office ProPlus themselves. Here
is how.

1. Make sure your users are licensed for Office ProPlus and have administrative rights on
   their workstations.

2. Provide them with the link to *https://portal.office.com* and have them log on to that site.

3. Have them click the Install Office 2016 button in the upper-right corner of the top section,
   as shown in Figure 16-28.

Figure 16-28 Portal landing page with Install Office 2016 link

The Office ProPlus install provides them with the instructions they need to follow. You still should provide instructions telling them that, in this case, it's okay for them to click the Run button at the bottom of the page, as shown in Figure 16-29.

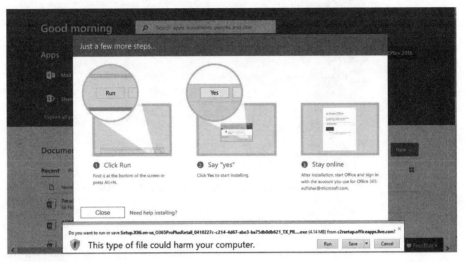

Figure 16-29 Install Office prompt

They can follow along from there; the application completes automatically. However, if you just want them to install the Skype for Business client, give them these instructions.

1. Log on to the Office 365 portal at *https://portal.office.com*.

2. At the top of the page, in the upper right, click the question mark icon, type **install software**, and then press Enter, as shown in Figure 16-30.

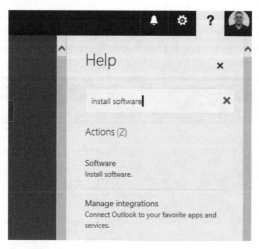

Figure 16-30 Locating the Skype for Business client install

3. Click the first result, Software.

4. On the Software page, choose to deploy Office ProPlus, Tools & Add-Ins, Project, Visio, Skype For Business, and Phone & Tablet, as shown in Figure 16-31.

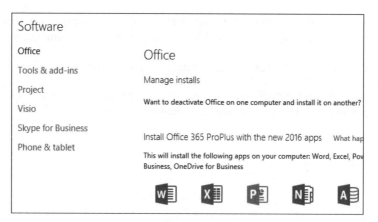

Figure 16-31: Software installation options

5. On the left side, click Skype For Business.

This opens the page to install the client. It's recommended that you install the Skype for Business client that matches your Office install. Usually, that is the Skype for Business 2016 client in 32 bit.

6. Follow the install instructions to the end.

NOTE

The Skype for Business client installs the Skype Meeting add-in for Microsoft Office as long as Office is already installed. This add-in enables you to add Skype meetings to Outlook meeting invites with a single button press. Make sure that if you are not installing Office ProPlus, Office is installed before you install the Skype for Business client. If that is not possible, you can either reinstall Skype for Business after you install Office or refer to *https://support.microsoft.com/en-us/help/3097122/skype-meeting-control-is-not-displayed-on-outlook-2016*.

For rollout to your entire organization, you want an approach that is more scalable and can be automated. You can use the Office Deployment Tool, available at *https://www.microsoft.com/en-us/download/details.aspx?id=49117*, to customize the deployment of Office ProPlus, including the Skype for Business client. You then use the output of this tool to control a manual installation or a push installation by using Microsoft System Center Configuration Manager or other third-party software management tool that your organization uses.

Keep in mind that no matter which Skype for Business client you choose, you must maintain it as updates are released for security or other issues. To take advantage of new features and ensure that your users keep current, the click-to-run (C2R) version is the best choice.

Mobile clients

Skype for Business has mobile clients for iOS and Android, so you can use SBO from any mobile phone or tablet. Users can visit the application store appropriate for the platform, search for Skype for Business, and install the mobile client. In the iOS App Store, the Skype for Business client looks like the screenshot in Figure 16-32.

CHAPTER 16

Figure 16-32 Skype for Business for iOS in the App Store

If you use a Mobile Device Management (MDM) solution to manage mobile devices and deploy software to mobile clients, you must permit users to install this application themselves. Due to licensing agreements and restrictions in the app stores, Microsoft does not make the Skype for Business client available to deploy as a package through MDM. Users have to install it from the application store. Do not use one of the packaged installers available online. Microsoft does not support them, and in some cases they have been found to contain malware.

Managing the client

You want to manage your users' SBO experience by using the tenant settings and the various policies in the service. This is the most efficient way to do so and ensures that your users' experience is consistent whether they are using a managed Windows machine, a Mac, a mobile client, a tablet, or a personal computer. There are settings for the SBO client that can be managed through Group Policy, but those only apply to domain-joined Windows systems.

You can download the Office 2016 Administrative Template files (ADMX/ADML) from *https://www.microsoft.com/en-us/download/details.aspx?id=49030*, import them into Active Directory, and use them to manage some client settings. Thirteen machine settings and 14 user settings are available for you to configure, but don't think that you need to. Most of these settings apply only when you are using an on-premises instance of Skype for Business.

Logging on

The first time a user launches the Skype for Business client, it asks them for their sign-in address, which is their SIP address. That will look like Figure 16-33.

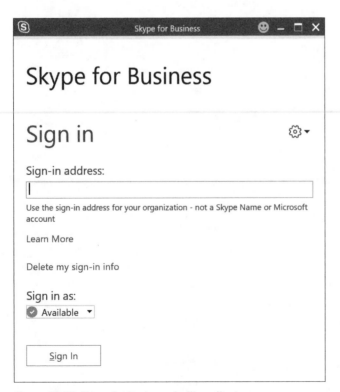

Figure 16-33 Skype for Business desktop client app

If a user's sign-in address (also known as their SIP address) is the same as their User Principal Name (UPN) and primary SMTP address, you need only tell them to enter their email address when prompted and click Sign In. The Skype for Business client uses Modern Authentication, so your users will be automatically signed in to the service.

However, if you have decided to use a different value for UPN than the SIP address, users must go through an additional step before they can authenticate to the service. Their initial attempt to connect to the service will fail because their SIP address does not match their UPN, and they will be prompted a second time to authenticate, with an additional prompt for their password, as shown in Figure 16-34.

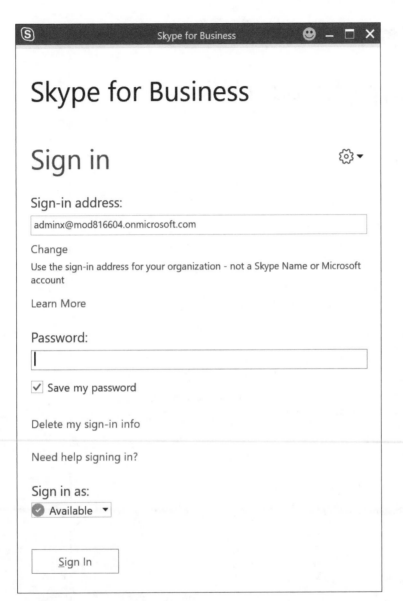

Figure 16-34 Prompt for password

When they enter their password and click Sign In, this authentication attempt will also fail, and they will finally be presented with options in the user interface to submit one value for Sign-In address, which is their SIP address, and another for User Name, which is their UPN, and then Password, as shown in Figure 16-35.

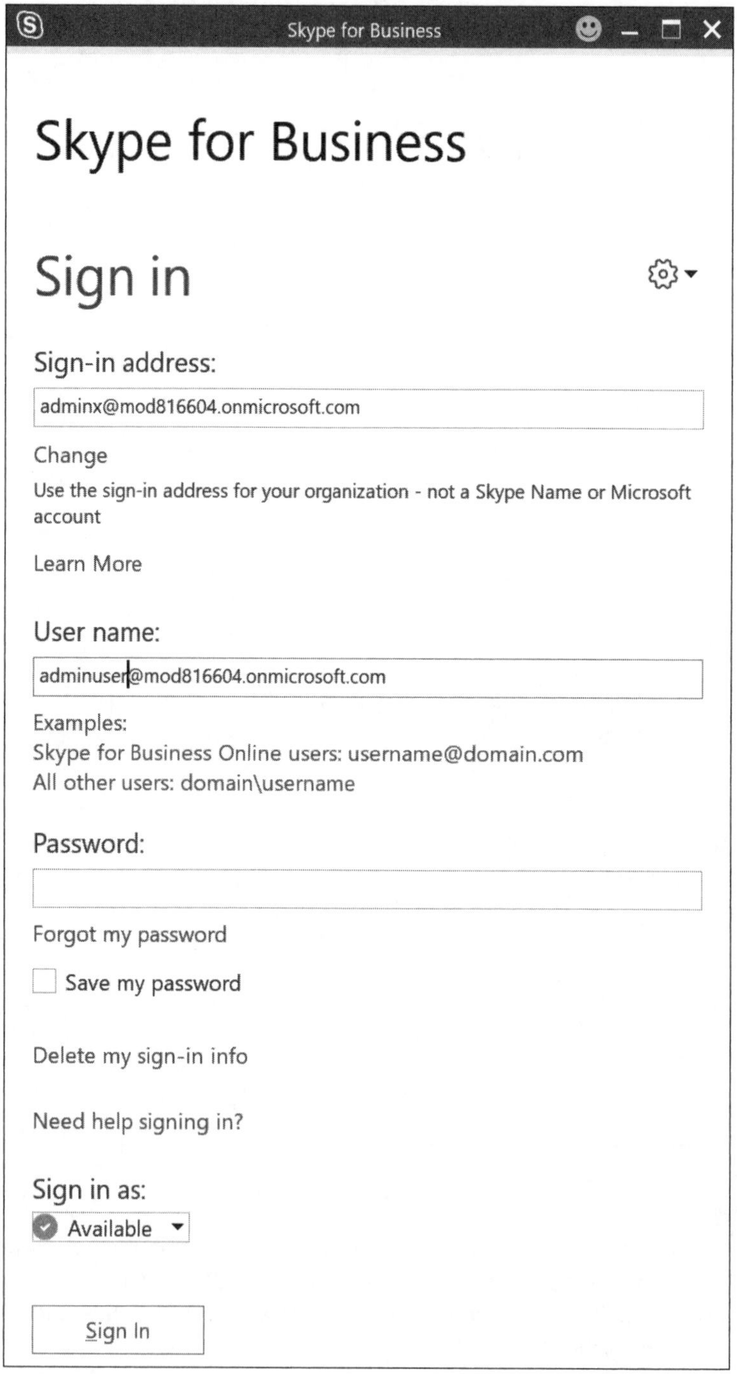

Figure 16-35 Prompt for User Name

Although users only have to do this the first time on their workstation, they have to do it each time they log on to a new workstation. The client behavior this mismatch causes might elicit a significant number of help desk calls, so consider carefully whether any perceived security benefit from using a different value for UPN than for SIP and primary SMTP addresses outweighs the user experience.

INSIDE OUT

UserPrincipalName and SMTP Address parity

As previously mentioned, best practices are to ensure that users' UPN, SIP, and primary SMTP addresses all match. Although the experience when logging on for the first time is significant, that has more impact on the user experience than any technical reasons. There are two other considerations when using SBO and making these values match. If your primary SMTP and SIP do not match, viewing presence for a user with a mismatch in email and viewing SharePoint Online will not work unless the user is saved as a contact where the primary SMTP and SIP are both saved. Most organizations ensure that these match, so you might also encounter challenges with partners or customers with whom you have set up external Skype federation, because their users cannot use Skype with your users unless they know the SIP address is different and add that to their contacts. If your security team is concerned that making these values match presents risk, consider the following.

- Most victims of phishing attacks provide both their user name and their password to the attacker, making any mismatch pointless. Users are providing their user names whether they match or not.

- Unless UPNs are truly random, knowing any one user's UPN enables an attacker to infer another user's UPN.

- Multi-factor authentication, such as is available through Azure Active Directory, prevents attackers who have both the user name and the password of a user from being able to use those to access services.

- Soft lockout in Active Directory Federation Services (AD FS) prevents denial-of-service attacks against users by blocking attempts to brute-force or lock out Active Directory accounts by blocking repeated authentication attempts from the same source without locking out the account in Active Directory.

CHAPTER 16

Deploying Skype for Business Online

With the clients' software deployed, the service configured, and testing complete, it's now time to deploy Skype for Business Online. Many companies elect to deploy SBO as the first major workload after they have identity and authentication set up. Whether you have an existing SIP solution in place or not, the amount of work needed to deploy SBO is much less than is required for Exchange Online or SharePoint Online, and it's a quick and easy way to start using the cloud and show management some return on its investment to move the company to the cloud.

The two most common ways to do this can be referred to as a rollout and a cutover. Companies that do not have an existing SIP solution can do either, whereas companies that want to switch from an existing but older on-premises SIP solution, such as Lync Server or Skype for Business, to Skype for Business Online, perform a cutover.

Rollout

A rollout deployment can be done on whatever schedule you wish. After you have configured the service to meet your organization's needs, you can enable users to use SBO in small groups or all at once. All you need to do is license them and they can begin to use the service. If you have not fully assessed or prepared your network for the additional bandwidth SBO uses, you might want to enable users in small groups, or one site at a time, until you get a feel for things. Otherwise, you can license everyone all at once and let them all start using the service together.

Cutover

A cutover becomes necessary when you have an existing SIP-based solution you intend to stop using and replace with Skype for Business Online. A SIP namespace cannot exist in two SIP infrastructures at the same time, so you need to stop using it in the one so you can start using it in the other. This sort of cutover is usually done over a weekend. When users stop using the existing system at the end of the day on Friday, IT makes the required changes and tests them to confirm all is well, and users come in on Monday and start using the new system.

Cutovers are fairly easy to perform, with minimal risk involved. However, they are cutovers; you stop using one system and start using another. For users, this means they start with an empty contact list. For many users, this is a minor inconvenience, but for some, it is a major issue. Whereas there are third-party solutions that can export a contact list to a file and then reimport contacts from that file after the cutover, there is no way to move contacts from an older system to SBO or to export contacts centrally.

To perform a cutover, perform the following steps.

- Start informing your users ahead of the planned cutover date that the change is coming, and that services might be unavailable or only available intermittently during the scheduled weekend.

- Make sure you notify any partners with which you have SIP federation set up that you are changing to SBO, in case they need to update their federation settings to use SRV records and update any firewall rules they might have. Refer them to *http://aka.ms/ipaddrs* for the list of endpoints SBO uses.

- Reduce the time-to-live (TTL) for your SIP records in DNS ahead of the change; 30 seconds is a good value to facilitate a quick change (and, if necessary, a quick fallback) during the cutover. As a refresher, that includes the SRV records and any hostnames or CNAMEs you might have in place.

- At the end of the business day on the date of the cutover, disable access to the older system. You can stop services or disconnect the server from the network, but keep things running in case you need to fall back.

- Update the DNS records for your SIP domain to refer to the SBO services. Refer to the portal, Setup | Domains | DNS settings and make sure the two CNAMEs and two SRV records for SBO are all added to your DNS for both your Internet and internal DNS.

- For each system you want to use to test with to confirm everything is ready, clear the DNS cache, launch the Skype for Business client, authenticate, and perform your testing.

- When all testers agree that testing passes, you can close your change and be ready for Monday.

- If you cannot resolve any issues and the decision is made to fall back, you simply restart the services or reconnect the older servers to the network, revert your DNS changes, clear your DNS caches and restart the clients, and confirm that you are back on the original system. Before you do that, though, you might want to open a support case with Microsoft to help you quickly identify and resolve any issue you are encountering.

TROUBLESHOOTING

Issues during a cutover

Any testing you did during the initial configuration should have identified all possible blockers to using SBO, but there are a few things that come up frequently that you might not encounter until you begin the cutover. Here are the things you will want to check to confirm.

- **Service health** Check the dashboard in the Office 365 Admin Center portal to ensure that there are no service issues. The likelihood that there is a service issue is practically nonexistent, but it's a good habit to develop to take the five seconds to confirm rather than spending hours trying to run down an issue that is out of your control.

- **Cached data** Both Lync and Skype clients cache data under AppData\Local to improve performance. Sometimes clients seem to stick to the older system and try to connect to it even after you update DNS. Clear out the SIP profile(s) cached on your client machine, restart the client, and try again. You can find these in one of the following locations, depending on version.

```
Lync 2010: %UserProfile%\AppData\Local\Microsoft\Communicator\
Lync 2013: %UserProfile%\AppData\Local\Microsoft\Office\15.0\Lync
Skype for Business: %UserProfile%\AppData\Local\Microsoft\Office\16.0\Lync
```

It's safe to delete these completely. Any data the client needs is pulled from the service, and the client will re-create the profile for any data it needs to cache. You can also deploy a script to remove the cached data, such as *https://gallery.technet .microsoft.com/Delete-Skype-and-Lync-9d8cf887*.

- **DNS**   Clients must resolve both CNAMEs and both SRV records on both the internal and external networks for users to use SBO. Use NSLOOKUP or DIG to confirm internal name resolution and those or one of the various Internet web portals to confirm external resolution, and have a second person confirm that there are no typos in your records. Query more than just your primary DNS server to make sure your DNS infrastructure is replicating changes correctly. Remember that if you didn't reduce the TTL of your records before the change, you might have to wait a much longer period of time before caches expire and you can resolve the new records.

- **Testing**   Make sure that you are testing from both the internal network, and the external one. Use a Mi-Fi device, test from home, or use a Wi-Fi hotspot to confirm that everything works from both inside and outside the corporate network. If you start testing on the inside network, a quick check to determine whether a proxy or firewall might be the cause of any issue is to move to an external network and test again. If it works externally, you can focus on your network internally.

- **Proxies**   If you are using forward web proxies, confirm that they are permitting outbound connections to *all* the endpoints listed at *http://aka.ms/ipaddrs* in the "Skype for Business Online," "Office 365 Portal and Shared," and Office 365 Authentication and Identity" sections. Also confirm that the proxies are not prompting for authentication before permitting outbound connections to the Office 365 services. A network analyzer such as Microsoft Message Analyzer is very useful here.

- **Firewalls**   If you also control egress at the firewall, confirm that the access control lists permit outbound connectivity to all of the same endpoints listed as required in the sections "Skype for Business Online," "Office 365 Portal and Shared," and "Office 365 Authentication and Identity" of the article found at *http://aka.ms/ipaddrs*.

Testing your Skype for Business Online tenant

How much time you spend testing will vary from one organization to the next, and each company will have its own criteria for testing. At a minimum, test the primary functions of SBO. A high-level testing plan is available at *https://support.office.com/en-us/article/Test-your-Skype -for-Business-Online-installation-ae98aef4-5448-43c3-bab0-ba35ff541ca6*. It includes the steps a user needs to follow to test each function.

A much more detailed User Acceptance Testing (UAT) plan, with about 200 specific use cases, is included in a UAT spreadsheet published by Shane Hoey to the TechNet Gallery. You can find it at *https://gallery.technet.microsoft.com/lync/Skype-for-Business-User-fb20ff12*. It is very detailed and well thought out, and it provides tracking of all tests so you can generate a report at the end.

Administering Skype for Business Online

After your Skype for Business Online tenant is set up, tested, and deployed to your clients, the amount of administrative effort it takes to maintain SBO is relatively small. That's one of the reasons the only two administrative roles for SBO are the Global Admin role and the Skype for Business Administrator role, and there is no delegation or role-based access control (RBAC) in SBO.

If you use the default policies in SBO, there is nothing else you need to do when a user is licensed for SBO. However, if you are applying specific policies to users, then an SBO administrator will need to use Windows PowerShell to assign the appropriate policies, or you might choose to provide your help desk or provisioning team with scripts to do the same.

You might need to tune your policies as business needs evolve, but the primary administrative work includes the following.

- Managing Skype federation settings as you federate with new partners, vendors, or customer organizations

- Assigning phone numbers to new users

- Creating new auto attendants and call queues to support new business needs

- Monitoring the Call Quality dashboard to spot any trends that might indicate network performance or capacity issues

- Using Call Analytics to investigate specific users with any issues

If your organization does not deploy PSTN capabilities, you might go weeks at a time without needing to do anything in the SBO portal.

Integration with on-premises Skype

Up until now you have read about Skype for Business Online as a service wholly provided by Office 365. You can deploy a net new service to your users with a roll-out, or you can cutover your users from an existing but older solution to SBO. For organizations with an existing Lync or Skype for Business on-premises deployment, there is a third option.

Skype hybrid

Skype hybrid connects an existing on-premises Skype for Business Server or Lync Server to an Office 365 tenant and permits them to share a SIP namespace. Administrators can move users from the on-premises infrastructure to online in a staged fashion, enabling you to move to SBO at a more controlled pace. Moving users enables them to maintain their contact list, which might make it very appealing to both users and management because that avoids the most disruptive part of moving to SBO. However, Skype hybrid is not the best choice for many organizations. The amount of work required to set it up is considerable and might not be worth the effort if the goal is to move everyone to SBO and shut down the older on-premises system. The disparity in features between on-premises and online might become a problem for some users if they lose functionality that others keep.

Required infrastructure

The following on-premises topologies are supported when configuring Skype hybrid.

- A single on-premises deployment of Skype for Business Server or Lync Server is installed in one of the following supported topologies.

  - An on-premises deployment of Skype for Business Server 2015

  - An on-premises deployment of Lync Server 2013

  - An on-premises deployment of Lync Server 2010

  - A mixed Skype for Business Server 2015 and Lync Server 2013 on-premises deployment, with at least one site running Skype for Business Server 2015 with an edge pool associated with SIP federation for the site

  - A mixed Skype for Business Server 2015 and Lync Server 2010 on-premises deployment, with at least one site running Skype for Business Server 2015 with an edge pool associated with SIP federation for the site

  - A mixed Lync Server 2013 and Lync Server 2010 on-premises deployment with at least one site running Lync Server 2013 with an edge pool associated with SIP federation for the site

- The Skype for Business administrative tools, or the Lync 2013 administrative tools, is installed on an administrator workstation. You must use the version that supports the latest on-premises platform you have.

- An Office 365 tenant with Skype for Business Online installed.

Your on-premises infrastructure must be deployed in a way that supports external connectivity. You must have at least an Access Edge and an A/V Edge server in the perimeter network and permit connectivity to those servers from Office 365, and from those servers to Office 365.

NOTE

Whether you have the necessary servers already in place is one of the most important criteria for whether you deploy Skype hybrid. If you already have external connectivity and edge servers in place for your on-premises SIP environment, it's straightforward to configure Skype hybrid, but if your on-premises deployment is closed and does not support Internet connectivity, it might not make sense to buy and deploy the additional servers necessary for Skype hybrid. In addition, you must ensure that your on-premises servers are updated to the latest service packs and all post–service pack updates are applied, both for the operating system and for Skype or Lync Server as appropriate.

Connectivity requirements

Your on-premises environment and SBO must be able to communicate with each other. Table 16-1 lists the required connectivity that must be permitted.

Table 16-1 Required network connectivity for Skype hybrid environments

Protocol	TCP or UDP	Source IP	Destination IP	Source Port	Destination Port	Notes
SIP (MTLS)	TCP	Access Edge	Office 365	Any	5061	Signaling
SIP (MTLS)	TCP	Office 365	Access Edge	Any	5061	Signaling
STUN	TCP	A/V Edge	Office 365	50000–59999	443, 50000–59999	Open for audio, video, application-sharing sessions
STUN	TCP	Office 365	A/V Edge	443	50000–59999	Open for audio, video, application-sharing sessions
STUN	UDP	A/V Edge	Office 365	3478–3481	3478–3481	Open for audio, video sessions
STUN	UDP	Office 365	A/V Edge	3478–3481	3478–3481	Open for audio, video sessions

This is in addition to the connectivity required for SBO clients, as detailed at *http://aka.ms/ipaddrs*.

DNS settings

The Office 365 administrative portal only shows you DNS settings for using Skype for Business Online. In a Skype hybrid deployment, the DNS records must resolve to the on-premises infrastructure. Refer to *https://technet.microsoft.com/en-us/library/dn951397.aspx* for more information on the on-premises DNS requirements.

Federation configuration

Both the on-premises and the online services must be configured with the same settings for federation, and the same entries in the domain allow or deny lists. Even if you will not federate with any other domains, you must permit federation within the online tenant because Skype hybrid is a form of federation between your on-premises and your online organizations.

Online or hybrid user account limitations

There are differences between what you can provide users in your on-premises Skype for Business or Lync Server infrastructure and what you can provide them in Skype for Business Online. If you will deploy Skype hybrid, you need to consider this, because the following features available on-premises are not available to users you move online.

- Enhanced Presence: Use a photo from any public site for My Picture.

- Contacts: Search for response groups.

- IM Support: Persistent chat (group chat) integration.

- IM Support: Escalate a persistent chat room to a Skype for Business meeting with one click.

- External Users: Conduct two-party or multiparty calls with external users.

In addition, although a user's contact list will migrate, their existing meetings must be updated or rescheduled when moving the user from on-premises to online.

Setting up Skype hybrid

If your on-premises infrastructure meets the requirements and your online tenant is ready, you can set up Skype hybrid. Follow these steps.

1. In your on-premises environment, configure the edge server to enable federation by running the following command in Windows PowerShell on the edge server or an on-premises workstation on which the Skype for Business administration tools are installed.

   ```
   Set-CSAccessEdgeConfiguration -AllowOutsideUsers 1 1 -UseDnsSrvRouting
   -AllowFederatedUsers
   ```

2. Identify any existing hosting provider by using this command.

   ```
   Get-CsHostingProvider
   ```

3. Remove the existing hosting provider by using this command.

   ```
   Remove-CSHostingProvider -Identity "Skype for Business Online"
   ```

4. Add Skype for Business Online back as a hosting provider, but with the following additional parameters.

```
New-CSHostingProvider -Identity SkypeforBusinessOnline -ProxyFqdn "sipfed.online.
lync.com" -Enabled $true -EnabledSharedAddressSpace $true -HostsOCSUsers $true
-VerificationLevel UseSourceVerification -IsLocal $false -AutodiscoverUrl https://
webdir.online.lync.com/Autodiscover/AutodiscoverService.svc/root
```

5. Log on to the Skype for Business Online Admin Center and confirm that your SBO tenant is configured to permit external access, as shown in Figure 16-36.

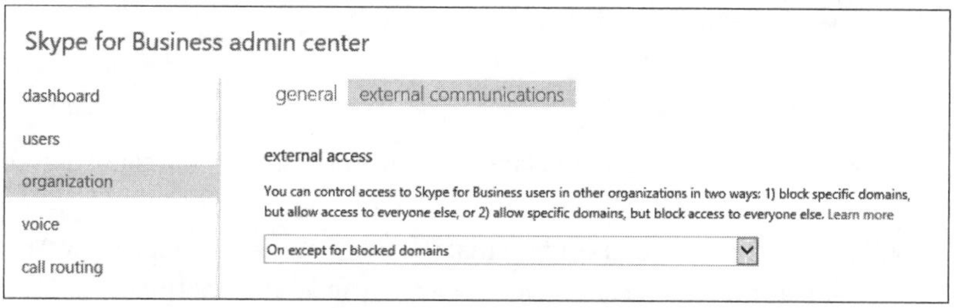

Figure 16-36 Skype for Business External Communications

6. Open the Skype for Business Server control panel for your on-premises organization and click the Set Up Hybrid With Skype For Business Online link.

7. Click Next.

8. When prompted, sign in to Office 365, using a Global Admin or Skype for Business Online admin account.

9. Click Next.

   The wizard confirms prerequisites and then configures hybrid.

10. Connect to Office 365 Skype for Business Online by using remote PowerShell.

11. Run the following command to enable sharing of the SIP namespace.

```
Set-CSTenantFederationConfiguration -SharedSipAddressSpace:$true
```

12. Confirm that the users you will use for testing are licensed for Skype for Business Online.

13. Use the Skype for Business control panel to move the test users from the on-premises infrastructure to SBO. From the Skype for Business control panel, click Users and right-click a test user to display Move Selected Users To Skype For Business Online, as shown in Figure 16-37.

Figure 16-37 A screenshot of the Action menu in Skype for Business Server 2015

14. Test functionality and confirm that the user has their contact list and can communicate with on-premises users as well as with any federation partners.

When you have confirmed that all features are working as expected, you can move users from on-premises to SBO as you need to or back again.

Summary

In this chapter, you learned how to deploy and administer Skype for Business Online as well as the Skype for Business clients. You learned how to configure the service by using both the Skype for Business Admin Center GUI and Windows PowerShell, how policies can be used to enforce settings or restrict features to meet your organization's needs, and how to deploy Skype for Business Online to your users. With this knowledge, you're ready to go! SBO is a great choice to deploy first to your users and enables them to start using Office 365 services while you are getting Exchange Online and SharePoint Online ready to go.

PART VI

SharePoint Online

SharePoint Online

SharePoint Online is both a collaboration tool and a platform. You can use it successfully as a tool to manage documents, lists, and tasks, or you can extend it as a platform with business analytics integrations, dashboards, and third-party plug-ins and applications.

SharePoint Online can function as an intranet or extranet, a document storage and collaboration platform, an enterprise search portal, a social platform, or a workflow engine. In addition, it can be used as a business intelligence platform, bringing in data sets from online or on-premises databases and displaying results in enterprise dashboards, charts, or pivot tables in a browser.

SharePoint Online concepts

SharePoint Online is organized into a hierarchy system of site collections, sites, and libraries. If you are familiar with administering SharePoint Server 2007 or later on-premises, you've undoubtedly used the Central Administration web application to manage SharePoint Server farm features.

SharePoint Online has many of the same features as SharePoint Server, although some notable things are hidden, presented differently, or not available.

One of the advantages of SharePoint Online (and, indeed, the entire Microsoft Office 365 experience) is that much of the underlying management tasks are removed, leaving you with purely application-level management. Microsoft handles tasks such as scheduling and updating, and you manage the content, plug-ins, and integration with your on-premises environments.

The following list shows some features that are re-abstracted, hidden, or not available from the user interface.

- Central Administration

- Service accounts

- Read-only databases

- Throttling

- SharePoint Health Analyzer

- Timer job management

- Wizards

- Individual server management and role distribution

- Content database management

- Access to service and web applications

- Access to server management for updating or service management

One notable exception that has been renamed is the Term Store. In SharePoint Server on-premises, you access this through the Metadata Management Service; in SharePoint Online, the Term Store is directly accessible from the SharePoint Admin Center. You can only have one term store (which can contain 200,000 terms) in SharePoint Online.

SharePoint Online capacities

When it was originally released as part of the Business Productivity Online Suite, SharePoint Online had a number of capacity limitations. As the cost for storage and bandwidth as gone down, the product group has been able to expand the storage capacity and limits for the service.

Overall service limits

Some overall limits apply to all subscriptions.

- **File sizes** The maximum size for a single file uploaded to a library is 15 GB. For files attached to a list item, the limit is 250 MB per file.

- **Groups** A user can belong to 5,000 groups, and each group can contain 5,000 members. You are limited to 10,000 groups per site collection.

- **Items and files** There are several item limits of which to be aware.

  - A list can have up to 30 million items.

  - A library can also have up to 30 million items (combined folders and files).

  - A view can have up to 12 lookup columns.

- A file name, including the path, must be fewer than 400 characters.

- A filename stored in SharePoint Online, OneDrive for Business on Office 365, and SharePoint Server 2016 cannot have any of the following characters: " * : < > ? / \ |

- SharePoint Online has no blocked files types, with the exception of certain executable web files: .aspx, .asmx, .ascx, .master, .xap, .swf, .jar, .xsf, .htc. Those files can be uploaded as long as scripting is enabled, per *https://support.office.com/en-us /article/Allow-or-prevent-custom-sc-1f2c515f-5d7e-448a-9fd7-835da935584f*.

- **Subsites**   You can create up to 2,000 sites per site collection.

- **Sync**   The OneDrive sync client can synchronize 100,000 items per OneDrive or team site library. The previous OneDrive sync client, Groove.exe, can sync 5,000 items per library.

- **Users**   You can have up to 2 million users per site collection.

- **Versions**   Each document can contain 5,000 major versions and 511 minor versions.

Individual service plan limits

In addition to the overall service limits, some limits are imposed on the various service plan levels, as shown in Table 17-1.

Table 17-1 SharePoint service plan limits

	Service Plans		
Feature	Office 365 Business Essentials and Office 365 Business Premium	Office 365 Enterprise E1, E3, E5 Office 365 Education, Office 365 E5 Education, Office 365 U.S. Government Office 365 Germany and Office 365 operated by 21Vianet SharePoint Online stand-alone plans (Plan 1 and Plan 2)	Office 365 Enterprise K1 (kiosk)
Storage	1 TB per organization base, plus 500 MB per subscribed user	1 TB per organization base plus 500 MB per user license purchased	10 GB per organization, with no additional storage per kiosk user
Terms in term store	200,000	200,000	200,000

	Service Plans		
Site collection and Office 365 Groups storage	Up to 25 TB per site collection or group	Up to 25 TB per site collection or group	Up to 25 TB per site collection or group. Kiosk workers cannot administer site collections. Administration requires one enterprise user license.
Site collections and Office 365 Groups	500,000 per organization, not including OneDrive for Business sites	500,000 per organization, not including OneDrive for Business sites	500,000 per organization
OneDrive storage	1 TB per user	1 TB per user by default; users with a OneDrive P2 license have unlimited storage.	2 GB per user
Number of users	Up to 300	1–500,000+	1–500,000+

For updated capacity information, please see *https://support.office.com/en-us/article /SharePoint-Online-limits-and-quotas-8f34ff47-b749-408b-abc0-b605e1f6d498*, "SharePoint Online limits and quotas," and *https://technet.microsoft.com/EN-US/library/sharepoint-online -service-description.aspx*, "SharePoint Online Service Description."

SharePoint Online features

SharePoint Online contains a number of features, ranging from very basic to very complex and advanced. It includes the following features.

- One Drive for Business

- Office Online

- Delve

- Yammer

- Enterprise Search

- Office Store Apps

- Business Connectivity Services

OneDrive for Business

Formerly known as SkyDrive Pro, OneDrive for Business is a personal SharePoint site collection. Similar in function to a home directory on a file share, a user can use the OneDrive for Business site to create and store online content, sync content between folders on-premises, or provide a collaboration space for external users. See Figure 17-1.

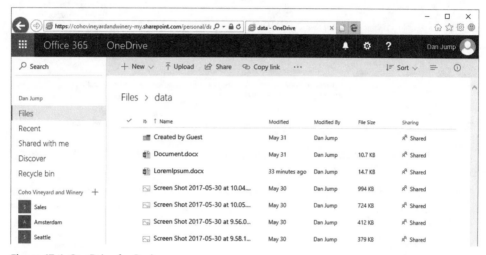

Figure 17-1 OneDrive for Business

A user is enabled for OneDrive for Business when a license for SharePoint Online is assigned. Normally, the user's OneDrive for Business site is provisioned the first time the user accesses the site, although you can provision sites ahead of time by using Windows PowerShell.

For more information about configuring and managing hybrid OneDrive for Business, see Chapter 18, "SharePoint Online Hybrid." For more information about deploying and managing OneDrive for Business, see Chapter 19, "OneDrive for Business."

Office Online

The Office Online apps are web-enabled versions of the popular Office desktop software. Applications, including Word Online, Excel Online, and PowerPoint Online, enable your users to create, view, and update documents through any browser, with no desktop software installed.

When a document is stored in either a SharePoint Online document library or a user's OneDrive site, the document is immediately available for co-authoring. Co-authoring is an Office 365 feature that enables multiple people to view and edit a document at the same time. Users can edit documents with a web browser and the Office Online apps or by choosing to open the documents in their desktop application, as shown in Figure 17-2.

CHAPTER 17

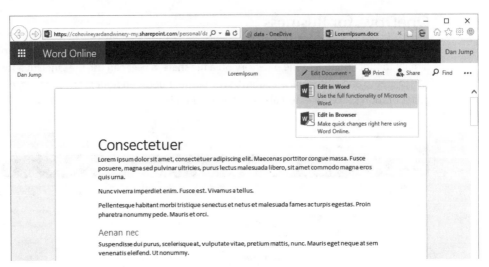

Figure 17-2 Choosing to edit a document in application or browser

The Office Online apps are enabled automatically when a user is licensed for a SharePoint Online plan.

Delve

Delve is an Office Graph API-based application integrated with Microsoft SharePoint and is used to display the contents of your user profile in SharePoint Online. Data in Delve is arranged on cards and displays data based on your usage as well as documents that your peers are working on. Delve cannot change permissions on any content and can only display content that you can access already. Delve discovers and displays information and documents that it thinks might be relevant to your work, based on its analysis of data stored in the Office Graph. You can disable access to the Office Graph in SharePoint settings. Your Delve profile also shows recently accessed documents and generates a list of users with whom you've recently interacted, as shown in Figure 17-3.

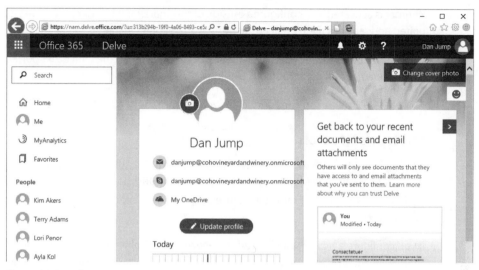

Figure 17-3 Delve

Delve is enabled automatically when a user is licensed for SharePoint Online.

Yammer

Yammer is a post and feed–style collaboration solution, purchased by Microsoft in 2012 and integrated with Office 365. Yammer enables users to post and reply to messages and supports files and polls. See Figure 17-4.

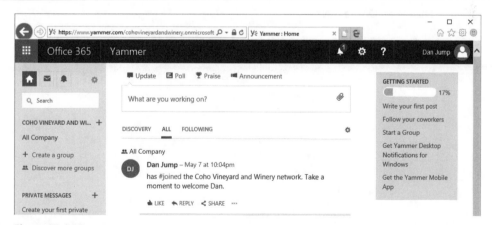

Figure 17-4 Yammer

Yammer is activated and configured outside of the SharePoint interface; however, it can be integrated and replaces the Newsfeeds feature of SharePoint Online.

Access to Yammer is controlled by an individual user license in the Office 365 portal. Yammer is administered separately through its own portal as well.

For more information on configuring and managing Yammer, see Chapter 20, "Yammer."

Enterprise search

Although search is important to organizations of all sizes, it is vital to those with hundreds of thousands or millions of documents scattered among sites and file shares. As documents stored in file shares and sites are moved to Office 365, search indexes them and makes them available for discovery.

If you configure a hybrid search solution between SharePoint Online and your on-premises SharePoint Server farm, you can present a single pane-of-glass view for content—whether your users are looking in cloud or on the local network.

For more information about hybrid search options and configuration, see Chapter 18.

SharePoint Store apps

The SharePoint Online platform naturally lends itself to development. Your organization can develop its own application solutions and publish them in an app catalog available to your SharePoint Online users or sell them in the Office.com marketplace. Your organization can also purchase applications from the SharePoint Store (Figure 17-5) and deploy them to your SharePoint Online users.

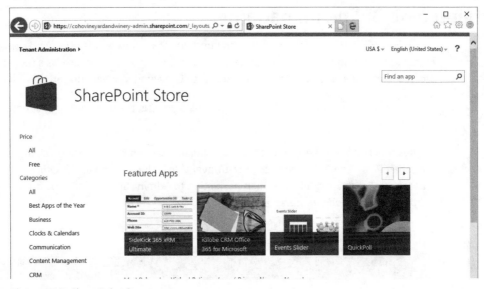

Figure 17-5 SharePoint Store

Business Connectivity Services

Through the use of Business Connectivity Services, you can make data in other locations available in SharePoint Online for consumption, processing, visualization, and updating. External data sources might include another SharePoint Online repository, an OData source on the Internet, or a database instance available in your on-premises environment or a partner's.

Depending on configuration of the Business Connectivity Services data connector, data might be read-only or potentially written back to the data sources. With a Business Connectivity Services connector, SharePoint Online becomes a client to an external data source.

SharePoint Online hybrid

You can configure hybrid coexistence and integration between an on-premises SharePoint Server farm and SharePoint Online. Some of the features of a SharePoint hybrid configuration include on-premises OneDrive redirection to Office 365 and cross-environment hybrid search.

For more information about configuring SharePoint Online hybrid, please see Chapter 18.

CHAPTER 17

SharePoint Online management

SharePoint Online is a large product, with hundreds of settings and features and configurations ranging from simple deployment to deep enterprise integration. Because it's a service, a repository, and an application platform, there really isn't any limit to what you can do with the service.

There are, however, some configurations that help you get the most out of your enterprise subscription.

Unless otherwise specified, you perform all management and configuration changes inside the SharePoint Admin Center (Figure 17-6), available by logging on to the Office 365 portal, selecting the Admin tile, and then navigating to Admin | SharePoint or by browsing to *https://<tenant>-admin.sharepoint.com*.

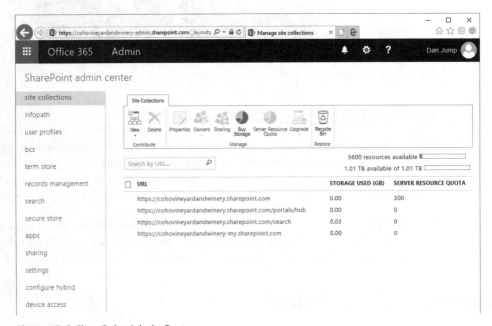

Figure 17-6 SharePoint Admin Center

Site collections

The top-level administrative unit in SharePoint Online is the site collection. Site collections hold sites, and sites can contain pages, applications, lists, document libraries, and other sites.

You administer site collections from the Site Collections page in the SharePoint Admin Center. The Site Collections page, shown in Figure 17-7, is where you can create and manage the resources for site collections, purchase additional storage, assign ownership, and restore deleted items.

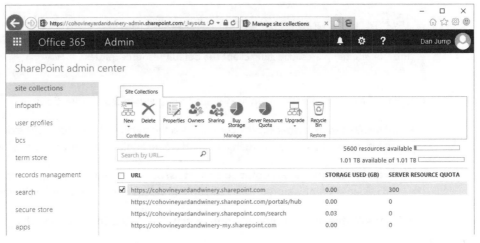

Figure 17-7 Site Collections page

SERVER RESOURCE QUOTA

The Server Resource Quota column indicates the number of server resources allocated to sandboxed solutions. Adjusting the server resource quotas might be necessary if you have custom code solutions that use more server resources. You use this setting to limit the risk to availability that sandboxed solutions can have on other site collections. When you reach your quota, sandboxed solutions are turned off. You can configure the quota to notify you when you reach a threshold, so you can make modifications to the application code or the quota, as shown in Figure 17-8.

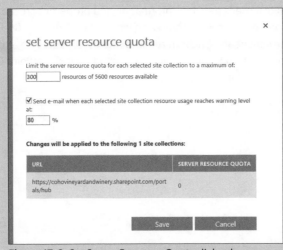

Figure 17-8 Set Server Resource Quota dialog box

CHAPTER 17

> The total number of server resources available to allocate is based on the number of licenses available in your tenant. If the majority of the sites in your site collections are using out-of-the-box site templates, you can accept the default resource quotas.

Out of the box, your SharePoint Online tenant comes with four site collections.

- **https://<tenant>.sharepoint.com**   This is the default site collection. The default team site is created here. You can manage it and create additional sites or subsites inside it.

- **https://<tenant>.sharepoint.com/portals/hub**   This site collection is where Office 365 video content is stored. Users can upload videos directly and create channels.

- **https://<tenant>.sharepoint.com/search**   This is the enterprise search portal.

- **https://<tenant>-my.sharepoint.com**   Users' OneDrive for Business sites are automatically provisioned into thsite collection.

Infopath

The Infopath page enables you to configure the SharePoint Online Infopath Forms Services. From this page, you can enable or disable browser-based forms (which would require clients to complete forms by using the Infopath desktop application). You can also configure user agent exemptions for indexing. Configuring user agent exemptions causes search indexers with matching user agents to index the Infopath form as XML text instead of as a web form.

User profiles

The user profile is where all of a user's personal information and properties are stored for SharePoint Online. If your organization is synchronizing with Active Directory, user attributes from the on-premises environment are synchronized into Microsoft Azure Active Directory, and then the User Profile Synchronization Service (which is not exposed in SharePoint Online) synchronizes that data into the individual user profiles. See Figure 17-9.

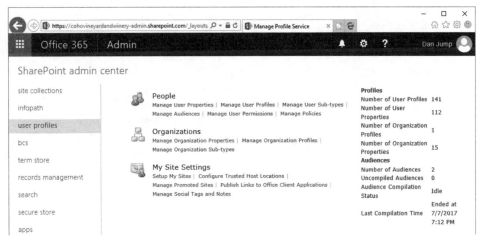

Figure 17-9 User Profiles page

People

The People area of User Profiles contains management tasks related to users. Tasks in this area include configuring additional user properties and audiences—both of which can be used to make SharePoint Online deliver customized value to your organization.

Managing user properties

By creating additional property fields, you give users the ability to enter data in their SharePoint profile that might not otherwise be captured in other systems. This can be useful for creating audiences (SharePoint terminology for groups that can be created based on certain properties) or for enabling user discovery through search. For example, you might create a property field called Previous Departments to provide users a way to indicate what other roles they might have had in an organization. See Figure 17-10.

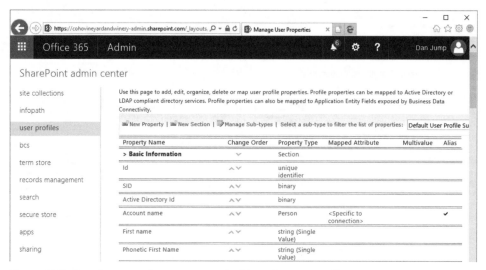

Figure 17-10 Page for managing user properties Managing user profiles

In User Profiles, you find options to manage the individual user profiles of users in your organization, as shown in Figure 17-11.

Figure 17-11 Manage user profiles

From this page, you can use Edit My Profile to modify the individual properties associated with a user. If you are synchronizing data from Active Directory, fields might be overwritten during the next profile synchronization process. You can also delete the user profile or update settings for the user's OneDrive for Business site by selecting either Manage Personal Site or Manage Site Collection Owners.

Managing user subtypes

User subtypes are classifications that you can apply to user profile properties. You can use subtypes to configure which profile fields are available for various user types. For example, you might create a subtype for employees and contractors and then restrict a profile field such as Office Phone to be available to employees only.

Managing audiences

Audiences are groups of users that can be created based on user profile properties. For example, you might choose to create an audience that contains all members whose department is Marketing and whose work phone contains the digits 555.

Manage user permissions

You can use Manage User Permissions to adjust the permissions users have for the User Profile service. You can use this, for example, to restrict OneDrive for Business provisioning (for more information, see Chapter 19) or access other User Profile Service features.

Managing policies

You can manage the policies to configure which profile fields are required or optional for the User Profile Service as well as to configure visibility of those profile fields.

Organizations

You can use the Organizations area to manage more global-facing settings of the User Profile Service.

Managing organization properties

In Manage Organization Properties, you can control additional global profile properties. You can map profile properties to Active Directory or other LDAP directory service properties as well as Application Entity fields from Business Data Connectivity.

Managing organization profile

Just as users have profiles, your organization can have a profile as well. You can use the Manage Organization Profile page to create and maintain properties about your organization.

CHAPTER 17

Managing organization subtypes

You can create subtypes for your organization profile by selecting Manage Organization Sub-types.

My Site Settings

The My Site Settings area contains settings by which you manage My Sites (OneDrive for Business) sites across your organization.

Setting up My Sites

You can modify the settings in Set Up My Sites to configure the behavior of the sites the User Profile Service application manages, as shown in Figure 17-12.

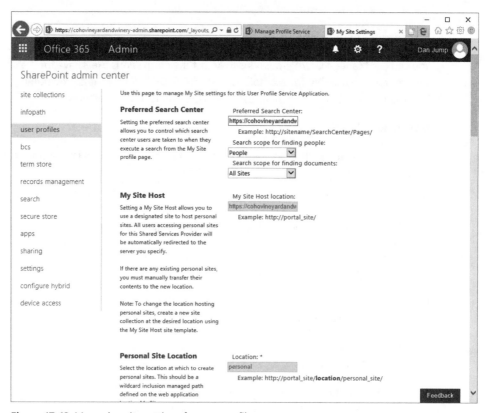

Figure 17-12 Managing site settings for user profiles

Some of the settings, such as My Site Host and Personal Site Location, cannot be changed, because they were configured when the User Profile Service for your tenant was created.

Configuring trusted host locations

You can use this feature to manage a list of other My Site hosts in your organization. Most organizations cannot use this feature because Office 365 has only one User Profile Service application per tenant.

Managing promoted sites

You can configure promoted sites to appear on the Sites page in a user's My Sites (OneDrive for Business). You can restrict promoted sites by audiences.

Publishing links to Office client applications

You can create and manage links for saving documents in Office client applications with Publish Links To Office Client Applications. These links show up in Favorite Links when users perform a Save As operation in an Office client application connected to Office 365.

Managing social tags and notes

You can use Manage Social Tags And Notes to manage the social items of users. This only affects data stored in SharePoint Online and does not connect to Yammer, regardless of the setting for the enterprise social platform in general settings.

You can learn more about planning for user profiles at *https://technet.microsoft.com/en-us /library/ee721054.aspx*, "Plan user profiles in SharePoint Server 2013."

Business Connectivity Services

Business Connectivity Services enables you to connect to data sets outside of SharePoint Online and then make them available for use. The Business Connectivity Services page enables you to configure connections to external data sources, as shown in Figure 17-13.

CHAPTER 17

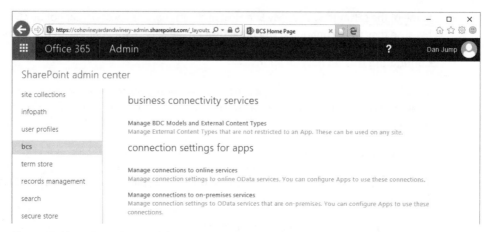

Figure 17-13 Business Connectivity Services page

To configure Business Connectivity Services fully, configure permissions, configure a Secure Store credential mapping, create an external content type, configure a connection to a data source, create an output (such as an External List), and then grant permissions to view and manage the external content type.

Before you begin configuring Business Connectivity Services, use the Manage BDC Models And External Content Types page to configure permissions on the Business Connectivity Metadata Store.

Select the Set Metadata Store Permissions button on the ribbon and then add the administrators for the application to the list, selecting the appropriate permissions, and then click OK. See Figure 17-14.

You must create an external content type (ECT) by using Visual Studio or SharePoint Designer 2010. SharePoint Designer 2010 is available as a free download from the Microsoft Download Center at *https://www.microsoft.com/download/en/details.aspx?id=16573*.

For an example of how to create an ECT and build an external list that retrieves data from a SQL Azure table, see *https://support.office.com/en-us/article/Make-an-External-List-from-a-SQL-Azure-table-with-Business-Connectivity-Services-and-Secure-Store-466f3809-fde7-41f2-87f7-77d9fdadfc95*, "Make an External List from a SQL Azure Table with Business Connectivity Services and Secure Store."

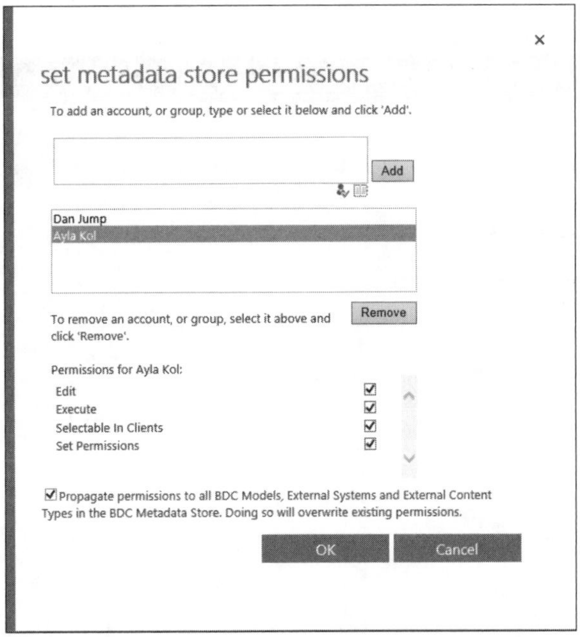

Figure 17-14 Set Metadata Store Permissions dialog box

You can configure connections to online services by using the Manage Connections To Online Services setting. Connections might be used by apps that you develop or purchase from the SharePoint Store.

You can configure connections to on-premises data services by using the Manage Connections To On-Premises Services setting. If you configure an on-premises data service, you can use a credential stored in a target application (configured on the Secure Store page).

Term Store

SharePoint Online enables you to tag and categorize data for standardization purposes. You can use data contained in the Term Store to achieve this.

For example, if your organization is a winery and you are cataloging products in your inventory, you might want to create a set of standard terms describing flavor characteristics, such as strawberry or vanilla (Figure 17-15). If your organization produces vehicles, you might want to create categories and terms describing passenger vehicles, trucks, or trailers.

CHAPTER 17

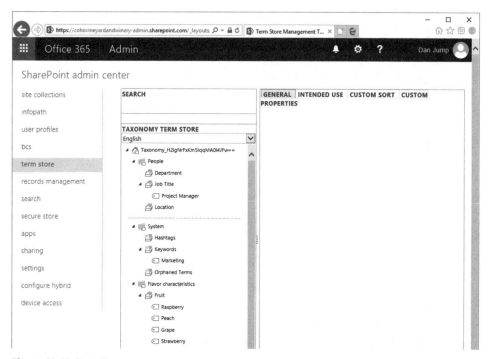

Figure 17-15   Term Store

To manage the term store, you must be granted permissions to do so. Select the top level of the Term Store (Taxonomy_*<ID>*) and add administrators in the Term Store Administrators area.

For more information about term sets, see *https://technet.microsoft.com/en-us/library /ee519604.aspx*, "Plan terms and term sets in SharePoint Server 2013."

Records management

You can configure SharePoint Online to manage records in place or send them to a records management center. The Records Management page enables you to configure a Send To connection for records management that the Content Organizer can use.

Before implementing a records management plan, you should work with business owners and content experts to develop a file plan to describe the types of items and documents to acknowledge as records and where the records will be stored.

The following example can be used to set up a Records Management site collection and configure a site to route documents there automatically. To do so, follow these steps.

1.   From the SharePoint Admin Center, select Site Collections.

2. Click New | Private Site Collection.

3. Fill out the page details, including Title, Address, Template Selection, Time Zone, Administrator, and Server Resource Quota details. For the template, select the Enterprise tab and then select Records Center. See Figure 17-16.

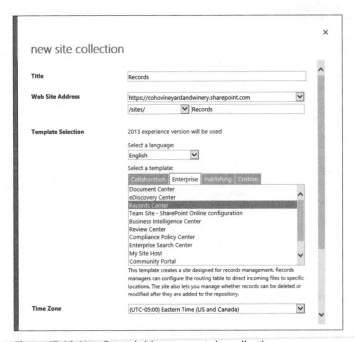

Figure 17-16 New Records Management site collection

4. Click OK to create the site collection.

5. After the site collection has been created, you can navigate to it and examine the structure. See Figure 17-17.

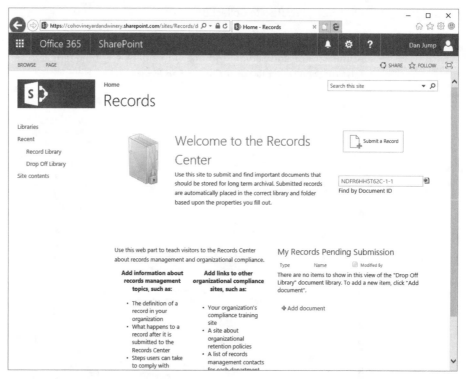

Figure 17-17   SharePoint Records Center page

When your records center has been configured, you can configure libraries and lists to manage and contain records. Content types are associated with libraries, which ultimately enable documents to be routed to the correct libraries. Follow these steps.

1.   On the Records Center site, click Libraries in the navigation pane.

2.   Click New and then select Document Library.

3.   In the Create Document Library fly-out, type a name and click Create.

Content types enable the Records Center to process documents automatically. Follow these steps to add content to a library.

1.   Select the new library you just created in the navigation pane and then, on the ribbon, select Library. See Figure 17-18.

Figure 17-18 Library settings

2. In the Settings group, select Library Settings.

3. In the Content Types section, click Add From Existing Site Content Types.

4. Select a content type from the list, click Add, and then click OK.

TROUBLESHOOTING

Content types not available?

If you cannot see the Content Type settings, select Advanced Settings and then select the Yes button under Allow Management Of Content Types. Scroll to the end of the page and click OK. For more information, see *https://support.office.com/en-us/article/Turn-on -support-for-multiple-content-types-in-a-list-or-library-80506b54-361d-4847-bce3 -67e30f497256*, "Turn on support for multiple content types in a list or library."

Finally, create an information management policy to route documents to the library.

1. On the Records Center site, click the gear icon and select Site Settings.

2. In the Web Designer Galleries *https://technet.microsoft.com/en-us/library/ee519604.aspx* section, click Site Content Types.

3. Select the content type to which you want to apply the policy settings, such as Document.

4. Select Information Management Policy Settings.

5. Type a description, a policy statement, enable one or more policy settings, and then click OK.

CHAPTER 17

For more information about configuring a records center and management policies, see *https://support.office.com/en-us/article/Implement-Records-Management-0BFE419E-EB1D -421A-BECD-5BE9FED1E479*, "Implement Records Management."

Now that a Records Center has been created, you can configure the Send To connection in the SharePoint Admin Center. To do so, follow these steps.

1.   In the SharePoint Admin Center, select Records Management.

2.   Configure Send To Connections by typing a name for the connection and a Send To URL. The Send To URL can be obtained from the Records Center site in Site Settings | Content Organizer Settings. See Figure 17-19.

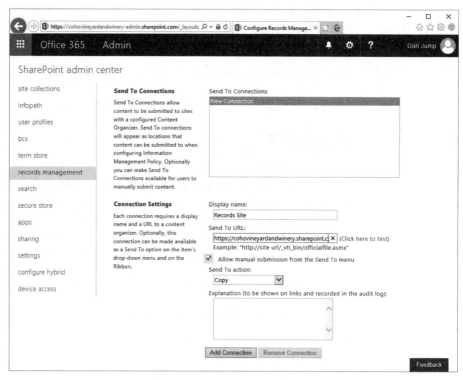

Figure 17-19 Configuring the Send To connection

3.   Click Add Connection.

Your organization might also use the combination of a records management site and preservation or retention policies (configured through the Security & Compliance Center) to label and preserve important business data. See Chapter 8, "Inside the Security & Compliance Center: Data Classification, Loss Prevention, Governance, and Discovery," for more information.

Search

The Search Administration page enables you to customize Search for your organization.

- **Manage Search Schema**   The search schema enables you to control which properties of users, documents, and other objects are indexed for search.

- **Manage Search Dictionaries**   This option opens the term store, enabling you to create and manage term sets.

- **Manage Authoritative Pages**   Use the Authoritative Pages settings to tune the order and weight of returned documents. For example, if you have a document called Procedures.docx in /sites/active and a copy from several years ago with outdated historical content in /sites/archive, you can choose return results so that the item in /sites/active is ranked higher.

- **Query Suggestion Settings**   Use these settings to enable or disable search suggestions. You can also pre-populate common search phrases from a text file.

- **Manage Result Sources**   Configure locations that search queries.

- **Manage Query Rules**   Create rules to promote important or preferred results and tune search ranking.

- **Manage Query Client Types**   Use Client Types to manage the sources of queries and rank them in priority for performance.

- **Remove Search Results**   Use this to remove specific URLs from the search results. URLs are re-added upon the next crawl. To remove a result from search permanently, change permissions on the item or remove it completely.

- **View Usage Reports**   View usage reports to get information about how often your users are using search as well as what types of queries are being run.

- **Search Center Settings**   Use this setting to point to the URL of the enterprise search portal. By default, it points to *https://<tenant>.sharepoint.com/search/Pages*.

- **Export Search Configuration**   Create an export file containing the query rules, ranking models, and settings.

CHAPTER 17

- **Import Search Configuration**   Import a search configuration file.

- **Crawl Log Permissions**   Type the email addresses of users to whom you wish to grant permissions to read the crawl log.

Secure Store

The Secure Store management page is in the SharePoint Admin Center. On that page, you can create a new target application (see Figure 17-20) and configure which users are mapped to this application and credential.

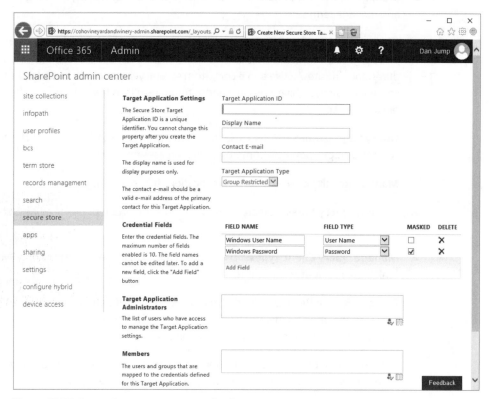

Figure 17-20 Secure Store new target application

After a target application has been configured, you can configure credentials. They are encrypted and enable you to store them in SharePoint Online for usage by Business Connectivity Services or apps.

Apps

You can enable the use of apps in your SharePoint Online environment to extend the capabilities of the platform further. See Figure 17-21.

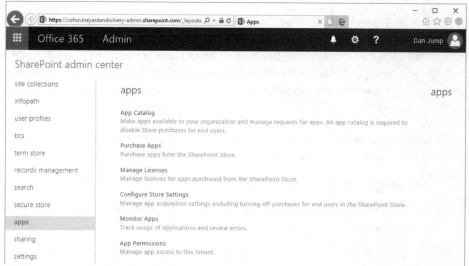

Figure 17-21 Apps page in the SharePoint Admin Center

App catalog

You can configure an app catalog to make apps available to your users. The first time you select the App Catalog link, you are prompted to create a new app catalog site or use an existing site. When you have provisioned or connected to an app catalog, it appears as a new site collection.

Purchase apps

You can click the Purchase Apps link to launch the SharePoint Store. When the SharePoint Store opens, you can navigate to an app and click Add It. If purchase details are needed, you can input those.

> **TROUBLESHOOTING**
>
> **Sorry, this site does not support apps**
>
> **Selecting Purchase Apps from the SharePoint Admin site results in the error shown in Figure 17-22.**

Figure 17-22 SharePoint Store warning

The error, "Sorry, this site does not support apps but you can still acquire them and add them on other sites," appears because you cannot install apps to the SharePoint Admin Center site. You can purchase the apps here, but you have to install them directly into sites.

After you have acquired an app, you receive a notification that the app has been made available to everyone in your organization. Site administrators can then add the app to their sites.

Manage licenses

Use the Manage Licenses page (Figure 17-23) to view information about apps for your organization.

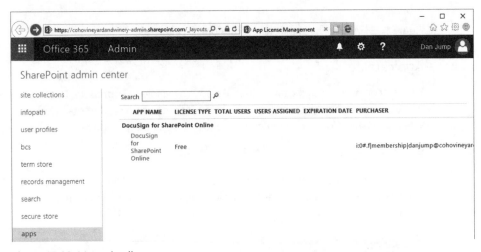

Figure 17-23 Managing licenses

You can select an individual app to display licensing details (Figure 17-24) as well as revoke individual licenses and assign a license manager.

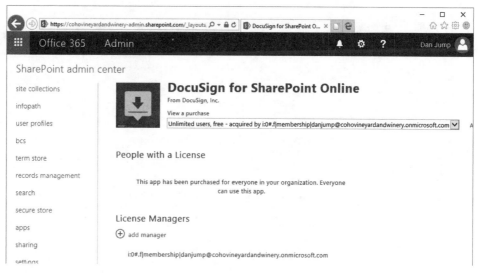

Figure 17-24 App details

Configure Store settings

Use the settings in Configure Store Settings to control store behavior and app requests. See Figure 17-25. Clicking the Click Here To View App Requests link redirects you to the App catalog site.

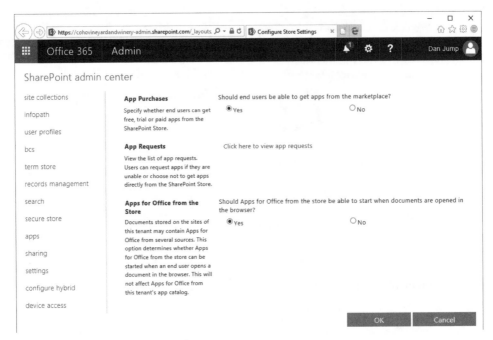

Figure 17-25 Configuring Store settings

Monitor apps

Configure app monitoring in Monitor Apps. This enables you to track usage of apps across your tenant. To configure an app for monitoring, click Add App from the ribbon and select the app from the list.

App permissions

Use the app permissions page to remove permissions granted to apps. By default, the only app permission listed is Office 365 Exchange Online. As you add more apps to your organization and they request access to data on behalf of your users, they appear here.

Sharing

Use the Sharing page to manage whether and how content can be shared outside your organization, as shown in Figure 17-26. These settings are global and apply to OneDrive for Business sites as well.

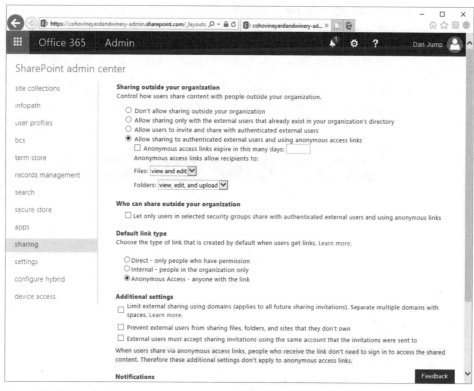

Figure 17-26 Sharing page

A number of restrictions are available, such as prohibiting all external sharing, only allowing sharing with certain domains, or preventing users from using sharing invitations with addresses other than the intended recipient.

Sharing activities can be audited through the Security & Compliance Center. For more information about auditing, see Chapter 7, "Inside the Security & Compliance Center: Alerting, Threat Management, and Reporting."

Settings

The Settings page contains a number of options that can be configured to change the experience and capabilities of SharePoint Online.

- **Show Or Hide Options** This option contains buttons to show or hide OneDrive For Business and Sites tiles. This setting removes the tiles from the App Launcher but does not disable the services. If users have bookmarked the URLs or otherwise know how to navigate to them, they can still access them. The default setting is Show for both OneDrive for Business and Sites.

CHAPTER 17

- **Site Collection Store Management** This setting has two options—automatic and manual. Manual storage operation means you as the administrator must update quotas for site collections as they grow, whereas the automatic setting automatically grows the size of the site collection as it nears its limit. The default is Automatic.

- **OneDrive for Business Experience** You can enable the New Experience or Classic Experience user interface. The default is New Experience, as shown in Figure 17-27.

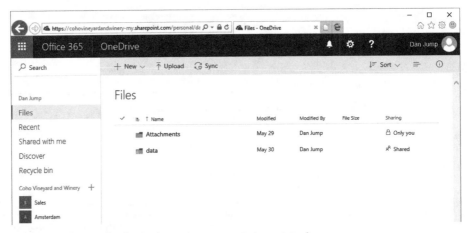

Figure 17-27 OneDrive for Business new user experience interface

You can also switch to the Classic Experience, as shown in Figure 17-28.

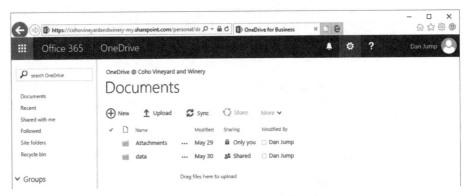

Figure 17-28 OneDrive for Business classic user experience interface

- **OneDrive Sync Button** You can use this option to show or hide the Sync button in the OneDrive user interface. The default is Show The Sync Button.

- **Sync Client for SharePoint**   This option selects which sync client to start when a user clicks the Sync button in a SharePoint library. The recommended option is to use the new client by selecting the Start The New Client button. The default setting, however, is Start The Old Client.

- **SharePoint Lists and Libraries Experience**   This option enables you to toggle the user interface experience between the newer interface and the classic interface. This affects the default view of the site, and users can switch between the user interface experiences. The default setting is New Experience (Auto Detect).

- **Admin Center Experience**   This setting controls whether to show a minimal set of configuration options or all options. The default setting is Use Advanced.

- **Office Graph**   Use this setting to enable or disable access to Office Graph. Office Graph analyzes the relationships between users and data in Office 365 and presents it through interfaces such as Delve. Disabling Office Graph disables applications that rely on it, such as Delve. The default setting is Allow Access To The Office Graph (Default).

- **Enterprise Social Collaboration**   You can select whether to use Yammer or SharePoint Newsfeed as the social platform. Yammer is currently not covered in the Office 365 Trust Center. The default setting is Use SharePoint Newsfeed (Default).

- **Streaming Video Service**   This option determines whether the Azure Media Service is available and enables or disables the video portal. The default option is Enable Streaming Video Through Azure Media Services And Enable The Video Portal.

- **Site Pages**   Modifying this option enables you to control whether users can create site pages by using the authoring canvas. The default setting is Allow Users To Create Site Pages.

- **Global Experience Version Settings**   This option controls which version of a site collection users can create and whether users can upgrade site collections. The default option is Prevent Creation Of Old Version Site Collections, But Allow Creation Of New Version Site Collections. Allow Opt-In Upgrade To The New Version Site Collections.

- **Information Rights Management (IRM)**   Enable or disable Information Rights Management for your tenant. To enable Information Rights Management, you must have a subscription that includes Azure Rights Management and enable Information Rights management in your Office 365 tenant before enabling IRM in SharePoint Online. For more information about deploying Azure Rights Management, see *https://docs.microsoft. com/en-us/information-protection/deploy-use/activate-service*. The default setting is Do Not Use IRM For This Tenant.

INSIDE OUT

Information rights management

You can use information rights management to encrypt documents and make them available only to users who have access to the Azure Rights Management Service and have been granted permissions to a file. IRM can be applied to libraries and lists, protecting all documents contained within them. Typical restrictions include making a document read-only or prohibiting the use of screen-capture tools or printing. Using IRM to protect documents can help prevent distribution of documents outside your organization. SharePoint Online encryption supports PDF, XPS, and Office documents created in Word, Microsoft Excel, and Microsoft PowerPoint from version 97 onward.

- **Site Creation**   There are multiple settings groups under this option.
    - The first settings group is to hide or show the Create Site command. Only users who have permission to create sites see the command in SharePoint Online. The default option is Show The Create Site Command To Users Who Have Permissions To Create Sites.
    - The second settings group takes effect when a user creates a site. Because Office 365 groups can be integrated with SharePoint Sites, you can control whether the Create Site command still functions normally if Office 365 group creation is disabled. The three options are:
        - **A Site With An Office 365 Group Or A Classic Site**   This setting enables users to create a SharePoint site even if Office 365 groups creation is disabled. This is the default setting.
        - **A Site With An Office 365 Group**   This setting shows the Create Site command and enables users to create sites only if they also have permissions to create Office 365 groups.
        - **A Classic Site**   Choose this option if you want to enable users to create only a classic site or sites from a custom form.
- **Use The Form At This URL**   You can specify a URL that contains a custom form for all user-provisioned sites.
- **Custom Script**   There are two settings under this option. Use this option to enable or disable custom scripting on personal and self-service created sites. The default settings are Prevent Users From Running Custom Script On Personal Sites and Prevent Users From Running Custom Script On Self-Service Created Sites.
- **Preview Features**   This option enables whether preview features are enabled in SharePoint Online. The default setting is Enable Preview Features.

- **Connected Services**   This option limits SharePoint Online features that attempt to connect to other services. The Block SharePoint 2013 Workflows check box is cleared by default.

- **Access Apps**   Use this option to enable or disable access apps in the cloud. This setting is set to Disable Access Apps by default. Access apps are a deprecated feature in SharePoint Online. Starting in June 2017, users can no longer create new access apps. See *https://support.office.com/en-us/article/Access-Services-in-SharePoint-Roadmap-497fd86b-e982-43c4-8318-81e6d3e711e8* for more information.

- **Mobile Push Notifications – OneDrive for Business**   This setting enables whether users can get push notifications for the OneDrive for Business mobile app. The default setting is Allow Notifications.

- **Mobile Push Notifications – SharePoint**   This setting enables whether users can get push notifications for SharePoint content. The default setting is Allow Notifications.

- **Comments on Site Pages**   You can use this setting to enable whether users can leave comments on site pages. Users who have access to view a page can leave comments. The default setting is Enable Comments On Site Pages.

After making any changes to settings, click OK at the bottom of the page to commit changes.

Configure hybrid

The Configure Hybrid page, shown in Figure 17-29, provides information about hybrid configuration options available between SharePoint Server and SharePoint Online as well as a link to the Hybrid Picker. The Hybrid Picker is a wizard designed to assist in configuring some SharePoint hybrid features.

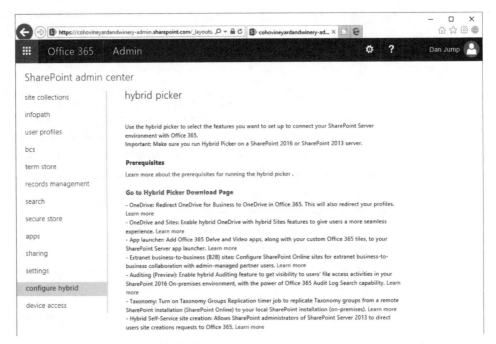

Figure 17-29 Configure Hybrid page

For more information about SharePoint hybrid configurations, see Chapter 18.

Device access

You can use the settings on the Device Access page to restrict locations from which users can connect to SharePoint Online–based services. These settings apply to SharePoint sites, OneDrive for Business sites, and Office 365 groups (because they have a SharePoint component). See Figure 17-30.

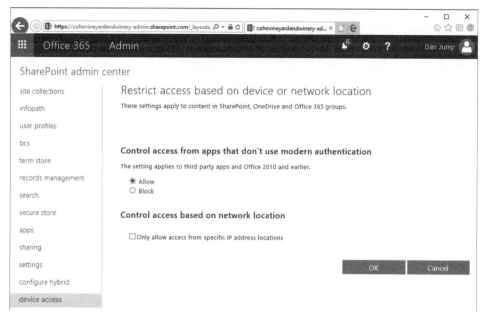

Figure 17-30 Device Access page

INSIDE OUT

Location-based access settings

The location-based access controls apply to all clients, regardless of platform. Configuring the IP address restrictions to only an organization's corporate IP address ranges, for example, prohibits mobile devices from synchronizing OneDrive for Business content when they are on cellular data networks.

Depending on your organization's requirements, there might be a number of ways to control access for your environment. You can use Active Directory Federation Services claims to restrict access as well as InTune's Conditional Access feature.

Summary

This chapter discussed SharePoint Online concepts and features as well as how to manage the settings in the SharePoint Online Admin Center. SharePoint Online can be configured in a variety of hybrid modes, as discussed in Chapter 18. In addition, OneDrive for Business is a SharePoint Online feature and is discussed in Chapter 19. Finally, Yammer can also be integrated with SharePoint Online, replacing the Newsfeed feature with Yammer groups. For more information on configuring Yammer, see Chapter 20.

CHAPTER 17

SharePoint Online Hybrid

Planning 857   Configuration 863

SharePoint Online, as discussed in Chapter 17, "Overview of SharePoint Online," is a cloud-based collaboration platform comprising sites, storage, and apps. In a SharePoint hybrid configuration scenario, you can connect your on-premises Microsoft SharePoint deployment to Office 365 in a number of ways to extend your infrastructure into the cloud.

SharePoint Online Hybrid has four core components.

- **Hybrid OneDrive for Business**   Redirect SharePoint on-premises storage for user files to Office 365 OneDrive for Business.

- **Hybrid Search**   Enable users to search for content in both on-premises and online systems.

- **Hybrid Taxonomy**   Create managed metadata that can be shared and updated between SharePoint 2016 on-premises and SharePoint Online systems.

- **Hybrid Auditing (SharePoint 2016 Preview Feature)**   Configure auditing to provide insights into users' online and on-premises file access activities.

Two additional types of configurations exist to complete a robust collaboration space experience.

- **App launcher**   Configure the Office 365 app launcher to help users navigate between on-premises and online environments.

- **Business-to-business extranet**   Create partner sites to allow external users access to relevant online content in a members-only site.

Planning

In planning any SharePoint topology, the first questions you should be asking are about the business goal you're trying to achieve and how you will manage it. In the case of a hybrid OneDrive for Business configuration, maybe it's transitioning on-premises storage to the cloud. For hybrid search, maybe it's providing an integrated search platform so users can locate content on either platform. After you have identified the organizational goals and capabilities of the platforms, it's important to become familiar with the process and prerequisites of any implementation.

General

After you have decided on the hybrid features to implement, make sure you meet the prerequisites for the services you intend to configure. Some services have specific requirements, whereas others are more general and apply regardless.

- Configuring any hybrid service scenario that includes SharePoint Server 2013 requires SharePoint Server Service Pack 1 (*https://go.microsoft.com/fwlink/p/?LinkId=521936*). Without it, site redirection features are unavailable.

- The Subscription Settings service application must be configured.

- The User Profile service application must be configured and Active Directory synchronized with the User Profile service.

- The App Management service application must be configured.

- My Sites must be configured.

- The Managed Metadata service application must be configured.

- Identity synchronization between Active Directory and Microsoft Azure Active Directory must be configured. For more information about configuring identity synchronization, see Chapter 4, "Directory Synchronization Basics," and Chapter 5, "Installing Azure AD Connect."

OneDrive for Business

Hybrid OneDrive for Business enables you to shift data consumption and sharing from your Microsoft OneDrive on-premises deployment (if it exists) to OneDrive for Business in Office 365. Hybrid OneDrive for Business enables your users to continue using on-premises SharePoint sites and services in addition to cloud-based OneDrive.

Although configuring hybrid OneDrive for Business does enable you to redirect users accessing their OneDrive to Office 365, it's important to note that the data migration process is *separate*. Data migration must be performed outside of the hybrid configuration process.

Also, because there's no link or synchronization between OneDrive for Business in SharePoint Server and OneDrive for Business in Office 365, the Shared With Me list in Office 365 won't populate with documents shared with a user in the on-premises environment or vice versa.

Hybrid OneDrive for Business configuration also configures hybrid user profiles, so that when users view a profile in SharePoint Server, they are redirected to the user's Office 365 profile.

If you want to pilot hybrid OneDrive for Business, consider creating an audience in SharePoint to identify those users.

Search

Two types of search are available in SharePoint hybrid configuration: cloud hybrid search and hybrid federated search.

Cloud hybrid search is the simplest to configure and stores the search index for all crawled content in Office 365. This single index exposes all SharePoint content (including on-premises) to the Office Graph, so your users can discover content inside Office 365 applications such as Delve. Results are ranked based on their relevance, regardless of the source of the content, and presented in a single result.

Hybrid federated search returns content from two indices (Office 365 and SharePoint Server on-premises). Results are grouped and ranked independently according to their source and then displayed in separate result blocks.

For most organizations, cloud hybrid search is recommended. Cloud hybrid search has the following advantages.

- Users see unified search results from multiple sources.

- Your organization can begin using the updated SharePoint experience without upgrading on-premises servers to SharePoint Server 2016.

- You don't need to upgrade on-premises servers past the required updates to enable hybrid functionality.

- You don't have to upgrade your search index.

- Your organization will have a lower total cost of ownership for search, *because* no additional on-premises hardware or capacity needs to be deployed moving forward; the enterprise search index is stored in Office 365.

- Office Graph applications such as Delve can present content to users.

- Cloud hybrid search is simpler to deploy and maintain.

This chapter focuses on configuring cloud hybrid search, although you might wish to implement hybrid federated search or use a combination of hybrid federated search and cloud hybrid search (such as for sensitive content sets or unavailable features).

CHAPTER 18

When planning a hybrid search, it's important to understand what's different or unavailable, what has been replaced with newer features, or additional configurations you might need to perform to provide the best experience for your users.

- **Site search** SharePoint Server does not automatically return results for content that has been moved to Office 365. To return Office 365 results in your SharePoint on-premises environment, you must configure your on-premises environment to retrieve search results from the Office 365 Search service application (SSA).

- **Search verticals** If you currently use search verticals in your on-premises SharePoint Server environment, you must re-create it in your search center in Office 365.

- **eDiscovery** eDiscovery for Office 365 is managed in the Search & Compliance Center. Office 365 eDiscovery cannot index or search content in SharePoint Server on-premises; eDiscovery managers might have to perform searches in multiple places to return all relevant data.

- **Cross-site publishing search** Cross-site publishing search is not available with hybrid search.

- **Custom security trimming** Custom security trimming is not supported in Office 365.

- **Usage reports** Usage reports are based on information stored in SharePoint Online. The SSA in SharePoint Server doesn't communicate with SharePoint Online, so the SharePoint Online usage reports do not contain information regarding on-premises user activity.

- **Custom Search Scopes** Custom Search Scopes is a SharePoint Server 2010 feature. Use result sources in SharePoint Online.

- **Best Bets** Best Bets is a SharePoint Server 2010 feature. Use result sources in SharePoint Online.

- **Multitenancy** SharePoint Online cannot preserve tenant isolation in a multitenant SharePoint Server 2013 or SharePoint Server 2016 farm.

- **Thesaurus** SharePoint Online does not support thesauruses.

- **Content Enrichment web service** The Content Enrichment web service is not available in SharePoint Online.

- **Custom entity extraction** SharePoint Online does not support custom entity extraction.

- **Index reset for on-premises content**   It is not possible to clear search results for on-premises content. To remove on-premises content from search results, remove the on-premises content source or create an on-premises crawl rule to exclude the content from the search.

When configuring cloud hybrid search, your on-premises SharePoint server that hosts the cloud SSA needs at least 100 GB of storage space. From a cloud planning perspective, SharePoint Online can index 1 million items for every 1 TB of space. If you need to index more than 20 million items, you must open a case with Microsoft Support.

Taxonomy

Hybrid Taxonomy is the idea that you can define a single SharePoint taxonomy to span SharePoint Server on-premises and SharePoint Online. The benefit is that you can use a single metadata set between both platforms.

Unlike other hybrid configurations, Taxonomy is different in that it is mastered *online*. With other hybrid solutions (such as Active Directory and Exchange), the on-premises system is the source of authority, and then the cloud derives its data set from what is synchronized from the on-premises environment.

When you configure hybrid taxonomy and content types, you copy your on-premises term store configuration and available content types to SharePoint Online and then configure the on-premises environment to update its taxonomy and content types through a timer job.

Auditing

Hybrid auditing enables users to upload their SharePoint diagnostic and usage logs and have reports generated for them in Office 365. Administrators have visibility into users' on-premises file access activities.

Hybrid auditing is only available for SharePoint 2016 server farms and requires SharePoint Server 2016 Feature Pack 1, available for download at *https://support.microsoft.com/en-us /help/3127940/november-8,-2016,-update-for-sharepoint-server-2016-kb3127940*.

App launcher

The hybrid app launcher enables you to create a more seamless experience for users moving between the SharePoint on-premises and SharePoint Online environments. Originally available only with SharePoint Server 2016, the extensible app launcher is available with the July 2016 public update for SharePoint Server 2013. Go to *https://support.microsoft.com/kb/3115286* for more information.

The app launcher experience exposes Office 365 apps through the on-premises SharePoint Server app launcher interface.

Business-to-business extranet

An extranet is a restricted site that enables your organization to share information with external users while prohibiting them from accessing other corporate content. In a SharePoint hybrid configuration, you can direct external users to a members-only site in Office 365.

There are many advantages to configuring extranet sites in SharePoint Online.

- Site collections can be configured to allow all users to invite partner users.

- Site collections can be configured to allow only site owners to invite partner users.

- Admins can control the list of partner domains to which the organization allows sharing.

- Office 365 activity reports can be used to track partner site access and usage.

- Guests or partner users can be restricted to only a single site, preventing access to unauthorized resources.

- Guests or partner users can be restricted to be able only to accept invitations from the address that received the email, preventing sharing with additional accounts or accounts from unapproved domains.

In planning your extranet model, you need to make decisions around three core areas.

- **Invitation model**   This determines how users get access to sites—whether all users or only site collection owners can invite users, or an admin-managed model by which you import partner users from a directory.

- **Licensing**   By default, SharePoint guest users have limited capabilities in SharePoint Online and are limited to the restrictions governing the group into which they are placed. Authenticated external users can use Office Online to view and edit documents, but further features (such as installing Office ProPlus or being able to create and manage sites) require assignment of a SharePoint license.

- **Account life cycle management**   At some point, external users might no longer require access to an extranet resource, or the project an extranet site supports will end. In either case, plan for managing and archiving sites as well as for removing partner user accounts and site permissions. If licenses are assigned to some external users, plan for a way that licenses can be assigned to external users (denoted as #EXT# in the directory) and reclaimed when the partner user account is no longer in use.

INSIDE OUT

Is a SharePoint hybrid architecture right for me?

Hybrid deployments can provide a path to the cloud for many workloads. Although this chapter gives you the knowledge to configure hybrid solutions for a variety of scenarios, you still need to work with your organization's service desk managers, call center representatives, application integration specialists, users, or enterprise architects to determine which portions of your SharePoint environment are well-suited for a hybrid topology.

If your organization has developed custom Infopath forms, configured integrations with other on-premises data sources, or deployed plug-ins to interact with other on-premises applications, you'll need input from the individuals or teams responsible for managing those solutions. If you have deployed custom solutions but want to explore commercial products, you can explore add-ins and solutions available at *https://store.office.com/en-us /appshome.aspx?productgroup=sharepoint*.

However, if your SharePoint environment is underused or hasn't undergone a lot of customization, it might be more worthwhile to migrate content directly to SharePoint Online and bypass hybrid configurations altogether.

Configuration

When the prerequisites have been met for the set of hybrid configuration options you want to perform, you can configure the individual services.

Set up SharePoint services for hybrid integration

For all SharePoint hybrid services, you must at least ensure that the base services are configured. The shared services requirements are as follows.

- Managed Metadata service application

- User Profile service application

- My Sites service application

- Apps Management service application

- SharePoint Foundation Subscription Settings service

If you already have a fully deployed SharePoint farm, chances are you've already configured these services and won't have to configure additional instances of them. However, if your

SharePoint farm is new or you haven't provisioned these services, you can use these abbreviated steps to configure them to the minimal level necessary for hybrid configuration. If you are installing SharePoint 2013 with SP1, these services are already enabled and configured.

Managed metadata service

The managed metadata service application enables metadata and content type sharing across site collections and applications. A farm can have multiple managed metadata service applications, and each one can publish a term store and content types to be consumed by a managed metadata connection.

For more information about managed metadata, see *https://technet.microsoft.com/en-us/library/ee424402.aspx*, "Overview of managed metadata in SharePoint Server 2013."

To configure the managed metadata service, follow these steps.

1. Launch SharePoint Central Administration.

2. Select System Settings and then click Manage Services On Server, as shown in Figure 18-1.

Figure 18-1 SharePoint Central Administration System Settings

3. If you have more than one server, select the server that you want to run the managed metadata service.

4. On the Services page, scroll to the Managed Metadata web service and click Start.

5. In Central Administration, select Application Management and then, under Service Applications, click Manage Service Applications.

6. If a service isn't currently listed for Managed Metadata, click New from the menu and select Managed Metadata Services from the list.

7. Type a name, database server, and new database name for the managed metadata database. See Figure 18-2.

Figure 18-2 Create New Managed Metadata Service page

8. Scroll to the bottom of the page, select the Use Existing Application Pool button, select SharePoint Web Services Default from the drop-down list, and then click OK.

My Sites

Use My Sites to provision and store individual user data sites. Users can create sites and store files in My Sites and synchronize the content through the OneDrive desktop application.

If My Sites is not configured, you can follow these steps to configure the minimum settings necessary to complete the hybrid configuration of SharePoint Server.

1. In Central Administration, select Application Management and then select Manage Web Applications.

2. Select New on the ribbon.

3. Select the Create A New IIS Web Site button and then type a name in the Name box.

4. Under Public URL, type a URL or accept the default (*http://servername:port*).

5. Under Application Pool, select the Create New Application Pool button and type a name for the IIS application pool.

6. Scroll to the bottom of the page and click OK.

7. Click OK to dismiss the dialog box after the web application has been created.

8. Click Application Management.

9. Under Site Collections, click Create Site Collections.

CHAPTER 18

10. Under Web Application, click the drop-down arrow and select Change Web Application. See Figure 18-3.

Figure 18-3 Create Site Collection Choose Web Application drop-down list

11. Select the newly created web application.

12. Type a title and description for the site collection.

13. Under Web Site Address, leave the default root ("/") URL set.

14. Under Template Selection, select the Enterprise tab and then select My Site Host.

15. Under Primary Site Collection Administrator, type a user name or choose one from the People Picker.

16. Click OK.

17. Click OK to dismiss the completion dialog box.

User Profile service

The User Profile service contains individual user data. It must be enabled on at least one server in your SharePoint farm. If you have not configured the User Profile Service, follow these steps.

1. In SharePoint Central Administration, select System Settings and then click Manage Services On Server.

2. If you have more than one server in the farm, select which server to configure.

3. In the Service List, locate User Profile Service and click Start.

NOTE

Do not start the User Profile Synchronization Service at this time, because it will cause the rest of the configuration steps to fail.

4. Click Application Management and then, under Service Applications, select Manage Service Applications.

5. Click New and then click User Profile Service Application.

6. Type a name for the service application, such as User Profile Service, in the name box.

7. Under Application Pool, select the Use Existing Application Pool button and then select SharePoint Web Services Default.

8. In the Profile Synchronization Instance drop-down list, choose the server to run the User Profile Synchronization Service.

9. In the My Site URL Host, type the URL of the My Site Host site collection that you created previously and click OK.

10. Click OK to dismiss the dialog box.

11. Select System Settings from the SharePoint Central Administration navigation pane and then select System Settings.

12. Click Manage Services On Server. If you have more than one server in your SharePoint farm, select the server that will run the User Profile Synchronization Service.

13. In the services list, locate User Profile Synchronization Service and click Start.

14. On the User Profile Synchronization Service page, type the password for the service account that will be used to run the User Profile Synchronization Service and click OK. See Figure 18-4.

Figure 18-4 User Profile Synchronization Service

After you configure the User Profile service, connect on-premises Active Directory to the User Profile service. If it has not already been configured in your environment, follow these steps.

1.   In SharePoint Central Administration, select Application Management and then click Manage Service Applications.

2.   Click the User Profile service application.

3.   On the Manage Profile Service: User Profile Service Application page, under Synchronization, click Configure Synchronization Connections, as shown in Figure 18-5.

Figure 18-5 Configure Synchronization Connections

4.   Click Create New Connection.

5. Type a name for the new connection, such as Active Directory.

6. Ensure that the type is set to Active Directory.

7. Under Connection Settings, type your Active Directory fully qualified forest name, such as contoso.com.

8. Under Account Name, enter credentials for a user account that is a member of Domain Admins or is granted the Replication Directory Changes and Replication Directory Changes All rights (to be able to replicate secure account details).

9. Click the Populate Containers button.

10. Expand the domain node and select the containers where your user objects are located.

11. Click OK.

To synchronize user profiles, follow these steps.

1. In SharePoint Central Administration, select Application Management and then click Manage Service Applications.

2. Click the User Profile service application.

3. On the Manage Profile Service: User Profile Service Application page, under Synchronization, click Start Profile Synchronization.

4. On the Start Profile Synchronization page, select the Start Incremental Synchronization button and then click OK.

App management service

The App Management service stores information regarding SharePoint app licenses and permissions. Licenses downloaded from the Marketplace are stored in the Apps Management service application. The App Management service must be running on at least one server in the SharePoint Farm.

To configure the App Management service, follow these steps.

1. In SharePoint Central Administration, select System Settings and then click Manage Services On Server.

2. If you have more than one server in your SharePoint farm, click Change Server and select the server you wish to configure.

3. In the Service list, locate App Management Service and click Start.

CHAPTER 18

4. In the SharePoint Central Administration navigation pane, select Application Management and then click Manage Service Applications.

5. On the ribbon, click New and then click App Management Service.

6. In the Service Application Name box, type a name for the service, such as App Management Service.

7. Under Application Pool, select the Use Existing Application Pool button and then select SharePoint Web Services Default from the drop-down list.

8. Click OK.

9. Click OK to close the confirmation dialog box.

SharePoint Foundation Subscription Settings

The SharePoint Foundation Subscription Settings service stores configuration information for site subscriptions. It must be configured with SharePoint PowerShell.

1. In SharePoint Central Administration, select System Settings and then click Manage Services On Server.

2. If you have more than one server in your SharePoint farm, click Change Server and select the server you wish to configure.

3. In the Service list, locate Microsoft SharePoint Foundation Subscription Settings Service and click Start.

4. Click Start, type **SharePoint**, right-click Management Shell, and select Run As Administrator to launch an elevated console.

5. Copy and paste the following commands into the Windows PowerShell window to create the SharePoint Foundation Subscription settings.

```
$AppPool = New-SPServiceApplicationPool -Name SettingsServiceAppPool -Account
(Get-SPManagedAccount <DOMAIN\SharePointServiceAccount>)

$App = New-SPSubscriptionSettingsServiceApplication -ApplicationPool $appPool
-Name SettingsServiceApp -DatabaseName SettingsServiceDB

$proxy = New-SPSubscriptionSettingsServiceApplicationProxy -ServiceApplication
$App

Get-SPServiceInstance | where{$_.TypeName -eq "Microsoft SharePoint Foundation
Subscription Settings Service"} | Start-SPServiceInstance
```

After the required components for SharePoint hybrid services have been configured, you can begin configuring individual services or settings.

Server-to-server authentication

For a SharePoint Server farm to consume resources and content from SharePoint Online or Office 365, you must configure server-to-server authentication, which enables features to work cross-premises, such as search or other web applications.

Any on-premises application that is currently configured to use Integrated Windows Authentication (IWA) with NTLM can pass claims to Office 365. IWA using NTLM is required for the SharePoint authentication service to pass user claims to SharePoint Online using OAuth. If your existing web application isn't configured to use IWA with NTLM, you can update it or configure a new web application.

For example, you can create a new website in Internet Information Services (IIS) and connect it to an existing content database and web application, or you can create an entirely new web application and an empty content database. For more information about extending an existing application, see *https://technet.microsoft.com/en-us/library/gg276325.aspx*, "Extend claims-based web applications in SharePoint 2013."

OneDrive for Business and hybrid sites

Hybrid OneDrive for Business is part of a bundle option that enables you to configure Hybrid Sites also. Hybrid OneDrive for Business performs redirection for users' OneDrive for Business sites, whereas Hybrid Sites configures site-following parameters. Hybrid Sites combines the followed sites from SharePoint Online and SharePoint Server into a consolidated list in SharePoint Online. If a user selects the followed-sites link in SharePoint Server on-premises, they are redirected to the followed-sites lists in SharePoint Online.

Configuring hybrid OneDrive for Business can be broken down into three main sections.

- Configure Office 365 for SharePoint hybrid

- Ensure proper permissions

- Redirect OneDrive to Office 365

Prerequisites

To configure hybrid OneDrive for Business and Sites, you must meet the following prerequisites.

- Users with SharePoint Online license in Office 365

- Administration account with SharePoint Online admin role privileges

- SharePoint Online My Sites URL

- Administration account with membership in the Farm Administrators group

Configure Office 365 for SharePoint hybrid

To make hybrid services available for SharePoint Online, you must subscribe to an Office 365 plan that contains SharePoint Online and then connect your on-premises directory to Office 365.

See Chapter 1, "Office 365 Deployment Milestones," and Chapter 2, "Preparing Your Environment for the Cloud," for more information about setting up your Office 365 subscription and domains.

Ensure proper permissions

To use OneDrive for Business in Office 365, users must have the Create Personal Site and Follow People and Edit Profile permissions.

To confirm or configure these permissions, follow these steps.

1.   Log on to the Office 365 portal with a global admin account and select the Admin tile.

2.   Expand Admin Centers and then click SharePoint.

3.   In the navigation pane, click User Profiles.

4.   Under People, click Manage User Permissions.

5.   In the Permissions For User Profile Service Application dialog box, select Everyone Except External Users or add a specific audience if you are piloting.

      Everyone Except External Users is selected by default, with all permissions selected. Click OK.

PILOTING ONEDRIVE FOR A SPECIFIC GROUP

If you decide you want to conduct a pilot of hybrid OneDrive for Business for a small group of users, you can create an audience for your pilot users. Copy and paste the following script into an elevated SharePoint PowerShell console, editing the values for the variables such as $mySiteHostUrl, $audienceName, and $audienceDescription. If you intend to use that pilot group for other activities in SharePoint Online, you might want to repeat the process by updating $mySiteHostUrl to the SharePoint Online My Sites URL and running this from the SharePoint Online PowerShell console. In this example, you create an audience where the members are in the IT department.

You can also perform this action in SharePoint Server on-premises by going to Central Administration | Manage Service Applications | User Profile Service | Manage Audiences or in SharePoint Online by going to SharePoint Admin Center| User Profiles | Manage.

```
## Settings you might want to change for Audience Name and Description ##
$mySiteHostUrl = "https://www.my.contoso.com"
$audienceName = "OneDrive Pilot Users"
$audienceDescription = "OneDrive Pilot Users"
$audienceRules = @()
$audienceRules += New-Object Microsoft.Office.Server.Audience.AudienceRuleComponent("
Department", "Contains", "IT")
#Get the My Site Host's SPSite object
$site = Get-SPSite $mySiteHostUrl
$ctx = [Microsoft.Office.Server.ServerContext]::GetContext($site)
$audMan = New-Object Microsoft.Office.Server.Audience.AudienceManager($ctx)
#Create a new audience object for the given Audience Manager
$aud = $audMan.Audiences.Create($audienceName, $audienceDescription)
$aud.AudienceRules = New-Object System.Collections.ArrayList
$audienceRules | ForEach-Object { $aud.AudienceRules.Add($_) }
#Save the new Audience
$aud.Commit()
#Compile the new Audience
$upa = Get-SPServiceApplication | Where-Object {$_.DisplayName -eq "User Profile Ser-
vice Application"}
$audJob = [Microsoft.Office.Server.Audience.AudienceJob]::RunAudienceJob(($upa.
Id.Guid.ToString(), "1", "1", $aud.AudienceName))
```

6. Verify that the Create Personal Site And Follow People and Edit Profile boxes are selected.

7. Click OK.

Redirect OneDrive to Office 365

Before you begin these steps, ensure that users have a SharePoint Online license in Office 365. (SharePoint Online includes OneDrive for Business.) In addition, you might want to follow the procedure to pre-provision OneDrive for Business sites in Office 365 you find in Chapter 19, "OneDrive for Business."

To perform the redirection, you need the My Sites URL in Office 365. You can locate it by navigating to the SharePoint Online Admin Center, selecting Site Collections, and then looking for the site collection that matches *https://<tenant>-my.sharepoint.com*, as shown in Figure 18-6.

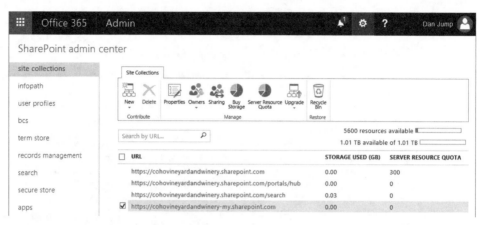

Figure 18-6 Locating the My Sites site collection URL

When you have your tenant's My Sites URL, you can follow these steps to configure OneDrive for Business redirection.

1. Log on to Central Administration, using a Farm Administrator account.

2. In the navigation pane, select Office 365.

3. Click Configure OneDrive Sites And Sites Links (SharePoint Server 2013), as shown in Figure 18-7.

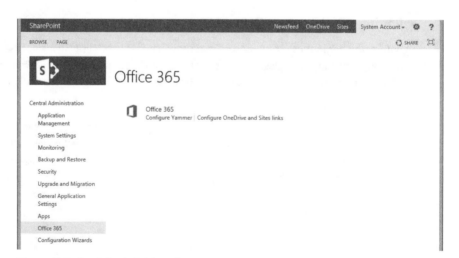

Figure 18-7 OneDrive hybrid configuration in SharePoint Server 2013

If you are using SharePoint Server 2016, the interface is a little different. Click Configure Hybrid OneDrive And Sites Features, as shown in Figure 18-8.

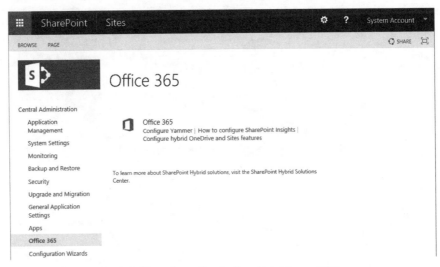

Figure 18-8 OneDrive hybrid configuration in SharePoint Server 2016

4. In the My Site URL box, type the URL obtained from SharePoint Online for the My Sites site collection.

5. Under Set The Audience For The Connection, select the Everyone button to perform redirection for all users or select the Use A Specific Audience button to select a pilot audience group.

6. Select the site redirection feature. Depending on your version of SharePoint server, you might see a different interface. If you are using SharePoint Server 2013, select the Redirect The Sites Page check box, as depicted in Figure 18-9.

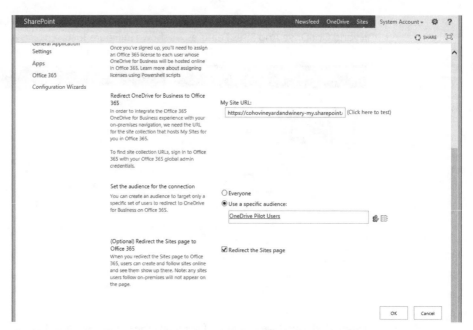

Figure 18-9 Hybrid OneDrive for Business configuration in SharePoint Server 2013

If you are using SharePoint Server 2016, select the OneDrive And Sites button to configure both features, as shown in Figure 18-10.

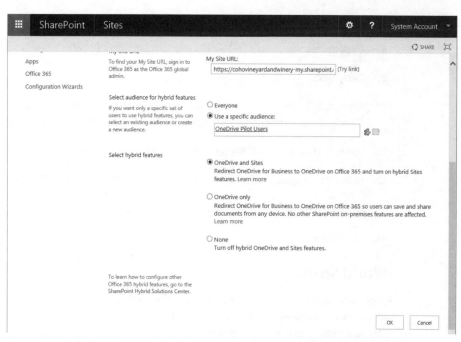

Figure 18-10 Hybrid OneDrive for Business configuration in SharePoint Server 2016

7. Click OK to complete the configuration.

Hybrid Picker

Hybrid Picker is a new option that enables you to configure hybrid OneDrive for Business and Hybrid Sites from a wizard-driven interface. It does not allow the flexibility of the manual control and enables hybrid OneDrive for Business for all users.

To use Hybrid Picker to configure hybrid OneDrive for Business, follow these steps.

1. Log on to SharePoint Server 2016 with an account meeting the prerequisites. If SharePoint Hybrid Picker has already been run, you can execute it by double-clicking it on the desktop and skipping to step 9.

2. Open Microsoft Internet Explorer and log on to the Office 365 portal.

3. Click the Admin tile to launch the Office 365 Admin Center dashboard.

4. In the Office 365 Admin Center, expand Admin and then select SharePoint.

5. In the navigation pane, select Configure Hybrid.

6. On the Hybrid Picker page, click Go To Hybrid Picker Download Page.

7. Click the Click Here link to start SharePoint Hybrid Picker.

8. Click Install.

9. Click Next.

10. Type your credentials for both the local Active Directory environment and Office 365. Click Validate Credentials and click Next when the button becomes available.

11. Verify that all prerequisites pass. Resolve any errors. Click Next to continue.

12. Select the Hybrid OneDrive and Hybrid Sites check boxes and click Next.

13. After reviewing the configuration summary page, click Next.

14. Click Close.

Hybrid Search

As mentioned previously, there are two hybrid search possibilities—cloud hybrid search, where users perform searches and are returned results from a single, consolidated index, and hybrid federated search, where users perform one search and results are returned from both the cloud and on-premises indices.

Microsoft recommends using cloud hybrid search. The default search configuration is recommended for most organizations.

For information about hybrid federated search, please see *https://support.office.com/en-us /article/Learn-about-hybrid-federated-search-for-SharePoint-4ee4b876-1673-4d1f-ba47 -d9a0ef4474a9?ui=en-US&rs=en-US&ad=US*, "Learn about hybrid federated search for SharePoint."

Prerequisites

Prior to configuring a hybrid search option for SharePoint, verify that you meet the following prerequisites.

- SharePoint Server 2013 Service Pack 1 and the January 2016 Public Update (*https:// technet.microsoft.com/library/mt715807.aspx*)

- Account with Office 365 Global Administrator role

- Account that is a member of Domain Admins in the on-premises Active Directory environment

- Account that is a member of the SharePoint Farm Administrators group

- Account must have the securityadmin server role in the farm's SQL server instance.

- Account must be a member of the db_owner fixed database role on SharePoint databases.

- Account must be a member of the local Administrators group on the server where tasks will be performed.

- CreateCloudSSA.ps1 and Onboard-CloudHybridSearch.ps1 scripts, located in the Microsoft Download Center (*https://go.microsoft.com/fwlink/?LinkId=717902*)

- Microsoft Online Services Sign-In Assistant for IT Professionals RTW (*https://go.microsoft.com/fwlink/?LinkID=286152*) installed on the search server

- Azure Active Directory Module for Windows PowerShell (*http://connect.microsoft.com/site1164/Downloads/DownloadDetails.aspx?DownloadID=59185*) installed on the search server

- URL of Office 365 SharePoint Online site collection (*https://<tenant>.sharepoint.com*)

Configure Office 365 for SharePoint hybrid

To make hybrid services available for SharePoint Online, you must subscribe to an Office 365 plan that contains SharePoint Online and then connect your on-premises directory to Office 365.

See Chapter 1 and Chapter 2 for more information about setting up your Office 365 subscription and domains.

Create a cloud Search service application

The cloud Search service application will be used to configure result sets for SharePoint searches.

1. On the server that will host Search, launch an elevated SharePoint Management Shell.

2. Run CreateCloudSSA.ps1 and follow the prompts to provide the necessary values, as shown in Figure 18-11. You might need to unblock the script after downloading it before it will run.

    - **SearchServerName**   Server that will run the cloud Search service application

    - **SearchServiceAccount**   The Search service account (in DOMAIN\Username format)

    - **SearchServiceAppName**   Name for the cloud Search service application that will be created

    - **DatabaseServerName**   Name of the server where the cloud Search service application database will be created

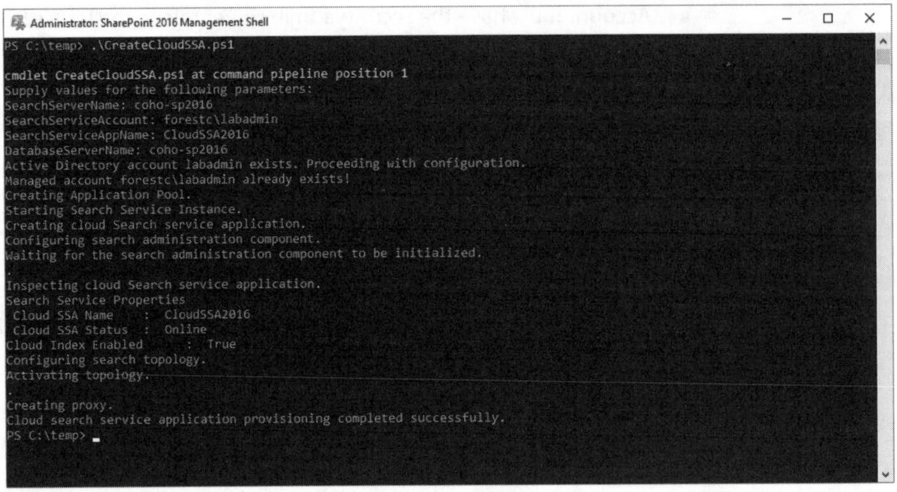

Figure 18-11 Create the cloud Search service application

> **TROUBLESHOOTING**
>
> **CreateCloudSSA.PS1 fails due to Internet connectivity**
>
> The CreateCloudSSA.ps1 script requires access to Office 365. If your environment is behind a proxy, please try to bypass the proxy server or appliances to reach Office 365. If bypassing the proxy is not possible, you may need to configure the WinHTTP proxy via NetSh. If you have proxy settings configured correctly in Internet Explorer, you can run the following command to import those settings into the WinHTTP proxy configuration:

```
netsh winhttp import proxy source=ie
```

Connect the cloud Search service application to Office 365

After you have created the cloud Search service application, you can proceed with connecting it to Office 365.

1. From the SharePoint Management Shell, run the following command and enter your Office 365 Global Admin credential when prompted.

```
$Credential = Get-Credential
```

2. Run the following command, using your organization's SharePoint Online URL and the name of the cloud Search service application you used when running the CreateCloudSSA.ps1 script. See Figure 18-12.

```
.\Onboard-CloudHybridSearch.ps1 -CloudSsaId <CloudSsaID> -PortalUrl
https://<tenant>.sharepoint.com -Credential $Credential
```

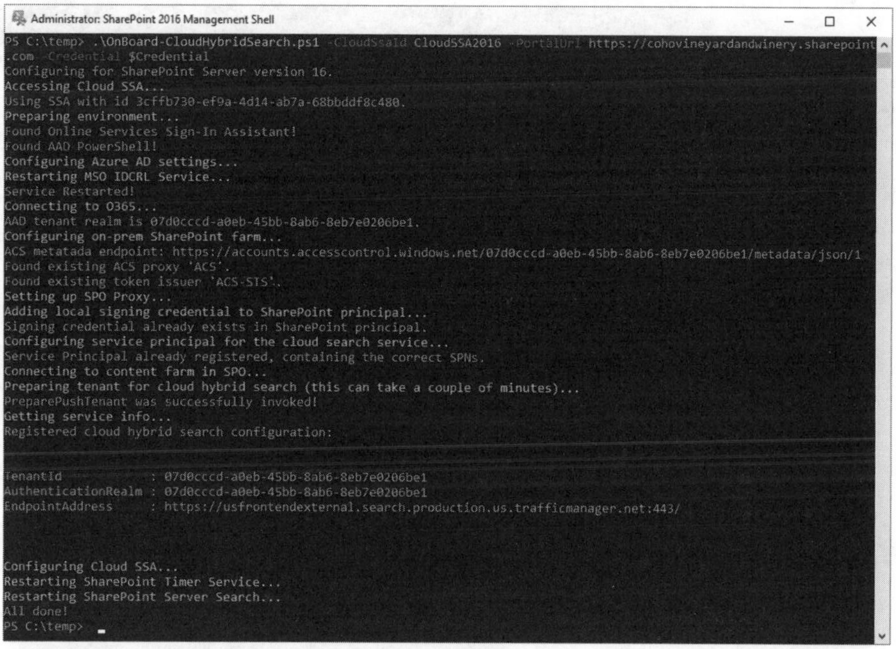

Figure 18-12 Run Onboard-CloudHybridSearch.ps1

Create a content source for cloud hybrid search

After the cloud search application has been created and connected to Office 365, you must create a content source to be incorporated into the Office 365 search index.

1. From Central Administration in your SharePoint Server farm, under Application Management, select Manage Service Applications.

2. On the Manage Service Applications page, click the cloud SSA that you created earlier. See Figure 18-13.

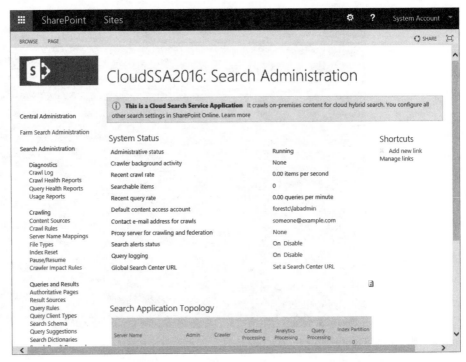

Figure 18-13 Cloud Search service application page

3. Under Crawling, select Content Sources.

4. Click New Content Source to create a selection of content to crawl.

5. Under Name, type a name for the content source.

6. Under Content Source Type, select the type of content that will be crawled. Options include SharePoint Sites, Web Sites, File Shares, Exchange Public Folders, Line Of Business Data, or Custom Repository.

7. Under Start Address, enter the addresses that will be included in the content search. If you are searching SharePoint Sites or Web Sites, for example, you can type *http://server*. If you intend to crawl file shares, type addresses as *server**share*.

8. Under Crawl Settings, select the behavior for crawling—either the folder and all subfolders or just the top-level folder.

9. Under Crawl Schedules, configure a schedule for full and incremental crawls.

10. Under Content Source Priority, configure whether this content source will be High or Normal priority. Selecting High priority prioritizes this content source's processing over content sources with Normal priority.

11. Click OK to create the content source.

12. Right-click the content source and select Start Full Crawl.

13. After the content source crawls are completed, navigate to Office 365 and perform a search for IsExternalContent:true.

    The IsExternalContent:true property shows content that is external to the operating environment (in this case, content external to SharePoint Online). In the example in Figure 18-14, a search was executed in SharePoint Online, and the data set shows results from the local SharePoint environment, confirming that the cloud hybrid search is working correctly.

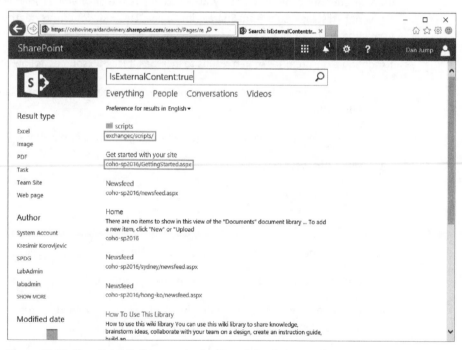

Figure 18-14 SharePoint Online search with SharePoint Server results returned

TROUBLESHOOTING

Why isn't my cloud hybrid search returning expected results?

There can be a number of reasons, but the most common one is that the data source you're indexing on-premises (SharePoint sites, file shares, and so on) only has permissions granted to the Domain Users group. AAD Connect does not synchronize user objects with the IsCriticalSystemObject attribute set to True. Domain Users, among other built-in groups, has that attribute set to True, blocking it from synchronization. Check the content sources you're indexing—if Domain Users is the only security principal granted access, update the access control list for the object to a group that is synchronized to Office 365.

Configure on-premises Search to display results from SharePoint Online

When you have configured cloud hybrid search so that SharePoint Online can return results from on-premises content sources, you can configure the on-premises SharePoint Server environment to display results from SharePoint Online. This way, your users get the same results from either environment.

To configure on-premises search results to include Office 365 sources, follow these steps.

1. Using an account that is a member of the Farm Administrators group, launch Central Administration.

2. Under Application Management, select Manage Service Applications.

3. Select the cloud SSA.

4. Under Queries And Results, click Result Sources.

5. Select New Result Source.

6. Under General Information, type a name of the result source, such as SharePoint Online.

7. Under Protocol, select the Remote SharePoint button.

8. Under Remote Service URL, enter the top-level URL of your SharePoint Online tenant (*https://<tenant>.sharepoint.com*). See Figure 18-15.

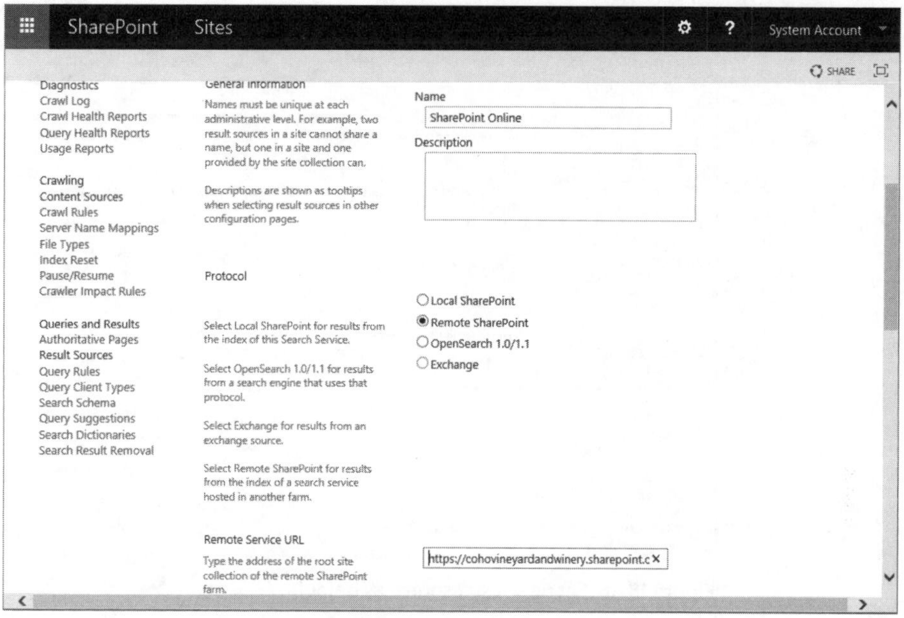

Figure 18-15 Configuring result source for cloud SSA

9. Under Type, ensure that the SharePoint Search Results button is selected.

10. Under Query Transform, leave the default transform value, `{searchTerms}`.

11. Under Credentials Information, ensure that the Default Authentication button is selected.

12. Click Save.

13. Point to the newly created result source, select the down arrow, and then select Set As Default, as shown in Figure 18-16.

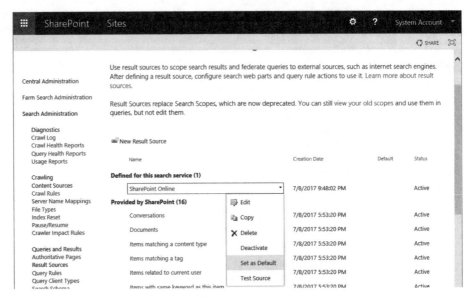

Figure 18-16 Set new result source as default

14. Log on to the SharePoint Server search site with an identity that is federated and licensed in Office 365 for SharePoint Online and perform a search, using the `IsExternalContent:true` search term.

Hybrid taxonomy

Originally available only for SharePoint Server 2016, hybrid taxonomy and content types are available for both SharePoint Server 2013 and SharePoint Server 2016 with the appropriate public updates.

Prerequisites

- November 2016 or later public update for hybrid taxonomy (*https://support.microsoft .com/kb/3127940*)

- June 2017 or later public update for hybrid content types (*https://support.microsoft.com /help/3203432*)

- Access to the Copy-SPTaxonomyGroups and Copy-SPContentTypes cmdlets

- Hybrid Picker, which has the following requirements:
    - Account that is a member of the Farm Administrators group
    - Service application administrator (Full Control) for the User Profile service

- Account that is an Office 365 global administrator
- Ability to run elevated (local administrator) commands on SharePoint server
- Appropriate SharePoint version
- Availability of SPO365LinkSettings cmdlet

Update term store permissions

For the SharePoint Timer job to complete successfully, the Timer service account must be made a member of the Managed Metadata Service administrators. To do this, follow this procedure.

1. Launch an elevated SharePoint Management Shell.

2. Run the following script:

```
$SPTimerServiceAccount = (Get-WmiObject win32_service | ? { $_.Name -eq (Get-
Service | ? { $_.Displayname -eq "SharePoint Timer Service"}).Name }).StartName

$SPSite = "http://coho-2016"

$SPTermStoreName = "Managed Metadata Service"

$Web = Get-SPWeb -Site $SPSite

$TaxonomySession = Get-SPTaxonomySession -Site $Web.Site

$TermStore = $TaxonomySession.TermStores[$SPTermStoreName]

$TermStore.AddTermStoreAdministrator($SPTimerServiceAccount)

$TermStore.CommitAll()
```

Copy on-premises taxonomy to SharePoint Online

If you have configured taxonomy groups, terms, and content types on-premises, export and copy those to Office 365 before beginning the hybrid configuration.

1. Log on to SharePoint Server with a Farm Administrator account.

   The Farm Administrator account should have access by default to view the content stored in the managed metadata service application.

2. Launch the SharePoint Management Shell.

3. Run the following script to copy the non-default taxonomy groups and terms to SharePoint Online.

   The Copy-SPTaxonomyGroups command will fail if your group contains special term sets. In this example, the default groups People, Search Dictionaries, and System have been excluded because they contain special term sets that cannot be replicated. If you have additional term sets or the term store is stored in another managed metadata service instance name, you must update those parameters accordingly.

```
$SPOCredential = Get-Credential

$SPOSite = "https://<tenant>.sharepoint.com"

$SPSite = "http://<SharePoint Site URL>r"

$SPTermStoreName = "Managed Metadata Service"

$Web = Get-SPWeb -Site $SPSite

$TaxonomySession = Get-SPTaxonomySession -Site $Web.Site

$TermStore = $TaxonomySession.TermStores[$SPTermStoreName]

[array]$GroupNames = $TermStore.Groups.Name -notmatch ("People|Search
Dictionaries|System")

Copy-SPTaxonomyGroups -LocalTermStoreName $SPTermStoreName -LocalSiteURL $SPSite
-RemoteSiteURL $SPOSite -GroupNames $GroupNames -Credential $SPOCredential
```

4.   Gather a list of the content types you wish to copy to SharePoint Online. To list all of the content types for a particular site, run the following script from the SharePoint Management Shell. Note any custom content types.

```
$SPSite = "http://coho-2016"

$Web = Get-SPWeb -Site $SPSite

[array]$ContentTypeNames = $Web.ContentTypes.Name
```

5.   Review the values stored in $ContentTypeNames. When you have determined the content types to copy from Office 365, use the following script to copy them.

```
$SPOCredential = Get-Credential

$SPOSite = "https://<tenant>.sharepoint.com"

$SPSite = "http://<Sharepoint Site Url>"

Copy-SPContentTypes -LocalSiteUrl $SPSite -LocalTermStoreName $SPContentTermStore-
Name -RemoteSiteUrl $SPOSite -ContentTypeName @("Content Type 1 Name","Content
Type 2 Name") -Credential $SPOCredential
```

Configure hybrid taxonomy with Hybrid Picker

When you are ready to set up hybrid taxonomy, you can run Hybrid Picker to complete the configuration.

1. Log on to the SharePoint server with an account meeting the prerequisites. If SharePoint Hybrid Picker has already been run, you can run it by double-clicking it on the desktop and skipping to step 9.

2. Open Internet Explorer and log on to the Office 365 portal.

3. Click the Admin tile to launch the Office 365 Admin Center dashboard.

4. In the Office 365 Admin Center, expand Admin and then select SharePoint.

5. In the navigation pane, select Configure Hybrid.

6. On the Hybrid Picker page, click Go To Hybrid Picker Download Page. See Figure 18-17.

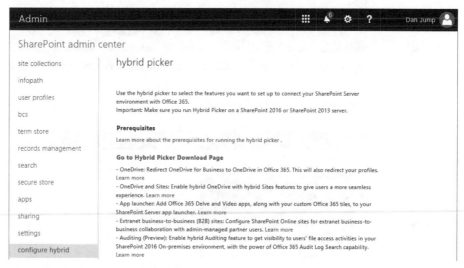

Figure 18-17 SharePoint Hybrid Picker page

7. Click the Click Here link to start the SharePoint Hybrid Picker, as shown in Figure 18-18.

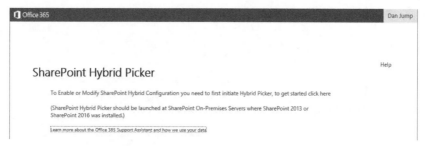

Figure 18-18 Launching SharePoint Hybrid Picker

8. Click Install, as shown in Figure 18-19.

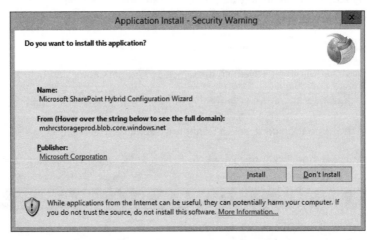

Figure 18-19 SharePoint Hybrid Configuration Wizard application installation

9. Click Next, as shown in Figure 18-20.

Figure 18-20 SharePoint Hybrid Picker initial page

10. Type your credentials for both the local Active Directory environment as well as Office 365. See Figure 18-21. Click Validate Credentials and click Next when the button becomes available.

Figure 18-21 SharePoint Hybrid Configuration Wizard Credentials page

11. Verify that all prerequisites pass. Resolve any errors. See Figure 18-22. Click Next to continue.

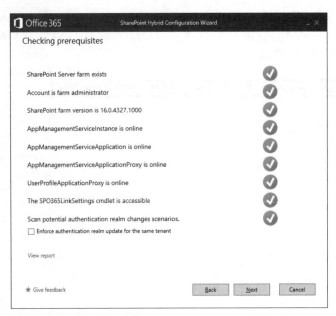

Figure 18-22 SharePoint Hybrid Configuration Wizard Checking Prerequisites page

12. Select the Hybrid Taxonomy And Content Type check box and click Next.

13. Enter data for the following values:

   - **SharePoint Server root site**   http://<SharePoint Server URL>.

   - **SharePoint Managed Metadata Application**   For most organizations, the default name is Managed Metadata Application. If you are unsure of the Managed Metadata Application Service name, launch Central Administration and select Manage Service Application under Application Management. Look for an entry with type Managed Metadata Service and use the value in the Name column in Hybrid Picker.

   - **Groups**   Type the names of the taxonomy groups you wish to replicate. You can use the list from the previous task, where you copied the taxonomy groups to Office 365, or you can leave it blank to replicate all groups except the system and default special groups.

14. After reviewing the Configuration Summary page, click Next.

15. Click Close.

Hybrid auditing

The SharePoint Hybrid Auditing feature is only available with SharePoint Server 2016. It is currently in Preview and is not supported in production environments.

Prerequisites

Before configuring SharePoint Hybrid Auditing, you must verify that you meet the prerequisites.

- SharePoint Server 2016

- An account with membership in the Farm Administrators group

- An account with the Office 365 Global Admin role

- Local administrator privileges on SharePoint Server where the configuration will be performed

- An account granted service application administrator privileges for the User Profile service

- Ability to browse to SharePoint Online from SharePoint Server where the configuration will be performed

Enable Audit Log Search Recording

To make auditing data available from Office 365, enable the recording of activity. These next steps enable logging in Office 365.

1. Log on to SharePoint Server 2016 with an account meeting the prerequisites.

2. Open Internet Explorer and log on to the Office 365 Security & Compliance Center at *https://protection.office.com* with an account that is a member of the Global Admin role.

3. In the navigation pane, select Search & Investigation and then click Audit Log Search.

4. Under Audit Log Search, click Start Recording User And Admin Activities and then select Turn On.

   If the Start Recording User And Admin Activities link is not available, then recording is already enabled. For more information about Audit Log Search capabilities, see Chapter 8, "Inside the Security & Compliance Center: Data Classification, Loss Prevention, Governance, and Discovery."

Enable SharePoint hybrid auditing

After cloud logging has been enabled, you can proceed to the configuration of hybrid auditing. Hybrid auditing is only available for SharePoint Server 2016.

1. Log on to SharePoint Server 2016 with an account meeting the prerequisites. If the SharePoint Hybrid Configuration Picker has already been run, you can run it again by double-clicking it on the desktop and skipping to step 9.

2. Open Internet Explorer and log on to the Office 365 portal.

3. Click the Admin tile to launch the Office 365 Admin Center dashboard.

4. In the Office 365 Admin Center, expand Admin and then select SharePoint.

5. In the navigation pane, select Configure Hybrid.

6. On the Hybrid Picker page, click Go To Hybrid Picker Download Page.

7. Click the Click Here link to start the SharePoint Hybrid Picker.

8. Click Install.

9. Click Next.

10. Enter your credentials for both the local Active Directory environment as well as Office 365. Click Validate Credentials and click Next when the button becomes available.

11. Verify that all prerequisites pass. Resolve any errors. Click Next to continue.

12. Select the Hybrid Auditing (Preview) check box and click Next.

13. After reviewing the Configuration Summary page, click Next.

14. Click Close.

After the hybrid configuration has been completed, logs are uploaded to SharePoint Online through a timer job. The logs that will be uploaded are stored by default in the *%ProgramFiles%\Common Files\Microsoft Shared\Web Server Extensions\16\LOGS \SPUnifiedAuditEntry* folder.

App launcher

The hybrid app launcher configures the SharePoint Server App Launcher experience to integrate with Office 365. You configure the app launcher with the SharePoint Hybrid Picker.

Prerequisites

Before configuring the SharePoint Hybrid app launcher, you must verify that you meet the prerequisites.

- SharePoint Server 2013 July 2016 Cumulative Update

- SharePoint Server 2016 RTM

- An account with membership in the Farm Administrators group

- An account with Office 365 global admin role

- Local administrator privileges on SharePoint Server where the configuration will be performed

Enable the hybrid app launcher

To configure the SharePoint Hybrid app launcher, follow these steps.

1. Log on to SharePoint Server 2016 with an account meeting the prerequisites. If the SharePoint Hybrid Configuration Picker has already been run, you can run it again by double-clicking it on the desktop and skipping to step 9.

2. Open Internet Explorer and log on to the Office 365 portal.

3. Click the Admin tile to launch the Office 365 Admin Center dashboard.

4. In the Office 365 Admin Center, expand Admin and then select SharePoint.

5. In the navigation pane, select Configure Hybrid.

6. On the Hybrid Picker page, click Go To Hybrid Picker Download Page.

7. Click the Click Here link to start SharePoint Hybrid Picker.

8. Click Install.

9. Click Next.

10. Type your credentials for both the local Active Directory environment as well as Office 365. Click Validate Credentials and click Next when the button becomes available.

11. Verify that all prerequisites pass. Resolve any errors. Click Next to continue.

12. Select the Hybrid App Launcher check box, as shown in Figure 18-23.

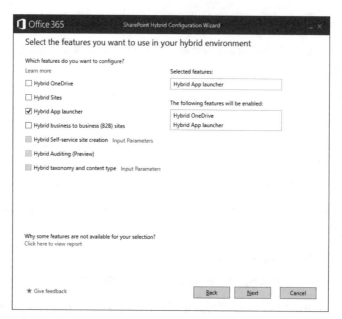

Figure 18-23 Hybrid App launcher configuration

13. Review the Configuration Summary page, as shown in Figure 18-24.

Figure 18-24 Hybrid App Launcher Configuration Summary page

14. Click Next.

15. Click Close.

Business-to-business extranet

Although business-to-business extranets are configured in Office 365, you can configure an optional integration component to enable integrated authentication by using OAuth so that users can navigate seamlessly between local intranet sites on-premises and extranet sites stored in SharePoint Online.

Prerequisites

Before configuring SharePoint hybrid business-to-business sites, you must verify that you meet the prerequisites.

- SharePoint Server 2013 September 2015 cumulative update

- SharePoint Server 2016 RTM

- An account with membership in the Farm Administrators group

- An account with the Office 365 Global Administrator role

- Local administrator privileges on SharePoint Server where the configuration will be performed

Enable hybrid business-to-business (B2B) sites

Use the following steps to enable the integrated authentication between on-premises SharePoint sites and Office 365 sites.

1. Log on to SharePoint Server 2016 with an account meeting the prerequisites. If the SharePoint Hybrid Configuration Picker has already been run, you can run it again by double-clicking it on the desktop and skipping to step 9.

2. Open Internet Explorer and log on to the Office 365 portal.

3. Click the Admin tile to launch the Office 365 Admin Center dashboard.

4. In the Office 365 Admin Center, expand Admin and then select SharePoint.

5. In the navigation pane, select Configure Hybrid.

6. On the Hybrid Picker page, click Go To Hybrid Picker Download Page.

7. Click the Click Here link to start SharePoint Hybrid Picker.

8.   Click Install.

9.   Click Next.

10. Type your credentials for both the local Active Directory environment as well as Office 365. Click Validate Credentials and click Next when the button becomes available.

11. Verify that all prerequisites pass. Resolve any errors. Click Next to continue.

12. Select the Hybrid Business to Business (B2B) Sites check box, as shown in Figure 18-25.

Figure 18-25 Hybrid Business to Business (B2B) Sites configuration

13. Review the Configuration Summary page, as shown in Figure 18-26.

Figure 18-26 Hybrid Business To Business (B2B) Sites Configuration Summary page

14. Click Next.

15. Click Close.

After OAuth has been configured, you can create extranet sites in SharePoint Online and share the sites with external entities.

Summary

In this chapter, you learned about the various kinds of hybrid configurations available for SharePoint Server 2013 and SharePoint Server 2016 environments. Hybrid SharePoint configurations enable you to give your users the ability to move between on-premises and cloud environments. In addition, you might want to explore configuring other SharePoint Online components, such as OneDrive for Business or Yammer. You can find information on OneDrive in Chapter 19, "OneDrive for Business," and deployment, planning, and configuration information for Yammer in Chapter 20, "Yammer."

CHAPTER 18

OneDrive for Business

OneDrive for Business is a personalized Microsoft SharePoint library designed to give you a space to store, share, and synchronize content. It's a multiplatform collaboration tool, accessible through apps for Windows, iOS, Mac OS, and Android as well as a web browser.

OneDrive for Business allows synchronization and offline editing of files on Windows and Mac. Because it's built on SharePoint Server, it also provides coauthoring capabilities for documents stored in OneDrive for Business libraries.

Accessing OneDrive for Business

To access OneDrive for Business Online, you must have a license that includes SharePoint Online or OneDrive for Business.

Online

You can access OneDrive for Business Online by opening a web browser and navigating to *https://portal.office.com*.

Upon logon, the dashboard appears, similar to what is depicted in Figure 19-1, and includes a OneDrive tile.

Figure 19-1 Office 365 portal dashboard

The first time you click the OneDrive tile, you see the splash page, shown in Figure 19-2, while your OneDrive for Business site is provisioned. After it's provisioned (which usually takes about 30 seconds), a Your OneDrive Is Ready link appears, and you're ready to start using OneDrive for Business.

Figure 19-2 OneDrive splash page

Click Your OneDrive Is Ready to access OneDrive for Business. If the Welcome to OneDrive Wizard opens, click Not Now to cancel it.

The navigation pane on the left enables you to upload and create Office documents (Word, Microsoft PowerPoint, Microsoft Excel, Microsoft OneNote) from the New menu. See Figure 19-3.

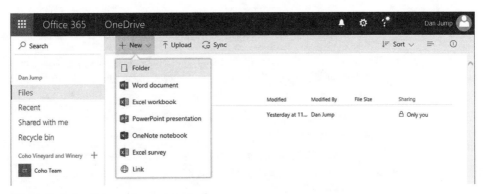

Figure 19-3 OneDrive web user interface

In the navigation pane, you also see links to sites that have been created for any Office 365 groups that you are a member of.

OneDrive sync client for Windows

The new Microsoft OneDrive sync client (sometimes referred to as the next-generation sync client), built for Windows 10, Windows 8.1, Windows 8, and Windows 7, enables you to synchronize content between your computer and OneDrive for Business accounts. The OneDrive sync client also enables you to sync content from SharePoint Online sites.

Although OneDrive is a component of SharePoint on-premises deployments, the OneDrive sync client does not yet support OneDrive for Business when deployed on-premises.

INSIDE OUT

So many sync clients

If you're using a new computer with a fresh installation of Windows 10 and Office 2016, you probably have the new OneDrive sync client installed. However, if you're running a previous version of Windows or Office (or upgraded from a previous version), you could have one of the older clients, the new client, or multiple clients.

Because the versions and builds of the sync clients are continuously changing, look at the visual identifiers of the applications in the system tray to determine which client you're running, or check the actual file names.

To check visually, hover over the icon in the system tray and look for the text that appears.

- If you see a white cloud icon that says OneDrive – Personal or OneDrive, and you're running Windows 10, Windows 8.1, Windows 8, or Windows 7, you're using the new OneDrive sync client.

- If you see a blue cloud icon that says OneDrive - *<Company>*, you're using the new OneDrive sync client.

- If you see a white cloud icon that only says Files Are Up To Date and you're running Windows 8, Windows 8.1, or Windows RT 8.1, you're using the previous OneDrive for Business sync client.

- If you see a blue cloud icon that says OneDrive For Business, you're using the previous OneDrive for Business sync client.

To check the file name, locate the shortcut for OneDrive, right-click it, and select Properties. On the Target tab, look for the executable name.

- **OneDrive.exe** New OneDrive for Business sync client

- **Groove.exe** Previous OneDrive for Business sync client

- **SkyDrive.exe** Previous OneDrive personal client

For the purposes of this chapter, you need to be using the new OneDrive sync client.

To begin setup, you can initiate it from either your computer or the Office 365 portal. If you do not have the newest OneDrive sync client, you can download it from *https://go.microsoft.com/fwlink/?linkid=844652*.

To start OneDrive setup from your computer, follow these steps.

1. Click the Start button.

2. Type **OneDrive**, and select OneDrive for Business.

To start OneDrive setup from the Office 365 portal, follow these steps.

1. Sign in to the Office 365 portal, click App Launcher, click OneDrive, and then click Sync on the Files page, as shown in Figure 19-4.

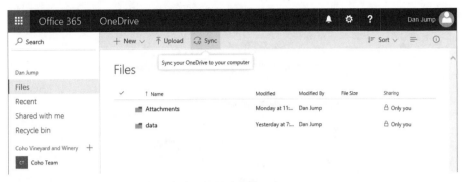

Figure 19-4 Clicking Sync to launch the OneDrive file sync

2. Click Allow to launch the OneDrive application, as shown in Figure 19-5.

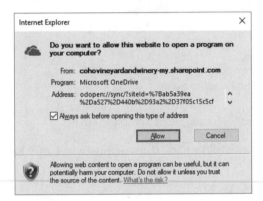

Figure 19-5 Internet Explorer confirmation dialog box after clicking Sync

To set up OneDrive, if your sign-in address isn't already populated, you might need to select a Work or School account, type your email address, and click Sign In. See Figure 19-6.

Figure 19-6 Microsoft OneDrive initial setup wizard

3. Confirm your address, enter your password, and click Sign In.

4. On the This Is Your OneDrive Folder page, shown in Figure 19-7, click Next.

Figure 19-7 This Is Your OneDrive Folder page

5. On the Sync Your OneDrive Files To This PC page, shown in Figure 19-8, choose the folders you want to sync or select the Sync All Files And Folders In OneDrive check box and click Next.

Figure 19-8 Selecting files and folders to sync to your computer

After sync setup completes, you can close the Microsoft OneDrive Wizard if you initiated OneDrive setup from the Office 365 portal. Your OneDrive for Business files appear in File Explorer as OneDrive – *<CompanyName>*.

OneDrive sync client for Mac OS X

The OneDrive client for Mac OS X is available in the App Store.

1.   Launch the App Store from the dock.

2.   In the App Store search box, type OneDrive.

3.   Click Get to download the app.

4.   After installation, press Cmd+Space to open Spotlight and type OneDrive to display the OneDrive application. Click OneDrive to initiate the OneDrive configuration.

5.   Type your Office 365 account name (usually your email address) and click Sign In.

6.   When the Office 365 sign-in dialog box appears, complete the sign-in process by entering your password and click Sign In.

7.   On the This Is Your OneDrive Folder page, click Choose OneDrive Folder Location, shown in Figure 19-9.

Figure 19-9 OneDrive This Is Your OneDrive Folder page

8.   Choose a folder on your computer, or create a new one to store synchronized OneDrive content, and then click Choose This Location. Click Next.

9.   On the Sync Files From Your OneDrive page, depicted in Figure 19-10, select which existing files and folders (if any) in your OneDrive for Business site you want to sync to your computer and click Next.

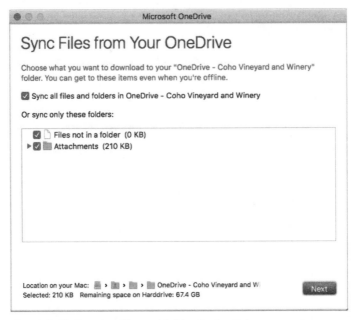

Figure 19-10 Choosing files and folders in OneDrive to sync to your computer

10. On the Your OneDrive Is Ready For You page, select the Open At Login So My Files Sync Automatically check box and then close the Microsoft OneDrive Wizard.

Your OneDrive for Business folder is accessible by clicking the OneDrive icon on the menu bar, as shown in Figure 19-11.

Figure 19-11 Choosing the OneDrive icon on the menu bar to access OneDrive for Business

Collaborating with OneDrive for Business

With OneDrive for Business, you make files available to share inside or outside your organization, depending on your organization's sharing settings. Office document files located in OneDrive support coauthoring and document versioning.

Sharing documents and folders

You can share documents and folders with both internal and external recipients. To share a document or folder, follow these steps.

1. Sign in to the Office 365 portal and click the OneDrive tile.

2. On the Files page, select a file or folder.

3. Click either the Get Link or Share buttons.

    If you click the Get Link button, Office 365 creates a link that you can share. If you select a file, the link grants the recipient the edit permission, which means they can modify the file. If you select a folder, the recipient can create folders, upload files, and download files unless you change the permissions. You can click Anyone With This Link Can Edit This Item to expose a fly-out that enables you to choose the permissions granted for the link as well as control who can access the link to prevent sharing outside your intended audience. If the users are external to your organization, they can be logged on using the Guest Contributor role.

    If you click the Share button, you can enter email addresses for recipients that you want to share the file or folder with. By default, users are granted Edit permissions. You can click Anyone With This Link Can Edit This Item to expose a fly-out that enables you to choose the permissions granted for the link as well as control who can access the link to prevent sharing outside your intended audience. If the users are external to your organization, they are logged on using the Guest Contributor role. See Figure 19-12 for permissions settings.

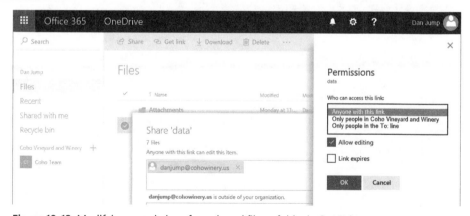

Figure 19-12 Modifying permissions for a shared file or folder in OneDrive

Coauthoring

Just like documents stored in other SharePoint libraries, documents stored in OneDrive for Business support coauthoring, so multiple users can work on a document simultaneously.

To coauthor a document from OneDrive for Business, follow these steps.

1. Place the file you want to coauthor in OneDrive for Business or create a new Office document in your OneDrive and distribute a link to other users.

2. Edit the document from the site by using one of the following methods.

    a. From OneDrive For Business in the Office 365 portal, left-click the document name to launch the associated Office Online app.

    b. From OneDrive For Business in the Office 365 portal, hover over the document to expose the ellipsis (...). Click the ellipsis and then select Open | Open In *<Office Online Application>* or Open | Open In *<Office Application>*.

    c. In the following example, because a Word document is selected, OneDrive for Business prompts you to use Word Online or the Word Office application installed on your computer. Figure 19-13 shows the application options.

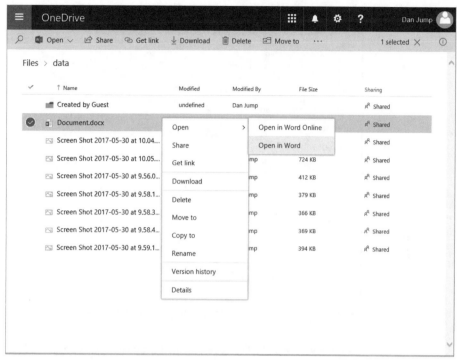

Figure 19-13 Opening a document from OneDrive for Business to enable coauthoring

Document versioning

Versioning in OneDrive for Business should already be turned on. However, it's always good to make sure.

To check whether your OneDrive site is configured for versioning, follow these steps.

1. Log on to the Office 365 portal and navigate to OneDrive For Business.

2. Select a document, right-click it, and look for Version History on the context menu, as shown in Figure 19-14.

Figure 19-14 Verifying presence of Version History on context menu

3. View the versions of a file by selecting Version History. See Figure 19-15.

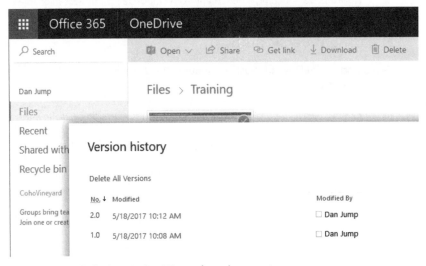

Figure 19-15 Displaying Version History for a document

If you don't have the version history properties for files, then versioning is not turned on for your OneDrive site. To configure versioning, follow these steps.

1. In OneDrive For Business, click the gear icon to open Settings. Click the Site Settings link.

2. On the Site Settings page, under Site Administration, click the Site Libraries And Lists link. See Figure 19-16.

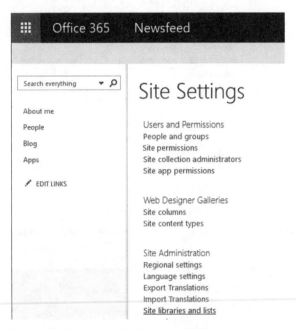

Figure 19-16 OneDrive for Business Site Settings page

3. Click the Customize "Documents" link, as shown in Figure 19-17.

Figure 19-17 Site Settings page for Site Libraries And Lists

4. Click the Versioning Settings link. See Figure 19-18.

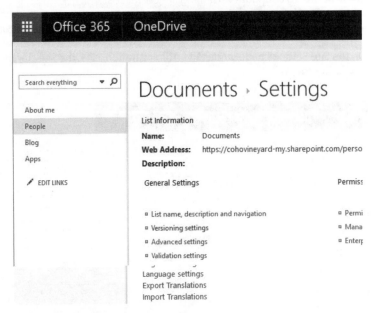

Figure 19-18 Editing Versioning Settings on the Documents Settings page

5. Next to Document Version History, select Create Major Versions.

6. Click OK.

Deploying OneDrive for Business to your users

OneDrive for Business is very simple to deploy—just enable the SharePoint Online license in Office 365, and OneDrive for Business is enabled automatically.

However, turning on OneDrive for Business doesn't necessarily mean it will be used according to your organization's needs. You might need to deploy settings in conjunction with the application and licensing to make sure your organization is getting the most out of it.

Group Policy

One of the best ways to ensure consistent deployment of OneDrive is to use Group Policy. OneDrive for Business can be managed through the Group Policy templates available in the OneDrive Deployment Package (*https://go.microsoft.com/fwlink/p/?LinkId=717805*).

A common request is to be able to configure users' Documents folder to redirect to OneDrive for Business. The next two tasks help you configure your environment to re-map users' Documents folder to OneDrive for Business and prevent users from changing the location of their OneDrive folder.

Create a GPO for OneDrive for Business

After you have downloaded the templates, follow these steps to import them into your Active Directory environment and create a policy that prevents users from changing the location of their OneDrive for Business folder.

1. Connect to Azure AD PowerShell by using the `Connect-AzureAD` cmdlet. If you don't have the Azure AD cmdlets, run `Install-Module AzureADPreview` to install them on your computer. For more information about the Azure AD Preview module, see *https://docs.microsoft.com/en-us/powershell/azure/install-adv2?view=azureadps-2.0*.

2. After you're connected, obtain your Azure Active Directory tenant ID by running the following cmdlet:

   ```
   Get-AzureADTenantDetail | Select ObjectID
   ```

3. Copy the tenant ID to the clipboard.

4. Edit the OneDrive.admx file with Notepad.

5. Select the Edit menu and then select Replace.

6. In the Find What box, type **INSERT YOUR TENANT'S GUID HERE**.

7. Paste your tenant ID in the Replace With box. Figure 19-19 shows the dialog box with these values populated.

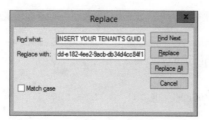

Figure 19-19 Replace dialog box

8. Click Replace All.

9. Save and close the file.

10. Copy the edited file OneDrive.admx to %systemroot%\PolicyDefinitions on a domain controller.

11. Copy the OneDrive.adml file to %systemroot%\PolicyDefinitions\<*language*> on a domain controller.

For example, if your system is using U.S. English, the folder path would be %systemroot%\PolicyDefinitions\en-us.

12. Launch the Group Policy Management console (gpmc.msc).

13. Navigate to the Group Policy Objects folder as shown in Figure 19-20, right-click it, and select New.

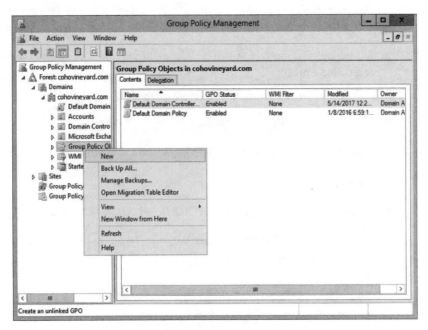

Figure 19-20 Group Policy Management console

14. Name the Group Policy object and click OK.

15. Edit the newly created Group Policy object.

16. Expand User Configuration | Policies | Administrative Templates and select OneDrive.

17. Configure the Prevent Users From Changing The Location Of Their OneDrive Folder setting to Enabled. See Figure 19-21 for the setting location.

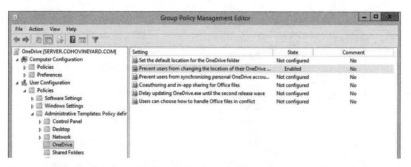

Figure 19-21 Configuring OneDrive Group Policy to prevent users from changing the location of their OneDrive for Business folder

18. Close the Group Policy Management Editor.

Configure documents redirection

To take advantage of OneDrive's storage and synchronization capabilities by default for users, you can configure the Windows Documents folder to be stored in OneDrive. To use Group Policy and folder redirection for OneDrive for Business, the OneDrive for Business folder must be installed in the default location.

1. Log on to a workstation or server with the OneDrive client installed and configure it using the default settings.

2. Click Start, type %userprofile%, and press Enter to open the current user's profile path. Copy the name of the OneDrive for Business folder (it should be OneDrive - <*Company Name*>), as pictured in Figure 19-22.

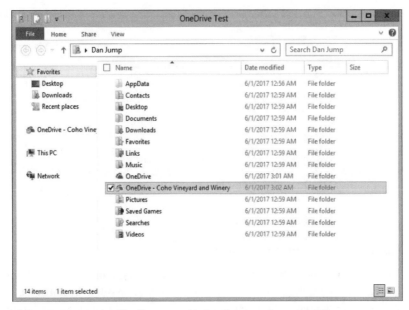

Figure 19-22 User profile directory with OneDrive - *<Company Name>*

3. Launch the Group Policy Management console (gpmc.msc).

4. Navigate to the Group Policy Objects node and create a new policy to configure the Documents folder redirection.

5. In the Group Policy Management Editor, navigate to User Configuration | Preferences | Windows Settings. Right-click Environment, select New, and select Environment Variable. See Figure 19-23.

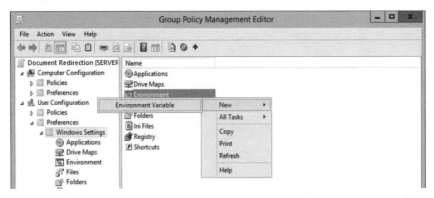

Figure 19-23 Creating a new environment variable in Group Policy Management Editor

6. Ensure that the User Variable button is selected.

7. In the Name box, type **OneDriveSync**.

8. In the Value box, type **%userprofile%\OneDrive** - *<Company Name>***.** Use the value you copied earlier, as shown in Figure 19-24.

Figure 19-24 New Environment Properties dialog box

9. On the Common tab, select the Item-Level Targeting check box and then click Targeting.

10. In the Targeting Editor, click New Item, click File Match, type **%userprofile%\OneDrive** - *<Company Name>* in the Path box, and then update the Match Type to Folder Exists, as shown in Figure 19-25.

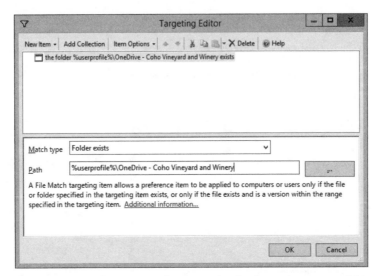

Figure 19-25 Configuring item-level targeting for the environment variable

11. Click OK twice.

12. Navigate to User Configuration | Policies | Windows Settings | Folder Redirection.

13. Right-click Documents and click Properties. See Figure 19-26.

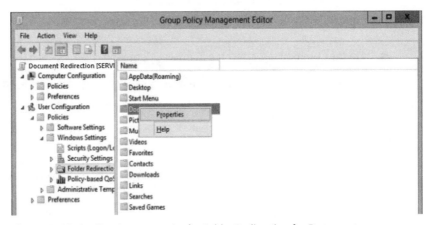

Figure 19-26 Configuring properties for Folder Redirection for Documents

14. On the Target tab, select Basic - Redirect Everyone's Folder To The Same Location.

15. Under Target Folder Location, select Redirect To The Following Location.

16. In the Root Path box, type **%OneDriveSync%\Documents**.

17. Confirm that the settings reflect what is shown in Figure 19-27.

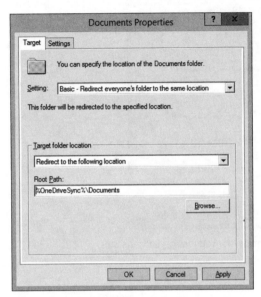

Figure 19-27 Documents folder target properties

18. Select the Settings tab.

19. Clear the Move The Contents Of Documents To The New Location check box (Figure 19-28) and click OK.

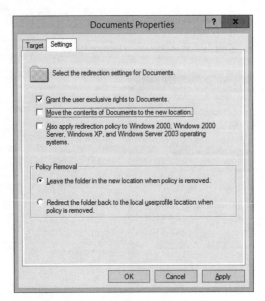

Figure 19-28 Documents folder redirection Settings tab

NOTE

What if you have already deployed OneDrive?

If your organization is new to OneDrive, you might want to select this check box to simplify your deployment. However, if you have had an inconsistent deployment or have some people using it already, it is recommended that you clear the check box to prevent items from Documents from overwriting existing files in their OneDrive folder. Most organizations will want to clear the check box for Move The Contents Of Documents To The New Location and plan to move document data manually.

20. Clickzto acknowledge the warning displayed in Figure 19-29.

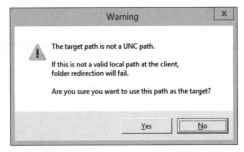

Figure 19-29 Warning dialog box because the target path is using an environment variable instead of a UNC path

21. Optional: Configure other well-known folders to follow the Documents folder redirection.

   a. Navigate to User Configuration | Policies | Windows Settings | Folder Redirection.

   b. Right-click Pictures, Music, or Video and select Properties.

   c. In the Setting drop-down list, choose Follow The Documents Folder and click OK. See Figure 19-30.

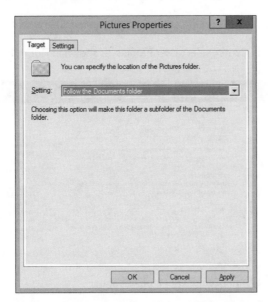

Figure 19-30 Configuring additional folders for redirection

22. Close the Group Policy Management Editor.

23. Link both policies to an organization unit and test.

Manage OneDrive for Business

There are a number of administrative and management tasks that you might need to perform in OneDrive for Business, depending on your organization's business requirements. Some of these might include granting access to other administrators or personnel for eDiscovery or management, preventing apps or clients outside your organization from synchronizing content, or even disabling the provisioning of OneDrive sites altogether.

Granting access to a secondary administrator

Some organizations require administrators to have access to everyone's content. By default, OneDrive permissions restrict access to only the owner. Office 365 automatically designates the owner as Site Collection Administrator.

Some features, such as eDiscovery, require all content to be discoverable. Enabling a secondary site collection administrator is one way to achieve that.

This process works only for OneDrive sites created after you designate a secondary site collection administrator (and does not work on existing OneDrive for Business sites).

1. Log on to Office 365 Admin Center with an account that has global admin privileges.

2. In the navigation pane, select Admin Centers and then select SharePoint.

3. In the SharePoint Admin Center, select User Profiles, as shown in Figure 19-31.

Figure 19-31 SharePoint Admin Center User Profiles page

4. Under My Site Settings, click Setup My Sites.

5. Scroll to My Site Secondary Admin, select the Enable My Site Secondary Admin check box, and type a user or group name to grant Site Collection Administrator privileges to a second security principal. See Figure 19-32.

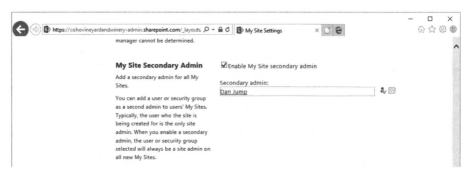

Figure 19-32 Granting My Site Secondary Admin privileges

6. Scroll to the bottom of the page and click OK.

As previously stated, this configuration only affects new sites, going forward. To grant access to existing sites, you must use the script and process described in *https://technet.microsoft.com /en-us/library/dn765092.aspx*.

Restricting devices that can synchronize OneDrive content

There are several settings you can use to control which devices can synchronize content, which might be important for your organization.

You can restrict PC synchronization to only PCs that are joined to specific domains. Follow these steps.

1. On a domain-joined computer with the Active Directory Remote Server Administration or Active Directory Domain Services installed, launch a Windows PowerShell session and run the following commands to retrieve a list of domain GUIDs.

    ```
    $domainGuids = @()

    [array]$domains = (Get-ADForest).Domains

    Foreach ($domain in $domains) {$domainGuids += Get-ADDomain -Identity $domain |
    Select ObjectGuid}

    $domainGuids.ObjectGuid.Guid | Clip
    ```

2. Log on to the OneDrive for Business Admin Center (*https://admin.onedrive.com*), using an account with global admin privileges.

3. Select Sync in the navigation pane and then select the Allow Syncing Only On PCs Joined To Specific Domains check box.

4. Click Edit Domains.

5. Paste the clipboard contents in the fly-out shown in Figure 19-33. Verify that the domain GUIDs are pasted in correctly, one per line.

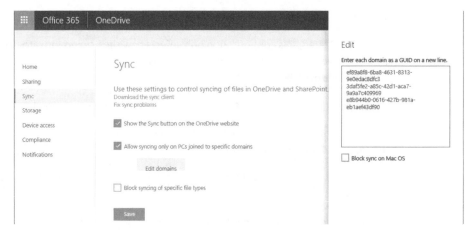

Figure 19-33 Editing list of domain GUIDs for domain-joined PCs that can sync content with OneDrive for Business

6. Optionally, choose whether you want to disable synchronization on the Mac OS OneDrive for Business client.

7. After you have entered all the domain GUIDs, click outside the fly-out on the Sync page.

   The list of domain GUIDs should appear next to the Edit Domains button shown in Figure 19-34.

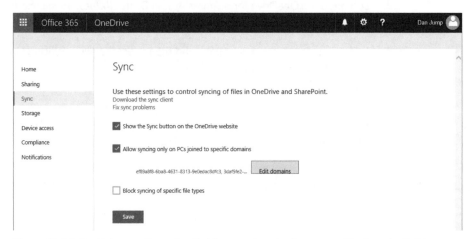

Figure 19-34 OneDrive configuration limiting synchronization to specific domain GUIDs

8. Click Save.

In addition to restricting sync capabilities, you can also restrict access capabilities as well as features available in the mobile clients.

1. Log on to the OneDrive for Business Admin Center (*https://admin.onedrive.com*) by using an account with global admin privileges.

2. Select Device Access in the navigation pane and review the available options, as shown in Figure 19-35.

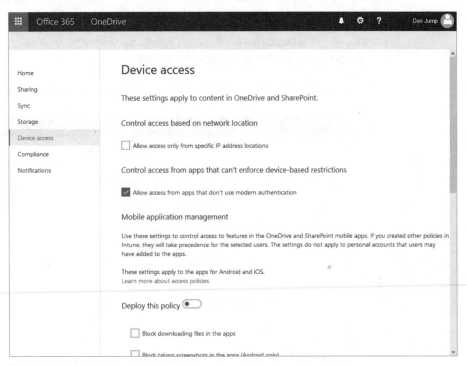

Figure 19-35 Device access management page

The following list explains the options on the Device Access page.

- **Control Access Based On Network Location**   Configuring this option enables you to restrict SharePoint and OneDrive for Business access to IP address ranges (such as your corporate network and VPN ranges). This blocks access from addresses outside this range altogether, such as mobile devices on carrier networks.

- **Control Access From Apps That Can't Enforce Device-Based Restrictions**   This option enables you to restrict access on devices or platforms that don't support conditional access policies or modern authentication.

- **Mobile Application Management**   These are additional policies that enable you to control the OneDrive for iOS and Android mobile applications, such as blocking the ability for users to synchronize and download content, take screenshots of documents, or print, and requiring re-authentication and passcodes.

Restricting sharing

OneDrive for Business enables you to restrict sharing outside your organization. Because OneDrive is a component of SharePoint, your OneDrive for Business site cannot have less restrictive sharing permissions than SharePoint online.

1. Log on to the **OneDrive for Business Admin Center** (*https://admin.onedrive.com*) by using an account with global admin privileges.

2. Select **Sharing** from the navigation pane to display the page shown in Figure 19-36.

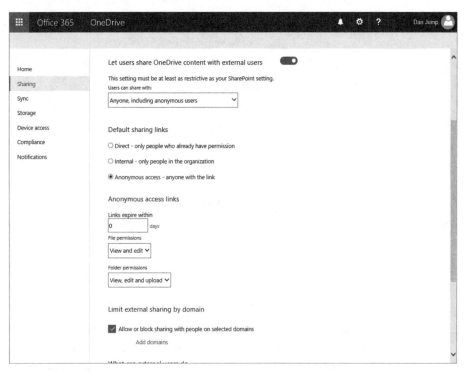

Figure 19-36 OneDrive Admin Sharing options

3. Use the Let Users Share OneDrive Content With External Users toggle to enable or disable external sharing.

4. Under Limit External Sharing By Domain, select the Allow Or Block Sharing With People On Selected Domains check box and then click the Add Domains link to control which external domains and organizations users can send OneDrive sharing links to.

NOTE

The list is binary in that you can choose only one action (block or allow) for all domains listed.

Disabling OneDrive provisioning

OneDrive is a feature of SharePoint Online. A OneDrive personal site collection (formerly known as My Sites) is provisioned for each user automatically the first time they attempt to access OneDrive.

However, some organizations might want to roll OneDrive out in phases, or start using SharePoint right away, but haven't yet had time to develop governance of how best to use OneDrive in their organizations. In those instances, you can disable automatic OneDrive provisioning or restrict OneDrive for Business provisioning to certain individuals or groups.

1. Log on to Office 365 Admin Center with an account that has global admin privileges.

2. In the navigation pane, select Admin Centers and then select SharePoint.

3. In the SharePoint Admin Center navigation pane, select User Profiles.

4. Under People, select Manage User Permissions.

5. To add users or a group of users you want to be able to provision OneDrive sites, type the user or group name and click Add.

NOTE

You can only add groups if they are mail-enabled security groups.

6. After you have added any users or groups you want to have permissions to provision their OneDrive sites to the list, select Everyone Except External Users in the user list and then clear the Create Personal Site check box. See Figure 19-37 for an example.

CHAPTER 19

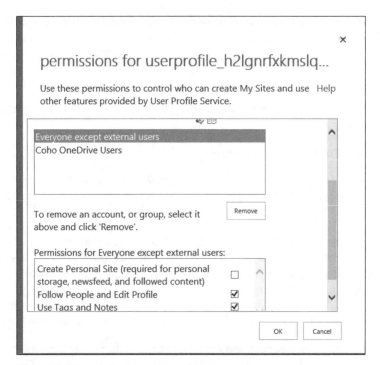

Figure 19-37 Updating permissions for users and groups

7. For every user or group you have added that you want to enable provisioning for, you must select the user or group from the permissions list and then select the Create Personal Site check box. When you are finished, click OK.

These steps affect only new OneDrive site provisioning, going forward—OneDrive sites that have already been provisioned are unaffected. To remove user access to those, you must either remove access to the individual user sites or remove the user's SharePoint license. Removing the user's SharePoint license could result in loss of data stored in the OneDrive site.

Troubleshooting

If you experience OneDrive synchronization problems, you might need to troubleshoot it. If the application seems not to be working, it might be simply a matter of restarting the OneDrive app or checking to see whether some files are preventing it from synchronizing properly.

OneDrive does have some limitations, which the following list describes.

- The OneDrive client can sync up to 20,000 files across all OneDrive and SharePoint libraries.

- The maximum file size that can be synchronized through the OneDrive sync client is 2 GB.

- Folder name and file combinations can have up to 400 characters. File paths longer than this will cause synchronization errors.

- You cannot synchronize file names with invalid characters: \ / : * ? " < > | # %.

- You cannot synchronize filenames that begin with a period (".").

- A folder named Forms cannot exist in the root of a OneDrive for Business library.

- OneNote notebooks cannot be synced because they have their own sync mechanism.

- Open files cannot be synced.

- Certain file types cannot be synced. Review the list of blocked file types at *http://office .microsoft.com/redir/HA101907868.aspx*.

Additional details about restrictions are available at *http://support.microsoft.com/kb/2933738* and *https://support.microsoft.com/en-us/help/3125202/restrictions-and-limitations-when -you-sync-files-and-folders*.

Yammer is a collaboration tool integrated with Office 365. It is formatted in a feed-style layout, with content arranged under topics (called Groups), and enables users to post updates, files, pictures, polls, and announcements as well as acknowledgements (praise) for others. Yammer is accessed by the Office 365 tile, shown in Figure 20-1, or by browsing to *http://www.yammer.com* and signing in with your Office 365 credentials.

Figure 20-1 Office 365 Yammer tile

Yammer's security and collaboration boundary is known as a network. From a subscription perspective, networks can be either stand-alone (basic) or Enterprise (integrated with Office 365 as part of an Office 365 subscription). From a configuration perspective, networks can be internal (corporate network or domains registered to the network) or external.

INSIDE OUT

Governance and security

Yammer is a product that is designed to give users freedom and flexibility in creating and publishing different types of discoverable content. There are some privacy settings that allow only certain individuals to create groups or post content, as well as moderator settings. Due to the open nature of the product, you might want to ask whether your organization has a governance policy in place to provide guidance in acceptable use and content. You might wish to restrict creation of groups and networks to a smaller set of administrative individuals until a governance policy is created.

In addition to governance of the types of content that can and should be posted or created, it is important also to think about governance surrounding external access to data resources. Because Yammer networks can be made up of both internal and external users, it is critical to ensure that users have access only to data that is applicable to them.

Concepts and administration

Before setting up your Yammer environment, familiarize yourself with the terminology, administrative roles, authentication methods, and the user interface elements and ways to add users to the environment.

Terminology

To design and structure a Yammer environment, you should understand the basic components that make up a Yammer deployment.

- **Networks**   A network is a collection of groups and users and is the top structural and administrative unit in the Yammer organization. The network is the collaboration space where other objects (groups and users) exist. Each Yammer organization can have one or more networks.

- **Internal network**   The internal network is the network associated with the organization's subscription. It's also known as the home network. Only users with a verified corporate address can join the home network and view its content.

- **External network**   An external network is a network made up of users who don't have one of an organization's verified corporate addresses. External networks can be used for collaboration among internal users, partners, vendors, and customers.

- **Groups**   All collaborative activities take place in groups. The group object is much like a bulletin or message board. Groups are typically formed around topics, products, teams, or services and contain posts and members. Collaboration can include posts and replies, polls, documents, and file uploads. You don't necessarily need to be a member to post to a group. However, if you join a group, it will show up on your navigation pane, and you will see notifications or badges that indicate new content.

- **Users**   A user is the basic security principal who logs on to a Yammer network and can post content or administer settings. Users can be members of one or more networks, zero or more groups, and hold zero or more administrative roles.

Roles

At some point, you might wish to delegate certain levels of administration to various users in the organization. Yammer has three types of admin roles: group admins, network admins, and verified admins.

Group admins can only administer certain options of groups for which they are delegated admin access or for groups that they have created (and own). Network admins have all the rights of group admins, but only for public groups, plus the ability to configure some organization-level settings. Verified admins can administer any group.

Office 365 global admins with a user principal name (UPN) that matches a domain configured in Yammer inherit the Yammer Verified Admin role. For group administrative tasks, group admins can perform any of the listed tasks for their respective groups, and network admins can perform any of the tasks listed for public groups and networks for which they have been granted the network admin role. Table 20-1 lists the rights associated with roles.

Table 20-1 Yammer roles and rights

Right	Group admin	Network admin	Verified admin
Configure network settings, features, and applications		X	X
Set network design, including logo and color scheme		X	X
Create Usage policy and require all users to accept it		X	X
Configure defaults for users who log on in the future		X	X
Configure user profile fields		X	X
Invite anyone, including outside guests		X	X

CHAPTER 20

Right	Group admin	Network admin	Verified admin
See all unlisted groups		X	X
Delete any message	X	X	X
Post announcements	X	X	X
Grant and revoke network admin privileges		X	X
Grant and revoke verified admin privileges			X
Remove or block any user	X	X	X
Manage user account activity			X
Perform integrations (such as for Microsoft SharePoint, Active Directory Sync)			X
Monitor keywords			X
Set data retention policy			X
Export data			X
Read messages in any private group			X
Configure security settings			X
Monitor private content in Yammer			X
Upload an image for a group	X	X	X
Set a group name	X	X	X
Set a group description	X	X	X
Add to a group or remove members from a group	X	X	X
Mark content official	X	X	X
Edit privacy of a group	X	X	X
Manage group membership options such as restricting membership	X	X	X

Yammer configuration

Deploying Yammer for your organization is straightforward. As soon as a verified admin logs on to Yammer the first time, the service is enabled. From that point forward, it is a matter of configuring it to fit your organization's requirements.

1. Log on to the Office 365 portal (*https://portal.office.com*) with a credential that has Global Admin rights.

2. Select the Admin tile from the landing page.

3. In the navigation pane, select Admin Centers, and then select Yammer, as shown in Figure 20-2.

   The Yammer administration landing page opens in a new tab.

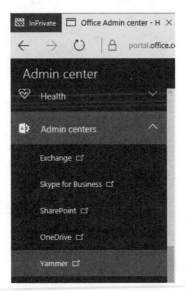

Figure 20-2 Yammer Admin Center link

INSIDE OUT

Administration shortcut

If at any time you are unable to find a way to navigate to the Yammer administration site, you can navigate to *https://yammer.com/admin/success* to open the configuration page or select the gear icon under the Office 365 header in the navigation bar on the left side of the page next to your user name (not the gear icon on the Office 365 toolbar).

4. Familiarize yourself with the Yammer Success page layout and complete the sections that are relevant to your configuration.

   The Yammer Success page, shown in Figure 20-3, is the landing page for configuring Yammer and getting the most out of your subscription.

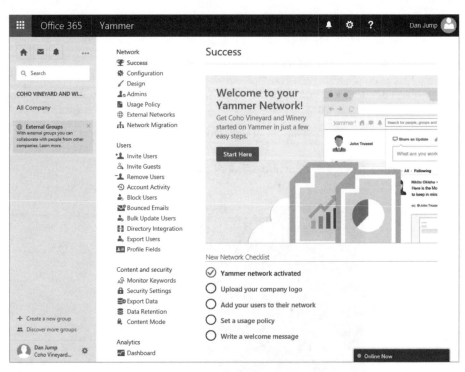

Figure 20-3 Yammer Success page

The following sections comprise the Yammer Success page.

- **Navigation pane** The navigation pane appears on the left side of the screen. A Yammer organization's home network contains a default group called All Company.

- **Network** The network section contains seven items relating to the network and organization configuration.

  - **Success** This is the landing page currently displayed.

  - **Configuration** This screen contains general configuration information about your networks and domains.

  - **Design** The Design screen enables you to select basic color schemes (background color, header background color, and header text color) as well as the images for the network, masthead, and Yammer-generated emails.

  - **Admins** In the Admins screen, you can assign additional network or verified administrators.

- **Usage Policy**   The usage policy settings can be used to display custom usage policy text and a URL to an existing corporate usage policy as well as require users to accept the usage policy during sign-up and every time changes are made to the policy.

- **External Networks**   Use the External Networks Settings screen to define who can create external networks (any user or admins), as well as settings related to discovery and joining external networks.

- **Network Migration**   If you have a stand-alone Yammer network or are merging with another organization that does, you can use the Network Migration screen to add those networks to the Office 365 tenant.

- **Users**   The Users section contains ten configuration items relating to adding, removing, importing, updating, and exporting users.

  - **Invite Users**   Use this screen to send invites to internal users.

  - **Invite Guests**   Use the Invite Guests screen to invite users with email domains external to the organization.

  - **Remove Users**   You can remove users from the network by using this screen.

  - **Account Activity**   Use the Account Activity screen to view user activity and disconnect sessions.

  - **Block Users**   Use the Block Users screen to prevent users from creating new accounts on the network by entering the email address of the user you wish to prevent.

  - **Bounced Emails**   Use the Bounced Emails screen to see which users might have invalid email addresses. Yammer sends periodic updates to enabled users; use this screen to track which users might no longer be part of the organization. You can deactivate users from this screen.

  - **Bulk Update Users**   You can upload a CSV through this screen to bulk update user information.

  - **Directory Integration**   Directory synchronization used to be a stand-alone product but has since been included in Azure AD Connect. Available configuration options include sending users a welcome message upon being added to the Yammer network or instructions on how to access it after they are synchronized.

  - **Export Users**   This screen enables you to export all or some of your users (based on date ranges) to a CSV file.

  - **Profile Fields**   Use this screen to select which attributes to show on member profiles in the network.

- **Content and Security**   The Content and Security section contains five options to manage and monitor content in your Yammer network.

  - **Monitor Keywords**   This screen enables you to monitor posts for certain keywords and email to the specified administrator.

  - **Security Settings**   This screen has several settings to control access to the service through IP ranges, configure password policies (if Office 365 Single Sign-On is not configured), enforce Exchange transport rules for messages leaving the Yammer environment, and enforce Office 365 identity. When Office 365 identity is enforced, and if your Office 365 tenant is associated with a single tenant, Connected Groups is enabled.

  - **Export Data**   This option enables you to export a date-limited range (including attachments, if selected) for your internal and external networks to a CSV file.

  - **Data Retention**   This setting controls how deleted data is handled (deleted permanently or stored in the Yammer environment until specifically removed with the Developer application programming interface [API]).

  - **Content Mode**   This setting controls content that is visible to your admin account.

    - **Default Mode**   See only content you normally have access to.

    - **Private Content Mode**   See private messages between people and posts in private groups that you are not a member of.

- **Analytics**   The Analytics section contains a single item, Dashboard, for reviewing data about your Office 365 Yammer subscription. The dashboard shows a variety of analytic information such as how many users your network has, number of messages posted, number of active groups, and how users are posting data.

- **New Network Checklist**   The new network checklist is a list of common items that you should configure to finish preparing your Yammer configuration.

  - **Yammer Network Activated**   This task is completed when you launch the Yammer Admin Center for the first time.

  - **Upload Your Company Logo**   This task links you to the Network > Design screen to set up color schemes and upload various logos and artwork to customize your network.

  - **Add Users To Their Network**   This task links you to the Users > Invite Users screen to add users to your network.

  - **Set A Usage Policy**   This task links you to the Users > Usage Policy section to create or link to a corporate acceptable-use policy.

  - **Write A Welcome Message**   This task links you to the All Company group so you can post a message for all new users to see.

Network administration tasks

To configure your Yammer network fully, you must complete each of the tasks in the Network section of the Admin Success page.

Configuration

The Configuration section, as shown in Figure 20-4, enables you to configure basic settings for the network, including the network display name, the default message prompt when you compose a new message, and network domains.

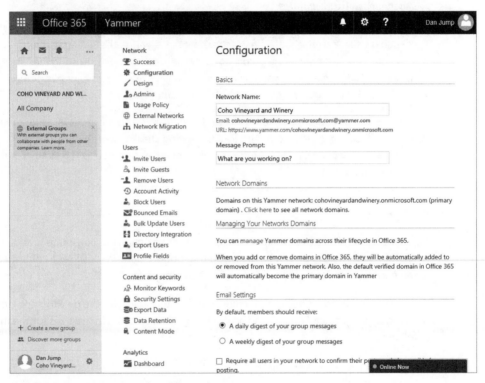

Figure 20-4 Yammer network configuration

The Network Name field controls how the network appears throughout the application, and the Message Prompt field denotes the initial text displayed in the text box area before a user begins typing a post.

Farther down the screen, you can manage email notification settings, as well as additional features enabled in the network, such as third-party applications, Org chart, and message translation.

Email Settings determines whether to require confirmation for posts made to a group through email.

The Yammer Org chart is built from the reporting relationships listed in a user's profile. Clearing the Org Chart check box disables the building and display of the Org chart in the Yammer user interface.

INSIDE OUT

Additional network features

Files and images can be attached to any message or reply, with a limit of 5 GB on each file. By default, file and image attachments are enabled. Clearing the File Attachment setting prohibits new files from being uploaded to the network; however, existing files are preserved and still accessible. Network admins can delete any file in any public group, and group admins can delete files in groups they manage.

Partners and developers have built a library of third-party applications by using the Yammer API. Clearing the 3rd Party Applications setting check box prohibits both the use of and access to the applications, although verified admins can continue to access any previously enabled applications.

Design

Customizing the Office 365 Yammer portal is a way to extend your corporate branding image into Office 365. The Design screen gives you that option. Here, you can set a color theme as well as the masthead and logo to be displayed on Yammer pages.

You can select a header background color, a header text color (for the desktop app), the network logo, the masthead image, and an email logo. The recommended sizes for the images are as follows.

- Network logo: 40 x 160 pixels

- Masthead image: 56 x 1200 pixels

- Email logo: 50 x 160 pixels

By default, the header text color is chosen automatically when you choose a background color to provide an optimal viewing experience. Yammer supports GIF, JPEG, or PNG images. Avoid images that have transparent portions.

Admins

The Admins screen enables you to create and manage admins in the Yammer network. To add a user as an admin, you either grant them Global Admin rights in the Office 365 portal (and the user will automatically be configured as a verified admin in the home network) or appoint them as an additional admin within the Yammer Admin Center.

In the following task sequence, you grant a user Network Admin privileges, elevate them to the Verified Admin level, revoke their Verified Admin level privileges (returning them to Network Admin), and finally, remove their administrative rights altogether.

Admin rights are granted in two ways—through inheritance by granting the Global Admin right in the Office 365 portal or by explicitly granting Network Admin or Verified Admin rights from the Admins screen in the Yammer Admin Center.

Yammer can have a mix of inherited and explicitly delegated admins. To make the admin tasks easier, the Change Status Of Office 365 Admins button appears in the Network Admins section. This button opens the Active Users screen in a new tab.

To add and remove admins, follow these steps.

1. If you are in Yammer and not the Yammer Admin Center, in the navigation pane, select the gear icon and then click Network Admin.

2. In the Yammer Admin Center, select Admins.

3. Under Appoint Additional Admins, type the name of a user in the tenant to whom you will grant admin privileges. See Figure 20-5.

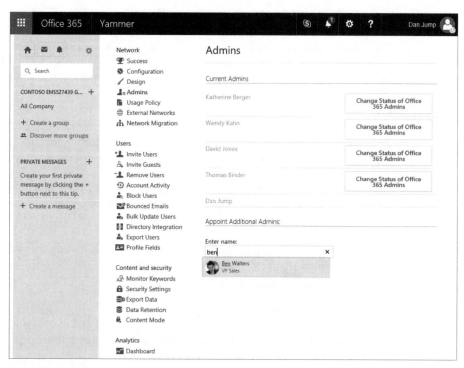

Figure 20-5 Yammer Admins page

4. Click Submit.

At this point, the user is now a Network Admin. To elevate privileges to Verified Admin, click the Grant Verified Admin button.

5. For users who were granted Verified Admin status (and not inherited from membership in Global Admins), you can confirm the grant by noticing the button text change to Revoke Verified Admin. See Figure 20-6.

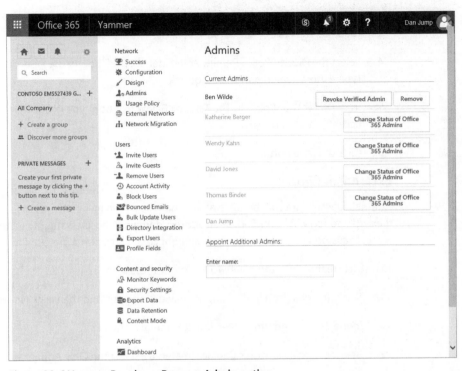

Figure 20-6 Yammer Revoke or Remove Admin option

6. Click Revoke Verified Admin for a user who was elevated to Verified Admin to return the user to a Network Admin Role.

   There is no confirmation dialog box for this task.

7. Click Remove to remove the Network Admin privileges of the user and then click OK to confirm the removal.

Usage policy

The Yammer Usage Policy settings offer a way to inform the site's users of the organization's acceptable use policy. You can force users to accept the usage policy upon signup and after changes are made, as well as display a reminder of the usage policy in the sidebar.

To configure a usage policy, follow these steps.

1. In the navigation pane in Yammer, select the gear icon and then click Network Admin.

2. In the Yammer Admin Center, select Usage Policy.

3.   Select the Require Users To Accept Policy During Sign Up And After Any Changes Are Made To The Policy check box.

4.   Select the Display Policy Reminder In Sidebar check box. In the Sidebar Message text box, type a short reminder of the usage policy.

5.   In the Enter Your Policy In The Textbox Below text box, type your organization's acceptable use policy.

6.   Click the Save button.

External networks

External networks are collaborative areas where users can invite others who are not members of the organization with a verified email address domain. A business might create this type of network for customers or vendors; a school might create an external network for alumni or parents.

To restrict creation of external networks, follow these steps.

1.   Select the gear icon in the Yammer navigation pane and then click Network Admin.

2.   In the Yammer Admin Center, select External Networks.

3.   Below External Networks Can Be Created By, select the Only Admins button and click Save.

To create an external network, follow these steps.

1.   Select the gear icon in the Yammer navigation pane and then click Create A New Network, as shown in Figure 20-7.

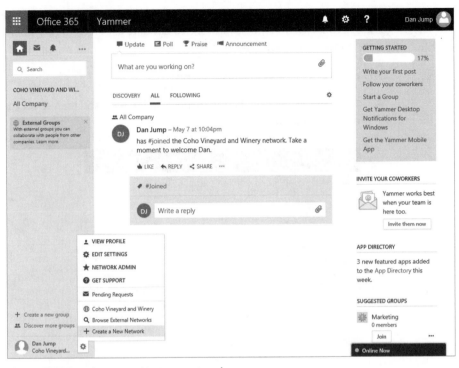

Figure 20-7 Creating a new Yammer network

2. Choose an image and a name for your external network, select any additional options, and click Create Network. See Figure 20-8.

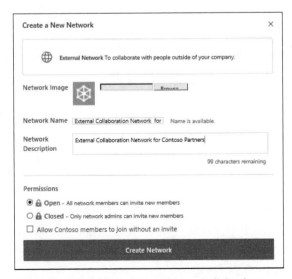

Figure 20-8 The Create A New Network dialog box

After creating the network, the new network appears. You can now create groups and administer this network like your home network. To navigate back to your home network, click the gear icon and then select your network name.

To delete an external network, follow these steps.

1. Select the gear icon in the Yammer navigation pane and then select your external network, as shown in Figure 20-9.

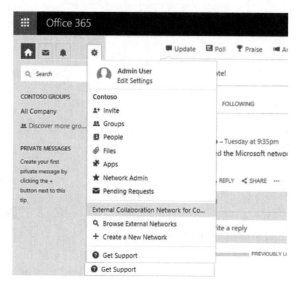

Figure 20-9 Selecting the external network

2. Select the gear icon in the Yammer navigation pane and then select Network Admin.

3. Under Network, select Configuration.

4. Scroll to the end of the page and, under External Network, click Delete External Network. See Figure 20-10.

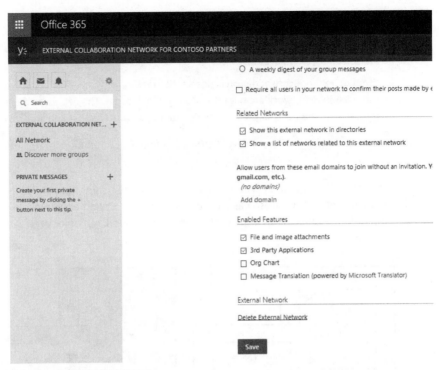

Figure 20-10 Deleting an external network

5. On the confirmation page, click Delete.

Network migration

If your organization acquires another organization with either a Yammer stand-alone network or enterprise network, you might want to consolidate networks. You can migrate one or more Yammer networks with their own email domains (a subsidiary network) into a Yammer Enterprise network. The network you migrate into is known as the parent network.

The subsidiary networks can be either stand-alone or enterprise, but the parent network must be enterprise activated.

INSIDE OUT

Yammer network migration

Yammer network consolidation is not a task to take lightly. In addition, only the users from the subsidiary network are migrated during this process. The groups and content are not migrated. If you need to preserve the content, you must export and archive the content.

Yammer networks that are part of Office 365 tenants cannot be migrated or consolidated.

In this example, depicted in Figure 20-11, Contoso is the parent network, and Fabrikam is the subsidiary network. Contoso has an Enterprise-activated Yammer network in its Office 365 subscription. Fabrikam has a stand-alone Yammer network not associated with an Office 365 subscription.

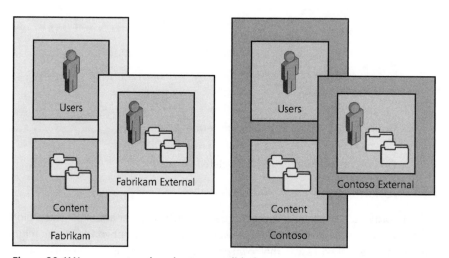

Figure 20-11 Yammer networks prior to consolidation

Post-migration, the Fabrikam users are relocated to the Contoso network, and the Fabrikam external network is reassigned to the Contoso network. See Figure 20-12.

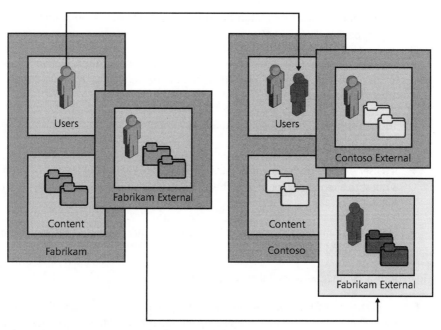

Figure 20-12 Yammer network after consolidation

The key factor is that although content from the subsidiary's external networks remains available, content from the subsidiary's internal network *will not* be.

INSIDE OUT

Network migration caveats

During a network migration, there are several prompts for you to log on to the source (subsidiary) network to export your data. This can lead you to think that you can restore your data after the network migration is complete.

At this time, you cannot import data (either through the user interface or the Yammer API) into a Yammer network. Data exports are just that—a backup that you can use to search for content at a later point in time. There is no way to import it into a Yammer network.

Given that caveat, it is important for you to communicate to the business that its data will be gone and not recoverable in the same format. Network migrations cannot be reversed—there is no undo button, so plan accordingly.

Before you begin a network migration, be sure you understand the requirements, limitations, and what happens in the event of errors.

- Only Office 365 global admins can perform a network migration. Network migrations involve retrieving the list of verified domains in the tenant, which is a task only a global admin can perform.

- You can start multiple network migrations without waiting for the previous migrations to finish.

- If a user exists in both networks, the account in the parent network will be promoted from a guest to a regular account, and the account in the migrating subsidiary network will be deleted.

- Network migrations can only be started from Yammer networks that have been enterprise activated from an Office 365 subscription.

To migrate a Yammer network, follow these steps.

1. Notify users and business owners that the Yammer subsidiary network will no longer be available after the migration is complete. Recommend that users back up any attachments, message threads, or private messages they wish to keep.

2. In the parent network, select the gear icon in the Yammer navigation pane and then click Network Admin.

3. Click Network Migration.

4. Verify that the subsidiary email domain is part of your tenant. If it is not, click the link to open the Office 365 Domain Administration page to verify that the new domain is in your tenant.

5. If all the domains you wish to migrate are present on the screen, click Next, as shown in Figure 20-13.

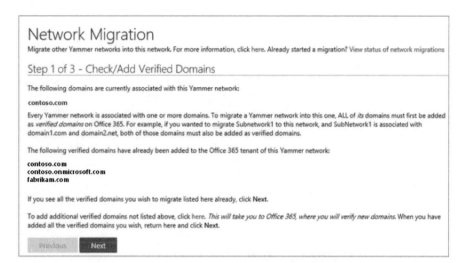

Figure 20-13 Yammer Network Migration page

6. Select the button, pictured in Figure 20-14, to confirm the Yammer network you are moving. If you don't see the network listed, confirm that the domain linked to the Yammer network is verified in your Office 365 tenant. If it is verified but the Yammer network is not showing up, contact support. Click Next.

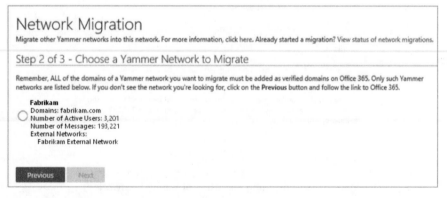

Figure 20-14 Selecting the Yammer network to migrate

7. Verify the migration details.

    The last step of the migration recommends that you export your data, which you might want to do. Remember—you cannot import the data back into the parent Yammer network, nor can you go back to the subsidiary network after it has been migrated.

CHAPTER 20

8.   Click Start Migration. See Figure 20-15.

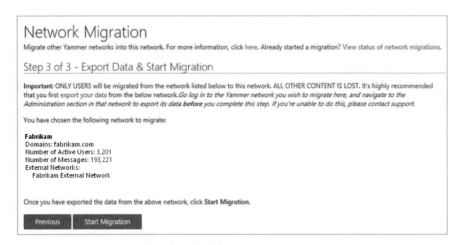

Figure 20-15 Starting Yammer network migration

9.   Confirm the start of the migration by typing the name of the network in the text box, shown in Figure 20-16, and click Migrate.

Figure 20-16 Confirming migration of Yammer network

Click View Status Of Network Migrations to view the status of the migration that you initiated. The status lists the network, domains, and which Office 365 administrator initiated the migration. Clicking the Show Details button gives more details about the network, including active users, messages, and external networks.

TROUBLESHOOTING

Network Migration Errors

If all or part of a migration fails, the status screen also displays details about those errors. Table 20-2 shows a list of potential errors.

Table 20-2 Network migration error messages

Error Message	Description
Failed to migrate source network <name>	The migration of the subsidiary network <network> to the parent network failed.
Failed to migrate user <email address>	The user account could not be migrated. Re-create the user in the parent network.
Failed to migrate external network <name>	The external network could not be migrated. The subsidiary network has been migrated. Contact support.

CHAPTER 20

User administration tasks

Managing users in your Yammer network consists of inviting, removing, blocking, and updating tasks. In addition, you can gather statistics and control the fields that users can edit within their own user profiles.

Users can be added in a number of ways.

Invite users

The most basic way to invite users to join your Yammer network is by inviting them. Only employees with a company email address can be invited by the Invite Users dialog box, as shown in Figure 20-17. Verified admins can import users in bulk from this dialog box by using an address book export created from an application such as Microsoft Outlook.

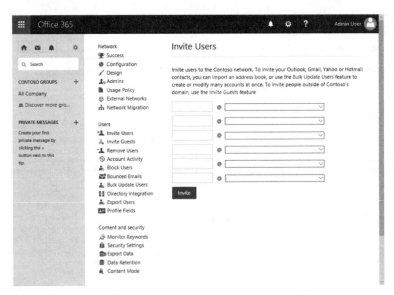

Figure 20-17: Invite Users

You can invite users individually by entering the user's alias and domain on the Invite Users page. As an alternative, you might invite users from an export of your email application. You can use Outlook to create a CSV export for this purpose. To do this, follow these steps to create a CSV export from an Outlook address book.

1. Launch Outlook.

2. Click the File tab.

3. Click Open & Export.

4. Click the Import/Export button.

5. Select Export To A File and click Next.

6. Select Comma Separated Values and click Next.

7. Select the Contacts folder, shown in Figure 20-18, that you wish to export to a CSV file and click Next.

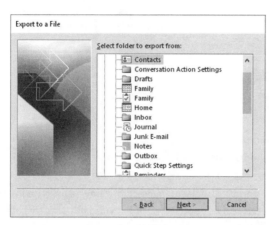

Figure 20-18 Selecting the Contacts folder in the Import/Export Wizard

8. Browse to a location in which to save the exported contacts CSV file and click Next.

9. Confirm the export action and click Finish.

With a CSV export file, you can import users through the Invite Users page in the Yammer Network Admin Center. To import them, follow these steps.

1. Select the gear icon in the Yammer navigation pane and then click Network Admin.

2. Under Users, click Invite Users.

3. On the Invite Users screen, click the Import An Address Book link, highlighted in Figure 20-19.

Figure 20-19 The Invite Users dialog box from an address book

4. Click Browse to locate an exported address book CSV file and then click the Preview button, shown in Figure 20-20.

CHAPTER 20

Figure 20-20 Import Address Book

5.   Select which users to import. Users with a check box have a valid verified domain in the tenant. Users with a red X do not and cannot be invited as users. Click the Send Invitation button at the bottom of the dialog box. See Figure 20-21.

Figure 20-21 Selecting users to whom you will send an invitation

Invite guests

If you want to invite users who are not members of one of your verified domains, you can use the Invite Guest dialog box. Guest users (including active and pending users who have not yet responded to their invitation) are listed on the Guests page.

To invite guests, follow these steps.

1.   Select the gear icon in the Yammer navigation pane and then click Network Admin.

2.   Under Users, select Invite Guests.

3.   Enter the email addresses of users outside of your verified networks that you wish to invite to your Yammer network and then click Invite.

Invited guests show up farther down the page, with either a pending or active status. See Figure 20-22.

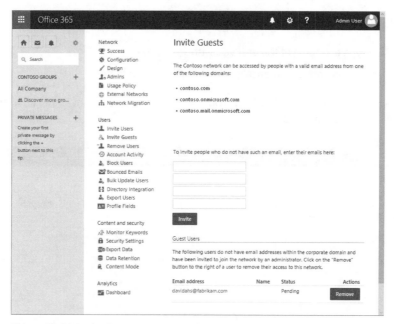

Figure 20-22 Invited guests

Remove users

At some point, it might become necessary to remove users from your Yammer network. You can remove users temporarily or permanently. After entering a name to delete, three options appear.

- **Deactivate This User (You Can Reactivate Their Account At Any Time)**   Deactivating a user blocks the user from logging on to the Yammer network until they verify their email address again. If you have removed access to their verified email address, they will not be able to reactivate their account. Deactivated accounts stay in this state for 90 days. After 90 days, the account is permanently deleted.

- **Permanently Remove This User But Retain Their Messages**   Selecting this option deletes the user account but retains the messages, replies, and attachments they posted.

- **Permanently Remove This User And Remove Their Messages**   Selecting this option removes the user as well as all the messages, replies, and attachments they have posted to the network.

CHAPTER 20

To remove or deactivate a user, follow these steps.

1.   Select the gear icon in the Yammer navigation pane and then click Network Admin.

2.   Under Users, select Remove Users.

3.   Type the name of the user you wish to remove.

     The text box automatically filters matching user names.

4.   Select Deactivate This User (you can reactivate the account at any time) and click Submit. See Figure 20-23.

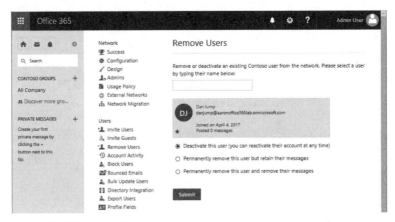

Figure 20-23 Deactivating a user

If you find that you need to reactivate a disabled user, you can do that from the Remove Users dialog box as well. To reactivate a user, follow these steps.

1.   Select the gear icon in the Yammer navigation pane and then click Network Admin.

2.   Under Users, select Remove Users.

3.   Review the list in Deactivated Users and click the Reactivate button for the user you wish to re-enable.

4.   Click OK in the confirmation dialog box.

If, however, you want to delete a deactivated user permanently, simply click the Delete button in the Deactivated Users list.

1.   Select the gear icon in the Yammer navigation pane and then click Network Admin.

2.   Under Users, select Remove Users.

3. Review the list in Deactivated Users and click the Reactivate button for the user you wish to delete.

4. Click the Delete button.

5. Click OK to confirm the permanent deletion.

Account activity

Sometimes, it is necessary to track a user's activity in a particular system. Yammer activity can be tracked through the Account Activity admin screen. You can perform session administration activities such as logging off individual user sessions on devices.

To log off an active user session, follow these steps.

1. Select the gear icon in the Yammer navigation pane and then click Network Admin.

2. Under Users, select Account Activity.

3. Search for the user to log off.

4. To cancel the session for a currently logged-on user, click the Logout link next to their name, as shown in Figure 20-24.

Figure 20-24 Account Activity page displaying actively logged-on user

5. After clicking the Logout button, the Account Activity page opens and a message appears, stating that it could take up to 2 minutes to log the user off from their session.

6. During this time, any activity the user performs (post, reply, screen refresh, clicking any link) returns them to the Yammer sign-in page.

7. After the user is logged off, the Account Activity page is updated to show remaining sessions for the user.

Block users

It may be necessary or desirable to block certain accounts from joining the Yammer network. Users with a blocked email address cannot join the network. You might do this for email addresses of shared mailboxes.

A blocked user can only register after an admin removes their address from the blocked user list. To block users from signing up for Yammer, perform these steps.

1. Select the gear icon in the Yammer navigation pane and then click Network Admin.

2. Under Users, select Block Users.

3. Enter one (or more) email addresses, separated by commas, into the text box and click Block.

    After blocking users, they appear in the list of blocked users, as shown in Figure 20-25.

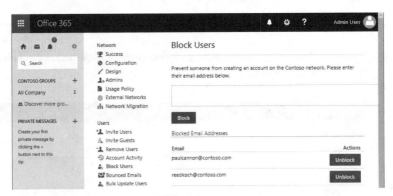

Figure 20-25 Blocked Email Addresses area after adding users to it

When a user with a blocked email address signs up using that address, they will be unable to complete the process.

Instead of being able to complete the signup process, they are just redirected to the same page and the Sign Up Free button changes to Retry.

Bounced emails

Yammer users receive periodic emails from the service, such as post notifications, digest emails, and service or system announcements. When a user's email address is disabled, the messages destined for their mailbox bounce, and the service records that as a bounced email address. Bounced emails might indicate users who have left the organization. You can view a list of users whose email addresses have returned non-delivery reports and deactivate them if necessary.

1. Select the gear icon in the Yammer navigation pane and then click Network Admin.

2. Under Users, select Bounced Emails.

3. If a user is listed as bouncing, you can click Deactivate, which deactivates the user account (similar to the option under Remove Users).

Bulk update users

If your organization is just starting to deploy Yammer or is acquiring another organization or business unit, you might want to configure many users at once. Conversely, if your organization is going through a divestiture, you might wish to remove many users at once. The Bulk Update feature enables you not only to add or remove several users; it also performs updates and deactivations.

NOTE

The Bulk Update feature is available to verified admins only.

To use this feature, you must place your users in a CSV-formatted table and include a header with the following fields from left to right: Action, Email Address, Full Name, Job Title, Password, New Email.

Place one of the following values in the action column.

- **New**   Provisions new users. If the password field for a user is left blank, the user is created as pending. If the password field is populated, the user is provisioned as active and is visible in the member directory.

- **Update**   Updates the existing account. The values in the populated fields overwrite the values on the user object. If you specify a new email address that is already in use, the previous user with that email address is suspended.

- **Suspend**   Deactivates the specified user account. The user must log on again to reactivate it.

- **Delete**   Deletes the user account if the action is specified as delete. The user account is deleted, but the messages and attachments remain.

CHAPTER 20

INSIDE OUT

Non-English bulk updates

Some applications, such as older versions of Microsoft Excel, do not encode non-English characters in text or CSV files correctly. If you need to put such characters in your update CSV, edit the file in Notepad and save it encoded in UTF-8 or use a version of an application that correctly encodes the characters for text output.

To bulk update users, prepare and upload a CSV as follows.

1. Launch Notepad.

2. Enter the data you wish to update, separating each field with a comma. Change the domain to match a verified domain in your network. See Figure 20-26 for an example of how an update file might look.

   ```
   Action,Email Address,Full Name,Job Title,Password,New Email
   ```

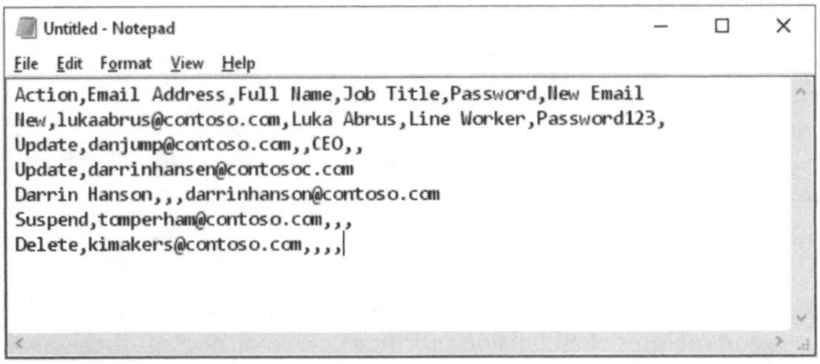

Figure 20-26 Notepad window containing users to add to a Yammer network from bulk update CSV

3. Click File | Save As and browse to a location.

4. Select All Files (*.*) in the Save As type, enter a file name in the file name box, select UTF-8 in the encoding drop-down list, and click Save.

5. Launch a web browser, navigate to the Yammer portal, and log on as a verified admin.

6. Select the gear icon in the Yammer navigation pane and then click Network Admin.

7. Under Users, select Bulk Update Users.

8. Scroll to the bottom of the window, click Browse, locate your CSV, and click Open.

9. Click Bulk Update.

    The screen refreshes, showing you the status of the updates in progress. Clicking the
    Show Failures button gives you details about any errors. If any errors occur, correct the
    errors in the CSV and re-import.

Directory integration

Use this page to manage users imported with the Directory Sync function. Yammer DSync has
been deprecated and replaced with Azure Active Directory Connect.

The Directory Integration page has three tabs. See Figure 20-27.

- **Directory Integration**   This tab has a link to the Yammer Admin documentation for
  configuring Directory Sync.

Figure 20-27 Yammer Directory Integration page

- **Email Invitation**   This tab has a customizable email template that can be sent to users
  as Directory Sync provisions them into the Yammer network. You can make changes to
  the From address and the email template in this dialog box and then click Save Changes
  to commit the configuration.

- **Welcome Message**   The welcome message is shown to users who have been provisioned by Directory Sync but navigated to the Yammer portal to begin the signup process.

Configuring Directory Synchronization and authentication is discussed later in the chapter.

Exporting users

The Export Users dialog box enables you to export a CSV of users in the Yammer network. The
fields exported include the User ID, Email Address, Name, Job Title, Location, and Joined On
(date the user joined the Yammer network). To export users, follow these steps.

1. Select the gear icon in the Yammer navigation pane and then click Network Admin.

2. Click Export Users.

3. Click either the button to export all users or the button to filter by a joined-on-date range.

4. Click Export.

Profile fields

The Profile Fields dialog box enables you to customize the profile page where users can update their information. Profile fields are searchable by other users in the Yammer network. Select or clear check boxes to make the fields appear when a user edits their profile.

1. Select the gear icon in the Yammer navigation pane and then click Network Admin.

2. Click Profile Fields.

3. Select or clear the check boxes shown in Figure 20-28 and then click Save.

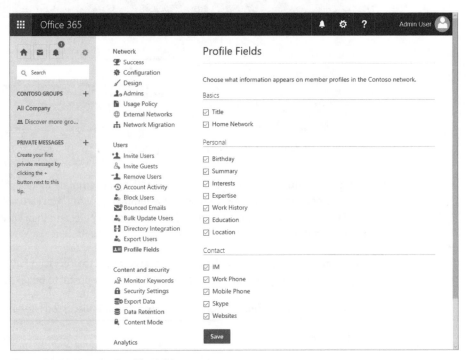

Figure 20-28 Yammer Profile Fields page

Content and security tasks

The Content and Security section of the Yammer Admin Center enables you to monitor and track potentially sensitive content, restrict access to content within certain IP ranges, configure password policies, route Yammer email notifications through your Exchange Online Transport Rules, and configure data retention policies.

Monitor keywords

It might be necessary to monitor posts for particular words or phrases. Your organization's usage policy or internal security and compliance policies might have guidelines about posting certain types of sensitive content such as social security numbers, credit card numbers, or other personally identifiable information (PII). You can use the Monitor Keywords setting to generate notifications to an administrator whenever content matching certain patterns is posted.

The Monitor Keywords setting uses regular expressions to search posts for content. Regular expressions are entered one per line and might span multiple lines.

Only verified admins can modify the patterns in the Monitor Keywords dialog box. To configure monitoring, follow these steps.

1. Select the gear icon in the Yammer navigation pane and then click Network Admin.

2. Click Monitor Keywords.

3. Type the email address to be notified when content matching the keywords, patterns, or phrases is detected.

4. Type keywords, phrases, or regular expressions to monitor in the text area.

5. Click Save.

    If there is a problem with the formatting of your regular expression, you are notified and must correct it before the save commits your changes. You might want to copy the content to the Clipboard or Notepad before clicking Save so you have a copy of your edits.

INSIDE OUT

Monitoring sensitive data

Depending on your organization guidelines and privacy requirements, you might want or need to put monitors in place to notify compliance officers about sensitive data that might be posted to Yammer. Such data can include social security numbers, credit card numbers, driver's license numbers, phone numbers, medical or other account records, or other personally identifiable data. There also might be pending legal cases, patents, or other internal project collateral whose circulation the organization deems it best to limit.

Although the Yammer interface supports both plaintext matching and regular expressions, try to use regular expressions whenever possible to account for the highest level of potential matches.

Security settings

Use the Security Settings page, shown in Figure 20-29, to configure IP address restrictions (such as allowing access to Yammer for your organization's internal and VPN subnets), password policies (password change frequency as well as complexity settings), whether Yammer email delivery flows through your organization's Office 365 tenant and is subject to its configured Exchange Transport Rules, and whether Office 365 Identity is enforced.

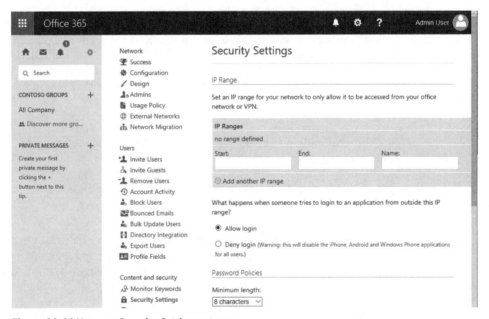

Figure 20-29 Yammer Security Settings page

IP ranges

IP range restrictions can be put in place to limit access to the Yammer network. If your organization has restrictive network access requirements, you might need to administer this setting.

INSIDE OUT

IP range restrictions

Controlling access to corporate resources is a foremost concern for many administrators, business owners, and security professionals. The IP range restriction policies can help achieve business goals.

IP range restrictions can affect all forms of client communication (desktop, browser, mobile client). However, something that isn't spelled out clearly is the "application" portion of the security restrictions screen.

After an IP range is entered, it affects browser-based logons. Typically, mobile device users will be using their platform's Yammer application. If the Allow Login button is selected, users will retain the ability to log on to mobile applications (such as Yammer for iOS) from mobile carrier or remote networks. However, if the Deny Login button is selected, mobile clients will also be restricted to the configured IP ranges and will need to be on a corporate VPN or corporate Wi-Fi network to access the Yammer network.

Before you set any IP ranges, be sure to check your external public IP and make sure it is included in the range. If you don't, you might just exclude yourself from managing your own network and will have to call support to fix it.

The following process will help you restrict access to corporate IP ranges.

1. Obtain the external public IP ranges from your network administration team for your corporate networks.

    If the network administrators supply you with a classless inter-domain routing (CIDR) network block such as 13.104.0.0/14, you must convert it to an IP range expressed as a starting IP and ending IP address (13.104.0.0–13.107.255.255). A number of online CIDR and subnet calculators can assist you in performing this task.

2. Select the gear icon in the Yammer navigation pane and then click Network Admin.

3. Click Security Settings and navigate to the IP Ranges section.

4. Enter the starting and ending IP addresses along with a description of the IP range.

5. Ensure that the Allow Login button is selected to allow mobile device applications to continue to access the service.

6. Scroll to the bottom of the page and click Save.

Password policies

Password policies can be used to enforce certain standards for your users, such as minimum password length, complexity, change frequency, and emergency forcing of password changes.

Selecting the option to force all users to change passwords immediately requires all users to change their passwords upon their next logon, regardless of the password change frequency policy.

Password policy settings are not available for external networks.

To set password restriction policies, follow these steps.

1. Select the gear icon in the Yammer navigation pane and then click Network Admin.

2. Click Security Settings and navigate to the Password Policies section.

3. Select nine characters from the Minimum Length drop-down list.

4. In the Required Complexity drop-down list, note the following options.

    No Requirements

    Must Include Both Letters And Numbers

    Must Include Letters, Numbers And Special Characters

    Must Include Upper- And Lower-Case Letters, Numbers, And Special Characters

5. Select Must Include Letters, Numbers And Special Characters.

6. In the Require Users To Change Their Passwords Every drop-down list, select 1 Month.

7. Scroll to the bottom of the page and click Save.

External messaging

External Messaging controls whether Yammer network messages are routed through your organization's Office 365 tenant. This option is not available for stand-alone or basic Yammer networks that are not part of an Office 365 subscription.

At any point in a conversation, an internal user can add an external user to a message thread by typing their email address in the Cc line.

When an external user participates in a Yammer conversation, they might receive notifications regarding replies to their post. Applying Exchange transport rules (ETRs) to Yammer messages helps protect the corporate IP by restricting the delivery of messages based on rules configured in Exchange Online Protection (EOP).

If Yammer is configured to use Exchange transport rules, it checks the message against the transport rules to see whether the message complies. If the message is found not to meet the transport rules, a notification is returned and the user cannot post the message with the external recipient added. See Figure 20-30.

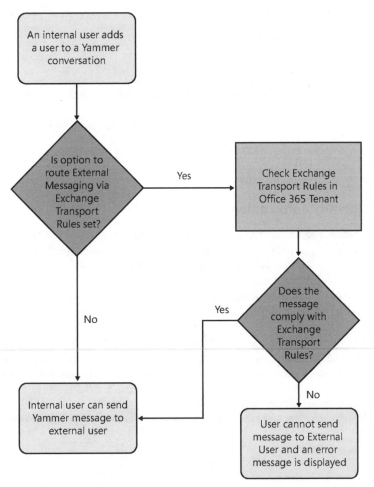

Figure 20-30 Flowchart showing Exchange Transport rules evaluation when an external user is added to a Yammer message

Not all ETRs work with Yammer. Yammer uses only Exchange Online transport rules and cannot be configured to integrate with on-premises Exchange transport rules. To use on-premises transport rules, ensure that you have an activated Office 365 subscription and at least one Exchange Online license. You can then export the transport rules from your Exchange on-premises environment and import them into Exchange Online.

Yammer ignores rules with the following conditions and actions.

- **Conditions**   MessageSizeOver, ContentCharacterSetContainsWord, MessageType-Matches, SCLOver, WithImportance

- **Actions**   SetSCL, PrependSubject, RemoveOME

To configure external messaging options, follow these steps.

1. Log on to Yammer as a verified admin.

2. Select the gear icon in the Yammer navigation pane and then click Network Admin.

3. Click Security Settings and navigate to the External Messaging section.

4. Select Enforce Your Exchange Online Exchange Transport Rules (ETRs) In Yammer.

5. Scroll to the bottom of the page and click Save.

Office 365 Identity enforcement

As your organization adopts Yammer as part of its enterprise social strategy, you might want to consider full integration with Office 365 Identity. Enforcing Office 365 Identity enables you to take advantage of a single identity source for your internal Yammer network.

With a Yammer stand-alone or Basic network or Yammer Enterprise with Yammer Identity, users are logged on with credentials in the Yammer network.

However, when Office 365 Identity Enforcement is selected for an enterprise network, only users with a valid Office 365 account can sign in. Users without a valid Office 365 Identity (either created manually or through directory synchronization) cannot log on to the Yammer network.

The authentication flow is shown in Figure 20-31.

CHAPTER 20

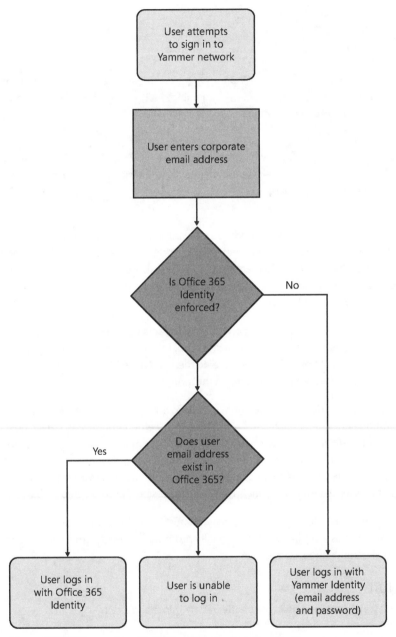

Figure 20-31 Yammer Identity and authentication flowchart

INSIDE OUT

Office 365 Identity

If your organization has not yet adopted Yammer, it might be worthwhile to consider enforcing Office 365 Identity from the beginning; that way, you never have to go through the planning and communications exercises to help your users prepare for the switch of identity models.

When Office 365 Identity is enabled and your Office 365 tenant is configured for federation (discussed in Chapter 3, "Federation Services and Authentication"), you can give your users a single sign-on (SSO) experience.

If you are currently using Yammer Identity and want to begin using Office 365 Identity, communicate the impending change to your network. In addition, make sure all of your Yammer users are represented by an Office 365 identity. After you enable Office 365 Identity enforcement, any previously configured Yammer network user who does not have a corresponding Office 365 identity will be unable to log on.

One possible exercise would be to open the Export Users page in Yammer to generate a list of all configured users and compare it against a list of Office 365 identities. If you have more users in Yammer than identities in Office 365, create them in Office 365 (either manually or through directory synchronization) prior to making the switch.

Enabling Office 365 Identity Enforcement overrides any previously configured single sign-on configuration and, when enabled in Committed Enforcement mode, is not reversible because enabling Office 365 Identity also enables Connected Yammer Groups. Thus, an Office 365 group is created for every new Yammer group, giving users access to SharePoint, Planner, and Microsoft OneNote features connected to the Office 365 group. Reverting the identity enforcement change blocks Yammer Identity users from accessing the connected resources.

To enable Office 365 Identity Enforcement, you must be a global admin who has been synchronized to Yammer as a verified admin. Manually promoted verified admins and network admins cannot make this change.

NOTE

Guests and external users are unaffected by this change.

When you are ready to make the change, the following steps enable Office 365 Identity in Yammer.

1. Log on to the Yammer network as a verified admin who has been synchronized from Office 365.

2. Select the gear icon in the Yammer navigation pane and then click Network Admin.

3. Click Security Settings and navigate to the Office 365 Identity Enforcement section.

4. Select the Enforce Office 365 Identity check box. See Figure 20-32.

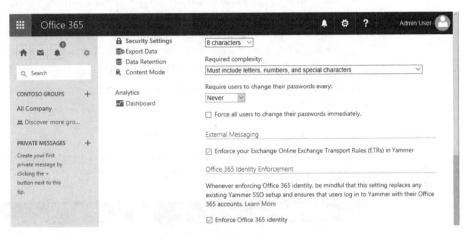

Figure 20-32 Yammer Office 365 Identity Enforcement

5. After you select the check box for identity enforcement, select your level of enforcement from one of the two options for enforcement, as shown in Figure 20-33.

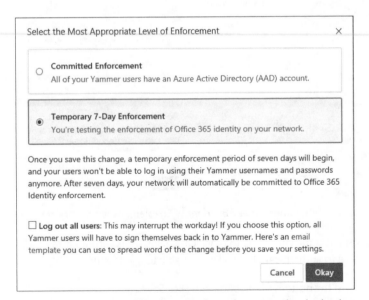

Figure 20-33 Yammer Office 365 Identity enforcement level selection

- **Committed Enforcement**   All of your Yammer users are represented by Azure Active Directory or Office 365 Identity. This is the default setting. This change cannot be reverted without assistance from support. Committed enforcement enables Office 365 Connected Yammer groups.

- **Temporary 7-Day Enforcement**   This is useful if you are testing Office 365 Identity with Yammer. If you do nothing after 7 days, the change is automatically committed. If you navigate back to the Settings page after saving the change, you can clear the Enforce Office 365 Identity check box. Temporary enforcement does not enable Office 365 Connected Yammer groups.

In addition, you can choose to force all your users to log out and then log back in using their Office 365 Identity.

6.   Select Temporary 7-Day Enforcement and click Okay.

The Enforce Office 365 Identity box is now selected, and an additional message appears below it. See Figure 20-34.

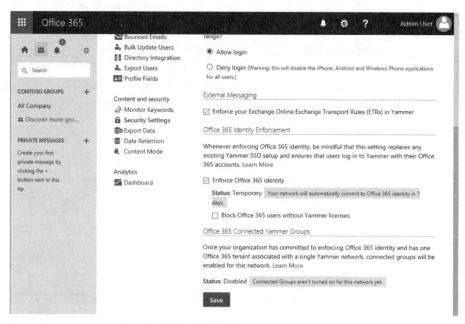

Figure 20-34 Yammer Office 365 Identity Enablement temporary status message

If you select the check box to block Office 365 users without a Yammer license, users will be able to authenticate but will not be able to use the service.

7.   Scroll to the bottom of the page and click Save.

If for some reason you need to undo your Office 365 Identity configuration during the temporary enforcement period, you can revert the configuration by using the following process.

1. Log on to the Yammer network as a verified admin who has been synchronized from Office 365.

2. Select the gear icon in the Yammer navigation pane and then click Network Admin.

3. Click Security Settings and navigate to the Office 365 Identity Enforcement section.

4. Clear the Enforce Office 365 Identity check box.

5. Click OK to acknowledge Stop Enforcing Office 365 Identity For This Network.

6. Scroll to the bottom of the page and click Save.

Export data

You might have a number of reasons to export your Yammer network's content, such as manipulating it inside a business analytics tool, for archival purposes, a divestiture, or a network merger. In any event, you can achieve this by using the Export Data dialog box in the Yammer Admin Center. Only verified admins can export data from a Yammer network.

NOTE

There is no way to import exported data from a Yammer network.

To export data from a Yammer network, follow these steps.

1. Select the gear icon in the Yammer navigation pane and then click Network Admin.

2. Click Export Data to open the Export Data page, shown in Figure 20-35.

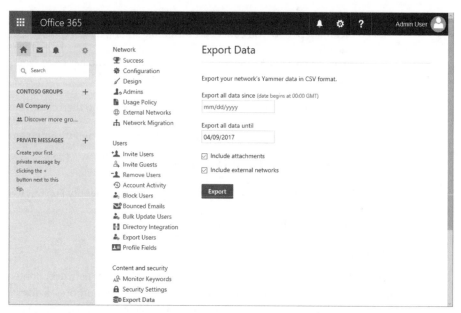

Figure 20-35 Export Data page

3.   Enter a starting and ending date.

4.   Select or clear check boxes to enable attachment export or exports from external networks.

5.   Click Export.

6.   After the content has been gathered, and the Download dialog box opens, click Save or Save As to save the download to your computer.

INSIDE OUT

The Export Data archive

An active Yammer network can have a lot of data to export. After you have clicked the Export button, you are prompted to download a file. The export is delivered as a ZIP archive file with several CSVs included.

The content is primarily stored in the following CSV files.

- **Messages.csv**   All the messages for the network

- **MessageVersions.csv**   All the revisions for messages for the network

If you have included file attachments in your export, information regarding them is stored in CSV Files.csv, and the attachment's object ID is referenced in the Attachments column of Messages.csv. The files are stored in a folder named Files inside the downloaded archive. File attachments are exported in their native source formats; notes, however, are exported as HTML.

The Yammer Developer Center (*https://developer.yammer.com*) has sample scripts for both Linux and Microsoft Windows that can be used to export data on a scheduled basis.

Data retention

The Yammer data retention policy focuses on how deleted content is handled. Two options are available.

- **Hard Delete**   This is the default option. When messages or data is deleted, it is deleted permanently and nothing is visible in the data exports.

- **Soft Delete**   Deleted data is no longer visible to users but can be accessed through the Export Data function. Permanently deleting data requires use of the Developer API.

Only verified admins can modify Data Retention settings. To configure the data retention policy, follow these steps.

1. Select the gear icon in the Yammer navigation pane and then click Network Admin.

2. Click Data Retention.

3. Select either the Hard Delete (Recommended) or Soft Delete button and click Save.

   If your organization has certain regulatory or eDiscovery compliance requirements, you might need to select Soft Delete so that the data is discoverable and exportable, even if it isn't visible to users.

Analytics

The Analytics view in the Yammer Admin Center does not have any exportable data. However, you can view a dashboard with graphs depicting engagement and client distribution. The Analytics page is shown in Figure 20-36.

CHAPTER 20

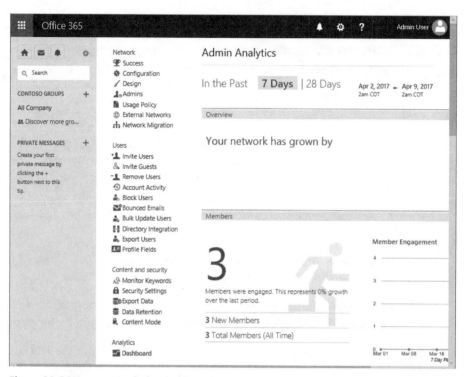

Figure 20-36 Yammer Analytics dashboard

Directory synchronization with Yammer

As of December 1, 2016, Yammer DSync and Yammer SSO were deprecated for use with Office 365. Their features and functionality have been replaced with Azure AD Connect and Office 365 Identity.

Office 365 Identity for Yammer works in the same fashion as the identity scenarios for the rest of the Office 365 product suite.

- **Cloud Identity**   Users are managed in Office 365 only.

- **Synchronized Identity**   On-premises Active Directory users are synchronized to Office 365 and Azure Active Directory, and users are managed on-premises. You can also choose to synchronize password hashes so that users can authenticate using the same passwords in the cloud as they do on-premises.

- **Federated Identity**   On-premises Active Directory users are synchronized to Office 365 and Azure Active Directory, and users are managed on-premises. User authentication is redirected to an on-premises identity provider (such as Active Directory) through a federation solution such as Active Directory Federation Services (AD FS).

More information about Azure Active Directory Connect (Azure AD Connect), Azure Active Directory synchronization, and federation is available starting in Chapter 2, "Preparing Your Environment for the Cloud."

Yammer directory synchronization is configured when you set up Azure AD Connect.

1. Review the server requirements for Azure AD Connect.

2. Install Azure AD Connect and synchronize your users to Office 365.

3. If you had an existing Yammer network, compare an export of your Yammer users with the users synchronized to Office 365 through Azure AD Connect. You can use a script such as this (save the following codeblock as CompareYammerToAzureAD.ps1) to assist you in comparing user sets.

```
<#
.SYNOPSIS
Compare Yammer User Export with Azure AD User list
.PARAMETER Credential
Standard PSCredential object for Office 365 Credential
.PARAMETER IncludeAllYammerUserStates
Include users in all Yammer activity states (active, soft_deleted, etc)
.PARAMETER InputFile
Yammer User Export file. Obtain from Network Admin | Export Users.
.PARAMETER OutputFile
Path to output file.
.PARAMETER UseExistingConnection
Use an existing Office 365 PowerShell session.
.EXAMPLE
.\CompareYammertoAzureAD.ps1 -InputFile .\YammerUsers.csv -OutputFile .\YammerA-
zureADCompare.csv
#>
Param (
        [System.Management.Automation.PSCredential]$Credential,
        [switch]$IncludeYammerInactiveUsers,
        [string]$InputFile,
        [string]$OutputFile = ".\YammerAzureADCompare.csv",
        [switch]$UseExistingConnection
        )
Import-Module MSOnline
If (!($UseExistingConnection))
        {
        Write-Host "Creating a new connection. Login with your Office 365 Global
Admin Credentials..."
        If (!($Credential))
                {
                $Credential = Get-Credential
```

```
                           }
               Connect-MsolService -Credential $Credential
               }
        If (!($InputFile))
               {
               Write-Host -ForegroundColor Red "Input file not specified. Exiting."
               Break
               }
        # Import users from AAD
        Write-Host "Getting all Office 365 users from Azure AD. This can take a while..."
        [array]$o365Users = Get-MsolUser -All | Select-Object UserPrincipalName, @{
               Name = "PrimarySmtpAddress"; '
               Expression = { ($_.ProxyAddresses -cmatch "SMTP:").Substring(5) } }
        Write-Host "$($o365Users.Count) users in Azure AD."
        # Import users from Yammer User Export CSV
        Write-Host "Importing Yammer Users from $($InputFile)..."
        If (!($IncludeYammerInactiveUsers)) { $State = "active" } Else { $State = "*" }
        [array]$YammerUsers = Import-Csv $InputFile | ? { $_.state -like $State }
        Write-Host "$($YammerUsers.Count) Active users in Yammer Export."
        # Add Yammer Users to Hash
        $YammerHash = @{}
        foreach ($obj in $YammerUsers) { $YammerHash[$obj.id] = $obj.Email }
        # Add AAD Users to Hash
        $o365UsersHash = @{}
        Foreach ($obj in $o365Users) { $o365UsersHash[$obj.UserPrincipalName] = $obj.Pri-
        marySmtpAddress }
        # Figure out the difference
        $YammerUsersNotInAAD = $YammerHash.Values | Where-Object { $_ -notin $o365User-
        sHash.Values }
        # Save the file
        Write-Host -ForegroundColor Green "Writing the output csv file..."
        $YammerUsersNotInAAD | Export-Csv $OutputFile -NoTypeInformation
```

4. Enable Enforce Office 365 Identity in Yammer Network Admin, using the steps earlier in this chapter.

Summary

In this chapter, you learned how to deploy and manage Yammer. Before deploying Yammer, develop a governance plan and determine whether the content retention policies and search tools available in the Yammer environment meet your organization's requirements. With some of the advances in group collaboration, you can integrate Yammer successfully and make it part of your Office 365 social strategy.

Index

About the Authors

DARRYL KEGG, senior consultant in the Microsoft cloud services team, is responsible for deployment of Office 365 and Microsoft Azure services to government, education, and Fortune® 100/500 customers. He has helped migrate over 10 million users to Azure.

AARON GUILMETTE, Senior Consultant at Microsoft, provides guidance and assistance to customers adopting Office 365, with a focus on messaging, identity, and scripting solutions.

LOU MANDICH, Senior Consultant at Microsoft, provides guidance and assistance to multiple customers adopting Office 365, with a focus on complex messaging and identity solutions.

ED FISHER is a Technology Solutions Professional at Microsoft, focusing on helping customers evaluate, deploy, and adopt Office 365 collaboration technologies, networking, and security solutions.

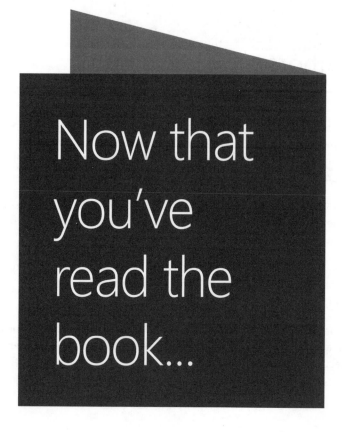

Now that you've read the book...

Tell us what you think!

Was it useful?
Did it teach you what you wanted to learn?
Was there room for improvement?

Let us know at http://aka.ms/tellpress

Your feedback goes directly to the staff at Microsoft Press,
and we read every one of your responses. Thanks in advance!